THE
VARIETIES
OF RELIGIOUS
EXPERIENCE

THE VARIETIES OF RELIGIOUS EXPERIENCE

A STUDY IN HUMAN NATURE

Being the Gifford Lectures on Natural Religion
Delivered at Edinburgh in 1901-1902

WILLIAM JAMES

ENLARGED EDITION WITH APPENDICES AND INTRODUCTION BY JOSEPH RATNER

UNIVERSITY BOOKS

New Hyde Park, New York

BIBLIOGRAPHICAL NOTE

First Edition June, 1902
Reprinted, with revisions, August, 1902
This was the final edition in the author's lifetime and all
impressions since then were from the August, 1902 edition
The present edition is the first to provide, in the
ten Appendices following James' text, James' other
writings bearing on the central idea of
THE VARIETIES

Acknowledgment is made to Paul R. Reynolds and Son for permission to
reprint selections from the following works: *Memories and Studies* by
William James, published by Longmans, Green & Co., Inc., copyright 1911
by Henry James, Jr.; *The Letters of William James*, edited by Henry James,
published by the Atlantic Monthly Press, copyright 1920 by Henry James;
The Thought and Character of William James, by Ralph Barton Perry,
published by Little, Brown & Co., copyright 1935 by Henry James; *Some
Problems of Philosophy* by William James, published by Longmans, Green
& Co., Inc., copyright 1911 by Henry James, Jr.; *A Pluralistic Universe:
Hibbert Lectures on the Present Situation on Philosophy*, by William James,
published by Longmans Green & Co., Inc., copyright 1909 by William
James; and *Collected Essays and Reviews* by William James, published by
Longmans, Green & Co., Inc., copyright 1920 by Henry James, Jr.
Acknowledgment is made to Yale University Press for permission to
reprint selections from *A Common Faith* by John Dewey and *Psychoan-
alysis and Religion* and *Man for Himself* by Erich Fromm

INTRODUCTION

THE VARIETIES OF RELIGIOUS EXPERIENCE is a pioneering work, the first of its kind and still the greatest.

During the sixty years since the VARIETIES was published, there has been an ever-increasing production of a certain kind of "psychologies of religion." Some of these "psychologies" are written by professional religionists of various persuasions and some by professional psychologists and psychoanalysts of various schools. Though the religionists and the secularists pursue different courses and reach different conclusions, they all start off from a common assumption: that there is something inherent in the very nature of religion of which there can be a "psychology." If the VARIETIES stimulated this kind of "psychological" study, it did so adventitiously for it is not, in this sense, a "psychology of religion" at all. Indeed, James clearly and explicitly denies the very possibility of any such thing.

The phrase "religious experience" is ambiguous. Its ambiguity is due to the fact that "experience" is, to use James's homespun terminology, a "double-barreled" word. One barrel is "subjective" and the other "objective." When fired from one barrel, the word means the psychological process, state or condition of experiencing; when fired from the other barrel it means the content or object experienced. Only of the first barrel, "experiencing" — a psychological happening — can there be a psychology; and only if there is something specifically "religious" about religious experiencing can there be, in the sense indicated above, a "psychology of religion." It is a basic finding of James's work that in religious experience there is "nothing whatever of a psychologically specific nature. There is religious fear, religious love, religious awe, religious joy and so forth. But religious love is only man's natural emotion of love directed to a religious object . . . and similarly of all the various sentiments which may be called into play in the lives of religious persons. As concrete states of mind, made up of a feeling *plus* a specific sort of object, religious emotions of course are psychic entities distinguished from other concrete emotions; but there is no ground for assuming a simple abstract "religious emotion" to exist as a distinct elementary mental affection by itself, present in every religious experience without

v

exception." (27)* What James here says is true of religious emotions he, in appropriate contexts, says is true of all other varieties of religious experience, from the simplest to the most complex, from the lowest to the highest, from ubiquitous religious conversion to the rarest and most rarefied religious mysticism. James highlighted his basic finding, upon which the whole of THE VARIETIES OF RELIGIOUS EXPERIENCE rests, by subtitling his work: "A Study in Human Nature." Those who misread or ignore essentials in his text of course have no difficulty giving his subtitle the same treatment.

That what makes an experience "religious" is not something in the nature of man but something in the nature of the object experienced is the profound difference between the VARIETIES and the productions of the religionists who deviously trick out ancient, modern or supermodern theological dogmas in fetching psychological styles; it is also the profound difference between James's work and the productions of the secularists who identify religious experience with this or that kind of psychological response, the stimulus or object evoking the response being this, that or anything at all — as long as the anything is not something distinctively religious.

James shows that the psychology of religious and non-religious experience is precisely the same by bringing together, under each classificatory head, examples of both. This procedure is anathema to the religionists: the sacred gulf between the religious and non-religious no classification may, without blasphemy, bridge. Presumably to help take the curse off his procedure, James, among other things, points out to his predominantly clerical audience at Edinburgh that "Probably a crab would be filled with a sense of personal outrage if it could hear us class it without ado or apology as a crustacean." (9) Did James really believe that comparing the tender feelings of the devoutly unenlightened religionist with those of a crab would help to mollify his audience? It is more credible that this is one of the thrusts in Edinburgh's evangelical "gizzard" James promised himself the pleasure of delivering. (534)

Not only did James offend by spanning the sacred gulf; he further offended by selecting as his case materials the most extreme examples of religious experience he could find. James was undoubtedly fascinated by the unusual, the extreme, the pathological types and repelled by "the clerico-academic-scientific type,

*All references to the VARIETIES and Appendices will be given as above; the number gives the page where the quotation or, when there is no quotation, where the idea or argument, begins. All italics are in the original unless otherwise stated.

the officially and conventionally 'correct' type, 'the deadly respectable' type." (109) However, sound scientific sense, not personal predilection, directed his selection of the evidence. If the
difference between the religious and non-religious experience is an
added quality in the concrete psychic condition induced or produced by the religious object experienced, then there is only one
sure way of clearly and unmistakably identifying that addition,
namely, by scrutinizing the most pronounced, or what is the same
thing, the most abnormal cases available. To try to discover the
characteristics distinctive of religious experience by hunting for
the "religious" ingredient in the hemisemidemireligious would be
absurd.

James believed in the ultimacy of individual experience in religious history. When the individuals are supreme religious geniuses, their experiences become the foundations of new religions;
when they are religious geniuses cf a lower order, their experiences
start new departures in old religions; and so on down the line
until we reach the broad undistinguished masses whose religious
experiences, in so far as they are genuine at all, provide the
ecclesiastical institutions with the vital juices necessary to keep
those corporations from complete putrefaction and death. As far
as James's work is concerned, it doesn't make any difference
whether his reading of religious history is true or false — and it is
certainly more false than true. Individuals have religious experiences, and whatever their role in the history of religion James
would have made them, not religious institutions, the subject
matter of his study. And the results of his study would have been
the same. What is decisive with James is not origin but value.
Even if individual religious experience is not the origin of all else
in religious history, it is nonetheless, for James, the supreme, if
not the only, value of religion.

James originally planned to devote the first ten Gifford Lectures
to the presentation and psychological analysis of case material,
the factual empirical evidences of religious experience; and the
second ten to the philosophical analysis of the value and validity
of religious experience. The latter he then thought of as his "last
will and testament, setting forth the philosophy best adapted to
normal religious needs."(533) But the case material grew bulkier
and bulkier, forcing a drastic revision of his original plan. But
not so drastically as to eliminate entirely the "last will and testament." He gives the substance of his views on "normal religious
needs" in Lectures XIV and XV ("The Value of Saintliness")
and he also manages to say, in sharply abbreviated form, all that

he was then ready to say on the philosophical ultimate of ultimates. This is evident from his letter to Starbuck, written some
two years after the publication of the VARIETIES, in which he tells
his friend: "I have frankly to confess that my VARIETIES carried
'theory' as far as I could then carry it, and that I can carry it no
farther today." (535) James never did carry it any farther. The
"theory," in the language of the letter, is about "the Higher
Powers" — most frequently designated in the VARIETIES by the
more neutral term "the divine." In subsequent writings — most
of all in PRAGMATISM and A PLURALISTIC UNIVERSE — James did
intensively examine rival theories, a task which, in the VARIETIES,
he could hardly do more than indicate was necessary (454), but
his own theory, concentrated in Lecture XX and the "Postscript"
and contextually foreshadowed in several other places, remained
in all significant particulars unchanged.

The question of validity — the ultimate of ultimates — is whether
or not the religious object, the divine, is real. James repeatedly
points out that to search for the answer to this question in the
theories or conceptions of the religious object that men have held
is to search for the answer where it cannot be found. All conceptions of the divine, from the vaguest primitive notions to the
most precise highly developed notions set forth in creeds, theodi-
cies, theologies and metaphysical systems, are secondary products; they are at best interpretations of religious experience — and
often they are not even that; being interpretations they necessarily
reflect the peculiar parochial intellectual habits and spiritual limitations of the individuals, peoples and cultures which produce them.
At different times and places, the divine has been conceived as
personal and impersonal; as localized and omnipresent; as monistic
and pluralistic; as busily interested in human welfare and as sub-
limely indifferent to all that concerns mankind; as finite and infinite; as deistic, pantheistic, monotheistic, polytheistic; as anthropomorphic, theriomorphic and amorphic; as incorruptibly barbarous and intermittently civilized; as static transcendental ideality
and dynamic supernatural power. All these conceptions—and there
are countless more — cannot all be true. And they may all be false
— as they must certainly all be if the religious object, the divine, is
in fact not a reality.

The crucial question of validity is not which theory or conception of the religious object is true; the crucial question is
whether there is any religious object at all. If we would find the
answer to this question we must put all secondary religious products to one side and investigate the primary religious phenomena,

the experiences of individuals who claim they have had immediate, firsthand commerce with the divine. That James should insist upon this procedure is of course in full harmony with his belief in the ultimacy of individual experience in religious history. It is also in full harmony with the basic principles of empirical philosophy which James calls "pragmatism" and others call "scientific method." Theories may illuminate or explain the facts; they do not establish or disestablish the facts. James treats of the primary religious phenomena in Lecture III ("The Reality of the Unseen") and again in Lectures XVI and XVII ("Mysticism"). On the first occasion he presents the factual data, the reported experiences of the religious object, and his psychological analysis of them; on the second, he gives his philosophical evaluation of the phenomena (with additional case material thrown in). That the two treatments are given on such widely separated occasions is a legacy of his original plan for the lecture series and not a very fortunate legacy. However, what James separated, the reader can always bring together. Even on a first reading. For nothing in "The Reality of the Unseen" is essential for understanding the contents between it and "Mysticism."

What is James's answer to the crucial question? After weighing the evidences for the reality of the religious object as conscientiously and sympathetically as he can, James reaches the verdict: NOT, PROVEN. Even when given the benefit of every qualification and doubt, "the utmost" that religious mysticism does is to "establish a presumption" in favor of the religious object's reality. James gives a number of reasons for his verdict. Undoubtedly the most far-reaching and impressive is the fact that "religious mysticism is only one half of mysticism. The other half has no accumulated traditions except those which the textbooks on insanity supply." Psychologically, both halves — the religious mysticisms and the non-religious mysticisms — are precisely the same; they both "spring from the same mental level, from that great subliminal or transmarginal region of which science is beginning to admit the existence, but of which so little is really known. That region contains every kind of matter: 'seraph and snake' abide there side by side. To come from thence is no infallible credential." Mystically, too, both are precisely the same: they enjoy in common the basic characteristics which define the mystical state; in the most pronounced forms of both, James finds, for example, "the same sense of ineffable importance," "the same controlling by extraneous powers" and the same noetic quality. (426) Indeed, "the inchoate sense of presence" which is typical of much religious

mysticism "is seldom equal to the evidence of hallucination."
(478) When religious mysticism does culminate in experience of
a definite sensorial image — the mystical objective, for example,
of Loyola's Spiritual Exercises — it is "a semi-hallucinatory mono-
ideism." (406) Since there is nothing in the intrinsic nature of a
mystical state that distinguishes the religious from the non-religious,
a real from a delusory content, what comes from the inner subliminal region "must be sifted and tested, and run the gauntlet of
confrontation with the total context of experience, just like what
comes from the outer world of sense." (426)

James does not do the sifting and testing (neither in the
VARIETIES nor in subsequent works). Some critics have, in consequence, charged him with failing to do his duty.* James had a
more modest conception of his powers than his critics have of
theirs. They are certain they know the ontological ultimates; therefore the problem of sifting and testing is, for them, quite simple,
something they can solve in a trice, out of hand. James was certain
he did not know the ontological ultimates and he did not believe
anyone else knew them either; therefore the job of sifting and
testing, as he saw it, was complex and difficult, and to get it even
partially done right would require the cooperation of many experts
over a long period of time. Mystical experiences and the experiences investigated by the Society for Psychical Research (of which
James was President) are not identical, but they do overlap. James
did not propose that a Society be formed for investigating mystical
experiences; he proposed instead that a "Science of Religions"
(433) be developed; his sketch of the purposes and procedures of
this "Science" reflects what he thought admirable in the purposes
and procedures of the Society for Psychical Research.

In the meantime, what? James has two answers, one for the
mystic and one for the non-mystic. Or, perhaps better said, James
has one answer consisting of two parts.

The answer for the mystic: "Mystical states, when well developed, usually are, and have the right to be, absolutely authoritative over the individuals to whom they come." (422) Why does
James defend as an "absolute right" the attitude mystics take as a
matter of psychological fact? Because James, like John Stuart Mill,
believed that society should support and safeguard, not undermine
and destroy, the liberty of the non-conforming individual. The
fearful consequences of the tyranny of the majority, so amply and
judiciously analyzed in Mill's essay "On Liberty," haunted James

*For example, James H. Leuba, *The Psychology of Religious Mysticism*:
293;307.

all his life. "If the mystical truth that comes to a man proves to be a force that he can live by" — James writes on the heels of the quotation above — "what mandate have we of the majority to order him to live in another way? We can throw him into a prison or a madhouse, but we cannot change his mind — we commonly attach it only the more stubbornly to its beliefs." (423) When James wrote this, the alternative "prison or madhouse" was more verbal than real; the transformation of "madhouse" into "mental hospital" — a transformation in which James played a notable part — was then hardly begun. The mystic is only one of the non-conformist types James gallantly championed, no matter what the cost or the odds. When he fought against legislative interference with "mind-curing," he was virtually an isolated figure in the academic community. Today, under the prestigeful term "psycho-somatic," the most conventionally correct inside and outside the academic precincts accept as a matter of course what James was given the pariah-treatment for espousing. His labors on behalf of the Society for Psychical Research, originally prompted by his "love of sportsmanlike fair play in science," is another example. Today, "parapsychology" is acquiring an academic status which even the deadly respectable type may not lightly scorn.

Granted that non-conformity should be supported and defended, is it necessary to go so far as to say that the religious mystic has the right to value his experiences as "absolutely authoritative" for himself? Would it not be better to advise the mystic to exercise some critical judgment? Viewed abstractly it might be, but the abstract view ignores the realities. To advise an ecstatic lover that he should be critical of the object of his love is always futile and it may also be heartless. If and when the ecstasy is gone, the poor wretch does not need *that* advice. The experience of the mystic and of the lover have much in common, James repeatedly points out.

James saw in the life of his father what a profound, well developed religious experience can do. He believed his father "was a religious prophet and genius, if ever prophet and genius there were"; nevertheless, upon reviewing his father's lifetime output, he found that his father "never analyzed his terms or his data beyond a certain point" with the result that his multifarious works were "the monotonous elaboration of one single bundle of truths." His father's "truths" were not true for James; that they were "absolutely authoritative" for his father was not merely a psychological fact but an essential of their religious value. For his father "his truths were his life; they were the companions of his death-bed;

and when all else had ebbed away, his grasp of them was still vigorous and sure."*

The non-mystics are in the majority; they assuredly have rights too. It is, however, not their rights as a "majority," but of the right of each individual in this majority, that James is concerned with in his religious philosophy. For "religion," as he defines it, means: "the feelings, acts and experiences of individual men in their solitude, so far as they apprehend themselves to stand in relation to whatever they may consider the divine." (31) Mystic and non-mystic are thus in one basic respect alike in their religious life: they are individual men responding "in their solitude" to the divine; and in the respect that both are alike, James's answer to the question is basically the same for both. Mystic and non-mystic, each after his own kind, has the right to accept as "absolutely authoritative" over his own life what each can or does believe. And each has no obligation to the other. The mystic has the right to believe his experience is an "infallible credential" and the non-mystic that it is not. As James repeatedly emphasizes: "non-mystics are under no obligation to acknowledge in mystical states a superior authority conferred on them by their intrinsic nature." (427)

The "right" of each individual to be himself is a social or political right and it does not change its character when carried into the religious sphere. James, as we have seen, is certainly concerned with defending this right against its enemy the "majority." But were this all he was concerned to defend he would simply be an individualistic liberal (which he was) and his doctrine would have to be evaluated in these terms alone. However, the "right" of the individual religious believer to cleave to his own religious belief is by no means the only "right" James seeks to uphold. He is far more deeply concerned with upholding or defending the "right" to have a religious belief at all. As he put it in the Preface to THE WILL TO BELIEVE, his deepest concern is "with defending the legitimacy of religious faith." *This* defense — one can say without outlandish exaggeration — is *the* concern or cause of his whole philosophic life. It is manifest, for example, in his 1879 essay on "The Sentiment of Rationality" and continues with increasing intensity, breadth and power to his "Faith and the Right to Believe" posthumously published in 1911.

For whom — according to the 1896 Preface just quoted — did James believe the legitimizing of religious faith was necessary? Most definitely not for everybody. "What mankind at large most

*From James's "Introduction" to his edition of his father's "Literary Remains."

2 lacks is criticism and caution, not faith. Its cardinal weakness is to let belief follow recklessly upon lively conception, especially when the conception has instinctive liking at its back." What mankind's reckless believers "most need is that their faiths be broken up and ventilated, that the northwest wind of science should get into them and blow their sickliness and barbarism away." Only for a very special group — and a very tiny group compared to the masses of mankind — is the legitimizing of faith necessary. It is necessary for the "academic," for those who have been "carefully instilled" with false, restrictive, inhibitory notions of "science" and "scientific evidence." Because of this misinstruction, the "forms of mental weakness" the academic suffer from are "paralysis of their native capacity for faith and timorous *abulia* in the religious field." (594)

It is always for the benefit of this special, limited, academic group that James labored to make religious faith legitimate. This group primarily consists of those who received their misinstruction in institutions of higher learning, but it of course also includes those who may have obtained it in some other way. James's 1896 diagnosis of the academic disease remains a constant in his thought. In the VARIETIES he restates it thus: "Inaptitude for religious faith may in some cases be intellectual in its origin. Their religious faculties may be checked in their natural tendency to expand by" — among other things — "the agnostic vetoes upon faith as something weak and shameful, under which so many of us today lie cowering, afraid to use our instincts. In many persons such inhibitions are never overcome." (204)

Obviously, "recklessness" and "paralysis" are two different diseases and require two different cures. The cure for "recklessness" is science; the cure for "paralysis" is an antidote for the false notions of science responsible for the "paralysis." James wrote out his prescription for the antidote in different forms on different occasions, but the basic ingredients remain always the same. His most famous effort is his essay "The Will to Believe." Nothing James ever wrote has been more widely identified with "the essence of James"; and nothing has been more violently misinterpreted or more obtusely criticized by more eminent men. What James clearly prescribes as an antidote for paralysis, his eminent critics self-righteously denounce as a booster for recklessness. James finally exploded: "I cry to Heaven to tell me of what insane root my 'leading contemporaries' have eaten, that they are so smitten with blindness as to the meaning of printed texts." If James could read Bertrand Russell's criticism of him in *A History of Western Philosophy* he well might 'cry to Heaven' again.

In "The Will to Believe" the principal example of misinstruction, the principal "agnostic veto" which James uses for hitching and flogging is provided by W. K. Clifford. It was James's favorite to the last; where it isn't explicit it is implicit, as in the VARIETIES. James uses a number of Clifford's statements; this one gives the vetoing substance of them all: "It is wrong always, everywhere, and for every one, to believe anything upon insufficient evidence." The awesome moral substance in Clifford's statements finds full voice, appropriately enough, when Clifford is stigmatizing violations of his veto: "belief is desecrated," "stolen," " a stain which can never be wiped out," "defiance of our duty to mankind."

James naturally agrees that "our first and great commandments as would-be knowers" are: *"We must know the truth:* and *we must avoid error."* But he does not agree that these two commandments are "an identical commandment" stated in two different ways, one in the positive and one in the negative mode. James sees them as "two materially different laws; and by choosing between them we may end by coloring differently our whole intellectual life." (605)

If we choose the negative commandment, then "the avoidance of error" becomes our paramount concern. And if we persist in this choice, then our whole intellectual life will wither with fear of the omnipresent danger of falling into error. This is to put it very mildly. For if we choose the negative commandment and are really and truly faithful to it we will sooner or later, and probably sooner than later, collapse in catatonic fright.

What if we choose the positive commandment? Then "the chase for truth" becomes our dominant concern. We will count "the risk of being in error" a small price for "the blessings of real knowledge." And if we persist in this choice, our whole intellectual being will flow with the sap of life — vigorous in the chase and joyful whenever the truth is bagged.

The term "hypothesis" is often used in a narrow sense, as denoting a piece of strictly scientific equipment. James uses the term in the broadest sense possible, as meaning "anything that may be proposed to our belief." This usage is neither arbitrary nor loose; it embodies a fundamental of what James then called his "radical empiricism" and nowadays would be called "the principle of fallibilism."

The choice between commandments is real. Which shall we choose to obey? James says: Neither — as an absolute, unvarying rule of life. In any given case, our choice should depend (as in fact it commonly does for all except one-eyed fanatical doctrinaires) upon the nature and importance of the particular hypothesis that is proposed to our belief. In one case the positive, in another case the negative commandment is the "right" one to choose. And how do we make our choice? On purely intellectual grounds? On purely "passional" or "non-intellectual" grounds? On some mixture of both?

It is a fundamental contention of "The Will to Believe" — a contention which became broader, deeper and more assured in the VARIETIES and subsequent works — that all our choices, beliefs, opinions, convictions, decisions are influenced by our "passional" nature; some influenced more, some influenced less but none wholly escaping — not even those which have the longest and noblest pedigree of immaculate intellectual conception. In 1962, this may be old hat; in 1896 (and for many years thereafter) it was *sans-culotte*.

Although James was certain of the ubiquitous influence of our passional nature, he does not rest his crucial argument on this general proposition. Instead, he proposes for consideration the most extreme kind of case theoretically possible: the kind which forces us to make a choice *"that cannot by its nature be decided on intellectual grounds."* (606) Since the choice is *forced,* there is no escaping it. No matter what our response, that response is a *decision.* And no matter what our decision, that decision is *not* made on intellectual grounds at all because what is before us *"by its nature"* excludes those grounds. Therefore, the decision which perforce we do make, be it negative or positive, *must* be made by our passional nature.

I have somewhat simplified James's crucial case. As he defines it, it is "living" and "momentous" as well as "forced." The characteristics I have omitted are essential for some of James's purposes, but not for the logic of his crucial argument. The fact that the choice is "forced" is the only thing that matters. To specify that it is also "living" and "momentous" obscures, rather than clarifies, the main issue at stake. For Clifford's veto implicitly asserts that for the virtuous mind no choice could possibly equal, let alone surpass, in life and momentousness the choice of not believing on insufficient evidence, or, what is the same thing, on insufficient intellectual grounds. That there are sinners is not in dispute; and it is surely obvious that for sinners the sinful choice is momentous and living and the virtuous choice, trivial and dead.

Is James's crucial case purely theoretical? The ubiquitous influence of our passional nature does not necessarily imply the ubiquitous influence of our intellectual nature. However, even if we can imagine a choice absolutely devoid of intellectual content and therefore one which has to be settled exclusively on passional or non-intellectual grounds, only for a total primitive can such be a "forced" choice; for an "academic" never. As James says in the VARIETIES: "We are thinking beings, and we cannot exclude the intellect from participating in any of our functions. Even in soliloquizing with ourselves, we construe our feelings intellectually." (432) The "we" in this and similar places may fortuitously embrace all men, but it intentionally embraces only some — the academic some — for whom, we should never forget, James always consciously wrote and hoped to influence.

For our passional nature to "participate" in the making of a decision and to be "wholly responsible" for the making of a decision are two quite different things. The difference, real as it is, nevertheless cuts no ice when the great issue between James and the Cliffordians is boiled down to the ultimate critical point. That point is not: "Do we have the 'right' to decide when we must? Nor is it: "Do we have the 'right' to decide on exclusively passional grounds when no other grounds exist?" The ultimate critical point is: "Do we have the 'right' to decide affirmatively — i.e. to believe — on insufficient evidence?" Clifford says we haven't. To decide that way is "sinful." Always, everywhere and by everyone, the decision should be negative — i.e. we should withhold belief or disbelieve. To do what we "should" is obviously the only "right" that we have.

James agrees that we have no "right" to sin. But he does not agree that it is a sin to decide affirmatively on insufficient evidence. Since it is conceded that the evidence — or intellectual ground — is insufficient for making the affirmative decision, if and when that affirmative decision is made our passional nature is and must be responsible for it. And wholly responsible for the affirmation or believing — when this is isolated and considered by itself. The function of isolating the passional element in the decision and demonstrating that it not only does but must have a role in the making of some decisions is the critical logical significance of the extreme case that James propounds.

Clifford's absolutistic veto has, as James says, "a thoroughly fantastic sound." If accepted ex animo science itself — not to speak of religion — would be impossible. For the scientific investigator always and necessarily starts out by believing "upon insufficient evidence" — otherwise he would not need to investigate. And oftentimes — probably more often than not — he believes or has faith in his hypothesis in spite of adverse evidence encountered in his search.

If the scientist has the "right" to believe in his scientific hypothesis (and he indubitably has) then the religious person has the "right" to believe in his religious hypothesis. In its most fundamental character "the right to believe" is the right to choose the positive instead of the negative commandment, the right to choose "the chase for truth" instead of "the avoidance of error" whenever we feel that the possible risks and compensations of the one outweigh the possible risks and compensations of the other. The chase for truth involves the risk of landing in error but also the lively hope of catching the truth. The avoidance of error involves the risk of letting the truth just pass us by, but also the unearthly satisfaction of having a mind of stainless beliefs. Consequently, we can alternatively say, as James in his writings frequently does, that "the right to believe" is in essence "the right to choose (our) own form of risk." This "right" holds for any hypothesis, for anything that may be proposed to our belief. James felt it necessary to defend this right on behalf of the religious hypothesis specifically because it was with respect to this hypothesis — for him the most "living" and "momentous" of all — that the right was specifically denied.

As for himself, James prefers to run the risks involved in believing the religious hypothesis, the compensations outweighing the risks. He will not surrender his right to this preference to the vetoing scientist. He finds, in fact, that "the queerest idol ever manufactured in the philosophic cave" is precisely this veto against religious belief because of insufficient evidence, "this command that we shall put a stopper on our heart, instincts, and courage, and *wait* — acting of course meanwhile more or less as if religion were *not* true — till doomsday, or till such time as our intellect and senses working together may have raked in evidence enough."*

In the VARIETIES James does not directly defend the right to religious faith but he engages in an intermittent, oblique, somewhat subterranean defense and it echoes the substance we have found in "The Will to Believe." The most important single conclusion in the VARIETIES is that the central, decisive fact of religious belief, the religious object's reality, is not proven. Whatever evidence there may be in favor of its reality, it is insufficient to justify belief on intellectual or scientific grounds. The search for evidence should continue therefore, more extensively, more persistently and scientifically than ever before. But in the meantime, what? Suspend

*THE WILL TO BELIEVE, 29.

religious belief, put it on ice, until sufficient evidence is, if ever, raked in? How absurd! The human race may wait till doomsday or the hardly less distant long run. The individual cannot. His run is short; his doomsday always near at hand. For him, belief in the religious hypothesis is now or never. It is for the now, not for the never, that religious faith must be legitimized, that the right for the academic to believe must be vindicated. James exercised that right for himself. In the VARIETIES he professes his belief in the reality of the religious object, despite the insufficiency of evidence. (519) What he has the right to do of course every academic also has the right to do. If only they knew it!

In the foregoing, we have been concerned with the "right" to believe. What about the "will" to believe? Does James use the terms "right" and "will" as equivalent or interchangeable? Or did he give his famous essay an incorrect or misleading title? James came to feel that he had. The title of his posthumously published "Faith and the Right to Believe" is the best testimony to this. It may be doubted, however, whether James was also justified in thinking that if he had called his famous essay "The Right to Believe" the incredible misinterpretations of his doctrine would not have been made. After all, in the opening paragraph of "The Will to Believe" he clearly states that his essay is "a defense of our *right* to adopt a believing attitude in religious matters" (italics mine); and in re-stating his purpose in the second paragraph he uses the term "lawful" which the reader soon finds out, if he does not get it immediately, is intended by James to carry the same meaning as "right." That the purpose of the argument is to defend the "right," the "lawfulness," the "legitimacy" of religious belief is stated, indicated, emphasized in manifold ways from one end of the essay to the other. James also emphasizes this, as we have seen, in the Preface to the volume in which "The Will to Believe" is the first and titular essay. What the Preface could not prevent, what the contents of the essay could not prevent,* it is hardly likely that a different title would have prevented. Even professional philosophers should be able to detect a discrepancy between title and content and to make due allowance for it.

John Dewey long ago observed that from the purely logical standpoint of pragmatic analysis of the fact or meaning of "belief" both "the right to believe" and "the will to believe" are, each in its different way, misleading formulations. Sound as Dewey's

---

*And we may add the contents of the next three essays; (596); also in each of these three the phrase "right to believe" and its equivalents are generously used.

observation is from the purely logical standpoint, it is, unfortunately, beside the point of James's concern. Which well may
explain why James was unpersuaded by it. The problem James
was concerned with was not even primarily, let alone purely,
logical. Primarily, it was a moral problem, set up by the Cliffordian
charge that it is morally wrong to believe on insufficient evidence.
To demolish the Cliffordian position and establish in its place that
it is morally right to believe on insufficient evidence is the problem
which occupied James. The pragmatic analysis of the logic of belief
is a necessary part of the solution James defends. It is not, and
cannot be, the whole solution; hence the irrelevance of what
Dewey said as far as James himself is concerned. The explanation
of Dewey's irrelevance may be found in the fact that although he
was reviewing James's PRAGMATISM, his purpose, as he said, was
"to review not so much Mr. James's book as the present status of
the pragmatic movement which is expressed in the book."*
Dewey's purpose, on the point in question, led him to ignore, not
to confront, James's purpose.

Every right is coupled with an obligation. The right to religious
belief, as James conceives and defends it, has its obligation too.
Indeed, its obligation is twofold. "Religious experience spontaneously and inevitably engenders myths, superstitions, dogmas,
creeds, and metaphysical theologies, and criticisms of one set of
these by the adherents of another." (433) The right to believe
carries with it the intellectual obligation to eliminate from religion's engenderings everything that is not "congruent" with the
best scientific knowledge of the time; and the moral obligation to
eliminate "the denunciations and anathemas" and everything else
in the religious life that violates the principle of tolerance which
is, in its deepest reaches, the principle of "respect for one another's
mental freedom." James was so profoundly outraged by the scientist's veto because of the intolerance he saw in it. For him, the
"spirit of inner tolerance without which all our outer tolerance is
soulless" is "empiricism's glory." For scientists to darken that glory
is as "sinful" in the eyes of James as it is "sinful" in the eyes of
Clifford to believe anything upon insufficient evidence. What it is
sinful for men of science to do is no less, if not more, sinful for
men of religion to do.

The intellectual task of making religion "congruent" with scientific knowledge falls upon the non-mystic. The mystic is relieved
of this obligation because he is incapable of discharging it, whether
because of his native constitution or his mystical experience or a

*Essays in Experimental Logic, 327.

combination of both really does not matter. It is enough that careful, sustained, thoroughgoing critical analysis and judgment are beyond him. Here, then, is the difference, alluded to earlier, between what James has to say to the mystic and to the non-mystic regarding their conduct of the religious life "in the meantime" — a stretch which reaches from now until doomsday or such other day, if it comes before, when the final revelation, coercive over all men's minds as well as irresistible to their hearts, is attained.

The intellectual task which James assigns to the non-mystic is manifold and conceivably endless. Within his competence, James took on this task himself. Throughout his life, he concentrated his great powers of mind and pen in a series of efforts dedicated to showing the "congruence" of some aspect or particular of religion with the best scientific knowledge available. In "Reflex Action and Theism" he is the psychologist, confining himself to the issues that fall within the boundaries of "the strictly natural-history point of view." His purpose is to show that "theism, whatever its objective warrant" has "a subjective anchorage in its congruity with our nature as thinkers"; that "the physiological view of mentality, so far from invalidating, can but give aid and comfort to the theistic attitude of mind." In HUMAN IMMORTALITY James is the logician and speculative philosopher. As logician, he analyzes the possible meanings of "function"; as speculative philosopher, he shows that when one of these meanings is taken, human immortality is "congruent" with accepting "the great psycho-physiological formula: *Thought is a function of the brain*" as a scientific fact "established absolutely, with no possibility of restriction." In the VARIETIES he is the psychologist and speculative philosopher; as psychologist, he points out that the subliminal, transmarginal or subconscious self, though at that time just beginning to be explored, is nevertheless "a well-accredited psychological entity" (511); as speculative philosopher he shows that this entity, in so far forth, makes belief in the religious object's reality "congruent" with scientific fact. In "The Sentiment of Rationality," "Is Life Worth Living?" and "The Will to Believe" (to name these in the order they were written) he is philosopher, moralist, psychologist and logician. In each of these capacities, singly and combined, he builds up his inclusive argument that religious faith is "congruent" with the rational demands of scientific methods of investigation and that the Cliffordian demands are "incongruent" or irrational. James characterizes these three essays and "Reflex Action and Theism" as those in THE WILL TO BELIEVE collection which are "largely concerned with defending the legitimacy of religious be-

lief." The intellectual tasks of showing "congruence" and of showing "legitimacy" are the same task stated or viewed in two different
ways. The classical method of "reconciling" science and religion
by distorting, evading, misinterpreting or otherwise falsifying
scientific knowledge does not "legitimize" religion; it degrades
religion and the "reconcilers" both. James's loyalty to the demands
of science is as deep and unwavering as his loyalty to the demands
of religious belief. Not to "reconcile" these two demands but to
make them "congruent" is his great enduring ambition.

James's efforts in the cases just reviewed are primarily negative
or critical; their purpose is not to defend the validity of old articles
of religious faith; their sole purpose is to remove alleged scientific
impediments or objections to their espousal. The constructive
task James takes up in the VARIETIES ("Conclusions" and "Postscript"). However, he gives only a thumbnail sketch of his fundamental over-beliefs. Although he kept promising himself in the
succeeding years to fill out this sketch, he never did. It is my
opinion that James allowed any and every secondary interest to
thwart the fulfillment of his avowed primary purpose because,
when he got right down to it, he really didn't have anything important to add. The letter to Starbuck proves this to be the case in
August, 1904. His letter to Charles Eliot Norton, in October, 1908,
proves that it is still the case then: "I am convinced as I can be
of anything that this experience of ours is only part of the experience that is, and with which it has something to do; but *what* or
where the other parts are, I cannot guess. It only enables one to
say, 'behind the veil, behind the veil!' more hopefully, however
interrogatively and vaguely, than would otherwise be the case."
Between the time of his letter to Norton and the time of his
death, James wrote considerably but no addition to his 1902 over-
beliefs.

The greater the number of over-beliefs and the more complex
their interrelationships the more difficult and complicated is the
critical task of determining whether or not they are "congruent"
with scientific knowledge. Sometimes the determination of "congruence" also depends upon "our instinctive sense of the dramatic
probabilities of nature." This is true not only in regard to "over-
beliefs" but also in regard to ordinary beliefs concerning this
mundane world. Witness, as one example, James's colleagues at
Harvard who propagated their "barbaric" conviction "that all the
fundamental conceptions of truth have already been found by
science, and that the future has only the details of the picture to
fill in." (597) Their dramatic sense was so shriveled, it might just

as well have been dead. Another example is the long, ignorant, silent treatment given Freud's *Interpretation of Dreams* by the academic know-it-alls throughout the world; and which they followed up with their long, ignorant, vituperative treatment of Freud's works.

Examples of smug obtuseness, quiescent and offensive, on the part of scientists and professed devotees of science are plentiful and James had firsthand experience of more than one. What aroused his indignation and scorn most was the offhand way the self-inflated scientific elite dismissed parapsychological phenomena as "bosh" — unworthy of any rational person's investigation. To deny the need to investigate is to deny the very spirit of science, the source of its life and rationality. It is the quintessence of irrationality. "Your genuine inquirer," James points out, "believes that 'bosh' is no more an ultimate element in Nature, or a really explanatory category in human life than 'dirt' is in chemistry. Every kind of 'bosh' has its own factors and laws; and patient study will bring them definitely to light."(580) To the complacent irrationalists masquerading as the guardians and oracles of scientific rationality, dreams were "bosh" and Freud's patient study of dreams was "bosh" compounded. To James, in whom the spirit of science, of the genuine inquirer, was incarnate, the objective need of continuing to explore the field Freud had opened up was immediately apparent — his own personal, subjective inability to follow properly counting as nothing in his estimate. After hearing and meeting Freud at Clark University, James wrote to Theodore Flournoy: "I hope that Freud and his pupils will push their ideas to their utmost limits, so that we may learn what they are. They can't fail to throw light on human nature; but I confess that he made on me personally the impression of a man obsessed with fixed ideas. I can make nothing in my own case with his dream theories, and obviously 'symbolism' is a most dangerous method." James's hope as to what Freud and his pupils would do expresses what James himself did when gathering materials for his Gifford Lectures: he searched for and selected records of religious experiences which had been "pushed to thir utmost limits, so that we may learn what they are."

James had no religious experience, as he understood it, for he had no commerce with the divine.(535) He was a non-mystic who had just enough of the "germ" of mysticism in him to make him responsive to the mystical experiences of others and to appreciate their importance for a total view of the universe. James had only one really fundamental over-belief; it is stated informally and somewhat incompletely in his letter to Norton and formally and completely in the VARIETIES: "that the world of our present consciousness is only one out of many worlds of consciousness that exist" and that between our world and those other worlds the subliminal, transmarginal or subconscious region constitutes "at certain points" a connection, a passageway through which "higher energies filter in." James never knew or even remotely implied that he knew "what the more characteristically divine facts are, apart from the actual inflow of energy in the faith-state and prayer-state" but he was ready, in 1902 as in the years thereafter, to make his "personal venture" on the over-belief "that they exist." (519)

But what if they don't exist? What if the religious object, the divine, as James or anyone else conceives it to be, is not real? In such case, only one conclusion can be honestly drawn and James draws it: "religion must on the whole be classed, not simply as containing elements of delusion — these undoubtedly everywhere exist — but as being rooted in delusion altogether, just as materialists and atheists have always said it was." (465)

James of course believes that this conclusion is false. Let us, however, assume that it is true and see what effect its truth would have on the VARIETIES — what it would leave standing and what it would destroy.

It would leave untouched all of James's phychological descriptions and analyses of religious experiences. Psychological facts are psychological facts and remain the same no matter how often we change our explanations of their origins or causes. We know this is true in ordinary psychology and psychoanalysis; it is equally true in the psychology of religious experience, though some may not be willing to see or admit it. What James says of the experiences of religious regeneration holds universally: the experiences "remain firm facts of human nature, no matter whether we adopt a theistic, a pantheistic-idealistic, or a medical-materialistic view of their ultimate causal explanation." (111) In sum, everything in the VARIETIES which is "a study in human nature" would stand.

However, though the phenomena of religious experience would remain the same phenomena, they would no longer be *religious* phenomena. For, according to James as we noted at the outset, what makes an experience distinctively religious is a quality which results from commerce with the divine. This quality of experience would of course remain a firm fact of human nature, but James's "ultimate causal explanation" of it would have to go. James uses the term "prayer" in an inclusive sense, as denoting "every kind of inward communion or conversation with the power recognized as divine." Prayer, in this sense, "is the very soul and essence of religion" and the very soul and essence of prayer is that *"something is transacting"* between the person praying and the divine. "The genuineness of religion is thus indissolubly bound up with the question whether the prayerful consciousness be or be not deceitful." If the divine does not exist, if it is not real, then "the direct experiences of prayer" are necessarily "false witnesses" and all sense of commerce with the divine necessarily is no more than "a feeling of what is illusory." (465)

James and Freud have precisely the same fundamental conception of the nature of religion, the same *sine qua non*. They both stand firm by the reality-principle. For religion to be real, they both maintain that the divine — however it be conceived and by whatever name it be called — must be objectively real, and something must be really transacting. James and Freud are in this respect quite old-fashioned. You may, if you like, think they are both 19th century fuddy-duddies. But you may not — or, better said, should not — criticize or judge them in total ignorance or total disregard of their peculiar views. As Erich Fromm does with Freud, for example. When he says that Freud's interpretation of religion "as a collective childhood neurosis of mankind" can be "reversed" he totally ignores what Freud means by religion and therefore is talking nonsense. When Fromm performs the "reversal" and says in italics: "We can interpret *neurosis as a private form of religion*" he is emphatically doubling up on his nonsense. For according to Erich Fromm, "neurosis itself is, in the last analysis, a symptom of moral failure" — which is about as far removed from Erich Fromm's own conception of "religion" as anything can be.* Fromm seemingly gives his nonsense some semblance of sense by dubbing his "private religion" a "lower form" of religion. But two mutually exclusive conceptions of "religion" (which is what Fromm has, if you take him seriously) cannot be brought within the same class as lower and higher or in any other way.

Fromm's elucidation of James and Dewey is on a par with his elucidation of Freud. Fromm couples James with Jung and says: "Like Jung he (James) compares the unconscious with the God concept of the theologian."* And as proof of this, Fromm quotes the following from the VARIETIES: "At the same time the theo-

---

*Psychoanalysis and Religion, 27; Man For Himself, viii.
*This and following quotations are from Psychoanalysis and Religion, 20.

logian's contention that the religious man is moved by an external power is vindicated, for it is one of the peculiarities of invasions from the subconscious region to take on objective appearances, and to suggest to the Subject an external control." James says: "In the religious life the control is felt as 'higher'; but since on *our hypothesis* it is primarily the higher faculties of *our own hidden mind which are controlling,* the sense of union with the power beyond us is a sense of something, not merely apparently, but literally true." (513; italics mine) Instead of James holding the same view as Jung, he holds just the opposite view. No where does James ever say that the subconscious, transmarginal or subliminal region is, with respect to the divine, anything more than a conduit, a passageway for "the actual inflow of energy in the faith-state and the prayer-state." James, as we know, believed that there really was such an "inflow" from the divine but James, as we also know, believed that the objective reality of the divine source of this "inflow" was not proven. This "not proven" is reflected in the sentence Fromm ignored. If the "invasions" or "inflow" did not come primarily from our own hidden mind, the sense of "an external control" instead of being *"literally* true" would be *"merely apparently* true."

The idea that James did, would or could compare the subconscious with the God concept of the theologian is hilarious. To dispose of Fromm's nonsense it is enough — or should be enough — to quote what James wrote to Leuba: "Of course the 'subliminal' theory is an inessential hypothesis." (538)

Fromm couples Dewey and Freud; their positions are "in essential points similar." An essential point in Dewey is his conception of "God." What Freud thinks of Dewey's kind of conception he has made quite clear in *The Future of an Illusion:* "Philosophers stretch the meaning of words until they retain scarcely anything of their original sense; by calling 'God' some vague abstraction which they have created for themselves, they pose as deists, as believers, before the world; they may even pride themselves on having attained a higher and purer idea of God, although their God is nothing but an insubstantial shadow and no longer the mighty personality of religious doctrine." Dewey stretches the word 'God' much farther than do the deists; whether he and they have the right to such stretching we need not decide. What is alone relevant here is that on this "essential point" Dewey and Freud are completely dissimilar, not similar.

Dewey and Freud are similar in that they both are opposed to religious creeds and would welcome their extinction. However, opposition to creeds is so wide a platform that an incalculable variety of thinkers can stand on it. For Dewey and Freud to be "similar" on this point is not a distinctive "essential" or a distinctive bond between them.

For Dewey there is an irremediable "opposition" between "religious values" (as he conceives them) and religious creeds. For Freud there is no such opposition at all because there are, for him, no "religious values" independent of the values of the creeds. On this truly "essential point" Dewey and Freud are entirely dissimilar, not similar.

Fromm quotes Dewey's statement: "Just because the release of these (religious) values is so important, their identification with the creeds and cults of religions must be dissolved." Dewey and Freud cannot stand together on this for the reasons given in the paragraph preceding. Dewey and James can and do because they both have non-creedal-related "religious values" and what Dewey says "must be dissolved" James had long since dissolved in the VARIETIES even as Dewey did in *A Common Faith*.

If religious experience is illusory or delusory, what happens to the *values* of religious experience described in the VARIETIES? Nothing happens — because to the believer, the experiences are genuine and to the non-believer religious experiences are impossible. But something does happen to James's *evaluation* of these values. Instead of the values having both an objective and subjective content, they would now have only a subjective content. Consequently, the objective half of James's evaluation would fall and the subjective half would stand. At this point, James and Freud seem to part company completely. Freud believes that the future of the Illusion should be its extinction; James does not. When the values of religion are given a "purely subjective rating" even then, says James, "Religion must be considered vindicated in a certain way from the attacks of her critics. It would seem that she cannot be a mere anachronism and survival, but must exert a permanent function, whether she be with or without intellectual content, and whether, if she have any, it be true or false." (507) And more specifically, in commenting on successful mind-cure cases: "it makes no difference whether you consider the patients to be deluded victims of their imagination or not. That they seemed to *themselves* to have been cured by the experiments tried was enough to make them converts to the system. And although it is evident that one must be of a certain mental mold to get such results . . . yet it would surely be pedantic and over-scrupulous for those who *can* get their savage and primitive philosophy of mental healing verified in such experimental ways as this, to give them up at word of command for more scientific therapeutics." (121)

James, no more than Freud, would want the "savage and primitive" to be a permanent class of men; but as long as there is such a class of men, James believes its members have the right to the therapeutics they can have faith in and the therapy they can take. Freud certainly agrees. It is the doctor's business to fit the cure to the disease — even to the extent of deliberately deluding the patient by administering a placebo. Whether any scientific spiritual healers — psychoanalysts, for example — ever administer a placebo in course of treatment of a patient, we need not trouble ourselves to decide. For championing the cause of mind-curing — an afterglow of his 1898 experience suffuses the argument in the VARIETIES — James was not concerned with what "scientific therapists" should do in their practice, but with what they should not do to the practice of others. Here again, James and Freud stand, in principle, solidly together. The motives of "Freud's crusade in favor of lay analysis"* are essentially the same as the motives of James's crusade in favor of mind-curing.

When going through his 1898 experience, James wrote to his friend James J. Putnam (later to become an important supporter of Freud): "I never did anything that required as much moral effort in my life." The afterglow of that experience not only suffuses his argument in the VARIETIES; it also confuses it. To force mind-curers to give up their healing "at word of (legislative) command" was the purpose of the "pedantic and over-scrupulous" medical profession. These traits it is manifestly impossible to squeeze in or squeeze out of the "mental mould" of the mind-curers whom James describes. When properly placed, "over-scrupulous" is an over-mild term. What James in 1898 thought of the medical profession is more faithfully revealed in the VARIETIES in his passionate exposition of the weakness of "learning and science" when pitted against "religious faith." (72) His most biting comment at the time was that members of the medical profession "had no more exact science in them than a fox terrier." And they were no better equipped with psychological insight. Since mind-curing, as James then pointed out, "is a religious or quasi-religious movement" the proposed legislation would in effect have required that the mind-curers "at word of command" abandon their religion. Freud's judgment on this kind of "command" is the

* Ernest Jones: *The Life and Work of Sigmund Freud*, vol. 3; quotation, 288; Freud's motives, 287-301; for James's motives see Letters, II, 66-72.

same as James's. In *The Future of an Illusion,* he writes: "It is a senseless proceeding to try and do away with religion by force and at one blow — more especially as it is a hopeless one. The believer will not let his faith be taken from him, neither by arguments nor by prohibitions. And even if it did succeed with some, it would be a cruel thing to do."

James and Freud seem to occupy completely opposite positions with regard to the future of the Illusion, but in reality their positions are not as far apart as they seem. The great difference between their real and apparent positions arises from the fact that by religion James means the experience of commerce with the divine which comes to the individual in his solitude; and Freud means by religion the institutionally developed and socially enforced "doctrines of religion." Leaving to one side Freud's psychoanalytic phraseology and content, there is nothing Freud says about "the burden" of religious doctrines with which James would disagree; indeed, which James has not said in his own more openly passionate way. And Freud and James agree on the remedy. James would have the "sickliness and barbarism" of religious doctrines (he specifically refers to Christian varieties but intentionally excludes none) blown away by the northwest wind of science; and Freud, in his more restrained, scientifically disciplined prose expresses the same desire.

Freud asserts that "in the long run nothing can withstand reason and experience." With this James would wholeheartedly agree. So would Dewey. All three would also agree that any religion which is in contradiction with reason and experience should, and in the long run hopefully will, become extinct.

Freud asserts that a religion would "relinquish the interest of men" if it did not "preserve anything of the consolation of religion," becoming so "purified" that it had nothing left but "the belief in a higher spiritual being, whose qualities are indefinable and whose intentions cannot be discerned." James thoroughly agrees (465). And Dewey, on this "essential point, thoroughly disagrees with both James and Freud. The "God" Dewey seriously proposes for mankind's belief, as capable of winning and holding "the interest of men," may have definable qualities (Dewey defines only one) but it certainly has no "intentions" since it is not any kind of "being" at all, let alone a "spiritual" one.

Freud asserts that "not even the purified religious ideas can escape" the fate of contradicting reason and experience "so long as they still try to preserve anything of the consolation of religion." James of course disagrees. So would Dewey. To be sure, Dewey, like Freud, and unlike James, does not believe there is any supernatural realm. But Dewey would not say what Freud says, namely, that any such realm whatever is impossible. And if not impossible, then necessarily not in contradiction with reason and experience, but necessarily "congruent" with them.

Freud unequivocally, even dogmatically, asserts his view; and yet, by his own avowal he is, strictly observed, entitled to no view at all. "It does not lie," he says, "within the scope of this inquiry to estimate the value of religious doctrines as truth."* His categorical assertion that it is an Illusion not only estimates the truth-value of all past and current religious doctrines, it estimates the truth-value of all possible future religious doctrines as well. And his estimate is wrong. James's religious doctrine may be false but it is congruent with reason and experience; it does not contradict them.

In the VARIETIES, James distinguishes between the religion of the sick soul and the religion of the healthy-minded, but he does not make any fundamental use of this distinction. Indeed, it would be true to say that outside the chapter devoted to the healthy-minded the religion of the sick soul is, in the VARIETIES, the one and only religion which James really considers. This is consistent with his finding: "Here is the real core of the religious problem: Help! Help!" (162) To the exploration and evaluation of this "real core" the VARIETIES is almost completely dedicated.

Many reasons for this curious imbalance in the VARIETIES can be found. There is the subjective reason that all the time James was working on the VARIETIES he was struggling with his ailing heart. (533) Although thoughts of impending death do not appear in his published letters of this period as they do with increasing frequency in the years following, James was acutely conscious from the very start that his Gifford Lectures might be his closing work, his "last will and testament." Another personal, subjective reason is the severe crisis James experienced in his late twenties, recorded in the VARIETIES as the experience of a French correspondent. (160) Before and after this crisis James was intermittently something of a sick soul, with marked somatic side-effects — eyestrain, backache, insomnia. Still another personal reason is that his father was a sick soul, rescued by his religion, his "bundle of truths." During the darkest hours of his own crisis, James saved himself from ultimate tragedy by resorting to the very method he had witnessed his father use to overcome recurrences of his soul

All quotations are from *The Future of an Illusion*. Doubleday. Anchor edition.

sickness. It is imitation of his father, not belief, that explains James's resort to highly charged Biblical quotations. Significantly, it is in connection with this saving method that James makes his only explicit reference to his father in the VARIETIES (161, foot-note).

However, when all personal, familial reasons are marshaled and given their proper weight (a task neither attempted nor ac-complished in the few preceding remarks), there remains the great impersonal reason, the objective fact that throughout history religion has been overwhelmingly, if not exclusively, identified as an antidote for evil, as the source of consolation, of salvation, first, last and always supremely.

If religious experience is illusory, then the value of religion predominant in the VARIETIES would be wholly psycho-therapeutic (ignoring the somatic side-effects and other material benefits which may incidentally accrue). Although Freud fully recognized the *de facto* psycho-therapeutic value of religion, he looked to a future when this mode of psycho-therapy would become extinct. James did not. Dewey's position on this point is, in one sense, more similar to Freud's than to James's, and, in another sense, it is just the other way round.

Dewey primarily means by religious value, by the quality in experience which he calls "religious," what is typified in an old-time religious conversion which sticks — as is the case with the one illustrative example of the "religious" which Dewey uses. It is the quality of experience resulting from changes in ourselves which are "inclusive and deep seated," that "pertain to our being in its entirety," "an orientation, that brings with it a sense of peace and security" and "is enduring."* This is a "religious" experience no matter how it happens to be brought about — and it can be brought about by anything at all. Not only does Dewey implicitly deny, he also explicitly denies that there is anything *sui generis* in the materials or causes of religious experience. On this essential, Dewey and James are fundamentally opposed. James stated the essence of Dewey's psychological position in criticizing Murisier who made "inner unification the mainspring of the whole religious life." The idea "that this formal condition was peculiarly charac-teristic of religion" James declared to be false: *"all* strongly ideal interests, religious or irreligious, unify the mind and tend to sub-ordinate everything to themselves." The truth is "that religion has plenty of material content which is characteristic, and which is

A Common Faith, 13, 16. All following quotations from this work. Some are abridged and conflated, as is the above.

more important by far than any general psychological form." (349)

Would James be able to maintain this "truth" if the direct experiences of prayer were incontestably deceitful? Obviously not. His distinction between religious and irreligious sources of unifying experiences would collapse. The "material content" peculiarly religious would be wholly delusory. The "general psychological form" would then of necessity be the only real, the only genuine characteristic differentiating religious from non-religious experiences. James would then have to agree with Dewey.

Conversion is a psycho-therapeutic experience. Dewey is not a dramatic writer like James, but the core of the religious experience, for him as for James, is predominantly the "Help! Help!" it gives the suffering soul of man, be it in "periods of darkness and despair" (14) or in periods less trying.

The basic ingredients Dewey finds in religious experience are on all essential points similar to, when not identical with, those James finds. For Fromm of course they are dissimilar. He quotes James's statement that the religious attitude is "both a helpless and a sacrificial attitude" toward the divine. Fromm does not quote the next sentence in which James explains: "That is, we shall have to confess to at least some amount of dependence on sheer mercy, and to practice some amount of renunciation, great or small, to save our souls alive." And then, to follow James along, "The constitution of the world we live in requires it: — [quoting five corroborating lines from Goethe]. For when all is said and done, we are in the end absolutely dependent on the universe; and into sacrifices and surrenders of some sort, deliberately looked at and accepted, we are drawn and pressed as into our only permanent positions of repose." (51)

And Dewey? "A religious attitude needs the sense of a connection of man, in the way of both dependence and support, with the enveloping world that the imagination feels is a universe." (53) "This attitude includes a note of submission. But it is voluntary, not externally imposed; and as voluntary it is something more than a mere Stoical resolution to endure unperturbed throughout the buffetings of fortune. It is more outgoing, more ready and glad, than the latter attitude, and it is more active than the former." (16)

And James? "Religion makes easy and felicitous what in any case is necessary" (51); "the service of the highest never is felt as a yoke. Dull submission — the drab discolored way of stoic resignation to necessity — is left far behind, and a mood of welcome, which may fill any place on the scale between cheerful serenity and enthusiastic gladness, has taken its place. The difference is as great as that between passivity and activity, as that between the defensive and the aggressive mood." (41)

James and Dewey not only differ greatly in their habitual literary styles; the purposes of their books on religion are also greatly different. Dewey's purpose is with the common form of religious experience, with the one common variety of faith that is fit for the normal needs of men, James's purpose is with the most extra-ordinary forms of religious experience, with the faith that is fit for the abnormal, pathological needs of men, the varieties most ecstatic, most exalted, most acute, most abandoned, the most heaven-storming and hell-defying. This difference in purpose also determines the difference in their language, and far more signifi-cantly than the mere difference in their habitual literary styles. Dewey in more than one book has his passionate outbursts, lyrical and otherwise. None in *A Common Faith*.

James says "a sacrificial attitude" is ingredient in religious ex-perience. Dewey says "any activity" on behalf of "an ideal end" believed to be of "general and enduring value is religious in quality" when that activity is pursued "against obstacles and in spite of threats of personal loss." (27)

James says "a helpless attitude" is ingredient in religious ex-perience, "some amount of dependence on sheer mercy." Dewey says: "All endeavor for the better is moved by faith in what is possible, not by adherence to the actual. The outcome, given our best endeavor, is not with us. When man, individually or collec-tively, has done his uttermost, conditions that at different times and places have given rise to the ideas of Fate and Fortune, of Chance and Providence, remain" (23, 24).

James says "we are all helpless failures in the last resort. The sanest and best of us are of one clay with lunatics and prison inmates, and death finally runs the robustest of us down. And whenever we feel this, such a sense of the vanity and provisionality of our voluntary career comes over us that all our morality appears but as a plaster hiding a sore it can never cure." (47) Dewey says: "every crisis, whether of the individual or of the community, reminds man of the precarious and partial nature of the control he exercises" and evokes the feeling of "dependence and the humility that accompanies it." (24, 25)

James says: "There is a state of mind, known to religious men, but to no others. In this state of mind, what we most dreaded has become the habitation of our safety, and the hour of our moral death has turned into our spiritual birthday. Fear is not held in abeyance as it is by mere morality, it is positively expunged and washed away [by] the excitement of a higher kind of emotion, in the presence of which no exertion of volition is necessary" (47, 46). Dewey says: The religious attitude which makes us ready and glad to go out and meet the buffetings of fortune "is voluntary, not externally imposed," but not voluntary in the sense "that it depends upon a particular resolve or volition. It is a change *of* will conceived as the organic plenitude of our being, rather than any special change *in* will." (17) This is more than mere morality. The religious attitude "is much broader than anything indicated by 'moral', in its usual sense" (22). "Moral faith in ideal ends" is religious "only when the ends of moral conviction arouse emotions that are not only intense but are actuated and supported by ends so inclusive that they unify the self" (22) and can "carry one through periods of darkness and despair to such an extent that they lose their usual depressive character." (14)

James says: We have the right to believe, to have faith, in spite of the evidence being insufficient to coerce intellectual assent; that we have the right to mount the rungs of the "faith-ladder" he constructed in his last years, from "it *might* have been true under certain conditions" to "it *shall* be true, at any rate for me." (608) Dewey says: "The idea of a whole, whether of the whole personal being or of the world, is an imaginative, not a literal, idea. The limited world of our observation and reflection becomes the Universe only through imaginative extension. It cannot be apprehended in knowledge nor realized in reflection. Neither observation, thought, nor practical activity can attain that complete unification of the self which is called a whole. The *whole* self is an ideal, an imaginative projection." (18) "An unseen power controlling our destiny becomes the power of an ideal. All possibilities, as possibilities, are ideal in character." (23) "There is a difference between belief that is a conviction that some end should be supreme over conduct, and belief that some object or being exists as a truth for the intellect. Conviction in the moral sense signifies being conquered, vanquished, in our active nature by an ideal end; [it] is practical, not primarily intellectual. The authority of an ideal over choice and conduct is the authority of an ideal, not of a fact. It goes beyond evidence that can be presented to *any* possible observer." (20)

In the VARIETIES, the real core of the religious problem is Help! Help! and religion is the answer to that desperate cry. Even in the double-chapter "The Value of Saintliness" the religion of the sick soul is pervasive and dominant. For there James's prescriptions for "normal religious needs" are, in essence, reduced, smaller, milder dosages of what abnormal religious needs require.

In PRAGMATISM, James sketches the basic principles of a religion for the healthy-minded. (See Appendix X.) To establish the genuineness of his pragmatistic or melioristic religion, James must minimize, almost to the point of practical obliteration, the distinction between "religion" and "moralism" he so passionately maintains in the VARIETIES. "Religion in the sense of self-surrender, and moralism in the sense of self-sufficingness, have been pitted against each other as incompatibles frequently enough in the history of human thought." To be sure, James never did this, in the VARIETIES or elsewhere. However, though moralism and religion are never incompatibles for James, the difference between them is in the VARIETIES the great orchestral theme. In his melioristic religion, his great theme is just the opposite.

The religion of the sick soul is the religion of "the prodigal-son" who wants the peace and rest, the security of the everlasting arms beneath. "I am willing to think," James now says, "that the prodigal-son attitude is not the right and final attitude towards the whole of life." "I find myself willing to take the universe to be really dangerous and adventurous" and "as a matter of fact countless human imaginations live in this moralistic and epic kind of a universe." These healthy human imaginations, these healthy-minded souls find that "reliance on possibilities that are not necessities" gives them religious security enough.

In their melioristic religions, James and Dewey are not merely similar on all essential points; they are identical.

Of course, as James says, "Of course as human beings we can be healthy minds on one day and sick souls on the next." In A PLURALISTIC UNIVERSE James returns to his old position. (See Appendix V.) Again the emphasis is on the vast difference between mere moralism and religion. The specifically religious experience is uniquely beyond the reach, indeed beyond the world, of merely moral man.

December 24, 1962

JOSEPH RATNER

PREFACE

THIS book would never have been written had I not been honored with an appointment as Gifford Lecturer on Natural Religion at the University of Edinburgh. In casting about me for subjects of the two courses of ten lectures each for which I thus became responsible, it seemed to me that the first course might well be a descriptive one on 'Man's Religious Appetites,' and the second a metaphysical one on ' Their Satisfaction through Philosophy.' But the unexpected growth of the psychological matter as I came to write it out has resulted in the second subject being postponed entirely, and the description of man's religious constitution now fills the twenty lectures. In Lecture XX I have suggested rather than stated my own philosophic conclusions, and the reader who desires immediately to know them should turn to pages 511–519, and to the ' Postscript ' of the book. I hope to be able at some later day to express them in more explicit form.

In my belief that a large acquaintance with particulars often makes us wiser than the possession of abstract formulas, however deep, I have loaded the lectures with concrete examples, and I have chosen these among the extremer expressions of the religious temperament. To some readers I may consequently seem, before they get beyond the middle of the book, to offer a caricature of the subject. Such convulsions of piety, they will say, are not sane. If, however, they will have the patience to read to the end, I believe that this unfavorable impression will disappear; for I there combine the religious impulses with other principles of common sense which serve as correctives of exaggeration, and allow the individual reader to draw as moderate conclusions as he will.

My thanks for help in writing these lectures are due to Edwin D. Starbuck, of Stanford University, who made over to me his large collection of manuscript material; to Henry W. Rankin, of East Northfield, a friend unseen but proved, to whom I owe precious information; to Theodore Flournoy, of Geneva, to Canning Schiller, of Oxford, and to my colleague Benjamin Rand, for documents; to my colleague Dickinson S. Miller, and to my friends, Thomas Wren Ward, of New York, and Wincenty Lutoslawski, late of Cracow, for important suggestions and advice. Finally, to conversations with the lamented Thomas Davidson and to the use of his books, at Glenmore, above Keene Valley, I owe more obligations than I can well express.

HARVARD UNIVERSITY,
    March, 1902.

CONTENTS

LECTURE I

LECTURE II

LECTURE III

LECTURE IX

LECTURE X

LECTURES XI, XII, AND XIII

LECTURE XVIII

Primacy of feeling in religion, philosophy being a secondary function, 430. Intellectualism professes to escape subjective standards in her theological constructions, 433. ' Dogmatic theology,' 436. Criticism of its account of God's attributes, 442. ' Pragmatism ' as a test of the value of conceptions, 444. God's metaphysical attributes have no practical significance, 445. His moral attributes are proved by bad arguments ; collapse of systematic theology, 448. Does transcendental idealism fare better? Its principles, 449. Quotations from John Caird, 450. They are good as restatements of religious experience, but uncoercive as reasoned proof, 453. What philosophy *can* do for religion by transforming herself into 'science of religions,' 455.

LECTURE XIX

Æsthetic elements in religion, 458. Contrast of Catholicism and Protestantism, 461. Sacrifice and Confession, 462. Prayer, 463. Religion holds that spiritual work is really effected in prayer, 465. Three degrees of opinion as to what is effected, 467. First degree, 468. Second degree, 472. Third degree, 474. Automatisms, their frequency among religious leaders, 478. Jewish cases, 479. Mohammed, 481. Joseph Smith, 482. Religion and the subconscious region in general, 483.

LECTURE XX

Summary of religious characteristics, 485. Men's religions need not be identical, 487. ' The science of religions ' can only suggest, not proclaim, a religious creed, 489. Is religion a 'survival' of primitive thought? 490. Modern science rules out the concept of personality, 491. Anthropomorphism and belief in the personal characterized pre-scientific thought, 493. Personal forces are real, in spite of this, 498. Scientific objects are abstractions, only individualized experiences are concrete, 498. Religion holds by the concrete, 500. Primarily religion is a biological reaction, 504. Its simplest terms are an uneasiness and a deliverance ; description of the deliverance, 508. Ques-

CONTENTS

THE VARIETIES
OF RELIGIOUS EXPERIENCE

LECTURE I

RELIGION AND NEUROLOGY

IT is with no small amount of trepidation that I take my place behind this desk, and face this learned audience. To us Americans, the experience of receiving instruction from the living voice, as well as from the books, of European scholars, is very familiar. At my own University of Harvard, not a winter passes without its harvest, large or small, of lectures from Scottish, English, French, or German representatives of the science or literature of their respective countries whom we have either induced to cross the ocean to address us, or captured on the wing as they were visiting our land. It seems the natural thing for us to listen whilst the Europeans talk. The contrary habit, of talking whilst the Europeans listen, we have not yet acquired; and in him who first makes the adventure it begets a certain sense of apology being due for so presumptuous an act. Particularly must this be the case on a soil as sacred to the American imagination as that of Edinburgh. The glories of the philosophic chair of this university were deeply impressed on my imagination in boyhood. Professor Fraser's Essays in Philosophy, then just published, was the first philosophic book I ever looked into, and I well remember the awe-struck feeling I received from the account of Sir William Hamilton's class-room therein contained. Hamilton's own lectures were the first philosophic writings I ever forced myself to study, and after that I was immersed in Dugald Stewart and Thomas Brown. Such juvenile emotions of reverence never get outgrown; and I confess that to find my humble self promoted from my native wilderness to be actually for the time an official here, and transmuted into a colleague of these illustrious names, carries with it a sense of dreamland quite as much as of reality.

But since I have received the honor of this appointment I have felt that it would never do to decline. The academic career also has its heroic obligations, so I stand here without further deprecatory words. Let me say only this, that now that the current, here and at Aberdeen, has begun to run from west to east, I hope it may continue to do so. As the years go by, I hope that many of my countrymen may be asked to lecture in the Scottish universities, changing places with Scotsmen lecturing in the United States; I hope that our people may become in all these higher matters even as one people; and that the peculiar philosophic temperament, as well as the peculiar political temperament, that goes with our English speech may more and more pervade and influence the world.

As regards the manner in which I shall have to administer this lectureship, I am neither a theologian, nor a scholar learned in the history of religions, nor an anthropologist. Psychology is the only branch of learning in which I am particularly versed. To the psychologist the religious propensities of man must be at least as interesting as any other of the facts pertaining to his mental constitution. It would seem, therefore, that, as a psychologist, the natural thing for me would be to invite you to a descriptive survey of those religious propensities.

If the inquiry be psychological, not religious institutions, but rather religious feelings and religious impulses must be its subject, and I must confine myself to those more developed subjective phenomena recorded in literature produced by articulate and fully self-conscious men, in works of piety and autobiography. Interesting as the origins and early stages of a subject always are, yet when one seeks earnestly for its full significance, one must always look to its more completely evolved and perfect forms. It follows from this that the documents that will most concern us will be those of the men who were most accomplished in the religious life and best able to give an intelligible account of their ideas and motives. These men, of course, are either comparatively modern writers, or else such earlier ones as have become religious classics. The *documents humains* which we shall find most instructive need not then be sought for in the haunts of special erudition — they lie along the beaten highway; and this circumstance, which flows so naturally from the character of our problem, suits admirably also your lecturer's lack of special theological learning. I may take my citations, my sentences and paragraphs of personal confession, from books that most of you at some time will have had already in your hands, and yet this will be no detriment to the value of my conclusions. It is true that some more adventurous reader and investigator, lecturing here in future, may unearth from the shelves of libraries documents that will make a more delectable and curious entertainment to listen to than mine. Yet I doubt whether he will necessarily, by his control of so much more out-of-the-way material, get much closer to the essence of the matter in hand.

The question, What are the religious propensities? and the question, What is their philosophic significance? are two entirely different orders of question from the logical point of view; and, as a failure to recognize this fact distinctly may breed confusion, I wish to insist upon the. point a little before we enter into the documents and materials to which I have referred.

In recent books on logic, distinction is made between two orders of inquiry concerning anything. First, what is the nature of it? how did it come about? what is its constitution, origin, and history? And second, What is its importance, meaning, or significance, now that it is once here? The answer to the one question is given in an *existential judgment* or proposition. The answer to the other is a *proposition of value,* what the Germans call a *Werthurtheil,* or what we may, if we like, denominate a *spiritual judgment.* Neither judgment can be deduced immediately from the other. They proceed from diverse intellectual preoccupations, and the mind combines them only by making them first separately, and then adding them together.

In the matter of religions it is particularly easy to distinguish the two orders of question. Every religious phenomenon has its history and its derivation from natural antecedents. What is nowadays called the higher criticism of the Bible is only a study of the Bible from this existential point of view, neglected too much by the earlier church. Under just what biographic conditions did the sacred writers bring forth their various contributions to the holy volume? And what had they exactly in their several individual minds, when they delivered their utterances? These are manifestly questions of historical fact, and one does not see how the answer to them can decide offhand the still further question: of what use should such a volume, with its manner of coming into existence so defined, be to us as a guide to life and a revelation ? To answer this other question we must have already in our mind some sort of a general theory as to what the peculiarities in a thing should be which give it value for purposes of revelation ; and this theory itself would be what I just called a spiritual judgment. Combining it with our existential judgment, we might indeed deduce another spiritual judgment as to the Bible's worth. Thus if our theory of revelation-value were to affirm that any book, to possess it, must have been composed automatically or not by the free caprice of the writer, or that it must exhibit no scientific and historic errors and express no local or personal passions, the Bible would probably fare ill at our hands. But if, on the other hand, our theory should allow that a book may well be a revelation in spite of errors and passions and deliberate human composition, if only it be a true record of the inner experiences of great-souled persons wrestling with the crises of their fate, then the verdict would be much more favorable. You see that the existential facts by themselves are insufficient for determining the value ; and the best adepts of the higher criticism accordingly never confound the existential with the spiritual problem. With the same conclusions of fact before them, some take one view, and some another, of the Bible's value as a revelation, according as their spiritual judgment as to the foundation of values differs.

I make these general remarks about the two sorts of judgment, because there are many religious persons — some of you now present, possibly, are among them — who do not yet make a working use of the distinction, and who may therefore feel at first a little startled at

the purely existential point of view from which in the
following lectures the phenomena of religious experience
must be considered. When I handle them biologically
and psychologically as if they were mere curious facts
of individual history, some of you may think it a degradation of so sublime a subject, and may even suspect
me, until my purpose gets more fully expressed, of deliberately seeking to discredit the religious side of life.

Such a result is of course absolutely alien to my intention; and since such a prejudice on your part would seriously obstruct the due effect of much of what I have to
relate, I will devote a few more words to the point.

There can be no doubt that as a matter of fact a religious life, exclusively pursued, does tend to make the person exceptional and eccentric. I speak not now of your
ordinary religious believer, who follows the conventional
observances of his country, whether it be Buddhist, Christian, or Mohammedan. His religion has been made for
him by others, communicated to him by tradition, determined to fixed forms by imitation, and retained by habit.
It would profit us little to study this second-hand religious life. We must make search rather for the original
experiences which were the pattern-setters to all this mass
of suggested feeling and imitated conduct. These experiences we can only find in individuals for whom religion
exists not as a dull habit, but as an acute fever rather.
But such individuals are 'geniuses' in the religious line;
and like many other geniuses who have brought forth
fruits effective enough for commemoration in the pages
of biography, such religious geniuses have often shown
symptoms of nervous instability. Even more perhaps
than other kinds of genius, religious leaders have been
subject to abnormal psychical visitations. Invariably
they have been creatures of exalted emotional sensibility.

Often they have led a discordant inner life, and had melancholy during a part of their career. They have known no measure, been liable to obsessions and fixed ideas; and frequently they have fallen into trances, heard voices, seen visions, and presented all sorts of peculiarities which are ordinarily classed as pathological. Often, moreover, these pathological features in their career have helped to give them their religious authority and influence.

If you ask for a concrete example, there can be no better one than is furnished by the person of George Fox. The Quaker religion which he founded is something which it is impossible to overpraise. In a day of shams, it was a religion of veracity rooted in spiritual inwardness, and a return to something more like the original gospel truth than men had ever known in England. So far as our Christian sects to-day are evolving into liberality, they are simply reverting in essence to the position which Fox and the early Quakers so long ago assumed. No one can pretend for a moment that in point of spiritual sagacity and capacity, Fox's mind was unsound. Every one who confronted him personally, from Oliver Cromwell down to county magistrates and jailers, seems to have acknowledged his superior power. Yet from the point of view of his nervous constitution, Fox was a psychopath or *détraqué* of the deepest dye. His Journal abounds in entries of this sort : —

" As I was walking with several friends, I lifted up my head, and saw three steeple-house spires, and they struck at my life. I asked them what place that was? They said, Lichfield. Immediately the word of the Lord came to me, that I must go thither. Being come to the house we were going to, I wished the friends to walk into the house, saying nothing to them of whither I was to go. As soon as they were gone I stept away, and went by my eye over hedge and ditch till I came within a mile of Lichfield; where, in a great field, shepherds were keeping their sheep. Then was I commanded by the Lord to pull off my shoes. I stood still, for it was winter : but the word of the Lord was like a fire in me. So I put off my shoes, and left them with the shepherds ; and the poor shepherds trembled, and were astonished. Then I walked on about a mile, and as soon as I was got within the city, the word of the Lord came to me again, saying : Cry, ' Wo to the bloody city of Lichfield ! ' So I went up and down the streets, crying with a loud voice, Wo to the bloody city of Lichfield ! It being market day, I went into the market-place, and to and fro in the several parts of it, and made stands, crying as before, Wo to the bloody city of Lichfield ! And no one laid hands on me. As I went thus crying through the streets, there seemed to me to be a channel of blood running down the streets, and the market-place appeared like a pool of blood. When I had declared what was upon me, and felt myself clear, I went out of the town in peace ; and returning to the shepherds gave them some money, and took my shoes of them again. But the fire of the Lord was so on my feet, and all over me, that I did not matter to put on my shoes again, and was at a stand whether I should or no, till I felt freedom from the Lord so to do : then, after I had washed my feet, I put on my shoes again. After this a deep consideration came upon me, for what reason I should be sent to cry against that city, and call it The bloody city ! For though the parliament had the minister one while, and the king another, and much blood had been shed in the town during the wars between them, yet there was no more than had befallen many other places. But afterwards I came to understand, that in the Emperor Diocletian's time a thousand Christians were martyr'd in Lichfield. So I was to go, without my shoes, through the channel of their blood, and into the pool of their blood in the market-place, that I might raise up the memorial of the blood of those martyrs, which had been shed above a thousand years before, and lay cold in their streets. So the sense of this blood was upon me, and I obeyed the word of the Lord."

Bent as we are on studying religion's existential conditions, we cannot possibly ignore these pathological aspects of the subject. We must describe and name them just as if they occurred in non-religious men. It is true that we instinctively recoil from seeing an object to which our emotions and affections are committed handled by the intellect as any other object is handled. The first thing the intellect does with an object is to class it along with something else. But any object that is infinitely important to us and awakens our devotion feels to us also as if it must be *sui generis* and unique. Probably a crab would be filled with a sense of personal outrage if it could hear us class it without ado or apology as a crustacean, and thus dispose of it. " I am no such thing," it would say ; " I am MYSELF, MYSELF alone."

The next thing the intellect does is to lay bare the causes in which the thing originates. Spinoza says : " I will analyze the actions and appetites of men as if it were a question of lines, of planes, and of solids." And elsewhere he remarks that he will consider our passions and their properties with the same eye with which he looks on all other natural things, since the consequences of our affections flow from their nature with the same necessity as it results from the nature of a triangle that its three angles should be equal to two right angles. Similarly M. Taine, in the introduction to his history of English literature, has written : " Whether facts be moral or physical, it makes no matter. They always have their causes. There are causes for ambition, courage, veracity, just as there are for digestion, muscular movement, animal heat. Vice and virtue are products like vitriol and sugar." When we read such proclamations of the intellect bent on showing the existential conditions of absolutely everything, we feel — quite apart from our legitimate impatience at the somewhat ridiculous swagger of the program, in view of what the authors are actually able to perform — menaced and negated in the springs of our innermost life. Such cold-blooded assimilations threaten, we think, to undo our soul's vital secrets, as if the same breath which should succeed in explaining their origin would simultaneously explain away their significance, and make them appear of no more preciousness, either, than the useful groceries of which M. Taine speaks.

Perhaps the commonest expression of this assumption that spiritual value is undone if lowly origin be asserted is seen in those comments which unsentimental people so often pass on their more sentimental acquaintances. Alfred believes in immortality so strongly because his temperament is so emotional. Fanny's extraordinary conscientiousness is merely a matter of over-instigated nerves. William's melancholy about the universe is due to bad digestion — probably his liver is torpid. Eliza's delight in her church is a symptom of her hysterical constitution. Peter would be less troubled about his soul if he would take more exercise in the open air, etc. A more fully developed example of the same kind of reasoning is the fashion, quite common nowadays among certain writers, of criticising the religious emotions by showing a connection between them and the sexual life. Conversion is a crisis of puberty and adolescence. The macerations of saints, and the devotion of missionaries, are only instances of the parental instinct of self-sacrifice gone astray. For the hysterical nun, starving for natural life, Christ is but an imaginary substitute for a more earthly object of affection. And the like.[1]

[1] As with many ideas that float in the air of one's time, this notion

We are surely all familiar in a general way with this
method of discrediting states of mind for which we have

shrinks from dogmatic general statement and expresses itself only partially
and by innuendo. It seems to me that few conceptions are less instructive
than this re-interpretation of religion as perverted sexuality. It reminds
one, so crudely is it often employed, of the famous Catholic taunt, that the
Reformation may be best understood by remembering that its *fons et origo*
was Luther's wish to marry a nun : — the effects are infinitely wider than
the alleged causes, and for the most part opposite in nature. It is true
that in the vast collection of religious phenomena, some are undisguisedly
amatory — e. g., sex-deities and obscene rites in polytheism, and ecstatic
feelings of union with the Saviour in a few Christian mystics. But then
why not equally call religion an aberration of the digestive function, and
prove one's point by the worship of Bacchus and Ceres, or by the ecstatic
feelings of some other saints about the Eucharist ? Religious language
clothes itself in such poor symbols as our life affords, and the whole organism gives overtones of comment whenever the mind is strongly stirred to
expression. Language drawn from eating and drinking is probably as common in religious literature as is language drawn from the sexual life. We
'hunger and thirst' after righteousness ; we 'find the Lord a sweet savor ;'
we 'taste and see that he is good.' 'Spiritual milk for American babes,
drawn from the breasts of both testaments,' is a sub-title of the once famous
New England Primer, and Christian devotional literature indeed quite floats
in milk, thought of from the point of view, not of the mother, but of the
greedy babe.

Saint François de Sales, for instance, thus describes the 'orison of
quietude ': "In this state the soul is like a little child still at the breast,
whose mother, to caress him whilst he is still in her arms, makes her milk
distill into his mouth without his even moving his lips. So it is here. . . .
Our Lord desires that our will should be satisfied with sucking the milk
which His Majesty pours into our mouth, and that we should relish the
sweetness without even knowing that it cometh from the Lord." And
again : "Consider the little infants, united and joined to the breasts of
their nursing mothers. you will see that from time to time they press themselves closer by little starts to which the pleasure of sucking prompts them.
Even so, during its orison, the heart united to its God oftentimes makes
attempts at closer union by movements during which it presses closer upon
the divine sweetness." Chemin de la Perfection, ch. xxxi. ; Amour de Dieu,
vii. ch. i.

In fact, one might almost as well interpret religion as a perversion of
the respiratory function. The Bible is full of the language of respiratory
oppression : "Hide not thine ear at my breathing ; my groaning is not hid
from thee ; my heart panteth, my strength faileth me ; my bones are hot
with my roaring all the night long ; as the hart panteth after the water-

an antipathy. We all use it to some degree in criticising persons whose states of mind we regard as overstrained. But when other people criticise our own more exalted soul-flights by calling them 'nothing but' expressions of our organic disposition, we feel outraged and hurt, for we know that, whatever be our organism's peculiarities, our mental states have their substantive value as revela-

brooks, so my soul panteth after thee, O my God." *God's Breath in Man* is the title of the chief work of our best known American mystic (Thomas Lake Harris) ; and in certain non-Christian countries the foundation of all religious discipline consists in regulation of the inspiration and expiration.

These arguments are as good as much of the reasoning one hears in favor of the sexual theory. But the champions of the latter will then say that their chief argument has no analogue elsewhere. The two main phenomena of religion, namely, melancholy and conversion, they will say, are essentially phenomena of adolescence, and therefore synchronous with the development of sexual life. To which the retort again is easy. Even were the asserted synchrony unrestrictedly true as a fact (which it is not), it is not only the sexual life, but the entire higher mental life which awakens during adolescence. One might then as well set up the thesis that the interest in mechanics, physics, chemistry, logic, philosophy, and sociology, which springs up during adolescent years along with that in poetry and religion, is also a perversion of the sexual instinct : — but that would be too absurd. Moreover, if the argument from synchrony is to decide, what is to be done with the fact that the religious age *par excellence* would seem to be old age, when the uproar of the sexual life is past ?

The plain truth is that to interpret religion one must in the end look at the immediate content of the religious consciousness. The moment one does this, one sees how wholly disconnected it is in the main from the content of the sexual consciousness. Everything about the two things differs, objects, moods, faculties concerned, and acts impelled to. Any *general* assimilation is simply impossible : what we find most often is complete hostility and contrast. If now the defenders of the sex-theory say that this makes no difference to their thesis ; that without the chemical contributions which the sex-organs make to the blood, the brain would not be nourished so as to carry on religious activities, this final proposition may be true or not true ; but at any rate it has become profoundly uninstructive : we can deduce no consequences from it which help us to interpret religion's meaning or value. In this sense the religious life depends just as much upon the spleen, the pancreas, and the kidneys as on the sexual apparatus, and the whole theory has lost its point in evaporating into a vague general assertion of the dependence, *somehow*, of the mind upon the body.

tions of the living truth ; and we wish that all this medical materialism could be made to hold its tongue.

Medical materialism seems indeed a good appellation for the too simple-minded system of thought which we are considering. Medical materialism finishes up Saint Paul by calling his vision on the road to Damascus a discharging lesion of the occipital cortex, he being an epileptic. It snuffs out Saint Teresa as an hysteric, Saint Francis of Assisi as an hereditary degenerate. George Fox's discontent with the shams of his age, and his pining for spiritual veracity, it treats as a symptom of a disordered colon. Carlyle's organ-tones of misery it accounts for by a gastro-duodenal catarrh. All such mental over-tensions, it says, are, when you come to the bottom of the matter, mere affairs of diathesis (auto-intoxications most probably), due to the perverted action of various glands which physiology will yet discover.

And medical materialism then thinks that the spiritual authority of all such personages is successfully undermined.[1]

Let us ourselves look at the matter in the largest possible way. Modern psychology, finding definite psycho-physical connections to hold good, assumes as a convenient hypothesis that the dependence of mental states upon bodily conditions must be thorough-going and complete. If we adopt the assumption, then of course what medical materialism insists on must be true in a general way, if not in every detail : Saint Paul certainly had once an epileptoid, if not an epileptic seizure ; George Fox was an hereditary degenerate ; Carlyle was undoubtedly auto-intoxicated by some organ or other, no matter which,

---

[1] For a first-rate example of medical-materialist reasoning, see an article on 'les Variétés du Type dévot,' by Dr. Binet-Sanglé, in the Revue de l'Hypnotisme, xiv. 161.

— and the rest. But now, I ask you, how can such an existential account of facts of mental history decide in one way or another upon their spiritual significance? According to the general postulate of psychology just referred to, there is not a single one of our states of mind, high or low, healthy or morbid, that has not some organic process as its condition. Scientific theories are organically conditioned just as much as religious emotions are; and if we only knew the facts intimately enough, we should doubtless see ' the liver' determining the dicta of the sturdy atheist as decisively as it does those of the Methodist under conviction anxious about his soul. When it alters in one way the blood that percolates it, we get the methodist, when in another way, we get the atheist form of mind. So of all our raptures and our drynesses, our longings and pantings, our questions and beliefs. They are equally organically founded, be they of religious or of non-religious content.

To plead the organic causation of a religious state of mind, then, in refutation of its claim to possess superior spiritual value, is quite illogical and arbitrary, unless one have already worked out in advance some psycho-physical theory connecting spiritual values in general with determinate sorts of physiological change. Otherwise none of our thoughts and feelings, not even our scientific doctrines, not even our *dis*-beliefs, could retain any value as revelations of the truth, for every one of them without exception flows from the state of their possessor's body at the time.

It is needless to say that medical materialism draws in point of fact no such sweeping skeptical conclusion. It is sure, just as every simple man is sure, that some states of mind are inwardly superior to others, and reveal to us more truth, and in this it simply makes use of an ordinary spiritual judgment. It has no physiological theory of the production of these its favorite states, by which it may accredit them; and its attempt to discredit the states which it dislikes, by vaguely associating them with nerves and liver, and connecting them with names connoting bodily affliction, is altogether illogical and inconsistent.

Let us play fair in this whole matter, and be quite candid with ourselves and with the facts. When we think certain states of mind superior to others, is it ever because of what we know concerning their organic antecedents? No! it is always for two entirely different reasons. It is either because we take an immediate delight in them; or else it is because we believe them to bring us good consequential fruits for life. When we speak disparagingly of 'feverish fancies,' surely the fever-process as such is not the ground of our disesteem — for aught we know to the contrary, 103° or 104° Fahrenheit might be a much more favorable temperature for truths to germinate and sprout in, than the more ordinary blood-heat of 97 or 98 degrees. It is either the disagreeableness itself of the fancies, or their inability to bear the criticisms of the convalescent hour. When we praise the thoughts which health brings, health's peculiar chemical metabolisms have nothing to do with determining our judgment. We know in fact almost nothing about these metabolisms. It is the character of inner happiness in the thoughts which stamps them as good, or else their consistency with our other opinions and their serviceability for our needs, which make them pass for true in our esteem.

Now the more intrinsic and the more remote of these criteria do not always hang together. Inner happiness and serviceability do not always agree. What immediately feels most 'good' is not always most 'true,' when measured by the verdict of the rest of experience. The difference between Philip drunk and Philip sober is the classic instance in corroboration. If merely 'feeling good' could decide, drunkenness would be the supremely valid human experience. But its revelations, however acutely satisfying at the moment, are inserted into an environment which refuses to bear them out for any length of time. The consequence of this discrepancy of the two criteria is the uncertainty which still prevails over so many of our spiritual judgments. There are moments of sentimental and mystical experience — we shall hereafter hear much of them — that carry an enormous sense of inner authority and illumination with them when they come. But they come seldom, and they do not come to every one; and the rest of life makes either no connection with them, or tends to contradict them more than it confirms them. Some persons follow more the voice of the moment in these cases, some prefer to be guided by the average results. Hence the sad discordancy of so many of the spiritual judgments of human beings ; a discordancy which will be brought home to us acutely enough before these lectures end.

It is, however, a discordancy that can never be resolved by any merely medical test. A good example of the impossibility of holding strictly to the medical tests is seen in the theory of the pathological causation of genius promulgated by recent authors. "Genius," said Dr. Moreau, "is but one of the many branches of the neuropathic tree." "Genius," says Dr. Lombroso, "is a symptom of hereditary degeneration of the epileptoid variety, and is allied to moral insanity." "Whenever a man's life," writes Mr. Nisbet, "is at once sufficiently illustrious and recorded with sufficient fullness to be a subject of profit-

able study, he inevitably falls into the morbid category.
. . . And it is worthy of remark that, as a rule, the
greater the genius, the greater the unsoundness." [1]

Now do these authors, after having succeeded in estab-
lishing to their own satisfaction that the works of genius
are fruits of disease, consistently proceed thereupon to
impugn the *value* of the fruits? Do they deduce a new
spiritual judgment from their new doctrine of existential
conditions? Do they frankly forbid us to admire the productions of genius from now onwards? and say outright
that no neuropath can ever be a revealer of new truth?

No! their immediate spiritual instincts are too strong
for them here, and hold their own against inferences
which, in mere love of logical consistency, medical materialism ought to be only too glad to draw. One disciple
of the school, indeed, has striven to impugn the value of
works of genius in a wholesale way (such works of contemporary art, namely, as he himself is unable to enjoy,
and they are many) by using medical arguments.[2] But
for the most part the masterpieces are left unchallenged;
and the medical line of attack either confines itself to
such secular productions as every one admits to be intrinsically eccentric, or else addresses itself exclusively to
religious manifestations. And then it is because the
religious manifestations have been already condemned
because the critic dislikes them on internal or spiritual
grounds.

In the natural sciences and industrial arts it never
occurs to any one to try to refute opinions by showing up their author's neurotic constitution. Opinions
here are invariably tested by logic and by experiment, no

---

[1] J. F. NISBET: The Insanity of Genius, 3d ed., London, 1893, pp. xvi,
xxiv.

[2] MAX NORDAU, in his bulky book entitled *Degeneration.*

matter what may be their author's neurological type. It should be no otherwise with religious opinions. Their value can only be ascertained by spiritual judgments directly passed upon them, judgments based on our own immediate feeling primarily; and secondarily on what we can ascertain of their experiential relations to our moral needs and to the rest of what we hold as true.

Immediate luminousness, in short, *philosophical reasonableness,* and *moral helpfulness* are the only available criteria. Saint Teresa might have had the nervous system of the placidest cow, and it would not now save her theology, if the trial of the theology by these other tests should show it to be contemptible. And conversely if her theology can stand these other tests, it will make no difference how hysterical or nervously off her balance Saint Teresa may have been when she was with us here below.

You see that at bottom we are thrown back upon the general principles by which the empirical philosophy has always contended that we must be guided in our search for truth. Dogmatic philosophies have sought for tests for truth which might dispense us from appealing to the future. Some direct mark, by noting which we can be protected immediately and absolutely, now and forever, against all mistake — such has been the darling dream of philosophic dogmatists. It is clear that the *origin* of the truth would be an admirable criterion of this sort, if only the various origins could be discriminated from one another from this point of view, and the history of dogmatic opinion shows that origin has always been a favorite test. Origin in immediate intuition; origin in pontifical authority; origin in supernatural revelation, as by vision, hearing, or unaccountable impression; origin in direct possession by a higher spirit, expressing itself in prophecy and warning; origin in automatic utterance generally, — these origins have been stock warrants for the truth of one opinion after another which we find represented in religious history. The medical materialists are therefore only so many belated dogmatists, neatly turning the tables on their predecessors by using the criterion of origin in a destructive instead of an accreditive way.

They are effective with their talk of pathological origin only so long as supernatural origin is pleaded by the other side, and nothing but the argument from origin is under discussion. But the argument from origin has seldom been used alone, for it is too obviously insufficient. Dr. Maudsley is perhaps the cleverest of the rebutters of supernatural religion on grounds of origin. Yet he finds himself forced to write : —

" What right have we to believe Nature under any obligation to do her work by means of complete minds only ? She may find an incomplete mind a more suitable instrument for a particular purpose. It is the work that is done, and the quality in the worker by which it was done, that is alone of moment ; and it may be no great matter from a cosmical standpoint, if in other qualities of character he was singularly defective — if indeed he were hypocrite, adulterer, eccentric, or lunatic. . . . Home we come again, then, to the old and last resort of certitude, — namely the common assent of mankind, or of the competent by instruction and training among mankind." [1]

In other words, not its origin, but *the way in which it works on the whole*, is Dr. Maudsley's final test of a belief. This is our own empiricist criterion ; and this cri-

[1] H. MAUDSLEY : Natural Causes and Supernatural Seemings, 1886, pp. 257, 256.

terion the stoutest insisters on supernatural origin have also been forced to use in the end. Among the visions and messages some have always been too patently silly, among the trances and convulsive seizures some have been too fruitless for conduct and character, to pass themselves off as significant, still less as divine. In the history of Christian mysticism the problem how to discriminate between such messages and experiences as were really divine miracles, and such others as the demon in his malice was able to counterfeit, thus making the religious person twofold more the child of hell he was before, has always been a difficult one to solve, needing all the sagacity and experience of the best directors of conscience. In the end it had to come to our empiricist criterion : By their fruits ye shall know them, not by their roots. Jonathan Edwards's Treatise on Religious Affections is an elaborate working out of this thesis. The *roots* of a man's virtue are inaccessible to us. No appearances whatever are infallible proofs of grace. Our practice is the only sure evidence, even to ourselves, that we are genuinely Christians.

" In forming a judgment of ourselves now," Edwards writes, " we should certainly adopt that evidence which our supreme Judge will chiefly make use of when we come to stand before him at the last day. . . . There is not one grace of the Spirit of God, of the existence of which, in any professor of religion, Christian practice is not the most decisive evidence. . . . The degree in which our experience is productive of practice shows the degree in which our experience is spiritual and divine."

Catholic writers are equally emphatic. The good dispositions which a vision, or voice, or other apparent heavenly favor leave behind them are the only marks by which we may be sure they are not possible deceptions of the tempter. Says Saint Teresa : —

" Like imperfect sleep which, instead of giving more strength to the head, doth but leave it the more exhausted, the result of mere operations of the imagination is but to weaken the soul. Instead of nourishment and energy she reaps only lassitude and disgust : whereas a genuine heavenly vision yields to her a harvest of ineffable spiritual riches, and an admirable renewal of bodily strength. I alleged these reasons to those who so often accused my visions of being the work of the enemy of mankind and the sport of my imagination. . . . I showed them the jewels which the divine hand had left with me : — they were my actual dispositions. All those who knew me saw that I was changed ; my confessor bore witness to the fact ; this improvement, palpable in all respects, far from being hidden, was brilliantly evident to all men. As for myself, it was impossible to believe that if the demon were its author, he could have used, in order to lose me and lead me to hell, an expedient so contrary to his own interests as that of uprooting my vices, and filling me with masculine courage and other virtues instead, for I saw clearly that a single one of these visions was enough to enrich me with all that wealth." [1]

I fear I may have made a longer excursus than was necessary, and that fewer words would have dispelled the uneasiness which may have arisen among some of you as I announced my pathological programme. At any rate you must all be ready now to judge the religious life by its results exclusively, and I shall assume that the bugaboo of morbid origin will scandalize your piety no more.

Still, you may ask me, if its results are to be the ground of our final spiritual estimate of a religious phenomenon, why threaten us at all with so much existential study of its conditions ? Why not simply leave pathological questions out ?

To this I reply in two ways : First, I say, irrepressible curiosity imperiously leads one on ; and I say, secondly,

[1] Autobiography, ch. xxviii.

that it always leads to a better understanding of a thing's significance to consider its exaggerations and perversions, its equivalents and substitutes and nearest relatives elsewhere. Not that we may thereby swamp the thing in the wholesale condemnation which we pass on its inferior congeners, but rather that we may by contrast ascertain the more precisely in what its merits consist, by learning at the same time to what particular dangers of corruption it may also be exposed.

Insane conditions have this advantage, that they isolate special factors of the mental life, and enable us to inspect them unmasked by their more usual surroundings. They play the part in mental anatomy which the scalpel and the microscope play in the anatomy of the body. To understand a thing rightly we need to see it both out of its environment and in it, and to have acquaintance with the whole range of its variations. The study of hallucinations has in this way been for psychologists the key to their comprehension of normal sensation, that of illusions has been the key to the right comprehension of perception. Morbid impulses and imperative conceptions, 'fixed ideas,' so called, have thrown a flood of light on the psychology of the normal will; and obsessions and delusions have performed the same service for that of the normal faculty of belief.

Similarly, the nature of genius has been illuminated by the attempts, of which I already made mention, to class it with psychopathical phenomena. Borderland insanity, crankiness, insane temperament, loss of mental balance, psychopathic degeneration (to use a few of the many synonyms by which it has been called), has certain peculiarities and liabilities which, when combined with a superior quality of intellect in an individual, make it more probable that he will make his mark and affect his age, than if his temperament were less neurotic. There is of course no special affinity between crankiness as such and superior intellect,[1] for most psychopaths have feeble intellects, and superior intellects more commonly . have normal nervous systems. But the psychopathic temperament, whatever be the intellect with which it finds itself paired, often brings with it ardor and excitability of character. The cranky person has extraordinary emotional susceptibility. He is liable to fixed ideas and obsessions. His conceptions tend to pass immediately into belief and action ; and when he gets a new idea, he has no rest till he proclaims it, or in some way ' works it off.' "What shall I think of it?" a common person says to himself about a vexed question ; but in a ' cranky ' mind " What must I do about it?" is the form the question tends to take. In the autobiography of that high-souled woman, Mrs. Annie Besant, I read the following passage : " Plenty of people wish well to any good cause, but very few care to exert themselves to help it, and still fewer will risk anything in its support. 'Some one ought to do it, but why should I?' is the ever reëchoed phrase of weak-kneed amiability. 'Some one ought to do it, so why not I?' is the cry of some earnest servant of man, eagerly forward springing to face some perilous duty. Between these two sentences lie whole centuries of moral evolution." True enough! and between these two sentences lie also the different destinies of the ordinary sluggard and the psychopathic man. Thus, when a superior intellect and a psychopathic temperament coalesce — as in the endless permutations and combinations of human faculty, they are bound to coalesce often enough — in the same individual, we have

[1] Superior intellect, as Professor Bain has admirably shown, seems to consist in nothing so much as in a large development of the faculty of association by similarity.

the best possible condition for the kind of effective genius that gets into the biographical dictionaries. Such men do not remain mere critics and understanders with their intellect. Their ideas possess them, they inflict them, for better or worse, upon their companions or their age. It is they who get counted when Messrs Lombroso, Nisbet, and others invoke statistics to defend their paradox.

To pass now to religious phenomena, take the melancholy which, as we shall see, constitutes an essential moment in every complete religious evolution. Take the happiness which achieved religious belief confers. Take the trance-like states of insight into truth which all religious mystics report.[1] These are each and all of them special cases of kinds of human experience of much wider scope. Religious melancholy, whatever peculiarities it may have _quâ_ religious, is at any rate melancholy. Religious happiness is happiness. Religious trance is trance. And the moment we renounce the absurd notion that a thing is exploded away as soon as it is classed with others, or its origin is shown; the moment we agree to stand by experimental results and inner quality, in judging of values, — who does not see that we are likely to ascertain the distinctive significance of religious melancholy and happiness, or of religious trances, far better by comparing them as conscientiously as we can with other varieties of melancholy, happiness, and trance, than by refusing to consider their place in any more general series, and treating them as if they were outside of nature's order altogether?

I hope that the course of these lectures will confirm us in this supposition. As regards the psychopathic origin of so many religious phenomena, that would not be

[1] I may refer to a criticism of the insanity theory of genius in the Psychological Review, ii. 287 (1895).

in the least surprising or disconcerting, even were such phenomena certified from on high to be the most precious of human experiences. No one organism can possibly 'yield to its owner the whole body of truth. Few of us are not in some way infirm, or even diseased; and our very infirmities help us unexpectedly. In the psychopathic temperament we have the emotionality which is the *sine quâ non* of moral perception; we have the intensity and tendency to emphasis which are the essence of practical moral vigor; and we have the love of metaphysics and mysticism which carry one's interests beyond the surface of the sensible world. What, then, is more natural than that this temperament should introduce one to regions of religious truth, to corners of the universe, which your robust Philistine type of nervous system, forever offering its biceps to be felt, thumping its breast, and thanking Heaven that it has n't a single morbid fibre in its composition, would be sure to hide forever from its self-satisfied possessors?

If there were such a thing as inspiration from a higher realm, it might well be that the neurotic temperament would furnish the chief condition of the requisite receptivity. And having said thus much, I think that I may let the matter of religion and neuroticism drop.

The mass of collateral phenomena, morbid or healthy, with which the various religious phenomena must be compared in order to understand them better, forms what in the slang of pedagogics is termed 'the apperceiving mass' by which we comprehend them. The only novelty that I can imagine this course of lectures to possess lies in the breadth of the apperceiving mass. I may succeed in discussing religious experiences in a wider context than has been usual in university courses.

LECTURE II

CIRCUMSCRIPTION OF THE TOPIC

MOST books on the philosophy of religion try to begin with a precise definition of what its essence consists of. Some of these would-be definitions may possibly come before us in later portions of this course, and I shall not be pedantic enough to enumerate any of them to you now. Meanwhile the very fact that they are so many and so different from one another is enough to prove that the word 'religion' cannot stand for any single principle or essence, but is rather a collective name. The theorizing mind tends always to the over-simplification of its materials. This is the root of all that absolutism and one-sided dogmatism by which both philosophy and religion have been infested. Let us not fall immediately into a one-sided view of our subject, but let us rather admit freely at the outset that we may very likely find no one essence, but many characters which may alternately be equally important in religion. If we should inquire for the essence of 'government,' for example, one man might tell us it was authority, another submission, another police, another an army, another an assembly, another a system of laws; yet all the while it would be true that no concrete government can exist without all these things, one of which is more important at one moment and others at another. The man who knows governments most completely is he who troubles himself least about a definition which shall give their essence. Enjoying an intimate acquaintance with all their particularities in turn, he would naturally regard an abstract conception in which these were unified as a thing more misleading than enlightening. And why may not religion be a conception equally complex ? [1]

Consider also the ' religious sentiment ' which we see referred to in so many books, as if it were a single sort of mental entity.

In the psychologies and in the philosophies of religion, we find the authors attempting to specify just what entity it is. One man allies it to the feeling of dependence ; one makes it a derivative from fear ; others connect it with the sexual life ; others still identify it with the feeling of the infinite ; and so on. Such different ways of conceiving it ought of themselves to arouse doubt as to whether it possibly can be one specific thing ; and the moment we are willing to treat the term ' religious sentiment ' as a collective name for the many sentiments which religious objects may arouse in alternation, we see that it probably contains nothing whatever of a psychologically specific nature. There is religious fear, religious love, religious awe, religious joy, and so forth. But religious love is only man's natural emotion of love directed to a religious object ; religious fear is only the ordinary fear of commerce, so to speak, the common quaking of the human breast, in so far as the notion of divine retribution may arouse it ; religious awe is the same organic thrill which we feel in a forest at twilight, or in a mountain gorge ; only this time it comes over us at the thought of our supernatural relations ; and similarly of all the various sentiments which may be called into play in the lives of

---

[1] I can do no better here than refer my readers to the extended and admirable remarks on the futility of all these definitions of religion, in an article by Professor Leuba, published in the Monist for January, 1901, after my own text was written.

religious persons.   As concrete states of mind, made up
of a feeling *plus* a specific sort of object, religious emotions of course are psychic entities distinguishable from
other concrete emotions; but there is no ground for
assuming a simple abstract 'religious emotion' to exist
as a distinct elementary mental affection by itself, present
in every religious experience without exception.

As there thus seems to be no one elementary religious
emotion, but only a common storehouse of emotions upon
which religious objects may draw, so there might conceivably also prove to be no one specific and essential
kind of religious object, and no one specific and essential
kind of religious act.

The field of religion being as wide as this, it is manifestly impossible that I should pretend to cover it.   My
lectures must be limited to a fraction of the subject.
And, although it would indeed be foolish to set up an
abstract definition of religion's essence, and then proceed
to defend that definition against all comers, yet this need
not prevent me from taking my own narrow view of what
religion shall consist in *for the purpose of these lectures,*
or, out of the many meanings of the word, from choosing the one meaning in which I wish to interest you particularly, and proclaiming arbitrarily that when I say
'religion' I mean *that*.   This, in fact, is what I must do,
and I will now preliminarily seek to mark out the field I
choose.

One way to mark it out easily is to say what aspects
of the subject we leave out.   At the outset we are struck
by one great partition which divides the religious field.
On the one side of it lies institutional, on the other personal religion.   As M. P. Sabatier says, one branch of
religion keeps the divinity, another keeps man most in

view. Worship and sacrifice, procedures for working on
the dispositions of the deity, theology and ceremony and
ecclesiastical organization, are the essentials of religion
in the institutional branch. Were we to limit our view
to it, we should have to define religion as an external
art, the art of winning the favor of the gods. In the
more personal branch of religion it is on the contrary the
inner dispositions of man himself which form the centre
of interest, his conscience, his deserts, his helplessness,
his incompleteness. And although the favor of the God,
as forfeited or gained, is still an essential feature of the
story, and theology plays a vital part therein, yet the acts
to which this sort of religion prompts are personal not
ritual acts, the individual transacts the business by himself alone, and the ecclesiastical organization, with its
priests and sacraments and other go-betweens, sinks to
an altogether secondary place. The relation goes direct
from heart to heart, from soul to soul, between man and
his maker.

Now in these lectures I propose to ignore the institutional branch entirely, to say nothing of the ecclesiastical
organization, to consider as little as possible the systematic theology and the ideas about the gods themselves,
and to confine myself as far as I can to personal religion
pure and simple. To some of you personal religion,
thus nakedly considered, will no doubt seem too incomplete a thing to wear the general name. "It is a part
of religion," you will say, "but only its unorganized
rudiment; if we are to name it by itself, we had better
call it man's conscience or morality than his religion.
The name 'religion' should be reserved for the fully
organized system of feeling, thought, and institution,
for the Church, in short, of which this personal religion,
so called, is but a fractional element."

But if you say this, it will only show the more plainly how much the question of definition tends to become a dispute about names. Rather than prolong such a dispute, I am willing to accept almost any name for the personal religion of which I propose to treat. Call it conscience or morality, if you yourselves prefer, and not religion — under either name it will be equally worthy of our study. As for myself, I think it will prove to contain some elements which morality pure and simple does not contain, and these elements I shall soon seek to point out; so I will myself continue to apply the word 'religion' to it; and in the last lecture of all, I will bring in the theologies and the ecclesiasticisms, and say something of its relation to them.

In one sense at least the personal religion will prove itself more fundamental than either theology or ecclesiasticism. Churches, when once established, live at secondhand upon tradition; but the *founders* of every church owed their power originally to the fact of their direct personal communion with the divine. Not only the superhuman founders, the Christ, the Buddha, Mahomet, but all the originators of Christian sects have been in this case; — so personal religion should still seem the primordial thing, even to those who continue to esteem it incomplete.

There are, it is true, other things in religion chronologically more primordial than personal devoutness in the moral sense. Fetishism and magic seem to have preceded inward piety historically — at least our records of inward piety do not reach back so far. And if fetishism and magic be regarded as stages of religion, one may say that personal religion in the inward sense and the genuinely spiritual ecclesiasticisms which it founds are phenomena of secondary or even tertiary order. But, quite apart from the fact that many anthropologists — for instance, Jevons and Frazer — expressly oppose 'religion' and 'magic' to each other, it is certain that the whole system of thought which leads to magic, fetishism, and the lower superstitions may just as well be called primitive science as called primitive religion. The question thus becomes a verbal one again; and our knowledge of all these early stages of thought and feeling is in any case so conjectural and imperfect that farther discussion would not be worth while.

Religion, therefore, as I now ask you arbitrarily to take it, shall mean for us *the feelings, acts, and experiences of individual men in their solitude, so far as they apprehend themselves to stand in relation to whatever they may consider the divine.* Since the relation may be either moral, physical, or ritual, it is evident that out of religion in the sense in which we take it, theologies, philosophies, and ecclesiastical organizations may secondarily grow. In these lectures, however, as I have already said, the immediate personal experiences will amply fill our time, and we shall hardly consider theology or ecclesiasticism at all.

We escape much controversial matter by this arbitrary definition of our field. But, still, a chance of controversy comes up over the word 'divine,' if we take it in the definition in too narrow a sense. There are systems of thought which the world usually calls religious, and yet which do not positively assume a God. Buddhism is in this case. Popularly, of course, the Buddha himself stands in place of a God; but in strictness the Buddhistic system is atheistic. Modern transcendental idealism, Emersonianism, for instance, also seems to let God evaporate into abstract Ideality. Not a deity *in concreto*, not a superhuman person, but the immanent divinity in things, the essentially spiritual structure of the universe, is the object of the transcendentalist cult. In that address to the graduating class at Divinity College in 1838 which made Emerson famous, the frank expression of this worship of mere abstract laws was what made the scandal of the performance.

" These laws," said the speaker, " execute themselves. They are out of time, out of space, and not subject to circumstance : Thus, in the soul of man there is a justice whose retributions are instant and entire. He who does a good deed is instantly ennobled. He who does a mean deed is by the action itself contracted. He who puts off impurity thereby puts on purity. If a man is at heart just, then in so far is he God; the safety of God, the immortality of God, the majesty of God, do enter into that man with justice. If a man dissemble, deceive, he deceives himself, and goes out of acquaintance with his own being. Character is always known. Thefts never enrich; alms never impoverish; murder will speak out of stone walls. The least admixture of a lie — for example, the taint of vanity, any attempt to make a good impression, a favorable appearance — will instantly vitiate the effect. But speak the truth, and all things alive or brute are vouchers, and the very roots of the grass underground there do seem to stir and move to bear your witness. For all things proceed out of the same spirit, which is differently named love, justice, temperance, in its different applications, just as the ocean receives different names on the several shores which it washes. In so far as he roves from these ends, a man bereaves himself of power, of auxiliaries. His being shrinks . . . he becomes less and less, a mote, a point, until absolute badness is absolute death. The perception of this law awakens in the mind a sentiment which we call the religious sentiment, and which makes our highest happiness. Wonderful is its power to charm and to command. It is a mountain air. It is the embalmer of the world. It makes the sky and the hills sublime, and the silent song of the stars is it. It is the beatitude of man. It makes him illimitable. When he says ' I ought '; when love warns him ; when he chooses, warned from on high, the good and great deed; then, deep melodies wander through his soul from supreme wisdom. Then he can worship, and be enlarged by his worship; for he can never go behind this sentiment. All the expressions of this sentiment are sacred and permanent in proportion to their purity. [They] affect us more than all other compositions. The sentences of the olden time, which ejaculate this piety, are still fresh and fragrant. And the unique impression of Jesus upon mankind, whose name is not so much written as ploughed into the history of this world, is proof of the subtle virtue of this infusion." [1]

Such is the Emersonian religion. The universe has a divine soul of order, which soul is moral, being also the soul within the soul of man. But whether this soul of the universe be a mere quality like the eye's brilliancy or the skin's softness, or whether it be a self-conscious life like the eye's seeing or the skin's feeling, is a decision that never unmistakably appears in Emerson's pages. It quivers on the boundary of these things, sometimes leaning one way, sometimes the other, to suit the literary rather than the philosophic need. Whatever it is, though, it is active. As much as if it were a God, we can trust it to protect all ideal interests and keep the world's balance straight. The sentences in which Emerson, to the very end, gave utterance to this faith are as fine as anything in literature : "If you love and serve men, you cannot by any hiding or stratagem escape the remuneration. Secret retributions are always restoring the level, when disturbed, of the divine justice. It is impossible to tilt the beam. All the tyrants and proprietors and monopolists of the world in vain set their shoulders to heave the bar. Settles forevermore the ponderous equator to its line, and man and mote, and star and sun, must range to it, or be pulverized by the recoil." [2]

[1] Miscellanies, 1868, p. 120 (abridged).
[2] Lectures and Biographical Sketches, 1868, p. 186.

Now it would be too absurd to say that the inner experiences that underlie such expressions of faith as this and impel the writer to their utterance are quite unworthy to be called religious experiences. The sort of appeal that Emersonian optimism, on the one hand, and Buddhistic pessimism, on the other, make to the individual and the sort of response which he makes to them in his life are in fact indistinguishable from, and in many respects identical with, the best Christian appeal and response. We must therefore, from the experiential point of view, call these godless or quasi-godless creeds ' religions ' ; and accordingly when in our definition of religion we speak of the individual's relation to ' what he considers the divine,' we must interpret the term ' divine ' very broadly, as denoting any object that is god*like*, whether it be a concrete deity or not.

But the term ' godlike,' if thus treated as a floating general quality, becomes exceedingly vague, for many gods have flourished in religious history, and their attributes have been discrepant enough. What then is that essentially godlike quality — be it embodied in a concrete deity or not — our relation to which determines our character as religious men ? It will repay us to seek some answer to this question before we proceed farther.

For one thing, gods are conceived to be first things in the way of being and power. They overarch and envelop, and from them there is no escape. What relates to them is the first and last word in the way of truth. Whatever then were most primal and enveloping and deeply true might at this rate be treated as godlike, and a man's religion might thus be identified with his attitude, whatever it might be, towards what he felt to be the primal truth.

Such a definition as this would in a way be defensible. Religion, whatever it is, is a man's total reaction upon life, so why not say that any total reaction upon life is a religion? Total reactions are different from casual reactions, and total attitudes are different from usual or professional attitudes. To get at them you must go behind the foreground of existence and reach down to that curious sense of the whole residual cosmos as an everlasting presence, intimate or alien, terrible or amusing, lovable or odious, which in some degree every one possesses. This sense of the world's presence, appealing as it does to our peculiar individual temperament, makes us either strenuous or careless, devout or blasphemous, gloomy or exultant, about life at large; and our reaction, involuntary and inarticulate and often half unconscious as it is, is the completest of all our answers to the question, "What is the character of this universe in which we dwell?" It expresses our individual sense of it in the most definite way. Why then not call these reactions our religion, no matter what specific character they may have? Non-religious as some of these reactions may be, in one sense of the word 'religious,' they yet belong to *the general sphere of the religious life,* and so should generically be classed as religious reactions. "He believes in No-God, and he worships him," said a colleague of mine of a student who was manifesting a fine atheistic ardor; and the more fervent opponents of Christian doctrine have often enough shown a temper which, psychologically considered, is indistinguishable from religious zeal.

But so very broad a use of the word 'religion' would be inconvenient, however defensible it might remain on logical grounds. There are trifling, sneering attitudes even towards the whole of life; and in some men these attitudes are final and systematic. It would strain the ordinary use of language too much to call such attitudes religious, even though, from the point of view of an unbiased critical philosophy, they might conceivably be perfectly reasonable ways of looking upon life. Voltaire, for example, writes thus to a friend, at the age of seventy-three : " As for myself," he says, "weak as I am, I carry on the war to the last moment, I get a hundred pike-thrusts, I return two hundred, and I laugh. I see near my door Geneva on fire with quarrels over nothing, and I laugh again ; and, thank God, I can look upon the world as a farce even when it becomes as tragic as it sometimes does. All comes out even at the end of the day, and all comes out still more even when all the days are over."

Much as we may admire such a robust old gamecock spirit in a valetudinarian, to call it a religious spirit would be odd. Yet it is for the moment Voltaire's reaction on the whole of life. *Je m'en fiche* is the vulgar French equivalent for our English ejaculation ' Who cares ? ' And the happy term *je m'en fichisme* recently has been invented to designate the systematic determination not to take anything in life too solemnly. ' All is vanity ' is the relieving word in all difficult crises for this mode of thought, which that exquisite literary genius Renan took pleasure, in his later days of sweet decay, in putting into coquettishly sacrilegious forms which remain to us as excellent expressions of the ' all is vanity ' state of mind. Take the following passage, for example, — we must hold to duty, even against the evidence, Renan says, — but he then goes on : —

" There are many chances that the world may be nothing but a fairy pantomime of which no God has care. We must therefore arrange ourselves so that on neither hypothesis we shall be completely wrong. We must listen to the superior voices, but in such a way that if the second hypothesis were true we should not have been too completely duped. If in effect the world be not a serious thing, it is the dogmatic people who will be the shallow ones, and the worldly minded whom the theologians now call frivolous will be those who are really wise.

"*In utrumque paratus*, then. Be ready for anything — that perhaps is wisdom. Give ourselves up, according to the hour, to confidence, to skepticism, to optimism, to irony, and we may be sure that at certain moments at least we shall be with the truth. . . . Good-humor is a philosophic state of mind; it seems to say to Nature that we take her no more seriously than she takes us. I maintain that one should always talk of philosophy with a smile. We owe it to the Eternal to be virtuous; but we have the right to add to this tribute our irony as a sort of personal reprisal. In this way we return to the right quarter jest for jest; we play the trick that has been played on us. Saint Augustine's phrase: *Lord, if we are deceived, it is by thee!* remains a fine one, well suited to our modern feeling. Only we wish the Eternal to know that if we accept the fraud, we accept it knowingly and willingly. We are resigned in advance to losing the interest on our investments of virtue, but we wish not to appear ridiculous by having counted on them too securely." [1]

Surely all the usual associations of the word 'religion' would have to be stripped away if such a systematic *parti pris* of irony were also to be denoted by the name. For common men 'religion,' whatever more special meanings it may have, signifies always a *serious* state of mind. If any one phrase could gather its universal message, that phrase would be, 'All is *not* vanity in this Universe, whatever the appearances may suggest.' If it can stop anything, religion as commonly apprehended can stop just such chaffing talk as Renan's. It favors gravity, not pertness; it says 'hush' to all vain chatter and smart wit.

[1] Feuilles détachées, pp. 394–398 (abridged).

But if hostile to light irony, religion is equally hostile to heavy grumbling and complaint. The world appears tragic enough in some religions, but the tragedy is realized as purging, and a way of deliverance is held to exist. We shall see enough of the religious melancholy in a future lecture; but melancholy, according to our ordinary use of language, forfeits all title to be called religious when, in Marcus Aurelius's racy words, the sufferer simply lies kicking and screaming after the fashion of a sacrificed pig. The mood of a Schopenhauer or a Nietzsche, — and in a less degree one may sometimes say the same of our own sad Carlyle, — though often an ennobling sadness, is almost as often only peevishness running away with the bit between its teeth. The sallies of the two German authors remind one, half the time, of the sick shriekings of two dying rats. They lack the purgatorial note which religious sadness gives forth.

There must be something solemn, serious, and tender about any attitude which we denominate religious. If glad, it must not grin or snicker; if sad, it must not scream or curse. It is precisely as being *solemn* experiences that I wish to interest you in religious experiences. So I propose — arbitrarily again, if you please — to narrow our definition once more by saying that the word ' divine,' as employed therein, shall mean for us not merely the primal and enveloping and real, for that meaning if taken without restriction might well prove too broad. The divine shall mean for us only such a primal reality as the individual feels impelled to respond to solemnly and gravely, and neither by a curse nor a jest.

But solemnity, and gravity, and all such emotional attributes, admit of various shades; and, do what we will with our defining, the truth must at last be confronted

that we are dealing with a field of experience where there
is not a single conception that can be sharply drawn.
The pretension, under such conditions, to be rigorously
'scientific' or 'exact' in our terms would only stamp
us as lacking in understanding of our task.   Things are
more or less divine, states of mind are more or less religious, reactions are more or less total, but the boundaries are always misty, and it is everywhere a question
of amount and degree.   Nevertheless, at their extreme of
development, there can never be any question as to what
experiences are religious.   The divinity of the object
and the solemnity of the reaction are too well marked
for doubt.   Hesitation as to whether a state of mind is
'religious,' or 'irreligious,' or 'moral,' or 'philosophical,' is only likely to arise when the state of mind is
weakly characterized, but in that case it will be hardly
worthy of our study at all.   With states that can only
by courtesy be called religious we need have nothing to
do, our only profitable business being with what nobody
can possibly feel tempted to call anything else.   I said
in my former lecture that we learn most about a thing
when we view it under a microscope, as it were, or in its
most exaggerated form.   This is as true of religious
phenomena as of any other kind of fact.   The only cases
likely to be profitable enough to repay our attention will
therefore be cases where the religious spirit is unmistakable and extreme.   Its fainter manifestations we may
tranquilly pass by.   Here, for example, is the total reaction upon life of Frederick Locker Lampson, whose autobiography, entitled 'Confidences,' proves him to have
been a most amiable man.

"I am so far resigned to my lot that I feel small pain at the
thought of having to part from what has been called the pleasant habit of existence, the sweet fable of life.   I would not

care to live my wasted life over again, and so to prolong my span. Strange to say, I have but little wish to be younger. I submit with a chill at my heart. I humbly submit because it is the Divine Will, and my appointed destiny. I dread the increase of infirmities that will make me a burden to those around me, those dear to me. No! let me slip away as quietly and comfortably as I can. Let the end come, if peace come with it.

"I do not know that there is a great deal to be said for this world, or our sojourn here upon it; but it has pleased God so to place us, and it must please me also. I ask you, what is human life? Is not it a maimed happiness — care and weariness, weariness and care, with the baseless expectation, the strange cozenage of a brighter to-morrow? At best it is but a froward child, that must be played with and humored, to keep it quiet till it falls asleep, and then the care is over." [1]

This is a complex, a tender, a submissive, and a graceful state of mind. For myself, I should have no objection to calling it on the whole a religious state of mind, although I dare say that to many of you it may seem too listless and half-hearted to merit so good a name. But what matters it in the end whether we call such a state of mind religious or not? It is too insignificant for our instruction in any case; and its very possessor wrote it down in terms which he would not have used unless he had been thinking of more energetically religious moods in others, with which he found himself unable to compete. It is with these more energetic states that our sole business lies, and we can perfectly well afford to let the minor notes and the uncertain border go.

It was the extremer cases that I had in mind a little while ago when I said that personal religion, even without theology or ritual, would prove to embody some elements that morality pure and simple does not contain. You may remember that I promised shortly to point out

[1] Op. cit., pp. 314, 313.

what those elements were. In a general way I can now say what I had in mind.

" I accept the universe " is reported to have been a favorite utterance of our New England transcendentalist, Margaret Fuller; and when some one repeated this phrase to Thomas Carlyle, his sardonic comment is said to have been : " Gad ! she 'd better ! " At bottom the whole concern of both morality and religion is with the manner of our acceptance of the universe. Do we accept it only in part and grudgingly, or heartily and altogether? Shall our protests against certain things in it be radical and unforgiving, or shall we think that, even with evil, there are ways of living that must lead to good? If we accept the whole, shall we do so as if stunned into submission, — as Carlyle would have us — " Gad ! we 'd better ! " — or shall we do so with enthusiastic assent? Morality pure and simple accepts the law of the whole which it finds reigning, so far as to acknowledge and obey it, but it may obey it with the heaviest and coldest heart, and never cease to feel it as a yoke. But for religion, in its strong and fully developed manifestations, the service of the highest never is felt as a yoke. Dull submission is left far behind, and a mood of welcome, which may fill any place on the scale between cheerful serenity and enthusiastic gladness, has taken its place.

It makes a tremendous emotional and practical difference to one whether one accept the universe in the drab discolored way of stoic resignation to necessity, or with the passionate happiness of Christian saints. The difference is as great as that between passivity and activity, as that between the defensive and the aggressive mood. Gradual as are the steps by which an individual may grow from one state into the other, many as are the intermediate stages which different individuals represent, yet when you place the typical extremes beside each other for comparison, you feel that two discontinuous psychological universes confront you, and that in passing from one to the other a 'critical point' has been overcome.

If we compare stoic with Christian ejaculations we see much more than a difference of doctrine; rather is it a difference of emotional mood that parts them. When Marcus Aurelius reflects on the eternal reason that has ordered things, there is a frosty chill about his words which you rarely find in a Jewish, and never in a Christian piece of religious writing. The universe is 'accepted' by all these writers; but how devoid of passion or exultation the spirit of the Roman Emperor is! Compare his fine sentence: "If gods care not for me or my children, here is a reason for it," with Job's cry: "Though he slay me, yet will I trust in him!" and you immediately see the difference I mean. The *anima mundi*, to whose disposal of his own personal destiny the Stoic consents, is there to be respected and submitted to, but the Christian God is there to be loved; and the difference of emotional atmosphere is like that between an arctic climate and the tropics, though the outcome in the way of accepting actual conditions uncomplainingly may seem in abstract terms to be much the same.

"It is a man's duty," says Marcus Aurelius, "to comfort himself and wait for the natural dissolution, and not to be vexed, but to find refreshment solely in these thoughts — first that nothing will happen to me which is not conformable to the nature of the universe; and secondly that I need do nothing contrary to the God and deity within me; for there is no man who can compel me to transgress.[1] He is an abscess on the

----
[1] Book V. ch x. (abridged).

universe who withdraws and separates himself from the reason
of our common nature, through being displeased with the things
which happen.   For the same nature produces these, and has
produced thee too.   And so accept everything which happens,
even if it seem disagreeable, because it leads to this, the health
of the universe and to the prosperity and felicity of Zeus.   For
he would not have brought on any man what he has brought,
if it were not useful for the whole.   The integrity of the whole
is mutilated if thou cuttest off anything.   And thou dost cut
off, as far as it is in thy power, when thou art dissatisfied, and
in a manner triest to put anything out of the way." [1]

Compare now this mood with that of the old Christian
author of the Theologia Germanica : —

" Where men are enlightened witk the true light, they renounce all desire and choice, and commit and commend themselves and all things to the eternal Goodness, so that every
enlightened man could say : ' I would fain be to the Eternal
Goodness what his own hand is to a man.'   Such men are in
a state of freedom, because they have lost the fear of pain or
hell, and the hope of reward or heaven, and are living in pure
submission to the eternal Goodness, in the perfect freedom of
fervent love.   When a man truly perceiveth and considereth
himself, who and what he is, and findeth himself utterly vile
and wicked and unworthy, he falleth into such a deep abase-
ment that it seemeth to him reasonable that all creatures in
heaven and earth should rise up against him.   And therefore
he will not and dare not desire any consolation and release ;
but he is willing to be unconsoled and unreleased ; and he doth
not grieve over his sufferings, for they are right in his eyes, and
he hath nothing to say against them.   This is what is meant
by true repentance for sin ; and he who in this present time
entereth into this hell, none may console him.   Now God hath
not forsaken a man in this hell, but He is laying his hand upon
him, that the man may not desire nor regard anything but the
eternal Good only.   And then, when the man neither careth
for nor desireth anything but the eternal Good alone, and seek-

[1] Book V., ch. ix. (abridged).

eth not himself nor his own things, but the honour of God only, he is made a partaker of all manner of joy, bliss, peace, rest, and consolation, and so the man is henceforth in the kingdom of heaven. This hell and this heaven are two good safe ways for a man, and happy is he who truly findeth them." [1]

How much more active and positive the impulse of the Christian writer to accept his place in the universe is! Marcus Aurelius agrees *to* the scheme — the German theologian agrees *with* it. He literally *abounds* in agreement, he runs out to embrace the divine decrees.

Occasionally, it is true, the Stoic rises to something like a Christian warmth of sentiment, as in the often quoted passage of Marcus Aurelius : —

"Everything harmonizes with me which is harmonious to thee, O Universe. Nothing for me is too early nor too late, which is in due time for thee. Everything is fruit to me which thy seasons bring, O Nature : from thee are all things, in thee are all things, to thee all things return. The poet says, Dear City of Cecrops ; and wilt thou not say, Dear City of Zeus ? " [2]

But compare even as devout a passage as this with a genuine Christian outpouring, and it seems a little cold. Turn, for instance, to the Imitation of Christ : —

"Lord, thou knowest what is best; let this or that be according as thou wilt. Give what thou wilt, so much as thou wilt, when thou wilt. Do with me as thou knowest best, and as shall be most to thine honour. Place me where thou wilt, and freely work thy will with me in all things. . . . When could it be evil when thou wert near ? I had rather be poor for thy sake than rich without thee. I choose rather to be a pilgrim upon the earth with thee, than without thee to possess heaven. Where thou art, there is heaven ; and where thou art not, behold there death and hell." [3]

[1] Chaps. x., xi. (abridged): Winkworth's translation.
[2] Book IV., § 23.
[3] Benham's translation : Book III., chaps. xv., lix. Compare Mary Moody Emerson: " Let me be a blot on this fair world, the obscurest, the

It is a good rule in physiology, when we are studying the meaning of an organ, to ask after its most peculiar and characteristic sort of performance, and to seek its office in that one of its functions which no other organ can possibly exert. Surely the same maxim holds good in our present quest. The essence of religious experiences, the thing by which we finally must judge them, must be that element or quality in them which we can meet nowhere else. And such a quality will be of course most prominent and easy to notice in those religious experiences which are most one-sided, exaggerated, and intense.

Now when we compare these intenser experiences with the experiences of tamer minds, so cool and reasonable that we are tempted to call them philosophical rather than religious, we find a character that is perfectly distinct. That character, it seems to me, should be regarded as the practically important *differentia* of religion for our purpose ; and just what it is can easily be brought out by comparing the mind of an abstractly conceived Christian with that of a moralist similarly conceived.

A life is manly, stoical, moral, or philosophical, we say, in proportion as it is less swayed by paltry personal considerations and more by objective ends that call for energy, even though that energy bring personal loss and pain. This is the good side of war, in so far as it calls for ' volunteers.' And for morality life is a war, and the service of the highest is a sort of cosmic patriotism which also calls for volunteers. Even a sick man, unable to be militant outwardly, can carry on the moral warfare. He can willfully turn his attention away from his own

loneliest sufferer, with one proviso, — that I know it is His agency. I will love Him though He shed frost and darkness on every way of mine." R. W. EMERSON : Lectures and Biographical Sketches, p. 188.

future, whether in this world or the next. He can train himself to indifference to his present drawbacks and immerse himself in whatever objective interests still remain accessible. He can follow public news, and sympathize with other people's affairs. He can cultivate cheerful manners, and be silent about his miseries. He can contemplate whatever ideal aspects of existence his philosophy is able to present to him, and practice whatever duties, such as patience, resignation, trust, his ethical system requires. Such a man lives on his loftiest, largest plane. He is a high-hearted freeman and no pining slave. And yet he lacks something which the Christian *par excellence*, the mystic and ascetic saint, for example, has in abundant measure, and which makes of him a human being of an altogether different denomination.

The Christian also spurns the pinched and mumping sick-room attitude, and the lives of saints are full of a kind of callousness to diseased conditions of body which probably no other human records show. But whereas the merely moralistic spurning takes an effort of volition, the Christian spurning is the result of the excitement of a higher kind of emotion, in the presence of which no exertion of volition is required. The moralist must hold his breath and keep his muscles tense ; and so long as this athletic attitude is possible all goes well — morality suffices. But the athletic attitude tends ever to break down, and it inevitably does break down even in the most stalwart when the organism begins to decay, or when morbid fears invade the mind. To suggest personal will and effort to one all sicklied o'er with the sense of irremediable impotence is to suggest the most impossible of things. What he craves is to be consoled in his very powerlessness, to feel that the spirit of the universe recognizes and secures him, all decaying and failing as he is. Well, we are all such helpless failures in the last resort. The sanest and best of us are of one clay with lunatics and prison inmates, and death finally runs the robustest of us down. And whenever we feel this, such a sense of the vanity and provisionality of our voluntary career comes over us that all our morality appears but as a plaster hiding a sore it can never cure, and all our well-doing as the hollowest substitute for that well-*being* that our lives ought to be grounded in, but, alas! are not.

And here religion comes to our rescue and takes our fate into her hands. There is a state of mind, known to religious men, but to no others, in which the will to assert ourselves and hold our own has been displaced by a willingness to close our mouths and be as nothing in the floods and waterspouts of God. In this state of mind, what we most dreaded has become the habitation of our safety, and the hour of our moral death has turned into our spiritual birthday. The time for tension in our soul is over, and that of happy relaxation, of calm deep breathing, of an eternal present, with no discordant future to be anxious about, has arrived. Fear is not held in abeyance as it is by mere morality, it is positively expunged and washed away.

We shall see abundant examples of this happy state of mind in later lectures of this course. We shall see how infinitely passionate a thing religion at its highest flights can be. Like love, like wrath, like hope, ambition, jealousy, like every other instinctive eagerness and impulse, it adds to life an enchantment which is not rationally or logically deducible from anything else. This enchantment, coming as a gift when it does come, — a gift of our organism, the physiologists will tell us, a gift of God's grace, the theologians say, — is either there or not there for us, and there are persons who can no more become possessed by it than they can fall in love with a given woman by mere word of command. Religious feeling is thus an absolute addition to the Subject's range of life. It gives him a new sphere of power. When the outward battle is lost, and the outer world disowns him, it redeems and vivifies an interior world which otherwise would be an empty waste.

If religion is to mean anything definite for us, it seems to me that we ought to take it as meaning this added dimension of emotion, this enthusiastic temper of espousal, in regions where morality strictly so called can at best but bow its head and acquiesce. It ought to mean nothing short of this new reach of freedom for us, with the struggle over, the keynote of the universe sounding in our ears, and everlasting possession spread before our eyes.[1]

This sort of happiness in the absolute and everlasting is what we find nowhere but in religion. It is parted off from all mere animal happiness, all mere enjoyment of the present, by that element of solemnity of which I have already made so much account. Solemnity is a hard thing to define abstractly, but certain of its marks are patent enough. A solemn state of mind is never crude or simple — it seems to contain a certain measure of its own opposite in solution. A solemn joy preserves a sort of bitter in its sweetness; a solemn sorrow is one to which we intimately consent. But there are writers who, realizing that happiness of a supreme sort is the prerogative of religion, forget this complication, and call all happiness, as such, religious. Mr. Havelock Ellis, for exam-

---

[1] Once more, there are plenty of men, constitutionally sombre men, in whose religious life this rapturousness is lacking. They are religious in the wider sense; yet in this acutest of all senses they are not so, and it is religion in the acutest sense that I wish, without disputing about words, to study first, so as to get at its typical *differentia*.

ple, identifies religion with the entire field of the soul's liberation from oppressive moods.

"The simplest functions of physiological life," he writes, "may be its ministers. Every one who is at all acquainted with the Persian mystics knows how wine may be regarded as an instrument of religion. Indeed, in all countries and in all ages, some form of physical enlargement — singing, dancing, drinking, sexual excitement — has been intimately associated with worship. Even the momentary expansion of the soul in laughter is, to however slight an extent, a religious exercise. . . . Whenever an impulse from the world strikes against the organism, and the resultant is not discomfort or pain, not even the muscular contraction of strenuous manhood, but a joyous expansion or aspiration of the whole soul — there is religion. It is the infinite for which we hunger, and we ride gladly on every little wave that promises to bear us towards it." [1]

But such a straight identification of religion with any and every form of happiness leaves the essential peculiarity of religious happiness out. The more commonplace happinesses which we get are 'reliefs,' occasioned by our momentary escapes from evils either experienced or threatened. But in its most characteristic embodiments, religious happiness is no mere feeling of escape. It cares no longer to escape. It consents to the evil outwardly as a form of sacrifice — inwardly it knows it to be permanently overcome. If you ask *how* religion thus falls on the thorns and faces death, and in the very act annuls annihilation, I cannot explain the matter, for it is religion's secret, and to understand it you must yourself have been a religious man of the extremer type. In our future examples, even of the simplest and healthiest-minded type of religious consciousness, we shall find this complex sacrificial constitution, in which a higher happiness holds a lower unhappiness in check. In the Louvre there is a

[1] The New Spirit, p. 232.

picture, by Guido Reni, of St. Michael with his foot on Satan's neck. The richness of the picture is in large part due to the fiend's figure being there. The richness of its allegorical meaning also is due to his being there — that is, the world is all the richer for having a devil in it, *so long as we keep our foot upon his neck*. In the religious consciousness, that is just the position in which the fiend, the negative or tragic principle, is found ; and for that very reason the religious consciousness is so rich from the emotional point of view.[1] We shall see how in certain men and women it takes on a monstrously ascetic form. There are saints who have literally fed on the negative principle, on humiliation and privation, and the thought of suffering and death, — their souls growing in happiness just in proportion as their outward state grew more intolerable. No other emotion than religious emotion can bring a man to this peculiar pass. And it is for that reason that when we ask our question about the value of religion for human life, I think we ought to look for the answer among these violenter examples rather than among those of a more moderate hue.

Having the phenomenon of our study in its acutest possible form to start with, we can shade down as much as we please later. And if in these cases, repulsive as they are to our ordinary worldly way of judging, we find ourselves compelled to acknowledge religion's value and treat it with respect, it will have proved in some way its value for life at large. By subtracting and toning down extravagances we may thereupon proceed to trace the boundaries of its legitimate sway.

To be sure, it makes our task difficult to have to deal so much with eccentricities and extremes. " How *can*

---

[1] I owe this allegorical illustration to my lamented colleague and friend, Charles Carroll Everett.

religion on the whole be the most important of all human functions," you may ask, " if every several manifestation of it in turn have to be corrected and sobered down and pruned away?" Such a thesis seems a paradox impossible to sustain reasonably, — yet I believe that something like it will have to be our final contention. That personal attitude which the individual finds himself impelled to take up towards what he apprehends to be the divine — and you will remember that this was our definition — will prove to be both a helpless and a sacrificial attitude. That is, we shall have to confess to at least some amount of dependence on sheer mercy, and to practice some amount of renunciation, great or small, to save our souls alive. The constitution of the world we live in requires it : —

> " Entbehren sollst du ! sollst entbehren !
> Das ist der ewige Gesang
> Der jedem an die Ohren klingt,
> Den, unser ganzes Leben lang
> Uns heiser jede Stunde singt."

For when all is said and done, we are in the end absolutely dependent on the universe ; and into sacrifices and surrenders of some sort, deliberately looked at and accepted, we are drawn and pressed as into our only permanent positions of repose. Now in those states of mind which fall short of religion, the surrender is submitted to as an imposition of necessity, and the sacrifice is undergone at the very best without complaint. In the religious life, on the contrary, surrender and sacrifice are positively espoused : even unnecessary givings-up are added in order that the happiness may increase. *Religion thus makes easy and felicitous what in any case is necessary ;* and if it be the only agency that can accomplish this result, its vital importance as a human faculty stands vindicated beyond dispute.   It becomes an essential organ of our life, performing a function which no other portion of our nature can so successfully fulfill. From the merely biological point of view, so to call it, this is a conclusion to which, so far as I can now see, we shall inevitably be led, and led moreover by following the purely empirical method of demonstration which I sketched to you in the first lecture.   Of the farther office of religion as a metaphysical revelation I will say nothing now.

But to foreshadow the terminus of one's investigations is one thing, and to arrive there safely is another.   In the next lecture, abandoning the extreme generalities which have engrossed us hitherto, I propose that we begin our actual journey by addressing ourselves directly to the concrete facts.

LECTURE III

THE REALITY OF THE UNSEEN

WERE one asked to characterize the life of religion in the broadest and most general terms possible, one might say that it consists of the belief that there is an unseen order, and that our supreme good lies in harmoniously adjusting ourselves thereto. This belief and this adjustment are the religious attitude in the soul. I wish during this hour to call your attention to some of the psychological peculiarities of such an attitude as this, of belief in an object which we cannot see. All our attitudes, moral, practical, or emotional, as well as religious, are due to the ' objects ' of our consciousness, the things which we believe to exist, whether really or ideally, along with ourselves. Such objects may be present to our senses, or they may be present only to our thought. In either case they elicit from us a *reaction ;* and the reaction due to things of thought is notoriously in many cases as strong as that due to sensible presences. It may be even stronger. The memory of an insult may make us angrier than the insult did when we received it. We are frequently more ashamed of our blunders afterwards than we were at the moment of making them ; and in general our whole higher prudential and moral life is based on the fact that material sensations actually present may have a weaker influence on our action than ideas of remoter facts.

The more concrete objects of most men's religion, the deities whom they worship, are known to them only in idea. It has been vouchsafed, for example, to very few Christian believers to have had a sensible vision of their Saviour; though enough appearances of this sort are on record, by way of miraculous exception, to merit our attention later. The whole force of the Christian religion, therefore, so far as belief in the divine personages determines the prevalent attitude of the believer, is in general exerted by the instrumentality of pure ideas, of which nothing in the individual's past experience directly serves as a model.

But in addition to these ideas of the more concrete religious objects, religion is full of abstract objects which prove to have an equal power. God's attributes as such, his holiness, his justice, his mercy, his absoluteness, his infinity, his omniscience, his tri-unity, the various mysteries of the redemptive process, the operation of the sacraments, etc., have proved fertile wells of inspiring meditation for Christian believers.[1] We shall see later that the absence of definite sensible images is positively insisted on by the mystical authorities in all religions as the *sine qua non* of a successful orison, or contemplation of the higher divine truths. Such contemplations are expected (and abundantly verify the expectation, as we shall also see) to influence the believer's subsequent attitude very powerfully for good.

Immanuel Kant held a curious doctrine about such objects of belief as God, the design of creation, the soul, its freedom, and the life hereafter. These things, he said,

---

[1] Example : "I have had much comfort lately in meditating on the passages which show the personality of the Holy Ghost, and his distinctness from the Father and the Son. It is a subject that requires searching into to find out, but, when realized, gives one so much more true and lively a sense of the fullness of the Godhead, and its work in us and to us, than when only thinking of the Spirit in its effect on us." AUGUSTUS HARE: Memorials, i. 244, Maria Hare to Lucy H. Hare.

are properly not objects of knowledge at all. Our conceptions always require a sense-content to work with, and as the words 'soul,' 'God,' 'immortality,' cover no distinctive sense-content whatever, it follows that theoretically speaking they are words devoid of any significance. Yet strangely enough they have a definite meaning *for our practice*. We can act *as if* there were a God; feel *as if* we were free; consider Nature *as if* she were full of special designs; lay plans *as if* we were to be immortal; and we find then that these words do make a genuine difference in our moral life. Our faith *that* these unintelligible objects actually exist proves thus to be a full equivalent in *praktischer Hinsicht*, as Kant calls it, or from the point of view of our action, for a knowledge of *what* they might be, in case we were permitted positively to conceive them. So we have the strange phenomenon, as Kant assures us, of a mind believing with all its strength in the real presence of a set of things of no one of which it can form any notion whatsoever.

My object in thus recalling Kant's doctrine to your mind is not to express any opinion as to the accuracy of this particularly uncouth part of his philosophy, but only to illustrate the characteristic of human nature which we are considering, by an example so classical in its exaggeration. The sentiment of reality can indeed attach itself so strongly to our object of belief that our whole life is polarized through and through, so to speak, by its sense of the existence of the thing believed in, and yet that thing, for purpose of definite description, can hardly be said to be present to our mind at all. It is as if a bar of iron, without touch or sight, with no representative faculty whatever, might nevertheless be strongly endowed with an inner capacity for magnetic feeling; and as if, through the various arousals of its magnetism by magnets coming and going in its neighborhood, it might be consciously determined to different attitudes and tendencies. Such a bar of iron could never give you an outward description of the agencies that had the power of stirring it so strongly; yet of their presence, and of their significance for its life, it would be intensely aware through every fibre of its being.

It is not only the Ideas of pure Reason, as Kant styled them, that have this power of making us vitally feel presences that we are impotent articulately to describe. All sorts of higher abstractions bring with them the same kind of impalpable appeal. Remember those passages from Emerson which I read at my last lecture. The whole universe of concrete objects, as we know them, swims, not only for such a transcendentalist writer, but for all of us, in a wider and higher universe of abstract ideas, that lend it its significance. As time, space, and the ether soak through all things, so (we feel) do abstract and essential goodness, beauty, strength, significance, justice, soak through all things good, strong, significant, and just.

Such ideas, and others equally abstract, form the background for all our facts, the fountain-head of all the possibilities we conceive of. They give its 'nature,' as we call it, to every special thing. Everything we know is 'what' it is by sharing in the nature of one of these abstractions. We can never look directly at them, for they are bodiless and featureless and footless, but we grasp all other things by their means, and in handling the real world we should be stricken with helplessness in just so far forth as we might lose these mental objects, these adjectives and adverbs and predicates and heads of classification and conception.

This absolute determinability of our mind by abstractions is one of the cardinal facts in our human constitution. Polarizing and magnetizing us as they do, we turn towards them and from them, we seek them, hold them, hate them, bless them, just as if they were so many concrete beings. And beings they are, beings as real in the realm which they inhabit as the changing things of sense are in the realm of space.

Plato gave so brilliant and impressive a defense of this common human feeling, that the doctrine of the reality of abstract objects has been known as the platonic theory of ideas ever since. Abstract Beauty, for example, is for Plato a perfectly definite individual being, of which the intellect is aware as of something additional to all the perishing beauties of the earth. " The true order of going," he says, in the often quoted passage in his ' Banquet,' " is to use the beauties of earth as steps along which one mounts upwards for the sake of that other Beauty, going from one to two, and from two to all fair forms, and from fair forms to fair actions, and from fair actions to fair notions, until from fair notions he arrives at the notion of absolute Beauty, and at last knows what the essence of Beauty is." [1] In our last lecture we had a glimpse of the way in which a platonizing writer like Emerson may treat the abstract divineness of things, the moral structure of the universe, as a fact worthy of worship. In those various churches without a God which to-day are spreading through the world under the name of ethical societies, we have a similar worship of the abstract divine, the moral law believed in as an ultimate object. ' Science ' in many minds is genuinely taking the place of a religion. Where this is so, the scientist treats the ' Laws of Nature ' as objective facts to be revered. A brilliant school of interpretation of Greek mythology

[1] Symposium, Jowett, 1871, i. 527.

would have it that in their origin the Greek gods were only half-metaphoric personifications of those great spheres of abstract law and order into which the natural world falls apart — the sky-sphere, the ocean-sphere, the earth-sphere, and the like ; just as even now we may speak of the smile of the morning, the kiss of the breeze, or the bite of the cold, without really meaning that these phenomena of nature actually wear a human face.[1]

As regards the origin of the Greek gods, we need not at present seek an opinion. But the whole array of our instances leads to a conclusion something like this : It is as if there were in the human consciousness a *sense of reality, a feeling of objective presence, a perception* of what we may call ' *something there,*' more deep and more general than any of the special and particular ' senses ' by which the current psychology supposes existent realities to be originally revealed. If this were so, we might suppose the senses to waken our attitudes and conduct as they so habitually do, by first exciting this sense of reality ; but anything else, any idea, for example, that might similarly excite it, would have that same prerogative of appearing real which objects of sense normally possess. So far as religious conceptions were able to touch this reality-feeling, they would be believed in in spite of criticism, even though they might be so vague and remote as to be almost unimaginable, even though they might be such non-entities in point of *whatness*, as Kant makes the objects of his moral theology to be.

The most curious proofs of the existence of such an undifferentiated sense of reality as this are found in experiences of hallucination. It often happens that an

---

[1] Example : "Nature is always so interesting, under whatever aspect she shows herself, that when it rains, I seem to see a beautiful woman weeping. She appears the more beautiful, the more afflicted she is." B. de St. Pierre.

hallucination is imperfectly developed : the person affected will feel a 'presence' in the room, definitely localized, facing in one particular way, real in the most emphatic sense of the word, often coming suddenly, and as suddenly gone ; and yet neither seen, heard, touched, nor cognized in any of the usual 'sensible' ways. Let me give you an example of this, before I pass to the objects with whose presence religion is more peculiarly concerned.

An intimate friend of mine, one of the keenest intellects I know, has had several experiences of this sort. He writes as follows in response to my inquiries : —

"I have several times within the past few years felt the so-called 'consciousness of a presence.' The experiences which I have in mind are clearly distinguishable from another kind of experience which I have had very frequently, and which I fancy many persons would also call the 'consciousness of a presence.' But the difference for me between the two sets of experience is as great as the difference between feeling a slight warmth originating I know not where, and standing in the midst of a conflagration with all the ordinary senses alert.

"It was about September, 1884, when I had the first experience. On the previous night I had had, after getting into bed at my rooms in College, a vivid tactile hallucination of being grasped by the arm, which made me get up and search the room for an intruder; but the sense of presence properly so called came on the next night. After I had got into bed and blown out the candle, I lay awake awhile thinking on the previous night's experience, when suddenly I *felt* something come into the room and stay close to my bed. It remained only a minute or two. I did not recognize it by any ordinary sense, and yet there was a horribly unpleasant 'sensation' connected with it. It stirred something more at the roots of my being than any ordinary perception. The feeling had something of the quality of a very large tearing vital pain spreading chiefly over the chest, but within the organism — and yet the feeling was not *pain* so much as *abhorrence.* At all events, something was present with me, and I knew its presence far more surely than I have ever known the presence of any fleshly living creature. I was conscious of its departure as of its coming: an almost instantaneously swift going through the door, and the ' horrible sensation ' disappeared.

" On the third night when I retired my mind was absorbed in some lectures which I was preparing, and I was still absorbed in these when I became aware of the actual presence (though not of the *coming*) of the thing that was there the night before, and of the ' horrible sensation.' I then mentally concentrated all my effort to charge this 'thing,' if it was evil, to depart, if it was *not* evil, to tell me who or what it was, and if it could not explain itself, to go, and that I would compel it to go. It went as on the previous night, and my body quickly recovered its normal state.

" On two other occasions in my life I have had precisely the same ' horrible sensation.' Once it lasted a full quarter of an hour. In all three instances the certainty that there in outward space there stood *something* was indescribably *stronger* than the ordinary certainty of companionship when we are in the close presence of ordinary living people. The something seemed close to me, and intensely more real than any ordinary perception. Although I felt it to be like unto myself, so to speak, or finite, small, and distressful, as it were, I did n't recognize it as any individual being or person."

Of course such an experience as this does not connect itself with the religious sphere. Yet it may upon occasion do so ; and the same correspondent informs me that at more than one other conjuncture he had the sense of presence developed with equal intensity and abruptness, only then it was filled with a quality of joy.

" There was not a mere consciousness of something there, but fused in the central happiness of it, a startling awareness of some ineffable good. Not vague either, not like the emotional effect of some poem, or scene, or blossom, of music, but the sure knowledge of the close presence of a sort of mighty person, and after it went, the memory persisted as the one perception of reality. Everything else might be a dream, but not that."

My friend, as it oddly happens, does not interpret these latter experiences theistically, as signifying the presence of God. But it would clearly not have been unnatural to interpret them as a revelation of the deity's existence. When we reach the subject of mysticism, we shall have much more to say upon this head.

Lest the oddity of these phenomena should disconcert you, I will venture to read you a couple of similar narratives, much shorter, merely to show that we are dealing with a well-marked natural kind of fact. In the first case, which I take from the Journal of the Society for Psychical Research, the sense of presence developed in a few moments into a distinctly visualized hallucination, — but I leave that part of the story out.

" I had read," the narrator says, " some twenty minutes or so, was thoroughly absorbed in the book, my mind was perfectly quiet, and for the time being my friends were quite forgotten, when suddenly without a moment's warning my whole being seemed roused to the highest state of tension or aliveness, and I was aware, with an intenseness not easily imagined by those who had never experienced it, that another being or presence was not only in the room, but quite close to me. I put my book down, and although my excitement was great, I felt quite collected, and not conscious of any sense of fear. Without changing my position, and looking straight at the fire, I knew somehow that my friend A. H. was standing at my left elbow, but so far behind me as to be hidden by the armchair in which I was leaning back. Moving my eyes round slightly without otherwise changing my position, the lower portion of one leg became visible, and I instantly recognized the gray-blue material of trousers he often wore, but the stuff appeared semi-transparent, reminding me of tobacco smoke in consistency," [1] — and hereupon the visual hallucination came.

[1] Journal of the S. P. R., February, 1895, p. 26.

Another informant writes : —

" Quite early in the night I was awakened. . . . I felt as if I had been aroused intentionally, and at first thought some one was breaking into the house. . . . I then turned on my side to go to sleep again, and immediately felt a consciousness of a presence in the room, and singular to state, it was not the con-sciousness of a live person, but of a spiritual presence. This may provoke a smile, but I can only tell you the facts as they occurred to me. I do not know how to better describe my sensations than by simply stating that I felt a consciousness of a spiritual presence. . . . I felt also at the same time a strong feeling of superstitious dread, as if something strange and fear-ful were about to happen." [1]

Professor Flournoy of Geneva gives me the following testimony of a friend of his, a lady, who has the gift of automatic or involuntary writing : —

" Whenever I practice automatic writing, what makes me feel that it is not due to a subconscious self is the feeling I always have of a foreign presence, external to my body. It is some-times so definitely characterized that I could point to its exact position. This impression of presence is impossible to describe. It varies in intensity and clearness according to the personality from whom the writing professes to come. If it is some one whom I love, I feel it immediately, before any writing has come. My heart seems to recognize it."

In an earlier book of mine I have cited at full length a curious case of presence felt by a blind man. The presence was that of the figure of a gray-bearded man dressed in a pepper and salt suit, squeezing himself under the crack of the door and moving across the floor of the room towards a sofa. The blind subject of this quasi-hallucination is an exceptionally intelligent reporter. He is entirely without internal visual imagery and cannot represent light or colors to himself, and is positive that

[1] E. GURNEY: Phantasms of the Living, i. 384.

his other senses, hearing, etc., were not involved in this false perception. It seems to have been an abstract conception rather, with the feelings of reality and spatial outwardness directly attached to it — in other words, a fully objectified and exteriorized *idea*.

Such cases, taken along with others which would be too tedious for quotation, seem sufficiently to prove the existence in our mental machinery of a sense of present reality more diffused and general than that which our special senses yield. For the pyschologists the tracing of the organic seat of such a feeling would form a pretty problem — nothing could be more natural than to connect it with the muscular sense, with the feeling that our muscles were innervating themselves for action. Whatsoever thus innervated our activity, or 'made our flesh creep,' — our senses are what do so oftenest, — might then appear real and present, even though it were but an abstract idea. But with such vague conjectures we have no concern at present, for our interest lies with the faculty rather than with its organic seat.

Like all positive affections of consciousness, the sense of reality has its negative counterpart in the shape of a feeling of unreality by which persons may be haunted, and of which one sometimes hears complaint : —

"When I reflect on the fact that I have made my appearance by accident upon a globe itself whirled through space as the sport of the catastrophes of the heavens," says Madame Ackermann; "when I see myself surrounded by beings as ephemeral and incomprehensible as I am myself, and all excitedly pursuing pure chimeras, I experience a strange feeling of being in a dream. It seems to me as if I have loved and suffered and that erelong I shall die, in a dream. My last word will be, 'I have been dreaming.'" [1]

[1] Pensées d'un Solitaire, p. 66.

In another lecture we shall see how in morbid melancholy this sense of the unreality of things may become a carking pain, and even lead to suicide.

We may now lay it down as certain that in the distinctively religious sphere of experience, many persons (how many we cannot tell) possess the objects of their belief, not in the form of mere conceptions which their intellect accepts as true, but rather in the form of quasi-sensible realities directly apprehended. As his sense of the real presence of these objects fluctuates, so the believer alternates between warmth and coldness in his faith. Other examples will bring this home to one better than abstract description, so I proceed immediately to cite some. The first example is a negative one, deploring the loss of the sense in question. I have extracted it from an account given me by a scientific man of my acquaintance, of his religious life. It seems to me to show clearly that the feeling of reality may be something more like a sensation than an intellectual operation properly so-called.

"Between twenty and thirty I gradually became more and more agnostic and irreligious, yet I cannot say that I ever lost that 'indefinite consciousness' which Herbert Spencer describes so well, of an Absolute Reality behind phenomena. For me this Reality was not the pure Unknowable of Spencer's philosophy, for although I had ceased my childish prayers to God, and never prayed to *It* in a formal manner, yet my more recent experience shows me to have been in a relation to *It* which practically was the same thing as prayer. Whenever I had any trouble, especially when I had conflict with other people, either domestically or in the way of business, or when I was depressed in spirits or anxious about affairs, I now recognize that I used to fall back for support upon this curious relation I felt myself to be in to this fundamental cosmical *It*. It was on my side, or I was on Its side, however you please to term it, in the particular trouble, and it always strengthened me and seemed to give me endless vitality to feel its underlying and supporting presence. In fact, it was an unfailing fountain of living justice, truth, and strength, to which I instinctively turned at times of weakness, and it always brought me out. I know now that it was a personal relation I was in to it, because of late years the power of communicating with it has left me, and I am conscious of a perfectly definite loss. I used never to fail to find it when I turned to it. Then came a set of years when sometimes I found it, and then again I would be wholly unable to make connection with it. I remember many occasions on which at night in bed, I would be unable to get to sleep on account of worry. I turned this way and that in the darkness, and groped mentally for the familiar sense of that higher mind of my mind which had always seemed to be close at hand as it were, closing the passage, and yielding support, but there was no electric current. A blank was there instead of *It:* I couldn't find anything. Now, at the age of nearly fifty, my power of getting into connection with it has entirely left me; and I have to confess that a great help has gone out of my life. Life has become curiously dead and indifferent; and I can now see that my old experience was probably exactly the same thing as the prayers of the orthodox, only I did not call them by that name. What I have spoken of as 'It' was practically not Spencer's Unknowable, but just my own instinctive and individual God, whom I relied upon for higher sympathy, but whom somehow I have lost."

Nothing is more common in the pages of religious biography than the way in which seasons of lively and of difficult faith are described as alternating. Probably every religious person has the recollection of particular crises in which a directer vision of the truth, a direct perception, perhaps, of a living God's existence, swept in and overwhelmed the languor of the more ordinary belief. In James Russell Lowell's correspondence there is a brief memorandum of an experience of this kind: —

"I had a revelation last Friday evening. I was at Mary's, and happening to say something of the presence of spirits (of whom, I said, I was often dimly aware), Mr. Putnam entered into an argument with me on spiritual matters. As I was speaking, the whole system rose up before me like a vague destiny looming from the Abyss. I never before so clearly felt the Spirit of God in me and around me. The whole room seemed to me full of God. The air seemed to waver to and fro with the presence of Something I knew not what. I spoke with the calmness and clearness of a prophet. I cannot tell you what this revelation was. I have not yet studied it enough. But I shall perfect it one day, and then you shall hear it and acknowledge its grandeur." [1]

Here is a longer and more developed experience from a manuscript communication by a clergyman, — I take it from Starbuck's manuscript collection : —

" I remember the night, and almost the very spot on the hill-top, where my soul opened out, as it were, into the Infinite, and there was a rushing together of the two worlds, the inner and the outer. It was deep calling unto deep, — the deep that my own struggle had opened up within being answered by the unfathomable deep without, reaching beyond the stars. I stood alone with Him who had made me, and all the beauty of the world, and love, and sorrow, and even temptation. I did not seek Him, but felt the perfect unison of my spirit with His. The ordinary sense of things around me faded. For the moment nothing but an ineffable joy and exaltation remained. It is impossible fully to describe the experience. It was like the effect of some great orchestra when all the separate notes have melted into one swelling harmony that leaves the listener conscious of nothing save that his soul is being wafted upwards, and almost bursting with its own emotion. The perfect stillness of the night was thrilled by a more solemn silence. The darkness held a presence that was all the more felt because it was not seen. I could not any more have doubted that *He* was

[1] Letters of Lowell, i. 75.

there than that I was. Indeed, I felt myself to be, if possible, the less real of the two.

" My highest faith in God and truest idea of him were then born in me. I have stood upon the Mount of Vision since, and felt the Eternal round about me. But never since has there come quite the same stirring of the heart. Then, if ever, I believe, I stood face to face with God, and was born anew of his spirit. There was, as I recall it, no sudden change of thought or of belief, except that my early crude conception had, as it were, burst into flower. There was no destruction of the old, but a rapid, wonderful unfolding. Since that time no discussion that I have heard of the proofs of God's existence has been able to shake my faith. Having once felt the presence of God's spirit, I have never lost it again for long. My most assuring evidence of his existence is deeply rooted in that hour of vision, in the memory of that supreme experience, and in the conviction, gained from reading and reflection, that something the same has come to all who have found God. I am aware that it may justly be called mystical. I am not enough acquainted with philosophy to defend it from that or any other charge. I feel that in writing of it I have overlaid it with words rather than put it clearly to your thought. But, such as it is, I have described it as carefully as I now am able to do."

Here is another document, even more definite in character, which, the writer being a Swiss, I translate from the French original.[1]

" I was in perfect health : we were on our sixth day of tramping, and in good training. We had come the day before from Sixt to Trient by Buet. I felt neither fatigue, hunger, nor thirst, and my state of mind was equally healthy. I had had at Forlaz good news from home ; I was subject to no anxiety, either near or remote, for we had a good guide, and there was not a shadow of uncertainty about the road we should follow. I can best describe the condition in which I was by calling it a

[1] I borrow it, with Professor Flournoy's permission, from his rich collection of psychological documents.

state of equilibrium. When all at once I experienced a feeling of being raised above myself, I felt the presence of God — I tell of the thing just as I was conscious of it — as if his goodness and his power were penetrating me altogether. The throb of emotion was so violent that I could barely tell the boys to pass on and not wait for me. I then sat down on a stone, unable to stand any longer, and my eyes overflowed with tears. I thanked God that in the course of my life he had taught me to know him, that he sustained my life and took pity both on the insignificant creature and on the sinner that I was. I begged him ardently that my life might be consecrated to the doing of his will. I felt his reply, which was that I should do his will from day to day, in humility and poverty, leaving him, the Almighty God, to be judge of whether I should some time be called to bear witness more conspicuously. Then, slowly, the ecstasy left my heart; that is, I felt that God had withdrawn the communion which he had granted, and I was able to walk on, but very slowly, so strongly was I still possessed by the interior emotion. Besides, I had wept uninterruptedly for several minutes, my eyes were swollen, and I did not wish my companions to see me. The state of ecstasy may have lasted four or five minutes, although it seemed at the time to last much longer. My comrades waited for me ten minutes at the cross of Barine, but I took about twenty-five or thirty minutes to join them, for as well as I can remember, they said that I had kept them back for about half an hour. The impression had been so profound that in climbing slowly the slope I asked myself if it were possible that Moses on Sinai could have had a more intimate communication with God. I think it well to add that in this ecstasy of mine God had neither form, color, odor, nor taste; moreover, that the feeling of his presence was accompanied with no determinate localization. It was rather as if my personality had been transformed by the presence of a *spiritual spirit*. But the more I seek words to express this intimate intercourse, the more I feel the impossibility of describing the thing by any of our usual images. At bottom the expression most apt to render what I felt is this: God was present, though invisible; he fell under no one of my senses, yet my consciousness perceived him."

The adjective 'mystical' is technically applied, most often, to states that are of brief duration. Of course such hours of rapture as the last two persons describe are mystical experiences, of which in a later lecture I shall have much to say. Meanwhile here is the abridged record of another mystical or semi-mystical experience, in a mind evidently framed by nature for ardent piety. I owe it to Starbuck's collection. The lady who gives the account is the daughter of a man well known in his time as a writer against Christianity. The suddenness of her conversion shows well how native the sense of God's presence must be to certain minds. She relates that she was brought up in entire ignorance of Christian doctrine, but, when in Germany, after being talked to by Christian friends, she read the Bible and prayed, and finally the plan of salvation flashed upon her like a stream of light.

"To this day," she writes, "I cannot understand dallying with religion and the commands of God. The very instant I heard my Father's cry calling unto me, my heart bounded in recognition. I ran, I stretched forth my arms, I cried aloud, 'Here, here I am, my Father.' Oh, happy child, what should I do? 'Love me,' answered my God. 'I do, I do,' I cried passionately. 'Come unto me,' called my Father. 'I will,' my heart panted. Did I stop to ask a single question? Not one. It never occurred to me to ask whether I was good enough, or to hesitate over my unfitness, or to find out what I thought of his church, or . . . to wait until I should be satisfied. Satisfied! I was satisfied. Had I not found my God and my Father? Did he not love me? Had he not called me? Was there not a Church into which I might enter? . . . Since then I have had direct answers to prayer — so significant as to be almost like talking with God and hearing his answer. The idea of God's reality has never left me for one moment."

Here is still another case, the writer being a man aged

twenty-seven, in which the experience, probably almost as characteristic, is less vividly described : —

" I have on a number of occasions felt that I had enjoyed a period of intimate communion with the divine. These meetings came unasked and unexpected, and seemed to consist merely in the temporary obliteration of the conventionalities which usually surround and cover my life. . . . Once it was when from the summit of a high mountain I looked over a gashed and corrugated landscape extending to a long convex of ocean that ascended to the horizon, and again from the same point when I could see nothing beneath me but a boundless expanse of white cloud, on the blown surface of which a few high peaks, including the one I was on, seemed plunging about as if they were dragging their anchors. What I felt on these occasions was a temporary loss of my own identity, accompanied by an illumination which revealed to me a deeper significance than I had been wont to attach to life. It is in this that I find my justification for saying that I have enjoyed communication with God. Of course the absence of such a being as this would be chaos. I cannot conceive of life without its presence."

Of the more habitual and so to speak chronic sense of God's presence the following sample from Professor Starbuck's manuscript collection may serve to give an idea. It is from a man aged forty-nine, — probably thousands of unpretending Christians would write an almost identical account.

" God is more real to me than any thought or thing or person. I feel his presence positively, and the more as I live in closer harmony with his laws as written in my body and mind. I feel him in the sunshine or rain ; and awe mingled with a delicious restfulness most nearly describes my feelings. I talk to him as to a companion in prayer and praise, and our communion is delightful. He answers me again and again, often in words so clearly spoken that it seems my outer ear must have carried the tone, but generally in strong mental impressions. Usually a text of Scripture, unfolding some new view of him and his love for me, and care for my safety. I could give hundreds of instances, in school matters, social problems, financial difficulties, etc. That he is mine and I am his never leaves me, it is an abiding joy. Without it life would be a blank, a desert, a shoreless, trackless waste."

I subjoin some more examples from writers of different ages and sexes. They are also from Professor Starbuck's collection, and their number might be greatly multiplied. The first is from a man twenty-seven years old : —

"God is quite real to me. I talk to him and often get answers. Thoughts sudden and distinct from any I have been entertaining come to my mind after asking God for his direction. Something over a year ago I was for some weeks in the direst perplexity. When the trouble first appeared before me I was dazed, but before long (two or three hours) I could hear distinctly a passage of Scripture : ‘ My grace is sufficient for thee.’ Every time my thoughts turned to the trouble I could hear this quotation. I don’t think I ever doubted the existence of God, or had him drop out of my consciousness. God has frequently stepped into my affairs very perceptibly, and I feel that he directs many little details all the time. But on two or three occasions he has ordered ways for me very contrary to my ambitions and plans."

Another statement (none the less valuable psychologically for being so decidedly childish) is that of a boy of seventeen : —

"Sometimes as I go to church, I sit down, join in the service, and before I go out I feel as if God was with me, right side of me, singing and reading the Psalms with me. . . . And then again I feel as if I could sit beside him, and put my arms around him, kiss him, etc. When I am taking Holy Communion at the altar, I try to get with him and generally feel his presence."

I let a few other cases follow at random : —

"God surrounds me like the physical atmosphere. He is

closer to me than my own breath. In him literally I live and
move and have my being." —

"There are times when I seem to stand in his very presence,
to talk with him. Answers to prayer have come, sometimes
direct and overwhelming in their revelation of his presence and
powers. There are times when God seems far off, but this is
always my own fault." —

"I have the sense of a presence, strong, and at the same time
soothing, which hovers over me. Sometimes it seems to enwrap
me with sustaining arms."

Such is the human ontological imagination, and such
is the convincingness of what it brings to birth. Unpic-
turable beings are realized, and realized with an intensity
almost like that of an hallucination. They determine
our vital attitude as decisively as the vital attitude of
lovers is determined by the habitual sense, by which each
is haunted, of the other being in the world. A lover has
notoriously this sense of the continuous being of his
idol, even when his attention is addressed to other matters and he no longer represents her features. He cannot forget her; she uninterruptedly affects him through
and through.

I spoke of the convincingness of these feelings of
reality, and I must dwell a moment longer on that point.
They are as convincing to those who have them as any
direct sensible experiences can be, and they are, as a rule,
much more convincing than results established by mere
logic ever are. One may indeed be entirely without
them; probably more than one of you here present is
without them in any marked degree; but if you do have
them, and have them at all strongly, the probability is
that you cannot help regarding them as genuine perceptions of truth, as revelations of a kind of reality which
no adverse argument, however unanswerable by you in

words, can expel from your belief. The opinion opposed to mysticism in philosophy is sometimes spoken of as *rationalism*. Rationalism insists that all our beliefs ought ultimately to find for themselves articulate grounds. Such grounds, for rationalism, must consist of four things : (1) definitely statable abstract principles ; (2) definite facts of sensation ; (3) definite hypotheses based on such facts ; and (4) definite inferences logically drawn. Vague impressions of something indefinable have no place in the rationalistic system, which on its positive side is surely a splendid intellectual tendency, for not only are all our philosophies fruits of it, but physical science (amongst other good things) is its result.

Nevertheless, if we look on man's whole mental life as it exists, on the life of men that lies in them apart from their learning and science, and that they inwardly and privately follow, we have to confess that the part of it of which rationalism can give an account is relatively superficial. It is the part that has the *prestige* undoubtedly, for it has the loquacity, it can challenge you for proofs, and chop logic, and put you down with words. But it will fail to convince or convert you all the same, if your dumb intuitions are opposed to its conclusions. If you have intuitions at all, they come from a deeper level of your nature than the loquacious level which rationalism inhabits. Your whole subconscious life, your impulses, your faiths, your needs, your divinations, have prepared the premises, of which your consciousness now feels the weight of the result ; and something in you absolutely *knows* that that result must be truer than any logic-chopping rationalistic talk, however clever, that may contradict it. This inferiority of the rationalistic level in founding belief is just as manifest when rationalism argues for religion as when it argues against it. That vast literature of proofs of God's existence drawn from the order of nature, which a century ago seemed so overwhelmingly convincing, to-day does little more than gather dust in libraries, for the simple reason that our generation has ceased to believe in the kind of God it argued for. Whatever sort of a being God may be, we *know* to-day that he is nevermore that mere external inventor of ' contrivances ' intended to make manifest his ' glory ' in which our great-grandfathers took such satisfaction, though just how we know this we cannot possibly make clear by words either to others or to ourselves. I defy any of you here fully to account for your persuasion that if a God exist he must be a more cosmic and tragic personage than that Being.

The truth is that in the metaphysical and religious sphere, articulate reasons are cogent for us only when our inarticulate feelings of reality have already been impressed in favor of the same conclusion. Then, indeed, our intuitions and our reason work together, and great world-ruling systems, like that of the Buddhist or of the Catholic philosophy, may grow up. Our impulsive belief is here always what sets up the original body of truth, and our articulately verbalized philosophy is but its showy translation into formulas. The unreasoned and immediate assurance is the deep thing in us, the reasoned argument is but a surface exhibition. Instinct leads, intelligence does but follow. If a person feels the presence of a living God after the fashion shown by my quotations, your critical arguments, be they never so superior, will vainly set themselves to change his faith.

Please observe, however, that I do not yet say that it is *better* that the subconscious and non-rational should thus hold primacy in the religious realm. I confine myself to simply pointing out that they do so hold it as a matter of fact.

So much for our sense of the reality of the religious objects. Let me now say a brief word more about the attitudes they characteristically awaken.

We have already agreed that they are *solemn ;* and we have seen reason to think that the most distinctive of them is the sort of joy which may result in extreme cases from absolute self-surrender. The sense of the kind of object to which the surrender is made has much to do with determining the precise complexion of the joy ; and the whole phenomenon is more complex than any simple formula allows. In the literature of the subject, sadness and gladness have each been emphasized in turn. The ancient saying that the first maker of the Gods was fear receives voluminous corroboration from every age of religious history ; but none the less does religious history show the part which joy has evermore tended to play. Sometimes the joy has been primary ; sometimes secondary, being the gladness of deliverance from the fear. This latter state of things, being the more complex, is also the more complete ; and as we proceed, I think we shall have abundant reason for refusing to leave out either the sadness or the gladness, if we look at religion with the breadth of view which it demands. Stated in the completest possible terms, a man's religion involves both moods of contraction and moods of expansion of his being. But the quantitative mixture and order of these moods vary so much from one age of the world, from one system of thought, and from one individual to another, that you may insist either on the dread and the submission, or on the peace and the freedom as the essence of the matter, and still remain materially within the limits of the truth. The constitutionally sombre and the constitutionally sanguine onlooker are bound to emphasize opposite aspects of what lies before their eyes.

The constitutionally sombre religious person makes even of his religious peace a very sober thing. Danger still hovers in the air about it. Flexion and contraction are not wholly checked. It were sparrowlike and childish after our deliverance to explode into twittering laughter and caper-cutting, and utterly to forget the imminent hawk on bough. Lie low, rather, lie low; for you are in the hands of a living God. In the Book of Job, for example, the impotence of man and the omnipotence of God is the exclusive burden of its author's mind. " It is as high as heaven; what canst thou do? — deeper than hell; what canst thou know?" There is an astringent relish about the truth of this conviction which some men can feel, and which for them is as near an approach as can be made to the feeling of religious joy.

"In Job," says that coldly truthful writer, the author of Mark Rutherford, "God reminds us that man is not the measure of his creation. The world is immense, constructed on no plan or theory which the intellect of man can grasp. It is *transcendent* everywhere. This is the burden of every verse, and is the secret, if there be one, of the poem. Sufficient or insufficient, there is nothing more. . . . God is great, we know not his ways. He takes from us all we have, but yet if we possess our souls in patience, we *may* pass the valley of the shadow, and come out in sunlight again. We may or we may not! . . . What more have we to say now than God said from the whirlwind over two thousand five hundred years ago?"[1]

If we turn to the sanguine onlooker, on the other hand, we find that deliverance is felt as incomplete unless the burden be altogether overcome and the danger forgotten. Such onlookers give us definitions that seem to the sombre minds of whom we have just been speaking to leave out all the solemnity that makes religious peace so different from merely animal joys. In the opinion of some

[1] Mark Rutherford's Deliverance, London, 1885, pp. 196, 198.

writers an attitude might be called religious, though no touch were left in it of sacrifice or submission, no tendency to flexion, no bowing of the head. Any "habitual and regulated admiration," says Professor J. R. Seeley,[1] "is worthy to be called a religion"; and accordingly he thinks that our Music, our Science, and our so-called ' Civilization,' as these things are now organized and admiringly believed in, form the more genuine religions of our time. Certainly the unhesitating and unreasoning way in which we feel that we must inflict our civilization upon ' lower' races, by means of Hotchkiss guns, etc., reminds one of nothing so much as of the early spirit of Islam spreading its religion by the sword.

In my last lecture I quoted to you the ultra-radical opinion of Mr. Havelock Ellis, that laughter of any sort may be considered a religious exercise, for it bears witness to the soul's emancipation. I quoted this opinion in order to deny its adequacy. But we must now settle our scores more carefully with this whole optimistic way of thinking. It is far too complex to be decided off-hand. I propose accordingly that we make of religious optimism the theme of the next two lectures.

[1] In his book (too little read, I fear), Natural Religion, 3d edition, Boston, 1886, pp. 91, 122.

LECTURES IV AND V

THE RELIGION OF HEALTHY-MINDEDNESS

IF we were to ask the question: 'What is human life's chief concern?' one of the answers we should receive would be: 'It is happiness.' How to gain, how to keep, how to recover happiness, is in fact for most men at all times the secret motive of all they do, and of all they are willing to endure. The hedonistic school in ethics deduces the moral life wholly from the experiences of happiness and unhappiness which different kinds of conduct bring; and, even more in the religious life than in the moral life, happiness and unhappiness seem to be the poles round which the interest revolves. We need not go so far as to say with the author whom I lately quoted that any persistent enthusiasm is, as such, religion, nor need we call mere laughter a religious exercise; but we must admit that any persistent enjoyment may *produce* the sort of religion which consists in a grateful admiration of the gift of so happy an existence; and we must also acknowledge that the more complex ways of experiencing religion are new manners of producing happiness, wonderful inner paths to a supernatural kind of happiness, when the first gift of natural existence is unhappy, as it so often proves itself to be.

With such relations between religion and happiness, it is perhaps not surprising that men come to regard the happiness which a religious belief affords as a proof of its truth. If a creed makes a man feel happy, he almost inevitably adopts it. Such a belief ought to be true;

therefore it is true — such, rightly or wrongly, is one of the 'immediate inferences' of the religious logic used by ordinary men.

" The near presence of God's spirit," says a German writer,[1] " may be experienced in its reality — indeed *only* experienced. And the mark by which the spirit's existence and nearness are made irrefutably clear to those who have ever had the experience is the utterly incomparable *feeling of happiness* which is connected with the nearness, and which is therefore not only a possible and altogether proper feeling for us to have here below, but is the best and most indispensable proof of God's reality. No other proof is equally convincing, and therefore happiness is the point from which every efficacious new theology should start."

In the hour immediately before us, I shall invite you to consider the simpler kinds of religious happiness, leaving the more complex sorts to be treated on a later day.

In many persons, happiness is congenital and irreclaimable. 'Cosmic emotion' inevitably takes in them the form of enthusiasm and freedom. I speak not only of those who are animally happy. I mean those who, when unhappiness is offered or proposed to them, positively refuse to feel it, as if it were something mean and wrong. We find such persons in every age, passionately flinging themselves upon their sense of the goodness of life, in spite of the hardships of their own condition, and in spite of the sinister theologies into which they may be born. From the outset their religion is one of union with the divine. The heretics who went before the reformation are lavishly accused by the church writers of antinomian practices, just as the first Christians were accused of indulgence in orgies by the Romans. It is probable that there never has been a century in which the deliberate refusal to think ill of life has not been ideal-

_____
[1] C. HILTY : Glück, dritter Theil, 1900, p. 18.

ized by a sufficient number of persons to form sects, open or secret, who claimed all natural things to be permitted. Saint Augustine's maxim, *Dilige et quod vis fac,* — if you but love [God], you may do as you incline, — is morally one of the profoundest of observations, yet it is pregnant, for such persons, with passports beyond the bounds of conventional morality. According to their characters they have been refined or gross; but their belief has been at all times systematic enough to constitute a definite religious attitude. God was for them a giver of freedom, and the sting of evil was overcome. Saint Francis and his immediate disciples were, on the whole, of this company of spirits, of which there are of course infinite varieties. Rousseau in the earlier years of his writing, Diderot, B. de Saint Pierre, and many of the leaders of the eighteenth century anti-christian movement were of this optimistic type. They owed their influence to a certain authoritativeness in their feeling that Nature, if you will only trust her sufficiently, is absolutely good.

It is to be hoped that we all have some friend, perhaps more often feminine than masculine, and young than old, whose soul is of this sky-blue tint, whose affinities are rather with flowers and birds and all enchanting innocencies than with dark human passions, who can think no ill of man or God, and in whom religious gladness, being in possession from the outset, needs no deliverance from any antecedent burden.

" God has two families of children on this earth," says Francis W. Newman,[1] " *the once-born* and *the twice-born,*" and the once-born he describes as follows : "They see God, not as a strict Judge, not as a Glorious Potentate ; but as the animating Spirit of a beautiful harmonious world, Beneficent and Kind, Merciful as well as Pure. The same characters generally have

[1] The Soul ; its Sorrows and its Aspirations, 3d edition, 1852, pp. 89, 91.

no metaphysical tendencies: they do not look back into themselves. Hence they are not distressed by their own imperfections: yet it would be absurd to call them self-righteous; for
they hardly think of themselves *at all*. This childlike quality
of their nature makes the opening of religion very happy to
them: for they no more shrink from God, than a child from an
emperor, before whom the parent trembles: in fact, they have
no vivid conception of *any* of the qualities in which the severer
Majesty of God consists.[1] He is to them the impersonation
of Kindness and Beauty. They read his character, not in
the disordered world of man, but in romantic and harmonious
nature. Of human sin they know perhaps little in their own
hearts and not very much in the world; and human suffering
does but melt them to tenderness. Thus, when they approach
God, no inward disturbance ensues; and without being as yet
spiritual, they have a certain complacency and perhaps romantic
sense of excitement in their simple worship."

In the Romish Church such characters find a more
congenial soil to grow in than in Protestantism, whose
fashions of feeling have been set by minds of a decidedly
pessimistic order. But even in Protestantism they have
been abundant enough; and in its recent 'liberal' de-
velopments of Unitarianism and latitudinarianism generally, minds of this order have played and still are playing
leading and constructive parts. Emerson himself is an
admirable example. Theodore Parker is another, — here
are a couple of characteristic passages from Parker's correspondence.[2]

"Orthodox scholars say: 'In the heathen classics you find no
consciousness of sin.' It is very true — God be thanked for it.
They were conscious of wrath, of cruelty, avarice, drunkenness,
lust, sloth, cowardice, and other actual vices, and struggled
and got rid of the deformities, but they were not conscious of

[1] I once heard a lady describe the pleasure it gave her to think that she
"could always cuddle up to God."

[2] JOHN WEISS: Life of Theodore Parker, i. 152, 32.

'enmity against God,' and did n't sit down and whine and groan against non-existent evil.   I have done wrong things enough in my life, and do them now ; I miss the mark, draw bow, and try again.   But I am not conscious of hating God, or man, or right, or love, and I know there is much 'health in me' ; and in my body, even now, there dwelleth many a good thing, spite of consumption and Saint Paul."   In another letter Parker writes : "I have swum in clear sweet waters all my days ; and if sometimes they were a little cold, and the stream ran adverse and something rough, it was never too strong to be breasted and swum through.   From the days of earliest boyhood, when I went stumbling through the grass, . . . up to the gray-bearded manhood of this time, there is none but has left me honey in the hive of memory that I now feed on for present delight. When I recall the years . . . I am filled with a sense of sweet-ness and wonder that such little things can make a mortal so exceedingly rich.   But I must confess that the chiefest of all my delights is still the religious."

Another good expression of the ' once-born ' type of consciousness, developing straight and natural, with no element of morbid compunction or crisis, is contained in the answer of Dr. Edward Everett Hale, the eminent Unitarian preacher and writer, to one of Dr. Starbuck's circulars.   I quote a part of it : —

"I observe, with profound regret, the religious struggles which come into many biographies, as if almost essential to the formation of the hero.   I ought to speak of these, to say that any man has an advantage, not to be estimated, who is born, as I was, into a family where the religion is simple and rational ; who is trained in the theory of such a religion, so that he never knows, for an hour, what these religious or irreligious struggles are.   I always knew God loved me, and I was always grateful to him for the world he placed me in.   I always liked to tell him so, and was always glad to receive his suggestions to me. . . . I can remember perfectly that when I was coming to manhood, the half-philosophical novels of the time had a deal

to say about the young men and maidens who were facing the
'problem of life.' I had no idea whatever what the problem
of life was. To live with all my might seemed to me easy ; to
learn where there was so much to learn seemed pleasant and
almost of course ; to lend a hand, if one had a chance, natural; and if one did this, why, he enjoyed life because he could
not help it, and without proving to himself that he ought to enjoy it. . . . A child who is early taught that he is God's child,
that he may live and move and have his being in God, and that
he has, therefore, infinite strength at hand for the conquering
of any difficulty, will take life more easily, and probably will
make more of it, than one who is told that he is born the child
of wrath and wholly incapable of good." [1]

One can but recognize in such writers as these the
presence of a temperament organically weighted on the
side of cheer and fatally forbidden to linger, as those of
opposite temperament linger, over the darker aspects of
the universe. In some individuals optimism may become quasi-pathological. The capacity for even a transient sadness or a momentary humility seems cut off
from them as by a kind of congenital anæsthesia.[2]

---

[1] Starbuck : Psychology of Religion, pp. 305, 306.

[2] " I know not to what physical laws philosophers will some day refer the
feelings of melancholy. For myself, I find that they are the most volup-
tuous of all sensations," writes Saint Pierre, and accordingly he devotes a
series of sections of his work on Nature to the Plaisirs de la Ruine, Plaisirs
des Tombeaux, Ruines de la Nature, Plaisirs de la Solitude — each of them
more optimistic than the last.

This finding of a luxury in woe is very common during adolescence. The
truth-telling Marie Bashkirtseff expresses it well : —

" In this depression and dreadful uninterrupted suffering, I don't condemn life. On the contrary, I like it and find it good. Can you believe it ?
I find everything good and pleasant, even my tears, my grief. I enjoy
weeping, I enjoy my despair. I enjoy being exasperated and sad. I feel
as if these were so many diversions, and I love life in spite of them all. I
want to live on. It would be cruel to have me die when I am so accommo-
dating. I cry, I grieve, and at the same time I am pleased — no, not
exactly that — I know not how to express it. But everything in life pleases
me. I find everything agreeable, and in the very midst of my prayers for

The supreme contemporary example of such an inability to feel evil is of course Walt Whitman.

"His favorite occupation," writes his disciple, Dr. Bucke, "seemed to be strolling or sauntering about outdoors by himself, looking at the grass, the trees, the flowers, the vistas of light, the varying aspects of the sky, and listening to the birds, the crickets, the tree frogs, and all the hundreds of natural sounds. It was evident that these things gave him a pleasure far beyond what they give to ordinary people. Until I knew the man," continues Dr. Bucke, "it had not occurred to me that any one could derive so much absolute happiness from these things as he did. He was very fond of flowers, either wild or cultivated; liked all sorts. I think he admired lilacs and sunflowers just as much as roses. Perhaps, indeed, no man who ever lived liked so many things and disliked so few as Walt Whitman. All natural objects seemed to have a charm for him. All sights and sounds seemed to please him. He appeared to like (and I believe he did like) all the men, women, and children he saw (though I never knew him to say that he liked any one), but each who knew him felt that he liked him or her, and that he liked others also. I never knew him to argue or dispute, and he never spoke about money. He always justified, sometimes playfully, sometimes quite seriously, those who spoke harshly of himself or his writings, and I often thought he even took pleasure in the opposition of enemies. When I first knew [him], I used to think that he watched himself, and would not allow his tongue to give expression to fretfulness, antipathy, complaint, and remonstrance. It did not occur to me as possible that these mental states could be absent in him. After long observation, however, I satisfied myself that such absence or unconsciousness was entirely real. He never spoke deprecatingly of any nationality or class of men, or time in the world's history, or against any trades or occupations — not even against any animals, insects, or inanimate things, nor any of the

happiness, I find myself happy at being miserable. It is not I who undergo all this — my body weeps and cries; but something inside of me which is above me is glad of it all." Journal de Marie Bashkirtseff, i. 67.

laws of nature, nor any of the results of those laws, such as illness, deformity, and death. He never complained or grumbled either at the weather, pain, illness, or anything else. He never swore. He could not very well, since he never spoke in anger and apparently never was angry. He never exhibited fear, and I do not believe he ever felt it." [1]

Walt Whitman owes his importance in literature to the systematic expulsion from his writings of all contractile elements. The only sentiments he allowed himself to express were of the expansive order; and he expressed these in the first person, not as your mere monstrously conceited individual might so express them, but vicariously for all men, so that a passionate and mystic ontological emotion suffuses his words, and ends by persuading the reader that men and women, life and death, and all things are divinely good.

Thus it has come about that many persons to-day regard Walt Whitman as the restorer of the eternal natural religion. He has infected them with his own love of comrades, with his own gladness that he and they exist. Societies are actually formed for his cult; a periodical organ exists for its propagation, in which the lines of orthodoxy and heterodoxy are already beginning to be drawn; [2] hymns are written by others in his peculiar prosody; and he is even explicitly compared with the founder of the Christian religion, not altogether to the advantage of the latter.

Whitman is often spoken of as a 'pagan.' The word nowadays means sometimes the mere natural animal man without a sense of sin; sometimes it means a Greek or Roman with his own peculiar religious consciousness. In

[1] R. M. BUCKE : Cosmic Consciousness, pp. 182–186, abridged.
[2] I refer to The Conservator, edited by Horace Traubel, and published monthly at Philadelphia.

neither of these senses does it fitly define this poet. He is more than your mere animal man who has not tasted of the tree of good and evil. He is aware enough of sin for a swagger to be present in his indifference towards it, a conscious pride in his freedom from flexions and contractions, which your genuine pagan in the first sense of the word would never show.

"I could turn and live with animals, they are so placid and self-contained,
I stand and look at them long and long ;
They do not sweat and whine about their condition.
They do not lie awake in the dark and weep for their sins.
Not one is dissatisfied, not one is demented with the mania of owning
    things,
Not one kneels to another, nor to his kind that lived thousands of years
    ago,
Not one is respectable or unhappy over the whole earth." [1]

No natural pagan could have written these well-known lines. But on the other hand Whitman is less than a Greek or Roman ; for their consciousness, even in Homeric times, was full to the brim of the sad mortality of this sunlit world, and such a consciousness Walt Whitman resolutely refuses to adopt. When, for example, Achilles, about to slay Lycaon, Priam's young son, hears him sue for mercy, he stops to say : —

"Ah, friend, thou too must die: why thus lamentest thou? Patroclos too is dead, who was better far than thou. . . . Over me too hang death and forceful fate. There cometh morn or eve or some noonday when my life too some man shall take in battle, whether with spear he smite, or arrow from the string." [2]

Then Achilles savagely severs the poor boy's neck with his sword, heaves him by the foot into the Scamander, and calls to the fishes of the river to eat the white fat of Lycaon. Just as here the cruelty and the sympathy each

---

[1] Song of Myself, 32.
[2] Iliad, XXI., E. Myers's translation.

ring true, and do not mix or interfere with one another, so did the Greeks and Romans keep all their sadnesses and gladnesses unmingled and entire. Instinctive good they did not reckon sin ; nor had they any such desire to save the credit of the universe as to make them insist, as so many of *us* insist, that what immediately appears as evil must be ' good in the making,' or something equally ingenious. Good was good, and bad just bad, for the earlier Greeks. They neither denied the ills of nature, — Walt Whitman's verse, ' What is called good is perfect and what is called bad is just as perfect,' would have been mere silliness to them, — nor did they, in order to escape from those ills, invent ' another and a better world ' of the imagination, in which, along with the ills, the innocent goods of sense would also find no place. This integrity of the instinctive reactions, this freedom from all moral sophistry and strain, gives a pathetic dignity to ancient pagan feeling. And this quality Whitman's outpourings have not got. His optimism is too voluntary and defiant ; his gospel has a touch of bravado and an affected twist,[1] and this diminishes its effect on many readers who yet are well disposed towards optimism, and on the whole quite willing to admit that in important respects Whitman is of the genuine lineage of the prophets.

If, then, we give the name of healthy-mindedness to the tendency which looks on all things and sees that they are good, we find that we must distinguish between a more involuntary and a more voluntary or systematic way of being healthy-minded. In its involuntary variety, healthy-

---

[1] " God is afraid of me ! " remarked such a titanic-optimistic friend in my presence one morning when he was feeling particularly hearty and cannibalistic. The defiance of the phrase showed that a Christian education in humility still rankled in his breast.

mindedness is a way of feeling happy about things immediately. In its systematical variety, it is an abstract way of conceiving things as good. Every abstract way of conceiving things selects some one aspect of them as their essence for the time being, and disregards the other aspects. Systematic healthy-mindedness, conceiving good as the essential and universal aspect of being, deliberately excludes evil from its field of vision; and although, when thus nakedly stated, this might seem a difficult feat to perform for one who is intellectually sincere with himself and honest about facts, a little reflection shows that the situation is too complex to lie open to so simple a criticism.

In the first place, happiness, like every other emotional state, has blindness and insensibility to opposing facts given it as its instinctive weapon for self-protection against disturbance. When happiness is actually in possession, the thought of evil can no more acquire the feeling of reality than the thought of good can gain reality when melancholy rules. To the man actively happy, from whatever cause, evil simply cannot then and there be believed in. He must ignore it; and to the bystander he may then seem perversely to shut his eyes to it and hush it up.

But more than this: the hushing of it up may, in a perfectly candid and honest mind, grow into a deliberate religious policy, or *parti pris*. Much of what we call evil is due entirely to the way men take the phenomenon. It can so often be converted into a bracing and tonic good by a simple change of the sufferer's inner attitude from one of fear to one of fight; its sting so often departs and turns into a relish when, after vainly seeking to shun it, we agree to face about and bear it cheerfully, that a man is simply bound in honor, with reference to many of the facts that seem at first to disconcert his peace, to adopt this way of escape. Refuse to admit their badness; despise their power; ignore their presence; turn your attention the other way; and so far as you yourself are concerned at any rate, though the facts may still exist, their evil character exists no longer. Since you make them evil or good by your own thoughts about them, it is the ruling of your thoughts which proves to be your principal concern.

The deliberate adoption of an optimistic turn of mind thus makes its entrance into philosophy. And once in, it is hard to trace its lawful bounds. Not only does the human instinct for happiness, bent on self-protection by ignoring, keep working in its favor, but higher inner ideals have weighty words to say. The attitude of unhappiness is not only painful, it is mean and ugly. What can be more base and unworthy than the pining, puling, mumping mood, no matter by what outward ills it may have been engendered? What is more injurious to others? What less helpful as a way out of the difficulty? It but fastens and perpetuates the trouble which occasioned it, and increases the total evil of the situation. At all costs, then, we ought to reduce the sway of that mood; we ought to scout it in ourselves and others, and never show it tolerance. But it is impossible to carry on this discipline in the subjective sphere without zealously emphasizing the brighter and minimizing the darker aspects of the objective sphere of things at the same time. And thus our resolution not to indulge in misery, beginning at a comparatively small point within ourselves, may not stop until it has brought the entire frame of reality under a systematic conception optimistic enough to be congenial with its needs.

In all this I say nothing of any mystical insight or

persuasion that the total frame of things absolutely must be good. Such mystical persuasion plays an enormous part in the history of the religious consciousness, and we must look at it later with some care. But we need not go so far at present. More ordinary non-mystical conditions of rapture suffice for my immediate contention. All invasive moral states and passionate enthusiasms make one feelingless to evil in some direction. The common penalties cease to deter the patriot, the usual prudences are flung by the lover to the winds. When the passion is extreme, suffering may actually be gloried in, provided it be for the ideal cause, death may lose its sting, the grave its victory. In these states, the ordinary contrast of good and ill seems to be swallowed up in a higher denomination, an omnipotent excitement which engulfs the evil, and which the human being welcomes as the crowning experience of his life. This, he says, is truly to live, and I exult in the heroic opportunity and adventure.

The systematic cultivation of healthy-mindedness as a religious attitude is therefore consonant with important currents in human nature, and is anything but absurd. In fact, we all do cultivate it more or less, even when our professed theology should in consistency forbid it. We divert our attention from disease and death as much as we can ; and the slaughter-houses and indecencies without end on which our life is founded are huddled out of sight and never mentioned, so that the world we recognize officially in literature and in society is a poetic fiction far handsomer and cleaner and better than the world that really is.[1]

---

[1] " As I go on in this life, day by day, I become more of a bewildered child; I cannot get used to this world, to procreation, to heredity, to sight, to hearing ; the commonest things are a burthen. The prim, obliterated,

The advance of liberalism, so-called, in Christianity, during the past fifty years, may fairly be called a victory of healthy-mindedness within the church over the morbidness with which the old hell-fire theology was more harmoniously related. We have now whole congregations whose preachers, far from magnifying our consciousness of sin, seem devoted rather to making little of it. They ignore, or even deny, eternal punishment, and insist on the dignity rather than on the depravity of man. They look at the continual preoccupation of the old-fashioned Christian with the salvation of his soul as something sickly and reprehensible rather than admirable; and a sanguine and 'muscular' attitude, which to our forefathers would have seemed purely heathen, has become in their eyes an ideal element of Christian character. I am not asking whether or not they are right, I am only pointing out the change.

The persons to whom I refer have still retained for the most part their nominal connection with Christianity, in spite of their discarding of its more pessimistic theological elements. But in that 'theory of evolution' which, gathering momentum for a century, has within the past twenty-five years swept so rapidly over Europe and America, we see the ground laid for a new sort of religion of Nature, which has entirely displaced Christianity from the thought of a large part of our generation. The idea of a universal evolution lends itself to a doctrine of general meliorism and progress which fits the religious needs of the healthy-minded so well that it seems almost as if it might have been created for their use. Accordingly we find 'evolutionism' interpreted thus optimistically and

polite surface of life, and the broad, bawdy, and orgiastic — or mænadic — foundations, form a spectacle to which no habit reconciles me." R. L. STEVENSON: Letters, ii. 355.

embraced as a substitute for the religion they were born in, by a multitude of our contemporaries who have either been trained scientifically, or been fond of reading popular science, and who had already begun to be inwardly dissatisfied with what seemed to them the harshness and irrationality of the orthodox Christian scheme. As examples are better than descriptions, I will quote a document received in answer to Professor Starbuck's circular of questions. The writer's state of mind may by courtesy be called a religion, for it is his reaction on the whole nature of things, it is systematic and reflective, and it loyally binds him to certain inner ideals. I think you will recognize in him, coarse-meated and incapable of wounded spirit as he is, a sufficiently familiar contemporary type.

Q. *What does Religion mean to you?*

A. It means nothing; and it seems, so far as I can observe, useless to others. I am sixty-seven years of age and have resided in X. fifty years, and have been in business forty-five, consequently I have some little experience of life and men, and some women too, and I find that the most religious and pious people are as a rule those most lacking in uprightness and morality. The men who do not go to church or have any religious convictions are the best. Praying, singing of hymns, and sermonizing are pernicious — they teach us to rely on some supernatural power, when we ought to rely on ourselves. I *teetotally* disbelieve in a God. The God-idea was begotten in ignorance, fear, and a general lack of any knowledge of Nature. If I were to die now, being in a healthy condition for my age, both mentally and physically, I would just as lief, yes, rather, die with a hearty enjoyment of music, sport, or any other rational pastime. As a timepiece stops, we die — there being no immortality in either case.

Q. *What comes before your mind corresponding to the words God, Heaven, Angels, etc.?*

A. Nothing whatever. I am a man without a religion. These words mean so much mythic bosh.

Q. Have you had any experiences which appeared providential ?

A. None whatever. There is no agency of the superintending kind. A little judicious observation as well as knowledge of scientific law will convince any one of this fact.

Q. What things work most strongly on your emotions?

A. Lively songs and music; Pinafore instead of an Oratorio. I like Scott, Burns, Byron, Longfellow, especially Shakespeare, etc., etc. Of songs, the Star-spangled Banner, America, Marseillaise, and all moral and soul-stirring songs, but wishy-washy hymns are my detestation. I greatly enjoy nature, especially fine weather, and until within a few years used to walk Sundays into the country, twelve miles often, with no fatigue, and bicycle forty or fifty. I have dropped the bicycle. I never go to church, but attend lectures when there are any good ones. All of my thoughts and cogitations have been of a healthy and cheerful kind, for instead of doubts and fears I see things as they are, for I endeavor to adjust myself to my environment. This I regard as the deepest law. Mankind is a progressive animal. I am satisfied he will have made a great advance over his present status a thousand years hence.

Q. What is your notion of sin ?

A. It seems to me that sin is a condition, a disease, incidental to man's development not being yet advanced enough. Morbidness over it increases the disease. We should think that a million of years hence equity, justice, and mental and physical good order will be so fixed and organized that no one will have any idea of evil or sin.

Q. What is your temperament?

A. Nervous, active, wide-awake, mentally and physically. Sorry that Nature compels us to sleep at all.

If we are in search of a broken and a contrite heart, clearly we need not look to this brother. His contentment with the finite incases him like a lobster-shell and shields him from all morbid repining at his distance from the Infinite. We have in him an excellent example of the optimism which may be encouraged by popular science.

To my mind a current far more important and interesting religiously than that which sets in from natural
science towards healthy-mindedness is that which has
recently poured over America and seems to be gathering
force every day, — I am ignorant what foothold it may
yet have acquired in Great Britain, — and to which, for
the sake of having a brief designation, I will give the
title of the ' Mind-cure movement.'   There are various
sects of this ' New Thought,' to use another of the names
by which it calls itself ; but their agreements are so profound that their differences may be neglected for my
present purpose, and I will treat the movement, without
apology, as if it were a simple thing.

It is a deliberately optimistic scheme of life, with both
a speculative and a practical side.   In its gradual development during the last quarter of a century, it has taken
up into itself a number of contributory elements, and it
must now be reckoned with as a genuine religious power.
It has reached the stage, for example, when the demand
for its literature is great enough for insincere stuff,
mechanically produced for the market, to be to a certain
extent supplied by publishers, — a phenomenon never
observed, I imagine, until a religion has got well past
its earliest insecure beginnings.

One of the doctrinal sources of Mind-cure is the four
Gospels; another is Emersonianism or New England transcendentalism ; another is Berkeleyan idealism ; another
is spiritism, with its messages of ' law ' and ' progress '
and ' development ' ; another the optimistic popular science evolutionism of which I have recently spoken ; and,
finally, Hinduism has contributed a strain.   But the
most characteristic feature of the mind-cure movement
is an inspiration much more direct.   The leaders in this
faith have had an intuitive belief in the all-saving power

of healthy-minded attitudes as such, in the conquering efficacy of courage, hope, and trust, and a correlative contempt for doubt, fear, worry, and all nervously precautionary states of mind.[1] Their belief has in a general way been corroborated by the practical experience of their disciples; and this experience forms to-day a mass imposing in amount.

The blind have been made to see, the halt to walk; lifelong invalids have had their health restored. The moral fruits have been no less remarkable. The deliberate adoption of a healthy-minded attitude has proved possible to many who never supposed they had it in them; regeneration of character has gone on on an extensive scale; and cheerfulness has been restored to countless homes. The indirect influence of this has been great. The mind-cure principles are beginning so to pervade the air that one catches their spirit at second-hand. One hears of the 'Gospel of Relaxation,' of the 'Don't Worry Movement,' of people who repeat to themselves, 'Youth, health, vigor!' when dressing in the morning, as their motto for the day. Complaints of the weather are getting to be forbidden in many households; and more and more people are recognizing it to be bad form to speak of disagreeable sensations, or to make much of the ordinary inconveniences and ailments of life. These general tonic effects on public opinion would be good even if the more striking results were non-existent. But the latter abound so that we can afford to overlook the

[1] 'Cautionary Verses for Children': this title of a much used work, published early in the nineteenth century, shows how far the muse of evangelical protestantism in England, with her mind fixed on the idea of danger, had at last drifted away from the original gospel freedom. Mind-cure might be briefly called a reaction against all that religion of chronic anxiety which marked the earlier part of our century in the evangelical circles of England and America.

innumerable failures and self-deceptions that are mixed in with them (for in everything human failure is a matter of course), and we can also overlook the verbiage of a good deal of the mind-cure literature, some of which is so moonstruck with optimism and so vaguely expressed that an academically trained intellect finds it almost impossible to read it at all.

The plain fact remains that the spread of the movement has been due to practical fruits, and the extremely practical turn of character of the American people has never been better shown than by the fact that this, their only decidedly original contribution to the systematic philosophy of life, should be so intimately knit up with concrete therapeutics. To the importance of mind-cure the medical and clerical professions in the United States are beginning, though with much recalcitrancy and protesting, to open their eyes. It is evidently bound to develop still farther, both speculatively and practically, and its latest writers are far and away the ablest of the group.[1] It matters nothing that, just as there are hosts of persons who cannot pray, so there are greater hosts who cannot by any possibility be influenced by the mind-curers' ideas. For our immediate purpose, the important point is that so large a number should exist who *can* be so influenced. They form a psychic type to be studied with respect.[2]

---

[1] I refer to Mr. Horatio W. Dresser and Mr. Henry Wood, especially the former. Mr. Dresser's works are published by G. P. Putnam's Sons, New York and London ; Mr. Wood's by Lee & Shepard, Boston.

[2] Lest my own testimony be suspected, I will quote another reporter, Dr. H. H. Goddard, of Clark University, whose thesis on "the Effects of Mind on Body as evidenced by Faith Cures" is published in the American Journal of Psychology for 1899 (vol. x.). This critic, after a wide study of the facts, concludes that the cures by mind-cure exist, but are in no respect different from those now officially recognized in medicine as cures by suggestion ; and the end of his essay contains an interesting physiological

To come now to a little closer quarters with their creed. The fundamental pillar on which it rests is nothing more than the general basis of all religious experience, the fact that man has a dual nature, and is connected with two spheres of thought, a shallower and a profounder sphere, in either of which he may learn to live more habitually. The shallower and lower sphere is that of the fleshly sensations, instincts, and desires, of egotism, doubt, and the lower personal interests. But whereas Christian theology has always considered *fro-*

speculation as to the way in which the suggestive ideas may work (p. 67 of the reprint). As regards the general phenomenon of mental cure itself, Dr. Goddard writes : " In spite of the severe criticism we have made of reports of cure, there still remains a vast amount of material, showing a powerful influence of the mind in disease. Many cases are of diseases that have been diagnosed and treated by the best physicians of the country, or which prominent hospitals have tried their hand at curing, but without success. People of culture and education have been treated by this method with satisfactory results. Diseases of long standing have been ameliorated, and even cured. . . . We have traced the mental element through primitive medicine and folk-medicine of to-day, patent medicine, and witchcraft. We are convinced that it is impossible to account for the existence of these practices, if they did not cure disease, and that if they cured disease, it must have been the mental element that was effective. The same argument applies to those modern schools of mental therapeutics — Divine Healing and Christian Science. It is hardly conceivable that the large body of intelligent people who comprise the body known distinctively as Mental Scientists should continue to exist if the whole thing were a delusion. It is not a thing of a day ; it is not confined to a few ; it is not local. It is true that many failures are recorded, but that only adds to the argument. There must be many and striking successes to counterbalance the failures, otherwise the failures would have ended the delusion. . . . Christian Science, Divine Healing, or Mental Science do not, and never can in the very nature of things, cure all diseases ; nevertheless, the practical applications of the general principles of the broadest mental science will tend to prevent disease. . . . We do find sufficient evidence to convince us that the proper reform in mental attitude would relieve many a sufferer of ills that the ordinary physician cannot touch ; would even delay the approach of death to many a victim beyond the power of absolute cure, and the faithful adherence to a truer philosophy of life will keep many a man well, and give the doctor time to devote to alleviating ills that are unpreventable " (pp. 33, 34 of reprint).

wardness to be the essential vice of this part of human nature, the mind-curers say that the mark of the beast in it is *fear ;* and this is what gives such an entirely new religious turn to their persuasion.

" Fear," to quote a writer of the school, " has had its uses in the evolutionary process, and seems to constitute the whole of forethought in most animals ; but that it should remain any part of the mental equipment of human civilized life is an absurdity. I find that the fear element of forethought is not stimulating to those more civilized persons to whom duty and attraction are the natural motives, but is weakening and deterrent. As soon as it becomes unnecessary, fear becomes a positive deterrent, and should be entirely removed, as dead flesh is removed from living tissue. To assist in the analysis of fear, and in the denunciation of its expressions, I have coined the word *fearthought* to stand for the unprofitable element of forethought, and have defined the word ' worry ' as *fearthought in contradistinction to forethought.* I have also defined fearthought as *the self-imposed or self-permitted suggestion of inferiority*, in order to place it where it really belongs, in the category of harmful, unnecessary, and therefore not respectable things." [1]

The ' misery-habit,' the ' martyr-habit,' engendered by the prevalent ' fearthought,' get pungent criticism from the mind-cure writers : —

" Consider for a moment the habits of life into which we are born. There are certain social conventions or customs and alleged requirements, there is a theological bias, a general view of the world. There are conservative ideas in regard to our early training, our education, marriage, and occupation in life. Following close upon this, there is a long series of anticipations, namely, that we shall suffer certain children's diseases, diseases of middle life, and of old age ; the thought that we shall grow

[1] HORACE FLETCHER : Happiness as found in Forethought *minus* Fearthought, Menticulture Series, ii. Chicago and New York, Stone, 1897, pp. 21–25, abridged.

old, lose our faculties, and again become childlike; while crowning all is the fear of death. Then there is a long line of particular fears and trouble-bearing expectations, such, for example, as ideas associated with certain articles of food, the dread of the east wind, the terrors of hot weather, the aches and pains associated with cold weather, the fear of catching cold if one sits in a draught, the coming of hay-fever upon the 14th of August in the middle of the day, and so on through a long list of fears, dreads, worriments, anxieties, anticipations, expectations, pessimisms, morbidities, and the whole ghostly train of fateful shapes which our fellow-men, and especially physicians, are ready to help us conjure up, an array worthy to rank with Bradley's ' unearthly ballet of bloodless categories.'

" Yet this is not all. This vast array is swelled by innumerable volunteers from daily life, — the fear of accident, the possibility of calamity, the loss of property, the chance of robbery, of fire, or the outbreak of war. And it is not deemed sufficient to fear for ourselves. When a friend is taken ill, we must forthwith fear the worst and apprehend death. If one meets with sorrow . . . sympathy means to enter into and increase the suffering." [1]

" Man," to quote another writer, " often has fear stamped upon him before his entrance into the outer world; he is reared in fear; all his life is passed in bondage to fear of disease and death, and thus his whole mentality becomes cramped, limited, and depressed, and his body follows its shrunken pattern and specification. . . . Think of the millions of sensitive and responsive souls among our ancestors who have been under the dominion of such a perpetual nightmare! Is it not surprising that health exists at all? Nothing but the boundless divine love, exuberance, and vitality, constantly poured in, even though unconsciously to us, could in some degree neutralize such an ocean of morbidity." [2]

Although the disciples of the mind-cure often use Christian terminology, one sees from such quotations

[1] H. W. DRESSER: Voices of Freedom, New York, 1899, p. 38.

[2] HENRY WOOD : Ideal Suggestion through Mental Photography, Boston, 1899, p. 54.

how widely their notion of the fall of man diverges from that of ordinary Christians.[1]

Their notion of man's higher nature is hardly less divergent, being decidedly pantheistic. The spiritual in man appears in the mind-cure philosophy as partly conscious, but chiefly subconscious; and through the subconscious part of it we are already one with the Divine without any miracle of grace, or abrupt creation of a new inner man. As this view is variously expressed by different writers, we find in it traces of Christian mysticism, of transcendental idealism, of vedantism, and of the modern psychology of the subliminal self. A quotation or two will put us at the central point of view : —

"The great central fact of the universe is that spirit of infinite life and power that is back of all, that manifests itself in and through all. This spirit of infinite life and power that is back of all is what I call God. I care not what term you may use, be it Kindly Light, Providence, the Over-Soul, Omnipo-

[1] Whether it differs so much from Christ's own notion is for the exegetists to decide. According to Harnack, Jesus felt about evil and disease much as our mind-curers do. "What is the answer which Jesus sends to John the Baptist ?" asks Harnack, and says it is this : "'The blind see, and the lame walk, the lepers are cleansed, and the deaf hear, the dead rise up, and the gospel is preached to the poor.' That is the 'coming of the kingdom,' or rather in these saving works the kingdom is already there. By the overcoming and removal of misery, of need, of sickness, by these actual effects John is to see that the new time has arrived. The casting out of devils is only a part of this work of redemption, *but Jesus points to that as the sense and seal of his mission.* Thus to the wretched, sick, and poor did he address himself, but not as a moralist, and without a trace of sentimentalism. He never makes groups and departments of the ills ; he never spends time in asking whether the sick one 'deserves' to be cured ; and it never occurs to him to sympathize with the pain or the death. He nowhere says that sickness is a beneficent infliction, and that evil has a healthy use. No, he calls sickness sickness and health health. All evil, all wretchedness, is for him something dreadful ; it is of the great kingdom of Satan ; but he feels the power of the Saviour within him. He knows that advance is possible only when weakness is overcome when sickness is made well." Das Wesen des Christenthums, 1900, p. 39.

tence, or whatever term may be most convenient, so long as we are agreed in regard to the great central fact itself. God then fills the universe alone, so that all is from Him and in Him, and there is nothing that is outside. He is the life of our life, our very life itself. We are partakers of the life of God; and though we differ from Him in that we are individualized spirits, while He is the Infinite Spirit, including us, as well as all else beside, yet in essence the life of God and the life of man are identically the same, and so are one. They differ not in essence or quality; they differ in degree.

"The great central fact in human life is the coming into a conscious vital realization of our oneness with this Infinite Life, and the opening of ourselves fully to this divine inflow. In just the degree that we come into a conscious realization of our oneness with the Infinite Life, and open ourselves to this divine inflow, do we actualize in ourselves the qualities and powers of the Infinite Life, do we make ourselves channels through which the Infinite Intelligence and Power can work. In just the degree in which you realize your oneness with the Infinite Spirit, you will exchange dis-ease for ease, inharmony for harmony, suffering and pain for abounding health and strength. To recognize our own divinity, and our intimate relation to the Universal, is to attach the belts of our machinery to the powerhouse of the Universe. One need remain in hell no longer than one chooses to; we can rise to any heaven we ourselves choose; and when we choose so to rise, all the higher powers of the Universe combine to help us heavenward." [1]

Let me now pass from these abstracter statements to some more concrete accounts of experience with the mind-cure religion. I have many answers from correspondents — the only difficulty is to choose. The first two whom I shall quote are my personal friends. One of them, a woman, writing as follows, expresses well the feeling of continuity with the Infinite Power, by which all mind-cure disciples are inspired.

[1] R. W. TRINE: In Tune with the Infinite, 26th thousand, N. Y., 1899. I have strung scattered passages together.

"The first underlying cause of all sickness, weakness, or depression is the *human sense of separateness* from that Divine Energy which we call God. The soul which can feel and affirm in serene but jubilant confidence, as did the Nazarene: 'I and my Father are one,' has no further need of healer, or of healing. This is the whole truth in a nutshell, and other foundation for wholeness can no man lay than this fact of impregnable divine union. Disease can no longer attack one whose feet are planted on this rock, who feels hourly, momently, the influx of the Deific Breath. If one with Omnipotence, how can weariness enter the consciousness, how illness assail that indomitable spark?

"This possibility of annulling forever the law of fatigue has been abundantly proven in my own case; for my earlier life bears a record of many, many years of bedridden invalidism, with spine and lower limbs paralyzed. My thoughts were no more impure than they are to-day, although my belief in the necessity of illness was dense and unenlightened; but since my resurrection in the flesh, I have worked as a healer unceasingly for fourteen years without a vacation, and can truthfully assert that I have never known a moment of fatigue or pain, although coming in touch constantly with excessive weakness, illness, and disease of all kinds. For how can a conscious part of Deity be sick? — since 'Greater is he that is *with* us than all that can strive against us.'"

My second correspondent, also a woman, sends me the following statement: —

"Life seemed difficult to me at one time. I was always breaking down, and had several attacks of what is called nervous prostration, with terrible insomnia, being on the verge of insanity; besides having many other troubles, especially of the digestive organs. I had been sent away from home in charge of doctors, had taken all the narcotics, stopped all work, been fed up, and in fact knew all the doctors within reach. But I never recovered permanently till this New Thought took possession of me.

"I think that the one thing which impressed me most was

learning the fact that we must be in absolutely constant relation or mental touch (this word is to me very expressive) with that essence of life which permeates all and which we call God. This is almost unrecognizable unless we live it into ourselves *actually*, that is, by a constant turning to the very innermost, deepest consciousness of our real selves or of God in us, for illumination from within, just as we turn to the sun for light, warmth, and invigoration without. When you do this consciously, realizing that to turn inward to the light within you is to live in the presence of God or your divine self, you soon discover the unreality of the objects to which you have hitherto been turning and which have engrossed you without.

" I have come to disregard the meaning of this attitude for bodily health *as such*, because that comes of itself, as an incidental result, and cannot be found by any special mental act or desire to have it, beyond that general attitude of mind I have referred to above. That which we usually make the object of life, those outer things we are all so wildly seeking, which we so often live and die for, but which then do not give us peace and happiness, they should all come of themselves as accessory, and as the mere outcome or natural result of a far higher life sunk deep in the bosom of the spirit. This life is the real seeking of the kingdom of God, the desire for his supremacy in our hearts, so that all else comes as that which shall be ' added unto you ' — as quite incidental and as a surprise to us, perhaps ; and yet it is the proof of the reality of the perfect poise in the very centre of our being.

" When I say that we commonly make the object of our life that which we should not work for primarily, I mean many things which the world considers praiseworthy and excellent, such as success in business, fame as author or artist, physician or lawyer, or renown in philanthropic undertakings. Such things should be results, not objects. I would also include pleasures of many kinds which seem harmless and good at the time, and are pursued because many accept them — I mean conventionalities, sociabilities, and fashions in their various development, these being mostly approved by the masses, although they may be unreal, and even unhealthy superfluities."

Here is another case, more concrete, also that of a woman. I read you these cases without comment,—they express so many varieties of the state of mind we are studying.

"I had been a sufferer from my childhood till my fortieth year. [Details of ill-health are given which I omit.] I had been in Vermont several months hoping for good from the change of air, but steadily growing weaker, when one day during the latter part of October, while resting in the afternoon, I suddenly heard as it were these words : ' You will be healed and do a work you never dreamed of.' These words were impressed upon my mind with such power I said at once that only God could have put them there. I believed them in spite of myself and of my suffering and weakness, which continued until Christmas, when I returned to Boston. Within two days a young friend offered to take me to a mental healer (this was January 7, 1881). The healer said : ' There is nothing but Mind ; we are expressions of the One Mind ; body is only a mortal belief ; as a man thinketh so is he.' I could not accept all she said, but I translated all that was there for *me* in this way : ' There is nothing but God ; I am created by Him, and am absolutely dependent upon Him ; mind is given me to use ; and by just so much of it as I will put upon the thought of right action in body I shall be lifted out of bondage to my ignorance and fear and past experience.' That day I commenced accordingly to take a little of every food provided for the family, constantly saying to myself : ' The Power that created the stomach must take care of what I have eaten.' By holding these suggestions through the evening I went to bed and fell asleep, saying : ' I am soul, spirit, just one with God's Thought of me,' and slept all night without waking, for the first time in several years [the distress-turns had usually recurred about two o'clock in the night]. I felt the next day like an escaped prisoner, and believed I had found the secret that would in time give me perfect health. Within ten days I was able to eat anything provided for others, and after two weeks I began to have my own positive mental suggestions of Truth, which were to me like stepping-stones. I will note a few of them; they came about two weeks apart.

"1st. I am Soul, therefore it is well with me.

"2d. I am Soul, therefore I *am* well.

"3d. A sort of inner vision of myself as a four-footed beast with a protuberance on every part of my body where I had suffering, with my own face, begging me to acknowledge it as myself. I resolutely fixed my attention on being well, and refused to even look at my old self in this form.

"4th. Again the vision of the beast far in the background, with faint voice. Again refusal to acknowledge.

"5th. Once more the vision, but only of my eyes with the longing look; and again the refusal. Then came the conviction, the inner consciousness, that I was perfectly well and always had been, for I was Soul, an expression of God's Perfect Thought. That was to me the perfect and completed separation between what I was and what I appeared to be. I succeeded in never losing sight after this of my real being, by constantly affirming this truth, and by degrees (though it took me two years of hard work to get there) *I expressed health continuously throughout my whole body.*

"In my subsequent nineteen years' experience I have never known this Truth to fail when I applied it, though in my ignorance I have often failed to apply it, but through my failures I have learned the simplicity and trustfulness of the little child."

But I fear that I risk tiring you by so many examples, and I must lead you back to philosophic generalities again. You see already by such records of experience how impossible it is not to class mind-cure as primarily a religious movement. Its doctrine of the oneness of our life with God's life is in fact quite indistinguishable from an interpretation of Christ's message which in these very Gifford lectures has been defended by some of your very ablest Scottish religious philosophers.[1]

[1] The Cairds, for example. In EDWARD CAIRD's Glasgow Lectures of 1890–92 passages like this abound : —

"The declaration made in the beginning of the ministry of Jesus that

But philosophers usually profess to give a quasi-logical explanation of the existence of evil, whereas of the general fact of evil in the world, the existence of the selfish, suffering, timorous finite consciousness, the mind-curers, so far as I am acquainted with them, profess to give no speculative explanation.   Evil is empirically there for them as it is for everybody, but the practical point of view predominates, and it would ill agree with the spirit of their system to spend time in worrying over it as a ' mystery ' or ' problem,' or in ' laying to heart' the lesson of its experience, after the manner of the Evangelicals.   Don't reason about it, as Dante says, but give a glance and pass beyond!   It is Avidhya, ignorance ! something merely to be outgrown and left behind, transcended and forgotten.   Christian Science so-called, the sect of Mrs. Eddy, is the most radical branch of mind-cure in its dealings with evil.   For it evil is simply a *lie*,

'the time is fulfilled, and the kingdom of heaven is at hand,' passes with scarce a break into the announcement that ' the kingdom of God is among you ' ; and the importance of this announcement is asserted to be such that it makes, so to speak, a difference *in kind* between the greatest saints and prophets who lived under the previous reign of division, and 'the least in the kingdom of heaven.'   The highest ideal is brought close to men and declared to be within their reach, they are called on to be ' perfect as their Father in heaven is perfect.'   The sense of alienation and distance from God which had grown upon the pious in Israel just in proportion as they had learned to look upon Him as no mere national divinity, but as a God of justice who would punish Israel for its sin as certainly as Edom or Moab, is declared to be no longer in place ; and the typical form of Christian prayer points to the abolition of the contrast between this world and the next which through all the history of the Jews had continually been growing wider : ' As in heaven, so on earth.'   The sense of the division of man from God, as a finite being from the Infinite, as weak and sinful from the Omnipotent Goodness, is not indeed lost ; but it can no longer overpower the consciousness of oneness.   The terms ' Son ' and ' Father ' at once state the opposition and mark its limit.   They show that it is not an absolute opposition, but one which presupposes an indestructible principle of unity, that can and must become a principle of reconciliation."   The Evolution of Religion, ii. pp. 146, 147.

and any one who mentions it is a liar. The optimistic ideal of duty forbids us to pay it the compliment even of explicit attention. Of course, as our next lectures will show us, this is a bad speculative omission, but it is intimately linked with the practical merits of the system we are examining. Why regret a philosophy of evil, a mind-curer would ask us, if I can put you in possession of a life of good?

After all, it is the life that tells ; and mind-cure has developed a living system of mental hygiene which may well claim to have thrown all previous literature of the *Diätetik der Seele* into the shade. This system is wholly and exclusively compacted of optimism : ' Pessimism leads to weakness. Optimism leads to power.' ' Thoughts are things,' as one of the most vigorous mind-cure writers prints in bold type at the bottom of each of his pages ; and if your thoughts are of health, youth, vigor, and success, before you know it these things will also be your outward portion. No one can fail of the regenerative influence of optimistic thinking, pertinaciously pursued. Every man owns indefeasibly this inlet to the divine. Fear, on the contrary, and all the contracted and egoistic modes of thought, are inlets to destruction. Most mind-curers here bring in a doctrine that thoughts are ' forces,' and that, by virtue of a law that like attracts like, one man's thoughts draw to themselves as allies all the thoughts of the same character that exist the world over. Thus one gets, by one's thinking, reinforcements from elsewhere for the realization of one's desires ; and the great point in the conduct of life is to get the heavenly forces on one's side by opening one's own mind to their influx.

On the whole, one is struck by a psychological similarity between the mind-cure movement and the Lutheran

and Wesleyan movements. To the believer in moralism
and works, with his anxious query, ' What shall I do to
be saved?' Luther and Wesley replied : ' You are saved
now, if you would but believe it.'   And the mind-curers
come with precisely similar words of emancipation.   They
speak, it is true, to persons for whom the conception of
salvation has lost its ancient theological meaning, but who
labor nevertheless with the same eternal human difficulty.
Things are wrong with them; and 'What shall I do to
be clear, right, sound, whole, well?' is the form of their
question.   And the answer is : ' You *are* well, sound,
and clear already, if you did but know it.'   " The whole
matter may be summed up in one sentence," says one of
the authors whom I have already quoted, " *God is well,
and so are you.*   You must awaken to the knowledge of
your real being."

The adequacy of their message to the mental needs of
a large fraction of mankind is what gave force to those
earlier gospels.   Exactly the same adequacy holds in the
case of the mind-cure message, foolish as it may sound
upon its surface ; and seeing its rapid growth in influence, and its therapeutic triumphs, one is tempted to ask
whether it may not be destined (probably by very reason
of the crudity and extravagance of many of its manifestations [1]) to play a part almost as great in the evolution
of the popular religion of the future as did those earlier
movements in their day.

But I here fear that I may begin to ' jar upon the
nerves ' of some of the members of this academic audience.   Such contemporary vagaries, you may think,

---

[1] It remains to be seen whether the school of Mr. Dresser, which assumes
more and more the form of mind-cure experience and academic philosophy
mutually impregnating each other, will score the practical triumphs of the
less critical and rational sects.

should hardly take so large a place in dignified Gifford lectures. I can only beseech you to have patience. The whole outcome of these lectures will, I imagine, be the emphasizing to your mind of the enormous diversities which the spiritual lives of different men exhibit. Their wants, their susceptibilities, and their capacities all vary and must be classed under different heads. The result is that we have really different types of religious experience; and, seeking in these lectures closer acquaintance with the healthy-minded type, we must take it where we find it in most radical form. The psychology of individual types of character has hardly begun even to be sketched as yet — our lectures may possibly serve as a crumb-like contribution to the structure. The first thing to bear in mind (especially if we ourselves belong to the clerico-academic-scientific type, the officially and conventionally 'correct' type, 'the deadly respectable' type, for which to ignore others is a besetting temptation) is that nothing can be more stupid than to bar out phenomena from our notice, merely because we are incapable of taking part in anything like them ourselves.

Now the history of Lutheran salvation by faith, of methodistic conversions, and of what I call the mind-cure movement seems to prove the existence of numerous persons in whom — at any rate at a certain stage in their development — a change of character for the better, so far from being facilitated by the rules laid down by official moralists, will take place all the more successfully if those rules be exactly reversed. Official moralists advise us never to relax our strenuousness. " Be vigilant, day and night," they adjure us; "hold your passive tendencies in check; shrink from no effort; keep your will like a bow always bent." But the persons I speak of find that all this conscious effort leads to nothing but failure

and vexation in their hands, and only makes them twofold more the children of hell they were before. The
tense and voluntary attitude becomes in them an impossible fever and torment. Their machinery refuses to run
at all when the bearings are made so hot and the belts
so tight.

Under these circumstances the way to success, as
vouched for by innumerable authentic personal narra-
tions, is by an anti-moralistic method, by the ' surrender '
of which I spoke in my second lecture. Passivity, not
activity ; relaxation, not intentness, should be now the
rule. Give up the feeling of responsibility, let go your
hold, resign the care of your destiny to higher powers,
be genuinely indifferent as to what becomes of it all, and
you will find not only that you gain a perfect inward relief, but often also, in addition, the particular goods you
sincerely thought you were renouncing. This is the salvation through self-despair, the dying to be truly born,
of Lutheran theology, the passage into *nothing* of which
Jacob Behmen writes. To get to it, a critical point must
usually be passed, a corner turned within one. Something must give way, a native hardness must break down
and liquefy ; and this event (as we shall abundantly see
hereafter) is frequently sudden and automatic, and leaves
on the Subject an impression that he has been wrought
on by an external power.

Whatever its ultimate significance may prove to be,
this is certainly one fundamental form of human experience. Some say that the capacity or incapacity for it
is what divides the religious from the merely moralistic
character. With those who undergo it in its fullness, no
criticism avails to cast doubt on its reality. They *know* ;
for they have actually *felt* the higher powers, in giving
up the tension of their personal will.

A story which revivalist preachers often tell is that of a man who found himself at night slipping down the side of a precipice. At last he caught a branch which stopped his fall, and remained clinging to it in misery for hours. But finally his fingers had to loose their hold, and with a despairing farewell to life, he let himself drop. He fell just six inches. If he had given up the struggle earlier, his agony would have been spared. As the mother earth received him, so, the preachers tell us, will the everlasting arms receive *us* if we confide absolutely in them, and give up the hereditary habit of relying on our personal strength, with its precautions that cannot shelter and safeguards that never save.

The mind-curers have given the widest scope to this sort of experience. They have demonstrated that a form of regeneration by relaxing, by letting go, psychologically indistinguishable from the Lutheran justification by faith and the Wesleyan acceptance of free grace, is within the reach of persons who have no conviction of sin and care nothing for the Lutheran theology. It is but giving your little private convulsive self a rest, and finding that a greater Self is there. The results, slow or sudden, or great or small, of the combined optimism and expectancy, the regenerative phenomena which ensue on the abandonment of effort, remain firm facts of human nature, no matter whether we adopt a theistic, a pantheistic-idealistic, or a medical-materialistic view of their ultimate causal explanation.[1]

[1] The theistic explanation is by divine grace, which creates a new nature within one the moment the old nature is sincerely given up. The pantheistic explanation (which is that of most mind-curers) is by the merging of the narrower private self into the wider or greater self, the spirit of the universe (which is your own 'subconscious' self), the moment the isolating barriers of mistrust and anxiety are removed. The medico-materialistic explanation is that simpler cerebral processes act more freely where they are left to act automatically by the shunting-out of physiologically (though

When we take up the phenomena of revivalistic conversion, we shall learn something more about all this. Meanwhile I will say a brief word about the mind-curer's *methods*.

They are of course largely suggestive. The suggestive influence of environment plays an enormous part in all spiritual education. But the word 'suggestion,' having acquired official status, is unfortunately already beginning to play in many quarters the part of a wet blanket upon investigation, being used to fend off all inquiry into the varying susceptibilities of individual cases. 'Suggestion' is only another name for the power of ideas, *so far as they prove efficacious over belief and conduct.* Ideas efficacious over some people prove inefficacious over others. Ideas efficacious at some times and in some human surroundings are not so at other times and elsewhere. The ideas of Christian churches are not efficacious in the therapeutic direction to-day, whatever they may have been in earlier centuries; and when the whole question is as to why the salt has lost its savor here or gained it there, the mere blank waving of the word 'suggestion' as if it were a banner gives no light. Dr. Goddard, whose candid psychological essay on Faith Cures ascribes them to nothing but ordinary suggestion, concludes by saying that "Religion [and by this he seems to mean our popular Christianity] has in it all there is in mental therapeutics, and has it in its best form. Living up to [our religious] ideas will do anything for us that can be done." And this in spite of the actual fact that the popular Christianity does abso-

in this instance not spiritually) 'higher' ones which, seeking to regulate, only succeed in inhibiting results. — Whether this third explanation might, in a psycho-physical account of the universe, be combined with either of the others may be left an open question here.

lutely *nothing,* or did nothing until mind-cure came to the rescue.[1]

An idea, to be suggestive, must come to the individual with the force of a revelation. The mind-cure with its gospel of healthy-mindedness has come as a revelation to many whose hearts the church Christianity had left hardened. It has let loose their springs of higher life.

[1] Within the churches a disposition has always prevailed to regard sickness as a visitation; something sent by God for our good, either as chastisement, as warning, or as opportunity for exercising virtue, and, in the Catholic Church, of earning 'merit.' "Illness," says a good Catholic writer (P. LEJEUNE : Introd. a la Vie Mystique, 1899, p. 218), "is the most excellent of corporeal mortifications, the mortification which one has not one's self chosen, which is imposed directly by God, and is the direct expression of his will. 'If other mortifications are of silver,' Mgr. Gay says, ' this one is of gold ; since although it comes of ourselves, coming as it does of original sin, still on its greater side, as coming (like all that happens) from the providence of God, it is of divine manufacture. And how just are its blows ! And how efficacious it is ! . . . I do not hesitate to say that patience in a long illness is mortification's very masterpiece, and consequently the triumph of mortified souls.'" According to this view, disease should in any case be submissively accepted, and it might under certain circumstances even be blasphemous to wish it away.

Of course there have been exceptions to this, and cures by special miracle have at all times been recognized within the church's pale, almost all the great saints having more or less performed them. It was one of the heresies of Edward Irving, to maintain them still to be possible. An extremely pure faculty of healing after confession and conversion on the patient's part, and prayer on the priest's, was quite spontaneously developed in the German pastor, Joh. Christoph Blumhardt, in the early forties and exerted during nearly thirty years. Blumhardt's Life by Zündel (5th edition, Zurich, 1887) gives in chapters ix., x., xi., and xvii. a pretty full account of his healing activity, which he invariably ascribed to direct divine interposition. Blumhardt was a singularly pure, simple, and non-fanatical character, and in this part of his work followed no previous model. In Chicago to-day we have the case of Dr. J. A. Dowie, a Scottish Baptist preacher, whose weekly ' Leaves of Healing' were in the year of grace 1900 in their sixth volume, and who, although he denounces the cures wrought in other sects as 'diabolical counterfeits' of his own exclusively 'Divine Healing,' must on the whole be counted into the mind-cure movement. In mind-cure circles the fundamental article of faith is that disease should never be accepted. It is wholly of the pit. God wants us to be absolutely healthy, and we should not tolerate ourselves on any lower terms.

In what can the originality of any religious movement consist, save in finding a channel, until then sealed up, through which those springs may be set free in some group of human beings ?

The force of personal faith, enthusiasm, and example, and above all the force of novelty, are always the prime suggestive agency in this kind of success. If mind-cure should ever become official, respectable, and intrenched, these elements of suggestive efficacy will be lost. In its acuter stages every religion must be a homeless Arab of the desert. The church knows this well enough, with its everlasting inner struggle of the acute religion of the few against the chronic religion of the many, indurated into an obstructiveness worse than that which irreligion opposes to the movings of the Spirit. "We may pray," says Jonathan Edwards, "concerning all those saints that are not lively Christians, that they may either be enlivened, or taken away ; if that be true that is often said by some at this day, that these cold dead saints do more hurt than natural men, and lead more souls to hell, and that it would be well for mankind if they were all dead."[1]

The next condition of success is the apparent existence, in large numbers, of minds who unite healthy-mindedness with readiness for regeneration by letting go. Protestantism has been too pessimistic as regards the natural man, Catholicism has been too legalistic and moralistic, for either the one or the other to appeal in any generous way to the type of character formed of this peculiar mingling of elements. However few of us here present may belong to such a type, it is now evident that

[1] Edwards, from whose book on the Revival in New England I quote these words, dissuades from such a use of prayer, but it is easy to see that he enjoys making his thrust at the cold dead church members.

it forms a specific moral combination, well represented in the world.

Finally, mind-cure has made what in our protestant countries is an unprecedentedly great use of the subconscious life. To their reasoned advice and dogmatic assertion, its founders have added systematic exercise in passive relaxation, concentration, and meditation, and have even invoked something like hypnotic practice. I quote some passages at random : —

"The value, the potency of ideals is the great practical truth on which the New Thought most strongly insists, — the development namely from within outward, from small to great.[1] Consequently one's thought should be centred on the ideal outcome, even though this trust be literally like a step in the dark.[2] To attain the ability thus effectively to direct the mind, the New Thought advises the practice of concentration, or in other words, the attainment of self-control. One is to learn to marshal the tendencies of the mind, so that they may be held together as a unit by the chosen ideal. To this end, one should set apart times for silent meditation, by one's self, preferably in a room where the surroundings are favorable to spiritual thought. In New Thought terms, this is called 'entering the silence.'"[3]

"The time will come when in the busy office or on the noisy street you can enter into the silence by simply drawing the mantle of your own thoughts about you and realizing that there and everywhere the Spirit of Infinite Life, Love, Wisdom, Peace, Power, and Plenty is guiding, keeping, protecting, leading you. This is the spirit of continual prayer.[4] One of the most intuitive men we ever met had a desk at a city office where several other gentlemen were doing business constantly, and often talking loudly. Entirely undisturbed by the many various sounds about him, this self-centred faithful man would,

[1] H. W. DRESSER : Voices of Freedom, 46.
[2] DRESSER : Living by the Spirit, 58.
[3] DRESSER : Voices of Freedom, 33.
[4] TRINE : In Tune with the Infinite, p. 214.

in any moment of perplexity, draw the curtains of privacy so
completely about him that he would be as fully inclosed in his
own psychic aura, and thereby as effectually removed from all
distractions, as though he were alone in some primeval wood.
Taking his difficulty with him into the mystic silence in the
form of a direct question, to which he expected a certain answer, he would remain utterly passive until the reply came,
and never once through many years' experience did he find
himself disappointed or misled." [1]

Wherein, I should like to know, does this *intrinsically*
differ from the practice of ' recollection ' which plays so
great a part in Catholic discipline ?   Otherwise called the
practice of the presence of God (and so known among
ourselves, as for instance in Jeremy Taylor), it is thus
defined by the eminent teacher Alvarez de Paz in his
work on Contemplation.

" It is the recollection of God, the thought of God, which in
all places and circumstances makes us see him present, lets us
commune respectfully and lovingly with him, and fills us with
desire and affection for him. . . . Would you escape from
every ill ?   Never lose this recollection of God, neither in prosperity nor in adversity, nor on any occasion whichsoever it be.
Invoke not, to excuse yourself from this duty, either the difficulty or the importance of your business, for you can always
remember that God sees you, that you are under his eye.   If a
thousand times an hour you forget him, reanimate a thousand
times the recollection.   If you cannot practice this exercise
continuously, at least make yourself as familiar with it as possible ; and, like unto those who in a rigorous winter draw near
the fire as often as they can, go as often as you can to that
ardent fire which will warm your soul." [2]

All the external associations of the Catholic discipline
are of course unlike anything in mind-cure thought, but
the purely spiritual part of the exercise is identical in

[1] TRINE : p. 117.

[2] Quoted by LEJEUNE : Introd. à la Vie Mystique, 1899, p. 66.

both communions, and in both communions those who urge it write with authority, for they have evidently experienced in their own persons that whereof they tell. Compare again some mind-cure utterances : —

"High, healthful, pure thinking can be encouraged, promoted, and strengthened. Its current can be turned upon grand ideals until it forms a habit and wears a channel. By means of such discipline the mental horizon can be flooded with the sunshine of beauty, wholeness, and harmony. To inaugurate pure and lofty thinking may at first seem difficult, even almost mechanical, but perseverance will at length render it easy, then pleasant, and finally delightful.

"The soul's real world is that which it has built of its thoughts, mental states, and imaginations. If we *will*, we can turn our backs upon the lower and sensuous plane, and lift ourselves into the realm of the spiritual and Real, and there gain a residence. The assumption of states of expectancy and receptivity will attract spiritual sunshine, and it will flow in as naturally as air inclines to a vacuum. . . . Whenever the thought is not occupied with one's daily duty or profession, it should be sent aloft into the spiritual atmosphere. There are quiet leisure moments by day, and wakeful hours at night, when this wholesome and delightful exercise may be engaged in to great advantage. If one who has never made any systematic effort to lift and control the thought-forces will, for a single month, earnestly pursue the course here suggested, he will be surprised and delighted at the result, and nothing will induce him to go back to careless, aimless, and superficial thinking. At such favorable seasons the outside world, with all its current of daily events, is barred out, and one goes into the silent sanctuary of the inner temple of soul to commune and aspire. The spiritual hearing becomes delicately sensitive, so that the 'still, small voice' is audible, the tumultuous waves of external sense are hushed, and there is a great calm. The ego gradually becomes conscious that it is face to face with the Divine Presence ; that mighty, healing, loving, Fatherly life which is nearer to us than we are to ourselves. There is soul-contact with the Parent-Soul, and an influx of life, love, virtue, health, and happiness from the Inexhaustible Fountain." [1]

When we reach the subject of mysticism, you will undergo so deep an immersion into these exalted states of consciousness as to be wet all over, if I may so express myself; and the cold shiver of doubt with which this little sprinkling may affect you will have long since passed away — doubt, I mean, as to whether all such writing be not mere abstract talk and rhetoric set down *pour encourager les autres.* You will then be convinced, I trust, that these states of consciousness of ' union ' form a perfectly definite class of experiences, of which the soul may occasionally partake, and which certain persons may live by in a deeper sense than they live by anything else with which they have acquaintance. This brings me to a general philosophical reflection with which I should like to pass from the subject of healthy-mindedness, and close a topic which I fear is already only too long drawn out. It concerns the relation of all this systematized healthy-mindedness and mind-cure religion to scientific method and the scientific life.

In a later lecture I shall have to treat explicitly of the relation of religion to science on the one hand, and to primeval savage thought on the other. There are plenty of persons to-day — ' scientists ' or ' positivists,' they are fond of calling themselves — who will tell you that religious thought is a mere survival, an atavistic reversion to a type of consciousness which humanity in its more enlightened examples has long since left behind and outgrown. If you ask them to explain themselves more fully, they will probably say that for primitive thought

[1] HENRY WOOD : Ideal Suggestion through Mental Photography, pp. 51, 70 (abridged).

everything is conceived of under the form of personality. The savage thinks that things operate by personal forces, and for the sake of individual ends. For him, even external nature obeys individual needs and claims, just as if these were so many elementary powers. Now science, on the other hand, these positivists say, has proved that personality, so far from being an elementary force in nature, is but a passive resultant of the really elementary forces, physical, chemical, physiological, and psycho-physical, which are all impersonal and general in character. Nothing individual accomplishes anything in the universe save in so far as it obeys and exemplifies some universal law. Should you then inquire of them by what means science has thus supplanted primitive thought, and discredited its personal way of looking at things, they would undoubtedly say it has been by the strict use of the method of experimental verification. Follow out science's conceptions practically, they will say, the conceptions that ignore personality altogether, and you will always be corroborated. The world is so made that all your expectations will be experientially verified so long, and only so long, as you keep the terms from which you infer them impersonal and universal.

But here we have mind-cure, with her diametrically opposite philosophy, setting up an exactly identical claim. Live as if I were true, she says, and every day will practically prove you right. That the controlling energies of nature are personal, that your own personal thoughts are forces, that the powers of the universe will directly respond to your individual appeals and needs, are propositions which your whole bodily and mental experience will verify. And that experience does largely verify these primeval religious ideas is proved by the fact that the mind-cure movement spreads as it does, not by proclamation and assertion simply, but by palpable experiential results. Here, in the very heyday of science's authority, it carries on an aggressive warfare against the scientific philosophy, and succeeds by using science's own peculiar methods and weapons. Believing that a higher power will take care of us in certain ways better than we can take care of ourselves, if we only genuinely throw ourselves upon it and consent to use it, it finds the belief, not only not impugned, but corroborated by its observation.

How conversions are thus made, and converts confirmed, is evident enough from the narratives which I have quoted. I will quote yet another couple of shorter ones to give the matter a perfectly concrete turn. Here is one : —

"One of my first experiences in applying my teaching was two months after I first saw the healer. I fell, spraining my right ankle, which I had done once four years before, having then had to use a crutch and elastic anklet for some months, and carefully guarding it ever since. As soon as I was on my feet I made the positive suggestion (and felt it through all my being) : 'There is nothing but God, all life comes from him perfectly. I cannot be sprained or hurt, I will let him take care of it.' Well, I never had a sensation in it, and I walked two miles that day."

The next case not only illustrates experiment and verification, but also the element of passivity and surrender of which awhile ago I made such account.

"I went into town to do some shopping one morning, and I had not been gone long before I began to feel ill. The ill feeling increased rapidly, until I had pains in all my bones, nausea and faintness, headache, all the symptoms in short that precede an attack of influenza. I thought that I was going to have the grippe, epidemic then in Boston, or something worse. The mind-cure teachings that I had been listening to all the winter thereupon came into my mind, and I thought that here was an opportunity to test myself. On my way home I met a friend, and I refrained with some effort from telling her how I felt. That was the first step gained. I went to bed immediately, and my husband wished to send for the doctor. But I told him that I would rather wait until morning and see how I felt. Then followed one of the most beautiful experiences of my life.

"I cannot express it in any other way than to say that I did ' lie down in the stream of life and let it flow over me.' I gave up all fear of any impending disease; I was perfectly willing and obedient. There was no intellectual effort, or train of thought. My dominant idea was: 'Behold the handmaid of the Lord : be it unto me even as thou wilt,' and a perfect confidence that all would be well, that all *was* well. The creative life was flowing into me every instant, and I felt myself allied with the Infinite, in harmony, and full of the peace that passeth understanding. There was no place in my mind for a jarring body. I had no consciousness of time or space or persons ; but only of love and happiness and faith.

"I do not know how long this state lasted, nor when I fell asleep ; but when I woke up in the morning, *I was well.*"

These are exceedingly trivial instances,[1] but in them, if we have anything at all, we have the method of experiment and verification. For the point I am driving at now, it makes no difference whether you consider the patients to be deluded victims of their imagination or not. That they seemed to *themselves* to have been cured by the experiments tried was enough to make them converts to the system. And although it is evident that one must be of a certain mental mould to get such results (for not every one can get thus cured to his own satisfaction any more than every one can be cured by the first regular practitioner whom he calls in), yet it would surely be pedantic and over-scrupulous for those who *can* get their savage and primitive philosophy of mental healing veri-

[1] See Appendix to this lecture for two other cases furnished me by friends.

fied in such experimental ways as this, to give them up
at word of command for more scientific therapeutics.
What are we to think of all this ?   Has science made
too wide a claim ?

I believe that the claims of the sectarian scientist are,
to say the least, premature.   The experiences which we
have been studying during this hour (and a great many
other kinds of religious experiences are like them) plainly
show the universe to be a more many-sided affair than
any sect, even the scientific sect, allows for.   What, in
the end, are all our verifications but experiences that
agree with more or less isolated systems of ideas (conceptual systems) that our minds have framed?   But why in
the name of common sense need we assume that only
one such system of ideas can be true?   The obvious outcome of our total experience is that the world can be
handled according to many systems of ideas, and is so
handled by different men, and will each time give some
characteristic kind of profit, for which he cares, to the
handler, while at the same time some other kind of profit
has to be omitted or postponed.   Science gives to all of
us telegraphy, electric lighting, and diagnosis, and succeeds in preventing and curing a certain amount of disease.   Religion in the shape of mind-cure gives to some
of us serenity, moral poise, and happiness, and prevents
certain forms of disease as well as science does, or even
better in a certain class of persons.   Evidently, then, the
science and the religion are both of them genuine keys
for unlocking the world's treasure-house to him who can
use either of them practically.   Just as evidently neither
is exhaustive or exclusive of the other's simultaneous use.
And why, after all, may not the world be so complex as
to consist of many interpenetrating spheres of reality,
which we can thus approach in alternation by using dif-

ferent conceptions and assuming different attitudes, just as mathematicians handle the same numerical and spatial facts by geometry, by analytical geometry, by algebra, by the calculus, or by quaternions, and each time come out right?   On this view religion and science, each verified in its own way from hour to hour and from life to life, would be co-eternal. Primitive thought, with its belief in individualized personal forces, seems at any rate as far as ever from being driven by science from the field to-day.   Numbers of educated people still find it the directest experimental channel by which to carry on their intercourse with reality.[1]

The case of mind-cure lay so ready to my hand that I could not resist the temptation of using it to bring these last truths home to your attention, but I must content myself to-day with this very brief indication.   In a later lecture the relations of religion both to science and to primitive thought will have to receive much more explicit attention.

APPENDIX

(See note to p. 121.)

CASE I. " My own experience is this : I had long been ill, and one of the first results of my illness, a dozen years before, had been a diplopia which deprived me of the use of my eyes for reading and writing almost entirely, while a later one had been to shut me out from exercise of any kind under penalty of

---

[1] Whether the various spheres or systems are ever to fuse integrally into one absolute conception, as most philosophers assume that they must, and how, if so, that conception may best be reached, are questions that only the future can answer.   What is certain now is the fact of lines of disparate conception, each corresponding to some part of the world's truth, each verified in some degree, each leaving out some part of real experience.

immediate and great exhaustion. I had been under the care of doctors of the highest standing both in Europe and America, men in whose power to help me I had had great faith, with no or ill result. Then, at a time when I seemed to be rather rapidly losing ground, I heard some things that gave me interest enough in mental healing to make me try it; I had no great hope of getting any good from it — it was a *chance* I tried, partly because my thought was interested by the new possibility it seemed to open, partly because it was the only chance I then could see. I went to X. in Boston, from whom some friends of mine had got, or thought that they had got, great help; the treatment was a silent one; little was said, and that little carried no conviction to my mind; whatever influence was exerted was that of another person's thought or feeling silently projected on to my unconscious mind, into my nervous system as it were, as we sat still together. I believed from the start in the *possibility* of such action, for I knew the power of the mind to shape, helping or hindering, the body's nerve-activities, and I thought telepathy probable, although unproved, but I had no belief in it as more than a possibility, and no strong conviction nor any mystic or religious faith connected with my thought of it that might have brought imagination strongly into play.

"I sat quietly with the healer for half an hour each day, at first with no result; then, after ten days or so, I became quite suddenly and swiftly conscious of a tide of new energy rising within me, a sense of power to pass beyond old halting-places, of power to break the bounds that, though often tried before, had long been veritable walls about my life, too high to climb. I began to read and walk as I had not done for years, and the change was sudden, marked, and unmistakable. This tide seemed to mount for some weeks, three or four perhaps, when, summer having come, I came away, taking the treatment up again a few months later. The lift I got proved permanent, and left me slowly gaining ground instead of losing it, but with this lift the influence seemed in a way to have spent itself, and, though my confidence in the reality of the power had gained immensely from this first experience, and should have helped me to make further gain in health and strength if my belief in it had been the potent factor there, I never after this got any result at all as striking or as clearly marked as this which came when I made trial of it first, with little faith and doubtful expectation. It is difficult to put all the evidence in such a matter into words, to gather up into a distinct statement all that one bases one's conclusions on, but I have always felt that I had abundant evidence to justify (to myself, at least) the conclusion that I came to then, and since have held to, that the physical change which came at that time was, first, the result of a change wrought within me by a change of mental state ; and, secondly, that that change of mental state was not, save in a very secondary way, brought about through the influence of an excited imagination, or a *consciously* received suggestion of an hypnotic sort. Lastly, I believe that this change was the result of my receiving telepathically, and upon a mental stratum quite below the level of immediate consciousness, a healthier and more energetic attitude, receiving it from another person whose thought was directed upon me with the intention of impressing the idea of this attitude upon me. In my case the disease was distinctly what would be classed as nervous, not organic ; but from such opportunities as I have had of observing, I have come to the conclusion that the dividing line that has been drawn is an arbitrary one, the nerves controlling the internal activities and the nutrition of the body throughout ; and I believe that the central nervous system, by starting and inhibiting local centres, can exercise a vast influence upon disease of any kind, if it can be brought to bear. In my judgment the question is simply how to bring it to bear, and I think that the uncertainty and remarkable differences in the results obtained through mental healing do but show how ignorant we are as yet of the forces at work and of the means we should take to make them effective. That these results are not due to chance coincidences my observation of myself and others makes me sure ; that the conscious mind, the imagination, enters into them as a factor in many cases is doubtless true, but in many others, and sometimes very extraordinary ones, it hardly seems to enter in at all. On the whole I am inclined to think that as the healing action, like the morbid one, springs from the plane of the normally *unconscious* mind, so the strongest and most effective impressions are those which *it* receives, in some as yet unknown, subtle way, *directly* from a healthier mind whose state, through a hidden law of sympathy, it reproduces."

CASE II. "At the urgent request of friends, and with no faith and hardly any hope (possibly owing to a previous unsuccessful experience with a Christian Scientist), our little daughter was placed under the care of a healer, and cured of a trouble about which the physician had been very discouraging in his diagnosis. This interested me, and I began studying earnestly the method and philosophy of this method of healing. Gradually an inner peace and tranquillity came to me in so positive a way that my manner changed greatly. My children and friends noticed the change and commented upon it. All feelings of irritability disappeared. Even the expression of my face changed noticeably.

"I had been bigoted, aggressive, and intolerant in discussion, both in public and private. I grew broadly tolerant and receptive toward the views of others. I had been nervous and irritable, coming home two or three times a week with a sick headache induced, as I then supposed, by dyspepsia and catarrh. I grew serene and gentle, and the physical troubles entirely disappeared. I had been in the habit of approaching every business interview with an almost morbid dread. I now meet every one with confidence and inner calm.

"I may say that the growth has all been toward the elimination of selfishness. I do not mean simply the grosser, more sensual forms, but those subtler and generally unrecognized kinds, such as express themselves in sorrow, grief, regret, envy, etc. It has been in the direction of a practical, working realization of the immanence of God and the Divinity of man's true, inner self."

LECTURES VI AND VII

THE SICK SOUL

AT our last meeting, we considered the healthy-minded temperament, the temperament which has a constitutional incapacity for prolonged suffering, and in which the tendency to see things optimistically is like a water of crystallization in which the individual's character is set. We saw how this temperament may become the basis for a peculiar type of religion, a religion in which good, even the good of this world's life, is regarded as the essential thing for a rational being to attend to. This religion directs him to settle his scores with the more evil aspects of the universe by systematically declining to lay them to heart or make much of them, by ignoring them in his reflective calculations, or even, on occasion, by denying outright that they exist. Evil is a disease; and worry over disease is itself an additional form of disease, which only adds to the original complaint. Even repentance and remorse, affections which come in the character of ministers of good, may be but sickly and relaxing impulses. The best repentance is to up and act for righteousness, and forget that you ever had relations with sin.

Spinoza's philosophy has this sort of healthy-mindedness woven into the heart of it, and this has been one secret of its fascination. He whom Reason leads, according to Spinoza, is led altogether by the influence over his mind of good. Knowledge of evil is an 'inadequate' knowledge, fit only for slavish minds. So Spi-

noza categorically condemns repentance. When men
make mistakes, he says, —

"One might perhaps expect gnawings of conscience and
repentance to help to bring them on the right path, and might
thereupon conclude (as every one does conclude) that these
affections are good things. Yet when we look at the matter
closely, we shall find that not only are they not good, but on
the contrary deleterious and evil passions. For it is manifest
that we can always get along better by reason and love of truth
than by worry of conscience and remorse. Harmful are these
and evil, inasmuch as they form a particular kind of sadness ;
and the disadvantages of sadness," he continues, " I have already proved, and shown that we should strive to keep it from
our life. Just so we should endeavor, since uneasiness of conscience and remorse are of this kind of complexion, to flee and
shun these states of mind." [1]

Within the Christian body, for which repentance of
sins has from the beginning been the critical religious
act, healthy-mindedness has always come forward with
its milder interpretation. Repentance according to such
healthy-minded Christians means *getting away from* the
sin, not groaning and writhing over its commission. The
Catholic practice of confession and absolution is in one
of its aspects little more than a systematic method of
keeping healthy-mindedness on top. By it a man's
accounts with evil are periodically squared and audited,
so that he may start the clean page with no old debts
inscribed. Any Catholic will tell us how clean and fresh
and free he feels after the purging operation. Martin
Luther by no means belonged to the healthy-minded
type in the radical sense in which we have discussed it,
and he repudiated priestly absolution for sin. Yet in this
matter of repentance he had some very healthy-minded

[1] Tract on God, Man, and Happiness, Book ii. ch. x.

ideas, due in the main to the largeness of his conception of God.

" When I was a monk," he says, " I thought that I was utterly cast away, if at any time I felt the lust of the flesh : that is to say, if I felt any evil motion, fleshly lust, wrath, hatred, or envy against any brother. I assayed many ways to help to quiet my conscience, but it would not be ; for the concupiscence and lust of my flesh did always return, so that I could not rest, but was continually vexed with these thoughts : This or that sin thou hast committed : thou art infected with envy, with impatiency, and such other sins : therefore thou art entered into this holy order in vain, and all thy good works are unprofitable. But if then I had rightly understood these sentences of Paul : ' The flesh lusteth contrary to the Spirit, and the Spirit contrary to the flesh ; and these two are one against another, so that ye cannot do the things that ye would do,' I should not have so miserably tormented myself, but should have thought and said to myself, as now commonly I do, ' Martin, thou shalt not utterly be without sin, for thou hast flesh ; thou shalt therefore feel the battle thereof.' I remember that Staupitz was wont to say, ' I have vowed unto God above a thousand times that I would become a better man : but I never performed that which I vowed. Hereafter I will make no such vow : for I have now learned by experience that I am not able to perform it. Unless, therefore, God be favorable and merciful unto me for Christ's sake, I shall not be able, with all my vows and all my good deeds, to stand before him.' This (of Staupitz's) was not only a true, but also a godly and a holy desperation ; and this must they all confess, both with mouth and heart, who will be saved. For the godly trust not to their own righteousness. They look unto Christ their reconciler, who gave his life for their sins. Moreover, they know that the remnant of sin which is in their flesh is not laid to their charge, but freely pardoned. Notwithstanding, in the mean while they fight in spirit against the flesh, lest they should *fulfill* the lusts thereof ; and although they feel the flesh to rage and rebel, and themselves also do fall sometimes into sin through infirmity, yet are they not discouraged, nor think therefore that their state and kind of life, and the works which are done according to their calling, displease God; but they raise up themselves by faith." [1]

One of the heresies for which the Jesuits got that spiritual genius, Molinos, the founder of Quietism, so abominably condemned was his healthy-minded opinion of repentance : —

" When thou fallest into a fault, in what matter soever it be, do not trouble nor afflict thyself for it. For they are effects of our frail Nature, stained by Original Sin. The common enemy will make thee believe, as soon as thou fallest into any fault, that thou walkest in error, and therefore art out of God and his favor, and herewith would he make thee distrust of the divine Grace, telling thee of thy misery, and making a giant of it; and putting it into thy head that every day thy soul grows worse instead of better, whilst it so often repeats these failings. O blessed Soul, open thine eyes ; and shut the gate against these diabolical suggestions, knowing thy misery, and trusting in the mercy divine. Would not he be a mere fool who, running at tournament with others, and falling in the best of the career, should lie weeping on the ground and afflicting himself with discourses upon his fall ? Man (they would tell him), lose no time, get up and take the course again, for he that rises again quickly and continues his race is as if he had never fallen. If thou seest thyself fallen once and a thousand times, thou oughtest to make use of the remedy which I have given thee, that is, a loving confidence in the divine mercy. These are the weapons with which thou must fight and conquer cowardice and vain thoughts. This is the means thou oughtest to use — not to lose time, not to disturb thyself, and reap no good." [2]

Now in contrast with such healthy-minded views as these, if we treat them as a way of deliberately minimizing evil, stands a radically opposite view, a way of max-

[1] Commentary on Galatians, Philadelphia, 1891, pp. 510–514 (abridged).
[2] MOLINOS : Spiritual Guide, Book II., chaps. xvii., xviii. (abridged).

imizing evil, if you please so to call it, based on the
persuasion that the evil aspects of our life are of its very
essence, and that the world's meaning most comes home
to us when we lay them most to heart. We have now
to address ourselves to this more morbid way of looking
at the situation. But as I closed our last hour with a
general philosophical reflection on the healthy-minded
way of taking life, I should like at this point to make
another philosophical reflection upon it before turning
to that heavier task. You will excuse the brief delay.

If we admit that evil is an essential part of our being
and the key to the interpretation of our life, we load ourselves down with a difficulty that has always proved bur-
densome in philosophies of religion. Theism, whenever
it has erected itself into a systematic philosophy of the
universe, has shown a reluctance to let God be anything
less than All-in-All. In other words, philosophic theism
has always shown a tendency to become pantheistic and
monistic, and to consider the world as one unit of absolute fact; and this has been at variance with popular or
practical theism, which latter has ever been more or less
frankly pluralistic, not to say polytheistic, and shown
itself perfectly well satisfied with a universe composed
of many original principles, provided we be only allowed
to believe that the divine principle remains supreme, and
that the others are subordinate. In this latter case God
is not necessarily responsible for the existence of evil;
he would only be responsible if it were not finally overcome. But on the monistic or pantheistic view, evil, like
everything else, must have its foundation in God; and
the difficulty is to see how this can possibly be the case
if God be absolutely good. This difficulty faces us in
every form of philosophy in which the world appears as
one flawless unit of fact. Such a unit is an *Individual*,

and in it the worst parts must be as essential as the best, must be as necessary to make the individual what he is; since if any part whatever in an individual were to vanish or alter, it would no longer be *that* individual at all. The philosophy of absolute idealism, so vigorously represented both in Scotland and America to-day, has to struggle with this difficulty quite as much as scholastic theism struggled in its time; and although it would be premature to say that there is no speculative issue whatever from the puzzle, it is perfectly fair to say that there is no clear or easy issue, and that the only *obvious* escape from paradox here is to cut loose from the monistic assumption altogether, and to allow the world to have existed from its origin in pluralistic form, as an aggregate or collection of higher and lower things and principles, rather than an absolutely unitary fact. For then evil would not need to be essential; it might be, and may always have been, an independent portion that had no rational or absolute right to live with the rest, and which we might conceivably hope to see got rid of at last.

Now the gospel of healthy-mindedness, as we have described it, casts its vote distinctly for this pluralistic view. Whereas the monistic philosopher finds himself more or less bound to say, as Hegel said, that everything actual is rational, and that evil, as an element dialectically required, must be pinned in and kept and consecrated and have a function awarded to it in the final system of truth, healthy-mindedness refuses to say anything of the sort.[1] Evil, it says, is emphatically irrational,

[1] I say this in spite of the monistic utterances of many mind-cure writers; for these utterances are really inconsistent with their attitude towards disease, and can easily be shown not to be logically involved in the experiences of union with a higher Presence with which they connect themselves. The higher Presence, namely, need not be the absolute whole of things, it is quite sufficient for the life of religious experience to regard it as a part, if only it be the most ideal part.

and *not* to be pinned in, or preserved, or consecrated in any final system of truth. It is a pure abomination to the Lord, an alien unreality, a waste element, to be sloughed off and negated, and the very memory of it, if possible, wiped out and forgotten. The ideal, so far from being co-extensive with the whole actual, is a mere *extract* from the actual, marked by its deliverance from all contact with this diseased, inferior, and excrementitious stuff.

Here we have the interesting notion fairly and squarely presented to us, of there being elements of the universe which may make no rational whole in conjunction with the other elements, and which, from the point of view of any system which those other elements make up, can only be considered so much irrelevance and accident — so much ' dirt,' as it were, and matter out of place. I ask you now not to forget this notion; for although most philosophers seem either to forget it or to disdain it too much ever to mention it, I believe that we shall have to admit it ourselves in the end as containing an element of truth. The mind-cure gospel thus once more appears to us as having dignity and importance. We have seen it to be a genuine religion, and no mere silly appeal to imagination to cure disease; we have seen its method of experimental verification to be not unlike the method of all science; and now here we find mind-cure as the champion of a perfectly definite conception of the metaphysical structure of the world. I hope that, in view of all this, you will not regret my having pressed it upon your attention at such length.

Let us now say good-by for a while to all this way of thinking, and turn towards those persons who cannot so swiftly throw off the burden of the consciousness of evil, but are congenitally fated to suffer from its presence. Just as we saw that in healthy-mindedness there are shallower and profounder levels, happiness like that of the mere animal, and more regenerate sorts of happiness, so also are there different levels of the morbid mind, and the one is much more formidable than the other. There are people for whom evil means only a mal-adjustment with *things*, a wrong correspondence of one's life with the environment. Such evil as this is curable, in principle at least, upon the natural plane, for merely by modifying either the self or the things, or both at once, the two terms may be made to fit, and all go merry as a marriage bell again. But there are others for whom evil is no mere relation of the subject to particular outer things, but something more radical and general, a wrongness or vice in his essential nature, which no alteration of the environment, or any superficial rearrangement of the inner self, can cure, and which requires a supernatural remedy. On the whole, the Latin races have leaned more towards the former way of looking upon evil, as made up of ills and sins in the plural, removable in detail; while the Germanic races have tended rather to think of Sin in the singular, and with a capital S, as of something ineradicably ingrained in our natural subjectivity, and never to be removed by any superficial piecemeal operations.[1] These comparisons of races are always open to exception, but undoubtedly the northern tone in religion has inclined to the more intimately pessimistic persuasion, and this way of feeling, being the more extreme, we shall find by far the more instructive for our study.

Recent psychology has found great use for the word 'threshold' as a symbolic designation for the point at which one state of mind passes into another. Thus we

[1] Cf. J. MILSAND : Luther et le Serf-Arbitre, 1884, *passim*.

speak of the threshold of a man's consciousness in general, to indicate the amount of noise, pressure, or other outer stimulus which it takes to arouse his attention at all. One with a high threshold will doze through an amount of racket by which one with a low threshold would be immediately waked. Similarly, when one is sensitive to small differences in any order of sensation, we say he has a low ' difference-threshold ' — his mind easily steps over it into the consciousness of the differences in question. And just so we might speak of a ' pain-threshold,' a ' fear-threshold,' a ' misery-threshold,' and find it quickly overpassed by the consciousness of some individuals, but lying too high in others to be often reached by their consciousness. The sanguine and healthy-minded live habitually on the sunny side of their misery-line, the depressed and melancholy live beyond it, in darkness and apprehension. There are men who seem to have started in life with a bottle or two of champagne inscribed to their credit ; whilst others seem to have been born close to the pain-threshold, which the slightest irritants fatally send them over.

Does it not appear as if one who lived more habitually on one side of the pain-threshold might need a different sort of religion from one who habitually lived on the other ? This question, of the relativity of different types of religion to different types of need, arises naturally at this point, and will become a serious problem ere we have done. But before we confront it in general terms, we must address ourselves to the unpleasant task of hearing what the sick souls, as we may call them in contrast to the healthy-minded, have to say of the secrets of their prison-house, their own peculiar form of consciousness. Let us then resolutely turn our backs on the once-born and their sky-blue optimistic gospel ; let us not simply cry out, in spite of all appearances, "Hurrah for the Universe! — God's in his Heaven, all's right with the world." Let us see rather whether pity, pain, and fear, and the sentiment of human helplessness may not open a profounder view and put into our hands a more complicated key to the meaning of the situation.

To begin with, how *can* things so insecure as the successful experiences of this world afford a stable anchorage? A chain is no stronger than its weakest link, and life is after all a chain. In the healthiest and most prosperous existence, how many links of illness, danger, and disaster are always interposed? Unsuspectedly from the bottom of every fountain of pleasure, as the old poet said, something bitter rises up : a touch of nausea, a falling dead of the delight, a whiff of melancholy, things that sound a knell, for fugitive as they may be, they bring a feeling of coming from a deeper region and often have an appalling convincingness. The buzz of life ceases at their touch as a piano-string stops sounding when the damper falls upon it.

Of course the music can commence again ; — and again and again, — at intervals. But with this the healthy-minded consciousness is left with an irremediable sense of precariousness. It is a bell with a crack ; it draws its breath on sufferance and by an accident.

Even if we suppose a man so packed with healthy-mindedness as never to have experienced in his own person any of these sobering intervals, still, if he is a reflecting being, he must generalize and class his own lot with that of others ; and, doing so, he must see that his escape is just a lucky chance and no essential difference. He might just as well have been born to an entirely different fortune. And then indeed the hollow security! What kind of a frame of things is it of which the best you can say is, " Thank God, it has let me off clear this time ! " Is not its blessedness a fragile fiction ? Is not your joy in it a very vulgar glee, not much unlike the snicker of any rogue at his success ? If indeed it were all success, even on such terms as that ! But take the happiest man, the one most envied by the world, and in nine cases out of ten his inmost consciousness is one of failure. Either his ideals in the line of his achievements are pitched far higher than the achievements themselves, or else he has secret ideals of which the world knows nothing, and in regard to which he inwardly knows himself to be found wanting.

When such a conquering optimist as Goethe can express himself in this wise, how must it be with less successful men ?

" I will say nothing," writes Goethe in 1824, " against the course of my existence. But at bottom it has been nothing but pain and burden, and I can affirm that during the whole of my 75 years, I have not had four weeks of genuine well-being. It is but the perpetual rolling of a rock that must be raised up again forever."

What single-handed man was ever on the whole as successful as Luther ? yet when he had grown old, he looked back on his life as if it were an absolute failure.

" I am utterly weary of life. I pray the Lord will come forthwith and carry me hence. Let him come, above all, with his last Judgment: I will stretch out my neck, the thunder will burst forth, and I shall be at rest." — And having a necklace of white agates in his hand at the time he added : " O God, grant that it may come without delay. I would readily eat up this necklace to-day, for the Judgment to come to-morrow." — The Electress Dowager, one day when Luther was dining with her, said to him : " Doctor, I wish you may live forty years to come." " Madam," replied he, " rather than live forty years more, I would give up my chance of Paradise."

Failure, then, failure! so the world stamps us at every turn. We strew it with our blunders, our misdeeds, our lost opportunities, with all the memorials of our inadequacy to our vocation. And with what a damning emphasis does it then blot us out! No easy fine, no mere apology or formal expiation, will satisfy the world's demands, but every pound of flesh exacted is soaked with all its blood. The subtlest forms of suffering known to man are connected with the poisonous humiliations incidental to these results.

And they are pivotal human experiences. A process so ubiquitous and everlasting is evidently an integral part of life. "There is indeed one element in human destiny," Robert Louis Stevenson writes, " that not blindness itself can controvert. Whatever else we are intended to do, we are not intended to succeed; failure is the fate allotted." [1] And our nature being thus rooted in failure, is it any wonder that theologians should have held it to be essential, and thought that only through the personal experience of humiliation which it engenders the deeper sense of life's significance is reached? [2]

---

[1] He adds with characteristic healthy-mindedness: "Our business is to continue to fail in good spirits."

[2] The God of many men is little more than their court of appeal against the damnatory judgment passed on their failures by the opinion of this world. To our own consciousness there is usually a residuum of worth left over after our sins and errors have been told off — our capacity of acknowledging and regretting them is the germ of a better self *in posse* at least. But the world deals with us *in actu* and not *in posse:* and of this hidden germ, not to be guessed at from without, it never takes account. Then we turn to the All-knower, who knows our bad, but knows this good in us also, and who is just. We cast ourselves with our repentance on his mercy: only by an All-knower can we finally be judged. So the need of a God very definitely emerges from this sort of experience of life.

But this is only the first stage of the world-sickness. Make the human being's sensitiveness a little greater, carry him a little farther over the misery-threshold, and the good quality of the successful moments themselves when they occur is spoiled and vitiated. All natural goods perish. Riches take wings; fame is a breath; love is a cheat; youth and health and pleasure vanish. Can things whose end is always dust and disappointment be the real goods which our souls require? Back of everything is the great spectre of universal death, the all-encompassing blackness : —

" What profit hath a man of all his labour which he taketh under the Sun? I looked on all the works that my hands had wrought, and behold, all was vanity and vexation of spirit. For that which befalleth the sons of men befalleth beasts ; as the one dieth, so dieth the other ; all are of the dust, and all turn to dust again. . . . The dead know not anything, neither have they any more a reward ; for the memory of them is forgotten. Also their love and their hatred and their envy is now perished ; neither have they any more a portion for ever in anything that is done under the Sun. . . . Truly the light is sweet, and a pleasant thing it is for the eyes to behold the Sun : but if a man live many years and rejoice in them all, yet let him remember the days of darkness ; for they shall be many."

In short, life and its negation are beaten up inextricably together. But if the life be good, the negation of it must be bad. Yet the two are equally essential facts of existence ; and all natural happiness thus seems infected with a contradiction. The breath of the sepulchre surrounds it.

To a mind attentive to this state of things and rightly subject to the joy-destroying chill which such a contemplation engenders, the only relief that healthy-mindedness can give is by saying: 'Stuff and nonsense, get out into the open air!' or 'Cheer up, old fellow, you 'll be all right erelong, if you will only drop your morbidness!' But in all seriousness, can such bald animal talk as that be treated as a rational answer? To ascribe religious value to mere happy-go-lucky contentment with one's brief chance at natural good is but the very consecration of forgetfulness and superficiality. Our troubles lie indeed too deep for *that* cure. The fact that we *can* die, that we *can* be ill at all, is what perplexes us; the fact that we now for a moment live and are well is irrelevant to that perplexity. We need a life not correlated with death, a health not liable to illness, a kind of good that will not perish, a good in fact that flies beyond the Goods of nature.

It all depends on how sensitive the soul may become to discords. " The trouble with me is that I believe too much in common happiness and goodness," said a friend of mine whose consciousness was of this sort, " and nothing can console me for their transiency. I am appalled and disconcerted at its being possible." And so with most of us: a little cooling down of animal excitability and instinct, a little loss of animal toughness, a little irritable weakness and descent of the pain-threshold, will bring the worm at the core of all our usual springs of delight into full view, and turn us into melancholy metaphysicians. The pride of life and glory of the world will shrivel. It is after all but the standing quarrel of hot youth and hoary eld. Old age has the last word: the purely naturalistic look at life, however enthusiastically it may begin, is sure to end in sadness.

This sadness lies at the heart of every merely positivistic, agnostic, or naturalistic scheme of philosophy. Let sanguine healthy-mindedness do its best with its strange power of living in the moment and ignoring and forgetting, still the evil background is really there to be thought of, and the skull will grin in at the banquet. In the practical life of the individual, we know how his whole gloom or glee about any present fact depends on the remoter schemes and hopes with which it stands related. Its significance and framing give it the chief part of its value. Let it be known to lead nowhere, and however agreeable it may be in its immediacy, its glow and gilding vanish. The old man, sick with an insidious internal disease, may laugh and quaff his wine at first as well as ever, but he knows his fate now, for the doctors have revealed it; and the knowledge knocks the satisfaction out of all these functions. They are partners of death and the worm is their brother, and they turn to a mere flatness.

The lustre of the present hour is always borrowed from the background of possibilities it goes with. Let our common experiences be enveloped in an eternal moral order; let our suffering have an immortal significance; let Heaven smile upon the earth, and deities pay their visits; let faith and hope be the atmosphere which man breathes in; — and his days pass by with zest; they stir with prospects, they thrill with remoter values. Place round them on the contrary the curdling cold and gloom and absence of all permanent meaning which for pure naturalism and the popular science evolutionism of our time are all that is visible ultimately, and the thrill stops short, or turns rather to an anxious trembling.

For naturalism, fed on recent cosmological speculations, mankind is in a position similar to that of a set of people living on a frozen lake, surrounded by cliffs over which there is no escape, yet knowing that little by little the ice is melting, and the inevitable day drawing near when the last film of it will disappear, and to be drowned ignominiously will be the human creature's portion. The

merrier the skating, the warmer and more sparkling the
sun by day, and the ruddier the bonfires at night, the
more poignant the sadness with which one must take in
the meaning of the total situation.

The early Greeks are continually held up to us in literary works as models of the healthy-minded joyousness
which the religion of nature may engender. There was
indeed much joyousness among the Greeks — Homer's
flow of enthusiasm for most things that the sun shines
upon is steady. But even in Homer the reflective passages are cheerless,[1] and the moment the Greeks grew
systematically pensive and thought of ultimates, they
became unmitigated pessimists.[2] The jealousy of the
gods, the nemesis that follows too much happiness, the
all-encompassing death, fate's dark opacity, the ultimate
and unintelligible cruelty, were the fixed background of

[1] E. g., Iliad, XVII. 446 : "Nothing then is more wretched anywhere
than man of all that breathes and creeps upon this earth."

[2] E. g., Theognis, 425–428 : " Best of all for all things upon earth is it
not to be born nor to behold the splendors of the Sun ; next best to traverse
as soon as possible the gates of Hades." See also the almost identical
passage in Œdipus in Colonus, 1225. — The Anthology is full of pessimistic utterances : "Naked came I upon the earth, naked I go below the
ground — why then do I vainly toil when I see the end naked before me ? "
— " How did I come to be ? Whence am I ? Wherefore did I come ? To
pass away. How can I learn aught when naught I know ? Being naught I
came to life : once more shall I be what I was. Nothing and nothingness
is the whole race of mortals." — " For death we are all cherished and fat-
tened like a herd of hogs that is wantonly butchered."
The difference between Greek pessimism and the oriental and modern
variety is that the Greeks had not made the discovery that the pathetic
mood may be idealized, and figure as a higher form of sensibility. Their
spirit was still too essentially masculine for pessimism to be elaborated or
lengthily dwelt on in their classic literature. They would have despised a
life set wholly in a minor key, and summoned it to keep within the proper
bounds of lachrymosity. The discovery that the enduring emphasis, so far
as this world goes, may be laid on its pain and failure, was reserved for
races more complex, and (so to speak) more feminine than the Hellenes
had attained to being in the classic period. But all the same was the outlook of those Hellenes blackly pessimistic.

their imagination. The beautiful joyousness of their polytheism is only a poetic modern fiction. They knew no joys comparable in quality of preciousness to those which we shall erelong see that Brahmans, Buddhists, Christians, Mohammedans, twice-born people whose religion is non-naturalistic, get from their several creeds of mysticism and renunciation.

Stoic insensibility and Epicurean resignation were the farthest advance which the Greek mind made in that direction. The Epicurean said : " Seek not to be happy, but rather to escape unhappiness ; strong happiness is always linked with pain ; therefore hug the safe shore, and do not tempt the deeper raptures. Avoid disappointment by expecting little, and by aiming low ; and above all do not fret." The Stoic said : " The only genuine good that life can yield a man is the free possession of his own soul ; all other goods are lies." Each of these philosophies is in its degree a philosophy of despair in nature's boons. Trustful self-abandonment to the joys that freely offer has entirely departed from both Epicurean and Stoic ; and what each proposes is a way of rescue from the resultant dust-and-ashes state of mind. The Epicurean still awaits results from economy of indulgence and damping of desire. The Stoic hopes for no results, and gives up natural good altogether. There is dignity in both these forms of resignation. They represent distinct stages in the sobering process which man's primitive intoxication with sense-happiness is sure to undergo. In the one the hot blood has grown cool, in the other it has become quite cold ; and although I have spoken of them in the past tense, as if they were merely historic, yet Stoicism and Epicureanism will probably be to all time typical attitudes, marking a certain definite stage accomplished in the evolution of the world-sick soul.[1] They mark the conclusion of what we call the once-born period, and represent the highest flights of what twice-born religion would call the purely natural man — Epicureanism, which can only by great courtesy be called a religion, showing his refinement, and Stoicism exhibiting his moral will. They leave the world in the shape of an unreconciled contradiction, and seek no higher unity. Compared with the complex ecstasies which the supernaturally regenerated Christian may enjoy, or the oriental pantheist indulge in, their receipts for equanimity are expedients which seem almost crude in their simplicity.

Please observe, however, that I am not yet pretending finally to *judge* any of these attitudes. I am only describing their variety.

The securest way to the rapturous sorts of happiness of which the twice-born make report has as an historic matter of fact been through a more radical pessimism than anything that we have yet considered. We have seen how the lustre and enchantment may be rubbed off from the goods of nature. But there is a pitch of unhappiness so great that the goods of nature may be entirely forgotten, and all sentiment of their existence vanish from the mental field. For this extremity of pessimism to be reached, something more is needed than observation of

[1] For instance, on the very day on which I write this page, the post brings me some aphorisms from a worldly-wise old friend in Heidelberg which may serve as a good contemporaneous expression of Epicureanism : " By the word 'happiness' every human being understands something different. It is a phantom pursued only by weaker minds. The wise man is satisfied with the more modest but much more definite term *contentment*. What education should chiefly aim at is to save us from a discontented life. Health is one favoring condition, but by no means an indispensable one, of contentment. Woman's heart and love are a shrewd device of Nature, a trap which she sets for the average man, to force him into working. But the wise man will always prefer work chosen by himself."

life and reflection upon death. The individual must in his own person become the prey of a pathological melancholy. As the healthy-minded enthusiast succeeds in ignoring evil's very existence, so the subject of melancholy is forced in spite of himself to ignore that of all good whatever : for him it may no longer have the least reality. Such sensitiveness and susceptibility to mental pain is a rare occurrence where the nervous constitution is entirely normal ; one seldom finds it in a healthy subject even where he is the victim of the most atrocious cruelties of outward fortune. So we note here the neurotic constitution, of which I said so much in my first lecture, making its active entrance on our scene, and destined to play a part in much that follows. Since these experiences of melancholy are in the first instance absolutely private and individual, I can now help myself out with personal documents. Painful indeed they will be to listen to, and there is almost an indecency in handling them in public. Yet they lie right in the middle of our path ; and if we are to touch the psychology of religion at all seriously, we must be willing to forget conventionalities, and dive below the smooth and lying official conversational surface.

One can distinguish many kinds of pathological depression. Sometimes it is mere passive joylessness and dreariness, discouragement, dejection, lack of taste and zest and spring. Professor Ribot has proposed the name *anhedonia* to designate this condition.

"The state of *anhedonia*, if I may coin a new word to pair off with *analgesia*," he writes, "has been very little studied, but it exists. A young girl was smitten with a liver disease which for some time altered her constitution. She felt no longer any affection for her father and mother. She would have played with her doll, but it was impossible to find the least pleasure in the act. The same things which formerly convulsed her with laughter entirely failed to interest her now. Esquirol observed the case of a very intelligent magistrate who was also a prey to hepatic disease. Every emotion appeared dead within him. He manifested neither perversion nor violence, but complete absence of emotional reaction. If he went to the theatre, which he did out of habit, he could find no pleasure there. The thought of his house, of his home, of his wife, and of his absent children moved him as little, he said, as a theorem of Euclid." [1]

Prolonged seasickness will in most persons produce a temporary condition of anhedonia. Every good, terrestrial or celestial, is imagined only to be turned from with disgust. A temporary condition of this sort, connected with the religious evolution of a singularly lofty character, both intellectual and moral, is well described by the Catholic philosopher, Father Gratry, in his autobiographical recollections. In consequence of mental isolation and excessive study at the Polytechnic school, young Gratry fell into a state of nervous exhaustion with symptoms which he thus describes: —

"I had such a universal terror that I woke at night with a start, thinking that the Pantheon was tumbling on the Polytechnic school, or that the school was in flames, or that the Seine was pouring into the Catacombs, and that Paris was being swallowed up. And when these impressions were past, all day long without respite I suffered an incurable and intolerable desolation, verging on despair. I thought myself, in fact, rejected by God, lost, damned! I felt something like the suffering of hell. Before that I had never even thought of hell. My mind had never turned in that direction. Neither discourses nor reflections had impressed me in that way. I took no account of hell. Now, and all at once, I suffered in a measure what is suffered there.

"But what was perhaps still more dreadful is that every idea of heaven was taken away from me: I could no longer conceive

[1] RIBOT: Psychologie des sentiments, p. 54.

of anything of the sort. Heaven did not seem to me worth going to. It was like a vacuum; a mythological elysium, an abode of shadows less real than the earth. I could conceive no joy, no pleasure in inhabiting it. Happiness, joy, light, affection, love — all these words were now devoid of sense. Without doubt I could still have talked of all these things, but I had become incapable of feeling anything in them, of understanding anything about them, of hoping anything from them, or of believing them to exist. There was my great and inconsolable grief! I neither perceived nor conceived any longer the existence of happiness or perfection. An abstract heaven over a naked rock. Such was my present abode for eternity." [1]

So much for melancholy in the sense of incapacity for joyous feeling. A much worse form of it is positive and active anguish, a sort of psychical neuralgia wholly unknown to healthy life. Such anguish may partake of various characters, having sometimes more the quality of loathing; sometimes that of irritation and exasperation; or again of self-mistrust and self-despair; or of suspicion, anxiety, trepidation, fear. The patient may rebel or sub-

---

[1] A. GRATRY: Souvenirs de ma jeunesse, 1880, pp. 119–121, abridged. Some persons are affected with anhedonia permanently, or at any rate with a loss of the usual appetite for life. The annals of suicide supply such examples as the following : —

An uneducated domestic servant, aged nineteen, poisons herself, and leaves two letters expressing her motive for the act. To her parents she writes : —

"Life is sweet perhaps to some, but I prefer what is sweeter than life, and that is death. So good-by forever, my dear parents. It is nobody's fault, but a strong desire of my own which I have longed to fulfill for three or four years. I have always had a hope that some day I might have an opportunity of fulfilling it, and now it has come. . . . It is a wonder I have put this off so long, but I thought perhaps I should cheer up a bit and put all thought out of my head." To her brother she writes : "Good-by forever, my own dearest brother. By the time you get this I shall be gone forever. I know, dear love, there is no forgiveness for what I am going to do. . . . I am tired of living, so am willing to die. . . . Life may be sweet to some, but death to me is sweeter." S. A. K. STRAHAN : Suicide and Insanity, 2d edition, London, 1894, p. 131.

mit; may accuse himself, or accuse outside powers; and he may or he may not be tormented by the theoretical mystery of why he should so have to suffer. Most cases are mixed cases, and we should not treat our classifications with too much respect. Moreover, it is only a relatively small proportion of cases that connect themselves with the religious sphere of experience at all. Exasperated cases, for instance, as a rule do not. I quote now literally from the first case of melancholy on which I lay my hand. It is a letter from a patient in a French asylum.

" I suffer too much in this hospital, both physically and morally. Besides the burnings and the sleeplessness (for I no longer sleep since I am shut up here, and the little rest I get is broken by bad dreams, and I am waked with a jump by nightmares, dreadful visions, lightning, thunder, and the rest), fear, atrocious fear, presses me down, holds me without respite, never lets me go. Where is the justice in it all! What have I done to deserve this excess of severity? Under what form will this fear crush me? What would I not owe to any one who would rid me of my life! Eat, drink, lie awake all night, suffer without interruption — such is the fine legacy I have received from my mother! What I fail to understand is this abuse of power. There are limits to everything, there is a middle way. But God knows neither middle way nor limits. I say God, but why? All I have known so far has been the devil. After all, I am afraid of God as much as of the devil, so I drift along, thinking of nothing but suicide, but with neither courage nor means here to execute the act. As you read this, it will easily prove to you my insanity. The style and the ideas are incoherent enough — I can see that myself. But I cannot keep myself from being either crazy or an idiot; and, as things are, from whom should I ask pity? I am defenseless against the invisible enemy who is tightening his coils around me. I should be no better armed against him even if I saw him, or had seen him. Oh, if he would but kill me, devil take him! Death,

death, once for all! But I stop. I have raved to you long
enough. I say raved, for I can write no otherwise, having
neither brain nor thoughts left. O God! what a misfortune
to be born! Born like a mushroom, doubtless between an
evening and a morning ; and how true and right I was when in
our philosophy-year in college I chewed the cud of bitterness
with the pessimists. Yes, indeed, there is more pain in life than
gladness — it is one long agony until the grave. Think how
gay it makes me to remember that this horrible misery of mine,
coupled with this unspeakable fear, may last fifty, one hundred,
who knows how many more years! " [1]

This letter shows two things. First, you see how the
entire consciousness of the poor man is so choked with
the feeling of evil that the sense of there being any good
in the world is lost for him altogether. His attention
excludes it, cannot admit it: the sun has left his heaven.
And secondly you see how the querulous temper of his
misery keeps his mind from taking a religious direction.
Querulousness of mind tends in fact rather towards irreligion ; and it has played, so far as I know, no part
whatever in the construction of religious systems.

Religious melancholy must be cast in a more melting
mood. Tolstoy has left us, in his book called My Confession, a wonderful account of the attack of melancholy
which led him to his own religious conclusions. The
latter in some respects are peculiar ; but the melancholy
presents two characters which make it a typical document
for our present purpose. First it is a well-marked case
of anhedonia, of passive loss of appetite for all life's
values; and second, it shows how the altered and es-
tranged aspect which the world assumed in consequence
of this stimulated Tolstoy's intellect to a gnawing, carking questioning and effort for philosophic relief. I mean

[1] Roubinovitch et Toulouse : La Mélancolie, 1897, p. 170, abridged.

to quote Tolstoy at some length ; but before doing so, I will make a general remark on each of these two points.

First on our spiritual judgments and the sense of value in general.

It is notorious that facts are compatible with opposite emotional comments, since the same fact will inspire entirely different feelings in different persons, and at different times in the same person ; and there is no rationally deducible connection between any outer fact and the sentiments it may happen to provoke. These have their source in another sphere of existence altogether, in the animal and spiritual region of the subject's being. Conceive yourself, if possible, suddenly stripped of all the emotion with which your world now inspires you, and try to imagine it *as it exists*, purely by itself, without your favorable or unfavorable, hopeful or apprehensive comment. It will be almost impossible for you to realize such a condition of negativity and deadness. No one portion of the universe would then have importance beyond another ; and the whole collection of its things and series of its events would be without significance, character, expression, or perspective. Whatever of value, interest, or meaning our respective worlds may appear endued with are thus pure gifts of the spectator's mind. The passion of love is the most familiar and extreme example of this fact. If it comes, it comes ; if it does not come, no process of reasoning can force it. Yet it transforms the value of the creature loved as utterly as the sunrise transforms Mont Blanc from a corpse-like gray to a rosy enchantment ; and it sets the whole world to a new tune for the lover and gives a new issue to his life. So with fear, with indignation, jealousy, ambition, worship. If they are there, life changes. And whether they shall be there or not depends almost always upon non-logical, often on organic conditions. And as the excited interest which these passions put into the world is our gift to the world, just so are the passions themselves *gifts*, — gifts to us, from sources sometimes low and sometimes high; but almost always non-logical and beyond our control. How can the moribund old man reason back to himself the romance, the mystery, the imminence of great things with which our old earth tingled for him in the days when he was young and well? Gifts, either of the flesh or of the spirit; and the spirit bloweth where it listeth; and the world's materials lend their surface passively to all the gifts alike, as the stage-setting receives indifferently whatever alternating colored lights may be shed upon it from the optical apparatus in the gallery.

Meanwhile the practically real world for each one of us, the effective world of the individual, is the compound world, the physical facts and emotional values in indistinguishable combination. Withdraw or: pervert either factor of this complex resultant, and the kind of experience we call pathological ensues.

In Tolstoy's case the sense that life had any meaning whatever was for a time wholly withdrawn. The result was a transformation in the whole expression of reality. When we come to study the phenomenon of conversion or religious regeneration, we shall see that a not infrequent consequence of the change operated in the subject is a transfiguration of the face of nature in his eyes. A new heaven seems to shine upon a new earth. In melancholiacs there is usually a similar change, only it is in the reverse direction. The world now looks remote, strange, sinister, uncanny. Its color is gone, its breath is cold, there is no speculation in the eyes it glares with. " It is as if I lived in another century," says one asylum patient.

— "I see everything through a cloud," says another, "things are not as they were, and I am changed." — " I see," says a third, " I touch, but the things do not come near me, a thick veil alters the hue and look of everything." — " Persons move like shadows, and sounds seem to come from a distant world." — " There is no longer any past for me ; people appear so strange ; it is as if I could not see any reality, as if I were in a theatre ; as if people were actors, and everything were scenery ; I can no longer find myself; I walk, but why? Everything floats before my eyes, but leaves no impression." — " I weep false tears, I have unreal hands : the things I see are not real things." — Such are expressions that naturally rise to the lips of melancholy subjects describing their changed state.[1]

Now there are some subjects whom all this leaves a prey to the profoundest astonishment. The strangeness is wrong. The unreality cannot be. A mystery is concealed, and a metaphysical solution must exist. If the natural world is so double-faced and unhomelike, what world, what thing is real ? An urgent wondering and questioning is set up, a poring theoretic activity, and in the desperate effort to get into right relations with the matter, the sufferer is often led to what becomes for him a satisfying religious solution.

At about the age of fifty, Tolstoy relates that he began to have moments of perplexity, of what he calls arrest, as if he knew not ' how to live,' or what to do. It is obvious that these were moments in which the excitement and interest which our functions naturally bring had ceased. Life had been enchanting, it was now flat sober, more than sober, dead. Things were meaningless whose

[1] I cull these examples from the work of G. DUMAS : La Tristesse et la Joie, 1900.

meaning had always been self-evident. The questions
'Why?' and 'What next?' began to beset him more
and more frequently. At first it seemed as if such questions must be answerable, and as if he could easily find
the answers if he would take the time; but as they ever
became more urgent, he perceived that it was like those
first discomforts of a sick man, to which he pays but little
attention till they run into one continuous suffering, and
then he realizes that what he took for a passing disorder
means the most momentous thing in the world for him,
means his death.

These questions 'Why?' 'Wherefore?' 'What for?'
found no response.

"I felt," says Tolstoy, "that something had broken within
me on which my life had always rested, that I had nothing
left to hold on to, and that morally my life had stopped. An
invincible force impelled me to get rid of my existence, in one
way or another. It cannot be said exactly that I *wished* to kill
myself, for the force which drew me away from life was fuller,
more powerful, more general than any mere desire. It was a
force like my old aspiration to live, only it impelled me in the
opposite direction. It was an aspiration of my whole being to
get out of life.

"Behold me then, a man happy and in good health, hiding
the rope in order not to hang myself to the rafters of the room
where every night I went to sleep alone; behold me no longer
going shooting, lest I should yield to the too easy temptation of
putting an end to myself with my gun.

"I did not know what I wanted. I was afraid of life; I
was driven to leave it; and in spite of that I still hoped something from it.

"All this took place at a time when so far as all my outer
circumstances went, I ought to have been completely happy. I
had a good wife who loved me and whom I loved; good children and a large property which was increasing with no pains
taken on my part. I was more respected by my kinsfolk and

acquaintance than I had ever been; I was loaded with praise by strangers; and without exaggeration I could believe my name already famous. Moreover I was neither insane nor ill. On the contrary, I possessed a physical and mental strength which I have rarely met in persons of my age. I could mow as well as the peasants, I could work with my brain eight hours uninterruptedly and feel no bad effects.

" And yet I could give no reasonable meaning to any actions of my life. And I was surprised that I had not understood this from the very beginning. My state of mind was as if some wicked and stupid jest was being played upon me by some one. One can live only so long as one is intoxicated, drunk with life; but when one grows sober one cannot fail to see that it is all a stupid cheat. What is truest about it is that there is nothing even funny or silly in it; it is cruel and stupid, purely and simply.

" The oriental fable of the traveler surprised in the desert by a wild beast is very old.

" Seeking to save himself from the fierce animal, the traveler jumps into a well with no water in it; but at the bottom of this well he sees a dragon waiting with open mouth to devour him. And the unhappy man, not daring to go out lest he should be the prey of the beast, not daring to jump to the bottom lest he should be devoured by the dragon, clings to the branches of a wild bush which grows out of one of the cracks of the well. His hands weaken, and he feels that he must soon give way to certain fate; but still he clings, and sees two mice, one white, the other black, evenly moving round the bush to which he hangs, and gnawing off its roots.

" The traveler sees this and knows that he must inevitably perish; but while thus hanging he looks about him and finds on the leaves of the bush some drops of honey. These he reaches with his tongue and licks them off with rapture.

" Thus I hang upon the boughs of life, knowing that the inevitable dragon of death is waiting ready to tear me, and I cannot comprehend why I am thus made a martyr. I try to suck the honey which formerly consoled me; but the honey pleases me no longer, and day and night the white mouse and

the black mouse gnaw the branch to which I cling. I can see
but one thing : the inevitable dragon and the mice — I cannot
turn my gaze away from them.

"This is no fable, but the literal incontestable truth which
every one may understand. What will be the outcome of what
I do to-day ? Of what I shall do to-morrow ? What will be
the outcome of all my life ? Why should I live ? Why should
I do anything ? Is there in life any purpose which the inevitable death which awaits me does not undo and destroy ?

"These questions are the simplest in the world. From the
stupid child to the wisest old man, they are in the soul of every
human being. Without an answer to them, it is impossible, as
I experienced, for life to go on.

"'But perhaps,' I often said to myself, 'there may be something I have failed to notice or to comprehend. It is not
possible that this condition of despair should be natural to
mankind.' And I sought for an explanation in all the branches
of knowledge acquired by men. I questioned painfully and
protractedly and with no idle curiosity. I sought, not with
indolence, but laboriously and obstinately for days and nights
together. I sought like a man who is lost and seeks to save
himself, — and I found nothing. I became convinced, moreover, that all those who before me had sought for an answer in
the sciences have also found nothing. And not only this, but
that they have recognized that the very thing which was leading me to despair — the meaningless absurdity of life — is the
only incontestable knowledge accessible to man."

To prove this point, Tolstoy quotes the Buddha, Solo-
mon, and Schopenhauer. And he finds only four ways
in which men of his own class and society are accustomed
to meet the situation. Either mere animal blindness,
sucking the honey without seeing the dragon or the
mice, — "and from such a way," he says, "I can learn
nothing, after what I now know ; " or reflective epicureanism, snatching what it can while the day lasts, — which is
only a more deliberate sort of stupefaction than the first ;

or manly suicide; or seeing the mice and dragon and yet weakly and plaintively clinging to the bush of life.

Suicide was naturally the consistent course dictated by the logical intellect.

"Yet," says Tolstoy, "whilst my intellect was working, something else in me was working too, and kept me from the deed — a consciousness of life, as I may call it, which was like a force that obliged my mind to fix itself in another direction and draw me out of my situation of despair. . . . During the whole course of this year, when I almost unceasingly kept asking myself how to end the business, whether by the rope or by the bullet, during all that time, alongside of all those movements of my ideas and observations, my heart kept languishing with another pining emotion. I can call this by no other name than that of a thirst for God. This craving for God had nothing to do with the movement of my ideas, — in fact, it was the direct contrary of that movement, — but it came from my heart. It was like a feeling of dread that made me seem like an orphan and isolated in the midst of all these things that were so foreign. And this feeling of dread was mitigated by the hope of finding the assistance of some one." [1]

Of the process, intellectual as well as emotional, which, starting from this idea of God, led to Tolstoy's recovery, I will say nothing in this lecture, reserving it for a later hour. The only thing that need interest us now is the phenomenon of his absolute disenchantment with ordinary life, and the fact that the whole range of habitual values may, to a man as powerful and full of faculty as he was, come to appear so ghastly a mockery.

When disillusionment has gone as far as this, there is seldom a *restitutio ad integrum*. One has tasted of the fruit of the tree, and the happiness of Eden never comes again. The happiness that comes, when any does come,

[1] My extracts are from the French translation by 'ZONIA.' In abridging I have taken the liberty of transposing one passage.

— and often enough it fails to return in an acute form, though its form is sometimes very acute, — is not the simple ignorance of ill, but something vastly more complex, including natural evil as one of its elements, but finding natural evil no such stumbling-block and terror because it now sees it swallowed up in supernatural good. The process is one of redemption, not of mere reversion to natural health, and the sufferer, when saved, is saved by what seems to him a second birth, a deeper kind of conscious being than he could enjoy before.

We find a somewhat different type of religious melancholy enshrined in literature in John Bunyan's autobiography. Tolstoy's preoccupations were largely objective, for the purpose and meaning of life in general was what so troubled him; but poor Bunyan's troubles were over the condition of his own personal self. He was a typical case of the psychopathic temperament, sensitive of conscience to a diseased degree, beset by doubts, fears, and insistent ideas, and a victim of verbal automatisms, both motor and sensory. These were usually texts of Scripture which, sometimes damnatory and sometimes favorable, would come in a half-hallucinatory form as if they were voices, and fasten on his mind and buffet it between them like a shuttlecock. Added to this were a fearful melancholy self-contempt and despair.

"Nay, thought I, now I grow worse and worse; now I am farther from conversion than ever I was before. If now I should have burned at the stake, I could not believe that Christ had love for me; alas, I could neither hear him, nor see him, nor feel him, nor savor any of his things. Sometimes I would tell my condition to the people of God, which, when they heard, they would pity me, and would tell of the Promises. But they had as good have told me that I must reach the Sun with my finger as have bidden me receive or rely upon the Promise

[Yet] all this while as to the act of sinning, I never was more tender than now; I durst not take a pin or stick, though but so big as a straw, for my conscience now was sore, and would smart at every touch; I could not tell how to speak my words, for fear I should misplace them. Oh, how gingerly did I then go, in all I did or said! I found myself as on a miry bog that shook if I did but stir; and was as there left both by God and Christ, and the spirit, and all good things.

" But my original and inward pollution, that was my plague and my affliction. By reason of that, I was more loathsome in my own eyes than was a toad; and I thought I was so in God's eyes too. Sin and corruption, I said, would as naturally bubble out of my heart as water would bubble out of a fountain. I could have changed heart with anybody. I thought none but the Devil himself could equal me for inward wickedness and pollution of mind. Sure, thought I, I am forsaken of God; and thus I continued a long while, even for some years together.

" And now I was sorry that God had made me a man. The beasts, birds, fishes, etc., I blessed their condition, for they had not a sinful nature; they were not obnoxious to the wrath of God; they were not to go to hell-fire after death. I could therefore have rejoiced, had my condition been as any of theirs. Now I blessed the condition of the dog and toad, yea, gladly would I have been in the condition of the dog or horse, for I knew they had no soul to perish under the everlasting weight of Hell or Sin, as mine was like to do. Nay, and though I saw this, felt this, and was broken to pieces with it, yet that which added to my sorrow was, that I could not find with all my soul that I did desire deliverance. My heart was at times exceedingly hard. If I would have given a thousand pounds for a tear, I could not shed one; no, nor sometimes scarce desire to shed one.

" I was both a burthen and a terror to myself; nor did I ever so know, as now, what it was to be weary of my life, and yet afraid to die. How gladly would I have been anything but myself! Anything but a man! and in any condition but my own." [1]

[1] Grace abounding to the Chief of Sinners : I have printed a number of detached passages continuously.

Poor patient Bunyan, like Tolstoy, saw the light again, but we must also postpone that part of his story to another hour. In a later lecture I will also give the end of the experience of Henry Alline, a devoted evangelist who worked in Nova Scotia a hundred years ago, and who thus vividly describes the high-water mark of the religious melancholy which formed its beginning. The type was not unlike Bunyan's.

" Everything I saw seemed to be a burden to me ; the earth seemed accursed for my sake : all trees, plants, rocks, hills, and vales seemed to be dressed in mourning and groaning, under the weight of the curse, and everything around me seemed to be conspiring my ruin. My sins seemed to be laid open ; so that I thought that every one I saw knew them, and sometimes I was almost ready to acknowledge many things, which I thought they knew : yea sometimes it seemed to me as if every one was pointing me out as the most guilty wretch upon earth. I had now so great a sense of the vanity and emptiness of all things here below, that I knew the whole world could not possibly make me happy, no, nor the whole system of creation. When I waked in the morning, the first thought would be, Oh, my wretched soul, what shall I do, where shall I go ? And when I laid down, would say, I shall be perhaps in hell before morning. I would many times look on the beasts with envy, wishing with all my heart I was in their place, that I might have no soul to lose ; and when I have seen birds flying over my head, have often thought within myself, Oh, that I could fly away from my danger and distress ! Oh, how happy should I be, if I were in their place ! " [1]

Envy of the placid beasts seems to be a very widespread affection in this type of sadness.

The worst kind of melancholy is that which takes the

[1] The Life and Journal of the Rev. Mr. Henry Alline, Boston, 1806, pp. 25, 26. I owe my acquaintance with this book to my colleague, Dr. Benjamin Rand.

form of panic fear. Here is an excellent example, for permission to print which I have to thank the sufferer. The original is in French, and though the subject was evidently in a bad nervous condition at the time of which he writes, his case has otherwise the merit of extreme simplicity. I translate freely.

" Whilst in this state of philosophic pessimism and general depression of spirits about my prospects, I went one evening into a dressing-room in the twilight to procure some article that was there ; when suddenly there fell upon me without any warning, just as if it came out of the darkness, a horrible fear of my own existence. Simultaneously there arose in my mind the image of an epileptic patient whom I had seen in the asylum, a black-haired youth with greenish skin, entirely idiotic, who used to sit all day on one of the benches, or rather shelves against the wall, with his knees drawn up against his chin, and the coarse gray undershirt, which was his only garment, drawn over them inclosing his entire figure. He sat there like a sort of sculptured Egyptian cat or Peruvian mummy, moving nothing but his black eyes and looking absolutely non-human. This image and my fear entered into a species of combination with each other. *That shape am I*, I felt, potentially. Nothing that I possess can defend me against that fate, if the hour for it should strike for me as it struck for him. There was such a horror of him, and such a perception of my own merely momentary discrepancy from him, that it was as if something hitherto solid within my breast gave way entirely, and I became a mass of quivering fear. After this the universe was changed for me altogether. I awoke morning after morning with a horrible dread at the pit of my stomach, and with a sense of the insecurity of life that I never knew before, and that I have never felt since.[1] It was like a revelation ; and although the imme-

[1] Compare Bunyan : "There was I struck into a very great trembling, insomuch that at some times I could, for days together, feel my very body, as well as my mind, to shake and totter under the sense of the dreadful judgment of God, that should fall on those that have sinned that most fearful and unpardonable sin. I felt also such clogging and heat at my stom-

diate feelings passed away, the experience has made me sympathetic with the morbid feelings of others ever since. It gradually faded, but for months I was unable to go out into the
dark alone.

"In general I dreaded to be left alone. I remember wondering how other people could live, how I myself had ever
lived, so unconscious of that pit of insecurity beneath the surface of life. My mother in particular, a very cheerful person, seemed to me a perfect paradox in her unconsciousness of
danger, which you may well believe I was very careful not to
disturb by revelations of my own state of mind. I have always
thought that this experience of melancholia of mine had a religious bearing."

On asking this correspondent to explain more fully
what he meant by these last words, the answer he wrote
was this : —

" I mean that the fear was so invasive and powerful that if I
had not clung to scripture-texts like ' The eternal God is my
refuge,' etc., ' Come unto me, all ye that labor and are heavy-
laden,' etc., ' I am the resurrection and the life,' etc., I think I
should have grown really insane." [1]

There is no need of more examples. The cases we
have looked at are enough. One of them gives us the
vanity of mortal things ; another the sense of sin ; and
the remaining one describes the fear of the universe ; —
and in one or other of these three ways it always is that
man's original optimism and self-satisfaction get leveled
with the dust.

In none of these cases was there any intellectual insan-

ach, by reason of this my terror, that I was, especially at some times, as if
my breast-bone would have split asunder. . . . Thus did I wind, and twine,
and shrink, under the burden that was upon me ; which burden also did
so oppress me that I could neither stand, nor go, nor lie, either at rest or
quiet."

[1] For another case of fear equally sudden, see HENRY JAMES : Society
the Redeemed Form of Man, Boston, 1879, pp. 43 ff.

ity or delusion about matters of fact; but were we disposed to open the chapter of really insane melancholia, with its hallucinations and delusions, it would be a worse story still — desperation absolute and complete, the whole universe coagulating about the sufferer into a material of overwhelming horror, surrounding him without opening or end. Not the conception or intellectual perception of evil, but the grisly blood-freezing heart-palsying sensation of it close upon one, and no other conception or sensation able to live for a moment in its presence. How irrelevantly remote seem all our usual refined optimisms and intellectual and moral consolations in presence of a need of help like this! Here is the real core of the religious problem: Help! help! No prophet can claim to bring a final message unless he says things that will have a sound of reality in the ears of victims such as these. But the deliverance must come in as strong a form as the complaint, if it is to take effect; and that seems a reason why the coarser religions, revivalistic, orgiastic, with blood and miracles and supernatural operations, may possibly never be displaced. Some constitutions need them too much.

Arrived at this point, we can see how great an antagonism may naturally arise between the healthy-minded way of viewing life and the way that takes all this experience of evil as something essential. To this latter way, the morbid-minded way, as we might call it, healthy-mindedness pure and simple seems unspeakably blind and shallow. To the healthy-minded way, on the other hand, the way of the sick soul seems unmanly and diseased. With their grubbing in rat-holes instead of living in the light; with their manufacture of fears, and preoccupation with every unwholesome kind of misery, there is something almost obscene about these children of wrath and cravers of a second birth. If religious intolerance and hanging and burning could again become the order of the day, there is little doubt that, however it may have been in the past, the healthy-minded would at present show themselves the less indulgent party of the two.

In our own attitude, not yet abandoned, of impartial onlookers, what are we to say of this quarrel? It seems to me that we are bound to say that morbid-mindedness ranges over the wider scale of experience, and that its survey is the one that overlaps. The method of averting one's attention from evil, and living simply in the light of good is splendid as long as it will work. It will work with many persons; it will work far more generally than most of us are ready to suppose; and within the sphere of its successful operation there is nothing to be said against it as a religious solution. But it breaks down impotently as soon as melancholy comes; and even though one be quite free from melancholy one's self, there is no doubt that healthy-mindedness is inadequate as a philosophical doctrine, because the evil facts which it refuses positively to account for are a genuine portion of reality; and they may after all be the best key to life's significance, and possibly the only openers of our eyes to the deepest levels of truth.

The normal process of life contains moments as bad as any of those which insane melancholy is filled with, moments in which radical evil gets its innings and takes its solid turn. The lunatic's visions of horror are all drawn from the material of daily fact. Our civilization is founded on the shambles, and every individual existence goes out in a lonely spasm of helpless agony. If you protest, my friend, wait till you arrive there yourself! To believe in the carnivorous reptiles of geologic times is hard for our imagination — they seem too much like mere museum specimens. Yet there is no tooth in any one of those museum-skulls that did not daily through long years of the foretime hold fast to the body struggling in despair of some fated living victim. Forms of horror just as dreadful to their victims, if on a smaller spatial scale, fill the world about us to-day. Here on our very hearths and in our gardens the infernal cat plays with the panting mouse, or holds the hot bird fluttering in her jaws. Crocodiles and rattlesnakes and pythons are at this moment vessels of life as real as we are ; their loathsome existence fills every minute of every day that drags its length along ; and whenever they or other wild beasts clutch their living prey, the deadly horror which an agitated melancholiac feels is the literally right reaction on the situation.[1]

It may indeed be that no religious reconciliation with the absolute totality of things is possible. Some evils, indeed, are ministerial to higher forms of good ; but it

[1] Example : " It was about eleven o'clock at night . . . but I strolled on still with the people. . . . Suddenly upon the left side of our road, a crackling was heard among the bushes ; all of us were alarmed, and in an instant a tiger, rushing out of the jungle, pounced upon the one of the party that was foremost, and carried him off in the twinkling of an eye. The rush of the animal, and the crush of the poor victim's bones in his mouth, and his last cry of distress, ' Ho hai ! ' involuntarily reëchoed by all of us, was over in three seconds ; and then I know not what happened till I returned to my senses, when I found myself and companions lying down on the ground as if prepared to be devoured by our enemy, the sovereign of the forest. I find my pen incapable of describing the terror of that dreadful moment. Our limbs stiffened, our power of speech ceased, and our hearts beat violently, and only a whisper of the same ' Ho hai ! ' was heard from us. In this state we crept on all fours for some distance back, and then ran for life with the speed of an Arab horse for about half an hour, and fortunately happened to come to a small village. . . . After this every one of us was attacked with fever, attended with shivering, in which deplorable state we remained till morning." — Autobiography of Lutfullah, a Mohammedan Gentleman, Leipzig, 1857, p. 112.

may be that there are forms of evil so extreme as to enter into no good system whatsoever, and that, in respect of such evil, dumb submission or neglect to notice is the only practical resource. This question must confront us on a later day. But provisionally, and as a mere matter of program and method, since the evil facts are as genuine parts of nature as the good ones, the philosophic presumption should be that they have some rational significance, and that systematic healthy-mindedness, failing as it does to accord to sorrow, pain, and death any positive and active attention whatever, is formally less complete than systems that try at least to include these elements in their scope.

The completest religions would therefore seem to be those in which the pessimistic elements are best developed. Buddhism, of course, and Christianity are the best known to us of these. They are essentially religions of deliverance : the man must die to an unreal life before he can be born into the real life. In my next lecture, I will try to discuss some of the psychological conditions of this second birth. Fortunately from now onward we shall have to deal with more cheerful subjects than those which we have recently been dwelling on.

LECTURE VIII

THE DIVIDED SELF, AND THE PROCESS OF ITS UNIFICATION

THE last lecture was a painful one, dealing as it did with evil as a pervasive element of the world we live in. At the close of it we were brought into full view of the contrast between the two ways of looking at life which are characteristic respectively of what we called the healthy-minded, who need to be born only once, and of the sick souls, who must be twice-born in order to be happy. The result is two different conceptions of the universe of our experience. In the religion of the once-born the world is a sort of rectilinear or one-storied affair, whose accounts are kept in one denomination, whose parts have just the values which naturally they appear to have, and of which a simple algebraic sum of pluses and minuses will give the total worth. Happiness and religious peace consist in living on the plus side of the account. In the religion of the twice-born, on the other hand, the world is a double-storied mystery. Peace cannot be reached by the simple addition of pluses and elimination of minuses from life. Natural good is not simply insufficient in amount and transient, there lurks a falsity in its very being. Cancelled as it all is by death if not by earlier enemies, it gives no final balance, and can never be the thing intended for our lasting worship. It keeps us from our real good, rather; and renunciation and despair of it are our first step in the direction of the truth. There are two lives, the natural and the spiritual, and we must lose the one before we can participate in the other.

In their extreme forms, of pure naturalism and pure salvationism, the two types are violently contrasted; though here as in most other current classifications, the radical extremes are somewhat ideal abstractions, and the concrete human beings whom we oftenest meet are intermediate varieties and mixtures. Practically, however, you all recognize the difference : you understand, for example, the disdain of the methodist convert for the mere sky-blue healthy-minded moralist; and you likewise enter into the aversion of the latter to what seems to him the diseased subjectivism of the Methodist, dying to live, as he calls it, and making of paradox and the inversion of natural appearances the essence of God's truth.[1]

The psychological basis of the twice-born character seems to be a certain discordancy or heterogeneity in the native temperament of the subject, an incompletely unified moral and intellectual constitution.

"Homo duplex, homo duplex!" writes Alphonse Daudet. "The first time that I perceived that I was two was at the death of my brother Henri, when my father cried out so dramatically, 'He is dead, he is dead!' While my first self wept, my second self thought, 'How truly given was that cry, how fine it would be at the theatre.' I was then fourteen years old.

"This horrible duality has often given me matter for reflection. Oh, this terrible second me, always seated whilst the other is on foot, acting, living, suffering, bestirring itself. This

[1] E. g., "Our young people are diseased with the theological problems of original sin, origin of evil, predestination, and the like. These never presented a practical difficulty to any man — never darkened across any man's road, who did not go out of his way to seek them. These are the soul's mumps, and measles, and whooping-coughs," etc. EMERSON : 'Spiritual Laws.'

second me that I have never been able to intoxicate, to make shed tears, or put to sleep. And how it sees into things, and how it mocks!"[1]

Recent works on the psychology of character have had much to say upon this point.[2] Some persons are born with an inner constitution which is harmonious and well balanced from the outset. Their impulses are consistent with one another, their will follows without trouble the guidance of their intellect, their passions are not excessive, and their lives are little haunted by regrets. Others are oppositely constituted; and are so in degrees which may vary from something so slight as to result in a merely odd or whimsical inconsistency, to a discordancy of which the consequences may be inconvenient in the extreme. Of the more innocent kinds of heterogeneity I find a good example in Mrs. Annie Besant's autobiography.

"I have ever been the queerest mixture of weakness and strength, and have paid heavily for the weakness. As a child I used to suffer tortures of shyness, and if my shoe-lace was untied would feel shamefacedly that every eye was fixed on the unlucky string; as a girl I would shrink away from strangers and think myself unwanted and unliked, so that I was full of eager gratitude to any one who noticed me kindly; as the young mistress of a house I was afraid of my servants, and would let careless work pass rather than bear the pain of reproving the ill-doer; when I have been lecturing and debating with no lack of spirit on the platform, I have preferred to go without what I wanted at the hotel rather than to ring and make the waiter fetch it. Combative on the platform in defense of any cause I cared for, I shrink from quarrel or disapproval in the house, and am a coward at heart in private while a good

---

[1] Notes sur la Vie, p. 1.

[2] See, for example, F. Paulhan, in his book Les Caractères, 1894, who contrasts les Equilibrés, les Unifiés, with les Inquiets, les Contrariants, les Incohérents, les Emiettés, as so many diverse psychic types.

fighter in public. How often have I passed unhappy quarters of an hour screwing up my courage to find fault with some subordinate whom my duty compelled me to reprove, and how often have I jeered at myself for a fraud as the doughty platform combatant, when shrinking from blaming some lad or lass for doing their work badly. An unkind look or word has availed to make me shrink into myself as a snail into its shell, while, on the platform, opposition makes me speak my best." [1]

This amount of inconsistency will only count as amiable weakness; but a stronger degree of heterogeneity may make havoc of the subject's life. There are persons whose existence is little more than a series of zigzags, as now one tendency and now another gets the upper hand. Their spirit wars with their flesh, they wish for incompatibles, wayward impulses interrupt their most deliberate plans, and their lives are one long drama of repentance and of effort to repair misdemeanors and mistakes.

Heterogeneous personality has been explained as the result of inheritance — the traits of character of incompatible and antagonistic ancestors are supposed to be preserved alongside of each other.[2] This explanation may pass for what it is worth — it certainly needs corroboration. But whatever the cause of heterogeneous personality may be, we find the extreme examples of it in the psychopathic temperament, of which I spoke in my first lecture. All writers about that temperament make the inner heterogeneity prominent in their descriptions. Frequently, indeed, it is only this trait that leads us to ascribe that temperament to a man at all. A ' dégénéré supérieur ' is simply a man of sensibility in many directions, who finds more difficulty than is common in

---

[1] ANNIE BESANT : an Autobiography, p. 82.

[2] SMITH BAKER, in Journal of Nervous and Mental Diseases, September, 1893.

keeping his spiritual house in order and running his fur-
row straight, because his feelings and impulses are too
keen and too discrepant mutually.   In the haunting and
insistent ideas, in the irrational impulses, the morbid
scruples, dreads, and inhibitions which beset the psychopathic temperament when it is thoroughly pronounced,
we have exquisite examples of heterogeneous personality.
Bunyan had an obsession of the words, "Sell Christ for
this, sell him for that, sell him, sell him!" which would
run through his mind a hundred times together, until one
day out of breath with retorting, "I will not, I will not,"
he impulsively said, "Let him go if he will," and this
loss of the battle kept him in despair for over a year.
The lives of the saints are full of such blasphemous
obsessions, ascribed invariably to the direct agency of
Satan.   The phenomenon connects itself with the life of
the subconscious self, so-called, of which we must erelong speak more directly.

Now in all of us, however constituted, but to a degree
the greater in proportion as we are intense and sensitive
and subject to diversified temptations, and to the greatest
possible degree if we are decidedly psychopathic, does
the normal evolution of character chiefly consist in the
straightening out and unifying of the inner self.   The
higher and the lower feelings, the useful and the erring
impulses, begin by being a comparative chaos within us —
they must end by forming a stable system of functions
in right subordination.   Unhappiness is apt to characterize the period of order-making and struggle.   If the individual be of tender conscience and religiously quickened,
the unhappiness will take the form of moral remorse and
compunction, of feeling inwardly vile and wrong, and of
standing in false relations to the author of one's being
and appointer of one's spiritual fate.   This is the reli-

gious melancholy and 'conviction of sin' that have played
so large a part in the history of Protestant Christianity.
The man's interior is a battle-ground for what he feels to
be two deadly hostile selves, one actual, the other ideal.
As Victor Hugo makes his Mahomet say : —

> " Je suis le champ vil des sublimes combats :
>   Tantôt l'homme d'en haut, et tantôt l'homme d'en bas ;
>   Et le mal dans ma bouche avec le bien alterne,
>   Comme dans le désert le sable et la citerne."

Wrong living, impotent aspirations ; " What I would, that
do I not ; but what I hate, that do I," as Saint Paul says ;
self-loathing, self-despair ; an unintelligible and intolerable burden to which one is mysteriously the heir.

Let me quote from some typical cases of discordant
personality, with melancholy in the form of self-condem-
nation and sense of sin. Saint Augustine's case is a classic
example. You all remember his half-pagan, half-Chris-
tian bringing up at Carthage, his emigration to Rome and
Milan, his adoption of Manicheism and subsequent skepticism, and his restless search for truth and purity of life ;
and finally how, distracted by the struggle between the
two souls in his breast, and ashamed of his own weakness of will, when so many others whom he knew and
knew of had thrown off the shackles of sensuality and
dedicated themselves to chastity and the higher life, he
heard a voice in the garden say, " *Sume, lege* " (take and
read), and opening the Bible at random, saw the text,
"not in chambering and wantonness," etc., which seemed
directly sent to his address, and laid the inner storm
to rest forever.[1] Augustine's psychological genius has

[1] Louis GOURDON (Essai sur la Conversion de Saint Augustine, Paris,
Fischbacher, 1900) has shown by an analysis of Augustine's writings immediately after the date of his conversion (A. D. 386) that the account he gives
in the Confessions is premature. The crisis in the garden marked a definitive conversion from his former life, but it was to the neo-platonic spiritualism

given an account of the trouble of having a divided self which has never been surpassed.

" The new will which I began to have was not yet strong enough to overcome that other will, strengthened by long indulgence. So these two wills, one old, one new, one carnal, the other spiritual, contended with each other and disturbed my soul. I understood by my own experience what I had read, 'flesh lusteth against spirit, and spirit against flesh.' It was myself indeed in both the wills, yet more myself in that which I approved in myself than in that which I disapproved in myself. Yet it was through myself that habit had attained so fierce a mastery over me, because I had willingly come whither I willed not. Still bound to earth, I refused, O God, to fight on thy side, as much afraid to be freed from all bonds, as I ought to have feared being trammeled by them.

" Thus the thoughts by which I meditated upon thee were like the efforts of one who would awake, but being overpowered with sleepiness is soon asleep again. Often does a man when heavy sleepiness is on his limbs defer to shake it off, and though not approving it, encourage it ; even so I was sure it was better to surrender to thy love than to yield to my own lusts, yet, though the former course convinced me, the latter pleased and held me bound. There was naught in me to answer thy call, 'Awake, thou sleeper,' but only drawling, drowsy words, ' Presently ; yes, presently ; wait a little while.' But the 'presently' had no 'present,' and the 'little while' grew long. . . . For I was afraid thou wouldst hear me too soon, and heal me at once of my disease of lust, which I wished to satiate rather than to see extinguished. With what lashes of words did I not scourge my own soul. Yet it shrank back ; it refused, though it had no excuse to offer. . . . I said within myself : ' Come, let it be done now,' and as I said it, I was on the point of the resolve. I all but did it, yet I did not do it. And I made another effort, and almost succeeded, yet I did not reach it, and did not grasp it, hesitating to die to death, and live to life ; and the evil to which

and only a halfway stage toward Christianity. The latter he appears not fully and radically to have embraced until four years more had passed.

I was so wonted held me more than the better life I had not
tried." [1]

There could be no more perfect description of the
divided will, when the higher wishes lack just that last
acuteness, that touch of explosive intensity, of dynamogenic quality (to use the slang of the psychologists), that
enables them to burst their shell, and make irruption
efficaciously into life and quell the lower tendencies forever.   In a later lecture we shall have much to say
about this higher excitability.

I find another good description of the divided will in
the autobiography of Henry Alline, the Nova Scotian
evangelist, of whose melancholy I read a brief account in
my last lecture.   The poor youth's sins were, as you will
see, of the most harmless order, yet they interfered with
what proved to be his truest vocation, so they gave him
great distress.

" I was now very moral in my life, but found no rest of conscience.   I now began to be esteemed in young company, who
knew nothing of my mind all this while, and their esteem began
to be a snare to my soul, for I soon began to be fond of carnal
mirth, though I still flattered myself that if I did not get drunk,
nor curse, nor swear, there would be no sin in frolicking and
carnal mirth, and I thought God would indulge young people
with some (what I called simple or civil) recreation.   I still
kept a round of duties, and would not suffer myself to run into
any open vices, and so got along very well in time of health
and prosperity, but when I was distressed or threatened by
sickness, death, or heavy storms of thunder, my religion would
not do, and I found there was something wanting, and would
begin to repent my going so much to frolics, but when the
distress was over, the devil and my own wicked heart, with the
solicitations of my associates, and my fondness for young com-

[1] Confessions, Book VIII., chaps. v., vii., xi., abridged.

pany, were such strong allurements, I would again give way, and thus I got to be very wild and rude, at the same time kept up my rounds of secret prayer and reading; but God, not willing I should destroy myself, still followed me with his calls, and moved with such power upon my conscience, that I could not satisfy myself with my diversions, and in the midst of my mirth sometimes would have such a sense of my lost and undone condition, that I would wish myself from the company, and after it was over, when I went home, would make many promises that I would attend no more on these frolics, and would beg forgiveness for hours and hours; but when I came to have the temptation again, I would give way: no sooner would I hear the music and drink a glass of wine, but I would find my mind elevated and soon proceed to any sort of merriment or diversion, that I thought was not debauched or openly vicious; but when I returned from my carnal mirth I felt as guilty as ever, and could sometimes not close my eyes for some hours after I had gone to my bed.   I was one of the most unhappy creatures on earth.

"Sometimes I would leave the company (often speaking to the fiddler to cease from playing, as if I was tired), and go out and walk about crying and praying, as if my very heart would break, and beseeching God that he would not cut me off, nor give me up to hardness of heart.   Oh, what unhappy hours and nights I thus wore away!   When I met sometimes with merry companions, and my heart was ready to sink, I would labor to put on as cheerful a countenance as possible, that they might not distrust anything, and sometimes would begin some discourse with young men or young women on purpose, or propose a merry song, lest the distress of my soul would be discovered, or mistrusted, when at the same time I would then rather have been in a wilderness in exile, than with them or any of their pleasures or enjoyments.   Thus for many months when I was in company, I would act the hypocrite and feign a merry heart, but at the same time would endeavor as much as I could to shun their company, oh wretched and unhappy mortal that I was!   Everything I did, and wherever I went, I was still in a storm, and yet I continued to be the chief contriver and ring-

leader of the frolics for many months after; though it was a
toil and torment to attend them; but the devil and my own
wicked heart drove me about like a slave, telling me that I
must do this and do that, and bear this and bear that, and turn
here and turn there, to keep my credit up, and retain the
esteem of my associates: and all this while I continued as strict
as possible in my duties, and left no stone unturned to pacify
my conscience, watching even against my thoughts, and praying
continually wherever I went: for I did not think there was any
sin in my conduct, when I was among carnal company, because
I did not take any satisfaction there, but only followed it, I
thought, for sufficient reasons.

"But still, all that I did or could do, conscience would roar
night and day."

Saint Augustine and Alline both emerged into the
smooth waters of inner unity and peace, and I shall next
ask you to consider more closely some of the peculiarities
of the process of unification, when it occurs. It may
come gradually, or it may occur abruptly; it may come
through altered feelings, or through altered powers of
action; or it may come through new intellectual insights,
or through experiences which we shall later have to designate as 'mystical.' However it come, it brings a characteristic sort of relief; and never such extreme relief as
when it is cast into the religious mould. Happiness!
happiness! religion is only one of the ways in which men
gain that gift. Easily, permanently, and successfully,
it often transforms the most intolerable misery into the
profoundest and most enduring happiness.

But to find religion is only one out of many ways
of reaching unity; and the process of remedying inner
incompleteness and reducing inner discord is a general
psychological process, which may take place with any sort
of mental material, and need not necessarily assume the
religious form. In judging of the religious types of

regeneration which we are about to study, it is important to recognize that they are only one species of a genus that contains other types as well.   For example, the new birth may be away from religion into incredulity; or it may be from moral scrupulosity into freedom and license; or it may be produced by the irruption into the individual's life of some new stimulus or passion, such as love, ambition, cupidity, revenge, or patriotic devotion.   In all these instances we have precisely the same psychological form of event, — a firmness, stability, and equilibrium succeeding a period of storm and stress and inconsistency. In these non-religious cases the new man may also be born either gradually or suddenly.

The French philosopher Jouffroy has left an eloquent memorial of his own 'counter-conversion,' as the transition from orthodoxy to infidelity has been well styled by Mr. Starbuck.   Jouffroy's doubts had long harassed him; but he dates his final crisis from a certain night when his disbelief grew fixed and stable, and where the immediate result was sadness at the illusions he had lost.

" I shall never forget that night of December," writes Jouffroy, " in which the veil that concealed from me my own incredulity was torn.   I hear again my steps in that narrow naked chamber where long after the hour of sleep had come I had the habit of walking up and down.   I see again that moon, half-veiled by clouds, which now and again illuminated the frigid window-panes.   The hours of the night flowed on and I did not note their passage.   Anxiously I followed my thoughts, as from layer to layer they descended towards the foundation of my consciousness, and, scattering one by one all the illusions which until then had screened its windings from my view, made them every moment more clearly visible.

" Vainly I clung to these last beliefs as a shipwrecked sailor clings to the fragments of his vessel; vainly, frightened at the unknown void in which I was about to float, I turned with them towards my childhood, my family, my country, all that was dear and sacred to me: the inflexible current of my thought was too strong, — parents, family, memory, beliefs, it forced me to let go of everything. The investigation went on more obstinate and more severe as it drew near its term, and did not stop until the end was reached. I knew then that in the depth of my mind nothing was left that stood erect.

"This moment was a frightful one; and when towards morning I threw myself exhausted on my bed, I seemed to feel my earlier life, so smiling and so full, go out like a fire, and before me another life opened, sombre and unpeopled, where in future I must live alone, alone with my fatal thought which had exiled me thither, and which I was tempted to curse. The days which followed this discovery were the saddest of my life." [1]

[1] TH. JOUFFROY: Nouveaux Mélanges philosophiques, 2me édition, p. 83. I add two other cases of counter-conversion dating from a certain moment. The first is from Professor Starbuck's manuscript collection, and the narrator is a woman.

"Away down in the bottom of my heart, I believe I was always more or less skeptical about 'God;' skepticism grew as an undercurrent, all through my early youth, but it was controlled and covered by the emotional elements in my religious growth. When I was sixteen I joined the church and was asked if I loved God. I replied 'Yes,' as was customary and expected. But instantly with a flash something spoke within me, 'No, you do not.' I was haunted for a long time with shame and remorse for my falsehood and for my wickedness in not loving God, mingled with fear that there might be an avenging God who would punish me in some terrible way. . . . At nineteen, I had an attack of tonsilitis. Before I had quite recovered, I heard told a story of a brute who had kicked his wife downstairs, and then continued the operation until she became insensible. I felt the horror of the thing keenly. Instantly this thought flashed through my mind: 'I have no use for a God who permits such things.' This experience was followed by months of stoical indifference to the God of my previous life, mingled with feelings of positive dislike and a somewhat proud defiance of him. I still thought there might be a God. If so he would probably damn me, but I should have to stand it. I felt very little fear and no desire to propitiate him. I have never had any personal relations with him since this painful experience."

The second case exemplifies how small an additional stimulus will overthrow the mind into a new state of equilibrium when the process of preparation and incubation has proceeded far enough. It is like the proverbial last straw added to the camel's burden, or that touch of a needle which

In John Foster's Essay on Decision of Character, there is an account of a case of sudden conversion to avarice, which is illustrative enough to quote : —

A young man, it appears, " wasted, in two or three years, a large patrimony in profligate revels with a number of worthless associates who called themselves his friends, and who, when his last means were exhausted, treated him of course with neglect or contempt. Reduced to absolute want, he one day went out of the house with an intention to put an end to his life; but wandering awhile almost unconsciously, he came to the brow of an eminence which overlooked what were lately his estates. Here he sat down, and remained fixed in thought a number of hours, at the end of which he sprang from the ground with a vehement, exulting emotion. He had formed his resolution, which was, that all these estates should be his again ; he had formed his plan, too, which he instantly began to execute. He walked hastily forward, determined to seize the first opportunity, of however humble a kind, to gain any money, though it were ever so despicable a trifle, and resolved absolutely not to

makes the salt in a supersaturated fluid suddenly begin to crystallize out.

Tolstoy writes : " S., a frank and intelligent man, told me as follows how he ceased to believe : —

" He was twenty-six years old when one day on a hunting expedition, the time for sleep having come, he set himself to pray according to the custom he had held from childhood.

" His brother, who was hunting with him, lay upon the hay and looked at him. When S. had finished his prayer and was turning to sleep, the brother said, ' Do you still keep up that thing ? ' Nothing more was said. But since that day, now more than thirty years ago, S. has never prayed again ; he never takes communion, and does not go to church. All this, not because he became acquainted with convictions of his brother which he then and there adopted ; not because he made any new resolution in his soul, but merely because the words spoken by his brother were like the light push of a finger against a leaning wall already about to tumble by its own weight. These words but showed him that the place wherein he supposed religion dwelt in him had long been empty, and that the sentences he uttered, the crosses and bows which he made during his prayer, were actions with no inner sense. Having once seized their absurdity, he could no longer keep them up." Ma Confession, p. 8.

spend, if he could help it, a farthing of whatever he might obtain. The first thing that drew his attention was a heap of coals shot out of carts on the pavement before a house. He offered himself to shovel or wheel them into the place where they were to be laid, and was employed. He received a few pence for the labor; and then, in pursuance of the saving part of his plan, requested some small gratuity of meat and drink, which was given him. He then looked out for the next thing that might chance; and went, with indefatigable industry, through a succession of servile employments in different places, of longer and shorter duration, still scrupulous in avoiding, as far as possible, the expense of a penny. He promptly seized every opportunity which could advance his design, without regarding the meanness of occupation or appearance. By this method he had gained, after a considerable time, money enough to purchase in order to sell again a few cattle, of which he had taken pains to understand the value. He speedily but cautiously turned his first gains into second advantages; retained without a single deviation his extreme parsimony; and thus advanced by degrees into larger transactions and incipient wealth. I did not hear, or have forgotten, the continued course of his life, but the final result was, that he more than recovered his lost possessions, and died an inveterate miser, worth £60,000." [1]

[1] Op. cit., Letter III., abridged.

I subjoin an additional document which has come into my possession, and which represents in a vivid way what is probably a very frequent sort of conversion, if the opposite of ‘falling in love,’ falling out of love, may be so termed. Falling in love also conforms frequently to this type, a latent process of unconscious preparation often preceding a sudden awakening to the fact that the mischief is irretrievably done. The free and easy tone in this narrative gives it a sincerity that speaks for itself.

"For two years of this time I went through a very bad experience, which almost drove me mad. I had fallen violently in love with a girl who, young as she was, had a spirit of coquetry like a cat. As I look back on her now, I hate her, and wonder how I could ever have fallen so low as to be worked upon to such an extent by her attractions. Nevertheless, I fell into a regular fever, could think of nothing else; whenever I was alone, I pictured her attractions, and spent most of the time when I should have been working, in recalling our previous interviews, and imagining future conversations. She was very pretty, good humored, and jolly to the last

Let me turn now to the kind of case, the religious case, namely, that immediately concerns us. Here is one of

degree, and intensely pleased with my admiration. Would give me no decided answer yes or no, and the queer thing about it was that whilst pursuing her for her hand, I secretly knew all along that she was unfit to be a wife for me, and that she never would say yes. Although for a year we took our meals at the same boarding-house, so that I saw her continually and familiarly, our closer relations had to be largely on the sly, and this fact, together with my jealousy of another one of her male admirers, and my own conscience despising me for my uncontrollable weakness, made me so nervous and sleepless that I really thought I should become insane. I understand well those young men murdering their sweethearts, which appear so often in the papers. Nevertheless I did love her passionately, and in some ways she did deserve it.

"The queer thing was the sudden and unexpected way in which it all stopped. I was going to my work after breakfast one morning, thinking as usual of her and of my misery, when, just as if some outside power laid hold of me, I found myself turning round and almost running to my room, where I immediately got out all the relics of her which I possessed, including some hair, all her notes and letters, and ambrotypes on glass. The former I made a fire of, the latter I actually crushed beneath my heel, in a sort of fierce joy of revenge and punishment. I now loathed and despised her altogether, and as for myself I felt as if a load of disease had suddenly been removed from me. That was the end. I never spoke to her or wrote to her again in all the subsequent years, and I have never had a single moment of loving thought towards one who for so many months entirely filled my heart. In fact, I have always rather hated her memory, though now I can see that I had gone unnecessarily far in that direction. At any rate, from that happy morning onward I regained possession of my own proper soul, and have never since fallen into any similar trap."

This seems to me an unusually clear example of two different levels of personality, inconsistent in their dictates, yet so well balanced against each other as for a long time to fill the life with discord and dissatisfaction. At last, not gradually, but in a sudden crisis, the unstable equilibrium is resolved, and this happens so unexpectedly that it is as if, to use the writer's words, "some outside power laid hold."

Professor Starbuck gives an analogous case, and a converse case of hatred suddenly turning into love, in his Psychology of Religion, p. 141. Compare the other highly curious instances which he gives on pp. 137–144, of sudden non-religious alterations of habit or character. He seems right in conceiving all such sudden changes as results of special cerebral functions unconsciously developing until they are ready to play a controlling part, when they make irruption into the conscious life. When we treat of sudden 'conversion,' I shall make as much use as I can of this hypothesis of subconscious incubation.

the simplest possible type, an account of the conversion to the systematic religion of healthy-mindedness of a man who must already have been naturally of the healthy-minded type. It shows how, when the fruit is ripe, a touch will make it fall.

Mr. Horace Fletcher, in his little book called Menti-culture, relates that a friend with whom he was talking of the self-control attained by the Japanese through their practice of the Buddhist discipline said : —

" ' You must first get rid of anger and worry.' ' But,' said I, ' is that possible?' ' Yes,' replied he ; ' it is possible to the Japanese, and ought to be possible to us.'

" On my way back I could think of nothing else but the words ' get rid, get rid ' ; and the idea must have continued to possess me during my sleeping hours, for the first consciousness in the morning brought back the same thought, with the revelation of a discovery, which framed itself into the reasoning, ' If it is possible to get rid of anger and worry, why is it necessary to have them at all ?' I felt the strength of the argument, and at once accepted the reasoning. The baby had discovered that it could walk. It would scorn to creep any longer.

" From the instant I realized that these cancer spots of worry and anger were removable, they left me. With the discovery of their weakness they were exorcised. From that time life has had an entirely different aspect.

" Although from that moment the possibility and desirability of freedom from the depressing passions has been a reality to me, it took me some months to feel absolute security in my new position ; but, as the usual occasions for worry and anger have presented themselves over and over again, and I have been unable to feel them in the slightest degree, I no longer dread or guard against them, and I am amazed at my increased energy and vigor of mind ; at my strength to meet situations of all kinds, and at my disposition to love and appreciate everything.

" I have had occasion to travel more than ten thousand miles by rail since that morning. The same Pullman porter, con-ductor, hotel-waiter, peddler, book-agent, cabman, and others who were formerly a source of annoyance and irritation have been met, but I am not conscious of a single incivility. All at once the whole world has turned good to me. I have become, as it were, sensitive only to the rays of good.

"I could recount many experiences which prove a brand-new condition of mind, but one will be sufficient. Without the slightest feeling of annoyance or impatience, I have seen a train that I had planned to take with a good deal of interested and pleasurable anticipation move out of the station without me, because my baggage did not arrive. The porter from the hotel came running and panting into the station just as the train pulled out of sight. When he saw me, he looked as if he feared a scolding, and began to tell of being blocked in a crowded street and unable to get out. When he had finished, I said to him: 'It does n't matter at all, you could n't help it, so we will try again to-morrow. Here is your fee, I am sorry you had all this trouble in earning it.' The look of surprise that came over his face was so filled with pleasure that I was repaid on the spot for the delay in my departure. Next day he would not accept a cent for the service, and he and I are friends for life.

"During the first weeks of my experience I was on guard only against worry and anger; but, in the mean time, having noticed the absence of the other depressing and dwarfing passions, I began to trace a relationship, until I was convinced that they are all growths from the two roots I have specified. I have felt the freedom now for so long a time that I am sure of my relation toward it; and I could no more harbor any of the thieving and depressing influences that once I nursed as a heritage of humanity than a fop would voluntarily wallow in a filthy gutter.

"There is no doubt in my mind that pure Christianity and pure Buddhism, and the Mental Sciences and all Religions, fundamentally teach what has been a discovery to me; but none of them have presented it in the light of a simple and easy process of elimination. At one time I wondered if the elimination would not yield to indifference and sloth. In my experience, the contrary is the result. I feel such an increased desire to do something useful that it seems as if I were a boy again and the energy for play had returned. I could fight as readily as (and better than) ever, if there were occasion for it. It does not make one a coward. It can't, since fear is one of the things eliminated. I notice the absence of timidity in the presence of any audience. When a boy, I was standing under a tree which was struck by lightning, and received a shock from the effects of which I never knew exemption until I had dissolved partnership with worry. Since then, lightning and thunder have been encountered under conditions which would formerly have caused great depression and discomfort, without [my] experiencing a trace of either. Surprise is also greatly modified, and one is less liable to become startled by unexpected sights or noises.

" As far as I am individually concerned, I am not bothering myself at present as to what the results of this emancipated condition may be. I have no doubt that the perfect health aimed at by Christian Science may be one of the possibilities, for I note a marked improvement in the way my stomach does its duty in assimilating the food I give it to handle, and I am sure it works better to the sound of a song than under the friction of a frown. Neither am I wasting any of this precious time formulating an idea of a future existence or a future Heaven. The Heaven that I have within myself is as attractive as any that has been promised or that I can imagine; and I am willing to let the growth lead where it will, as long as the anger and their brood have no part in misguiding it." [1]

The older medicine used to speak of two ways, *lysis* and *crisis*, one gradual, the other abrupt, in which one might recover from a bodily disease. In the spiritual realm there are also two ways, one gradual, the other sudden, in which inner unification may occur. Tolstoy and Bunyan may again serve us as examples, examples, as it happens, of the gradual way, though it must be confessed at the outset that it is hard to follow these wind-

[1] H. FLETCHER : Menticulture, or the A-B-C of True Living, New York and Chicago, 1899, pp. 26–36, abridged.

ings of the hearts of others, and one feels that their words do not reveal their total secret.

Howe'er this be, Tolstoy, pursuing his unending questioning, seemed to come to one insight after another. First he perceived that his conviction that life was meaningless took only this finite life into account. He was looking for the value of one finite term in that of another, and the whole result could only be one of those indeterminate equations in mathematics which end with $0=0$. Yet this is as far as the reasoning intellect by itself can go, unless irrational sentiment or faith brings in the infinite. Believe in the infinite as common people do, and life grows possible again.

" Since mankind has existed, wherever life has been, there also has been the faith that gave the possibility of living. Faith is the sense of life, that sense by virtue of which man does not destroy himself, but continues to live on. It is the force whereby we live. If Man did not believe that he must live for something, he would not live at all. The idea of an infinite God, of the divinity of the soul, of the union of men's actions with God — these are ideas elaborated in the infinite secret depths of human thought. They are ideas without which there would be no life, without which I myself," said Tolstoy, " would not exist. I began to see that I had no right to rely on my individual reasoning and neglect these answers given by faith, for they are the only answers to the question."

Yet how believe as the common people believe, steeped as they are in grossest superstition ? It is impossible, — but yet their life ! their life ! It is normal. It is happy ! It is an answer to the question !

Little by little, Tolstoy came to the settled conviction — he says it took him two years to arrive there — that his trouble had not been with life in general, not with the common life of common men, but with the life of the upper, intellectual, artistic classes, the life which he had

personally always led, the cerebral life, the life of conventionality, artificiality, and personal ambition.   He had
been living wrongly and must change.   To work for
animal needs, to abjure lies and vanities, to relieve common wants, to be simple, to believe in God, therein lay
happiness again.

" I remember," he says, " one day in early spring, I was alone
in the forest, lending my ear to its mysterious noises.   I listened,
and my thought went back .to what for these three years it
always was busy with — the quest of God.   But the idea of
him, I said, how did I ever come by the idea?

" And again there arose in me, with this thought, glad aspirations towards life.   Everything in me awoke and received
a meaning. . . . Why do I look farther? a voice within me
asked.   He is there: he, without whom one cannot live.   To
acknowledge God and to live are one and the same thing.   God
is what life is.   Well, then! live, seek God, and there will be
no life without him. . . .

" After this, things cleared up within me and about me better than ever, and the light has never wholly died away.   I was
saved from suicide.   Just how or when the change took place I
cannot tell.   But as insensibly and gradually as the force of
life had been annulled within me, and I had reached my moral
death-bed, just as gradually and imperceptibly did the energy
of life come back.   And what was strange was that this energy
that came back was nothing new.   It was my ancient juvenile
force of faith, the belief that the sole purpose of my life was to
be *better*.   I gave up the life of the conventional world, recognizing it to be no life, but a parody on life, which its superfluities
simply keep us from comprehending," — and Tolstoy thereupon
embraced the life of the peasants, and has felt right and happy,
or at least relatively so, ever since.[1]

As I interpret his melancholy, then, it was not merely
an accidental vitiation of his humors, though it was doubtless also that.   It was logically called for by the clash

[1] I have considerably abridged Tolstoy's words in my translation.

between his inner character and his outer activities and aims. Although a literary artist, Tolstoy was one of those primitive oaks of men to whom the superfluities and insincerities, the cupidities, complications, and cruelties of our polite civilization are profoundly unsatisfying, and for whom the eternal veracities lie with more natural and animal things. His crisis was the getting of his soul in order, the discovery of its genuine habitat and vocation, the escape from falsehoods into what for him were ways of truth. It was a case of heterogeneous personality tardily and slowly finding its unity and level. And though not many of us can imitate Tolstoy, not having enough, perhaps, of the aboriginal human marrow in our bones, most of us may at least feel as if it might be better for us if we could.

Bunyan's recovery seems to have been even slower. For years together he was alternately haunted with texts of Scripture, now up and now down, but at last with an ever growing relief in his salvation through the blood of Christ.

" My peace would be in and out twenty times a day; comfort now and trouble presently; peace now and before I could go a furlong as full of guilt and fear as ever heart could hold." When a good text comes home to him, " This," he writes, " gave me good encouragement for the space of two or three hours " ; or " This was a good day to me, I hope I shall not forget it " ; or " The glory of these words was then so weighty on me that I was ready to swoon as I sat; yet not with grief and trouble, but with solid joy and peace " ; or " This made a strange seizure on my spirit ; it brought light with it, and commanded a silence in my heart of all those tumultuous thoughts that before did use, like masterless hell-hounds, to roar and bellow and make a hideous noise within me. It showed me that Jesus Christ had not quite forsaken and cast off my Soul."

Such periods accumulate until he can write : " And now

remained only the hinder part of the tempest, for the thunder was gone beyond me, only some drops would still remain, that now and then would fall upon me " ; — and at last : " Now did my chains fall off my legs indeed ; I was loosed from my afflictions and irons ; my temptations also fled away ; so that from that time, those dreadful Scriptures of God left off to trouble me ; now went I also home rejoicing, for the grace and love of God. . . . Now could I see myself in Heaven and Earth at once ; in Heaven by my Christ, by my Head, by my Righteousness and Life, though on Earth by my body or person. . . . Christ was a precious Christ to my soul that night ; I could scarce lie in my bed for joy and peace and triumph through Christ."

Bunyan became a minister of the gospel, and in spite of his neurotic constitution, and of the twelve years he lay in prison for his non-conformity, his life was turned to active use. He was a peacemaker and doer of good, and the immortal Allegory which he wrote has brought the very spirit of religious patience home to English hearts.

But neither Bunyan nor Tolstoy could become what we have called healthy-minded. They had drunk too deeply of the cup of bitterness ever to forget its taste, and their redemption is into a universe two stories deep. Each of them realized a good which broke the effective edge of his sadness ; yet the sadness was preserved as a minor ingredient in the heart of the faith by which it was overcome. The fact of interest for us is that as a matter of fact they could and did find *something* welling up in the inner reaches of their consciousness, by which such extreme sadness could be overcome. Tolstoy does well to talk of it as *that by which men live ;* for that is exactly what it is, a stimulus, an excitement, a faith, a force that re-infuses the positive willingness to live, even in full presence of the evil perceptions that erewhile made life seem unbearable. For Tolstoy's perceptions of evil appear within their sphere to have remained unmodified. His later works show him implacable to the whole system of official values : the ignobility of fashionable life ; the infamies of empire; the spuriousness of the church, the vain conceit of the professions ; the meannesses and cruelties that go with great success ; and every other pompous crime and lying institution of this world.   To all patience with such things his experience has been for him a permanent ministry of death.

Bunyan also leaves this world to the enemy.

" I must first pass a sentence of death," he says, "upon everything that can properly be called a thing of this life, even to reckon myself, my wife, my children, my health, my enjoyments, and all, as dead to me, and myself as dead to them ; to trust in God through Christ, as touching the world to come ; and as touching this world, to count the grave my house, to make my bed in darkness, and to say to corruption, Thou art my father, and to the worm, Thou art my mother and sister. . . . The parting with my wife and my poor children hath often been to me as the pulling of my flesh from my bones, especially my poor blind child who lay nearer my heart than all I had besides.   Poor child, thought I, what sorrow art thou like to have for thy portion in this world !   Thou must be beaten, must beg, suffer hunger, cold, nakedness, and a thousand calamities, though I cannot now endure that the wind should blow upon thee.   But yet I must venture you all with God, though it goeth to the quick to leave you." [1]

The ' hue of resolution ' is there, but the full flood of ecstatic liberation seems never to have poured over poor John Bunyan's soul.

These examples may suffice to acquaint us in a general way with the phenomenon technically called ' Conversion.'   In the next lecture I shall invite you to study its peculiarities and concomitants in some detail.

[1] In my quotations from Bunyan I have omitted certain intervening portions of the text.

LECTURE IX

CONVERSION

TO be converted, to be regenerated, to receive grace, to experience religion, to gain an assurance, are so many phrases which denote the process, gradual or sudden, by which a self hitherto divided, and consciously wrong inferior and unhappy, becomes unified and consciously right superior and happy, in consequence of its firmer hold upon religious realities. This at least is what conversion signifies in general terms, whether or not we believe that a direct divine operation is needed to bring such a moral change about.

Before entering upon a minuter study of the process, let me enliven our understanding of the definition by a concrete example. I choose the quaint case of an unlettered man, Stephen H. Bradley, whose experience is related in a scarce American pamphlet.[1]

I select this case because it shows how in these inner alterations one may find one unsuspected depth below another, as if the possibilities of character lay disposed in a series of layers or shells, of whose existence we have no premonitory knowledge.

Bradley thought that he had been already fully converted at the age of fourteen.

"I thought I saw the Saviour, by faith, in human shape, for about one second in the room, with arms extended, appearing

---

[1] A sketch of the life of Stephen H. Bradley, from the age of five to twenty-four years, including his remarkable experience of the power of the Holy Spirit on the second evening of November, 1829. Madison, Connecticut, 1830.

to say to me, Come. The next day I rejoiced with trembling ; soon after, my happiness was so great that I said that I wanted to die ; this world had no place in my affections, as I knew of, and every day appeared as solemn to me as the Sabbath. I had an ardent desire that all mankind might feel as I did ; I wanted to have them all love God supremely. Previous to this time I was very selfish and self-righteous ; but now I desired the welfare of all mankind, and could with a feeling heart forgive my worst enemies, and I felt as if I should be willing to bear the scoffs and sneers of any person, and suffer anything for His sake, if I could be the means in the hands of God, of the conversion of one soul."

Nine years later, in 1829, Mr. Bradley heard of a revival of religion that had begun in his neighborhood. " Many of the young converts," he says, " would come to me when in meeting and ask me if I had religion, and my reply generally was, I hope I have. This did not appear to satisfy them ; they said they *knew they* had it. I requested them to pray for me, thinking with myself, that if I had not got religion now, after so long a time professing to be a Christian, that it was time I had, and hoped their prayers would be answered in my behalf.

" One Sabbath, I went to hear the Methodist at the Academy. He spoke of the ushering in of the day of general judgment ; and he set it forth in such a solemn and terrible manner as I never heard before. The scene of that day appeared to be taking place, and so awakened were all the powers of my mind that, like Felix, I trembled involuntarily on the bench where I was sitting, though I felt nothing at heart. The next day evening I went to hear him again. He took his text from Revelation : ' And I saw the dead, small and great, stand before God.' And he represented the terrors of that day in such a manner that it appeared as if it would melt the heart of stone. When he finished his discourse, an old gentleman turned to me and said, ' This is what I call preaching.' I thought the same ; but my feelings were still unmoved by what he said, and I did not enjoy religion, but I believe he did.

" I will now relate my experience of the power of the Holy Spirit which took place on the same night. Had any person told me previous to this that I could have experienced the power of the Holy Spirit in the manner which I did, I could not have believed it, and should have thought the person deluded that told me so. I went directly home after the meeting, and when I got home I wondered what made me feel so stupid. I retired to rest soon after I got home, and felt indifferent to the things of religion until I began to be exercised by the Holy Spirit, which began in about five minutes after, in the following manner : —

"At first, I began to feel my heart beat very quick all on a sudden, which made me at first think that perhaps something is going to ail me, though I was not alarmed, for I felt no pain. My heart increased in its beating, which soon convinced me that it was the Holy Spirit from the effect it had on me. I began to feel exceedingly happy and humble, and such a sense of unworthiness as I never felt before. I could not very well help speaking out, which I did, and said, Lord, I do not deserve this happiness, or words to that effect, while there was a stream (resembling air in feeling) came into my mouth and heart in a more sensible manner than that of drinking anything, which continued, as near as I could judge, five minutes or more, which appeared to be the cause of such a palpitation of my heart. It took complete possession of my soul, and I am certain that I desired the Lord, while in the midst of it, not to give me any more happiness, for it seemed as if I could not contain what I had got. My heart seemed as if it would burst, but it did not stop until I felt as if I was unutterably full of the love and grace of God. In the mean time while thus exercised, a thought arose in my mind, what can it mean? and all at once, as if to answer it, my memory became exceedingly clear, and it appeared to me just as if the New Testament was placed open before me, eighth chapter of Romans, and as light as if some candle lighted was held for me to read the 26th and 27th verses of that chapter, and I read these words: 'The Spirit helpeth our infirmities with groanings which cannot be uttered.' And all the time that my heart was a-beating, it made me groan like a person in distress, which was not very easy to stop, though I was in no pain at all, and my brother being in bed in another room came and opened the door, and asked me if I had got the toothache. I told him no, and that he might get to sleep. I tried to stop. I felt unwilling to go to sleep myself, I was so happy, fearing I should lose it — thinking within myself

'My willing soul would stay
In such a frame as this.'

And while I lay reflecting, after my heart stopped beating, feeling as if my soul was full of the Holy Spirit, I thought that perhaps there might be angels hovering round my bed. I felt just as if I wanted to converse with them, and finally I spoke, saying, ' O ye affectionate angels! how is it that ye can take so much interest in our welfare, and we take so little interest in our own.' After this, with difficulty I got to sleep; and when I awoke in the morning my first thoughts were: What has become of my happiness? and, feeling a degree of it in my heart, I asked for more, which was given to me as quick as thought. I then got up to dress myself, and found to my surprise that I could but just stand. It appeared to me as if it was a little heaven upon earth. My soul felt as completely raised above the fears of death as of going to sleep; and like a bird in a cage, I had a desire, if it was the will of God, to get released from my body and to dwell with Christ, though willing to live to do good to others, and to warn sinners to repent. I went downstairs feeling as solemn as if I had lost all my friends, and thinking with myself, that I would not let my parents know it until I had first looked into the Testament. I went directly to the shelf and looked into it, at the eighth chapter of Romans, and every verse seemed to almost speak and to confirm it to be truly the Word of God, and as if my feelings corresponded with the meaning of the word. I then told my parents of it, and told them that I thought that they must see that when I spoke, that it was not my own voice, for it appeared so to me. My speech seemed entirely under the control of the Spirit within me; I do not mean that the words which I spoke were not my own, for they were. I thought that I was influenced similar to the Apostles on the day of Pentecost (with the exception of having power to give it to others, and doing

what they did).   After breakfast I went round to converse
with my neighbors on religion, which I could not have been
hired to have done before this, and at their request I prayed
with them, though I had never prayed in public before.

"I now feel as if I had discharged my duty by telling the
truth, and hope by the blessing of God, it may do some good to
all who shall read it.   He has fulfilled his promise in sending
the Holy Spirit down into our hearts, or mine at least, and I
now defy all the Deists and Atheists in the world to shake my
faith in Christ."

So much for Mr. Bradley and his conversion, of the
effect of which upon his later life we gain no information.   Now for a minuter survey of the constituent elements of the conversion process.

If you open the chapter on Association, of any treatise
on Psychology, you will read that a man's ideas, aims,
and objects form diverse internal groups and systems,
relatively independent of one another.   Each ' aim ' which
he follows awakens a certain specific kind of interested
excitement, and gathers a certain group of ideas together
in subordination to it as its associates ; and if the aims
and excitements are distinct in kind, their groups of ideas
may have little in common.   When one group is present
and engrosses the interest, all the ideas connected with
other groups may be excluded from the mental field.
The President of the United States when, with paddle,
gun, and fishing-rod, he goes camping in the wilderness
for a vacation, changes his system of ideas from top to
bottom.   The presidential anxieties have lapsed into the
background entirely ; the official habits are replaced by
the habits of a son of nature, and those who knew the
man only as the strenuous magistrate would not ' know
him for the same person ' if they saw him as the camper.
If now he should never go back, and never again

suffer political interests to gain dominion over him, he would be for practical intents and purposes a permanently transformed being. Our ordinary alterations of character, as we pass from one of our aims to another, are not commonly called transformations, because each of them is so rapidly succeeded by another in the reverse direction ; but whenever one aim grows so stable as to expel definitively its previous rivals from the individual's life, we tend to speak of the phenomenon, and perhaps to wonder at it, as a ' transformation.'

These alternations are the completest of the ways in which a self may be divided. A less complete way is the simultaneous coexistence of two or more different groups of aims, of which one practically holds the right of way and instigates activity, whilst the others are only pious wishes, and never practically come to anything. Saint Augustine's aspirations to a purer life, in our last lecture, were for a while an example. Another would be the President in his full pride of office, wondering whether it were not all vanity, and whether the life of a wood-chopper were not the wholesomer destiny. Such fleeting aspirations are mere *velleitates*, whimsies. They exist on the remoter outskirts of the mind, and the real self of the man, the centre of his energies, is occupied with an entirely different system. As life goes on, there is a constant change of our interests, and a consequent change of place in our systems of ideas, from more central to more peripheral, and from more peripheral to more central parts of consciousness. I remember, for instance, that one evening when I was a youth, my father read aloud from a Boston newspaper that part of Lord Gifford's will which founded these four lectureships. At that time I did not think of being a teacher of philosophy : and what I listened to was as remote from my own life as if it related to the planet Mars. Yet here I am, with the Gifford system part and parcel of my very self, and all my energies, for the time being, devoted to successfully identifying myself with it. My soul stands now planted in what once was for it a practically unreal object, and speaks from it as from its proper habitat and centre.

When I say 'Soul,' you need not take me in the ontological sense unless you prefer to; for although ontological language is instinctive in such matters, yet Buddhists or Humians can perfectly well describe the facts in the phenomenal terms which are their favorites. For them the soul is only a succession of fields of consciousness: yet there is found in each field a part, or sub-field, which figures as focal and contains the excitement, and from which, as from a centre, the aim seems to be taken. Talking of this part, we involuntarily apply words of perspective to distinguish it from the rest, words like 'here,' 'this,' 'now,' 'mine,' or 'me'; and we ascribe to the other parts the positions 'there,' 'then,' 'that,' 'his' or 'thine,' 'it,' 'not me.' But a 'here' can change to a 'there,' and a 'there' become a 'here,' and what was 'mine' and what was 'not mine' change their places.

What brings such changes about is the way in which emotional excitement alters. Things hot and vital to us to-day are cold to-morrow. It is as if seen from the hot parts of the field that the other parts appear to us, and from these hot parts personal desire and volition make their sallies. They are in short the centres of our dynamic energy, whereas the cold parts leave us indifferent and passive in proportion to their coldness.

Whether such language be rigorously exact is for the present of no importance. It is exact enough, if you

recognize from your own experience the facts which I
seek to designate by it.

Now there may be great oscillation in the emotional
interest, and the hot places may shift before one almost
as rapidly as the sparks that run through burnt-up paper.
Then we have the wavering and divided self we heard so
much of in the previous lecture. Or the focus of excitement and heat, the point of view from which the aim is
taken, may come to lie permanently within a certain system ; and then, if the change be a religious one, we call
it a *conversion*, especially if it be by crisis, or sudden.

Let us hereafter, in speaking of the hot place in a
man's consciousness, the group of ideas to which he
devotes himself, and from which he works, call it *the
habitual centre of his personal energy*. It makes a great
difference to a man whether one set of his ideas, or another, be the centre of his energy; and it makes a great
difference, as regards any set of ideas which he may possess, whether they become central or remain peripheral in
him. To say that a man is 'converted' means, in these
terms, that religious ideas, previously peripheral in his consciousness, now take a central place, and that religious
aims form the habitual centre of his energy.

Now if you ask of psychology just *how* the excitement
shifts in a man's mental system, and *why* aims that were
peripheral become at a certain moment central, psychology
has to reply that although she can give a general description of what happens, she is unable in a given case
to account accurately for all the single forces at work.
Neither an outside observer nor the Subject who under-
goes the process can explain fully how particular experiences are able to change one's centre of energy so
decisively, or why they so often have to bide their hour
to do so. We have a thought, or we perform an act,

repeatedly, but on a certain day the real meaning of the
thought peals through us for the first time, or the act
has suddenly turned into a moral impossibility. All we
know is that there are dead feelings, dead ideas, and cold
beliefs, and there are hot and live ones; and when one
grows hot and alive within us, everything has to re-crystal-
lize about it. We may say that the heat and liveliness
mean only the ' motor efficacy,' long deferred but now
operative, of the idea; but such talk itself is only cir-
cumlocution, for whence the sudden motor efficacy?
And our explanations then get so vague and general
that one realizes all the more the intense individuality
of the whole phenomenon.

In the end we fall back on the hackneyed symbolism of
a mechanical equilibrium. A mind is a system of ideas,
each with the excitement it arouses, and with tendencies
impulsive and inhibitive, which mutually check or reinforce one another. The collection of ideas alters by subtraction or by addition in the course of experience, and
the tendencies alter as the organism gets more aged. A
mental system may be undermined or weakened by this
interstitial alteration just as a building is, and yet for a
time keep upright by dead habit. But a new perception, a
sudden emotional shock, or an occasion which lays bare
the organic alteration, will make the whole fabric fall
together; and then the centre of gravity sinks into an
attitude more stable, for the new ideas that reach the
centre in the rearrangement seem now to be locked there,
and the new structure remains permanent.

Formed associations of ideas and habits are usually
factors of retardation in such changes of equilibrium.
New information, however acquired, plays an accelerating
part in the changes; and the slow mutation of our instincts and propensities, under the ' unimaginable touch

of time' has an enormous influence. Moreover, all these influences may work subconsciously or half unconsciously.[1] And when you get a Subject in whom the subconscious life — of which I must speak more fully soon — is largely developed, and in whom motives habitually ripen in silence, you get a case of which you can never give a full account, and in which, both to the Subject and the onlookers, there may appear an element of marvel. Emotional occasions, especially violent ones, are extremely potent in precipitating mental rearrangements. The sudden and explosive ways in which love, jealousy, guilt, fear, remorse, or anger can seize upon one are known to everybody.[2] Hope, happiness, security, resolve, emotions characteristic of conversion, can be equally explosive. And emotions that come in this explosive way seldom leave things as they found them.

In his recent work on the Psychology of Religion, Professor Starbuck of California has shown by a statis-

---

[1] Jouffroy is an example : " Down this slope it was that my intelligence had glided, and little by little it had got far from its first faith. But this melancholy revolution had not taken place in the broad daylight of my consciousness ; too many scruples, too many guides and sacred affections had made it dreadful to me, so that I was far from avowing to myself the progress it had made. It had gone on in silence, by an involuntary elaboration of which I was not the accomplice ; and although I had in reality long ceased to be a Christian, yet, in the innocence of my intention, I should have shuddered to suspect it, and thought it calumny had I been accused of such a falling away." Then follows Jouffroy's account of his counter-conversion, quoted above on p. 176.

[2] One hardly needs examples ; but for love, see p. 179, note ; for fear, p. 162 ; for remorse, see Othello after the murder ; for anger, see Lear after Cordelia's first speech to him ; for resolve, see p. 178 (J. Foster case). Here is a pathological case in which *guilt* was the feeling that suddenly exploded: " One night I was seized on entering bed with a rigor, such as Swedenborg describes as coming over him with a sense of holiness, but over me with a sense of *guilt*. During that whole night I lay under the influence of the rigor, and from its inception I felt that I was under the curse of God. I have never done one act of duty in my life — sins against God and man, beginning as far as my memory goes back — a wildcat in human shape."

tical inquiry how closely parallel in its manifestations the ordinary 'conversion' which occurs in young people brought up in evangelical circles is to that growth into a larger spiritual life which is a normal phase of adolescence in every class of human beings. The age is the same, falling usually between fourteen and seventeen. The symptoms are the same, — sense of incompleteness and imperfection; brooding, depression, morbid introspection, and sense of sin; anxiety about the hereafter; distress over doubts, and the like. And the result is the same, — a happy relief and objectivity, as the confidence in self gets greater through the adjustment of the faculties to the wider outlook. In spontaneous religious awakening, apart from revivalistic examples, and in the ordinary storm and stress and moulting-time of adolescence, we also may meet with mystical experiences, astonishing the subjects by their suddenness, just as in revivalistic conversion. The analogy, in fact, is complete; and Starbuck's conclusion as to these ordinary youthful conversions would seem to be the only sound one: Conversion is in its essence a normal adolescent phenomenon, incidental to the passage from the child's small universe to the wider intellectual and spiritual life of maturity.

"Theology," says Dr. Starbuck, "takes the adolescent tendencies and builds upon them; it sees that the essential thing in adolescent growth is bringing the person out of childhood into the new life of maturity and personal insight. It accordingly brings those means to bear which will intensify the normal tendencies. It shortens up the period of duration of storm and stress." The conversion phenomena of 'conviction of sin' last, by this investigator's statistics, about one fifth as long as the periods of adolescent storm and stress phenomena of which he also got statistics, but they are very much more intense.

Bodily accompaniments, loss of sleep and appetite, for example, are much more frequent in them. " The essential distinction appears to be that conversion intensifies but shortens the period by bringing the person to a definite crisis." [1]

The conversions which Dr. Starbuck here has in mind are of course mainly those of very commonplace persons, kept true to a pre-appointed type by instruction, appeal, and example. The particular form which they affect is the result of suggestion and imitation.[2] If they went through their growth-crisis in other faiths and other countries, although the essence of the change would be the same (since it is one in the main so inevitable), its accidents would be different. In Catholic lands, for example, and in our own Episcopalian sects, no such anxiety and conviction of sin is usual as in sects that encourage revivals. The sacraments being more relied on in these more strictly ecclesiastical bodies, the individual's personal acceptance of salvation needs less to be accentuated and led up to.

---

[1] E. D. STARBUCK : The Psychology of Religion, pp. 224, 262.

[2] No one understands this better than Jonathan Edwards understood it already. Conversion narratives of the more commonplace sort must always be taken with the allowances which he suggests : " A rule received and established by common consent has a very great, though to many persons an insensible influence in forming their notions of the process of their own experience. I know very well how they proceed as to this matter, for I have had frequent opportunities of observing their conduct. Very often their experience at first appears like a confused chaos, but then those parts are selected which bear the nearest resemblance to such particular steps as are insisted on ; and these are dwelt upon in their thoughts, and spoken of from time to time, till they grow more and more conspicuous in their view, and other parts which are neglected grow more and more obscure. Thus what they have experienced is insensibly strained, so as to bring it to an exact conformity to the scheme already established in their minds. And it becomes natural also for ministers, who have to deal with those who insist upon distinctness and clearness of method, to do so too." Treatise on Religious Affections.

But every imitative phenomenon must once have had its original, and I propose that for the future we keep as close as may be to the more first-hand and original forms of experience. These are more likely to be found in sporadic adult cases.

Professor Leuba, in a valuable article on the psychology of conversion,[1] subordinates the theological aspect of the religious life almost entirely to its moral aspect. The religious sense he defines as " the feeling of unwholeness, of moral imperfection, of sin, to use the technical word, accompanied by the yearning after the peace of unity." " The word ' religion,' " he says, " is getting more and more to signify the conglomerate of desires and emotions springing from the sense of sin and its release "; and he gives a large number of examples, in which the sin ranges from drunkenness to spiritual pride, to show that the sense of it may beset one and crave relief as urgently as does the anguish of the sickened flesh or any form of physical misery.

Undoubtedly this conception covers an immense number of cases. A good one to use as an example is that of Mr. S. H. Hadley, who after his conversion became an active and useful rescuer of drunkards in New York. His experience runs as follows : —

" One Tuesday evening I sat in a saloon in Harlem, a homeless, friendless, dying drunkard. I had pawned or sold everything that would bring a drink. I could not sleep unless I was dead drunk. I had not eaten for days, and for four nights preceding I had suffered with delirium tremens, or the horrors, from midnight till morning. I had often said, ' I will never be a tramp. I will never be cornered, for when that time comes, if ever it comes, I will find a home in the bottom of the river.' But the Lord so ordered it that when that time did come I was

[1] Studies in the Psychology of Religious Phenomena, American Journal of Psychology, vii. 309 (1896).

not able to walk one quarter of the way to the river. As I sat there thinking, I seemed to feel some great and mighty presence. I did not know then what it was. I did learn afterwards that it was Jesus, the sinner's friend. I walked up to the bar and pounded it with my fist till I made the glasses rattle. Those who stood by drinking looked on with scornful curiosity. I said I would never take another drink, if I died on the street, and really I felt as though that would happen before morning. Something said, 'If you want to keep this promise, go and have yourself locked up.' I went to the nearest station-house and had myself locked up.

"I was placed in a narrow cell, and it seemed as though all the demons that could find room came in that place with me. This was not all the company I had, either. No, praise the Lord; that dear Spirit that came to me in the saloon was present, and said, Pray. I did pray, and though I did not feel any great help, I kept on praying. As soon as I was able to leave my cell I was taken to the police court and remanded back to the cell. I was finally released, and found my way to my brother's house, where every care was given me. While lying in bed the admonishing Spirit never left me, and when I arose the following Sabbath morning I felt that day would decide my fate, and toward evening it came into my head to go to Jerry M'Auley's Mission. I went. The house was packed, and with great difficulty I made my way to the space near the platform. There I saw the apostle to the drunkard and the outcast — that man of God, Jerry M'Auley. He rose, and amid deep silence told his experience. There was a sincerity about this man that carried conviction with it, and I found myself saying, ' I wonder if God can save *me* ? ' I listened to the testimony of twenty-five or thirty persons, every one of whom had been saved from rum, and I made up my mind that I would be saved or die right there. When the invitation was given, I knelt down with a crowd of drunkards. Jerry made the first prayer. Then Mrs. M'Auley prayed fervently for us. Oh, what a conflict was going on for my poor soul! A blessed whisper said, 'Come'; the devil said, 'Be careful.' I halted but a moment, and then, with a breaking heart, I said, 'Dear

Jesus, can you help me?' Never with mortal tongue can I describe that moment. Although up to that moment my soul had been filled with indescribable gloom, I felt the glorious brightness of the noonday sun shine into my heart. I felt I was a free man. Oh, the precious feeling of safety, of freedom, of resting on Jesus! I felt that Christ with all his brightness and power had come into my life; that, indeed, old things had passed away and all things had become new.

"From that moment till now I have never wanted a drink of whiskey, and I have never seen money enough to make me take one. I promised God that night that if he would take away the appetite for strong drink, I would work for him all my life. He has done his part, and I have been trying to do mine." [1]

Dr. Leuba rightly remarks that there is little doctrinal theology in such an experience, which starts with the absolute need of a higher helper, and ends with the sense that he has helped us. He gives other cases of drunk-ards' conversions which are purely ethical, containing, as recorded, no theological beliefs whatever. John B. Gough's case, for instance, is practically, says Dr. Leuba, the conversion of an atheist — neither God nor Jesus being mentioned.[2] But in spite of the importance of this type of regeneration, with little or no intellectual readjustment, this writer surely makes it too exclusive. It corresponds to the subjectively centred form of morbid melancholy, of which Bunyan and Alline were examples. But we saw in our seventh lecture that there are objective forms of melancholy also, in which the lack of rational

[1] I have abridged Mr. Hadley's account. For other conversions of drunk-ards, see his pamphlet, Rescue Mission Work, published at the Old Jerry M'Auley Water Street Mission, New York city. A striking collection of cases also appears in the appendix to Professor Leuba's article.

[2] A restaurant waiter served provisionally as Gough's 'Saviour.' General Booth, the founder of the Salvation Army, considers that the first vital step in saving outcasts consists in making them feel that some decent human being cares enough for them to take an interest in the question whether they are to rise or sink.

meaning of the universe, and of life anyhow, is the burden that weighs upon one — you remember Tolstoy's case.[1] So there are distinct elements in conversion, and their relations to individual lives deserve to be discriminated.[2]

Some persons, for instance, never are, and possibly never under any circumstances could be, converted. Religious ideas cannot become the centre of their spiritual energy. They may be excellent persons, servants of God in practical ways, but they are not children of his kingdom. They are either incapable of imagining the invisible; or else, in the language of devotion, they are life-long subjects of 'barrenness' and 'dryness.' Such inaptitude for religious faith may in some cases be intellectual in its origin. Their religious faculties may be checked in their natural tendency to expand, by beliefs about the world that are inhibitive, the pessimistic and materialistic beliefs, for example, within which so many good souls, who in former times would have freely indulged their religious propensities, find themselves nowadays, as it were, frozen; or the agnostic vetoes upon faith as something weak and shameful, under which so many of us to-day lie cowering, afraid to use our instincts. In many persons such inhibitions are never overcome. To the end of their days they refuse to believe, their personal energy never gets to its religious centre, and the latter remains inactive in perpetuity.

In other persons the trouble is profounder. There are men anæsthetic on the religious side, deficient in that

[1] The crisis of apathetic melancholy — no use in life — into which J. S. Mill records that he fell, and from which he emerged by the reading of Marmontel's Memoirs (Heaven save the mark!) and Wordsworth's poetry, is another intellectual and general metaphysical case. See Mill's Autobiography, New York, 1873, pp. 141, 148.

[2] Starbuck, in addition to 'escape from sin,' discriminates 'spiritual illumination' as a distinct type of conversion experience. Psychology of Religion, p. 85.

category of sensibility.   Just as a bloodless organism can
never, in spite of all its goodwill, attain to the reckless
'animal spirits' enjoyed by those of sanguine temperament; so the nature which is spiritually barren may
admire and envy faith in others, but can never compass
the enthusiasm and peace which those who are tempera-
mentally qualified for faith enjoy.   All this may, however,
turn out eventually to have been a matter of temporary
inhibition.   Even late in life some thaw, some release may
take place, some bolt be shot back in the barrenest
breast, and the man's hard heart may soften and break
into religious feeling.   Such cases more than any others
suggest the idea that sudden conversion is by miracle.
So long as they exist, we must not imagine ourselves to
deal with irretrievably fixed classes.

Now there are two forms of mental occurrence in
human beings, which lead to a striking difference in the
conversion process, a difference to which Professor Starbuck has called attention.   You know how it is when
you try to recollect a forgotten name.   Usually you help
the recall by working for it, by mentally running over
the places, persons, and things with which the word was
connected.   But sometimes this effort fails: you feel then
as if the harder you tried the less hope there would be,
as though the name were *jammed*, and pressure in its
direction only kept it all the more from rising.   And
then the opposite expedient often succeeds.   Give up the
effort entirely; think of something altogether different,
and in half an hour the lost name comes sauntering into
your mind, as Emerson says, as carelessly as if it had
never been invited.   Some hidden process was started in
you by the effort, which went on after the effort ceased,
and made the result come as if it came spontaneously.

A certain music teacher, says Dr. Starbuck, says to her pupils after the thing to be done has been clearly pointed out, and unsuccessfully attempted : "Stop trying and it will do itself ! " [1]

There is thus a conscious and voluntary way and an involuntary and unconscious way in which mental results may get accomplished ; and we find both ways exemplified in the history of conversion, giving us two types, which Starbuck calls the *volitional type* and the *type by self-surrender* respectively.

In the volitional type the regenerative change is usually gradual, and consists in the building up, piece by piece, of a new set of moral and spiritual habits. But there are always critical points here at which the movement forward seems much more rapid. This psychological fact is abundantly illustrated by Dr. Starbuck. Our education in any practical accomplishment proceeds apparently by jerks and starts, just as the growth of our physical bodies does.

"An athlete . . . sometimes awakens suddenly to an understanding of the fine points of the game and to a real enjoyment of it, just as the convert awakens to an appreciation of religion. If he keeps on engaging in the sport, there may come a day when all at once the game plays itself through him — when he loses himself in some great contest. In the same way, a musician may suddenly reach a point at which pleasure in the technique of the art entirely falls away, and in some moment of inspiration he becomes the instrument through which music flows. The writer has chanced to hear two different married persons, both of whose wedded lives had been beautiful from the beginning, relate that not until a year or more after marriage did they awake to the full blessedness of married life. So it is with the religious experience of these persons we are studying." [2]

[1] Psychology of Religion, p. 117.
[2] Psychology of Religion, p. 385. Compare, also, pp. 137–144 and 262.

We shall erelong hear still more remarkable illustrations of subconsciously maturing processes eventuating in results of which we suddenly grow conscious. Sir William Hamilton and Professor Laycock of Edinburgh were among the first to call attention to this class of effects; but Dr. Carpenter first, unless I am mistaken, introduced the term ' unconscious cerebration,' which has since then been a popular phrase of explanation. The facts are now known to us far more extensively than he could know them, and the adjective ' unconscious,' being for many of them almost certainly a misnomer, is better replaced by the vaguer term ' subconscious ' or ' subliminal.'

Of the volitional type of conversion it would be easy to give examples,[1] but they are as a rule less interesting

---

[1] For instance, C. G. Finney italicizes the volitional element : "Just at this point the whole question of Gospel salvation opened to my mind in a manner most marvelous to me at the time. I think I then saw, as clearly as I ever have in my life, the reality and fullness of the atonement of Christ. Gospel salvation seemed to me to be an offer of something to be accepted, and all that was necessary on my part was to get my own consent to give up my sins and accept Christ. After this distinct revelation had stood for some little time before my mind, the question seemed to be put, ' Will you accept it now, to-day?' I replied, ' Yes ; *I will accept it to-day, or I will die in the attempt !* '" He then went into the woods, where he describes his struggles. He could not pray, his heart was hardened in its pride. " I then reproached myself for having promised to give my heart to God before I left the woods. When I came to try, I found I could not. . . . My inward soul hung back, and there was no going out of my heart to God. The thought was pressing me, of the rashness of my promise that I would give my heart to God that day, or die in the attempt. It seemed to me as if that was binding on my soul ; and yet I was going to break my vow. A great sinking and discouragement came over me, and I felt almost too weak to stand upon my knees. Just at this moment I again thought I heard some one approach me, and I opened my eyes to see whether it were so. But right there the revelation of my pride of heart, as the great difficulty that stood in the way, was distinctly shown to me. An overwhelming sense of my wickedness in being ashamed to have a human being see me on my knees before God took such powerful possession of me, that *I cried at the top of my voice, and exclaimed that I would not leave that place if all the men on earth and all the devils in hell surrounded me.* ' What ! ' I said, ' such a degraded sinner

than those of the self-surrender type, in which the subconscious effects are more abundant and often startling.
I will therefore hurry to the latter, the more so because
the difference between the two types is after all not radical. Even in the most voluntarily built-up sort of regeneration there are passages of partial self-surrender interposed ; and in the great majority of all cases, when the
will has done its uttermost towards bringing one close to
the complete unification aspired after, it seems that the
very last step must be left to other forces and performed
without the help of its activity. In other words, self-
surrender becomes then indispensable. " The personal
will," says Dr. Starbuck, "must be given up. In many
cases relief persistently refuses to come until the person
ceases to resist, or to make an effort in the direction he
desires to go."

" I had said I would not give up ; but when my will was
broken, it was all over," writes one of Starbuck's correspondents. — Another says : " I simply said : ' Lord, I have done all
I can ; I leave the whole matter with Thee ; ' and immediately
there came to me a great peace." — Another : " All at once it
occurred to me that I might be saved, too, if I would stop trying to do it all myself, and follow Jesus : somehow I lost my
load." — Another : " I finally ceased to resist, and gave myself
up, though it was a hard struggle. Gradually the feeling came
over me that I had done my part, and God was willing to do
his." [1] — " Lord, Thy will be done ; damn or save ! " cries John
Nelson,[2] exhausted with the anxious struggle to escape damnation ; and at that moment his soul was filled with peace.

as I am, on my knees confessing my sins to the great and holy God ; and
ashamed to have any human being, and a sinner like myself, find me on my
knees endeavoring to make my peace with my offended God ! ' The sin
appeared awful, infinite. It broke me down before the Lord." Memoirs,
pp. 14–16, abridged.

    [1] STARBUCK : Op. cit., pp. 91, 114.
    [2] Extracts from the Journal of Mr. John Nelson, London, no date, p. 24.

Dr. Starbuck gives an interesting, and it seems to me a true, account — so far as conceptions so schematic can claim truth at all — of the reasons why self-surrender at the last moment should be so indispensable. To begin with, there are two things in the mind of the candidate for conversion : first, the present incompleteness or wrongness, the ' sin ' which he is eager to escape from ; and, second, the positive ideal which he longs to compass. Now with most of us the sense of our present wrongness is a far more distinct piece of our consciousness than is the imagination of any positive ideal we can aim at. In a majority of cases, indeed, the ' sin ' almost exclusively engrosses the attention, so that conversion is " *a process of struggling away from sin rather than of striving towards righteousness.*" [1] A man's conscious wit and will, so far as they strain towards the ideal, are aiming at something only dimly and inaccurately imagined. Yet all the while the forces of mere organic ripening within him are going on towards their own prefigured result, and his conscious strainings are letting loose subconscious allies behind the scenes, which in their way work towards rearrangement; and the rearrangement towards which all these deeper forces tend is pretty surely definite, and definitely different from what he consciously conceives and determines. It may consequently be actually interfered with (*jammed*, as it were, like the lost word when we seek too energetically to recall it), by his voluntary efforts slanting from the true direction.

Starbuck seems to put his finger on the root of the matter when he says that to exercise the personal will is still to live in the region where the imperfect self is the thing most emphasized. Where, on the contrary, the subconscious forces take the lead, it is more probably

[1] STARBUCK, p. 64.

the better self *in posse* which directs the operation. Instead of being clumsily and vaguely aimed at from without, it is then itself the organizing centre. What then must the person do? "He must relax," says Dr. Starbuck, — "that is, he must fall back on the larger Power that makes for righteousness, which has been welling up in his own being, and let it finish in its own way the work it has begun. . . . The act of yielding, in this point of view, is giving one's self over to the new life, making it the centre of a new personality, and living, from within, the truth of it which had before been viewed objectively." [1]

"Man's extremity is God's opportunity" is the theological way of putting this fact of the need of self-surrender; whilst the physiological way of stating it would be, "Let one do all in one's power, and one's nervous system will do the rest." Both statements acknowledge the same fact.[2]

To state it in terms of our own symbolism: When the new centre of personal energy has been subconsciously incubated so long as to be just ready to open into flower, 'hands off' is the only word for us, it must burst forth unaided!

We have used the vague and abstract language of psychology. But since, in any terms, the crisis described is the throwing of our conscious selves upon the mercy of powers which, whatever they may be, are more ideal than we are actually, and make for our redemption, you see why self-surrender has been and always must be regarded as the vital turning-point of the religious life, so far as the religious life is spiritual and no affair of outer works and ritual and sacraments. One may say that the whole development of Christianity in inwardness

[1] STARBUCK, p. 115.   [2] STARBUCK, p. 113.

has consisted in little more than the greater and greater emphasis attached to this crisis of self-surrender. From Catholicism to Lutheranism, and then to Calvinism; from that to Wesleyanism; and from this, outside of technical Christianity altogether, to pure 'liberalism' or transcendental idealism, whether or not of the mind-cure type, taking in the mediæval mystics, the quietists, the pietists, and quakers by the way, we can trace the stages of progress towards the idea of an immediate spiritual help, experienced by the individual in his forlornness and standing in no essential need of doctrinal apparatus or propitiatory machinery.

Psychology and religion are thus in perfect harmony up to this point, since both admit that there are forces seemingly outside of the conscious individual that bring redemption to his life. Nevertheless psychology, defining these forces as 'subconscious,' and speaking of their effects as due to 'incubation,' or 'cerebration,' implies that they do not transcend the individual's personality; and herein she diverges from Christian theology, which insists that they are direct supernatural operations of the Deity. I propose to you that we do not yet consider this divergence final, but leave the question for a while in abeyance — continued inquiry may enable us to get rid of some of the apparent discord.

Revert, then, for a moment more to the psychology of self-surrender.

When you find a man living on the ragged edge of his consciousness, pent in to his sin and want and incompleteness, and consequently inconsolable, and then simply tell him that all is well with him, that he must stop his worry, break with his discontent, and give up his anxiety, you seem to him to come with pure absurdities. The only positive consciousness he has tells him that all is *not* well, and the better way you offer sounds simply as if you proposed to him to assert cold-blooded falsehoods. ' The will to believe' cannot be stretched as far as that. We can make ourselves more faithful to a belief of which we have the rudiments, but we cannot create a belief out of whole cloth when our perception actively assures us of its opposite. The better mind proposed to us comes in that case in the form of a pure negation of the only mind we have, and we cannot actively will a pure negation.

There are only two ways in which it is possible to get rid of anger, worry, fear, despair, or other undesirable affections. One is that an opposite affection should over-poweringly break over us, and the other is by getting so exhausted with the struggle that we have to stop, — so we drop down, give up, and *don't care* any longer. Our emotional brain-centres strike work, and we lapse into a temporary apathy. Now there is documentary proof that this state of temporary exhaustion not infrequently forms part of the conversion crisis. So long as the egoistic worry of the sick soul guards the door, the expansive confidence of the soul of faith gains no presence. But let the former faint away, even but for a moment, and the latter can profit by the opportunity, and, having once acquired possession, may retain it. Carlyle's Teufelsdröckh passes from the everlasting No to the everlasting Yes through a ' Centre of Indifference.'

Let me give you a good illustration of this feature in the conversion process. That genuine saint, David Brainerd, describes his own crisis in the following words : —

" One morning, while I was walking in a solitary place as usual, I at once saw that all my contrivances and projects to effect or procure deliverance and salvation for myself were utterly in vain ; I was brought quite to a stand, as finding myself totally lost. I saw that it was forever impossible for me to do anything towards helping or delivering myself, that I had made all the pleas I ever could have made to all eternity ; and that all my pleas were vain, for I saw that self-interest had led me to pray, and that I had never once prayed from any respect to the glory of God. I saw that there was no necessary connection between my prayers and the bestowment of divine mercy ; that they laid not the least obligation upon God to bestow his grace upon me ; and that there was no more virtue or goodness in them than there would be in my paddling with my hand in the water. I saw that I had been heaping up my devotions before God, fasting, praying, etc., pretending, and indeed really thinking sometimes that I was aiming at the glory of God ; whereas I never once truly intended it, but only my own happiness. I saw that as I had never done anything for God, I had no claim on anything from him but perdition, on account of my hypocrisy and mockery. When I saw evidently that I had regard to nothing but self-interest, then my duties appeared a vile mockery and a continual course of lies, for the whole was nothing but self-worship, and an horrid abuse of God.

" I continued, as I remember, in this state of mind, from Friday morning till the Sabbath evening following (July 12, 1739), when I was walking again in the same solitary place. Here, in a mournful melancholy state *I was attempting to pray ; but found no heart to engage in that or any other duty ; my former concern, exercise, and religious affections were now gone. I thought that the Spirit of God had quite left me ; but still was not distressed ; yet disconsolate, as if there was nothing in heaven or earth could make me happy. Having been thus endeavoring to pray — though, as I thought, very stupid and senseless —* for near half an hour ; then, as I was walking in a thick grove, unspeakable glory seemed to open to the apprehension of my soul. I do not mean any external brightness, nor any imagination of a body of light, but it was a new inward apprehension or view that I had of God, such as I never had before, nor anything which had the least resemblance to it. I had no particular apprehension of any one person in the Trinity, either the Father, the Son, or the Holy Ghost; but it appeared to be Divine glory. My soul rejoiced with joy unspeakable, to see such a God, such a glorious Divine Being; and I was inwardly pleased and satisfied that he should be God over all for ever and ever. My soul was so captivated and delighted with the excellency of God that I was even swallowed up in him; at least to that degree that I had no thought about my own salvation, and scarce reflected that there was such a creature as myself. I continued in this state of inward joy, peace, and astonishing, till near dark without any sensible abatement; and then began to think and examine what I had seen; and felt sweetly composed in my mind all the evening following. I felt myself in a new world, and everything about me appeared with a different aspect from what it was wont to do. At this time, the way of salvation opened to me with such infinite wisdom, suitableness, and excellency, that I wondered I should ever think of any other way of salvation; was amazed that I had not dropped my own contrivances, and complied with this lovely, blessed, and excellent way before. If I could have been saved by my own duties or any other way that I had formerly contrived, my whole soul would now have refused it. I wondered that all the world did not see and comply with this way of salvation, entirely by the righteousness of Christ." [1]

I have italicized the passage which records the exhaustion of the anxious emotion hitherto habitual. In a large proportion, perhaps the majority, of reports, the writers speak as if the exhaustion of the lower and the entrance of the higher emotion were simultaneous,[2] yet

[1] EDWARD's and DWIGHT's Life of Brainerd, New Haven, 1822, pp. 45–47, abridged.

[2] Describing the whole phenomenon as a change of equilibrium, we might say that the movement of new psychic energies towards the personal centre and the recession of old ones towards the margin (or the rising of some objects above, and the sinking of others below the conscious threshold) were only two ways of describing an indivisible event. Doubtless this is often absolutely true, and Starbuck is right when he says that 'self-surrender' and 'new determination,' though seeming at first sight to be such different

often again they speak as if the higher actively drove the lower out. This is undoubtedly true in a great many instances, as we shall presently see. But often there seems little doubt that both conditions — subconscious ripening of the one affection and exhaustion of the other — must simultaneously have conspired, in order to produce the result.

T. W. B., a convert of Nettleton's, being brought to an acute paroxysm of conviction of sin, ate nothing all day, locked himself in his room in the evening in complete despair, crying aloud, "How long, O Lord, how long?" "After repeating this and similar language," he says, "several times, *I seemed to sink away into a state of insensibility*. When I came to myself again I was on my knees, praying not for myself but for others. I felt submission to the will of God, willing that he should do with me as should seem good in his sight. My concern seemed all lost in concern for others." [1]

Our great American revivalist Finney writes: "I said to myself: 'What is this? I must have grieved the Holy Ghost entirely away. I have lost all my conviction. I have not a particle of concern about my soul; and it must be that the Spirit has left me.' 'Why!' thought I, 'I never was so far from being concerned about my own salvation in my life.' . . . I tried to recall my convictions, to get back again the load of sin under which I had been laboring. I tried in vain to make myself anxious. I was so quiet and peaceful that I tried to feel concerned about that, lest it should be the result of my having grieved the Spirit away." [2]

But beyond all question there are persons in whom, quite independently of any exhaustion in the Subject's capacity for feeling, or even in the absence of any acute

experiences, are "really the same thing. Self-surrender sees the change in terms of the old self; determination sees it in terms of the new." Op. cit., p. 160.

[1] A. A. BONAR : Nettleton and his Labors, Edinburgh, 1854, p. 261.

[2] CHARLES G. FINNEY : Memoirs written by Himself, 1876, pp. 17, 18.

previous feeling, the higher condition, having reached the due degree of energy, bursts through all barriers and sweeps in like a sudden flood. These are the most striking and memorable cases, the cases of instantaneous conversion to which the conception of divine grace has been most peculiarly attached. I have given one of them at length — the case of Mr. Bradley. But I had better reserve the other cases and my comments on the rest of the subject for the following lecture.

LECTURE X

CONVERSION — *Concluded*

IN this lecture we have to finish the subject of Conversion, considering at first those striking instantaneous instances of which Saint Paul's is the most eminent, and in which, often amid tremendous emotional excitement or perturbation of the senses, a complete division is established in the twinkling of an eye between the old life and the new. Conversion of this type is an important phase of religious experience, owing to the part which it has played in Protestant theology, and it behooves us to study it conscientiously on that account.

I think I had better cite two or three of these cases before proceeding to a more generalized account. One must know concrete instances first; for, as Professor Agassiz used to say, one can see no farther into a generalization than just so far as one's previous acquaintance with particulars enables one to take it in. I will go back, then, to the case of our friend Henry Alline, and quote his report of the 26th of March, 1775, on which his poor divided mind became unified for good.

" As I was about sunset wandering in the fields lamenting my miserable lost and undone condition, and almost ready to sink under my burden, I thought I was in such a miserable case as never any man was before. I returned to the house, and when I got to the door, just as I was stepping off the threshold, the following impressions came into my mind like a powerful but small still voice. You have been seeking, praying, reforming, laboring, reading, hearing, and meditating, and what have you done by it towards your salvation? Are you any nearer to conversion now than when you first began? Are you any more prepared for heaven, or fitter to appear before the impartial bar of God, than when you first began to seek?

"It brought such conviction on me that I was obliged to say that I did not think I was one step nearer than at first, but as much condemned, as much exposed, and as miserable as before. I cried out within myself, O Lord God, I am lost, and if thou, O Lord, dost not find out some new way, I know nothing of, I shall never be saved, for the ways and methods I have prescribed to myself have all failed me, and I am willing they should fail. O Lord, have mercy! O Lord, have mercy!

"These discoveries continued until I went into the house and sat down. After I sat down, being all in confusion, like a drowning man that was just giving up to sink, and almost in an agony, I turned very suddenly round in my chair, and seeing part of an old Bible lying in one of the chairs, I caught hold of it in great haste; and opening it without any premeditation, cast my eyes on the 38th Psalm, which was the first time I ever saw the word of God: it took hold of me with such power that it seemed to go through my whole soul, so that it seemed as if God was praying in, with, and for me. About this time my father called the family to attend prayers; I attended, but paid no regard to what he said in his prayer, but continued praying in those words of the Psalm. Oh, help me, help me! cried I, thou Redeemer of souls, and save me, or I am gone forever; thou canst this night, if thou pleasest, with one drop of thy blood atone for my sins, and appease the wrath of an angry God. At that instant of time when I gave all up to him to do with me as he pleased, and was willing that God should rule over me at his pleasure, redeeming love broke into my soul with repeated scriptures, with such power that my whole soul seemed to be melted down with love; the burden of guilt and condemnation was gone, darkness was expelled, my heart humbled and filled with gratitude, and my whole soul, that was a few minutes ago groaning under mountains of death, and crying to an unknown God for help, was now filled with immortal love, soaring on the wings of faith, freed from the chains of death and darkness, and crying out, My Lord and my God; thou art my rock and my fortress, my shield and my high tower, my life, my joy, my present and my everlasting portion. Looking up, I thought I saw that same light [he had on more than one previous occasion seen subjectively a bright blaze of light], though it appeared different; and as soon as I saw it, the design was opened to me, according to his promise, and I was obliged to cry out: Enough, enough, O blessed God! The work of conversion, the change, and the manifestations of it are no more disputable than that light which I see, or anything that ever I saw.

" In the midst of all my joys, in less than half an hour after my soul was set at liberty, the Lord discovered to me my labor in the ministry and call to preach the gospel. I cried out, Amen, Lord, I 'll go; send me, send me. I spent the greatest part of the night in ecstasies of joy, praising and adoring the Ancient of Days for his free and unbounded grace. After I had been so long in this transport and heavenly frame that my nature seemed to require sleep, I thought to close my eyes for a few moments; then the devil stepped in, and told me that if I went to sleep, I should lose it all, and when I should awake in the morning I would find it to be nothing but a fancy and delusion. I immediately cried out, O Lord God, if I am deceived, undeceive me.

" I then closed my eyes for a few minutes, and seemed to be refreshed with sleep; and when I awoke, the first inquiry was, Where is my God? And in an instant of time, my soul seemed awake in and with God, and surrounded by the arms of everlasting love. About sunrise I arose with joy to relate to my parents what God had done for my soul, and declared to them the miracle of God's unbounded grace. I took a Bible to show them the words that were impressed by God on my soul the evening before; but when I came to open the Bible, it appeared all new to me.

" I so longed to be useful in the cause of Christ, in preaching the gospel, that it seemed as if I could not rest any longer, but go I must and tell the wonders of redeeming love. I lost all taste for carnal pleasures, and carnal company, and was enabled to forsake them." [1]

Young Mr. Alline, after the briefest of delays, and with no book-learning but his Bible, and no teaching save that of his own experience, became a Christian minister, and thenceforward his life was fit to rank, for its austerity and single-mindedness, with that of the most devoted saints. But happy as he became in his strenuous way, he never got his taste for even the most innocent carnal pleasures back. We must class him, like Bunyan and Tolstoy, amongst those upon whose soul the iron of melancholy left a permanent imprint. His redemption was into another universe than this mere natural world, and life remained for him a sad and patient trial. Years later we can find him making such an entry as this in his diary : " On Wednesday the 12th I preached at a wedding, and had the happiness thereby to be the means of excluding carnal mirth."

The next case I will give is that of a correspondent of Professor Leuba, printed in the latter's article, already cited, in vol. vi. of the American Journal of Psychology. This subject was an Oxford graduate, the son of a clergyman, and the story resembles in many points the classic case of Colonel Gardiner, which everybody may be supposed to know. Here it is, somewhat abridged : —

" Between the period of leaving Oxford and my conversion I never darkened the door of my father's church, although I lived with him for eight years, making what money I wanted by journalism, and spending it in high carousal with any one who would sit with me and drink it away. So I lived, sometimes drunk for a week together, and then a terrible repentance, and would not touch a drop for a whole month.

[1] Life and Journals, Boston, 1806, pp. 31–40, abridged.

" In all this period, that is, up to thirty-three years of age, I never had a desire to reform on religious grounds. But all my pangs were due to some terrible remorse I used to feel after a heavy carousal, the remorse taking the shape of regret after my folly in wasting my life in such a way — a man of superior talents and education. This terrible remorse turned me gray in one night, and whenever it came upon me I was perceptibly grayer the next morning. What I suffered in this way is beyond the expression of words. It was hell-fire in all its most dreadful tortures. Often did I vow that if I got over ' this time ' I would reform. Alas, in about three days I fully recovered, and was as happy as ever. So it went on for years, but, with a physique like a rhinoceros, I always recovered, and as long as I let drink alone, no man was as capable of enjoying life as I was.

" I was converted in my own bedroom in my father's rectory house at precisely three o'clock in the afternoon of a hot July day (July 13, 1886). I was in perfect health, having been off from the drink for nearly a month. I was in no way troubled about my soul. In fact, God was not in my thoughts that day. A young lady friend sent me a copy of Professor Drummond's Natural Law in the Spiritual World, asking me my opinion of it as a literary work only. Being proud of my critical talents and wishing to enhance myself in my new friend's esteem, I took the book to my bedroom for quiet, intending to give it a thorough study, and then write her what I thought of it. It was here that God met me face to face, and I shall never forget the meeting. ' He that hath the Son hath life eternal, he that hath not the Son hath not life.' I had read this scores of times before, but this made all the difference. I was now in God's presence and my attention was absolutely ' soldered ' on to this verse, and I was not allowed to proceed with the book till I had fairly considered what these words really involved. Only then was I allowed to proceed, feeling all the while that there was another being in my bedroom, though not seen by me. The stillness was very marvelous, and I felt supremely happy. It was most unquestionably shown me, in one second of time, that I had never touched the Eternal: and

that if I died then, I must inevitably be lost. I was undone.
I knew it as well as I now know I am saved. The Spirit of
God showed it me in ineffable love ; there was no terror in it;
I felt God's love so powerfully upon me that only a mighty sorrow crept over me that I had lost all through my own folly; and
what was I to do? What could I do? I did not repent even;
God never asked me to repent. All I felt was ' I am undone,'
and God cannot help it, although he loves me. No fault on
the part of the Almighty. All the time I was supremely
happy: I felt like a little child before his father. I had done
wrong, but my Father did not scold me, but loved me most
wondrously. Still my doom was sealed. I was lost to a certainty, and being naturally of a brave disposition I did not
quail under it, but deep sorrow for the past, mixed with regret
for what I had lost, took hold upon me, and my soul thrilled
within me to think it was all over. Then there crept in upon
me so gently, so lovingly, so unmistakably, a way of escape,
and what was it after all? The old, old story over again, told
in the simplest way: ' There is no name under heaven whereby
ye can be saved except that of the Lord Jesus Christ.' No
words were spoken to me; my soul seemed to see my Saviour
in the spirit, and from that hour to this, nearly nine years now,
there has never been in my life one doubt that the Lord Jesus
Christ and God the Father both worked upon me that afternoon in July, both differently, and both in the most perfect
love conceivable, and I rejoiced there and then in a conversion
so astounding that the whole village heard of it in less than
twenty-four hours.

  " But a time of trouble was yet to come. The day after
my conversion I went into the hay-field to lend a hand with
the harvest, and not having made any promise to God to abstain or drink in moderation only, I took too much and came
home drunk. My poor sister was heart-broken; and I felt
ashamed of myself and got to my bedroom at once, where she
followed me, weeping copiously. She said I had been converted and fallen away instantly. But although I was quite
full of drink (not muddled, however), I knew that God's work
begun in me was not going to be wasted. About midday I

made on my knees the first prayer before God for twenty years.
I did not ask to be forgiven; I felt that was no good, for I
would be sure to fall again. Well, what did I do? I committed myself to him in the profoundest belief that my individuality was going to be destroyed, that he would take all from
me, and I was willing. In such a surrender lies the secret of
a holy life. From that hour drink has had no terrors for me:
I never touch it, never want it. The same thing occurred with
my pipe: after being a regular smoker from my twelfth year
the desire for it went at once, and has never returned. So with
every known sin, the deliverance in each case being permanent
and complete. I have had no temptation since conversion, God
seemingly having shut out Satan from that course with me.
He gets a free hand in other ways, but never on sins of the
flesh. Since I gave up to God all ownership in my own life,
he has guided me in a thousand ways, and has opened my path
in a way almost incredible to those who do not enjoy the blessing of a truly surrendered life."

So much for our graduate of Oxford, in whom you
notice the complete abolition of an ancient appetite as
one of the conversion's fruits.

The most curious record of sudden conversion with
which I am acquainted is that of M. Alphonse Ratisbonne, a freethinking French Jew, to Catholicism, at
Rome in 1842. In a letter to a clerical friend, written a
few months later, the convert gives a palpitating account of
the circumstances.[1] The predisposing conditions appear
to have been slight. He had an elder brother who had
been converted and was a Catholic priest. He was himself irreligious, and nourished an antipathy to the apos-
tate brother and generally to his ' cloth.' Finding himself at Rome in his twenty-ninth year, he fell in with a

---

[1] My quotations are made from an Italian translation of this letter in the
Biografia del Sig. M. A. Ratisbonne, Ferrara, 1843, which I have to thank
Monsignore D. O'Connell of Rome for bringing to my notice. I abridge
the original.

French gentleman who tried to make a proselyte of him, but who succeeded no farther after two or three conversations than to get him to hang (half jocosely) a religious medal round his neck, and to accept and read a copy of a short prayer to the Virgin.   M. Ratisbonne represents his own part in the conversations as having been of a light and chaffing order ; but he notes the fact that for some days he was unable to banish the words of the prayer from his mind, and that the night before the crisis he had a sort of nightmare, in the imagery of which a black cross with no Christ upon it figured.   Nevertheless, until noon of the next day he was free in mind and spent the time in trivial conversations.   I now give his own words.

" If at this time any one had accosted me, saying : ' Alphonse, in a quarter of an hour you shall be adoring Jesus Christ as your God and Saviour ; you shall lie prostrate with your face upon the ground in a humble church ; you shall be smiting your breast at the foot of a priest ; you shall pass the carnival in a college of Jesuits to prepare yourself to receive baptism, ready to give your life for the Catholic faith ; you shall renounce the world and its pomps and pleasures ; renounce your fortune, your hopes, and if need be, your betrothed ; the affections of your family, the esteem of your friends, and your attachment to the Jewish people ; you shall have no other aspiration than to follow Christ and bear his cross till death ; ' — if, I say a prophet had come to me with such a prediction, I should have judged that only one person could be more mad than he, — whosoever, namely, might believe in the possibility of such senseless folly becoming true.   And yet that folly is at present my only wisdom, my sole happiness.

" Coming out of the café I met the carriage of Monsieur B. [the proselyting friend].   He stopped and invited me in for a drive, but first asked me to wait for a few minutes whilst he attended to some duty at the church of San Andrea delle Fratte. Instead of waiting in the carriage, I entered the church myself to look at it.   The church of San Andrea was poor, small, and

empty; I believe that I found myself there almost alone. No
work of art attracted my attention; and I passed my eyes
mechanically over its interior without being arrested by any
particular thought. I can only remember an entirely black
dog which went trotting and turning before me as I mused. In
an instant the dog had disappeared, the whole church had vanished, I no longer saw anything, . . . or more truly I saw, O
my God, one thing alone.

"Heavens, how can I speak of it? Oh no! human words
cannot attain to expressing the inexpressible. Any description,
however sublime it might be, could be but a profanation of the
unspeakable truth.

"I was there prostrate on the ground, bathed in my tears,
with my heart beside itself, when M. B. called me back to life.
I could not reply to the questions which followed from him one
upon the other. But finally I took the medal which I had on
my breast, and with all the effusion of my soul I kissed the
image of the Virgin, radiant with grace, which it bore. Oh,
indeed, it was She! It was indeed She! [What he had seen
had been a vision of the Virgin.]

"I did not know where I was: I did not know whether I
was Alphonse or another. I only felt myself changed and believed myself another me; I looked for myself in myself and
did not find myself. In the bottom of my soul I felt an explosion of the most ardent joy; I could not speak; I had no wish
to reveal what had happened. But I felt something solemn
and sacred within me which made me ask for a priest. I was
led to one; and there, alone, after he had given me the positive
order, I spoke as best I could, kneeling, and with my heart still
trembling. I could give no account to myself of the truth
of which I had acquired a knowledge and a faith. All that I
can say is that in an instant the bandage had fallen from my
eyes; and not one bandage only, but the whole manifold of
bandages in which I had been brought up. One after another
they rapidly disappeared, even as the mud and ice disappear
under the rays of the burning sun.

"I came out as from a sepulchre, from an abyss of darkness;
and I was living, perfectly living. But I wept, for at the bot-

tom of that gulf I saw the extreme of misery from which I had
been saved by an infinite mercy; and I shuddered at the sight
of my iniquities, stupefied, melted, overwhelmed with wonder
and with gratitude. You may ask me how I came to this new
insight, for truly I had never opened a book of religion nor
even read a single page of the Bible, and the dogma of original
sin is either entirely denied or forgotten by the Hebrews of
to-day, so that I had thought so little about it that I doubt
whether I ever knew its name. But how came I, then, to this
perception of it? I can answer nothing save this, that on entering that church I was in darkness altogether, and on coming out of it I saw the fullness of the light. I can explain the
change no better than by the simile of a profound sleep or the
analogy of one born blind who should suddenly open his eyes
to the day. He sees, but cannot define the light which bathes
him and by means of which he sees the objects which excite his
wonder. If we cannot explain physical light, how can we explain the light which is the truth itself? And I think I remain
within the limits of veracity when I say that without having any
knowledge of the letter of religious doctrine, I now intuitively
perceived its sense and spirit. Better than if I saw them, I
felt those hidden things; I felt them by the inexplicable effects
they produced in me. It all happened in my interior mind;
and those impressions, more rapid than thought, shook my soul,
revolved and turned it, as it were, in another direction, towards
other aims, by other paths. I express myself badly. But do
you wish, Lord, that I should inclose in poor and barren words
sentiments which the heart alone can understand?"

I might multiply cases almost indefinitely, but these
will suffice to show you how real, definite, and memorable an event a sudden conversion may be to him who
has the experience. Throughout the height of it he undoubtedly seems to himself a passive spectator or under-
goer of an astounding process performed upon him from
above. There is too much evidence of this for any doubt
of it to be possible. Theology, combining this fact with
the doctrines of election and grace, has concluded that

the spirit of God is with us at these dramatic moments in a peculiarly miraculous way, unlike what happens at any other juncture of our lives. At that moment, it believes, an absolutely new nature is breathed into us, and we become partakers of the very substance of the Deity.

That the conversion should be instantaneous seems called for on this view, and the Moravian Protestants appear to have been the first to see this logical consequence. The Methodists soon followed suit, practically if not dogmatically, and a short time ere his death, John Wesley wrote : —

" In London alone I found 652 members of our Society who were exceeding clear in their experience, and whose testimony I could see no reason to doubt. And every one of these (without a single exception) has declared that his deliverance from sin was instantaneous ; that the change was wrought in a moment. Had half of these, or one third, or one in twenty, declared it was *gradually* wrought in *them*, I should have believed this, with regard to *them*, and thought that *some* were gradually sanctified and some instantaneously. But as I have not found, in so long a space of time, a single person speaking thus, I cannot but believe that sanctification is commonly, if not always, an instantaneous work." Tyerman's Life of Wesley, i. 463.

All this while the more usual sects of Protestantism have set no such store by instantaneous conversion. For them as for the Catholic Church, Christ's blood, the sacraments, and the individual's ordinary religious duties are practically supposed to suffice to his salvation, even though no acute crisis of self-despair and surrender followed by relief should be experienced. For Methodism, on the contrary, unless there have been a crisis of this sort, salvation is only offered, not effectively received, and Christ's sacrifice in so far forth is incomplete. Methodism surely here follows, if not the healthier-minded, yet on the whole the profounder spiritual instinct. The individual models which it has set up as typical and worthy of imitation are not only the more interesting dramatically, but psychologically they have been the more complete.

In the fully evolved Revivalism of Great Britain and America we have, so to speak, the codified and stereotyped procedure to which this way of thinking has led. In spite of the unquestionable fact that saints of the once-born type exist, that there may be a gradual growth in holiness without a cataclysm; in spite of the obvious leakage (as one may say) of much mere natural goodness into the scheme of salvation; revivalism has always assumed that only its own type of religious experience can be perfect; you must first be nailed on the cross of natural despair and agony, and then in the twinkling of an eye be miraculously released.

It is natural that those who personally have traversed such an experience should carry away a feeling of its being a miracle rather than a natural process. Voices are often heard, lights seen, or visions witnessed; automatic motor phenomena occur; and it always seems, after the surrender of the personal will, as if an extraneous higher power had flooded in and taken possession. Moreover the sense of renovation, safety, cleanness, rightness, can be so marvelous and jubilant as well to warrant one's belief in a radically new substantial nature.

"Conversion," writes the New England Puritan, Joseph Alleine, "is not the putting in a patch of holiness; but with the true convert holiness is woven into all his powers, principles, and practice. The sincere Christian is quite a new fabric, from the foundation to the top-stone. He is a new man, a new creature."

And Jonathan Edwards says in the same strain: "Those gracious influences which are the effects of the Spirit of God are altogether supernatural — are quite different from anything that unregenerate men experience. They are what no improvement, or composition of natural qualifications or principles will ever produce ; because they not only differ from what is natural, and from everything that natural men experience in degree and circumstances, but also in kind, and are of a nature far more excellent. From hence it follows that in gracious affections there are [also] new perceptions and sensations entirely different in their nature and kind from anything experienced by the [same] saints before they were sanctified. . . . The conceptions which the saints have of the loveliness of God, and that kind of delight which they experience in it, are quite peculiar, and entirely different from anything which a natural man can possess, or of which he can form any proper notion."

And that such a glorious transformation as this ought of necessity to be preceded by despair is shown by Edwards in another passage.

"Surely it cannot be unreasonable," he says, "that before God delivers us from a state of sin and liability to everlasting woe, he should give us some considerable sense of the evil from which he delivers us, in order that we may know and feel the importance of salvation, and be enabled to appreciate the value of what God is pleased to do for us. As those who are saved are successively in two extremely different states — first in a state of condemnation and then in a state of justification and blessedness — and as God, in the salvation of men, deals with them as rational and intelligent creatures, it appears agreeable to this wisdom, that those who are saved should be made sensible of their Being, in those two different states. In the first place, that they should be made sensible of their state of condemnation ; and afterwards, of their state of deliverance and happiness."

Such quotations express sufficiently well for our purpose the doctrinal interpretation of these changes. Whatever part suggestion and imitation may have played in producing them in men and women in excited assemblies, they have at any rate been in countless individual instances an original and unborrowed experience. Were we writing the story of the mind from the purely natural-history point of view, with no religious interest whatever, we should still have to write down man's liability to sudden and complete conversion as one of his most curious peculiarities.

What, now, must we ourselves think of this question? Is an instantaneous conversion a miracle in which God is present as he is present in no change of heart less strikingly abrupt? Are there two classes of human beings, even among the apparently regenerate, of which the one class really partakes of Christ's nature while the other merely seems to do so? Or, on the contrary, may the whole phenomenon of regeneration, even in these startling instantaneous examples, possibly be a strictly natural process, divine in its fruits, of course, but in one case more and in another less so, and neither more nor less divine in its mere causation and mechanism than any other process, high or low, of man's interior life?

Before proceeding to answer this question, I must ask you to listen to some more psychological remarks. At our last lecture, I explained the shifting of men's centres of personal energy within them and the lighting up of new crises of emotion. I explained the phenomena as partly due to explicitly conscious processes of thought and will, but as due largely also to the subconscious incubation and maturing of motives deposited by the experiences of life. When ripe, the results hatch out, or burst into flower. I have now to speak of the subconscious region, in which such processes of flowering may occur, in a somewhat less vague way. I only regret that my limits of time here force me to be so short.

The expression 'field of consciousness' has but recently come into vogue in the psychology books. Until quite lately the unit of mental life which figured most was the single 'idea,' supposed to be a definitely outlined thing. But at present psychologists are tending, first, to admit that the actual unit is more probably the total mental state, the entire wave of consciousness or field of objects present to the thought at any time; and, second, to see that it is impossible to outline this wave, this field, with any definiteness.

As our mental fields succeed one another, each has its centre of interest, around which the objects of which we are less and less attentively conscious fade to a margin so faint that its limits are unassignable. Some fields are narrow fields and some are wide fields. Usually when we have a wide field we rejoice, for we then see masses of truth together, and often get glimpses of relations which we divine rather than see, for they shoot beyond the field into still remoter regions of objectivity, regions which we seem rather to be about to perceive than to perceive actually. At other times, of drowsiness, illness, or fatigue, our fields may narrow almost to a point, and we find ourselves correspondingly oppressed and contracted.

Different individuals present constitutional differences in this matter of width of field. Your great organizing geniuses are men with habitually vast fields of mental vision, in which a whole programme of future operations will appear dotted out at once, the rays shooting far ahead into definite directions of advance. In common people there is never this magnificent inclusive view of a topic. They stumble along, feeling their way, as it were, from point to point, and often stop entirely. In certain diseased conditions consciousness is a mere spark, without memory of the past or thought of the future, and with the present narrowed down to some one simple emotion or sensation of the body.

The important fact which this 'field' formula commemorates is the indetermination of the margin. Inattentively realized as is the matter which the margin contains, it is nevertheless there, and helps both to guide our behavior and to determine the next movement of our attention. It lies around us like a ' magnetic field,' inside of which our centre of energy turns like a compass-needle, as the present phase of consciousness alters into its successor. Our whole past store of memories floats beyond this margin, ready at a touch to come in; and the entire mass of residual powers, impulses, and knowledges that constitute our empirical self stretches continuously beyond it. So vaguely drawn are the outlines between what is actual and what is only potential at any moment of our conscious life, that it is always hard to say of certain mental elements whether we are conscious of them or not.

The ordinary psychology, admitting fully the difficulty of tracing the marginal outline, has nevertheless taken for granted, first, that all the consciousness the person now has, be the same focal or marginal, inattentive or attentive, is there in the 'field' of the moment, all dim and impossible to assign as the latter's outline may be; and, second, that what is absolutely extra-marginal is absolutely non-existent, and cannot be a fact of consciousness at all.

And having reached this point, I must now ask you to recall what I said in my last lecture about the subconscious life. I said, as you may recollect, that those who first laid stress upon these phenomena could not know the facts as we now know them. My first duty now is to tell you what I meant by such a statement.

I cannot but think that the most important step forward that has occurred in psychology since I have been a student of that science is the discovery, first made in 1886, that, in certain subjects at least, there is not only the consciousness of the ordinary field, with its usual centre and margin, but an addition thereto in the shape of a set of memories, thoughts, and feelings which are extra-marginal and outside of the primary consciousness altogether, but yet must be classed as conscious facts of some sort, able to reveal their presence by unmistakable signs. I call this the most important step forward because, unlike the other advances which psychology has made, this discovery has revealed to us an entirely unsuspected peculiarity in the constitution of human nature. No other step forward which psychology has made can proffer any such claim as this.

In particular this discovery of a consciousness existing beyond the field, or subliminally as Mr. Myers terms it, casts light on many phenomena of religious biography. That is why I have to advert to it now, although it is naturally impossible for me in this place to give you any account of the evidence on which the admission of such a consciousness is based. You will find it set forth in many recent books, Binet's Alterations of Personality [1] being perhaps as good a one as any to recommend.

The human material on which the demonstration has been made has so far been rather limited and, in part at least, eccentric, consisting of unusually suggestible hypnotic subjects, and of hysteric patients. Yet the elementary mechanisms of our life are presumably so uniform that what is shown to be true in a marked degree of some persons is probably true in some degree of all, and may in a few be true in an extraordinarily high degree.

[1] Published in the International Scientific Series.

The most important consequence of having a strongly developed ultra-marginal life of this sort is that one's ordinary fields of consciousness are liable to incursions from it of which the subject does not guess the source, and which, therefore, take for him the form of unaccountable impulses to act, or inhibitions of action, of obsessive ideas, or even of hallucinations of sight or hearing. The impulses may take the direction of automatic speech or writing, the meaning of which the subject himself may not understand even while he utters it; and generalizing this phenomenon, Mr. Myers has given the name of *automatism*, sensory or motor, emotional or intellectual, to this whole sphere of effects, due to ' uprushes ' into the ordinary consciousness of energies originating in the subliminal parts of the mind.

The simplest instance of an automatism is the phenomenon of post-hypnotic suggestion, so-called. You give to a hypnotized subject, adequately susceptible, an order to perform some designated act — usual or eccentric, it makes no difference — after he wakes from his hypnotic sleep. Punctually, when the signal comes or the time elapses upon which you have told him that the act must ensue, he performs it ; — but in so doing he has no recollection of your suggestion, and he always trumps up an improvised pretext for his behavior if the act be of an eccentric kind. It may even be suggested to a subject to have a vision or to hear a voice at a certain interval after waking, and when the time comes the vision is seen or the voice heard, with no inkling on the subject's part of its source. In the wonderful explorations by Binet, Janet, Breuer, Freud, Mason, Prince, and others, of the subliminal consciousness of patients with hysteria, we have revealed to us whole systems of underground life, in the shape of memories of a painful sort which lead a parasitic existence, buried outside of the primary fields of consciousness, and making irruptions thereinto with hallucinations, pains, convulsions, paralyses of feeling and of motion, and the whole procession of symptoms of hysteric disease of body and of mind. Alter or abolish by suggestion these subconscious memories, and the patient immediately gets well. His symptoms were automatisms, in Mr. Myers's sense of the word. These clinical records sound like fairy-tales when one first reads them, yet it is impossible to doubt their accuracy ; and, the path having been once opened by these first observers, similar observations have been made elsewhere. They throw, as I said, a wholly new light upon our natural constitution.

And it seems to me that they make a farther step inevitable. Interpreting the unknown after the analogy of the known, it seems to me that hereafter, wherever we meet with a phenomenon of automatism, be it motor impulses, or obsessive idea, or unaccountable caprice, or delusion, or hallucination, we are bound first of all to make search whether it be not an explosion, into the fields of ordinary consciousness, of ideas elaborated outside of those fields in subliminal regions of the mind. We should look, therefore, for its source in the Subject's subconscious life. In the hypnotic cases, we ourselves create the source by our suggestion, so we know it directly. In the hysteric cases, the lost memories which are the source have to be extracted from the patient's Subliminal by a number of ingenious methods, for an account of which you must consult the books. In other pathological cases, insane delusions, for example, or psychopathic obsessions, the source is yet to seek, but by analogy it also should be in subliminal regions which improvements in our methods may yet conceivably put on tap. There lies the mechanism logically to be assumed, — but the assumption

involves a vast program of work to be done in the way
of verification, in which the religious experiences of man
must play their part.[1]

And thus I return to our own specific subject of instantaneous conversions. You remember the cases of
Alline, Bradley, Brainerd, and the graduate of Oxford
converted at three in the afternoon. Similar occurrences
abound, some with and some without luminous visions,
all with a sense of astonished happiness, and of being
wrought on by a higher control. If, abstracting altogether from the question of their value for the future
spiritual life of the individual, we take them on their psy-

[1] The reader will here please notice that in my exclusive reliance in the
last lecture on the subconscious 'incubation' of motives deposited by a
growing experience, I followed the method of employing accepted principles of explanation as far as one can. The subliminal region, whatever else
it may be, is at any rate a place now admitted by psychologists to exist for
the accumulation of vestiges of sensible experience (whether inattentively
or attentively registered), and for their elaboration according to ordinary
psychological or logical laws into results that end by attaining such a 'tension' that they may at times enter consciousness with something like a burst.
It thus is 'scientific' to interpret all otherwise unaccountable invasive alterations of consciousness as results of the tension of subliminal memories reaching the bursting-point. But candor obliges me to confess that there are
occasional bursts into consciousness of results of which it is not easy to
demonstrate any prolonged subconscious incubation. Some of the cases I
used to illustrate the sense of presence of the unseen in Lecture III were of
this order (compare pages 59, 61, 62, 67) ; and we shall see other experiences
of the kind when we come to the subject of mysticism. The case of Mr.
Bradley, that of M. Ratisbonne, possibly that of Colonel Gardiner, possibly
that of Saint Paul, might not be so easily explained in this simple way.
The result, then, would have to be ascribed either to a merely physiological
nerve storm, a 'discharging lesion' like that of epilepsy ; or, in case it
were useful and rational, as in the two latter cases named, to some more
mystical or theological hypothesis. I make this remark in order that the
reader may realize that the subject is really complex. But I shall keep
myself as far as possible at present to the more 'scientific' view; and only
as the plot thickens in subsequent lectures shall I consider the question of
its absolute sufficiency as an explanation of all the facts. That subconscious
incubation explains a great number of them, there can be no doubt.

chological side exclusively, so many peculiarities in them remind us of what we find outside of conversion that we are tempted to class them along with other automatisms, and to suspect that what makes the difference between a sudden and a gradual convert is not necessarily the presence of divine miracle in the case of one and of something less divine in that of the other, but rather a simple psychological peculiarity, the fact, namely, that in the recipient of the more instantaneous grace we have one of those Subjects who are in possession of a large region in which mental work can go on subliminally, and from which invasive experiences, abruptly upsetting the equilibrium of the primary consciousness, may come.

I do not see why Methodists need object to such a view. Pray go back and recollect one of the conclusions to which I sought to lead you in my very first lecture. You may remember how I there argued against the notion that the worth of a thing can be decided by its origin. Our spiritual judgment, I said, our opinion of the significance and value of a human event or condition, must be decided on empirical grounds exclusively. If the *fruits for life* of the state of conversion are good, we ought to idealize and venerate it, even though it be a piece of natural psychology ; if not, we ought to make short work with it, no matter what supernatural being may have infused it.

Well, how is it with these fruits ? If we except the class of preëminent saints of whom the names illumine history, and consider only the usual run of ' saints,' the shopkeeping church-members and ordinary youthful or middle-aged recipients of instantaneous conversion, whether at revivals or in the spontaneous course of methodistic growth, you will probably agree that no splendor worthy of a wholly supernatural creature fulgurates from them, or sets them apart from the mortals who have never experienced that favor. Were it true that a suddenly converted man as such is, as Edwards says,[1] of an entirely different kind from a natural man, partaking as he does directly of Christ's substance, there surely ought to be some exquisite class-mark, some distinctive radiance attaching even to the lowliest specimen of this genus, to which no one of us could remain insensible, and which, so far as it went, would prove him more excellent than ever the most highly gifted among mere natural men. But notoriously there is no such radiance. Converted men as a class are indistinguishable from natural men; some natural men even excel some converted men in their fruits; and no one ignorant of doctrinal theology could guess by mere every-day inspection of the 'accidents' of the two groups of persons before him, that their substance differed as much as divine differs from human substance.

The believers in the non-natural character of sudden conversion have had practically to admit that there is no unmistakable class-mark distinctive of all true converts. The super-normal incidents, such as voices and visions and overpowering impressions of the meaning of suddenly presented scripture texts, the melting emotions and tumultuous affections connected with the crisis of change, may all come by way of nature, or worse still, be counterfeited by Satan. The real witness of the spirit to the second birth is to be found only in the disposition of the genuine child of God, the permanently patient heart, the love of self eradicated. And this, it has to be ad-

[1] Edwards says elsewhere : "I am bold to say that the work of God in the conversion of one soul, considered together with the source, foundation, and purchase of it, and also the benefit, end, and eternal issue of it, is a more glorious work of God than the creation of the whole material universe."

mitted, is also found in those who pass no crisis, and may even be found outside of Christianity altogether.

Throughout Jonathan Edwards's admirably rich and delicate description of the supernaturally infused condition, in his Treatise on Religious Affections, there is not one decisive trait, not one mark, that unmistakably parts it off from what may possibly be only an exceptionally high degree of natural goodness. In fact, one could hardly read a clearer argument than this book unwittingly offers in favor of the thesis that no chasm exists between the orders of human excellence, but that here as elsewhere, nature shows continuous differences, and generation and regeneration are matters of degree.

All which denial of two objective classes of human beings separated by a chasm must not leave us blind to the extraordinary momentousness of the fact of his conversion to the individual himself who gets converted. There are higher and lower limits of possibility set to each personal life. If a flood but goes above one's head, its absolute elevation becomes a matter of small importance; and when we touch our own upper limit and live in our own highest centre of energy, we may call ourselves saved, no matter how much higher some one else's centre may be. A small man's salvation will always be a great salvation and the greatest of all facts *for him*, and we should remember this when the fruits of our ordinary evangelicism look discouraging. Who knows how much less ideal still the lives of these spiritual grubs and earthworms, these Crumps and Stigginses, might have been, if such poor grace as they have received had never touched them at all? [1]

[1] Emerson writes : "When we see a soul whose acts are regal, graceful, and pleasant as roses, we must thank God that such things can be and are, and not turn sourly on the angel and say : Crump is a better man, with his grunting resistance to all his native devils." True enough. Yet Crump

If we roughly arrange human beings in classes, each class standing for a grade of spiritual excellence, I believe we shall find natural men and converts both sudden and gradual in all the classes. The forms which regenerative change effects have, then, no general spiritual significance, but only a psychological significance. We have seen how Starbuck's laborious statistical studies tend to assimilate conversion to ordinary spiritual growth. Another American psychologist, Prof. George A. Coe,[1] has analyzed the cases of seventy-seven converts or ex-candidates for conversion, known to him, and the results strikingly confirm the view that sudden conversion is connected with the possession of an active subliminal self. Examining his subjects with reference to their hypnotic sensibility and to such automatisms as hypnagogic hallucinations, odd impulses, religious dreams about the time of their conversion, etc., he found these relatively much more frequent in the group of converts whose transformation had been ' striking,' ' striking ' transformation being defined as a change which, though not necessarily instantaneous, seems to the subject of it to be distinctly different from a process of growth, however rapid." [2] Candidates for conversion at revivals are, as you know, often disappointed : they experience nothing striking. Professor Coe had a number of persons of this class among his seventy-seven subjects, and they almost all, when tested by hypnotism, proved to belong to a subclass which he

may really be the better *Crump*, for his inner discords and second birth ; and your once-born ' regal ' character, though indeed always better than poor Crump, may fall far short of what he individually might be had he only some Crump-like capacity for compunction over his own peculiar diabolisms, graceful and pleasant and invariably gentlemanly as these may be.

[1] In his book, The Spiritual Life, New York, 1900.
[2] Op. cit., p. 112.

calls ' spontaneous,' that is, fertile in self-suggestions, as distinguished from a ' passive ' subclass, to which most of the subjects of striking transformation belonged. His inference is that self-suggestion of impossibility had prevented the influence upon these persons of an environment which, on the more ' passive ' subjects, had easily brought forth the effects they looked for. Sharp distinctions are difficult in these regions, and Professor Coe's numbers are small. But his methods were careful, and the results tally with what one might expect; and they seem, on the whole, to justify his practical conclusion, which is that if you should expose to a converting influence a subject in whom three factors unite : first, pronounced emotional sensibility ; second, tendency to automatisms ; and third, suggestibility of the passive type ; you might then safely predict the result : there would be a sudden conversion, a transformation of the striking kind.

Does this temperamental origin diminish the significance of the sudden conversion when it has occurred ? Not in the least, as Professor Coe well says ; for " the ultimate test of religious values is nothing psychological, nothing definable in terms of *how it happens*, but something ethical, definable only in terms of *what is attained.*" [1]

As we proceed farther in our inquiry we shall see that what is attained is often an altogether new level of spiritual vitality, a relatively heroic level, in which impossible things have become possible, and new energies and endurances are shown. The personality is changed, the man *is* born anew, whether or not his psychological idiosyncrasies are what give the particular shape to his metamorphosis. ' Sanctification ' is the technical name of this result ; and erelong examples of it shall be brought

[1] Op. cit., p. 144.

before you. In this lecture I have still only to add a few remarks on the assurance and peace which fill the hour of change itself.

One word more, though, before proceeding to that point, lest the final purpose of my explanation of suddenness by subliminal activity be misunderstood. I do indeed believe that if the Subject have no liability to such subconscious activity, or if his conscious fields have a hard rind of a margin that resists incursions from beyond it, his conversion must be gradual if it occur, and must resemble any simple growth into new habits. His possession of a developed subliminal self, and of a leaky or pervious margin, is thus a *conditio sine qua non* of the Subject's becoming converted in the instantaneous way. But if you, being orthodox Christians, ask me as a psychologist whether the reference of a phenomenon to a subliminal self does not exclude the notion of the direct presence of the Deity altogether, I have to say frankly that as a psychologist I do not see why it necessarily should. The lower manifestations of the Subliminal, indeed, fall within the resources of the personal subject: his ordinary sense-material, inattentively taken in and subconsciously remembered and combined, will account for all his usual automatisms. But just as our primary wide-awake consciousness throws open our senses to the touch of things material, so it is logically conceivable that *if there be* higher spiritual agencies that can directly touch us, the psychological condition of their doing so *might be* our possession of a subconscious region which alone should yield access to them. The hubbub of the waking life might close a door which in the dreamy Subliminal might remain ajar or open.

Thus that perception of external control which is so

essential a feature in conversion might, in some cases at any rate, be interpreted as the orthodox interpret it : forces transcending the finite individual might impress him, on condition of his being what we may call a subliminal human specimen. But in any case the *value* of these forces would have to be determined by their effects, and the mere fact of their transcendency would of itself establish no presumption that they were more divine than diabolical.

I confess that this is the way in which I should rather see the topic left lying in your minds until I come to a much later lecture, when I hope once more to gather these dropped threads together into more definitive conclusions. The notion of a subconscious self certainly ought not at this point of our inquiry to be held to *exclude* all notion of a higher penetration. If there be higher powers able to impress us, they may get access to us only through the subliminal door. (See below, p. 515 ff.)

Let us turn now to the feelings which immediately fill the hour of the conversion experience. The first one to be noted is just this sense of higher control. It is not always, but it is very often present. We saw examples of it in Alline, Bradley, Brainerd, and elsewhere. The need of such a higher controlling agency is well expressed in the short reference which the eminent French Protestant Adolphe Monod makes to the crisis of his own conversion. It was at Naples in his early manhood, in the summer of 1827.

" My sadness," he says, " was without limit, and having got entire possession of me, it filled my life from the most indifferent external acts to the most secret thoughts, and corrupted at their source my feelings, my judgment, and my happiness. It was then that I saw that to expect to put a stop to this disorder by my reason and my will, which were themselves diseased, would be to act like a blind man who should pretend to correct one of his eyes by the aid of the other equally blind one. I had then no resource save in *some influence from without*. I remembered the promise of the Holy Ghost ; and what the positive declarations of the Gospel had never succeeded in bringing home to me, I learned at last from necessity, and believed, for the first time in my life, in this promise, in the only sense in which it answered the needs of my soul, in that, namely, of a real external supernatural action, capable of giving me thoughts, and taking them away from me, and exerted on me by a God as truly master of my heart as he is of the rest of nature.   Renouncing then all merit, all strength, abandoning all my personal resources, and acknowledging no other title to his mercy than my own utter misery, I went home and threw myself on my knees, and prayed as I never yet prayed in my life.   From this day onwards a new interior life began for me: not that my melancholy had disappeared, but it had lost its sting. Hope had entered into my heart, and once entered on the path, the God of Jesus Christ, to whom I then had learned to give myself up, little by little did the rest." [1]

It is needless to remind you once more of the admirable congruity of Protestant theology with the structure of the mind as shown in such experiences.   In the extreme of melancholy the self that consciously *is* can do absolutely nothing.   It is completely bankrupt and without resource, and no works it can accomplish will avail. Redemption from such subjective conditions must be a free gift or nothing, and grace through Christ's accomplished sacrifice is such a gift.

"God," says Luther, "is the God of the humble, the miserable, the oppressed, and the desperate, and of those that are brought even to nothing ; and his nature is to give sight to the

---

[1] I piece together a quotation made by W. Monod, in his book la Vie, and a letter printed in the work : Adolphe Monod : I., Souvenirs de sa Vie, 1885, p. 433.

blind, to comfort the broken-hearted, to justify sinners, to save the very desperate and damned. Now that pernicious and pestilent opinion of man's own righteousness, which will not be a sinner, unclean, miserable, and damnable, but righteous and holy, suffereth not God to come to his own natural and proper work. Therefore God must take this maul in hand (the law, I mean) to beat in pieces and bring to nothing this beast with her vain confidence, that she may so learn at length by her own misery that she is utterly forlorn and damned. But here lieth the difficulty, that when a man is terrified and cast down, he is so little able to raise himself up again and say, 'Now I am bruised and afflicted enough; now is the time of grace; now is the time to hear Christ.' The foolishness of man's heart is so great that then he rather seeketh to himself more laws to satisfy his conscience. 'If I live,' saith he, 'I will amend my life : I will do this, I will do that.' But here, except thou do the quite contrary, except thou send Moses away with his law, and in these terrors and this anguish lay hold upon Christ who died for thy sins, look for no salvation. Thy cowl, thy shaven crown, thy chastity, thy obedience, thy poverty, thy works, thy merits? what shall all these do? what shall the law of Moses avail? If I, wretched and damnable sinner, through works or merits could have loved the Son of God, and so come to him, what needed he to deliver himself for me? If I, being a wretch and damned sinner, could be redeemed by any other price, what needed the Son of God to be given? But because there was no other price, therefore he delivered neither sheep, ox, gold, nor silver, but even God himself, entirely and wholly ' for me,' even ' for me,' I say, a miserable, wretched sinner. Now, therefore, I take comfort and apply this to *myself*. And this manner of applying is the very true force and power of faith. For he died *not* to justify the righteous, but the *un*-righteous, and to make *them* the children of God." [1]

That is, the more literally lost you are, the more literally you are the very being whom Christ's sacrifice has already saved. Nothing in Catholic theology, I imagine,

[1] Commentary on Galatians, ch. iii. verse 19, and ch. ii. verse 20, abridged.

has ever spoken to sick souls as straight as this message from Luther's personal experience. As Protestants are not all sick souls, of course reliance on what Luther exults in calling the dung of one's merits, the filthy puddle of one's own righteousness, has come to the front again in their religion ; but the adequacy of his view of Christianity to the deeper parts of our human mental structure is shown by its wildfire contagiousness when it was a new and quickening thing.

Faith that Christ has genuinely done his work was part of what Luther meant by faith, which so far is faith in a fact intellectually conceived of. But this is only one part of Luther's faith, the other part being far more vital. This other part is something not intellectual but immediate and intuitive, the assurance, namely, that I, this individual I, just as I stand, without one plea, etc., am saved now and forever.[1]

Professor Leuba is undoubtedly right in contending that the conceptual belief about Christ's work, although so often efficacious and antecedent, is really accessory and non-essential, and that the ' joyous conviction ' can also

---

[1] In some conversions, both steps are distinct ; in this one, for example : —

"Whilst I was reading the evangelical treatise, I was soon struck by an expression : ' the finished work of Christ.' ' Why,' I asked of myself, ' does the author use these terms ? Why does he not say " the atoning work " ? ' Then these words, ' It is finished,' presented themselves to my mind. ' What is it that is finished ? ' I asked, and in an instant my mind replied : ' A perfect expiation for sin ; entire satisfaction has been given ; the debt has been paid by the Substitute. Christ has died for our sins ; not for ours only, but for those of all men. If, then, the entire work is finished, all the debt paid, what remains for me to do ? ' In another instant the light was shed through my mind by the Holy Ghost, and the joyous conviction was given me that nothing more was to be done, save to fall on my knees, to accept this Saviour and his love, to praise God forever." Autobiography of Hudson Taylor. I translate back into English from the French translation of Challand (Geneva, no date), the original not being accessible.

come by far other channels than this conception. It is to
the joyous conviction itself, the assurance that all is well
with one, that he would give the name of faith *par
excellence*.

"When the sense of estrangement," he writes, "fencing
man about in a narrowly limited ego, breaks down, the individual finds himself ' at one with all creation.' He lives in the
universal life ; he and man, he and nature, he and God, are
one. That state of confidence, trust, union with all things,
following upon the achievement of moral unity, is the *Faith-
state*. Various dogmatic beliefs suddenly, on the advent of
the faith-state, acquire a character of certainty, assume a new
reality, become an object of faith. As the ground of assurance
here is not rational, argumentation is irrelevant. But such
conviction being a mere casual offshoot of the faith-state, it is a
gross error to imagine that the chief practical value of the faith-
state is its power to stamp with the seal of reality certain particular theological conceptions.[1] On the contrary, its value
lies solely in the fact that it is the psychic correlate of a biological growth reducing contending desires to one direction ; a
growth which expresses itself in new affective states and new
reactions ; in larger, nobler, more Christ-like activities. The
ground of the specific assurance in religious dogmas is then an
affective experience. The objects of faith may even be preposterous ; the affective stream will float them along, and invest
them with unshakable certitude. The more startling the affective experience, the less explicable it seems, the easier it is
to make it the carrier of unsubstantiated notions." [2]

The characteristics of the affective experience which,
to avoid ambiguity, should, I think, be called the state of
assurance rather than the faith-state, can be easily enumerated, though it is probably difficult to realize their

---

[1] Tolstoy's case was a good comment on those words. There was almost
no theology in his conversion. His faith-state was the sense come back that
life was infinite in its moral significance.

[2] *American Journal of Psychology*, vii. 345–347, abridged.

intensity, unless one have been through the experience one's self.

The central one is the loss of all the worry, the sense that all is ultimately well with one, the peace, the harmony, the *willingness to be,* even though the outer conditions should remain the same. The certainty of God's ' grace,' of ' justification,' ' salvation,' is an objective belief that usually accompanies the change in Christians; but this may be entirely lacking and yet the affective peace remain the same — you will recollect the case of the Oxford graduate: and many might be given where the assurance of personal salvation was only a later result. A passion of willingness, of acquiescence, of admiration, is the glowing centre of this state of mind.

The second feature is the sense of perceiving truths not known before. The mysteries of life become lucid, as Professor Leuba says; and often, nay usually, the solution is more or less unutterable in words. But these more intellectual phenomena may be postponed until we treat of mysticism.

A third peculiarity of the assurance state is the objective change which the world often appears to undergo. ' An appearance of newness beautifies every object,' the precise opposite of that other sort of newness, that dreadful unreality and strangeness in the appearance of the world, which is experienced by melancholy patients, and of which you may recall my relating some examples.[1] This sense of clean and beautiful newness within and without is one of the commonest entries in conversion records. Jonathan Edwards thus describes it in himself: —

" After this my sense of divine things gradually increased and became more and more lively, and had more of that inward sweetness. The appearance of everything was altered; there

[1] Above, p. 152.

seemed to be, as it were, a calm, sweet cast, or appearance of divine glory, in almost everything. God's excellency, his wisdom, his purity and love, seemed to appear in everything; in the sun, moon, and stars; in the clouds and blue sky; in the grass, flowers, and trees; in the water and all nature; which used greatly to fix my mind. And scarce anything, among all the works of nature, was so sweet to me as thunder and lightning; formerly nothing had been so terrible to me. Before, I used to be uncommonly terrified with thunder, and to be struck with terror when I saw a thunderstorm rising; but now, on the contrary, it rejoices me." [1]

Billy Bray, an excellent little illiterate English evangelist, records his sense of newness thus : —

" I said to the Lord : ' Thou hast said, they that ask shall receive, they that seek shall find, and to them that knock the door shall be opened, and I have faith to believe it.' In an instant the Lord made me so happy that I cannot express what I felt. I shouted for joy. I praised God with my whole heart. . . . I think this was in November, 1823, but what day of the month I do not know. I remember this, that everything looked new to me, the people, the fields, the cattle, the trees. I was like a new man in a new world. I spent the greater part of my time in praising the Lord." [2]

Starbuck and Leuba both illustrate this sense of newness by quotations. I take the two following from Starbuck's manuscript collection. One, a woman, says : —

" I was taken to a camp-meeting, mother and religious friends seeking and praying for my conversion. My emotional nature was stirred to its depths; confessions of depravity and pleading with God for salvation from sin made me oblivious of all surroundings. I plead for mercy, and had a vivid realization of forgiveness and renewal of my nature. When rising from my knees I exclaimed, ' Old things have passed away, all things

---

[1] DWIGHT : Life of Edwards, New York, 1830, p. 61, abridged.

[2] W. F. BOURNE : The King's Son, a Memoir of Billy Bray, London Hamilton, Adams & Co., 1887, p. 9.

have become new.' It was like entering another world, a new
state of existence. Natural objects were glorified, my spiritual
vision was so clarified that I saw beauty in every material object in the universe, the woods were vocal with heavenly music ;
my soul exulted in the love of God, and I wanted everybody to
share in my joy."

The next case is that of a man : —

" I know not how I got back into the encampment, but found
myself staggering up to Rev. ——'s Holiness tent — and as it
was full of seekers and a terrible noise inside, some groaning,
some laughing, and some shouting, and by a large oak, ten feet
from the tent, I fell on my face by a bench, and tried to pray,
and every time I would call on God, something like a man's hand
would strangle me by choking. I don't know whether there
were any one around or near me or not. I thought I should
surely die if I did not get help, but just as often as I would
pray, that unseen hand was felt on my throat and my breath
squeezed off. Finally something said: ' Venture on the atonement, for you will die anyway if you don't.' So I made one final
struggle to call on God for mercy, with the same choking and
strangling, determined to finish the sentence of prayer for
Mercy, if I did strangle and die, and the last I remember that
time was falling back on the ground with the same unseen hand
on my throat. I don't know how long I lay there or what was
going on. None of my folks were present. When I came to
myself, there were a crowd around me praising God. The very
heavens seemed to open and pour down rays of light and glory.
Not for a moment only, but all day and night, floods of light
and glory seemed to pour through my soul, and oh, how I was
changed, and everything became new. My horses and hogs
and even everybody seemed changed."

This man's case introduces the feature of automatisms,
which in suggestible subjects have been so startling a
feature at revivals since, in Edwards's, Wesley's, and
Whitfield's time, these became a regular means of gospel-
propagation. They were at first supposed to be semi-

miraculous proofs of 'power' on the part of the Holy
Ghost; but great divergence of opinion quickly arose
concerning them. Edwards, in his Thoughts on the Revival of Religion in New England, has to defend them
against their critics; and their value has long been matter of debate even within the revivalistic denominations.[1]
They undoubtedly have no essential spiritual significance,
and although their presence makes his conversion more
memorable to the convert, it has never been proved that
converts who show them are more persevering or fertile
in good fruits than those whose change of heart has
had less violent accompaniments. On the whole, unconsciousness, convulsions, visions, involuntary vocal utterances, and suffocation, must be simply ascribed to the
subject's having a large subliminal region, involving
nervous instability. This is often the subject's own view
of the matter afterwards. One of Starbuck's correspondents writes, for instance : —

" I have been through the experience which is known as conversion. My explanation of it is this : the subject works his
emotions up to the breaking point, at the same time resisting
their physical manifestations, such as quickened pulse, etc., and
then suddenly lets them have their full sway over his body.
The relief is something wonderful, and the pleasurable effects
of the emotions are experienced to the highest degree."

There is one form of sensory automatism which possibly deserves special notice on account of its frequency.
I refer to hallucinatory or pseudo-hallucinatory luminous
phenomena, *photisms*, to use the term of the psychologists. Saint Paul's blinding heavenly vision seems to
have been a phenomen of this sort ; so does Constantine's

[1] Consult WILLIAM B. SPRAGUE : Lectures on Revivals of Religion, New
York, 1832, in the long Appendix to which the opinions of a large number
of ministers are given.

cross in the sky. The last case but one which I quoted mentions floods of light and glory. Henry Alline mentions a light, about whose externality he seems uncertain. Colonel Gardiner sees a blazing light. President Finney writes : —

" All at once the glory of God shone upon and round about me in a manner almost marvelous. . . . A light perfectly ineffable shone in my soul, that almost prostrated me on the ground. . . . This light seemed like the brightness of the sun in every direction. It was too intense for the eyes. . . . I think I knew something then, by actual experience, of that light that prostrated Paul on the way to Damascus. It was surely a light such as I could not have endured long." [1]

Such reports of photisms are indeed far from uncommon. Here is another from Starbuck's collection, where the light appeared evidently external : —

" I had attended a series of revival services for about two weeks off and on. Had been invited to the altar several times, all the time becoming more deeply impressed, when finally I decided I must do this, or I should be lost. Realization of conversion was very vivid, like a ton's weight being lifted from my heart ; a strange light which seemed to light up the whole room (for it was dark) ; a conscious supreme bliss which caused me to repeat ' Glory to God ' for a long time. Decided to be God's child for life, and to give up my pet ambition, wealth and social position. My former habits of life hindered my growth somewhat, but I set about overcoming these systematically, and in one year my whole nature was changed, i. e., my ambitions were of a different order."

Here is another one of Starbuck's cases, involving a luminous element : —

" I had been clearly converted twenty-three years before, or rather reclaimed. My experience in regeneration was then clear and spiritual, and I had not backslidden. But I expe-

[1] Memoirs, p. 34.

rienced entire sanctification on the 15th day of March, 1893, about eleven o'clock in the morning. The particular accompaniments of the experience were entirely unexpected. I was quietly sitting at home singing selections out of Pentecostal Hymns. Suddenly there seemed to be a something sweeping into me and inflating my entire being — such a sensation as I had never experienced before. When this experience came, I seemed to be conducted around a large, capacious, well-lighted room. As I walked with my invisible conductor and looked around, a clear thought was coined in my mind, ' They are not here, they are gone.' As soon as the thought was definitely formed in my mind, though no word was spoken, the Holy Spirit impressed me that I was surveying my own soul. Then, for the first time in all my life, did I know that I was cleansed from all sin, and filled with the fullness of God."

Leuba quotes the case of a Mr. Peek, where the luminous affection reminds one of the chromatic hallucinations produced by the intoxicant cactus buds called mescal by the Mexicans : —

" When I went in the morning into the fields to work, the glory of God appeared in all his visible creation. I well remember we reaped oats, and how every straw and head of the oats seemed, as it were, arrayed in a kind of rainbow glory, or to glow, if I may so express it, in the glory of God." [1]

[1] These reports of sensorial photism shade off into what are evidently only metaphorical accounts of the sense of new spiritual illumination, as, for instance, in Brainerd's statement : "As I was walking in a thick grove, unspeakable glory seemed to open to the apprehension of my soul. I do not mean any external brightness, for I saw no such thing, nor any imagination of a body of light in the third heavens, or anything of that nature, but it was a new inward apprehension or view that I had of God."

In a case like this next one from Starbuck's manuscript collection, the lighting up of the darkness is probably also metaphorical : —

" One Sunday night, I resolved that when I got home to the ranch where I was working, I would offer myself with my faculties and all to God to be used only by and for him. . . . It was raining and the roads were muddy ; but this desire grew so strong that I kneeled down by the side of the road and told God all about it, intending then to get up and go on. Such a thing as any special answer to my prayer never entered my mind, having

The most characteristic of all the elements of the con-version crisis, and the last one of which I shall speak, is the ecstasy of happiness produced. We have already heard several accounts of it, but I will add a couple more. President Finney's is so vivid that I give it at length : —

" All my feelings seemed to rise and flow out; and the ut-terance of my heart was, ' I want to pour my whole soul out to God.' The rising of my soul was so great that I rushed into the back room of the front office, to pray. There was no fire and no light in the room; nevertheless it appeared to me as if it were perfectly light. As I went in and shut the door after me, it seemed as if I met the Lord Jesus Christ face to face. It did not occur to me then, nor did it for some time afterwards, that it was wholly a mental state. On the contrary, it seemed to me that I saw him as I would see any other man. He said nothing, but looked at me in such a manner as to break me

been converted by faith, but still being most undoubtedly saved. Well, while I was praying, I remember holding out my hands to God and telling him they should work for him, my feet walk for him, my tongue speak for him, etc., etc., if he would only use me as his instrument and give me a satisfy-ing experience — when suddenly the darkness of the night seemed lit up — I felt, realized, knew, that God heard and answered my prayer. Deep hap-piness came over me ; I felt I was accepted into the inner circle of God's loved ones."

In the following case also the flash of light is metaphorical : —

" A prayer meeting had been called for at close of evening service. The minister supposed me impressed by his discourse (a mistake — he was dull). He came and, placing his hand upon my shoulder, said : ' Do you not want to give your heart to God ? ' I replied in the affirmative. Then said he, ' Come to the front seat.' They sang and prayed and talked with me. I experienced nothing but unaccountable wretchedness. They declared that the reason why I did not ' obtain peace ' was because I was not willing to give up all to God. After about two hours the minister said we would go home. As usual, on retiring, I prayed. In great distress, I at this time simply said, ' Lord, I have done all I can, I leave the whole matter with thee.' Immediately, like a flash of light, there came to me a great peace, and I arose and went into my parents' bedroom and said, ' I do feel so won-derfully happy.' This I regard as the hour of conversion. It was the hour in which I became assured of divine acceptance and favor. So far as my life was concerned, it made little immediate change."

right down at his feet. I have always since regarded this as a most remarkable state of mind; for it seemed to me a reality that he stood before me, and I fell down at his feet and poured out my soul to him. I wept aloud like a child, and made such confessions as I could with my choked utterance. It seemed to me that I bathed his feet with my tears; and yet I had no distinct impression that I touched him, that I recollect. I must have continued in this state for a good while; but my mind was too much absorbed with the interview to recollect anything that I said. But I know, as soon as my mind became calm enough to break off from the interview, I returned to the front office, and found that the fire that I had made of large wood was nearly burned out. But as I turned and was about to take a seat by the fire, I received a mighty baptism of the Holy Ghost. Without any expectation of it, without ever having the thought in my mind that there was any such thing for me, without any recollection that I had ever heard the thing mentioned by any person in the world, the Holy Spirit descended upon me in a manner that seemed to go through me, body and soul. I could feel the impression, like a wave of electricity, going through and through me. Indeed, it seemed to come in waves and waves of liquid love; for I could not express it in any other way. It seemed like the very breath of God. I can recollect distinctly that it seemed to fan me, like immense wings.

"No words can express the wonderful love that was shed abroad in my heart. I wept aloud with joy and love; and I do not know but I should say I literally bellowed out the unutterable gushings of my heart. These waves came over me, and over me, and over me, one after the other, until I recollect I cried out, 'I shall die if these waves continue to pass over me.' I said, 'Lord, I cannot bear any more;' yet I had no fear of death.

"How long I continued in this state, with this baptism continuing to roll over me and go through me, I do not know. But I know it was late in the evening when a member of my choir — for I was the leader of the choir — came into the office to see me. He was a member of the church. He found me in this state of loud weeping, and said to me, 'Mr. Finney, what ails you?' I could make him no answer for some time. He then said, 'Are you in pain?' I gathered myself up as best I could, and replied, 'No, but so happy that I cannot live.'"

I just now quoted Billy Bray; I cannot do better than give his own brief account of his post-conversion feelings : —

"I can't help praising the Lord. As I go along the street, I lift up one foot, and it seems to say 'Glory'; and I lift up the other, and it seems to say 'Amen'; and so they keep up like that all the time I am walking." [1]

One word, before I close this lecture, on the question of the transiency or permanence of these abrupt conversions. Some of you, I feel sure, knowing that numerous

---

[1] I add in a note a few more records : —

"One morning, being in deep distress, fearing every moment I should drop into hell, I was constrained to cry in earnest for mercy, and the Lord came to my relief, and delivered my soul from the burden and guilt of sin. My whole frame was in a tremor from head to foot, and my soul enjoyed sweet peace. The pleasure I then felt was indescribable. The happiness lasted about three days, during which time I never spoke to any person about my feelings." Autobiography of DAN YOUNG, edited by W. P. STRICKLAND, New York, 1860.

"In an instant there rose up in me such a sense of God's taking care of those who put their trust in him that for an hour all the world was crystalline, the heavens were lucid, and I sprang to my feet and began to cry and laugh." H. W. BEECHER, quoted by LEUBA.

"My tears of sorrow changed to joy, and I lay there praising God in such ecstasy of joy as only the soul who experiences it can realize." — "I cannot express how I felt. It was as if I had been in a dark dungeon and lifted into the light of the sun. I shouted and I sang praise unto him who loved me and washed me from my sins. I was forced to retire into a secret place, for the tears did flow, and I did not wish my shopmates to see me, and yet I could not keep it a secret." — "I experienced joy almost to weeping." — "I felt my face must have shone like that of Moses. I had a general feeling of buoyancy. It was the greatest joy it was ever my lot to experience." — "I wept and laughed alternately. I was as light as if walking on air. I felt as if I had gained greater peace and happiness than I had ever expected to experience." STARBUCK's correspondents.

backslidings and relapses take place, make of these their apperceiving mass for interpreting the whole subject, and dismiss it with a pitying smile at so much 'hysterics.' Psychologically, as well as religiously, however, this is shallow. It misses the point of serious interest, which is not so much the duration as the nature and quality of these shiftings of character to higher levels. Men lapse from every level — we need no statistics to tell us that. Love is, for instance, well known not to be irrevocable, yet, constant or inconstant, it reveals new flights and reaches of ideality while it lasts. These revelations form its significance to men and women, whatever be its duration. So with the conversion experience : that it should for even a short time show a human being what the high-water mark of his spiritual capacity is, this is what constitutes its importance, — an importance which backsliding cannot diminish, although persistence might increase it. As a matter of fact, all the more striking instances of conversion, all those, for instance, which I have quoted, *have* been permanent. The case of which there might be most doubt, on account of its suggesting so strongly an epileptoid seizure, was the case of M. Ratisbonne. Yet I am informed that Ratisbonne's whole future was shaped by those few minutes. He gave up his project of marriage, became a priest, founded at Jerusalem, where he went to dwell, a mission of nuns for the conversion of the Jews, showed no tendency to use for egotistic purposes the notoriety given him by the peculiar circumstances of his conversion, — which, for the rest, he could seldom refer to without tears, — and in short remained an exemplary son of the Church until he died, late in the 80's, if I remember rightly.

The only statistics I know of, on the subject of the duration of conversions, are those collected for Professor

Starbuck by Miss Johnston. They embrace only a hundred persons, evangelical church-members, more than half being Methodists. According to the statement of the subjects themselves, there had been backsliding of some sort in nearly all the cases, 93 per cent. of the women, 77 per cent. of the men. Discussing the returns more minutely, Starbuck finds that only 6 per cent. are relapses from the religious faith which the conversion confirmed, and that the backsliding complained of is in most only a fluctuation in the ardor of sentiment. Only six of the hundred cases report a change of faith. Starbuck's conclusion is that the effect of conversion is to bring with it " a changed attitude towards life, which is fairly constant and permanent, although the feelings fluctuate. . . . In other words, the persons who have passed through conversion, having once taken a stand for the religious life, tend to feel themselves identified with it, no matter how much their religious enthusiasm declines." [1]

[1] Psychology of Religion, pp. 360, 357.

LECTURES XI, XII, AND XIII

SAINTLINESS

THE last lecture left us in a state of expectancy. What may the practical fruits for life have been, of such movingly happy conversions as those we heard of? With this question the really important part of our task opens, for you remember that we began all this empirical inquiry not merely to open a curious chapter in the natural history of human consciousness, but rather to attain a spiritual judgment as to the total value and positive meaning of all the religious trouble and happiness which we have seen. We must, therefore, first describe the fruits of the religious life, and then we must judge them. This divides our inquiry into two distinct parts. Let us without further preamble proceed to the descriptive task.

It ought to be the pleasantest portion of our business in these lectures. Some small pieces of it, it is true, may be painful, or may show human nature in a pathetic light, but it will be mainly pleasant, because the best fruits of religious experience are the best things that history has to show. They have always been esteemed so ; here if anywhere is the genuinely strenuous life ; and to call to mind a succession of such examples as I have lately had to wander through, though it has been only in the reading of them, is to feel encouraged and uplifted and washed in better moral air.

The highest flights of charity, devotion, trust, patience, bravery to which the wings of human nature have spread themselves have been flown for religious ideals. I can do no better than quote, as to this, some remarks which Sainte-Beuve in his History of Port-Royal makes on the results of conversion or the state of grace.

" Even from the purely human point of view," Sainte-Beuve says, " the phenomenon of grace must still appear sufficiently extraordinary, eminent, and rare, both in its nature and in its effects, to deserve a closer study. For the soul arrives thereby at a certain fixed and invincible state, a state which is genuinely heroic, and from out of which the greatest deeds which it ever performs are executed. Through all the different forms of communion, and all the diversity of the means which help to produce this state, whether it be reached by a jubilee, by a general confession, by a solitary prayer and effusion, whatever in short be the place and the occasion, it is easy to recognize that it is fundamentally one state in spirit and in fruits. Penetrate a little beneath the diversity of circumstances, and it becomes evident that in Christians of different epochs it is always one and the same modification by which they are affected : there is veritably a single fundamental and identical spirit of piety and charity, common to those who have received grace ; an inner state which before all things is one of love and humility, of infinite confidence in God, and of severity for one's self, accompanied with tenderness for others. The fruits peculiar to this condition of the soul have the same savor in all, under distant suns and in different surroundings, in Saint Teresa of Avila just as in any Moravian brother of Herrnhut." [1]

Sainte-Beuve has here only the more eminent instances of regeneration in mind, and these are of course the instructive ones for us also to consider. These devotees

[1] SAINTE-BEUVE : Port-Royal, vol. i. pp. 95 and 106, abridged.

have often laid their course so differently from other men that, judging them by worldly law, we might be tempted to call them monstrous aberrations from the path of nature. I begin, therefore, by asking a general psychological question as to what the inner conditions are which may make one human character differ so extremely from another.

I reply at once that where the character, as something distinguished from the intellect, is concerned, the causes of human diversity lie chiefly in our *differing susceptibilities of emotional excitement*, and in the *different impulses and inhibitions* which these bring in their train. Let me make this more clear.

Speaking generally, our moral and practical attitude, at any given time, is always a resultant of two sets of forces within us, impulses pushing us one way and obstructions and inhibitions holding us back. "Yes! yes!" say the impulses; "No! no!" say the inhibitions. Few people who have not expressly reflected on the matter realize how constantly this factor of inhibition is upon us, how it contains and moulds us by its restrictive pressure almost as if we were fluids pent within the cavity of a jar. The influence is so incessant that it becomes subconscious. All of you, for example, sit here with a certain constraint at this moment, and entirely without express consciousness of the fact, because of the influence of the occasion. If left alone in the room, each of you would probably involuntarily rearrange himself, and make his attitude more 'free and easy.' But proprieties and their inhibitions snap like cobwebs if any great emotional excitement supervenes. I have seen a dandy appear in the street with his face covered with shaving-lather because a house across the way was on fire; and a woman will run among strangers in her nightgown if it be a question of saving her baby's life or her own. Take a self-indulgent woman's life in general. She will yield to every inhibition set by her disagreeable sensations, lie late in bed, live upon tea or bromides, keep indoors from the cold. Every difficulty finds her obedient to its ' no.' But make a mother of her, and what have you? Possessed by maternal excitement, she now confronts wakefulness, weariness, and toil without an instant of hesitation or a word of complaint. The inhibitive power of pain over her is extinguished wherever the baby's interests are at stake. The inconveniences which this creature occasions have become, as James Hinton says, the glowing heart of a great joy, and indeed are now the very conditions whereby the joy becomes most deep.

This is an example of what you have already heard of as the ' expulsive power of a higher affection.' But be the affection high or low, it makes no difference, so long as the excitement it brings be strong enough. In one of Henry Drummond's discourses he tells of an inundation in India where an eminence with a bungalow upon it remained unsubmerged, and became the refuge of a number of wild animals and reptiles in addition to the human beings who were there. At a certain moment a royal Bengal tiger appeared swimming towards it, reached it, and lay panting like a dog upon the ground in the midst of the people, still possessed by such an agony of terror that one of the Englishmen could calmly step up with a rifle and blow out its brains. The tiger's habitual ferocity was temporarily quelled by the emotion of fear, which became sovereign, and formed a new centre for his character.

Sometimes no emotional state is sovereign, but many contrary ones are mixed together. In that case one hears both 'yeses' and 'noes,' and the 'will' is called on then to solve the conflict. Take a soldier, for example, with his dread of cowardice impelling him to advance, his fears impelling him to run, and his propensities to imitation pushing him towards various courses if his comrades offer various examples. His person becomes the seat of a mass of interferences; and he may for a time simply waver, because no one emotion prevails. There is a pitch of intensity, though, which, if any emotion reach it, enthrones that one as alone effective and sweeps its antagonists and all their inhibitions away. The fury of his comrades' charge, once entered on, will give this pitch of courage to the soldier; the panic of their rout will give this pitch of fear. In these sovereign excitements, things ordinarily impossible grow natural because the inhibitions are annulled. Their 'no! no!' not only is not heard, it does not exist. Obstacles are then like tissue-paper hoops to the circus rider — no impediment; the flood is higher than the dam they make. "Lass sie betteln gehn wenn sie hungrig sind!" cries the grenadier, frantic over his Emperor's capture, when his wife and babes are suggested; and men pent into a burning theatre have been known to cut their way through the crowd with knives.[1]

---

[1] "'Love would not be love,' says Bourget, 'unless it could carry one to crime.' And so one may say that no passion would be a veritable passion unless it could carry one to crime." (SIGHELE : Psychologie des Sectes, p. 136.) In other words, great passions annul the ordinary inhibitions set by 'conscience.' And conversely, of all the criminal human beings, the false, cowardly, sensual, or cruel persons who actually live, there is perhaps not one whose criminal impulse may not be at some moment overpowered by the presence of some other emotion to which his character is also potentially liable, provided that other emotion be only made intense enough. Fear is usually the most available emotion for this result in this particular class of persons. It stands for conscience, and may here be classed appropriately as a 'higher affection.' If we are soon to die, or if we believe a day of judgment to be near at hand, how quickly do we put our moral house in order — we do not see how sin can evermore exert temptation over us! Old-

One mode of emotional excitability is exceedingly important in the composition of the energetic character, from its peculiarly destructive power over inhibitions. I mean what in its lower form is mere irascibility, susceptibility to wrath, the fighting temper; and what in subtler ways manifests itself as impatience, grimness, earnestness, severity of character. Earnestness means willingness to live with energy, though energy bring pain. The pain may be pain to other people or pain to one's self — it makes little difference; for when the strenuous mood is on one, the aim is to break something, no matter whose or what. Nothing annihilates an inhibition as irresistibly as anger does it; for, as Moltke says of war, destruction pure and simple is its essence. This is what makes it so invaluable an ally of every other passion. The sweetest delights are trampled on with a ferocious pleasure the moment they offer themselves as checks to a cause by which our higher indignations are elicited. It costs then nothing to drop friendships, to renounce long-rooted privileges and possessions, to break with social ties. Rather do we take a stern joy in the astringency and desolation; and what is called weakness of character seems in most cases to consist in the inaptitude for these sacrificial moods, of which one's own inferior self and its pet softnesses must often be the targets and the victims.[1]

fashioned hell-fire Christianity well knew how to extract from fear its full equivalent in the way of fruits for repentance, and its full conversion value.

[1] Example : Benjamin Constant was often marveled at as an extraordinary instance of superior intelligence with inferior character. He writes (Journal, Paris, 1895, p. 56), "I am tossed and dragged about by my miserable weakness. Never was anything so ridiculous as my indecision. Now marriage, now solitude; now Germany, now France, hesitation upon hesitation, and all because at bottom I am *unable to give up anything*." He can't 'get mad' at any of his alternatives; and the career of a man beset by such an all-round amiability is hopeless.

So far I have spoken of temporary alterations produced by shifting excitements in the same person. But the relatively fixed differences of character of different persons are explained in a precisely similar way. In a man with a liability to a special sort of emotion, whole ranges of inhibition habitually vanish, which in other men remain effective, and other sorts of inhibition take their place. When a person has an inborn genius for certain emotions, his life differs strangely from that of ordinary people, for none of their usual deterrents check him. Your mere aspirant to a type of character, on the contrary, only shows, when your natural lover, fighter, or reformer, with whom the passion is a gift of nature, comes along, the hopeless inferiority of voluntary to instinctive action. He has deliberately to overcome his inhibitions; the genius with the inborn passion seems not to feel them at all; he is free of all that inner friction and nervous waste. To a Fox, a Garibaldi, a General Booth, a John Brown, a Louise Michel, a Bradlaugh, the obstacles omnipotent over those around them are as if non-existent. Could the rest of us so disregard them, there might be many such heroes, for many have the wish to live for similar ideals, and only the adequate degree of inhibition-quenching fury is lacking.[1]

[1] The great thing which the higher excitabilities give is *courage;* and the addition or subtraction of a certain amount of this quality makes a different man, a different life. Various excitements let the courage loose. Trustful hope will do it; inspiring example will do it; love will do it; wrath will do it. In some people it is natively so high that the mere touch of danger does it, though danger is for most men the great inhibitor of action. 'Love of adventure' becomes in such persons a ruling passion. "I believe," says General Skobeleff, "that my bravery is simply the passion and at the same time the contempt of danger. The risk of life fills me with an exaggerated rapture. The fewer there are to share it, the more I like it. The participation of my body in the event is required to furnish me an adequate excitement. Everything intellectual appears to me to be reflex; but a meeting of man to man, a duel, a danger into which I can

The difference between willing and merely wishing, between having ideals that are creative and ideals that are but pinings and regrets, thus depends solely either on the amount of steam-pressure chronically driving the character in the ideal direction, or on the amount of ideal excitement transiently acquired. Given a certain amount of love, indignation, generosity, magnanimity, admiration, loyalty, or enthusiasm of self-surrender, the result is always the same. That whole raft of cowardly obstructions, which in tame persons and dull moods are sovereign impediments to action, sinks away at once. Our conventionality,[1] our shyness, laziness, and stingi- ness, our demands for precedent and permission, for guar- antee and surety, our small suspicions, timidities, despairs, where are they now? Severed like cobwebs, broken like bubbles in the sun —

> " Wo sind die Sorge nun und Noth
> Die mich noch gestern wollt' erschlaffen ?
> Ich schäm' mich dess' im Morgenroth."

The flood we are borne on rolls them so lightly under that their very contact is unfelt. Set free of them, we float and soar and sing. This auroral openness and

throw myself headforemost, attracts me, moves me, intoxicates me. I am crazy for it, I love it, I adore it. I run after danger as one runs after women ; I wish it never to stop. Were it always the same, it would always bring me a new pleasure. When I throw myself into an adventure in which I hope to find it, my heart palpitates with the uncertainty ; I could wish at once to have it appear and yet to delay. A sort of painful and delicious shiver shakes me ; my entire nature runs to meet the peril with an impetus that my will would in vain try to resist." (JULIETTE ADAM : Le Général Skobeleff, Nouvelle Revue, 1886, abridged.) Skobeleff seems to have been a cruel egoist ; but the disinterested Garibaldi, if one may judge by his ' Memorie,' lived in an unflagging emotion of similar danger- seeking excitement.

[1] See the case on p. 70, above, where the writer describes his experiences of communion with the Divine as consisting " merely in the *temporary oblit- eration of the conventionalities* which usually cover my life."

uplift gives to all creative ideal levels a bright and carol-
ing quality, which is nowhere more marked than where
the controlling emotion is religious. " The true monk,"
writes an Italian mystic, " takes nothing with him but
his lyre."

We may now turn from these psychological generalities to those fruits of the religious state which form the
special subject of our present lecture. The man who
lives in his religious centre of personal energy, and is
actuated by spiritual enthusiasms, differs from his previous carnal self in perfectly definite ways. The new ardor
which burns in his breast consumes in its glow the lower
'noes' which formerly beset him, and keeps him immune
against infection from the entire groveling portion of
his nature. Magnanimities once impossible are now easy;
paltry conventionalities and mean incentives once tyrannical hold no sway. The stone wall inside of him has
fallen, the hardness in his heart has broken down. The
rest of us can, I think, imagine this by recalling our
state of feeling in those temporary 'melting moods'
into which either the trials of real life, or the theatre,
or a novel sometimes throw us. Especially if we weep!
For it is then as if our tears broke through an inveterate
inner dam, and let all sorts of ancient peccancies and
moral stagnancies drain away, leaving us now washed
and soft of heart and open to every nobler leading.
With most of us the customary hardness quickly returns,
but not so with saintly persons. Many saints, even as
energetic ones as Teresa and Loyola, have possessed what
the church traditionally reveres as a special grace, the
so-called gift of tears. In these persons the melting
mood seems to have held almost uninterrupted control.
And as it is with tears and melting moods, so it is with

other exalted affections. Their reign may come by gradual growth or by a crisis; but in either case it may have ' come to stay.'

At the end of the last lecture we saw this permanence to be true of the general paramountcy of the higher insight, even though in the ebbs of emotional excitement meaner motives might temporarily prevail and backsliding might occur. But that lower temptations may remain completely annulled, apart from transient emotion and as if by alteration of the man's habitual nature, is also proved by documentary evidence in certain cases. Before embarking on the general natural history of the regenerate character, let me convince you of this curious fact by one or two examples. The most numerous are those of reformed drunkards. You recollect the case of Mr. Hadley in the last lecture; the Jerry McAuley Water Street Mission abounds in similar instances.[1] You also remember the graduate of Oxford, converted at three in the afternoon, and getting drunk in the hay-field the next day, but after that permanently cured of his appetite. "From that hour drink has had no terrors for me: I never touch it, never want it. The same thing occurred with my pipe, . . . the desire for it went at once and has never returned. So with every known sin, the deliverance in each case being permanent and complete. I have had no temptations since conversion."

Here is an analogous case from Starbuck's manuscript collection : —

" I went into the old Adelphi Theatre, where there was a Holiness meeting, . . . and I began saying, 'Lord, Lord, I must have this blessing.' Then what was to me an audible voice said : 'Are you willing to give up everything to the

[1] Above, p. 201. "The only radical remedy I know for dipsomania is religiomania," is a saying I have heard quoted from some medical man.

Lord?' and question after question kept coming up, to all of which I said : ' Yes, Lord ; yes, Lord ! ' until this came : ' Why do you not accept it *now* ? ' and I said : ' I do, Lord.' — I felt no particular joy, only a trust. Just then the meeting closed, and, as I went out on the street, I met a gentleman smoking a fine cigar, and a cloud of smoke came into my face, and I took a long, deep breath of it, and praise the Lord, all my appetite for it was gone. Then as I walked along the street, passing saloons where the fumes of liquor came out, I found that all my taste and longing for that accursed stuff was gone. Glory to God ! . . . [But] for ten or eleven long years [after that] I was in the wilderness with its ups and downs. My appetite for liquor never came back."

The classic case of Colonel Gardiner is that of a man cured of sexual temptation in a single hour. To Mr. Spears the colonel said, " I was effectually cured of all inclination to that sin I was so strongly addicted to that I thought nothing but shooting me through the head could have cured me of it ; and all desire and inclination to it was removed, as entirely as if I had been a sucking child ; nor did the temptation return to this day." Mr. Webster's words on the same subject are these : " One thing I have heard the colonel frequently say, that he was much addicted to impurity before his acquaintance with religion ; but that, so soon as he was enlightened from above, he felt the power of the Holy Ghost changing his nature so wonderfully that his sanctification in this respect seemed more remarkable than in any other." [1]

Such rapid abolition of ancient impulses and propensities reminds us so strongly of what has been observed as the result of hypnotic suggestion that it is difficult not to believe that subliminal influences play the decisive

[1] Doddridge's Life of Colonel James Gardiner, London Religious Tract Society, pp. 23–32.

part in these abrupt changes of heart, just as they do in hypnotism.[1] Suggestive therapeutics abound in records of cure, after a few sittings, of inveterate bad habits with which the patient, left to ordinary moral and physical influences, had struggled in vain. Both drunkenness and sexual vice have been cured in this way, action through the subliminal seeming thus in many individuals to have the prerogative of inducing relatively stable change. If the grace of God miraculously operates, it probably operates through the subliminal door, then. But just *how* anything operates in this region is still unexplained, and we shall do well now to say good-by to the *process* of transformation altogether, — leaving it, if you like, a good deal of a psychological or theological mystery, — and to turn our attention to the fruits of the religious condition, no matter in what way they may have been produced.[2]

[1] Here, for example, is a case, from Starbuck's book, in which a 'sensory automatism' brought about quickly what prayers and resolves had been unable to effect. The subject is a woman. She writes : —

"When I was about forty I tried to quit smoking, but the desire was on me, and had me in its power. I cried and prayed and promised God to quit, but could not. I had smoked for fifteen years. When I was fifty-three, as I sat by the fire one day smoking, a voice came to me. I did not hear it with my ears, but more as a dream or sort of double think. It said, 'Louisa, lay down smoking.' At once I replied, 'Will you take the desire away ? ' But it only kept saying : 'Louisa, lay down smoking.' Then I got up, laid my pipe on the mantel-shelf, and never smoked again or had any desire to. The desire was gone as though I had never known it or touched tobacco. The sight of others smoking and the smell of smoke never gave me the least wish to touch it again." The Psychology of Religion, p. 142.

[2] Professor Starbuck expresses the radical destruction of old influences physiologically, as a cutting off of the connection between higher and lower cerebral centres. "This condition," he says, "in which the association-centres connected with the spiritual life are cut off from the lower, is often reflected in the way correspondents describe their experiences. . . . For example : 'Temptations from without still assail me, but there is nothing *within* to respond to them.' The ego [here] is wholly identified with the

The collective name for the ripe fruits of religion in a character is Saintliness.[1] The saintly character is the character for which spiritual emotions are the habitual centre of the personal energy; and there is a certain composite photograph of universal saintliness, the same in all religions, of which the features can easily be traced.[2]

higher centres, whose quality of feeling is that of withinness. Another of the respondents says : ' Since then, although Satan tempts me, there is as it were a wall of brass around me, so that his darts cannot touch me.' " — Unquestionably, functional exclusions of this sort must occur in the cerebral organ. But on the side accessible to introspection, their causal condition is nothing but the degree of spiritual excitement, getting at last so high and strong as to be sovereign ; and it must be frankly confessed that we do not know just why or how such sovereignty comes about in one person and not in another. We can only give our imagination a certain delusive help by mechanical analogies.

If we should conceive, for example, that the human mind, with its different possibilities of equilibrium, might be like a many-sided solid with different surfaces on which it could lie flat, we might liken mental revolutions to the spatial revolutions of such a body. As it is pried up, say by a lever, from a position in which it lies on surface A, for instance, it will linger for a time unstably halfway up, and if the lever cease to urge it, it will tumble back or ' relapse ' under the continued pull of gravity. But if at last it rotate far enough for its centre of gravity to pass beyond surface A altogether, the body will fall over, on surface B, say, and abide there permanently. The pulls of gravity towards A have vanished, and may now be disregarded. The polyhedron has become immune against farther attraction from their direction.

In this figure of speech the lever may correspond to the emotional influences making for a new life, and the initial pull of gravity to the ancient drawbacks and inhibitions. So long as the emotional influence fails to reach a certain pitch of efficacy, the changes it produces are unstable, and the man relapses into his original attitude. But when a certain intensity is attained by the new emotion, a critical point is passed, and there then ensues an irreversible revolution, equivalent to the production of a new nature.

[1] I use this word in spite of a certain flavor of ' sanctimoniousness ' which sometimes clings to it, because no other word suggests as well the exact combination of affections which the text goes on to describe.

[2] " It will be found," says Dr. W. R. INGE (in his lectures on Christian Mysticism, London, 1899, p. 326), " that men of preëminent saintliness agree very closely in what they tell us. They tell us that they have arrived at an unshakable conviction, not based on inference but on immediate experience, that God is a spirit with whom the human spirit can hold intercourse ;

They are these : —

1. A feeling of being in a wider life than that of this world's selfish little interests ; and a conviction, not merely intellectual, but as it were sensible, of the existence of an Ideal Power.   In Christian saintliness this power is always personified as God ; but abstract moral ideals, civic or patriotic utopias, or inner visions of holiness or right may also be felt as the true lords and enlargers of our life, in ways which I described in the lecture on the Reality of the Unseen.[1]

that in him meet all that they can imagine of goodness, truth, and beauty ; that they can see his footprints everywhere in nature, and feel his presence within them as the very life of their life, so that in proportion as they come to themselves they come to him.   They tell us what separates us from him and from happiness is, first, self-seeking in all its forms ; and, secondly, sensuality in all its forms ; that these are the ways of darkness and death, which hide from us the face of God ; while the path of the just is like a shining light, which shineth more and more unto the perfect day."

[1] The 'enthusiasm of humanity' may lead to a life which coalesces in many respects with that of Christian saintliness.   Take the following rules proposed to members of the Union pour l'Action morale, in the Bulletin de l'Union, April 1–15, 1894.   See, also, Revue Bleue, August 13, 1892.

" We would make known in our own persons the usefulness of rule, of discipline, of resignation and renunciation ; we would teach the necessary perpetuity of suffering, and explain the creative part which it plays.   We would wage war upon false optimism ; on the base hope of happiness coming to us ready made ; on the notion of a salvation by knowledge alone, or by material civilization alone, vain symbol as this is of civilization, precarious external arrangement, ill-fitted to replace the intimate union and consent of souls.   We would wage war also on bad morals, whether in public or in private life ; on luxury, fastidiousness, and over-refinement ; on all that tends to increase the painful, immoral, and anti-social multiplication of our wants ; on all that excites envy and dislike in the soul of the common people, and confirms the notion that the chief end of life is freedom to enjoy.   We would preach by our example the respect of superiors and equals, the respect of all men ; affectionate simplicity in our relations with inferiors and insignificant persons ; indulgence where our own claims only are concerned, but firmness in our demands where they relate to duties towards others or towards the public.

" For the common people are what we help them to become ; their vices are our vices, gazed upon, envied, and imitated ; and if they come back with all their weight upon us, it is but just.

2. A sense of the friendly continuity of the ideal power with our own life, and a willing self-surrender to its control.

3. An immense elation and freedom, as the outlines of the confining selfhood melt down.

4. A shifting of the emotional centre towards loving and harmonious affections, towards ' yes, yes,' and away from ' no,' where the claims of the non-ego are concerned.

These fundamental inner conditions have characteristic practical consequences, as follows : —

a. Asceticism. — The self-surrender may become so passionate as to turn into self-immolation. It may then so overrule the ordinary inhibitions of the flesh that the saint finds positive pleasure in sacrifice and asceticism, measuring and expressing as they do the degree of his loyalty to the higher power.

b. Strength of Soul. — The sense of enlargement of life may be so uplifting that personal motives and inhibitions, commonly omnipotent, become too insignificant for notice, and new reaches of patience and fortitude open out. Fears and anxieties go, and blissful equanimity takes their place. Come heaven, come hell, it makes no difference now !

"We forbid ourselves all seeking after popularity, all ambition to appear important. We pledge ourselves to abstain from falsehood, in all its degrees. We promise not to create or encourage illusions as to what is possible, by what we say or write. We promise to one another active sincerity, which strives to see truth clearly, and which never fears to declare what it sees.

"We promise deliberate resistance to the tidal waves of fashion, to the ' booms ' and panics of the public mind, to all the forms of weakness and of fear.

"We forbid ourselves the use of sarcasm. Of serious things we will speak seriously and unsmilingly, without banter and without the appearance of banter ; — and even so of all things, for there are serious ways of being light of heart.

"We will put ourselves forward always for what we are, simply and without false humility, as well as without pedantry, affectation, or pride."

c. Purity. — The shifting of the emotional centre brings with it, first, increase of purity. The sensitiveness to spiritual discords is enhanced, and the cleansing of existence from brutal and sensual elements becomes imperative. Occasions of contact with such elements are avoided : the saintly life must deepen its spiritual consistency and keep unspotted from the world. In some temperaments this need of purity of spirit takes an ascetic turn, and weaknesses of the flesh are treated with relentless severity.

d. Charity. — The shifting of the emotional centre brings, secondly, increase of charity, tenderness for fellow-creatures. The ordinary motives to antipathy, which usually set such close bounds to tenderness among human beings, are inhibited. The saint loves his enemies, and treats loathsome beggars as his brothers.

I now have to give some concrete illustrations of these fruits of the spiritual tree. The only difficulty is to choose, for they are so abundant.

Since the sense of Presence of a higher and friendly Power seems to be the fundamental feature in the spiritual life, I will begin with that.

In our narratives of conversion we saw how the world might look shining and transfigured to the convert,[1] and, apart from anything acutely religious, we all have moments when the universal life seems to wrap us round with friendliness. In youth and health, in summer, in the woods or on the mountains, there come days when the weather seems all whispering with peace, hours when the goodness and beauty of existence enfold us like a dry warm climate, or chime through us as if our inner ears were subtly ringing with the world's security. Thoreau writes : —

[1] Above, pp. 248 ff.

"Once, a few weeks after I came to the woods, for an hour I doubted whether the near neighborhood of man was not essential to a serene and healthy life. To be alone was somewhat unpleasant. But, in the midst of a gentle rain, while these thoughts prevailed, I was suddenly sensible of such sweet and beneficent society in Nature, in the very pattering of the drops, and in every sight and sound around my house, an infinite and unaccountable friendliness all at once, like an atmosphere, sustaining me, as made the fancied advantages of human neighborhood insignificant, and I have never thought of them since. Every little pine-needle expanded and swelled with sympathy and befriended me. I was so distinctly made aware of the presence of something kindred to me, that I thought no place could ever be strange to me again." [1]

In the Christian consciousness this sense of the enveloping friendliness becomes most personal and definite. "The compensation," writes a German author, "for the loss of that sense of personal independence which man so unwillingly gives up, is the disappearance of all *fear* from one's life, the quite indescribable and inexplicable feeling of an inner *security*, which one can only experience, but which, once it has been experienced, one can never forget." [2]

I find an excellent description of this state of mind in a sermon by Mr. Voysey : —

"It is the experience of myriads of trustful souls, that this sense of God's unfailing presence with them in their going out and in their coming in, and by night and day, is a source of absolute repose and confident calmness. It drives away all fear of what may befall them. That nearness of God is a constant security against terror and anxiety. It is not that they are at all assured of physical safety, or deem themselves protected by a love which is denied to others, but that they are in a state of mind equally ready to be safe or to meet with injury. If injury

---

[1] H. THOREAU : Walden, Riverside edition, p. 206, abridged.
[2] C. H. HILTY : Glück, vol. i. p. 85.

befall them, they will be content to bear it because the Lord is their keeper, and nothing can befall them without his will. If it be his will, then injury is for them a blessing and no calamity at all. Thus and thus only is the trustful man protected and shielded from harm. And I for one — by no means a thick-skinned or hard-nerved man — am absolutely satisfied with this arrangement, and do not wish for any other kind of immunity from danger and catastrophe. Quite as sensitive to pain as the most highly strung organism, I yet feel that the worst of it is conquered, and the sting taken out of it altogether, by the thought that God is our loving and sleepless keeper, and that nothing can hurt us without his will." [1]

More excited expressions of this condition are abundant in religious literature. I could easily weary you with their monotony. Here is an account from Mrs. Jonathan Edwards: —

" Last night," Mrs. Edwards writes, " was the sweetest night I ever had in my life. I never before, for so long a time together, enjoyed so much of the light and rest and sweetness of heaven in my soul, but without the least agitation of body during the whole time. Part of the night I lay awake, sometimes asleep, and sometimes between sleeping and waking. But all night I continued in a constant, clear, and lively sense of the heavenly sweetness of Christ's excellent love, of his nearness to me, and of my dearness to him ; with an inexpressibly sweet calmness of soul in an entire rest in him. I seemed to myself to perceive a glow of divine love come down from the heart of Christ in heaven into my heart in a constant stream, like a stream or pencil of sweet light. At the same time my heart and soul all flowed out in love to Christ, so that there seemed to be a constant flowing and reflowing of heavenly love, and I appeared to myself to float or swim, in these bright, sweet beams, like the motes swimming in the beams of the sun, or the streams of his light which come in at the window. I think that what I felt each minute was worth more than all the outward comfort and pleasure which I had enjoyed in my whole life put

[1] The Mystery of Pain and Death, London, 1892, p. 258.

together. It was pleasure, without the least sting, or any interruption. It was a sweetness, which my soul was lost in; it
seemed to be all that my feeble frame could sustain. There was
but little difference, whether I was asleep or awake, but if there
was any difference, the sweetness was greatest while I was
asleep.[1] As I awoke early the next morning, it seemed to me
that I had entirely done with myself. I felt that the opinions
of the world concerning me were nothing, and that I had no
more to do with any outward interest of my own than with that
of a person whom I never saw. The glory of God seemed to
swallow up every wish and desire of my heart. . . . After retiring to rest and sleeping a little while, I awoke, and was led to
reflect on God's mercy to me, in giving me, for many years, a
willingness to die; and after that, in making me willing to
live, that I might do and suffer whatever he called me to here.
I also thought how God had graciously given me an entire
resignation to his will, with respect to the kind and manner of
death that I should die; having been made willing to die on
the rack, or at the stake, and if it were God's will, to die in
darkness. But now it occurred to me, I used to think of living
no longer than to the ordinary age of man. Upon this I was
led to ask myself, whether I was not willing to be kept out of
heaven even longer; and my whole heart seemed immediately
to reply: Yes, a thousand years, and a thousand in horror, if
it be most for the honor of God, the torment of my body being
so great, awful, and overwhelming that none could bear to live
in the country where the spectacle was seen, and the torment of
my mind being vastly greater. And it seemed to me that I
found a perfect willingness, quietness, and alacrity of soul in

[1] Compare Madame Guyon : " It was my practice to arise at midnight for
purposes of devotion. . . . It seemed to me that God came at the precise
time and woke me from sleep in order that I might enjoy him. When I
was out of health or greatly fatigued, he did not awake me, but at such
times I felt, even in my sleep, a singular possession of God. He loved me
so much that he seemed to pervade my being, at a time when I could be
only imperfectly conscious of his presence. My sleep is sometimes broken,
—a sort of half sleep ; but my soul seems to be awake enough to know
God, when it is hardly capable of knowing anything else." T. C. UPHAM :
The Life and Religious Experiences of Madame de la Mothe Guyon, New
York, 1877, vol. i. p. 260.

consenting that it should be so, if it were most for the glory of God, so that there was no hesitation, doubt, or darkness in my mind. The glory of God seemed to overcome me and swallow me up, and every conceivable suffering, and everything that was terrible to my nature, seemed to shrink to nothing before it. This resignation continued in its clearness and brightness the rest of the night, and all the next day, and the night following, and on Monday in the forenoon, without interruption or abatement." [1]

The annals of Catholic saintship abound in records as ecstatic or more ecstatic than this. " Often the assaults of the divine love," it is said of the Sister Séraphique de la Martinière, " reduced her almost to the point of death. She used tenderly to complain of this to God. ' I cannot support it,' she used to say. ' Bear gently with my weakness, or I shall expire under the violence of your love.' " [2]

Let me pass next to the Charity and Brotherly Love which are a usual fruit of saintliness, and have always been reckoned essential theological virtues, however limited may have been the kinds of service which the particular theology enjoined. Brotherly love would follow logically from the assurance of God's friendly presence, the notion of our brotherhood as men being an immediate inference from that of God's fatherhood of us all. When Christ utters the precepts : " Love your enemies, bless them that curse you, do good to them that hate you, and pray for them which despitefully use you, and persecute you," he gives for a reason : " That ye may be the children of your Father which is in heaven : for he maketh his sun to rise on the evil and on the good, and sendeth rain on the just and on the unjust." One might therefore

---

[1] I have considerably abridged the words of the original, which is given in EDWARDS's Narrative of the Revival in New England.

[2] BOUGAUD : Hist. de la Bienheureuse Marguerite Marie, 1894, p. 125.

be tempted to explain both the humility as to one's self
and the charity towards others which characterize spiritual excitement, as results of the all-leveling character of
theistic belief. But these affections are certainly not mere
derivatives of theism. We find them in Stoicism, in Hinduism, and in Buddhism in the highest possible degree.
They *harmonize* with paternal theism beautifully; but
they harmonize with all reflection whatever upon the dependence of mankind on general causes; and we must, I
think, consider them not subordinate but coordinate parts
of that great complex excitement in the study of which
we are engaged. Religious rapture, moral enthusiasm,
ontological wonder, cosmic emotion, are all unifying states
of mind, in which the sand and grit of the selfhood incline to disappear, and tenderness to rule. The best thing
is to describe the condition integrally as a characteristic
affection to which our nature is liable, a region in which
we find ourselves at home, a sea in which we swim; but
not to pretend to explain its parts by deriving them too
cleverly from one another. Like love or fear, the faith-
state is a natural psychic complex, and carries charity
with it by organic consequence. Jubilation is an expansive affection, and all expansive affections are self-forget-
ful and kindly so long as they endure.

We find this the case even when they are pathological
in origin. In his instructive work, la Tristesse et la Joie,[1]
M. Georges Dumas compares together the melancholy and
the joyous phase of circular insanity, and shows that,
while selfishness characterizes the one, the other is marked
by altruistic impulses. No human being so stingy and
useless as was Marie in her melancholy period! But the
moment the happy period begins, "sympathy and kindness become her characteristic sentiments. She displays

[1] Paris, 1900.

a universal goodwill, not only of intention, but in act.
. . . She becomes solicitous of the health of other patients, interested in getting them out, desirous to procure
wool to knit socks for some of them. Never since she
has been under my observation have I heard her in her
joyous period utter any but charitable opinions." [1] And
later, Dr. Dumas says of all such joyous conditions that
"unselfish sentiments and tender emotions are the only
affective states to be found in them. The subject's mind
is closed against envy, hatred, and vindictiveness, and
wholly transformed into benevolence, indulgence, and
mercy." [2]

There is thus an organic affinity between joyousness
and tenderness, and their companionship in the saintly
life need in no way occasion surprise. Along with the
happiness, this increase of tenderness is often noted in
narratives of conversion. " I began to work for others";
— "I had more tender feeling for my family and friends";
— "I spoke at once to a person with whom I had been
angry " ; — "I felt for every one, and loved my friends
better " ; — "I felt every one to be my friend " ; — these
are so many expressions from the records collected by
Professor Starbuck.[3]

"When," says Mrs. Edwards, continuing the narrative from
which I made quotation a moment ago, "I arose on the morning of the Sabbath, I felt a love to all mankind, wholly peculiar
in its strength and sweetness, far beyond all that I had ever
felt before. The power of that love seemed inexpressible. I
thought, if I were surrounded by enemies, who were venting
their malice and cruelty upon me, in tormenting me, it would
still be impossible that I should cherish any feelings towards
them but those of love, and pity, and ardent desires for their
happiness. I never before felt so far from a disposition to judge
and censure others, as I did that morning. I realized also, in

[1] Page 130.   [2] Page 167.   [3] Op. cit., p. 127.

an unusual and very lively manner, how great a part of Christianity lies in the performance of our social and relative duties to one another. The same joyful sense continued throughout the day — a sweet love to God and all mankind."

Whatever be the explanation of the charity, it may efface all usual human barriers.[1]

Here, for instance, is an example of Christian non-resistance from Richard Weaver's autobiography. Weaver was a collier, a semi-professional pugilist in his younger days, who became a much beloved evangelist. Fighting, after drinking, seems to have been the sin to which he originally felt his flesh most perversely inclined. After his first conversion he had a backsliding, which consisted in pounding a man who had insulted a girl. Feeling that, having once fallen, he might as well be hanged for a sheep as for a lamb, he got drunk and went and broke the jaw of another man who had lately challenged him to fight and taunted him with cowardice for refusing as a Christian man ; — I mention these incidents to show how genuine a change of heart is implied in the later conduct which he describes as follows : —

[1] The barrier between men and animals also. We read of Towianski, an eminent Polish patriot and mystic, that "one day one of his friends met him in the rain, caressing a big dog which was jumping upon him and covering him horribly with mud. On being asked why he permitted the animal thus to dirty his clothes, Towianski replied : ' This dog, whom I am now meeting for the first time, has shown a great fellow-feeling for me, and a great joy in my recognition and acceptance of his greetings. Were I to drive him off, I should wound his feelings and do him a moral injury. It would be an offense not only to him, but to all the spirits of the other world who are on the same level with him. The damage which he does to my coat is as nothing in comparison with the wrong which I should inflict upon him, in case I were to remain indifferent to the manifestations of his friendship. We ought,' he added, ' both to lighten the condition of animals, whenever we can, and at the same time to facilitate in ourselves that union of the world of all spirits, which the sacrifice of Christ has made possible.' " André Towianski, Traduction de l'Italien, Turin, 1897 (privately printed). I owe my knowledge of this book and of Towianski to my friend Professor W. Lutoslawski, author of ' Plato's Logic.'

"I went down the drift and found the boy crying because a fellow-workman was trying to take the wagon from him by force.   I said to him : —

" ' Tom, you must n't take that wagon.'

"He swore at me, and called me a Methodist devil.   I told him that God did not tell me to let him rob me.   He cursed again, and said he would push the wagon over me.

" ' Well,' I said, ' let us see whether the devil and thee are stronger than the Lord and me.'

"And the Lord and I proving stronger than the devil and he, he had to get out of the way, or the wagon would have gone over him.   So I gave the wagon to the boy.   Then said Tom : —

" ' I 've a good mind to smack thee on the face.'

" ' Well,' I said, ' if that will do thee any good, thou canst do it.'   So he struck me on the face.

"I turned the other cheek to him, and said, ' Strike again.'

"He struck again and again, till he had struck me five times. I turned my cheek for the sixth stroke ; but he turned away cursing.   I shouted after him : ' The Lord forgive thee, for I do, and the Lord save thee.'

"This was on a Saturday ; and when I went home from the coal-pit my wife saw my face was swollen, and asked what was the matter with it.   I said : ' I 've been fighting, and I 've given a man a good thrashing.'

"She burst out weeping, and said, ' O Richard, what made you fight ? '   Then I told her all about it ; and she thanked the Lord I had not struck back.

"But the Lord had struck, and his blows have more effect than man's.   Monday came.   The devil began to tempt me, saying : ' The other men will laugh at thee for allowing Tom to treat thee as he did on Saturday.'   I cried, ' Get thee behind me, Satan ; ' — and went on my way to the coal-pit.

"Tom was the first man I saw.   I said ' Good-morning,' but got no reply.

"He went down first.   When I got down, I was surprised to see him sitting on the wagon-road waiting for me.   When I came to him he burst into tears and said : ' Richard, will you forgive me for striking you ? '

" ' I have forgiven thee,' said I ; ' ask God to forgive thee. The Lord bless thee.' I gave him my hand, and we went each to his work." [1]

' Love your enemies ! ' Mark you, not simply those who happen not to be your friends, but your *enemies*, your positive and active enemies. Either this is a mere Oriental hyperbole, a bit of verbal extravagance, meaning only that we should, as far as we can, abate our animosities, or else it is sincere and literal. Outside of certain cases of intimate individual relation, it seldom has been taken literally. Yet it makes one ask the question : Can there in general be a level of emotion so unifying, so obliterative of differences between man and man, that even enmity may come to be an irrelevant circumstance and fail to inhibit the friendlier interests aroused ? If positive well-wishing could attain so supreme a degree of excitement, those who were swayed by it might well seem superhuman beings. Their life would be morally discrete from the life of other men, and there is no saying, in the absence of positive experience of an authentic kind, — for there are few active examples in our scriptures, and the Buddhistic examples are legendary,[2] — what the effects might be : they might conceivably transform the world.

Psychologically and in principle, the precept ' Love your enemies ' is not self-contradictory. It is merely the extreme limit of a kind of magnanimity with which, in the shape of pitying tolerance of our oppressors, we are fairly familiar. Yet if radically followed, it would involve such a breach with our instinctive springs of action as a whole, and with the present world's arrangements,

[1] J. PATTERSON's Life of Richard Weaver, pp. 66–68, abridged.

[2] As where the future Buddha, incarnated as a hare, jumps into the fire to cook himself for a meal for a beggar — having previously shaken himself three times, so that none of the insects in his fur should perish with him.

that a critical point would practically be passed, and we should be born into another kingdom of being. Religious emotion makes us feel that other kingdom to be close at hand, within our reach.

The inhibition of instinctive repugnance is proved not only by the showing of love to enemies, but by the showing of it to any one who is personally loathsome. In the annals of saintliness we find a curious mixture of motives impelling in this direction. Asceticism plays its part; and along with charity pure and simple, we find humility or the desire to disclaim distinction and to grovel on the common level before God. Certainly all three principles were at work when Francis of Assisi and Ignatius Loyola exchanged their garments with those of filthy beggars. All three are at work when religious persons consecrate their lives to the care of leprosy or other peculiarly unpleasant diseases. The nursing of the sick is a function to which the religious seem strongly drawn, even apart from the fact that church traditions set that way. But in the annals of this sort of charity we find fantastic excesses of devotion recorded which are only explicable by the frenzy of self-immolation simultaneously aroused. Francis of Assisi kisses his lepers; Margaret Mary Alacoque, Francis Xavier, St. John of God, and others are said to have cleansed the sores and ulcers of their patients with their respective tongues; and the lives of such saints as Elizabeth of Hungary and Madame de Chantal are full of a sort of reveling in hospital purulence, disagreeable to read of, and which makes us admire and shudder at the same time.

So much for the human love aroused by the faith-state. Let me next speak of the Equanimity, Resignation, Fortitude, and Patience which it brings.

'A paradise of inward tranquillity' seems to be faith's usual result; and it is easy, even without being religious one's self, to understand this. A moment back, in treating of the sense of God's presence, I spoke of the unaccountable feeling of safety which one may then have. And, indeed, how can it possibly fail to steady the nerves, to cool the fever, and appease the fret, if one be sensibly conscious that, no matter what one's difficulties for the moment may appear to be, one's life as a whole is in the keeping of a power whom one can absolutely trust? In deeply religious men the abandonment of self to this power is passionate. Whoever not only says, but *feels*, 'God's will be done,' is mailed against every weakness; and the whole historic array of martyrs, missionaries, and religious reformers is there to prove the tranquil-mindedness, under naturally agitating or distressing circumstances, which self-surrender brings.

The temper of the tranquil-mindedness differs, of course, according as the person is of a constitutionally sombre or of a constitutionally cheerful cast of mind. In the sombre it partakes more of resignation and submission; in the cheerful it is a joyous consent. As an example of the former temper, I quote part of a letter from Professor Lagneau, a venerated teacher of philosophy who lately died, a great invalid, at Paris: —

"My life, for the success of which you send good wishes, will be what it is able to be. I ask nothing from it, I expect nothing from it. For long years now I exist, think, and act, and am worth what I am worth, only through the despair which is my sole strength and my sole foundation. May it preserve for me, even in these last trials to which I am coming, the courage to do without the desire of deliverance. I ask nothing more from the Source whence all strength cometh, and if that is granted, your wishes will have been accomplished." [1]

[1] Bulletin de l'Union pour l'Action Morale, September, 1894.

There is something pathetic and fatalistic about this, but the power of such a tone as a protection against outward shocks is manifest. Pascal is another Frenchman of pessimistic natural temperament. He expresses still more amply the temper of self-surrendering submissiveness : —

"Deliver me, Lord," he writes in his prayers, "from the sadness at my proper suffering which self-love might give, but put into me a sadness like your own. Let my sufferings appease your choler. Make them an occasion for my conversion and salvation. I ask you neither for health nor for sickness, for life nor for death ; but that you may dispose of my health and my sickness, my life and my death, for your glory, for my salvation, and for the use of the Church and of your saints, of whom I would by your grace be one. You alone know what is expedient for me ; you are the sovereign master ; do with me according to your will. Give to me, or take away from me, only conform my will to yours. I know but one thing, Lord, that it is good to follow you, and bad to offend you. Apart from that, I know not what is good or bad in anything. I know not which is most profitable to me, health or sickness, wealth or poverty, nor anything else in the world. That discernment is beyond the power of men or angels, and is hidden among the secrets of your Providence, which I adore, but do not seek to fathom." [1]

When we reach more optimistic temperaments, the resignation grows less passive. Examples are sown so broadcast throughout history that I might well pass on without citation. As it is, I snatch at the first that occurs to my mind. Madame Guyon, a frail creature physically, was yet of a happy native disposition. She went through many perils with admirable serenity of soul. After being sent to prison for heresy, —

"Some of my friends," she writes, "wept bitterly at the hearing of it, but such was my state of acquiescence and resig-

---

[1] B. Pascal : Prières pour les Maladies, §§ xiii., xiv., abridged.

nation that it failed to draw any tears from me. . . . There appeared to be in me then, as I find it to be in me now, such an entire loss of what regards myself, that any of my own interests gave me little pain or pleasure ; ever wanting to will or wish for myself only the very thing which God does." In another place she writes : " We all of us came near perishing in a river which we found it necessary to pass. The carriage sank in the quicksand. Others who were with us threw themselves out in excessive fright. But I found my thoughts so much taken up with God that I had no distinct sense of danger. It is true that the thought of being drowned passed across my mind, but it cost no other sensation or reflection in me than this — that I felt quite contented and willing it were so, if it were my heavenly Father's choice." Sailing from Nice to Genoa, a storm keeps her eleven days at sea. " As the irritated waves dashed round us," she writes, " I could not help experiencing a certain degree of satisfaction in my mind. I pleased myself with thinking that those mutinous billows, under the command of Him who does all things rightly, might probably furnish me with a watery grave. Perhaps I carried the point too far, in the pleasure which I took in thus seeing myself beaten and bandied by the swelling waters. Those who were with me took notice of my intrepidity." [1]

The contempt of danger which religious enthusiasm produces may be even more buoyant still. I take an example from that charming recent autobiography, " With Christ at Sea," by Frank Bullen. A couple of days after he went through the conversion on shipboard of which he there gives an account, —

" It was blowing stiffly," he writes, " and we were carrying a press of canvas to get north out of the bad weather. Shortly after four bells we hauled down the flying-jib, and I sprang out astride the boom to furl it. I was sitting astride the boom when suddenly it gave way with me. The sail slipped through my fingers, and I fell backwards, hanging head downwards

---

[1] From THOMAS C. UPHAM's Life and Religious Opinions and Experiences of Madame de la Mothe Guyon, New York, 1877, ii. 48, i. 141, 413, abridged.

over the seething tumult of shining foam under the ship's bows, suspended by one foot.   But I felt only high exultation in my certainty of eternal life.   Although death was divided from me by a hair's breadth, and I was acutely conscious of the fact, it gave me no sensation but joy.   I suppose I could have hung there no longer than five seconds, but in that time I lived a whole age of delight.   But my body asserted itself, and with a desperate gymnastic effort I regained the boom.   How I furled the sail I don't know, but I sang at the utmost pitch of my voice praises to God that went pealing out over the dark waste of waters." [1]

The annals of martyrdom are of course the signal field of triumph for religious imperturbability.   Let me cite as an example the statement of a humble sufferer, persecuted as a Huguenot under Louis XIV. : —

"They shut all the doors," Blanche Gamond writes, " and I saw six women, each with a bunch of willow rods as thick as the hand could hold, and a yard long.   He gave me the order, 'Undress yourself,' which I did.   He said, 'You are leaving on your shift; you must take it off.'   They had so little patience that they took it off themselves, and I was naked from the waist up.   They brought a cord with which they tied me to a beam in the kitchen.   They drew the cord tight with all their strength and asked me, 'Does it hurt you?' and then they discharged their fury upon me, exclaiming as they struck me, 'Pray now to your God.'   It was the Roulette woman who held this language.   But at this moment I received the greatest consolation that I can ever receive in my life, since I had the honor of being whipped for the name of Christ, and in addition of being crowned with his mercy and his consolations.   Why can I not write down the inconceivable influences, consolations, and peace which I felt interiorly?   To understand them one must have passed by the same trial; they were so great that I was ravished, for there where afflictions abound grace is given superabundantly.   In vain the women cried, 'We must double our blows; she does not feel them, for she neither speaks nor

[1] Op. cit., London, 1901, p. 130.

cries.' And how should I have cried, since I was swooning with happiness within?"[1]

The transition from tenseness, self-responsibility, and worry, to equanimity, receptivity, and peace, is the most wonderful of all those shiftings of inner equilibrium, those changes of the personal centre of energy, which I have analyzed so often; and the chief wonder of it is that it so often comes about, not by doing, but by simply relaxing and throwing the burden down. This abandonment of self-responsibility seems to be the fundamental act in specifically religious, as distinguished from moral practice. It antedates theologies and is independent of philosophies. Mind-cure, theosophy, stoicism, ordinary neurological hygiene, insist on it as emphatically as Christianity does, and it is capable of entering into closest marriage with every speculative creed.[2] Christians who have it strongly live in what is called ' recollection,' and are never anxious about the future, nor worry over the outcome of the day. Of Saint Catharine of Genoa it is said that " she took cognizance of things, only as they were presented to her in succession, *moment by moment*." To her holy soul, " the divine moment was the present moment, . . . and when the present moment was estimated in itself and in its relations, and when the duty that was involved in it was accomplished, it was permitted to pass away as if it had never been, and to give way to the facts and duties of the moment which came after."[3]

[1] CLAPARÈDE et GOTY : Deux Héroines de la Foi, Paris, 1880, p. 112.

[2] Compare these three different statements of it : A. P. CALL : As a Matter of Course, Boston, 1894 ; H. W. DRESSER : Living by the Spirit, New York and London, 1900 ; H. W. SMITH : The Christian's Secret of a Happy Life, published by the Willard Tract Repository, and now in thousands of hands.

[3] T. C. UPHAM: Life of Madame Catharine Adorna, 3d ed., New York. 1864, pp. 158, 172–174.

Hinduism, mind-cure, and theosophy all lay great emphasis upon this concentration of the consciousness upon the moment at hand.

The next religious symptom which I will note is what I have called Purity of Life. The saintly person becomes exceedingly sensitive to inner inconsistency or discord, and mixture and confusion grow intolerable. All the mind's objects and occupations must be ordered with reference to the special spiritual excitement which is now its keynote. Whatever is unspiritual taints the pure water of the soul and is repugnant. Mixed with this exaltation of the moral sensibilities there is also an ardor of sacrifice, for the beloved deity's sake, of everything unworthy of him. Sometimes the spiritual ardor is so sovereign that purity is achieved at a stroke — we have seen examples. Usually it is a more gradual conquest. Billy Bray's account of his abandonment of tobacco is a good example of the latter form of achievement.

"I had been a smoker as well as a drunkard, and I used to love my tobacco as much as I loved my meat, and I would rather go down into the mine without my dinner than without my pipe. In the days of old, the Lord spoke by the mouths of his servants, the prophets; now he speaks to us by the spirit of his Son. I had not only the feeling part of religion, but I could hear the small, still voice within speaking to me. When I took the pipe to smoke, it would be applied within, 'It is an idol, a lust; worship the Lord with clean lips.' So, I felt it was not right to smoke. The Lord also sent a woman to convince me. I was one day in a house, and I took out my pipe to light it at the fire, and Mary Hawke — for that was the woman's name — said, 'Do you not feel it is wrong to smoke?' I said that I felt something inside telling me that it was an idol, a lust, and she said that was the Lord. Then I said, 'Now, I must give it up, for the Lord is telling me of it inside, and the woman outside, so the tobacco must go, love it as I may.' There and then I took the tobacco out of my pocket, and threw it into the fire, and put the pipe under my foot, 'ashes to ashes, dust to dust.' And I have not smoked since. I found it hard to break off old habits, but I cried to the Lord for help, and he gave me strength, for he has said, 'Call upon me in the day of trouble, and I will deliver thee.' The day after I gave up smoking I had the toothache so bad that I did not know what to do. I thought this was owing to giving up the pipe, but I said I would never smoke again, if I lost every tooth in my head. I said, 'Lord, thou hast told us My yoke is easy and my burden is light,' and when I said that, all the pain left me. Sometimes the thought of the pipe would come back to me very strong ; but the Lord strengthened me against the habit, and, bless his name, I have not smoked since."

Bray's biographer writes that after he had given up smoking, he thought that he would chew a little, but he conquered this dirty habit, too. "On one occasion," Bray said, "when at a prayer-meeting at Hicks Mill, I heard the Lord say to me, 'Worship me with clean lips.' So, when we got up from our knees, I took the quid out of my mouth and 'whipped 'en' [threw it] under the form. But, when we got on our knees again, I put another quid into my mouth. Then the Lord said to me again, 'Worship me with clean lips.' So I took the quid out of my mouth, and whipped 'en under the form again, and said, 'Yes, Lord, I will.' From that time I gave up chewing as well as smoking, and have been a free man."

The ascetic forms which the impulse for veracity and purity of life may take are often pathetic enough. The early Quakers, for example, had hard battles to wage against the worldliness and insincerity of the ecclesiastical Christianity of their time. Yet the battle that cost them most wounds was probably that which they fought in defense of their own right to social veracity and sincerity in their thee-ing and thou-ing, in not doffing the hat or giving titles of respect. It was laid on George Fox that these conventional customs were a lie and a sham, and the whole body of his followers thereupon renounced them, as a sacrifice to truth, and so that their acts and the spirit they professed might be more in accord.

" When the Lord sent me into the world," says Fox in his Journal, " he forbade me to put off my hat to any, high or low: and I was required to 'thee' and 'thou' all men and women, without any respect to rich or poor, great or small.   And as I traveled up and down, I was not to bid people Good-morning, or Good-evening, neither might I bow or scrape with my leg to any one.   This made the sects and professions rage.   Oh! the rage that was in the priests, magistrates, professors, and people of all sorts: and especially in priests and professors : for though ' thou ' to a single person was according to their accidence and grammar rules, and according to the Bible, yet they could not bear to hear it : and because I could not put off my hat to them, it set them all into a rage. . . . Oh! the scorn, heat, and fury that arose!   Oh! the blows, punchings, beatings, and imprison-ments that we underwent for not putting off our hats to men ! Some had their hats violently plucked off and thrown away, so that they quite lost them.   The bad language and evil usage we received on this account is hard to be expressed, besides the danger we were sometimes in of losing our lives for this mat-ter, and that by the great professors of Christianity, who thereby discovered they were not true believers.   And though it was but a small thing in the eye of man, yet a wonderful confusion it trought among all professors and priests : but, blessed be the Lord, many came to see the vanity of that custom of put-ting off hats to men, and felt the weight of Truth's testimony against it."

In the autobiography of Thomas Elwood, an early Quaker, who at one time was secretary to John Milton, we find an exquisitely quaint and candid account of the trials he underwent both at home and abroad, in following Fox's canons of sincerity. The anecdotes are too lengthy for citation ; but Elwood sets down his manner of feeling about these things in a shorter passage, which I will quote as a characteristic utterance of spiritual sensibility : —

"By this divine light, then," says Elwood, "I saw that though I had not the evil of the common uncleanliness, debauchery, profaneness, and pollutions of the world to put away, because I had, through the great goodness of God and a civil education, been preserved out of those grosser evils, yet I had many other evils to put away and to cease from ; some of which were not by the world, which lies in wickedness (1 John v. 19), accounted evils, but by the light of Christ were made manifest to me to be evils, and as such condemned in me.

"As particularly those fruits and effects of pride that discover themselves in the vanity and superfluity of apparel ; which I took too much delight in. This evil of my doings I was required to put away and cease from ; and judgment lay upon me till I did so.

"I took off from my apparel those unnecessary trimmings of lace, ribbons, and useless buttons, which had no real service, but were set on only for that which was by mistake called ornament ; and I ceased to wear rings.

"Again, the giving of flattering titles to men between whom and me there was not any relation to which such titles could be pretended to belong. This was an evil I had been much addicted to, and was accounted a ready artist in ; therefore this evil also was I required to put away and cease from. So that thenceforward I durst not say, Sir, Master, My Lord, Madam (or My Dame) ; or say Your Servant to any one to whom I did not stand in the real relation of a servant, which I had never done to any.

"Again, respect of persons, in uncovering the head and bowing the knee or body in salutation, was a practice I had been much in the use of ; and this, being one of the vain customs of the world, introduced by the spirit of the world, instead of the true honor which this is a false representation of, and used in deceit as a token of respect by persons one to another, who bear no real respect one to another ; and besides this, being a

type and a proper emblem of that divine honor which all ought
to pay to Almighty God, and which all of all sorts, who take
upon them the Christian name, appear in when they offer their
prayers to him, and therefore should not be given to men; — I
found this to be one of those evils which I had been too long
doing; therefore I was now required to put it away and cease
from it.

"Again, the corrupt and unsound form of speaking in the
plural number to a single person, *you* to one, instead of *thou*,
contrary to the pure, plain, and single language of truth, *thou*
to one, and *you* to more than one, which had always been used
by God to men, and men to God, as well as one to another,
from the oldest record of time till corrupt men, for corrupt
ends, in later and corrupt times, to flatter, fawn, and work
upon the corrupt nature in men, brought in that false and
senseless way of speaking *you* to one, which has since corrupted
the modern languages, and hath greatly debased the spirits and
depraved the manners of men; — this evil custom I had been
as forward in as others, and this I was now called out of and
required to cease from.

"These and many more evil customs which had sprung up
in the night of darkness and general apostasy from the truth
and true religion were now, by the inshining of this pure ray
of divine light in my conscience, gradually discovered to me to
be what I' ought to cease from, shun, and stand a witness
against." [1]

These early Quakers were Puritans indeed. The slightest inconsistency between profession and deed jarred some
of them to active protest. John Woolman writes in his
diary : —

"In these journeys I have been where much cloth hath been
dyed; and have at sundry times walked over ground where
much of their dyestuffs has drained away. This hath produced
a longing in my mind that people might come into cleanness
of spirit, cleanness of person, and cleanness about their houses

[1] The History of THOMAS ELWOOD, written by Himself, London, 1885,
pp. 32-34.

and garments. Dyes being invented partly to please the eye, and partly to hide dirt, I have felt in this weak state, when traveling in dirtiness, and affected with unwholesome scents, a strong desire that the nature of dyeing cloth to hide dirt may be more fully considered.

" Washing our garments to keep them sweet is cleanly, but it is the opposite to real cleanliness to hide dirt in them. Through giving way to hiding dirt in our garments a spirit which would conceal that which is disagreeable is strengthened. Real cleanliness becometh a holy people ; but hiding that which is not clean by coloring our garments seems contrary to the sweetness of sincerity. Through some sorts of dyes cloth is rendered less useful. And if the value of dyestuffs, and expense of dyeing, and the damage done to cloth, were all added together, and that cost applied to keeping all sweet and clean, how much more would real cleanliness prevail.

" Thinking often on these things, the use of hats and garments dyed with a dye hurtful to them, and wearing more clothes in summer than are useful, grew more uneasy to me ; believing them to be customs which have not their foundation in pure wisdom. The apprehension of being singular from my beloved friends was a strait upon me ; and thus I continued in the use of some things, contrary to my judgment, about nine months. Then I thought of getting a hat the natural color of the fur, but the apprehension of being looked upon as one affecting singularity felt uneasy to me. On this account I was under close exercise of mind in the time of our general spring meeting in 1762, greatly desiring to be rightly directed ; when, being deeply bowed in spirit before the Lord, I was made willing to submit to what I apprehended was required of me ; and when I returned home, got a hat of the natural color of the fur.

" In attending meetings, this singularity was a trial to me, and more especially at this time, as white hats were used by some who were fond of following the changeable modes of dress, and as some friends, who knew not from what motives I wore it, grew shy of me, I felt my way for a time shut up in the exercise of the ministry. Some friends were apprehensive that my wearing such a hat savored of an affected singularity :

those who spoke with me in a friendly way, I generally informed in a few words, that I believed my wearing it was not in my own will."

When the craving for moral consistency and purity is developed to this degree, the subject may well find the outer world too full of shocks to dwell in, and can unify his life and keep his soul unspotted only by withdrawing from it. That law which impels the artist to achieve harmony in his composition by simply dropping out whatever jars, or suggests a discord, rules also in the spiritual life. To omit, says Stevenson, is the one art in literature: "If I knew how to omit, I should ask no other knowledge." And life, when full of disorder and slackness and vague superfluity, can no more have what we call character than literature can have it under similar conditions. So monasteries and communities of sympathetic devotees open their doors, and in their changeless order, characterized by omissions quite as much as constituted of actions, the holy-minded person finds that inner smoothness and cleanness which it is torture to him to feel violated at every turn by the discordancy and brutality of secular existence.

That the scrupulosity of purity may be carried to a fantastic extreme must be admitted. In this it resembles Asceticism, to which further symptom of saintliness we had better turn next. The adjective 'ascetic' is applied to conduct originating on diverse psychological levels, which I might as well begin by distinguishing from one another.

1. Asceticism may be a mere expression of organic hardihood, disgusted with too much ease.

2. Temperance in meat and drink, simplicity of ap-

parel, chastity, and non-pampering of the body generally, may be fruits of the love of purity, shocked by whatever savors of the sensual.

3. They may also be fruits of love, that is, they may appeal to the subject in the light of sacrifices which he is happy in making to the Deity whom he acknowledges.

4. Again, ascetic mortifications and torments may be due to pessimistic feelings about the self, combined with theological beliefs concerning expiation. The devotee may feel that he is buying himself free, or escaping worse sufferings hereafter, by doing penance now.

5. In psychopathic persons, mortifications may be entered on irrationally, by a sort of obsession or fixed idea which comes as a challenge and must be worked off, because only thus does the subject get his interior consciousness feeling right again.

6. Finally, ascetic exercises may in rarer instances be prompted by genuine perversions of the bodily sensibility, in consequence of which normally pain-giving stimuli are actually felt as pleasures.

I will try to give an instance under each of these heads in turn; but it is not easy to get them pure, for in cases pronounced enough to be immediately classed as ascetic, several of the assigned motives usually work together. Moreover, before citing any examples at all, I must invite you to some general psychological considerations which apply to all of them alike.

A strange moral transformation has within the past century swept over our Western world. We no longer think that we are called on to face physical pain with equanimity. It is not expected of a man that he should either endure it or inflict much of it, and to listen to the recital of cases of it makes our flesh creep morally as well as physically. The way in which our ancestors looked upon pain as an eternal ingredient of the world's order, and both caused and suffered it as a matter-of-course portion of their day's work, fills us with amazement. We wonder that any human beings could have been so callous. The result of this historic alteration is that even in the Mother Church herself, where ascetic discipline has such a fixed traditional prestige as a factor of merit, it has largely come into desuetude, if not discredit. A believer who flagellates or 'macerates' himself to-day arouses more wonder and fear than emulation. Many Catholic writers who admit that the times have changed in this respect do so resignedly; and even add that perhaps it is as well not to waste feelings in regretting the matter, for to return to the heroic corporeal discipline of ancient days might be an extravagance.

Where to seek the easy and the pleasant seems instinctive — and instinctive it appears to be in man; any deliberate tendency to pursue the hard and painful as such and for their own sakes might well strike one as purely abnormal. Nevertheless, in moderate degrees it is natural and even usual to human nature to court the arduous. It is only the extreme manifestations of the tendency that can be regarded as a paradox.

The psychological reasons for this lie near the surface. When we drop abstractions and take what we call our will in the act, we see that it is a very complex function. It involves both stimulations and inhibitions; it follows generalized habits; it is escorted by reflective criticisms; and it leaves a good or a bad taste of itself behind, according to the manner of the performance. The result is that, quite apart from the immediate pleasure which any sensible experience may give us, our own general moral attitude in procuring or undergoing the experience brings with it a secondary satisfaction or distaste. Some

men and women, indeed, there are who can live on smiles
and the word 'yes' forever.   But for others (indeed for
most), this is too tepid and relaxed a moral climate.   Passive happiness is slack and insipid, and soon grows mawk-
ish and intolerable.   Some austerity and wintry negativity,
some roughness, danger, stringency, and effort, some
'no! no!' must be mixed in, to produce the sense of an
existence with character and texture and power.   The
range of individual differences in this respect is enormous; but whatever the mixture of yeses and noes may
be, the person is infallibly aware when he has struck it
in the right proportion *for him*.   This, he feels, is my
proper vocation, this is the *optimum*, the law, the life for
me to live.   Here I find the degree of equilibrium, safety,
calm, and leisure which I need, or here I find the challenge, passion, fight, and hardship without which my
soul's energy expires.

Every individual soul, in short, like every individual
machine or organism, has its own best conditions of efficiency.   A given machine will run best under a certain
steam-pressure, a certain amperage; an organism under a
certain diet, weight, or exercise.   You seem to do best,
I heard a doctor say to a patient, at about 140 milli-
meters of arterial tension.   And it is just so with our
sundry souls: some are happiest in calm weather; some
need the sense of tension, of strong volition, to make
them feel alive and well.   For these latter souls, whatever
is gained from day to day must be paid for by sacrifice
and inhibition, or else it comes too cheap and has no zest.

Now when characters of this latter sort become religious, they are apt to turn the edge of their need of effort
and negativity against their natural self; and the ascetic
life gets evolved as a consequence.

When Professor Tyndall in one of his lectures tells us

that Thomas Carlyle put him into his bath-tub every morning of a freezing Berlin winter, he proclaimed one of the lowest grades of asceticism.   Even without Carlyle, most of us find it necessary to our soul's health to start the day with a rather cool immersion.   A little farther along the scale we get such statements as this, from one of my correspondents, an agnostic : —

"Often at night in my warm bed I would feel ashamed to depend so on the warmth, and whenever the thought would come over me I would have to get up, no matter what time of night it was, and stand for a minute in the cold, just so as to prove my manhood."

Such cases as these belong simply to our head 1.   In the next case we probably have a mixture of heads 2 and 3 — the asceticism becomes far more systematic and pronounced.   The writer is a Protestant, whose sense of moral energy could doubtless be gratified on no lower terms, and I take his case from Starbuck's manuscript collection.

"I practiced fasting and mortification of the flesh.   I secretly made burlap shirts, and put the burrs next the skin, and wore pebbles in my shoes.   I would spend nights flat on my back on the floor without any covering."

The Roman Church has organized and codified all this sort of thing, and given it a market-value in the shape of ' merit.'   But we see the cultivation of hardship cropping out under every sky and in every faith, as a spontaneous need of character.   Thus we read of Channing, when first settled as a Unitarian minister, that —

"He was now more simple than ever, and seemed to have become incapable of any form of self-indulgence.   He took the smallest room in the house for his study, though he might easily have commanded one more light, airy, and in every way more suitable ; and chose for his sleeping chamber an attic which he shared with a younger brother. The furniture of the latter might have answered for the cell of an anchorite, and consisted of a hard mattress on a cot-bedstead, plain wooden chairs and table, with matting on the floor. It was without fire, and to cold he was throughout life extremely sensitive ; but he never complained or appeared in any way to be conscious of inconvenience. ' I recollect,' says his brother, ' after one most severe night, that in the morning he sportively thus alluded to his suffering : " If my bed were my country, I should be somewhat like Bonaparte : I have no control except over the part which I occupy ; the instant I move, frost takes possession." ' In sickness only would he change for the time his apartment and accept a few comforts. The dress too that he habitually adopted was of most inferior quality ; and garments were constantly worn which the world would call mean, though an almost feminine neatness preserved him from the least appearance of neglect." [1]

Channing's asceticism, such as it was, was evidently a compound of hardihood and love of purity. The democracy which is an offshoot of the enthusiasm of humanity, and of which I will speak later under the head of the cult of poverty, doubtless bore also a share. Certainly there was no pessimistic element in his case. In the next case we have a strongly pessimistic element, so that it belongs under head 4. John Cennick was Methodism's first lay preacher. In 1735 he was convicted of sin, while walking in Cheapside, —

" And at once left off song-singing, card-playing, and attending theatres. Sometimes he wished to go to a popish monastery, to spend his life in devout retirement. At other times he longed to live in a cave, sleeping on fallen leaves, and feeding on forest fruits. He fasted long and often, and prayed nine times a day. . . . Fancying dry bread too great an indulgence for so great a sinner as himself, he began to feed on potatoes, acorns, crabs, and grass ; and often wished that he could live on roots

[1] Memoirs of W. E. Channing, Boston, 1840, i. 196.

and herbs. At length, in 1737, he found peace with God, and went on his way rejoicing." [1]

In this poor man we have morbid melancholy and fear, and the sacrifices made are to purge out sin, and to buy safety. The hopelessness of Christian theology in respect of the flesh and the natural man generally has, in systematizing fear, made of it one tremendous incentive to self-mortification. It would be quite unfair, however, in spite of the fact that this incentive has often been worked in a mercenary way for hortatory purposes, to call it a mercenary incentive. The impulse to expiate and do penance is, in its first intention, far too immediate and spontaneous an expression of self-despair and anxiety to be obnoxious to any such reproach. In the form of loving sacrifice, of spending all we have to show our devotion, ascetic discipline of the severest sort may be the fruit of highly optimistic religious feeling.

M. Vianney, the curé of Ars, was a French country priest, whose holiness was exemplary. We read in his life the following account of his inner need of sacrifice : —

" ' On this path,' M. Vianney said, ' it is only the first step that costs. There is in mortification a balm and a savor without which one cannot live when once one has made their acquaintance. There is but one way in which to give one's self to God, — that is, to give one's self entirely, and to keep nothing for one's self. The little that one keeps is only good to trouble one and make one suffer.' Accordingly he imposed it on himself that he should never smell a flower, never drink when parched with thirst, never drive away a fly, never show disgust before a repugnant object, never complain of anything that had to do with his personal comfort, never sit down, never lean upon his elbows when he was kneeling. The Curé of Ars was very sensitive to cold, but he would never take means to pro-

[1] L. TYERMAN : The Life and Times of the Rev. John Wesley, i. 274.

tect himself against it. During a very severe winter, one of his missionaries contrived a false floor to his confessional and placed a metal case of hot water beneath. The trick succeeded, and the Saint was deceived: ' God is very good,' he said with emotion. ' This year, through all the cold, my feet have always been warm.' " [1]

In this case the spontaneous impulse to make sacrifices for the pure love of God was probably the uppermost conscious motive. We may class it, then, under our head 3. Some authors think that the impulse to sacrifice is the main religious phenomenon. It is a prominent, a universal phenomenon certainly, and lies deeper than any special creed. Here, for instance, is what seems to be a spontaneous example of it, simply expressing what seemed right at the time between the individual and his Maker. Cotton Mather, the New England Puritan divine, is generally reputed a rather grotesque pedant; yet what is more touchingly simple than his relation of what happened when his wife came to die?

" When I saw to what a point of resignation I was now called of the Lord," he says, " I resolved, with his help, therein to glorify him. So, two hours before my lovely consort expired, I kneeled by her bedside, and I took into my two hands a dear hand, the dearest in the world. With her thus in my hands, I solemnly and sincerely gave her up unto the Lord: and in token of my real *Resignation*, I gently put her out of my hands, and laid away a most lovely hand, resolving that I would never touch it more. This was the hardest, and perhaps the bravest action that ever I did. She . . . told me that she signed and sealed my act of resignation. And though before that she called for me continually, she after this never asked for me any more." [2]

[1] A. MOUNIN : Le Curé d'Ars, Vie de M. J. B. M. Vianney, 1864, p. 545, abridged.
[2] B. WENDELL : Cotton Mather, New York, no date, p. 198.

Father Vianney's asceticism taken in its totality was simply the result of a permanent flood of high spiritual enthusiasm, longing to make proof of itself. The Roman Church has, in its incomparable fashion, collected all the motives towards asceticism together, and so codified them that any one wishing to pursue Christian perfection may find a practical system mapped out for him in any one of a number of ready-made manuals.[1]   The dominant Church notion of perfection is of course the negative one of avoidance of sin. Sin proceeds from concupiscence, and concupiscence from our carnal passions and temptations, chief of which are pride, sensuality in all its forms, and the loves of worldly excitement and possession.   All these sources of sin must be resisted; and discipline and austerities are a most efficacious mode of meeting them. Hence there are always in these books chapters on self-mortification.   But whenever a procedure is codified, the more delicate spirit of it evaporates, and if we wish the undiluted ascetic spirit, — the passion of self-contempt wreaking itself on the poor flesh, the divine irrationality of devotion making a sacrificial gift of all it has (its sensibilities, namely) to the object of its adoration, — we must go to autobiographies, or other individual documents.

Saint John of the Cross, a Spanish mystic who flourished — or rather who existed, for there was little that suggested flourishing about him — in the sixteenth century, will supply a passage suitable for our purpose.

" First of all, carefully excite in yourself an habitual affectionate will in all things to imitate Jesus Christ. If anything agreeable offers itself to your senses, yet does not at the same

---

[1] That of the earlier Jesuit, RODRIGUEZ, which has been translated into all languages, is one of the best known. A convenient modern manual, very well put together, is L'Ascétique Chrétienne, by M. J. RIBET, Paris, Poussielgue, nouvelle édition, 1898.

time tend purely to the honor and glory of God, renounce it and separate yourself from it for the love of Christ, who all his life long had no other taste or wish than to do the will of his Father whom he called his meat and nourishment. For example, you take satisfaction in *hearing* of things in which the glory of God bears no part. Deny yourself this satisfaction, mortify your wish to listen. You take pleasure in *seeing* objects which do not raise your mind to God: refuse yourself this pleasure, and turn away your eyes. The same with conversations and all other things. Act similarly, so far as you are able, with all the operations of the senses, striving to make yourself free from their yokes.

" The radical remedy lies in the mortification of the four great natural passions, joy, hope, fear, and grief. You must seek to deprive these of every satisfaction and leave them as it were in darkness and the void. Let your soul therefore turn always :

" Not to what is most easy, but to what is hardest ;

" Not to what tastes best, but to what is most distasteful ;

" Not to what most pleases, but to what disgusts ;

" Not to matter of consolation, but to matter for desolation rather ;

" Not to rest, but to labor ;

" Not to desire the more, but the less ;

" Not to aspire to what is highest and most precious, but to what is lowest and most contemptible ;

" Not to will anything, but to will nothing ;

" Not to seek the best in everything, but to seek the worst, so that you may enter for the love of Christ into a complete destitution, a perfect poverty of spirit, and an absolute renunciation of everything in this world.

" Embrace these practices with all the energy of your soul and you will find in a short time great delights and unspeakable consolations.

" Despise yourself, and wish that others should despise you.

" Speak to your own disadvantage, and desire others to do the same ;

" Conceive a low opinion of yourself, and find it good when others hold the same ;

" To enjoy the taste of all things, have no taste for anything.

" To know all things, learn to know nothing.

" To possess all things, resolve to possess nothing.

" To be all things, be willing to be nothing.

" To get to where you have no taste for anything, go through whatever experiences you have no taste for.

" To learn to know nothing, go whither you are ignorant.

" To reach what you possess not, go whithersoever you own nothing.

" To be what you are not, experience what you are not."

These later verses play with that vertigo of self-contradiction which is so dear to mysticism. Those that come next are completely mystical, for in them Saint John passes from God to the more metaphysical notion of the All.

" When you stop at one thing, you cease to open yourself to the All.

" For to come to the All you must give up the All.

" And if you should attain to owning the All, you must own it, desiring Nothing.

" In this spoliation, the soul finds its tranquillity and rest. Profoundly established in the centre of its own nothingness, it can be assailed by naught that comes from below; and since it no longer desires anything, what comes from above cannot depress it; for its desires alone are the causes of its woes." [1]

And now, as a more concrete example of heads 4 and 5, in fact of all our heads together, and of the irrational extreme to which a psychopathic individual may go in the line of bodily austerity, I will quote the sincere Suso's account of his own self-tortures. Suso, you will remember, was one of the fourteenth century German mystics; his autobiography, written in the third person, is a classic religious document.

[1] SAINT JEAN DE LA CROIX, Vie et Œuvres, Paris, 1893, ii. 94, 99, abridged

" He was in his youth of a temperament full of fire and life ; and when this began to make itself felt, it was very grievous to him ; and he sought by many devices how he might bring his body into subjection. He wore for a long time a hair shirt and an iron chain, until the blood ran from him, so that he was obliged to leave them off. He secretly caused an undergarment to be made for him ; and in the undergarment he had strips of leather fixed, into which a hundred and fifty brass nails, pointed and filed sharp, were driven, and the points of the nails were always turned towards the flesh. He had this garment made very tight, and so arranged as to go round him and fasten in front, in order that it might fit the closer to his body, and the pointed nails might be driven into his flesh ; and it was high enough to reach upwards to his navel. In this he used to sleep at night. Now in summer, when it was hot, and he was very tired and ill from his journeyings, or when he held the office of lecturer, he would sometimes, as he lay thus in bonds, and oppressed with toil, and tormented also by noxious insects, cry aloud and give way to fretfulness, and twist round and round in agony, as a worm does when run through with a pointed needle. It often seemed to him as if he were lying upon an ant-hill, from the torture caused by the insects ; for if he wished to sleep, or when he had fallen asleep, they vied with one another.[1] Sometimes he cried to Almighty God in the fullness of his heart: Alas! Gentle God, what a dying is this! When a man is killed by murderers or strong beasts of prey it is soon over ; but I lie dying here under the cruel insects, and yet cannot die. The nights in winter were never so long, nor was the summer so hot, as to make him leave off this exercise. On the contrary, he devised something farther — two leathern loops into which he put his hands, and fastened one on each side his throat, and made the fastenings so secure that even if his cell had been

---

[1] 'Insects,' i. e. lice, were an unfailing token of mediæval sainthood. We read of Francis of Assisi's sheepskin that "often a companion of the saint would take it to the fire to clean and *dispediculate* it, doing so, as he said, because the seraphic father himself was no enemy of *pedocchi*, but on the contrary kept them on him (le portava adosso), and held it for an honor and a glory to wear these celestial pearls in his habit." Quoted by P. SABA-TIER : Speculum Perfectionis, etc., Paris, 1898, p. 231, note.

on fire about him, he could not have helped himself. This he continued until his hands and arms had become almost tremulous with the strain, and then he devised something else: two leather gloves; and he caused a brazier to fit them all over with sharp-pointed brass tacks, and he used to put them on at night, in order that if he should try while asleep to throw off the hair undergarment, or relieve himself from the gnawings of the vile insects, the tacks might then stick into his body. And so it came to pass. If ever he sought to help himself with his hands in his sleep, he drove the sharp tacks into his breast, and tore himself, so that his flesh festered. When after many weeks the wounds had healed, he tore himself again and made fresh wounds.

" He continued this tormenting exercise for about sixteen years. At the end of this time, when his blood was now chilled, and the fire of his temperament destroyed, there appeared to him in a vision on Whitsunday, a messenger from heaven, who told him that God required this of him no longer. Whereupon he discontinued it, and threw all these things away into a running stream."

Suso then tells how, to emulate the sorrows of his crucified Lord, he made himself a cross with thirty protruding iron needles and nails. This he bore on his bare back between his shoulders day and night. The first time that he stretched out this cross upon his back his tender frame was struck with terror at it, and blunted the sharp nails slightly against a stone. But soon, repenting of this womanly cowardice, he pointed them all again with a file, and placed once more the cross upon him. It made his back, where the bones are, bloody and seared. Whenever he sat down or stood up, it was as if a hedgehog-skin were on him. If any one touched him unawares, or pushed against his clothes, it tore him."

Suso next tells of his penitences by means of striking this cross and forcing the nails deeper into the flesh, and likewise of his self-scourgings, — a dreadful story, — and then goes on as follows: " At this same period the Servitor procured an old castaway door, and he used to lie upon it at night without any bedclothes to make him comfortable, except that he took off his shoes and wrapped a thick cloak round him. He thus secured for himself a most miserable bed; for hard pea-stalks lay in humps under his head, the cross with the sharp nails stuck into his back, his arms were locked fast in bonds, the horsehair undergarment was round his loins, and the cloak too was heavy and the door hard. Thus he lay in wretchedness, afraid to stir, just like a log, and he would send up many a sigh to God.

"In winter he suffered very much from the frost. If he stretched out his feet they lay bare on the floor and froze, if he gathered them up the blood became all on fire in his legs, and this was great pain. His feet were full of sores, his legs dropsical, his knees bloody and seared, his loins covered with scars from the horsehair, his body wasted, his mouth parched with intense thirst, and his hands tremulous from weakness. Amid these torments he spent his nights and days; and he endured them all out of the greatness of the love which he bore in his heart to the Divine and Eternal Wisdom, our Lord Jesus Christ, whose agonizing sufferings he sought to imitate. After a time he gave up this penitential exercise of the door, and instead of it he took up his abode in a very small cell, and used the bench, which was so narrow and short that he could not stretch himself upon it, as his bed. In this hole, or upon the door, he lay at night in his usual bonds, for about eight years. It was also his custom, during the space of twenty-five years, provided he was staying in the convent, never to go after compline in winter into any warm room, or to the convent stove to warm himself, no matter how cold it might be, unless he was obliged to do so for other reasons. Throughout all these years he never took a bath, either a water or a sweating bath; and this he did in order to mortify his comfort-seeking body. He practiced during a long time such rigid poverty that he would neither receive nor touch a penny, either with leave or without it. For a considerable time he strove to attain such a high degree of purity that he would neither scratch nor touch any part of his body, save only his hands and feet." [1]

[1] The Life of the Blessed HENRY SUSO, by Himself, translated by T. F. KNOX, London, 1865, pp. 56–80, abridged.

I spare you the recital of poor Suso's self-inflicted tortures from thirst. It is pleasant to know that after his fortieth year, God showed him by a series of visions that he had sufficiently broken down the natural man, and that he might leave these exercises off. His case is distinctly pathological, but he does not seem to have had the alleviation, which some ascetics have enjoyed, of an alteration of sensibility capable of actually turning torment into a perverse kind of pleasure. Of the founder of the Sacred Heart order, for example, we read that

" Her love of pain and suffering was insatiable. . . . She said that she could cheerfully live till the day of judgment, provided she might always have matter for suffering for God ; but that to live a single day without suffering would be intolerable. She said again that she was devoured with two unassuageable fevers, one for the holy communion, the other for suffering, humiliation, and annihilation. ' Nothing but pain,' she continually said in her letters, ' makes my life supportable.' " [1]

So much for the phenomena to which the ascetic impulse will in certain persons give rise. In the ecclesiastically consecrated character three minor branches of self-mortification have been recognized as indispensable pathways to perfection. I refer to the chastity, obedience, and poverty which the monk vows to observe; and upon the heads of obedience and poverty I will make a few remarks.

First, of Obedience. The secular life of our twentieth century opens with this virtue held in no high esteem. The duty of the individual to determine his own conduct and profit or suffer by the consequences seems, on the

[1] Bougaud : Hist. de la bienheureuse Marguerite Marie, Paris, 1894, pp. 265, 171. Compare, also, pp. 386, 387.

contrary, to be one of our best rooted contemporary Protestant social ideals. So much so that it is difficult even imaginatively to comprehend how men possessed of an inner life of their own could ever have come to think the subjection of its will to that of other finite creatures recommendable. I confess that to myself it seems something of a mystery. Yet it evidently corresponds to a profound interior need of many persons, and we must do our best to understand it.

On the lowest possible plane, one sees how the expediency of obedience in a firm ecclesiastical organization must have led to its being viewed as meritorious. Next, experience shows that there are times in every one's life when one can be better counseled by others than by one's self. Inability to decide is one of the commonest symptoms of fatigued nerves ; friends who see our troubles more broadly, often see them more wisely than we do ; so it is frequently an act of excellent virtue to consult and obey a doctor, a partner, or a wife. But, leaving these lower prudential regions, we find, in the nature of some of the spiritual excitements which we have been studying, good reasons for idealizing obedience. Obedience may spring from the general religious phenomenon of inner softening and self-surrender and throwing one's self on higher powers. So saving are these attitudes felt to be that in themselves, apart from utility, they become ideally consecrated ; and in obeying a man whose fallibility we see through thoroughly, we, nevertheless, may feel much as we do when we resign our will to that of infinite wisdom. Add self-despair and the passion of self-crucifixion to this, and obedience becomes an ascetic sacrifice, agreeable quite irrespective of whatever prudential uses it might have.

It is as a sacrifice, a mode of 'mortification,' that

obedience is primarily conceived by Catholic writers, a "sacrifice which man offers to God, and of which he is himself both the priest and the victim. By poverty he immolates his exterior possessions; by chastity he immolates his body; by obedience he completes the sacrifice, and gives to God all that he yet holds as his own, his two most precious goods, his intellect and his will. The sacrifice is then complete and unreserved, a genuine holocaust, for the entire victim is now consumed for the honor of God." [1] Accordingly, in Catholic discipline, we obey our superior not as mere man, but as the representative of Christ. Obeying God in him by our intention, obedience is easy. But when the text-book theologians marshal collectively all their reasons for recommending it, the mixture sounds to our ears rather odd.

" One of the great consolations of the monastic life," says a Jesuit authority, " is the assurance we have that in obeying we can commit no fault. The Superior may commit a fault in commanding you to do this thing or that, but you are certain that you commit no fault so long as you obey, because God will only ask you if you have duly performed what orders you received, and if you can furnish a clear account in that respect, you are absolved entirely. Whether the things you did were opportune, or whether there were not something better that might have been done, these are questions not asked of you, but rather of your Superior. The moment what you did was done obediently, God wipes it out of your account, and charges it to the Superior. So that Saint Jerome well exclaimed, in celebrating the advantages of obedience, ' Oh, sovereign liberty! Oh, holy and blessed security by which one becomes almost impeccable ! '

" Saint John Climachus is of the same sentiment when he calls obedience an excuse before God. In fact, when God asks why you have done this or that, and you reply, it is because I

---

[1] LEJEUNE : Introduction à la Vie Mystique, 1899, p. 277. The holocaust simile goes back at least as far as Ignatius Loyola.

was so ordered by my Superiors, God will ask for no other
excuse. As a passenger in a good vessel with a good pilot
need give himself no farther concern, but may go to sleep in
peace, because the pilot has charge over all, and ' watches for
him ' ; so a religious person who lives under the yoke of obedi-
ance goes to heaven as if while sleeping, that is, while leaning
entirely on the conduct of his Superiors, who are the pilots of
his vessel, and keep watch for him continually. It is no small
thing, of a truth, to be able to cross the stormy sea of life on
the shoulders and in the arms of another, yet that is just the
grace which God accords to those who live under the yoke of
obedience. Their Superior bears all their burdens. . . . A
certain grave doctor said that he would rather spend his life in
picking up straws by obedience, than by his own responsible
choice busy himself with the loftiest works of charity, because
one is certain of following the will of God in whatever one may
do from obedience, but never certain in the same degree of
anything which we may do of our own proper movement." [1]

One should read the letters in which Ignatius Loyola
recommends obedience as the backbone of his order, if
one would gain insight into the full spirit of its cult.[2]
They are too long to quote ; but Ignatius's belief is so
vividly expressed in a couple of sayings reported by companions that, though they have been so often cited, I
will ask your permission to copy them once more : —

" I ought," an early biographer reports him as saying, " on entering religion, and thereafter, to place myself entirely in the
hands of God, and of him who takes His place by His authority.
I ought to desire that my Superior should oblige me to give up
my own judgment, and conquer my own mind. I ought to set
up no difference between one Superior and another, . . . but
recognize them all as equal before God, whose place they fill.
For if I distinguish persons, I weaken the spirit of obedience.

---

[1] ALFONSO RODRIGUEZ, S. J.: Pratique de la Perfection Chrétienne, Part
iii., Treatise v., ch. x.

[2] Letters li. and cxx. of the collection translated into French by BOUIX,
Paris, 1870.

In the hands of my Superior, I must be a soft wax, a thing, from which he is to require whatever pleases him, be it to write or receive letters, to speak or not to speak to such a person, or the like ; and I must put all my fervor in executing zealously and exactly what I am ordered.   I must consider myself as a corpse which has neither intelligence nor will ; be like a mass of matter which without resistance lets itself be placed wherever it may please any one ; like a stick in the hand of an old man, who uses it according to his needs and places it where it suits him. So must I be under the hands of the Order, to serve it in the way it judges most useful.

"I must never ask of the Superior to be sent to a particular place, to be employed in a particular duty. . . . I must consider nothing as belonging to me personally, and as regards the things I use, be like a statue which lets itself be stripped and never opposes resistance."[1]

The other saying is reported by Rodriguez in the chapter from which I a moment ago made quotations.   When speaking of the Pope's authority, Rodriguez writes : —

"Saint Ignatius said, when general of his company, that if the Holy Father were to order him to set sail in the first bark which he might find in the port of Ostia, near Rome, and to abandon himself to the sea, without a mast, without sails, without oars or rudder or any of the things that are needful for navigation or subsistence, he would obey not only with alacrity, but without anxiety or repugnance, and even with a great internal satisfaction."[2]

With a solitary concrete example of the extravagance to which the virtue we are considering has been carried, I will pass to the topic next in order.

"Sister Marie Claire [of Port Royal] had been greatly imbued with the holiness and excellence of M. de Langres.   This prelate, soon after he came to Port Royal, said to her one day, seeing her so tenderly attached to Mother Angélique, that it

---

[1] BARTOLI-MICHEL, ii. 13.

[2] RODRIGUEZ : Op. cit., Part iii., Treatise v., ch. vi.

would perhaps be better not to speak to her again. Marie Claire, greedy of obedience, took this inconsiderate word for an oracle of God, and from that day forward remained for several years without once speaking to her sister." [1]

Our next topic shall be Poverty, felt at all times and under all creeds as one adornment of a saintly life. Since the instinct of ownership is fundamental in man's nature, this is one more example of the ascetic paradox. Yet it appears no paradox at all, but perfectly reasonable, the moment one recollects how easily higher excitements hold lower cupidities in check. Having just quoted the Jesuit Rodriguez on the subject of obedience, I will, to give immediately a concrete turn to our discussion of poverty, also read you a page from his chapter on this latter virtue. You must remember that he is writing instructions for monks of his own order, and bases them all on the text, " Blessed are the poor in spirit."

" If any one of you," he says, " will know whether or not he is really poor in spirit, let him consider whether he loves the ordinary consequences and effects of poverty, which are hunger, thirst, cold, fatigue, and the denudation of all conveniences. See if you are glad to wear a worn-out habit full of patches. See if you are glad when something is lacking to your meal, when you are passed by in serving it, when what you receive is distasteful to you, when your cell is out of repair. If you are not glad of these things, if instead of loving them you avoid them, then there is proof that you have not attained the perfection of poverty of spirit." Rodriguez then goes on to describe the practice of poverty in more detail. " The first point is that which Saint Ignatius proposes in his constitutions, when he says, ' Let no one use anything as if it were his private possession.' ' A religious person,' he says, ' ought in respect to all the things that he uses, to be like a statue which one may drape with clothing, but which feels no grief and makes no resistance when one

[1] SAINTE-BEUVE : Histoire de Port Royal, i. 346.

strips it again. It is in this way that you should feel towards
your clothes, your books, your cell, and everything else that
you make use of ; if ordered to quit them, or to exchange them
for others, have no more sorrow than if you were a statue being
uncovered. In this way you will avoid using them as if they
were your private possession. But if, when you give up your
cell, or yield possession of this or that object or exchange it for
another, you feel repugnance and are not like a statue, that
shows that you view these things as if they were your private
property.'

"And this is why our holy founder wished the superiors to
test their monks somewhat as God tested Abraham, and to put
their poverty and their obedience to trial, that by this means
they may become acquainted with the degree of their virtue,
and gain a chance to make ever farther progress in perfection,
. . . making the one move out of his room when he finds it
comfortable and is attached to it ; taking away from another a
book of which he is fond ; or obliging a third to exchange his
garment for a worse one. Otherwise we should end by acquiring a species of property in all these several objects, and little
by little the wall of poverty that surrounds us and constitutes
our principal defense would be thrown down. The ancient
fathers of the desert used often thus to treat their companions.
. . . Saint Dositheus, being sick-nurse, desired a certain knife,
and asked Saint Dorotheus for it, not for his private use, but
for employment in the infirmary of which he had charge.
Whereupon Saint Dorotheus answered him : ' Ha ! Dositheus,
so that knife pleases you so much ! Will you be the slave of a
knife or the slave of Jesus Christ? Do you not blush with
shame at wishing that a knife should be your master? I will
not let you touch it.' Which reproach and refusal had such
an effect upon the holy disciple that since that time he never
touched the knife again." . . .

"Therefore, in our rooms," Father Rodriguez continues,
"there must be no other furniture than a bed, a table, a bench,
and a candlestick, things purely necessary, and nothing more.
It is not allowed among us that our cells should be ornamented
with pictures or aught else, neither armchairs, carpets, curtains,

nor any sort of cabinet or bureau of any elegance. Neither is it allowed us to keep anything to eat, either for ourselves or for those who may come to visit us. We must ask permission to go to the refectory even for a glass of water; and finally we may not keep a book in which we can write a line, or which we may take away with us. One cannot deny that thus we are in great poverty. But this poverty is at the same time a great repose and a great perfection. For it would be inevitable, in case a religious person were allowed to own superfluous possessions, that these things would greatly occupy his mind, be it to acquire them, to preserve them, or to increase them; so that in not permitting us at all to own them, all these inconveniences are remedied. Among the various good reasons why the company forbids secular persons to enter our cells, the principal one is that thus we may the easier be kept in poverty. After all, we are all men, and if we were to receive people of the world into our rooms, we should not have the strength to remain within the bounds prescribed, but should at least wish to adorn them with some books to give the visitors a better opinion of our scholarship." [1]

Since Hindu fakirs, Buddhist monks, and Mohammedan dervishes unite with Jesuits and Franciscans in idealizing poverty as the loftiest individual state, it is worth while to examine into the spiritual grounds for such a seemingly unnatural opinion. And first, of those which lie closest to common human nature.

The opposition between the men who *have* and the men who *are* is immemorial. Though the gentleman, in the old-fashioned sense of the man who is well born, has usually in point of fact been predaceous and reveled in lands and goods, yet he has never identified his essence with these possessions, but rather with the personal superiorities, the courage, generosity, and pride supposed to be his birthright. To certain huckstering kinds of

---

[1] RODRIGUEZ: Op. cit., Part iii., Treatise iii., chaps. vi., vii.

consideration he thanked God he was forever inaccessible, and if in life's vicissitudes he should become destitute through their lack, he was glad to think that with his sheer valor he was all the freer to work out his salvation. "Wer nur selbst was hätte," says Lessing's Tempelherr, in Nathan the Wise, "mein Gott, mein Gott, ich habe nichts!" This ideal of the well-born man without possessions was embodied in knight-errantry and templardom ; and, hideously corrupted as it has always been, it still dominates sentimentally, if not practically, the military and aristocratic view of life. We glorify the soldier as the man absolutely unincumbered. Owning nothing but his bare life, and willing to toss that up at any moment when the cause commands him, he is the representative of unhampered freedom in ideal directions. The laborer who pays with his person day by day, and has no rights invested in the future, offers also much of this ideal detachment. Like the savage, he may make his bed wherever his right arm can support him, and from his simple and athletic attitude of observation, the property-owner seems buried and smothered in ignoble externalities and trammels, "wading in straw and rubbish to his knees." The claims which *things* make are corrupters of manhood, mortgages on the soul, and a drag anchor on our progress towards the empyrean.

"Everything I meet with," writes Whitefield, "seems to carry this voice with it, — 'Go thou and preach the Gospel; be a pilgrim on earth; have no party or certain dwelling place.' My heart echoes back, 'Lord Jesus, help me to do or suffer thy will. When thou seest me in danger of *nestling*, — in pity — in tender pity, — put a *thorn* in my nest to prevent me from it.'"[1]

[1] R. PHILIP: The Life and Times of George Whitefield, London, 1842, p. 366.

The loathing of 'capital' with which our laboring classes to-day are growing more and more infected seems largely composed of this sound sentiment of antipathy for lives based on mere having. As an anarchist poet writes : —

"Not by accumulating riches, but by giving away that which you have,

"Shall you become beautiful;

"You must undo the wrappings, not case yourself in fresh ones;

"Not by multiplying clothes shall you make your body sound and healthy, but rather by discarding them . . .

"For a soldier who is going on a campaign does not seek what fresh furniture he can carry on his back, but rather what he can leave behind;

"Knowing well that every additional thing which he cannot freely use and handle is an impediment." [1]

In short, lives based on having are less free than lives based either on doing or on being, and in the interest of action people subject to spiritual excitement throw away possessions as so many clogs. Only those who have no private interests can follow an ideal straight away. Sloth and cowardice creep in with every dollar or guinea we have to guard. When a brother novice came to Saint Francis, saying: "Father, it would be a great consolation to me to own a psalter, but even supposing that our general should concede to me this indulgence, still I should like also to have your consent," Francis put him off with the examples of Charlemagne, Roland, and Oliver, pursuing the infidels in sweat and labor, and finally dying on the field of battle. "So care not," he said, "for owning books and knowledge, but care rather for works of goodness." And when some weeks later the novice came

[1] EDWARD CARPENTER : Towards Democracy, p. 362, abridged.

again to talk of his craving for the psalter, Francis said : " After you have got your psalter you will crave a breviary ; and after you have got your breviary you will sit in your stall like a grand prelate, and will say to your brother : ' Hand me my breviary.' . . . And thenceforward he denied all such requests, saying : A man possesses of learning only so much as comes out of him in action, and a monk is a good preacher only so far as his deeds proclaim him such, for every tree is known by its fruits." [1]

But beyond this more worthily athletic attitude involved in doing and being, there is, in the desire of not having, something profounder still, something related to that fundamental mystery of religious experience, the satisfaction found in absolute surrender to the larger power. So long as any secular safeguard is retained, so long as any residual prudential guarantee is clung to, so long the surrender is incomplete, the vital crisis is not passed, fear still stands sentinel, and mistrust of the divine obtains : we hold by two anchors, looking to God, it is true, after a fashion, but also holding by our proper machinations. In certain medical experiences we have the same critical point to overcome. A drunkard, or a morphine or cocaine maniac, offers himself to be cured. He appeals to the doctor to wean him from his enemy, but he dares not face blank abstinence. The tyrannical drug is still an anchor to windward : he hides supplies of it among his clothing ; arranges secretly to have it smuggled in in case of need. Even so an incompletely regenerate man still trusts in his own expedients. His money is like the sleeping potion which the chronically wakeful patient keeps beside his bed ; he throws himself on God, but *if* he should need the other help, there it

[1] Speculum Perfectionis, ed. P. SABATIER, Paris, 1898, pp. 10, 13.

will be also.   Every one knows cases of this incomplete
and ineffective desire for reform, — drunkards whom,
with all their self-reproaches and resolves, one perceives
to be quite unwilling seriously to contemplate *never* being
drunk again !   Really to give up anything on which we
have relied, to give it up definitively, ' for good and all '
and forever, signifies one of those radical alterations of
character which came under our notice in the lectures on
conversion.   In it the inner man rolls over into an entirely
different position of equilibrium, lives in a new centre
of energy from this time on, and the turning-point and
hinge of all such operations seems usually to involve the
sincere acceptance of certain nakednesses and destitutions.

Accordingly, throughout the annals of the saintly life,
we find this ever-recurring note : Fling yourself upon
God's providence without making any reserve whatever,
— take no thought for the morrow, — sell all you have
and give it to the poor, — only when the sacrifice is
ruthless and reckless will the higher safety really arrive.
As a concrete example let me read a page from the
biography of Antoinette Bourignon, a good woman, much
persecuted in her day by both Protestants and Catholics,
because she would not take her religion at second hand.
When a young girl, in her father's house, —

" She spent whole nights in prayer, oft repeating : *Lord, what
wilt thou have me to do ?*   And being one night in a most profound penitence, she said from the bottom of her heart : ' O
my Lord !   What must I do to please thee ?   For I have nobody to teach me.   Speak to my soul and it will hear thee.'
At that instant she heard, as if another had spoke within her :
*Forsake all earthly things.   Separate thyself from the love of the
creatures.   Deny thyself.*   She was quite astonished, not understanding this language, and mused long on these three points,
thinking how she could fulfill them.   She thought she could
not live without earthly things, nor without loving the creatures,

nor without loving herself. Yet she said, 'By thy Grace I will do it, Lord!' But when she would perform her promise, she knew not where to begin. Having thought on the religious in monasteries, that they forsook all earthly things by being shut up in a cloister, and the love of themselves by subjecting of their wills, she asked leave of her father to enter into a cloister of the barefoot Carmelites, but he would not permit it, saying he would rather see her laid in her grave. This seemed to her a great cruelty, for she thought to find in the cloister the true Christians she had been seeking, but she found afterwards that he knew the cloisters better than she; for after he had forbidden her, and told her he would never permit her to be a religious, nor give her any money to enter there, yet she went to Father Laurens, the Director, and offered to serve in the monastery and work hard for her bread, and be content with little, if he would receive her. At which he smiled and said: *That cannot be. We must have money to build; we take no maids without money; you must find the way to get it, else there is no entry here.*

"This astonished her greatly, and she was thereby undeceived as to the cloisters, resolving to forsake all company and live alone till it should please God to show her what she ought to do and whither to go. She asked always earnestly, 'When shall I be perfectly thine, O my God?' And she thought he still answered her, *When thou shalt no longer possess anything, and shalt die to thyself.* 'And where shall I do that, Lord?' He answered her, *In the desert.* This made so strong an impression on her soul that she aspired after this; but being a maid of eighteen years only, she was afraid of unlucky chances, and was never used to travel, and knew no way. She laid aside all these doubts and said, 'Lord, thou wilt guide me how and where it shall please thee. It is for thee that I do it. I will lay aside my habit of a maid, and will take that of a hermit that I may pass unknown.' Having then secretly made ready this habit, while her parents thought to have married her, her father having promised her to a rich French merchant, she prevented the time, and on Easter evening, having cut her hair, put on the habit, and slept a little, she went out of her chamber

about four in the morning, taking nothing but one penny to
buy bread for that day. And it being said to her in the going
out, *Where is thy faith? in a penny?* she threw it away,
begging pardon of God for her fault, and saying, ' No, Lord,
my faith is not in a penny, but in thee alone.' Thus she went
away wholly delivered from the heavy burthen of the cares and
good things of this world, and found her soul so satisfied that
she no longer wished for anything upon earth, resting entirely
upon God, with this only fear lest she should be discovered and
be obliged to return home; for she felt already more content in
this poverty than she had done for all her life in all the delights
of the world." [1]

The penny was a small financial safeguard, but an effective spiritual obstacle. Not till it was thrown away could
the character settle into the new equilibrium completely.

Over and above the mystery of self-surrender, there are
in the cult of poverty other religious mysteries. There is

[1] An Apology for M. Antonia Bourignon, London, 1699, pp. 269, 270,
abridged.

Another example from Starbuck's MS. collection : —

" At a meeting held at six the next morning, I heard a man relate his
experience. He said : The Lord asked him if he would confess Christ
among the quarrymen with whom he worked, and he said he would. Then
he asked him if he would give up to be used of the Lord the four hundred
dollars he had laid up, and he said he would, and thus the Lord saved him.
The thought came to me at once that I had never made a real consecration
either of myself or of my property to the Lord, but had always tried to
serve the Lord in *my* way. Now the Lord asked me if I would serve him
in *his* way, and go out alone and penniless if he so ordered. The question
was pressed home, and I must decide : To forsake all and have him, or have
all and lose him ! I soon decided to take him ; and the blessed assurance
came, that he had taken me for his own, and my joy was full. I returned
home from the meeting with feelings as simple as a child. I thought all
would be glad to hear of the joy of the Lord that possessed me, and so I
began to tell the simple story. But to my great surprise, the pastors (for
I attended meetings in three churches) opposed the experience and said it
was fanaticism, and one told the members of his church to shun those that
professed it, and I soon found that my foes were those of my own household.'

the mystery of veracity: "Naked came I into the world,"
etc., — whoever first said that, possessed this mystery.
My own bare entity must fight the battle — shams cannot save me. There is also the mystery of democracy,
or sentiment of the equality before God of all his creatures. This sentiment (which seems in general to have
been more widespread in Mohammedan than in Christian
lands) tends to nullify man's usual acquisitiveness. Those
who have it spurn dignities and honors, privileges and
advantages, preferring, as I said in a former lecture, to
grovel on the common level before the face of God. It
is not exactly the sentiment of humility, though it comes
so close to it in practice. It is *humanity*, rather, refusing
to enjoy anything that others do not share. A profound
moralist, writing of Christ's saying, 'Sell all thou hast
and follow me,' proceeds as follows: —

" Christ may have meant: If you love mankind absolutely
you will as a result not care for any possessions whatever, and
this seems a very likely proposition. But it is one thing to
believe that a proposition is probably true; it is another thing
to see it as a fact. If you loved mankind as Christ loved them,
you would see his conclusion as a fact. It would be obvious.
You would sell your goods, and they would be no loss to you.
These truths, while literal to Christ, and to any mind that has
Christ's love for mankind, become parables to lesser natures.
There are in every generation people who, beginning innocently,
with no predetermined intention of becoming saints, find themselves drawn into the vortex by their interest in helping mankind, and by the understanding that comes from actually doing
it. The abandonment of their old mode of life is like dust in
the balance. It is done gradually, incidentally, imperceptibly.
Thus the whole question of the abandonment of luxury is no
question at all, but a mere incident to another question, namely,
the degree to which we abandon ourselves to the remorseless
logic of our love for others." [1]

[1] J. J. CHAPMAN, in the Political Nursery, vol. iv. p. 4, April, 1900,
abridged.

But in all these matters of sentiment one must have 'been there' one's self in order to understand them. No American can ever attain to understanding the loyalty of a Briton towards his king, of a German towards his emperor; nor can a Briton or German ever understand the peace of heart of an American in having no king, no Kaiser, no spurious nonsense, between him and the common God of all. If sentiments as simple as these are mysteries which one must receive as gifts of birth, how much more is this the case with those subtler religious sentiments which we have been considering! One can never fathom an emotion or divine its dictates by standing outside of it. In the glowing hour of excitement, however, all incomprehensibilities are solved, and what was so enigmatical from without becomes transparently obvious. Each emotion obeys a logic of its own, and makes deductions which no other logic can draw. Piety and charity live in a different universe from worldly lusts and fears, and form another centre of energy altogether. As in a supreme sorrow lesser vexations may become a consolation; as a supreme love may turn minor sacrifices into gain; so a supreme trust may render common safeguards odious, and in certain glows of generous excitement it may appear unspeakably mean to retain one's hold of personal possessions. The only sound plan, if we are ourselves outside the pale of such emotions, is to observe as well as we are able those who feel them, and to record faithfully what we observe; and this, I need hardly say, is what I have striven to do in these last two descriptive lectures, which I now hope will have covered the ground sufficiently for our present needs.

LECTURES XIV AND XV

THE VALUE OF SAINTLINESS

WE have now passed in review the more important of the phenomena which are regarded as fruits of genuine religion and characteristics of men who are devout. To-day we have to change our attitude from that of description to that of appreciation; we have to ask whether the fruits in question can help us to judge the absolute value of what religion adds to human life. Were I to parody Kant, I should say that a 'Critique of pure Saintliness' must be our theme.

If, in turning to this theme, we could descend upon our subject from above like Catholic theologians, with our fixed definitions of man and man's perfection and our positive dogmas about God, we should have an easy time of it. Man's perfection would be the fulfillment of his end; and his end would be union with his Maker. That union could be pursued by him along three paths, active, purgative, and contemplative, respectively; and progress along either path would be a simple matter to measure by the application of a limited number of theological and moral conceptions and definitions. The absolute significance and value of any bit of religious experience we might hear of would thus be given almost mathematically into our hands.

If convenience were everything, we ought now to grieve at finding ourselves cut off from so admirably convenient a method as this. But we did cut ourselves off from it deliberately in those remarks which you remember we

.made, in our first lecture, about the empirical method; and it must be confessed that after that act of renunciation we can never hope for clean-cut and scholastic results. *We* cannot divide man sharply into an animal and a rational part. *We* cannot distinguish natural from supernatural effects; nor among the latter know which are favors of God, and which are counterfeit operations of the demon. We have merely to collect things together without any special *a priori* theological system, and out of an aggregate of piecemeal judgments as to the value of this and that experience — judgments in which our general philosophic prejudices, our instincts, and our common sense are our only guides — decide that *on the whole* one type of religion is approved by its fruits, and another type condemned. 'On the whole,' — I fear we shall never escape complicity with that qualification, so dear to your practical man, so repugnant to your systematizer!

I also fear that as I make this frank confession, I may seem to some of you to throw our compass overboard, and to adopt caprice as our pilot. Skepticism or wayward choice, you may think, can be the only results of such a formless method as I have taken up. A few remarks in deprecation of such an opinion, and in farther explanation of the empiricist principles which I profess, may therefore appear at this point to be in place.

Abstractly, it would seem illogical to try to measure the worth of a religion's fruits in merely human terms of value. How *can* you measure their worth without considering whether the God really exists who is supposed to inspire them? If he really exists, then all the conduct instituted by men to meet his wants must necessarily be a reasonable fruit of his religion, — it would be unreasonable only in case he did not exist. If, for instance, you were to condemn a religion of human or animal sacrifices by virtue of your subjective sentiments, and if all the while a deity were really there demanding such sacrifices, you would be making a theoretical mistake by tacitly assuming that the deity must be non-existent; you would be setting up a theology of your own as much as if you were a scholastic philosopher.

To this extent, to the extent of disbelieving peremptorily in certain types of deity, I frankly confess that we must be theologians. If disbeliefs can be said to constitute a theology, then the prejudices, instincts, and common sense which I chose as our guides make theological partisans of us whenever they make certain beliefs abhorrent.

But such common-sense prejudices and instincts are themselves the fruit of an empirical evolution. Nothing is more striking than the secular alteration that goes on in the moral and religious tone of men, as their insight into nature and their social arrangements progressively develop. After an interval of a few generations the mental climate proves unfavorable to notions of the deity which at an earlier date were perfectly satisfactory : the older gods have fallen below the common secular level, and can no longer be believed in. To-day a deity who should require bleeding sacrifices to placate him would be too sanguinary to be taken seriously. Even if powerful historical credentials were put forward in his favor, we would not look at them. Once, on the contrary, his cruel appetites were of themselves credentials. They positively recommended him to men's imaginations in ages when such coarse signs of power were respected and no others could be understood. Such deities then were worshiped because such fruits were relished.

Doubtless historic accidents always played some later part, but the original factor in fixing the figure of the gods must always have been psychological. The deity to whom the prophets, seers, and devotees who founded the particular cult bore witness was worth something to them personally. They could use him. He guided their imagination, warranted their hopes, and controlled their will, — or else they required him as a safeguard against the demon and a curber of other people's crimes. In any case, they chose him for the value of the fruits he seemed to them to yield. So soon as the fruits began to seem quite worthless; so soon as they conflicted with indispensable human ideals, or thwarted too extensively other values; so soon as they appeared childish, contemptible, or immoral when reflected on, the deity grew discredited, and was erelong neglected and forgotten. It was in this way that the Greek and Roman gods ceased to be believed in by educated pagans; it is thus that we ourselves judge of the Hindu, Buddhist, and Mohammedan theologies; Protestants have so dealt with the Catholic notions of deity, and liberal Protestants with older Protestant notions; it is thus that Chinamen judge of us, and that all of us now living will be judged by our descendants. When we cease to admire or approve what the definition of a deity implies, we end by deeming that deity incredible.

Few historic changes are more curious than these mutations of theological opinion. The monarchical type of sovereignty was, for example, so ineradicably planted in the mind of our own forefathers that a dose of cruelty and arbitrariness in their deity seems positively to have been required by their imagination. They called the cruelty 'retributive justice,' and a God without it would certainly have struck them as not 'sovereign' enough. But to-day we abhor the very notion of eternal suffering inflicted; and that arbitrary dealing-out of salvation and damnation to selected individuals, of which Jonathan Edwards could persuade himself that he had not only a conviction, but a ' delightful conviction,' as of a doctrine ' exceeding pleasant, bright, and sweet,' appears to us, if sovereignly anything, sovereignly irrational and mean. Not only the cruelty, but the paltriness of character of the gods believed in by earlier centuries also strikes later centuries with surprise.   We shall see examples of it from the annals of Catholic saintship which make us rub our Protestant eyes.   Ritual worship in general appears to the modern transcendentalist, as well as to the ultra-puritanic type of mind, as if addressed to a deity of an almost absurdly childish character, taking delight in toy-shop furniture, tapers and tinsel, costume and mumbling and mummery, and finding his ' glory ' incomprehensibly enhanced thereby; — just as on the other hand the formless spaciousness of pantheism appears quite empty to ritualistic natures, and the gaunt theism of evangelical sects seems intolerably bald and chalky and bleak.   Luther, says Emerson, would have cut off his right hand rather than nail his theses to the door at Wittenberg, if he had supposed that they were destined to lead to the pale negations of Boston Unitarianism.

So far, then, although we are compelled, whatever may be our pretensions to empiricism, to employ some sort of a standard of theological probability of our own whenever we assume to estimate the fruits of other men's religion, yet this very standard has been begotten out of the drift of common life. It is the voice of human experience within us, judging and condemning all gods that stand athwart the pathway along which it feels itself to be advancing. Experience, if we take it in the largest sense, is thus the parent of those disbeliefs which, it was charged, were inconsistent with the experiential method. The inconsistency, you see, is immaterial, and the charge may be neglected.

If we pass from disbeliefs to positive beliefs, it seems to me that there is not even a formal inconsistency to be laid against our method. The gods we stand by are the gods we need and can use, the gods whose demands on us are reinforcements of our demands on ourselves and on one another. What I then propose to do is, briefly stated, to test saintliness by common sense, to use human standards to help us decide how far the religious life commends itself as an ideal kind of human activity. If it commends itself, then any theological beliefs that may inspire it, in so far forth will stand accredited. If not, then they will be discredited, and all without reference to anything but human working principles. It is but the elimination of the humanly unfit, and the survival of the humanly fittest, applied to religious beliefs; and if we look at history candidly and without prejudice, we have to admit that no religion has ever in the long run established or proved itself in any other way. Religions have *approved* themselves ; they have ministered to sundry vital needs which they found reigning. When they violated other needs too strongly, or when other faiths came which served the same needs better, the first religions were supplanted.

The needs were always many, and the tests were never sharp. So the reproach of vagueness and subjectivity and ' on the whole '-ness, which can with perfect legitimacy be addressed to the empirical method as we are forced to use it, is after all a reproach to which the entire life of man in dealing with these matters is obnoxious. No religion has ever yet owed its prevalence to ' apodictic certainty.' In a later lecture I will ask whether objective certainty can ever be added by theological reasoning to a religion that already empirically prevails.

One word, also, about the reproach that in following this sort of an empirical method we are handing ourselves over to systematic skepticism.

Since it is impossible to deny secular alterations in our sentiments and needs, it would be absurd to affirm that one's own age of the world can be beyond correction by the next age. Skepticism cannot, therefore, be ruled out by any set of thinkers as a possibility against which their conclusions are secure; and no empiricist ought to claim exemption from this universal liability. But to admit one's liability to correction is one thing, and to embark upon a sea of wanton doubt is another. Of willfully playing into the hands of skepticism we cannot be accused. He who acknowledges the imperfectness of his instrument, and makes allowance for it in discussing his observations, is in a much better position for gaining truth than if he claimed his instrument to be infallible. Or is dogmatic or scholastic theology less doubted in point of fact for claiming, as it does, to be in point of right undoubtable? And if not, what command over truth would this kind of theology really lose if, instead of absolute certainty, she only claimed reasonable probability for her conclusions? If *we* claim only reasonable probability, it will be as much as men who love the truth can ever at any given moment hope to have within their grasp. Pretty surely it will be more than we could have had, if we were unconscious of our liability to err.

Nevertheless, dogmatism will doubtless continue to condemn us for this confession. The mere outward form of inalterable certainty is so precious to some minds that to renounce it explicitly is for them out of the question. They will claim it even where the facts most patently pronounce its folly. But the safe thing is surely to recognize that all the insights of creatures of a day like ourselves must be provisional. The wisest of critics is an altering being, subject to the better insight of the morrow, and right at any moment, only 'up to date' and 'on the whole.' When larger ranges of truth open, it is surely best to be able to open ourselves to their reception, unfettered by our previous pretensions. "Heartily know, when half-gods go, the gods arrive."

The fact of diverse judgments about religious phenomena is therefore entirely unescapable, whatever may be one's own desire to attain the irreversible. But apart from that fact, a more fundamental question awaits us, the question whether men's opinions ought to be expected to be absolutely uniform in this field. Ought all men to have the same religion? Ought they to approve the same fruits and follow the same leadings? Are they so like in their inner needs that, for hard and soft, for proud and humble, for strenuous and lazy, for healthy-minded and despairing, exactly the same religious incentives are required? Or are different functions in the organism of humanity allotted to different types of man, so that some may really be the better for a religion of consolation and reassurance, whilst others are better for one of terror and reproof? It might conceivably be so ; and we shall, I think, more and more suspect it to be so as we go on. And if it be so, how can any possible judge or critic help being biased in favor of the religion by which his own needs are best met? He aspires to impartiality ; but he is too close to the struggle not to be to some degree a participant, and he is sure to approve most warmly those fruits of piety in others which taste most good and prove most nourishing to *him*.

I am well aware of how anarchic much of what I say may sound. Expressing myself thus abstractly and briefly, I may seem to despair of the very notion of truth. But I beseech you to reserve your judgment until we see it applied to the details which lie before us. I do indeed disbelieve that we or any other mortal men can attain on a given day to absolutely incorrigible and unimprovable truth about such matters of fact as those with which religions deal. But I reject this dogmatic ideal not out of a perverse delight in intellectual instability. I am no lover of disorder and doubt as such. Rather do I fear to lose truth by this pretension to possess it already wholly. That we can gain more and more of it by moving always in the right direction, I believe as much as any one, and I hope to bring you all to my way of thinking before the termination of these lectures. Till then, do not, I pray you, harden your minds irrevocably against the empiricism which I profess.

I will waste no more words, then, in abstract justification of my method, but seek immediately to use it upon the facts.

In critically judging of the value of religious phenomena, it is very important to insist on the distinction between religion as an individual personal function, and religion as an institutional, corporate, or tribal product. I drew this distinction, you may remember, in my second lecture. The word 'religion,' as ordinarily used, is equivocal. A survey of history shows us that, as a rule, religious geniuses attract disciples, and produce groups of sympathizers. When these groups get strong enough to 'organize' themselves, they become ecclesiastical institu-

tions with corporate ambitions of their own. The spirit
of politics and the lust of dogmatic rule are then apt to
enter and to contaminate the originally innocent thing;
so that when we hear the word 'religion' nowadays, we
think inevitably of some 'church' or other; and to some
persons the word 'church' suggests so much hypocrisy
and tyranny and meanness and tenacity of superstition
that in a wholesale undiscerning way they glory in saying that they are 'down' on religion altogether. Even
we who belong to churches do not exempt other churches
than our own from the general condemnation.

But in this course of lectures ecclesiastical institutions
hardly concern us at all. The religious experience which
we are studying is that which lives itself out within the
private breast. First-hand individual experience of this
kind has always appeared as a heretical sort of innova-
tion to those who witnessed its birth. Naked comes it
into the world and lonely; and it has always, for a time
at least, driven him who had it into the wilderness, often
into the literal wilderness out of doors, where the Buddha, Jesus, Mohammed, St. Francis, George Fox, and so
many others had to go. George Fox expresses well this
isolation; and I can do no better at this point than read
to you a page from his Journal, referring to the period
of his youth when religion began to ferment within him
seriously.

"I fasted much," Fox says, "walked abroad in solitary places
many days, and often took my Bible, and sat in hollow trees
and lonesome places until night came on; and frequently in
the night walked mournfully about by myself; for I was a
man of sorrows in the time of the first workings of the Lord
in me.

"During all this time I was never joined in profession of
religion with any, but gave up myself to the Lord, having for-

saken all evil company, taking leave of father and mother, and all other relations, and traveled up and down as a stranger on the earth, which way the Lord inclined my heart; taking a chamber to myself in the town where I came, and tarrying sometimes more, sometimes less in a place: for I durst not stay long in a place, being afraid both of professor and profane, lest, being a tender young man, I should be hurt by conversing much with either. For which reason I kept much as a stranger, seeking heavenly wisdom and getting knowledge from the Lord; and was brought off from outward things, to rely on the Lord alone. As I had forsaken the priests, so I left the separate preachers also, and those called the most experienced people; for I saw there was none among them all that could speak to my condition. And when all my hopes in them and in all men were gone so that I had nothing outwardly to help me, nor could tell what to do; then, oh then, I heard a voice which said, 'There is one, even Jesus Christ, that can speak to thy condition.' When I heard it, my heart did leap for joy. Then the Lord let me see why there was none upon the earth that could speak to my condition. I had not fellowship with any people, priests, nor professors, nor any sort of separated people. I was afraid of all carnal talk and talkers, for I could see nothing but corruptions. When I was in the deep, under all shut up, I could not believe that I should ever overcome; my troubles, my sorrows, and my temptations were so great that I often thought I should have despaired, I was so tempted. But when Christ opened to me how he was tempted by the same devil, and had overcome him, and had bruised his head; and that through him and his power, life, grace, and spirit, I should overcome also, I had confidence in him. If I had had a king's diet, palace, and attendance, all would have been as nothing; for nothing gave me comfort but the Lord by his power. I saw professors, priests, and people were whole and at ease in that condition which was my misery, and they loved that which I would have been rid of. But the Lord did stay my desires upon himself, and my care was cast upon him alone." [1]

[1] GEORGE FOX: Journal, Philadelphia, 1800, pp. 59–61, abridged.

A genuine first-hand religious experience like this is bound to be a heterodoxy to its witnesses, the prophet appearing as a mere lonely madman. If his doctrine prove contagious enough to spread to any others, it becomes a definite and labeled heresy. But if it then still prove contagious enough to triumph over persecution, it becomes itself an orthodoxy; and when a religion has become an orthodoxy, its day of inwardness is over: the spring is dry; the faithful live at second hand exclusively and stone the prophets in their turn. The new church, in spite of whatever human goodness it may foster, can be henceforth counted on as a staunch ally in every attempt to stifle the spontaneous religious spirit, and to stop all later bubblings of the fountain from which in purer days it drew its own supply of inspiration. Unless, indeed, by adopting new movements of the spirit it can make capital out of them and use them for its selfish corporate designs! Of protective action of this politic sort, promptly or tardily decided on, the dealings of the Roman ecclesiasticism with many individual saints and prophets yield examples enough for our instruction.

The plain fact is that men's minds are built, as has been often said, in water-tight compartments. Religious after a fashion, they yet have many other things in them beside their religion, and unholy entanglements and associations inevitably obtain. The basenesses so commonly charged to religion's account are thus, almost all of them, not chargeable at all to religion proper, but rather to religion's wicked practical partner, the spirit of corporate dominion. And the bigotries are most of them in their turn chargeable to religion's wicked intellectual partner, the spirit of dogmatic dominion, the passion for laying down the law in the form of an absolutely closed-in theoretic system. The ecclesiastical spirit in general is the

sum of these two spirits of dominion; and I beseech
you never to confound the phenomena of mere tribal
or corporate psychology which it presents with those
manifestations of the purely interior life which are the
exclusive object of our study. The baiting of Jews,
the hunting of Albigenses and Waldenses, the stoning
of Quakers and ducking of Methodists, the murdering
of Mormons and the massacring of Armenians, express
much rather that aboriginal human neophobia, that pug-
nacity of which we all share the vestiges, and that inborn
hatred of the alien and of eccentric and non-conforming
men as aliens, than they express the positive piety of the
various perpetrators. Piety is the mask, the inner force
is tribal instinct. You believe as little as I do, in spite
of the Christian unction with which the German emperor
addressed his troops upon their way to China, that the
conduct which he suggested, and in which other Christian
armies went beyond them, had anything whatever to do
with the interior religious life of those concerned in the
performance.

Well, no more for past atrocities than for this atrocity
should we make piety responsible. At most we may
blame piety for not availing to check our natural passions,
and sometimes for supplying them with hypocritical pre-
texts. But hypocrisy also imposes obligations, and with
the pretext usually couples some restriction; and when
the passion gust is over, the piety may bring a reaction
of repentance which the irreligious natural man would
not have shown.

For many of the historic aberrations which have been
laid to her charge, religion as such, then, is not to blame.
Yet of the charge that over-zealousness or fanaticism is
one of her liabilities we cannot wholly acquit her, so I
will next make a remark upon that point. But I will

preface it by a preliminary remark which connects itself with much that follows.

Our survey of the phenomena of saintliness has unquestionably produced in your minds an impression of extravagance. Is it necessary, some of you have asked, as one example after another came before us, to be quite so fantastically good as that? We who have no vocation for the extremer ranges of sanctity will surely be let off at the last day if our humility, asceticism, and devoutness prove of a less convulsive sort. This practically amounts to saying that much that it is legitimate to admire in this field need nevertheless not be imitated, and that religious phenomena, like all other human phenomena, are subject to the law of the golden mean. Political reformers accomplish their successive tasks in the history of nations by being blind for the time to other causes. Great schools of art work out the effects which it is their mission to reveal, at the cost of a one-sidedness for which other schools must make amends. We accept a John Howard, a Mazzini, a Botticelli, a Michael Angelo, with a kind of indulgence. We are glad they existed to show us that way, but we are glad there are also other ways of seeing and taking life. So of many of the saints whom we have looked at. We are proud of a human nature that could be so passionately extreme, but we shrink from advising others to follow the example. The conduct we blame ourselves for not following lies nearer to the middle line of human effort. It is less dependent on particular beliefs and doctrines. It is such as wears well in different ages, such as under different skies all judges are able to commend.

The fruits of religion, in other words, are, like all human products, liable to corruption by excess. Common sense must judge them. It need not blame the votary ; but it may be able to praise him only conditionally, as one who acts faithfully according to his lights. He shows us heroism in one way, but the unconditionally good way is that for which no indulgence need be asked.

We find that error by excess is exemplified by every saintly virtue. Excess, in human faculties, means usually one-sidedness or want of balance ; for it is hard to imagine an essential faculty too strong, if only other faculties equally strong be there to coöperate with it in action. Strong affections need a strong will ; strong active powers need a strong intellect ; strong intellect needs strong sympathies, to keep life steady. If the balance exist, no one faculty can possibly be too strong — we only get the stronger all-round character. In the life of saints, technically so called, the spiritual faculties are strong, but what gives the impression of extravagance proves usually on examination to be a relative deficiency of intellect. Spiritual excitement takes pathological forms whenever other interests are too few and the intellect too narrow. We find this exemplified by all the saintly attributes in turn — devout love of God, purity, charity, asceticism, all may lead astray. I will run over these virtues in succession.

First of all let us take Devoutness. When unbalanced, one of its vices is called Fanaticism. Fanaticism (when not a mere expression of ecclesiastical ambition) is only loyalty carried to a convulsive extreme. When an intensely loyal and narrow mind is once grasped by the feeling that a certain superhuman person is worthy of its exclusive devotion, one of the first things that happens is that it idealizes the devotion itself. To adequately realize the merits of the idol gets to be considered the

one great merit of the worshiper; and the sacrifices and
servilities by which savage tribesmen have from time
immemorial exhibited their faithfulness to chieftains are
now outbid in favor of the deity. Vocabularies are exhausted and languages altered in the attempt to praise
him enough; death is looked on as gain if it attract his
grateful notice; and the personal attitude of being his
devotee becomes what one might almost call a new and
exalted kind of professional specialty within the tribe.[1]
The legends that gather round the lives of holy persons
are fruits of this impulse to celebrate and glorify. The
Buddha[2] and Mohammed[3] and their companions and
many Christian saints are incrusted with a heavy jewelry

---

[1] Christian saints have had their specialties of devotion, Saint Francis to
Christ's wounds; Saint Anthony of Padua to Christ's childhood; Saint
Bernard to his humanity; Saint Teresa to Saint Joseph, etc. The Shi-ite
Mohammedans venerate Ali, the Prophet's son-in-law, instead of Abu-bekr,
his brother-in-law. Vambéry describes a dervish whom he met in Persia,
"who had solemnly vowed, thirty years before, that he would never employ his organs of speech otherwise but in uttering, everlastingly, the name
of his favorite, *Ali, Ali.* He thus wished to signify to the world that he
was the most devoted partisan of that Ali who had been dead a thousand
years. In his own home, speaking with his wife, children, and friends, no
other word but 'Ali!' ever passed his lips. If he wanted food or drink or
anything else, he expressed his wants still by repeating 'Ali!' Begging or
buying at the bazaar, it was always 'Ali!' Treated ill or generously, he
would still harp on his monotonous 'Ali!' Latterly his zeal assumed such
tremendous proportions that, like a madman, he would race, the whole day,
up and down the streets of the town, throwing his stick high up into the
air, and shriek out, all the while, at the top of his voice, 'Ali!' This dervish was venerated by everybody as a saint, and received everywhere with
the greatest distinction." ARMINIUS VAMBÉRY, his Life and Adventures,
written by Himself, London, 1889, p. 69. On the anniversary of the death
of Hussein, Ali's son, the Shi-ite Moslems still make the air resound with
cries of his name and Ali's.

[2] Compare H. C. WARREN: Buddhism in Translation, Cambridge, U. S.,
1898, passim.

[3] Compare J. L. MERRICK: The Life and Religion of Mohammed, as
contained in the Sheeah traditions of the Hyat-ul-Kuloob, Boston, 1850.
passim.

of anecdotes which are meant to be honorific, but are simply *abgeschmackt* and silly, and form a touching expression of man's misguided propensity to praise.

An immediate consequence of this condition of mind is jealousy for the deity's honor. How can the devotee show his loyalty better than by sensitiveness in this regard? The slightest affront or neglect must be resented, the deity's enemies must be put to shame. In exceedingly narrow minds and active wills, such a care may become an engrossing preoccupation; and crusades have been preached and massacres instigated for no other reason than to remove a fancied slight upon the God. Theologies representing the gods as mindful of their glory, and churches with imperialistic policies, have conspired to fan this temper to a glow, so that intolerance and persecution have come to be vices associated by some of us inseparably with the saintly mind. They are unquestionably its besetting sins. The saintly temper is a moral temper, and a moral temper has often to be cruel. It is a partisan temper, and that is cruel. Between his own and Jehovah's enemies a David knows no difference; a Catherine of Siena, panting to stop the warfare among Christians which was the scandal of her epoch, can think of no better method of union among them than a crusade to massacre the Turks; Luther finds no word of protest or regret over the atrocious tortures with which the Anabaptist leaders were put to death; and a Cromwell praises the Lord for delivering his enemies into his hands for 'execution.' Politics come in in all such cases; but piety finds the partnership not quite unnatural. So, when 'freethinkers' tell us that religion and fanaticism are twins, we cannot make an unqualified denial of the charge.

Fanaticism must then be inscribed on the wrong side

of religion's account, so long as the religious person's intellect is on the stage which the despotic kind of God satisfies. But as soon as the God is represented as less intent on his own honor and glory, it ceases to be a danger.

Fanaticism is found only where the character is masterful and aggressive. In gentle characters, where devoutness is intense and the intellect feeble, we have an imaginative absorption in the love of God to the exclusion of all practical human interests, which, though innocent enough, is too one-sided to be admirable. A mind too narrow has room but for one kind of affection. When the love of God takes possession of such a mind, it expels all human loves and human uses. There is no English name for such a sweet excess of devotion, so I will refer to it as a *theopathic* condition.

The blessed Margaret Mary Alacoque may serve as an example.

"To be loved here upon the earth," her recent biographer exclaims: "to be loved by a noble, elevated, distinguished being; to be loved with fidelity, with devotion, — what enchantment! But to be loved by God! and loved by him to distraction [aimé jusqù'à la folie]! — Margaret melted away with love at the thought of such a thing. Like Saint Philip of Neri in former times, or like Saint Francis Xavier, she said to God: 'Hold back, O my God, these torrents which overwhelm me, or else enlarge my capacity for their reception.'" [1]

The most signal proofs of God's love which Margaret Mary received were her hallucinations of sight, touch, and hearing, and the most signal in turn of these were the revelations of Christ's sacred heart, "surrounded with rays more brilliant than the Sun, and transparent like a crystal. The wound which he received on the cross visibly appeared upon it. There

[1] BOUGAUD: Hist. de la bienheureuse Marguerite Marie, Paris, 1894, p. 145.

was a crown of thorns round about this divine Heart, and a cross above it." At the same time Christ's voice told her that, unable longer to contain the flames of his love for mankind, he had chosen her by a miracle to spread the knowledge of them. He thereupon took out her mortal heart, placed it inside of his own and inflamed it, and then replaced it in her breast, adding: "Hitherto thou hast taken the name of my slave, hereafter thou shalt be called the well-beloved disciple of my Sacred Heart."

In a later vision the Saviour revealed to her in detail the 'great design' which he wished to establish through her instrumentality. "I ask of thee to bring it about that every first Friday after the week of holy Sacrament shall be made into a special holy day for honoring my Heart by a general communion and by services intended to make honorable amends for the indignities which it has received. And I promise thee that my Heart will dilate to shed with abundance the influences of its love upon all those who pay to it these honors, or who bring it about that others do the same."

"This revelation," says Mgr. Bougaud, "is unquestionably the most important of all the revelations which have illumined the Church since that of the Incarnation and of the Lord's Supper. . . . After the Eucharist, the supreme effort of the Sacred Heart." [1]   Well, what were its good fruits for Margaret Mary's life? Apparently little else but sufferings and prayers and absences of mind and swoons and ecstasies. She became increasingly useless about the convent, her absorption in Christ's love, —

"which grew upon her daily, rendering her more and more incapable of attending to external duties. They tried her in the infirmary, but without much success, although her kindness, zeal, and devotion were without bounds, and her charity rose to acts of such a heroism that our readers would not bear the recital

[1] BOUGAUD: Hist. de la bienheureuse Marguerite Marie, Paris, 1894, pp. 365, 241.

of them. They tried her in the kitchen, but were forced to give it up as hopeless — everything dropped out of her hands. The admirable humility with which she made amends for her clumsiness could not prevent this from being prejudicial to the order and regularity which must always reign in a community. They put her in the school, where the little girls cherished her, and cut pieces out of her clothes [for relics] as if she were already a saint, but where she was too absorbed inwardly to pay the necessary attention. Poor dear sister, even less after her visions than before them was she a denizen of earth, and they had to leave her in her heaven." [1]

Poor dear sister, indeed! Amiable and good, but so feeble of intellectual outlook that it would be too much to ask of us, with our Protestant and modern education, to feel anything but indulgent pity for the kind of saintship which she embodies. A lower example still of theopathic saintliness is that of Saint Gertrude, a Benedictine nun of the thirteenth century, whose 'Revelations,' a well-known mystical authority, consist mainly of proofs of Christ's partiality for her undeserving person. Assurances of his love, intimacies and caresses and compliments of the most absurd and puerile sort, addressed by Christ to Gertrude as an individual, form the tissue of this paltry-minded recital.[2] In reading such a narrative,

---

[1] BOUGAUD : Op. cit., p. 267.

[2] Examples : "Suffering from a headache, she sought, for the glory of God, to relieve herself by holding certain odoriferous substances in her mouth, when the Lord appeared to her to lean over towards her lovingly, and to find comfort Himself in these odors. After having gently breathed them in, He arose, and said with a gratified air to the Saints, as if contented with what He had done : 'See the new present which my betrothed has given Me !'

"One day, at chapel, she heard supernaturally sung the words, 'Sanctus, Sanctus, Sanctus.' The Son of God leaning towards her like a sweet lover, and giving to her soul the softest kiss, said to her at the second Sanctus : 'In this Sanctus addressed to my person, receive with this kiss all the sanctity of my divinity and of my humanity, and let it be to thee a sufficient preparation for approaching the communion table.' And the next follow-we realize the gap between the thirteenth and the twentieth century, and we feel that saintliness of character may yield almost absolutely worthless fruits if it be associated with such inferior intellectual sympathies. What with science, idealism, and democracy, our own imagination has grown to need a God of an entirely different temperament from that Being interested exclusively in dealing out personal favors, with whom our ancestors were so contented. Smitten as we are with the vision of social righteousness, a God indifferent to everything but adulation, and full of partiality for his individual favorites, lacks an essential element of largeness; and even the best professional sainthood of former centuries, pent in as it is to such a conception, seems to us curiously shallow and unedifying.

Take Saint Teresa, for example, one of the ablest women, in many respects, of whose life we have the record. She had a powerful intellect of the practical order. She wrote admirable descriptive psychology, possessed a will equal to any emergency, great talent for politics and business, a buoyant disposition, and a first-rate literary style. She was tenaciously aspiring, and put her whole life at the service of her religious ideals. Yet so paltry were these, according to our present way of thinking, that (although I know that others have been moved differently) I confess that my only feeling in

ing Sunday, while she was thanking God for this favor, behold the Son of God, more beauteous than thousands of angels, takes her in His arms as if He were proud of her, and presents her to God the Father, in that perfection of sanctity with which He had dowered her. And the Father took such delight in this soul thus presented by His only Son, that, as if unable longer to restrain Himself, He gave her, and the Holy Ghost gave her also, the Sanctity attributed to each by His own *Sanctus* — and thus she remained endowed with the plenary fullness of the blessing of *Sanctity*, bestowed on her by Omnipotence, by Wisdom, and by Love." Révélations de Sainte Gertrude, Paris, 1898, i. 44, 186.

reading her has been pity that so much vitality of soul should have found such poor employment.

In spite of the sufferings which she endured, there is a curious flavor of superficiality about her genius. A Birmingham anthropologist, Dr. Jordan, has divided the human race into two types, whom he calls 'shrews' and 'non-shrews' respectively.[1] The shrew-type is defined as possessing an 'active unimpassioned temperament.' In other words, shrews are the 'motors,' rather than the 'sensories,'[2] and their expressions are as a rule more energetic than the feelings which appear to prompt them. Saint Teresa, paradoxical as such a judgment may sound, was a typical shrew, in this sense of the term. The bustle of her style, as well as of her life, proves it. Not only must she receive unheard-of personal favors and spiritual graces from her Saviour, but she must immediately write about them and *exploiter* them professionally, and use her expertness to give instruction to those less privileged. Her voluble egotism; her sense, not of radical bad being, as the really contrite have it, but of her 'faults' and 'imperfections' in the plural; her stereotyped humility and return upon herself, as covered with 'confusion' at each new manifestation of God's singular partiality for a person so unworthy, are typical of shrewdom : a paramountly feeling nature would be objectively lost in gratitude, and silent. She had some public instincts, it is true; she hated the Lutherans, and longed for the church's triumph over them; but in the main her idea of religion seems to have been that of an endless amatory flirtation — if one may say so without irrever-

[1] FURNEAUX JORDAN : Character in Birth and Parentage, first edition. Later editions change the nomenclature.

[2] As to this distinction, see the admirably practical account in J. M. BALDWIN's little book, The Story of the Mind, 1898.

ence — between the devotee and the deity; and apart from helping younger nuns to go in this direction by the inspiration of her example and instruction, there is absolutely no human use in her, or sign of any general human interest. Yet the spirit of her age, far from rebuking her, exalted her as superhuman.

We have to pass a similar judgment on the whole notion of saintship based on merits. Any God who, on the one hand, can care to keep a pedantically minute account of individual shortcomings, and on the other can feel such partialities, and load particular creatures with such insipid marks of favor, is too small-minded a God for our credence. When Luther, in his immense manly way, swept off by a stroke of his hand the very notion of a debit and credit account kept with individuals by the Almighty, he stretched the soul's imagination and saved theology from puerility.

So much for mere devotion, divorced from the intellectual conceptions which might guide it towards bearing useful human fruit.

The next saintly virtue in which we find excess is Purity. In theopathic characters, like those whom we have just considered, the love of God must not be mixed with any other love. Father and mother, sisters, brothers, and friends are felt as interfering distractions; for sensitiveness and narrowness, when they occur together, as they often do, require above all things a simplified world to dwell in. Variety and confusion are too much for their powers of comfortable adaptation. But whereas your aggressive pietist reaches his unity objectively, by forcibly stamping disorder and divergence out, your retiring pietist reaches his subjectively, leaving disorder in the world at large, but making a smaller world in which he dwells himself and from which he eliminates it altogether. Thus, alongside of the church militant with its prisons, dragonnades, and inquisition methods, we have the church *fugient*, as one might call it, with its hermitages, monasteries, and sectarian organizations, both churches pursuing the same object — to unify the life,[1] and simplify the spectacle presented to the soul. A mind extremely sensitive to inner discords will drop one external relation after another, as interfering with the absorption of consciousness in spiritual things. Amusements must go first, then conventional ' society,' then business, then family duties, until at last seclusion, with a subdivision of the day into hours for stated religious acts, is the only thing that can be borne. The lives of saints are a history of successive renunciations of complication, one form of contact with the outer life being dropped after another, to save the purity of inner tone.[2] " Is it not better," a young sister

[1] On this subject I refer to the work of M. MURISIER (Les Maladies du Sentiment Religieux, Paris, 1901), who makes inner unification the mainspring of the whole religious life. But *all* strongly ideal interests, religious or irreligious, unify the mind and tend to subordinate everything to themselves. One would infer from M. Murisier's pages that this formal condition was peculiarly characteristic of religion, and that one might in comparison almost neglect material content, in studying the latter. I trust that the present work will convince the reader that religion has plenty of material content which is characteristic, and which is more important by far than any general psychological form. In spite of this criticism, I find M. Murisier's book highly instructive.

[2] Example : " At the first beginning of the Servitor's [Suso's] interior life, after he had purified his soul properly by confession, he marked out for himself, in thought, three circles, within which he shut himself up, as in a spiritual intrenchment. The first circle was his cell, his chapel, and the choir. When he was within this circle, he seemed to himself in complete security. The second circle was the whole monastery as far as the outer gate. The third and outermost circle was the gate itself, and here it was necessary for him to stand well upon his guard. When he went outside these circles, it seemed to him that he was in the plight of some wild animal which is outside its hole, and surrounded by the hunt, and therefore in need of all its cunning and watchfulness." The Life of the Blessed Henry Suso, by Himself, translated by KNOX, London, 1865, p. 168.

asks her Superior, " that I should not speak at all during the hour of recreation, so as not to run the risk, by speaking, of falling into some sin of which I might not be conscious ? " [1] If the life remains a social one at all, those who take part in it must follow one identical rule. Embosomed in this monotony, the zealot for purity feels clean and free once more. The minuteness of uniformity maintained in certain sectarian communities, whether monastic or not, is something almost inconceivable to a man of the world. Costume, phraseology, hours, and habits are absolutely stereotyped, and there is no doubt that some persons are so made as to find in this stability an incomparable kind of mental rest.

We have no time to multiply examples, so I will let the case of Saint Louis of Gonzaga serve as a type of excess in purification. I think you will agree that this youth carried the elimination of the external and dis- cordant to a point which we cannot unreservedly admire. At the age of ten, his biographer says : —

" The inspiration came to him to consecrate to the Mother of God his own virginity — that being to her the most agreeable of possible presents. Without delay, then, and with all the fervor there was in him, joyous of heart, and burning with love, he made his vow of perpetual chastity. Mary accepted the offering of his innocent heart, and obtained for him from God, as a recompense, the extraordinary grace of never feeling dur- ing his entire life the slightest touch of temptation against the virtue of purity. This was an altogether exceptional favor, rarely accorded even to Saints themselves, and all the more marvelous in that Louis dwelt always in courts and among great folks, where danger and opportunity are so unusually frequent. It is true that Louis from his earliest childhood had shown a natural repugnance for whatever might be impure or

[1] Vie des premières Religieuses Dominicaines de la Congrégation de St Dominique, à Nancy ; Nancy, 1896, p. 129.

unvirginal, and even for relations of any sort whatever between persons of opposite sex. But this made it all the more surprising that he should, especially since this vow, feel it necessary to have recourse to such a number of expedients for protecting against even the shadow of danger the virginity which he had thus consecrated. One might suppose that if any one could have contented himself with the ordinary precautions, prescribed for all Christians, it would assuredly have been he. But no! In the use of preservatives and means of defense, in flight from the most insignificant occasions, from every possibility of peril, just as in the mortification of his flesh, he went farther than the majority of saints. He, who by an extraordinary protection of God's grace was never tempted, measured all his steps as if he were threatened on every side by particular dangers. Thenceforward he never raised his eyes, either when walking in the streets, or when in society. Not only did he avoid all business with females even more scrupulously than before, but he renounced all conversation and every kind of social recreation with them, although his father tried to make him take part; and he commenced only too early to deliver his innocent body to austerities of every kind." [1]

At the age of twelve, we read of this young man that " if by chance his mother sent one of her maids of honor to him with a message, he never allowed her to come in, but listened to her through the barely opened door, and dismissed her immediately. He did not like to be alone with his own mother, whether at table or in conversation ; and when the rest of the company withdrew, he sought also a pretext for retiring. . . . Several great ladies, relatives of his, he avoided learning to know even by sight; and he made a sort of treaty with his father, engaging promptly and readily to accede to all his wishes, if he might only be excused from all visits to ladies." (Ibid., p. 71.)

[1] MESCHLER's Life of Saint Louis of Gonzaga, French translation by LEBRÉQUIER, 1891, p. 40.

When he was seventeen years old Louis joined the Jesuit order,[1] against his father's passionate entreaties, for he was heir of a princely house; and when a year later the father died, he took the loss as a ' particular attention ' to himself on God's part, and wrote letters of stilted good advice, as from a spiritual superior, to his grieving mother.   He soon became so good a monk that if any one asked him the number of his brothers and sisters, he had to reflect and count them over before replying. A Father asked him one day if he were never troubled by the thought of his family, to which, " I never think of them except when praying for them," was his only answer.   Never was he seen to hold in his hand a flower or anything perfumed, that he might take pleasure in it.   On the contrary, in the hospital, he used to seek for whatever was most disgusting, and eagerly snatch the bandages of ulcers, etc., from the hands of his companions. He avoided worldly talk, and immediately tried to turn every conversation on to pious subjects, or else he remained silent.   He systematically refused to notice his surroundings.   Being ordered one day to bring a book from the rector's seat in the refectory, he had to ask where the rector sat, for in the three months he had eaten bread there, so carefully did he guard his eyes that he had not noticed the place.   One day, during recess, having looked by chance on one of his companions, he reproached himself as for a grave sin against modesty. He cultivated silence, as preserving from sins of the tongue; and his greatest penance was the limit which his superiors set to his bodily penances.   He sought after

---

[1] In his boyish note-book he praises the monastic life for its freedom from sin, and for the imperishable treasures, which it enables us to store up, " of merit in God's eyes which makes of Him our debtor for all Eternity." Loc. cit., p. 62.

false accusations and unjust reprimands as opportunities of humility; and such was his obedience that, when a room-mate, having no more paper, asked him for a sheet, he did not feel free to give it to him without first obtaining the permission of the superior, who, as such, stood in the place of God, and transmitted his orders.

I can find no other sorts of fruit than these of Louis's saintship. He died in 1591, in his twenty-ninth year, and is known in the Church as the patron of all young people. On his festival, the altar in the chapel devoted to him in a certain church in Rome " is embosomed in flowers, arranged with exquisite taste; and a pile of letters may be seen at its foot, written to the Saint by young men and women, and directed to ' Paradiso.' They are supposed to be burnt unread except by San Luigi, who must find singular petitions in these pretty little missives, tied up now with a green ribbon, expressive of hope, now with a red one, emblematic of love," etc.[1]

---

[1] Mademoiselle Mori, a novel quoted in HARE's Walks in Rome, 1900, i. 55.

I cannot resist the temptation to quote from Starbuck's book, p. 388, another case of purification by elimination. It runs as follows : —

"The signs of abnormality which sanctified persons show are of frequent occurrence. They get out of tune with other people ; often they will have nothing to do with churches, which they regard as worldly ; they become hypercritical towards others ; they grow careless of their social, political, and financial obligations. As an instance of this type may be mentioned a woman of sixty-eight of whom the writer made a special study. She had been a member of one of the most active and progressive churches in a busy part of a large city. Her pastor described her as having reached the censorious stage. She had grown more and more out of sympathy with the church ; her connection with it finally consisted simply in attendance at prayer-meeting, at which her only message was that of reproof and condemnation of the others for living on a low plane. At last she withdrew from fellowship with any church. The writer found her living alone in a little room on the top story of a cheap boarding-house, quite out of touch with all human relations, but apparently happy in the enjoyment of her

Our final judgment of the worth of such a life as this will depend largely on our conception of God, and of the sort of conduct he is best pleased with in his creatures. The Catholicism of the sixteenth century paid little heed to social righteousness; and to leave the world to the devil whilst saving one's own soul was then accounted no discreditable scheme. To-day, rightly or wrongly, helpfulness in general human affairs is, in consequence of one of those secular mutations in moral sentiment of which I spoke, deemed an essential element of worth in character; and to be of some public or private use is also reckoned as a species of divine service. Other early Jesuits, especially the missionaries among them, the Xaviers, Brébeufs, Jogues, were objective minds, and fought in their way for the world's welfare; so their lives to-day inspire us. But when the intellect, as in this Louis, is originally no larger than a pin's head, and cherishes ideas of God of corresponding smallness, the result, notwithstanding the heroism put forth, is on the whole repulsive. Purity, we see in the object-lesson, is *not* the one thing needful; and it is better that a life should contract many a dirt-mark, than forfeit usefulness in its efforts to remain unspotted.

own spiritual blessings. Her time was occupied in writing booklets on sanctification — page after page of dreamy rhapsody. She proved to be one of a small group of persons who claim that entire salvation involves three steps instead of two ; not only must there be conversion and sanctification, but a third, which they call 'crucifixion' or 'perfect redemption,' and which seems to bear the same relation to sanctification that this bears to conversion. She related how the Spirit had said to her, 'Stop going to church. Stop going to holiness meetings. Go to your own room and I will teach you.' She professes to care nothing for colleges, or preachers, or churches, but only cares to listen to what God says to her. Her description of her experience seemed entirely consistent ; she is happy and contented, and her life is entirely satisfactory to herself. While listening to her own story, one was tempted to forget that it was from the life of a person who could not live by it in conjunction with her fellows.''

Proceeding onwards in our search of religious extravagance, we next come upon excesses of Tenderness and Charity. Here saintliness has to face the charge of preserving the unfit, and breeding parasites and beggars. ' Resist not evil,' ' Love your enemies,' these are saintly maxims of which men of this world find it hard to speak without impatience. Are the men of this world right, or are the saints in possession of the deeper range of truth ?

No simple answer is possible. Here, if anywhere, one feels the complexity of the moral life, and the mysteriousness of the way in which facts and ideals are interwoven.

Perfect conduct is a relation between three terms : the actor, the objects for which he acts, and the recipients of the action. In order that conduct should be abstractly perfect, all three terms, intention, execution, and reception, should be suited to one another. The best intention will fail if it either work by false means or address itself to the wrong recipient. Thus no critic or estimator of the value of conduct can confine himself to the actor's animus alone, apart from the other elements of the performance. As there is no worse lie than a truth misunderstood by those who hear it, so reasonable arguments, challenges to magnanimity, and appeals to sympathy or justice, are folly when we are dealing with human crocodiles and boa-constrictors. The saint may simply give the universe into the hands of the enemy by his trustfulness. He may by non-resistance cut off his own survival.

Herbert Spencer tells us that the perfect man's conduct will appear perfect only when the environment is perfect : to no inferior environment is it suitably adapted. We may paraphrase this by cordially admitting that saintly conduct would be the most perfect conduct conceivable in an environment where all were saints already; but by adding that in an environment where few are saints, and many the exact reverse of saints, it must be ill adapted. We must frankly confess, then, using our empirical common sense and ordinary practical prejudices, that in the world that actually is, the virtues of sympathy, charity, and non-resistance may be, and often have been, manifested in excess. The powers of darkness have systematically taken advantage of them. The whole modern scientific organization of charity is a consequence of the failure of simply giving alms. The whole history of constitutional government is a commentary on the excellence of resisting evil, and when one cheek is smitten, of smiting back and not turning the other cheek also.

You will agree to this in general, for in spite of the Gospel, in spite of Quakerism, in spite of Tolstoi, you believe in fighting fire with fire, in shooting down usurpers, locking up thieves, and freezing out vagabonds and swindlers.

And yet you are sure, as I am sure, that were the world confined to these hard-headed, hard-hearted, and hard-fisted methods exclusively, were there no one prompt to help a brother first, and find out afterwards whether he were worthy; no one willing to drown his private wrongs in pity for the wronger's person; no one ready to be duped many a time rather than live always on suspicion; no one glad to treat individuals passionately and impulsively rather than by general rules of prudence; the world would be an infinitely worse place than it is now to live in. The tender grace, not of a day that is dead, but of a day yet to be born somehow, with the golden rule grown natural, would be cut out from the perspective of our imaginations.

The saints, existing in this way, may, with their extravagances of human tenderness, be prophetic. Nay, innumerable times they have proved themselves prophetic. Treating those whom they met, in spite of the past, in spite of all appearances, as worthy, they have stimulated them to *be* worthy, miraculously transformed them by their radiant example and by the challenge of their expectation.

From this point of view we may admit the human charity which we find in all saints, and the great excess of it which we find in some saints, to be a genuinely creative social force, tending to make real a degree of virtue which it alone is ready to assume as possible. The saints are authors, *auctores*, increasers, of goodness. The potentialities of development in human souls are unfathomable. So many who seemed irretrievably hardened have in point of fact been softened, converted, regenerated, in ways that amazed the subjects even more than they surprised the spectators, that we never can be sure in advance of any man that his salvation by the way of love is hopeless. We have no right to speak of human crocodiles and boa-constrictors as of fixedly incurable beings. We know not the complexities of personality, the smouldering emotional fires, the other facets of the character-polyhedron, the resources of the subliminal region. St. Paul long ago made our ancestors familiar with the idea that every soul is virtually sacred. Since Christ died for us all without exception, St. Paul said, we must despair of no one. This belief in the essential sacredness of every one expresses itself to-day in all sorts of humane customs and reformatory institutions, and in a growing aversion to the death penalty and to brutality in punishment. The saints, with their extravagance of human tenderness, are the great torch-bearers of this belief, the tip of the wedge, the clearers of the darkness. Like the single drops which sparkle in the sun as they are flung far ahead of the advancing edge of a wave-crest or of a flood, they show the way and are forerunners. The world is not yet with them, so they often seem in the midst of the world's affairs to be preposterous. Yet they are impregnators of the world, vivifiers and animaters of potentialities of goodness which but for them would lie forever dormant. It is not possible to be quite as mean as we naturally are, when they have passed before us. One fire kindles another; and without that over-trust in human worth which they show, the rest of us would lie in spiritual stagnancy.

Momentarily considered, then, the saint may waste his tenderness and be the dupe and victim of his charitable fever, but the general function of his charity in social evolution is vital and essential. If things are ever to move upward, some one must be ready to take the first step, and assume the risk of it. No one who is not willing to try charity, to try non-resistance as the saint is always willing, can tell whether these methods will or will not succeed. When they do succeed, they are far more powerfully successful than force or worldly prudence. Force destroys enemies; and the best that can be said of prudence is that it keeps what we already have in safety. But non-resistance, when successful, turns enemies into friends; and charity regenerates its objects. These saintly methods are, as I said, creative energies; and genuine saints find in the elevated excitement with which their faith endows them an authority and impressiveness which makes them irresistible in situations where men of shallower nature cannot get on at all without the use of worldly prudence. This practical proof that worldly wisdom may be safely transcended is the saint's

magic gift to mankind.[1] Not only does his vision of a
better world console us for the generally prevailing prose

[1] The best missionary lives abound in the victorious combination of non-
resistance with personal authority.   John G. Paton, for example, in the
New Hebrides, among brutish Melanesian cannibals, preserves a charmed
life by dint of it.   When it comes to the point, no one ever dares actually
to strike him.   Native converts, inspired by him, showed analogous virtue.
" One of our chiefs, full of the Christ-kindled desire to seek and to save,
sent a message to an inland chief, that he and four attendants would come
on Sabbath and tell them the gospel of Jehovah God.   The reply came back
sternly forbidding their visit, and threatening with death any Christian
that approached their village.   Our chief sent in response a loving message,
telling them that Jehovah had taught the Christians to return good for
evil, and that they would come unarmed to tell them the story of how the
Son of God came into the world and died in order to bless and save his
enemies.   The heathen chief sent back a stern and prompt reply once
more : ' If you come, you will be killed.'   On Sabbath morn the Christian
chief and his four companions were met outside the village by the heathen
chief, who implored and threatened them once more.   But the former
said : —
   " ' We come to you without weapons of war !   We come only to tell you
about Jesus.   We believe that He will protect us to-day.'
   " As they pressed steadily forward towards the village, spears began to be
thrown at them.   Some they evaded, being all except one dexterous warriors ; and others they literally received with their bare hands, and turned
them aside in an incredible manner.   The heathen, apparently thunderstruck
at these men thus approaching them without weapons of war, and not even
flinging back their own spears which they had caught, after having thrown
what the old chief called ' a shower of spears,' desisted from mere surprise.   Our Christian chief called out, as he and his companions drew up in
the midst of them on the village public ground : —
   " ' Jehovah thus protects us.   He has given us all your spears !   Once we
would have thrown them back at you and killed you.   But now we come,
not to fight but to tell you about Jesus.   He has changed our dark hearts.
He asks you now to lay down all these your other weapons of war, and to
hear what we can tell you about the love of God, our great Father, the
only living God.'
   " The heathen were perfectly overawed.   They manifestly looked on these
Christians as protected by some Invisible One.   They listened for the first
time to the story of the Gospel and of the Cross.   We lived to see that
chief and all his tribe sitting in the school of Christ.   And there is perhaps
not an island in these southern seas, amongst all those won for Christ,
where similar acts of heroism on the part of converts cannot be recited."
JOHN G. PATON, Missionary to the New Hebrides, An Autobiography,
second part, London, 1890, p. 243.

and barrenness; but even when on the whole we have to confess him ill adapted, he makes some converts, and the environment gets better for his ministry. He is an effective ferment of goodness, a slow transmuter of the earthly into a more heavenly order.

In this respect the Utopian dreams of social justice in which many contemporary socialists and anarchists indulge are, in spite of their impracticability and non-adaptation to present environmental conditions, analogous to the saint's belief in an existent kingdom of heaven. They help to break the edge of the general reign of hardness, and are slow leavens of a better order.

The next topic in order is Asceticism, which I fancy you are all ready to consider without argument a virtue liable to extravagance and excess. The optimism and refinement of the modern imagination has, as I have already said elsewhere, changed the attitude of the church towards corporeal mortification, and a Suso or a Saint Peter of Alcantara [1] appear to us to-day rather in the

---

[1] Saint Peter, Saint Teresa tells us in her autobiography (French translation, p. 333), "had passed forty years without ever sleeping more than an hour and a half a day. Of all his mortifications, this was the one that had cost him the most. To compass it, he kept always on his knees or on his feet. The little sleep he allowed nature to take was snatched in a sitting posture, his head leaning against a piece of wood fixed in the wall. Even had he wished to lie down, it would have been impossible, because his cell was only four feet and a half long. In the course of all these years he never raised his hood, no matter what the ardor of the sun or the rain's strength. He never put on a shoe. He wore a garment of coarse sackcloth, with nothing else upon his skin. This garment was as scant as possible, and over it a little cloak of the same stuff. When the cold was great he took off the cloak and opened for a while the door and little window of his cell. Then he closed them and resumed the mantle, — his way, as he told us, of warming himself, and making his body feel a better temperature. It was a frequent thing with him to eat once only in three days; and when I expressed my surprise, he said that it was very easy if one once had acquired the habit. One of his companions has assured me that he has

light of tragic mountebanks than of sane men inspiring
us with respect. If the inner dispositions are right, we
ask, what need of all this torment, this violation of the
outer nature? It keeps the outer nature too important.
Any one who is genuinely emancipated from the flesh
will look on pleasures and pains, abundance and privation, as alike irrelevant and indifferent. He can engage
in actions and experience enjoyments without fear of
corruption or enslavement. As the Bhagavad-Gita says,
only those need renounce worldly actions who are still
inwardly attached thereto. If one be really unattached
to the fruits of action, one may mix in the world with
equanimity. I quoted in a former lecture Saint Augustine's antinomian saying: If you only love God enough,
you may safely follow all your inclinations. " He needs
no devotional practices," is one of Ramakrishna's maxims, " whose heart is moved to tears at the mere mention
of the name of Hari." [1] And the Buddha, in pointing
out what he called ' the middle way ' to his disciples,
told them to abstain from both extremes, excessive mortification being as unreal and unworthy as mere desire
and pleasure. The only perfect life, he said, is that of
inner wisdom, which makes one thing as indifferent to

gone sometimes eight days without food. . . . His poverty was extreme ;
and his mortification, even in his youth, was such that he told me he had
passed three years in a house of his order without knowing any of the
monks otherwise than by the sound of their voice, for he never raised his
eyes, and only found his way about by following the others. He showed
this same modesty on public highways. He spent many years without ever
laying eyes upon a woman ; but he confessed to me that at the age he had
reached it was indifferent to him whether he laid eyes on them or not. He
was very old when I first came to know him, and his body so attenuated
that it seemed formed of nothing so much as of so many roots of trees.
With all this sanctity he was very affable. He never spoke unless he was
questioned, but his intellectual right-mindedness and grace gave to all his
words an irresistible charm."

[1] F. Max Müller : Ramakrishna, his Life and Sayings, 1899, p. 180.

us as another, and thus leads to rest, to peace, and to Nirvâna.[1]

We find accordingly that as ascetic saints have grown older, and directors of conscience more experienced, they usually have shown a tendency to lay less stress on special bodily mortifications. Catholic teachers have always professed the rule that, since health is needed for efficiency in God's service, health must not be sacrificed to mortification. The general optimism and healthy-mindedness of liberal Protestant circles to-day makes mortification for mortification's sake repugnant to us. We can no longer sympathize with cruel deities, and the notion that God can take delight in the spectacle of sufferings self-inflicted in his honor is abhorrent. In consequence of all these motives you probably are disposed, unless some special utility can be shown in some individual's discipline, to treat the general tendency to asceticism as pathological.

Yet I believe that a more careful consideration of the whole matter, distinguishing between the general good intention of asceticism and the uselessness of some of the particular acts of which it may be guilty, ought to rehabilitate it in our esteem. For in its spiritual meaning asceticism stands for nothing less than for the essence of the twice-born philosophy. It symbolizes, lamely enough no doubt, but sincerely, the belief that there is an element of real wrongness in this world, which is neither to be ignored nor evaded, but which must be squarely met and overcome by an appeal to the soul's heroic resources, and neutralized and cleansed away by suffering. As against this view, the ultra-optimistic form of the once-born philosophy thinks we may treat evil by the method of ignoring. Let a man who, by fortunate health and cir-

[1] OLDENBERG: Buddha; translated by W. HOEY, London, 1882, p. 127

cumstances, escapes the suffering of any great amount of evil in his own person, also close his eyes to it as it exists in the wider universe outside his private experience, and he will be quit of it altogether, and can sail through life happily on a healthy-minded basis. But we saw in our lectures on melancholy how precarious this attempt necessarily is. Moreover it is but for the individual; and leaves the evil outside of him, unredeemed and unprovided for in his philosophy.

No such attempt can be a *general* solution of the problem; and to minds of sombre tinge, who naturally feel life as a tragic mystery, such optimism is a shallow dodge or mean evasion. It accepts, in lieu of a real deliverance, what is a lucky personal accident merely, a cranny to escape by. It leaves the general world unhelped and still in the clutch of Satan. The real deliverance, the twice-born folk insist, must be of universal application. Pain and wrong and death must be fairly met and overcome in higher excitement, or else their sting remains essentially unbroken. If one has ever taken the fact of the prevalence of tragic death in this world's history fairly into his mind, — freezing, drowning, entombment alive, wild beasts, worse men, and hideous diseases, — he can with difficulty, it seems to me, continue his own career of worldly prosperity without suspecting that he may all the while not be really inside the game, that he may lack the great initiation.

Well, this is exactly what asceticism thinks; and it voluntarily takes the initiation. Life is neither farce nor genteel comedy, it says, but something we must sit at in mourning garments, hoping its bitter taste will purge us of our folly. The wild and the heroic are indeed such rooted parts of it that healthy-mindedness pure and simple, with its sentimental optimism, can hardly be regarded by any thinking man as a serious solution. Phrases of neatness, cosiness, and comfort can never be an answer to the sphinx's riddle.

In these remarks I am leaning only upon mankind's common instinct for reality, which in point of fact has always held the world to be essentially a theatre for heroism. In heroism, we feel, life's supreme mystery is hidden. We tolerate no one who has no capacity whatever for it in any direction. On the other hand, no matter what a man's frailties otherwise may be, if he be willing to risk death, and still more if he suffer it heroically, in the service he has chosen, the fact consecrates him forever. Inferior to ourselves in this or that way, if yet we cling to life, and he is able ' to fling it away like a flower ' as caring nothing for it, we account him in the deepest way our born superior. Each of us in his own person feels that a high-hearted indifference to life would expiate all his shortcomings.

The metaphysical mystery, thus recognized by common sense, that he who feeds on death that feeds on men possesses life supereminently and excellently, and meets best the secret demands of the universe, is the truth of which asceticism has been the faithful champion. The folly of the cross, so inexplicable by the intellect, has yet its indestructible vital meaning.

Representatively, then, and symbolically, and apart from the vagaries into which the unenlightened intellect of former times may have let it wander, asceticism must, I believe, be acknowledged to go with the profounder way of handling the gift of existence. Naturalistic optimism is mere syllabub and flattery and sponge-cake in comparison. The practical course of action for us, as religious men, would therefore, it seems to me, not be simply to turn our backs upon the ascetic impulse, as most of us to-day turn them, but rather to discover some outlet for it of which the fruits in the way of privation and hardship might be objectively useful. The older monastic asceticism occupied itself with pathetic futilities, or terminated in the mere egotism of the individual, increasing his own perfection.[1] But is it not possible for us to discard most of these older forms of mortification, and yet find saner channels for the heroism which inspired them?

Does not, for example, the worship of material luxury and wealth, which constitutes so large a portion of the ' spirit ' of our age, make somewhat for effeminacy and unmanliness? Is not the exclusively sympathetic and facetious way in which most children are brought up to-day — so different from the education of a hundred years ago, especially in evangelical circles — in danger, in spite of its many advantages, of developing a certain trashiness of fibre? Are there not hereabouts some points of application for a renovated and revised ascetic discipline?

Many of you would recognize such dangers, but would point to athletics, militarism, and individual and national enterprise and adventure as the remedies. These contemporary ideals are quite as remarkable for the energy with which they make for heroic standards of life, as contemporary religion is remarkable for the way in which it neglects them.[2] War and adventure assuredly keep all who engage in them from treating themselves too tenderly. They demand such incredible efforts, depth

[1] " The vanities of all others may die out, but the vanity of a saint as regards his sainthood is hard indeed to wear away." Ramakrishna, his Life and Sayings, 1899, p. 172.

[2] " When a church has to be run by oysters, ice-cream, and fun," I read in an American religious paper, " you may be sure that it is running away from Christ." Such, if one may judge by appearances, is the present plight of many of our churches.

beyond depth of exertion, both in degree and in duration, that the whole scale of motivation alters. Discomfort and annoyance, hunger and wet, pain and cold, squalor and filth, cease to have any deterrent operation whatever. Death turns into a commonplace matter, and its usual power to check our action vanishes. With the annulling of these customary inhibitions, ranges of new energy are set free, and life seems cast upon a higher plane of power.

The beauty of war in this respect is that it is so congruous with ordinary human nature. Ancestral evolution has made us all potential warriors; so the most insignificant individual, when thrown into an army in the field, is weaned from whatever excess of tenderness towards his precious person he may bring with him, and may easily develop into a monster of insensibility.

But when we compare the military type of self-severity with that of the ascetic saint, we find a world-wide difference in all their spiritual concomitants.

" ' Live and let live,' " writes a clear-headed Austrian officer, " is no device for an army. Contempt for one's own comrades, for the troops of the enemy, and, above all, fierce contempt for one's own person, are what war demands of every one. Far better is it for an army to be too savage, too cruel, too barbarous, than to possess too much sentimentality and human reasonableness. If the soldier is to be good for anything as a soldier, he must be exactly the opposite of a reasoning and thinking man. The measure of goodness in him is his possible use in war. War, and even peace, require of the soldier absolutely peculiar standards of morality. The recruit brings with him common moral notions, of which he must seek immediately to get rid. For him victory, success, must be *everything*. The most barbaric tendencies in men come to life again in war, and for war's uses they are incommensurably good." [1]

These words are of course literally true. The immediate aim of the soldier's life is, as Moltke said, destruction, and nothing but destruction; and whatever constructions wars result in are remote and non-military. Consequently the soldier cannot train himself to be too feelingless to all those usual sympathies and respects, whether for persons or for things, that make for conservation. Yet the fact remains that war is a school of strenuous life and heroism; and, being in the line of aboriginal instinct, is the only school that as yet is universally available. But when we gravely ask ourselves whether this wholesale organization of irrationality and crime be our only bulwark against effeminacy, we stand aghast at the thought, and think more kindly of ascetic religion. One hears of the mechanical equivalent of heat. What we now need to discover in the social realm is the moral equivalent of war: something heroic that will speak to men as universally as war does, and yet will be as compatible with their spiritual selves as war has proved itself to be incompatible. I have often thought that in the old monkish poverty-worship, in spite of the pedantry which infested it, there might be something like that moral equivalent of war which we are seeking. May not voluntarily accepted poverty be 'the strenuous life,' without the need of crushing weaker peoples?

Poverty indeed *is* the strenuous life, — without brass bands or uniforms or hysteric popular applause or lies or circumlocutions; and when one sees the way in which wealth-getting enters as an ideal into the very bone and marrow of our generation, one wonders whether a revival

[1] C. V. B. K. : Friedens- und Kriegs-moral der Heere. Quoted by HAMON : Psychologie du Militaire professional, 1895, p. xli.

of the belief that poverty is a worthy religious vocation may not be 'the transformation of military courage,' and the spiritual reform which our time stands most in need of.

Among us English-speaking peoples especially do the praises of poverty need once more to be boldly sung. We have grown literally afraid to be poor. We despise any one who elects to be poor in order to simplify and save his inner life. If he does not join the general scramble and pant with the money-making street, we deem him spiritless and lacking in ambition. We have lost the power even of imagining what the ancient idealization of poverty could have meant : the liberation from material attachments, the unbribed soul, the manlier indifference, the paying our way by what we are or do and not by what we have, the right to fling away our life at any moment irresponsibly, — the more athletic trim, in short, the moral fighting shape. When we of the so-called better classes are scared as men were never scared in history at material ugliness and hardship ; when we put off marriage until our house can be artistic, and quake at the thought of having a child without a bank-account and doomed to manual labor, it is time for thinking men to protest against so unmanly and irreligious a state of opinion.

It is true that so far as wealth gives time for ideal ends and exercise to ideal energies, wealth is better than poverty and ought to be chosen. But wealth does this in only a portion of the actual cases. Elsewhere the desire to gain wealth and the fear to lose it are our chief breeders of cowardice and propagators of corruption. There are thousands of conjunctures in which a wealth-bound man must be a slave, whilst a man for whom poverty has no terrors becomes a freeman. Think of the strength which personal indifference to poverty would give us if we were devoted to unpopular causes. We need no longer hold our tongues or fear to vote the revolutionary or reformatory ticket. Our stocks might fall, our hopes of promotion vanish, our salaries stop, our club doors close in our faces; yet, while we lived, we would imperturbably bear witness to the spirit, and our example would help to set free our generation. The cause would need its funds, but we its servants would be potent in proportion as we personally were contented with our poverty.

I recommend this matter to your serious pondering, for it is certain that the prevalent fear of poverty among the educated classes is the worst moral disease from which our civilization suffers.

I have now said all that I can usefully say about the several fruits of religion as they are manifested in saintly lives, so I will make a brief review and pass to my more general conclusions.

Our question, you will remember, is as to whether religion stands approved by its fruits, as these are exhibited in the saintly type of character. Single attributes of saintliness may, it is true, be temperamental endowments, found in non-religious individuals. But the whole group of them forms a combination which, as such, is religious, for it seems to flow from the sense of the divine as from its psychological centre. Whoever possesses strongly this sense comes naturally to think that the smallest details of this world derive infinite significance from their relation to an unseen divine order. The thought of this order yields him a superior denomination of happiness, and a steadfastness of soul with which no other can compare. In social relations his serviceability is exemplary; he abounds in impulses to help. His help is in-

ward as well as outward, for his sympathy reaches souls
as well as bodies, and kindles unsuspected faculties therein.
Instead of placing happiness where common men place it,
in comfort, he places it in a higher kind of inner excitement, which converts discomforts into sources of cheer
and annuls unhappiness. So he turns his back upon
no duty, however thankless; and when we are in need of
assistance, we can count upon the saint lending his hand
with more certainty than we can count upon any other
person. Finally, his humble-mindedness and his ascetic
tendencies save him from the petty personal pretensions
which so obstruct our ordinary social intercourse, and
his purity gives us in him a clean man for a companion.
Felicity, purity, charity, patience, self-severity, — these
are splendid excellencies, and the saint of all men shows
them in the completest possible measure.

But, as we saw, all these things together do not make
saints infallible. When their intellectual outlook is narrow, they fall into all sorts of holy excesses, fanaticism
or theopathic absorption, self-torment, prudery, scrupulosity, gullibility, and morbid inability to meet the world.
By the very intensity of his fidelity to the paltry ideals
with which an inferior intellect may inspire him, a saint
can be even more objectionable and damnable than a
superficial carnal man would be in the same situation.
We must judge him not sentimentally only, and not
in isolation, but using our own intellectual standards,
placing him in his environment, and estimating his total
function.

Now in the matter of intellectual standards, we must
bear in mind that it is unfair, where we find narrowness
of mind, always to impute it as a vice to the individual,
for in religious and theological matters he probably absorbs his narrowness from his generation. Moreover, we

must not confound the essentials of saintliness, which are those general passions of which I have spoken, with its accidents, which are the special determinations of these passions at any historical moment. In these determinations the saints will usually be loyal to the temporary idols of their tribe. Taking refuge in monasteries was as much an idol of the tribe in the middle ages, as bearing a hand in the world's work is to-day. Saint Francis or Saint Bernard, were they living to-day, would undoubtedly be leading consecrated lives of some sort, but quite as undoubtedly they would not lead them in retirement. Our animosity to special historic manifestations must not lead us to give away the saintly impulses in their essential nature to the tender mercies of inimical critics.

The most inimical critic of the saintly impulses whom I know is Nietzsche. He contrasts them with the worldly passions as we find these embodied in the predaceous military character, altogether to the advantage of the latter. Your born saint, it must be confessed, has something about him which often makes the gorge of a carnal man rise, so it will be worth while to consider the contrast in question more fully.

Dislike of the saintly nature seems to be a negative result of the biologically useful instinct of welcoming leadership, and glorifying the chief of the tribe. The chief is the potential, if not the actual tyrant, the masterful, overpowering man of prey. We confess our inferiority and grovel before him. We quail under his glance, and are at the same time proud of owning so dangerous a lord. Such instinctive and submissive hero-worship must have been indispensable in primeval tribal life. In the endless wars of those times, leaders were absolutely needed for the tribe's survival. If there were any tribes who owned no leaders, they can have left no issue to narrate their doom. The leaders always had good consciences, for conscience in them coalesced with will, and those who looked on their face were as much smitten with wonder at their freedom from inner restraint as with awe at the energy of their outward performances.

Compared with these beaked and taloned graspers of the world, saints are herbivorous animals, tame and harmless barn-yard poultry. There are saints whose beard you may, if you ever care to, pull with impunity. Such a man excites no thrills of wonder veiled in terror; his conscience is full of scruples and returns; he stuns us neither by his inward freedom nor his outward power; and unless he found within us an altogether different faculty of admiration to appeal to, we should pass him by with contempt.

In point of fact, he does appeal to a different faculty. Reënacted in human nature is the fable of the wind, the sun, and the traveler. The sexes embody the discrepancy. The woman loves the man the more admiringly the stormier he shows himself, and the world deifies its rulers the more for being willful and unaccountable. But the woman in turn subjugates the man by the mystery of gentleness in beauty, and the saint has always charmed the world by something similar. Mankind is susceptible and suggestible in opposite directions, and the rivalry of influences is unsleeping. The saintly and the worldly ideal pursue their feud in literature as much as in real life.

For Nietzsche the saint represents little but sneakingness and slavishness. He is the sophisticated invalid, the degenerate *par excellence*, the man of insufficient vitality. His prevalence would put the human type in danger.

" The sick are the greatest danger for the well. The weaker, not the stronger, are the strong's undoing. It is not *fear* of our fellow-man, which we should wish to see diminished; for fear rouses those who are strong to become terrible in turn themselves, and preserves the hard-earned and successful type of humanity. What is to be dreaded by us more than any other doom is not fear, but rather the great disgust, not fear, but rather the great pity — disgust and pity for our human fellows. . . . The *morbid* are our greatest peril — not the 'bad' men, not the predatory beings. Those born wrong, the miscarried, the broken — they it is, the *weakest*, who are undermining the vitality of the race, poisoning our trust in life, and putting humanity in question. Every look of them is a sigh, — 'Would I were something other! I am sick and tired of what I am.' In this swamp-soil of self-contempt, every poisonous weed flourishes, and all so small, so secret, so dishonest, and so sweetly rotten. Here swarm the worms of sensitiveness and resentment; here the air smells odious with secrecy, with what is not to be acknowledged; here is woven endlessly the net of the meanest of conspiracies, the conspiracy of those who suffer against those who succeed and are victorious; here the very aspect of the victorious is hated — as if health, success, strength, pride, and the sense of power were in themselves things vicious, for which one ought eventually to make bitter expiation. Oh, how these people would themselves like to inflict the expiation, how they thirst to be the hangmen! And all the while their duplicity never confesses their hatred to be hatred." [1]

Poor Nietzsche's antipathy is itself sickly enough, but we all know what he means, and he expresses well the clash between the two ideals. The carnivorous-minded 'strong man,' the adult male and cannibal, can see nothing but mouldiness and morbidness in the saint's gentleness and self-severity, and regards him with pure loathing. The whole feud revolves essentially upon two pivots: Shall the seen world or the unseen world be our chief sphere of adaptation? and must our means of adaptation in this seen world be aggressiveness or non-resistance?

---

[1] Zur Genealogie der Moral, Dritte Abhandlung, § 14. I have abridged, and in one place transposed, a sentence.

The debate is serious. In some sense and to some degree both worlds must be acknowledged and taken account of; and in the seen world both aggressiveness and non-resistance are needful. It is a question of emphasis, of more or less. Is the saint's type or the strong-man's type the more ideal ?

It has often been supposed, and even now, I think, it is supposed by most persons, that there can be one intrinsically ideal type of human character. A certain kind of man, it is imagined, must be the best man absolutely and apart from the utility of his function, apart from economical considerations. The saint's type, and the knight's or gentleman's type, have always been rival claimants of this absolute ideality; and in the ideal of military religious orders both types were in a manner blended. According to the empirical philosophy, however, all ideals are matters of relation. It would be absurd, for example, to ask for a definition of 'the ideal horse,' so long as dragging drays and running races, bearing children, and jogging about with tradesmen's packages all remain as indispensable differentiations of equine function. You may take what you call a general all-round animal as a compromise, but he will be inferior to any horse of a more specialized type, in some one particular direction. We must not forget this now when, in discussing saintliness, we ask if it be an ideal type of manhood. We must test it by its economical relations.

I think that the method which Mr. Spencer uses in his Data of Ethics will help to fix our opinion. Ideality in conduct is altogether a matter of adaptation. A society where all were invariably aggressive would destroy itself by inner friction, and in a society where some are aggressive, others must be non-resistant, if there is to be any kind of order. This is the present constitution of society, and to the mixture we owe many of our blessings. But the aggressive members of society are always tending to become bullies, robbers, and swindlers ; and no one believes that such a state of things as we now live in is the millennium. It is meanwhile quite possible to conceive an imaginary society in which there should be no aggressiveness, but only sympathy and fairness, — any small community of true friends now realizes such a society. Abstractly considered, such a society on a large scale would be the millennium, for every good thing might be realized there with no expense of friction. To such a millennial society the saint would be entirely adapted. His peaceful modes of appeal would be efficacious over his companions, and there would be no one extant to take advantage of his non-resistance. The saint is therefore abstractly a higher type of man than the ' strong man,' because he is adapted to the highest society conceivable, whether that society ever be concretely possible or not. The strong man would immediately tend by his presence to make that society deteriorate. It would become inferior in everything save in a certain kind of bellicose excitement, dear to men as they now are.

But if we turn from the abstract question to the actual situation, we find that the individual saint may be well or ill adapted, according to particular circumstances. There is, in short, no absoluteness in the excellence of sainthood. It must be confessed that as far as this world goes, any one who makes an out-and-out saint of himself does so at his peril. If he is not a large enough man, he may appear more insignificant and contemptible, for all his saintship, than if he had remained a worldling.[1] Accordingly religion has seldom been so radically

[1] We all know *daft* saints, and they inspire a queer kind of aversion. But in comparing saints with strong men we must choose individuals on

taken in our Western world that the devotee could not mix it with some worldly temper. It has always found good men who could follow most of its impulses, but who stopped short when it came to non-resistance. Christ himself was fierce upon occasion. Cromwells, Stonewall Jacksons, Gordons, show that Christians can be strong men also.

How is success to be absolutely measured when there are so many environments and so many ways of looking at the adaptation? It cannot be measured absolutely; the verdict will vary according to the point of view adopted. From the biological point of view Saint Paul was a failure, because he was beheaded. Yet he was magnificently adapted to the larger environment of history; and so far as any saint's example is a leaven of righteousness in the world, and draws it in the direction of more prevalent habits of saintliness, he is a success, no matter what his immediate bad fortune may be. The greatest saints, the spiritual heroes whom every one acknowledges, the Francises, Bernards, Luthers, Loyolas, Wesleys, Channings, Moodys, Gratrys, the Phillips Brookses, the Agnes Joneses, Margaret Hallahans, and Dora Pattisons, are successes from the outset. They show themselves, and there is no question; every one perceives their strength and stature. Their sense of mystery in things, their passion, their goodness, irradiate about them and enlarge their outlines while they soften them. They are like pictures with an atmosphere and background; and, placed alongside of them, the strong men of this world and no other seem as dry as sticks, as hard and crude as blocks of stone or brickbats.

the same intellectual level. The under-witted strong man, homologous in his sphere with the under-witted saint, is the bully of the slums, the hooligan or rowdy. Surely on this level also the saint preserves a certain superiority.

In a general way, then, and 'on the whole,' [1] our abandonment of theological criteria, and our testing of religion by practical common sense and the empirical method, leave it in possession of its towering place in history. Economically, the saintly group of qualities is indispensable to the world's welfare. The great saints are immediate successes; the smaller ones are at least heralds and harbingers, and they may be leavens also, of a better mundane order. Let us be saints, then, if we can, whether or not we succeed visibly and temporally. But in our Father's house are many mansions, and each of us must discover for himself the kind of religion and the amount of saintship which best comports with what he believes to be his powers and feels to be his truest mission and vocation. There are no successes to be guaranteed and no set orders to be given to individuals, so long as we follow the methods of empirical philosophy.

This is my conclusion so far. I know that on some of your minds it leaves a feeling of wonder that such a method should have been applied to such a subject, and this in spite of all those remarks about empiricism which I made at the beginning of Lecture XIII. [2] How, you say, can religion, which believes in two worlds and an invisible order, be estimated by the adaptation of its fruits to this world's order alone? It is its *truth*, not its utility, you insist, upon which our verdict ought to depend. If religion is true, its fruits are good fruits, even though in this world they should prove uniformly ill adapted and full of naught but pathos. It goes back, then, after all, to the question of the truth of theology. The plot inevitably thickens upon us; we cannot escape theoretical considerations. I propose, then, that to some

---

[1] See above, p. 327.   [2] Above, pp. 327–334.

degree we face the responsibility. Religious persons have often, though not uniformly, professed to see truth in a special manner. That manner is known as mysticism. I will consequently now proceed to treat at some length of mystical phenomena, and after that, though more briefly, I will consider religious philosophy.

LECTURES XVI AND XVII

MYSTICISM

OVER and over again in these lectures I have raised points and left them open and unfinished until we should have come to the subject of Mysticism. Some of you, I fear, may have smiled as you noted my reiterated postponements. But now the hour has come when mysticism must be faced in good earnest, and those broken threads wound up together. One may say truly, I think, that personal religious experience has its root and centre in mystical states of consciousness; so for us, who in these lectures are treating personal experience as the exclusive subject of our study, such states of consciousness ought to form the vital chapter from which the other chapters get their light. Whether my treatment of mystical states will shed more light or darkness, I do not know, for my own constitution shuts me out from their enjoyment almost entirely, and I can speak of them only at second hand. But though forced to look upon the subject so externally, I will be as objective and receptive as I can; and I think I shall at least succeed in convincing you of the reality of the states in question, and of the paramount importance of their function.

First of all, then, I ask, What does the expression 'mystical states of consciousness' mean? How do we part off mystical states from other states?

The words 'mysticism' and 'mystical' are often used as terms of mere reproach, to throw at any opinion which we regard as vague and vast and sentimental, and with-

out a base in either facts or logic. For some writers a
' mystic ' is any person who believes in thought-transference, or spirit-return. Employed in this way the word
has little value : there are too many less ambiguous synonyms. So, to keep it useful by restricting it, I will do
what I did in the case of the word ' religion,' and simply
propose to you four marks which, when an experience
has them, may justify us in calling it mystical for the
purpose of the present lectures. In this way we shall
save verbal disputation, and the recriminations that generally go therewith.

1. *Ineffability.* — The handiest of the marks by which
I classify a state of mind as mystical is negative. The
subject of it immediately says that it defies expression,
that no adequate report of its contents can be given in
words. It follows from this that its quality must be
directly experienced ; it cannot be imparted or trans-
ferred to others. In this peculiarity mystical states are
more like states of feeling than like states of intellect.
No one can make clear to another who has never had a
certain feeling, in what the quality or worth of it consists. One must have musical ears to know the value of
a symphony ; one must have been in love one's self to
understand a lover's state of mind. Lacking the heart
or ear, we cannot interpret the musician or the lover
justly, and are even likely to consider him weak-minded
or absurd. The mystic finds that most of us accord to
his experiences an equally incompetent treatment.

2. *Noetic quality.* — Although so similar to states of
feeling, mystical states seem to those who experience
them to be also states of knowledge. They are states of
insight into depths of truth unplumbed by the discursive
intellect. They are illuminations, revelations, full of significance and importance, all inarticulate though they

remain; and as a rule they carry with them a curious sense of authority for after-time.

These two characters will entitle any state to be called mystical, in the sense in which I use the word. Two other qualities are less sharply marked, but are usually found. These are : —

3. *Transiency.* — Mystical states cannot be sustained for long. Except in rare instances, half an hour, or at most an hour or two, seems to be the limit beyond which they fade into the light of common day. Often, when faded, their quality can but imperfectly be reproduced in memory; but when they recur it is recognized; and from one recurrence to another it is susceptible of continuous development in what is felt as inner richness and importance.

4. *Passivity.* — Although the oncoming of mystical states may be facilitated by preliminary voluntary operations, as by fixing the attention, or going through certain bodily performances, or in other ways which manuals of mysticism prescribe; yet when the characteristic sort of consciousness once has set in, the mystic feels as if his own will were in abeyance, and indeed sometimes as if he were grasped and held by a superior power. This latter peculiarity connects mystical states with certain definite phenomena of secondary or alternative personality, such as prophetic speech, automatic writing, or the mediumistic trance. When these latter conditions are well pronounced, however, there may be no recollection whatever of the phenomenon, and it may have no significance for the subject's usual inner life, to which, as it were, it makes a mere interruption. Mystical states, strictly so called, are never merely interruptive. Some memory of their content always remains, and a profound sense of their importance. They modify the inner life

of the subject between the times of their recurrence. Sharp divisions in this region are, however, difficult to make, and we find all sorts of gradations and mixtures.

These four characteristics are sufficient to mark out a group of states of consciousness peculiar enough to deserve a special name and to call for careful study. Let it then be called the mystical group.

Our next step should be to gain acquaintance with some typical examples. Professional mystics at the height of their development have often elaborately organized experiences and a philosophy based thereupon. But you remember what I said in my first lecture: phenomena are best understood when placed within their series, studied in their germ and in their over-ripe decay, and compared with their exaggerated and degenerated kindred. The range of mystical experience is very wide, much too wide for us to cover in the time at our disposal. Yet the method of serial study is so essential for interpretation that if we really wish to reach conclusions we must use it. I will begin, therefore, with phenomena which claim no special religious significance, and end with those of which the religious pretensions are extreme.

The simplest rudiment of mystical experience would seem to be that deepened sense of the significance of a maxim or formula which occasionally sweeps over one. "I've heard that said all my life," we exclaim, "but I never realized its full meaning until now." "When a fellow-monk," said Luther, "one day repeated the words of the Creed : 'I believe in the forgiveness of sins,' I saw the Scripture in an entirely new light; and straightway I felt as if I were born anew. It was as if I had found the door of paradise thrown wide open." [1] This sense

[1] Newman's *Securus judicat orbis terrarum* is another instance.

of deeper significance is not confined to rational propositions. Single words,[1] and conjunctions of words, effects
of light on land and sea, odors and musical sounds, all
bring it when the mind is tuned aright. Most of us can
remember the strangely moving power of passages in certain poems read when we were young, irrational door-
ways as they were through which the mystery of fact,
the wildness and the pang of life, stole into our hearts
and thrilled them. The words have now perhaps become
mere polished surfaces for us; but lyric poetry and music
are alive and significant only in proportion as they fetch
these vague vistas of a life continuous with our own,
beckoning and inviting, yet ever eluding our pursuit.
We are alive or dead to the eternal inner message of the
arts according as we have kept or lost this mystical susceptibility.

A more pronounced step forward on the mystical ladder is found in an extremely frequent phenomenon, that
sudden feeling, namely, which sometimes sweeps over us,
of having ' been here before,' as if at some indefinite past
time, in just this place, with just these people, we were
already saying just these things. As Tennyson writes:

> " Moreover, something is or seems,
> That touches me with mystic gleams,
> Like glimpses of forgotten dreams —
>
> " Of something felt, like something here ;
> Of something done, I know not where ;
> Such as no language may declare." [2]

---

[1] 'Mesopotamia' is the stock comic instance. — An excellent old German
lady, who had done some traveling in her day, used to describe to me her
Sehnsucht that she might yet visit ' Philadelphiā,' whose wondrous name
had always haunted her imagination. Of John Foster it is said that " single
words (as *chalcedony*), or the names of ancient heroes, had a mighty fascination over him. ' At any time the word *hermit* was enough to transport
him.' The words *woods* and *forests* would produce the most powerful emotion." Foster's Life, by RYLAND, New York, 1846, p. 3.

[2] The Two Voices. In a letter to Mr. B. P. Blood, Tennyson reports of
himself as follows : —

Sir James Crichton-Browne has given the technical name of ' dreamy states ' to these sudden invasions of vaguely reminiscent consciousness.[1]   They bring a sense of mystery and of the metaphysical duality of things, and the feeling of an enlargement of perception which seems imminent but which never completes itself.   In Dr. Crichton-Browne's opinion they connect themselves with the perplexed and scared disturbances of self-consciousness which occasionally precede epileptic attacks.   I think that this learned alienist takes a rather absurdly alarmist view of an intrinsically insignificant phenomenon.   He follows it along the downward ladder, to insanity; our path pursues the upward ladder chiefly.   The divergence shows how important it is to neglect no part of a phenomenon's connections, for we make it appear admirable or dreadful according to the context by which we set it off.

Somewhat deeper plunges into mystical consciousness are met with in yet other dreamy states.   Such feelings

"I have never had any revelations through anæsthetics, but a kind of waking trance — this for lack of a better word — I have frequently had, quite up from boyhood, when I have been all alone.   This has come upon me through repeating my own name to myself silently, till all at once, as it were out of the intensity of the consciousness of individuality, individuality itself seemed to dissolve and fade away into boundless being, and this not a confused state but the clearest, the surest of the surest, utterly beyond words — where death was an almost laughable impossibility — the loss of personality (if so it were) seeming no extinction, but the only true life.   I am ashamed of my feeble description.   Have I not said the state is utterly beyond words ? "

Professor Tyndall, in a letter, recalls Tennyson saying of this condition : " By God Almighty ! there is no delusion in the matter !   It is no nebulous ecstasy, but a state of transcendent wonder, associated with absolute clearness of mind."   Memoirs of Alfred Tennyson, ii. 473.

[1] The Lancet, July 6 and 13, 1895, reprinted as the Cavendish Lecture, on Dreamy Mental States, London, Baillière, 1895.   They have been a good deal discussed of late by psychologists.   See, for example, BERNARD-LEROY : L'Illusion de Fausse Reconnaissance, Paris, 1898.

as these which Charles Kingsley describes are surely far from being uncommon, especially in youth : —

" When I walk the fields, I am oppressed now and then with an innate feeling that everything I see has a meaning, if I could but understand it. And this feeling of being surrounded with truths which I cannot grasp amounts to indescribable awe sometimes. . . . Have you not felt that your real soul was imperceptible to your mental vision, except in a few hallowed moments ? " [1]

A much more extreme state of mystical consciousness is described by J. A. Symonds; and probably more persons than we suspect could give parallels to it from their own experience.

" Suddenly," writes Symonds, " at church, or in company, or when I was reading, and always, I think, when my muscles were at rest, I felt the approach of the mood. Irresistibly it took possession of my mind and will, lasted what seemed an eternity, and disappeared in a series of rapid sensations which resembled the awakening from anæsthetic influence. One reason why I disliked this kind of trance was that I could not describe it to myself. I cannot even now find words to render it intelligible. It consisted in a gradual but swiftly progressive obliteration of space, time, sensation, and the multitudinous factors of experience which seem to qualify what we are pleased to call our Self. In proportion as these conditions of ordinary consciousness were subtracted, the sense of an underlying or essential consciousness acquired intensity. At last nothing remained but a pure, absolute, abstract Self. The universe became without form and void of content. But Self persisted, formidable in its vivid keenness, feeling the most poignant doubt about reality, ready, as it seemed, to find existence break as breaks a bubble round about it. And what then? The apprehension of a coming dissolution, the grim conviction that this state was the last state of the conscious Self, the sense that

[1] Charles Kingsley's Life, i. 55, quoted by INGE : Christian Mysticism, London, 1899, p. 341.

I had followed the last thread of being to the verge of the abyss, and had arrived at demonstration of eternal Maya or illusion, stirred or seemed to stir me up again. The return to ordinary conditions of sentient existence began by my first recovering the power of touch, and then by the gradual though rapid influx of familiar impressions and diurnal interests. At last I felt myself once more a human being; and though the riddle of what is meant by life remained unsolved, I was thankful for this return from the abyss — this deliverance from so awful an initiation into the mysteries of skepticism.

" This trance recurred with diminishing frequency until I reached the age of twenty-eight. It served to impress upon my growing nature the phantasmal unreality of all the circumstances which contribute to a merely phenomenal consciousness. Often have I asked myself with anguish, on waking from that formless state of denuded, keenly sentient being, Which is the unreality? — the trance of fiery, vacant, apprehensive, skeptical Self from which I issue, or these surrounding phenomena and habits which veil that inner Self and build a self of flesh-and-blood conventionality? Again, are men the factors of some dream, the dream-like unsubstantiality of which they comprehend at such eventful moments? What would happen if the final stage of the trance were reached? " [1]

In a recital like this there is certainly something suggestive of pathology.[2] The next step into mystical states carries us into a realm that public opinion and ethical philosophy have long since branded as pathological, though private practice and certain lyric strains of poetry

[1] H. F. Brown : J. A. Symonds, a Biography, London, 1895, pp. 29–31, abridged.

[2] Crichton-Browne expressly says that Symonds's " highest nerve centres were in some degree enfeebled or damaged by these dreamy mental states which afflicted him so grievously." Symonds was, however, a perfect monster of many-sided cerebral efficiency, and his critic gives no objective grounds whatever for his strange opinion, save that Symonds complained occasionally, as all susceptible and ambitious men complain, of lassitude and uncertainty as to his life's mission.

seem still to bear witness to its ideality. I refer to the consciousness produced by intoxicants and anæsthetics, especially by alcohol. The sway of alcohol over mankind is unquestionably due to its power to stimulate the mystical faculties of human nature, usually crushed to earth by the cold facts and dry criticisms of the sober hour. Sobriety diminishes, discriminates, and says no; drunkenness expands, unites, and says yes. It is in fact the great exciter of the *Yes* function in man. It brings its votary from the chill periphery of things to the radiant core. It makes him for the moment one with truth. Not through mere perversity do men run after it. To the poor and the unlettered it stands in the place of symphony concerts and of literature; and it is part of the deeper mystery and tragedy of life that whiffs and gleams of something that we immediately recognize as excellent should be vouchsafed to so many of us only in the fleeting earlier phases of what in its totality is so degrading a poisoning. The drunken consciousness is one bit of the mystic consciousness, and our total opinion of it must find its place in our opinion of that larger whole.

Nitrous oxide and ether, especially nitrous oxide, when sufficiently diluted with air, stimulate the mystical consciousness in an extraordinary degree. Depth beyond depth of truth seems revealed to the inhaler. This truth fades out, however, or escapes, at the moment of coming to; and if any words remain over in which it seemed to clothe itself, they prove to be the veriest nonsense. Nevertheless, the sense of a profound meaning having been there persists; and I know more than one person who is persuaded that in the nitrous oxide trance we have a genuine metaphysical revelation.

Some years ago I myself made some observations on this aspect of nitrous oxide intoxication, and reported them in print. One conclusion was forced upon my mind at that time, and my impression of its truth has ever since remained unshaken. It is that our normal waking consciousness, rational consciousness as we call it, is but one special type of consciousness, whilst all about it, parted from it by the filmiest of screens, there lie potential forms of consciousness entirely different. We may go through life without suspecting their existence; but apply the requisite stimulus, and at a touch they are there in all their completeness, definite types of mentality which probably somewhere have their field of application and adaptation. No account of the universe in its totality can be final which leaves these other forms of consciousness quite disregarded. How to regard them is the question, — for they are so discontinuous with ordinary consciousness. Yet they may determine attitudes though they cannot furnish formulas, and open a region though they fail to give a map. At any rate, they forbid a premature closing of our accounts with reality. Looking back on my own experiences, they all converge towards a kind of insight to which I cannot help ascribing some metaphysical significance. The keynote of it is invariably a reconciliation. It is as if the opposites of the world, whose contradictoriness and conflict make all our difficulties and troubles, were melted into unity. Not only do they, as contrasted species, belong to one and the same genus, but *one of the species*, the nobler and better one, *is itself the genus, and so soaks up and absorbs its opposite into itself*. This is a dark saying, I know, when thus expressed in terms of common logic, but I cannot wholly escape from its authority. I feel as if it must mean something, something like what the hegelian philosophy means, if one could only lay hold of it more clearly. Those who have ears to hear, let them hear;

to me the living sense of its reality only comes in the
artificial mystic state of mind.[1]

I just now spoke of friends who believe in the anæsthetic revelation. For them too it is a monistic insight,
in which the *other* in its various forms appears absorbed
into the One.

" Into this pervading genius," writes one of them, " we pass,
forgetting and forgotten, and thenceforth each is all, in God.
There is no higher, no deeper, no other, than the life in which
we are founded. ' The One remains, the many change and
pass ; ' and each and every one of us *is* the One that remains.
. . . This is the ultimatum. . . . As sure as being — whence
is all our care — so sure is content, beyond duplexity, antithesis,
or trouble, where I have triumphed in a solitude that God is
not above." [2]

---

[1] What reader of Hegel can doubt that that sense of a perfected Being
with all its otherness soaked up into itself, which dominates his whole
philosophy, must have come from the prominence in his consciousness of
mystical moods like this, in most persons kept subliminal ? The notion is
thoroughly characteristic of the mystical level, and the *Aufgabe* of making it
articulate was surely set to Hegel's intellect by mystical feeling.

[2] BENJAMIN PAUL BLOOD : The Anæsthetic Revelation and the Gist of
Philosophy, Amsterdam, N. Y., 1874, pp. 35, 36. Mr. Blood has made
several attempts to adumbrate the anæsthetic revelation, in pamphlets of
rare literary distinction, privately printed and distributed by himself at
Amsterdam. Xenos Clark, a philosopher, who died young at Amherst in
the '80's, much lamented by those who knew him, was also impressed by
the revelation. " In the first place," he once wrote to me, " Mr. Blood and
I agree that the revelation is, if anything, non-emotional. It is utterly flat.
It is, as Mr. Blood says, ' the one sole and sufficient insight why, or not
why, but how, the present is pushed on by the past, and sucked forward by
the vacuity of the future. Its inevitableness defeats all attempts at stop-
ping or accounting for it. It is all precedence and presupposition, and
questioning is in regard to it forever too late. It is an *initiation of the past.*'
The real secret would be the formula by which the ' now ' keeps exfoliating
out of itself, yet never escapes. What is it, indeed, that keeps existence
exfoliating ? The formal being of anything, the logical definition of it, is
static. For mere logic every question contains its own answer — we simply
fill the hole with the dirt we dug out. Why are twice two four ? Because,
in fact, four is twice two. Thus logic finds in life no propulsion, only a momentum. It goes because it is a-going. But the revelation adds : it goes

This has the genuine religious mystic ring! I just now quoted J. A. Symonds. He also records a mystical experience with chloroform, as follows: —

because it is and *was* a-going. You walk, as it were, round yourself in the revelation. Ordinary philosophy is like a hound hunting his own trail. The more he hunts the farther he has to go, and his nose never catches up with his heels, because it is forever ahead of them. So the present is already a foregone conclusion, and I am ever too late to understand it. But at the moment of recovery from anæsthesis, just then, *before starting on life*, I catch, so to speak, a glimpse of my heels, a glimpse of the eternal process just in the act of starting. The truth is that we travel on a journey that was accomplished before we set out ; and the real end of philosophy is accomplished, not when we arrive at, but when we remain in, our destination (being already there), — which may occur vicariously in this life when we cease our intellectual questioning. That is why there is a smile upon the face of the revelation, as we view it. It tells us that we are forever half a second too late — that's all. 'You could kiss your own lips, and have all the fun to yourself,' it says, if you only knew the trick. It would be perfectly easy if they would just stay there till you got round to them. Why don't you manage it somehow ? "

Dialectically minded readers of this farrago will at least recognize the region of thought of which Mr. Clark writes, as familiar. In his latest pamphlet, 'Tennyson's Trances and the Anæsthetic Revelation,' Mr. Blood describes its value for life as follows: —

" The Anæsthetic Revelation is the Initiation of Man into the Immemorial Mystery of the Open Secret of Being, revealed as the Inevitable Vortex of Continuity. Inevitable is the word. Its motive is inherent — it is what has to be. It is not for any love or hate, nor for joy nor sorrow, nor good nor ill. End, beginning, or purpose, it knows not of.

" It affords no particular of the multiplicity and variety of things ; but it fills appreciation of the historical and the sacred with a secular and intimately personal illumination of the nature and motive of existence, which then seems reminiscent — as if it should have appeared, or shall yet appear, to every participant thereof.

" Although it is at first startling in its solemnity, it becomes directly such a matter of course — so old-fashioned, and so akin to proverbs, that it inspires exultation rather than fear, and a sense of safety, as identified with the aboriginal and the universal. But no words may express the imposing certainty of the patient that he is realizing the primordial, Adamic surprise of Life.

" Repetition of the experience finds it ever the same, and as if it could not possibly be otherwise. The subject resumes his normal consciousness only to partially and fitfully remember its occurrence, and to try to formulate its baffling import, — with only this consolatory afterthought: that he

" After the choking and stifling had passed away, I seemed at first in a state of utter blankness; then came flashes of intense light, alternating with blackness, and with a keen vision of what was going on in the room around me, but no sensation of touch. I thought that I was near death; when, suddenly, my soul became aware of God, who was manifestly dealing with me, handling me, so to speak, in an intense personal present reality. I felt him streaming in like light upon me. . . . I cannot describe the ecstasy I felt. Then, as I gradually awoke from the influence of the anæsthetics, the old sense of my relation to the world began to return, the new sense of my relation to God began to fade. I suddenly leapt to my feet on the chair where I was sitting, and shrieked out, ' It is too horrible, it is too horrible, it is too horrible,' meaning that I could not bear this disillusionment. Then I flung myself on the ground, and at last awoke covered with blood, calling to the two surgeons (who were frightened), ' Why did you not kill me? Why would you not let me die?' Only think of it. To have felt for that long dateless ecstasy of vision the very God, in all purity and tenderness and truth and absolute love, and then to find that I had after all had no revelation, but that I had been tricked by the abnormal excitement of my brain.

has known the oldest truth, and that he has done with human theories as to the origin, meaning, or destiny of the race. He is beyond instruction in ' spiritual things.'

" The lesson is one of central safety : the Kingdom is within. All days are judgment days : but there can be no climacteric purpose of eternity, nor any scheme of the whole. The astronomer abridges the row of bewildering figures by increasing his unit of measurement : so may we reduce the distracting multiplicity of things to the unity for which each of us stands.

" This has been my moral sustenance since I have known of it. In my first printed mention of it I declared : ' The world is no more the alien terror that was taught me. Spurning the cloud-grimed and still sultry battlements whence so lately Jehovan thunders boomed, my gray gull lifts her wing against the nightfall, and takes the dim leagues with a fearless eye.' And now, after twenty-seven years of this experience, the wing is grayer, but the eye is fearless still, while I renew and doubly emphasize that declaration. I know — as having known — the meaning of Existence : the sane centre of the universe — at once the wonder and the assurance of the soul — for which the speech of reason has as yet no name but the Anæsthetic Revelation." — I have considerably abridged the quotation.

"Yet, this question remains, Is it possible that the inner sense of reality which succeeded, when my flesh was dead to impressions from without, to the ordinary sense of physical relations, was not a delusion but an actual experience? Is it possible that I, in that moment, felt what some of the saints have said they always felt, the undemonstrable but irrefragable certainty of God?"[1]

[1] Op. cit., pp. 78–80, abridged. I subjoin, also abridging it, another interesting anæsthetic revelation communicated to me in manuscript by a friend in England. The subject, a gifted woman, was taking ether for a surgical operation.

"I wondered if I was in a prison being tortured, and why I remembered having heard it said that people 'learn through suffering,' and in view of what I was seeing, the inadequacy of this saying struck me so much that I said, aloud, 'to suffer *is* to learn.'

"With that I became unconscious again, and my last dream immediately preceded my real coming to. It only lasted a few seconds, and was most vivid and real to me, though it may not be clear in words.

"A great Being or Power was traveling through the sky, his foot was on a kind of lightning as a wheel is on a rail, it was his pathway. The lightning was made entirely of the spirits of innumerable people close to one another, and I was one of them. He moved in a straight line, and each part of the streak or flash came into its short conscious existence only that he might travel. I seemed to be directly under the foot of God, and I thought he was grinding his own life up out of my pain. Then I saw that what he had been trying with all his might to do was to *change his course*, to *bend* the line of lightning to which he was tied, in the direction in which he wanted to go. I felt my flexibility and helplessness, and knew that he would succeed. He bended me, turning his corner by means of my hurt, hurting me more than I had ever been hurt in my life, and at the acutest point of this, as he passed, I *saw*. I understood for a moment things that I have now forgotten, things that no one could remember while retaining sanity. The angle was an obtuse angle, and I remember thinking as I woke that had he made it a right or acute angle, I should have both suffered and 'seen' still more, and should probably have died.

"He went on and I came to. In that moment the whole of my life passed before me, including each little meaningless piece of distress, and I *understood* them. *This* was what it had all meant, *this* was the piece of work it had all been contributing to do. I did not see God's purpose, I only saw his intentness and his entire relentlessness towards his means. He thought no more of me than a man thinks of hurting a cork when he is opening wine, or hurting a cartridge when he is firing. And yet, on waking, my first feeling was, and it came with tears, 'Domine non sum digna,' for I had been lifted into a position for which I was too small. I realized

With this we make connection with religious mysticism pure and simple. Symonds's question takes us back to those examples which you will remember my quoting in the lecture on the Reality of the Unseen, of sudden realization of the immediate presence of God. The phenomenon in one shape or another is not uncommon.

" I know," writes Mr. Trine, " an officer on our police force who has told me that many times when off duty, and on his way home in the evening, there comes to him such a vivid and vital realization of his oneness with this Infinite Power, and this Spirit of Infinite Peace so takes hold of and so fills him,

that in that half hour under ether I had served God more distinctly and purely than I had ever done in my life before, or than I am capable of desiring to do. I was the means of his achieving and revealing something, I know not what or to whom, and that, to the exact extent of my capacity for suffering.

" While regaining consciousness, I wondered why, since I had gone so deep, I had seen nothing of what the saints call the *love* of God, nothing but his relentlessness. And then I heard an answer, which I could only just catch, saying, 'Knowledge and Love are One, and the *measure* is suffering' — I give the words as they came to me. With that I came finally to (into what seemed a dream world compared with the reality of what I was leaving), and I saw that what would be called the 'cause' of my experience was a slight operation under insufficient ether, in a bed pushed up against a window, a common city window in a common city street. If I had to formulate a few of the things I then caught a glimpse of, they would run somewhat as follows : —

" The eternal necessity of suffering and its eternal vicariousness. The veiled and incommunicable nature of the worst sufferings ; — the passivity of genius, how it is essentially instrumental and defenseless, moved, not moving, it must do what it does ; — the impossibility of discovery without its price ; — finally, the excess of what the suffering 'seer' or genius pays over what his generation gains. (He seems like one who sweats his life out to earn enough to save a district from famine, and just as he staggers back, dying and satisfied, bringing a lac of rupees to buy grain with, God lifts the lac away, dropping *one* rupee, and says, ' That you may give them. That you have earned for them. The rest is for ME.') I perceived also in a way never to be forgotten, the excess of what we see over what we can demonstrate.

" And so on ! — these things may seem to you delusions, or truisms ; but for me they are dark truths, and the power to put them into even such words as these has been given me by an ether dream."

that it seems as if his feet could hardly keep to the pavement, so buoyant and so exhilarated does he become by reason of this inflowing tide." [1]

Certain aspects of nature seem to have a peculiar power of awakening such mystical moods.[2] Most of the striking cases which I have collected have occurred out of doors. Literature has commemorated this fact in many passages of great beauty — this extract, for example, from Amiel's Journal Intime : —

"Shall I ever again have any of those prodigious reveries which sometimes came to me in former days? One day, in

---

[1] In Tune with the Infinite, p. 137.

[2] The larger God may then swallow up the smaller one. I take this from Starbuck's manuscript collection : —

"I never lost the consciousness of the presence of God until I stood at the foot of the Horseshoe Falls, Niagara. Then I lost him in the immensity of what I saw. I also lost myself, feeling that I was an atom too small for the notice of Almighty God."

I subjoin another similar case from Starbuck's collection : —

"In that time the consciousness of God's nearness came to me sometimes. I say God, to describe what is indescribable. A presence, I might say, yet that is too suggestive of personality, and the moments of which I speak did not hold the consciousness of a personality, but something in myself made me feel myself a part of something bigger than I, that was controlling. I felt myself one with the grass, the trees, birds, insects, everything in Nature. I exulted in the mere fact of existence, of being a part of it all — the drizzling rain, the shadows of the clouds, the tree-trunks, and so on. In the years following, such moments continued to come, but I wanted them constantly. I knew so well the satisfaction of losing self in a perception of supreme power and love, that I was unhappy because that perception was not constant." The cases quoted in my third lecture, pp. 66, 67, 70, are still better ones of this type. In her essay, The Loss of Personality, in The Atlantic Monthly (vol. lxxxv. p. 195), Miss Ethel D. Puffer explains that the vanishing of the sense of self, and the feeling of immediate unity with the object, is due to the disappearance, in these rapturous experiences, of the motor adjustments which habitually intermediate between the constant background of consciousness (which is the Self) and the object in the foreground, whatever it may be. I must refer the reader to the highly instructive article, which seems to me to throw light upon the psychological conditions, though it fails to account for the rapture or the revelation-value of the experience in the Subject's eyes.

youth, at sunrise, sitting in the ruins of the castle of Faucigny;
and again in the mountains, under the noonday sun, above
Lavey, lying at the foot of a tree and visited by three butter-
flies; once more at night upon the shingly shore of the Northern
Ocean, my back upon the sand and my vision ranging through
the milky way; — such grand and spacious, immortal, cosmo-
gonic reveries, when one reaches to the stars, when one owns
the infinite! Moments divine, ecstatic hours; in which our
thought flies from world to world, pierces the great enigma,
breathes with a respiration broad, tranquil, and deep as the
respiration of the ocean, serene and limitless as the blue firmament; . . . instants of irresistible intuition in which one feels
one's self great as the universe, and calm as a god. . . . What
hours, what memories! The vestiges they leave behind are
enough to fill us with belief and enthusiasm, as if they were
visits of the Holy Ghost." [1]

Here is a similar record from the memoirs of that
interesting German idealist, Malwida von Meysenbug: —

" I was alone upon the seashore as all these thoughts flowed
over me, liberating and reconciling; and now again, as once
before in distant days in the Alps of Dauphiné, I was impelled
to kneel down, this time before the illimitable ocean, symbol of
the Infinite. I felt that I prayed as I had never prayed before,
and knew now what prayer really is: to return from the solitude of individuation into the consciousness of unity with all
that is, to kneel down as one that passes away, and to rise up as
one imperishable. Earth, heaven, and sea resounded as in one
vast world-encircling harmony. It was as if the chorus of all
the great who had ever lived were about me. I felt myself
one with them, and it appeared as if I heard their greeting:
' Thou too belongest to the company of those who overcome.' " [2]

The well-known passage from Walt Whitman is a
classical expression of this sporadic type of mystical experience.

[1] Op. cit., i. 43–44.
[2] Memoiren einer Idealistin, 5te Auflage, 1900, iii. 166. For years she
had been unable to pray, owing to materialistic belief.

" I believe in you, my Soul . . .
Loaf with me on the grass, loose the stop from your throat ; . . .
Only the lull I like, the hum of your valved voice.
I mind how once we lay, such a transparent summer morning.
Swiftly arose and spread around me the peace and knowledge that pass
     all the argument of the earth,
And I know that the hand of God is the promise of my own,
And I know that the spirit of God is the brother of my own,
And that all the men ever born are also my brothers and the women my
     sisters and lovers,
And that a kelson of the creation is love." [1]

I could easily give more instances, but one will suffice.
I take it from the Autobiography of J. Trevor.[2]

" One brilliant Sunday morning, my wife and boys went to
the Unitarian Chapel in Macclesfield.   I felt it impossible to
accompany them — as though to leave the sunshine on the hills,
and go down there to the chapel, would be for the time an act
of spiritual suicide.   And I felt such need for new inspiration
and expansion in my life.   So, very reluctantly and sadly, I left
my wife and boys to go down into the town, while I went
further up into the hills with my stick and my dog.   In the
loveliness of the morning, and the beauty of the hills and valleys, I soon lost my sense of sadness and regret.   For nearly
an hour I walked along the road to the ' Cat and Fiddle,' and
then returned.   On the way back, suddenly, without warning, I
felt that I was in Heaven — an inward state of peace and joy

---

[1] Whitman in another place expresses in a quieter way what was probably with him a chronic mystical perception : " There is," he writes, " apart
from mere intellect, in the make-up of every superior human identity, a
wondrous something that realizes without argument, frequently without
what is called education (though I think it the goal and apex of all education deserving the name), an intuition of the absolute balance, in time
and space, of the whole of this multifariousness, this revel of fools, and
incredible make-believe and general unsettledness, we call *the world ;* a soul-
sight of that divine clue and unseen thread which holds the whole congeries
of things, all history and time, and all events, however trivial, however momentous, like a leashed dog in the hand of the hunter. [Of] such soul-sight
and root-centre for the mind mere optimism explains only the surface."
Whitman charges it against Carlyle that he lacked this perception.   Specimen Days and Collect, Philadelphia, 1882, p. 174.

[2] My Quest for God, London, 1897, pp. 268, 269, abridged.

and assurance indescribably intense, accompanied with a sense
of being bathed in a warm glow of light, as though the external
condition had brought about the internal effect — a feeling of
having passed beyond the body, though the scene around me
stood out more clearly and as if nearer to me than before, by
reason of the illumination in the midst of which I seemed to be
placed. This deep emotion lasted, though with decreasing
strength, until I reached home, and for some time after, only
gradually passing away."

The writer adds that having had further experiences of
a similar sort, he now knows them well.

" The spiritual life," he writes, " justifies itself to those who
live it; but what can we say to those who do not understand?
This, at least, we can say, that it is a life whose experiences are
proved real to their possessor, because they remain with him
when brought closest into contact with the objective realities of
life. Dreams cannot stand this test. We wake from them to
find that they are but dreams. Wanderings of an overwrought
brain do not stand this test. These highest experiences that I
have had of God's presence have been rare and brief — flashes
of consciousness which have compelled me to exclaim with surprise — God is *here!* — or conditions of exaltation and insight,
less intense, and only gradually passing away. I have severely
questioned the worth of these moments. To no soul have I
named them, lest I should be building my life and work on
mere phantasies of the brain. But I find that, after every
questioning and test, they stand out to-day as the most real
experiences of my life, and experiences which have explained
and justified and unified all past experiences and all past
growth. Indeed, their reality and their far-reaching significance are ever becoming more clear and evident. When they
came, I was living the fullest, strongest, sanest, deepest life.
I was not seeking them. What I was seeking, with resolute
determination, was to live more intensely my own life, as
against what I knew would be the adverse judgment of the
world. It was in the most real seasons that the Real Presence

came, and I was aware that I was immersed in the infinite ocean of God." [1]

Even the least mystical of you must by this time be convinced of the existence of mystical moments as states of consciousness of an entirely specific quality, and of the deep impression which they make on those who have them. A Canadian psychiatrist, Dr. R. M. Bucke, gives to the more distinctly characterized of these phenomena the name of cosmic consciousness. "Cosmic consciousness in its more striking instances is not," Dr. Bucke says, "simply an expansion or extension of the self-conscious mind with which we are all familiar, but the superaddition of a function as distinct from any possessed by the average man as *self*-consciousness is distinct from any function possessed by one of the higher animals."

"The prime characteristic of cosmic consciousness is a consciousness of the cosmos, that is, of the life and order of the universe. Along with the consciousness of the cosmos there occurs an intellectual enlightenment which alone would place the individual on a new plane of existence — would make him almost a member of a new species. To this is added a state of moral exaltation, an indescribable feeling of elevation, elation, and joyousness, and a quickening of the moral sense, which is fully as striking, and more important than is the enhanced intellectual power. With these come what may be called a sense of immortality, a consciousness of eternal life, not a conviction that he shall have this, but the consciousness that he has it already." [2]

It was Dr. Bucke's own experience of a typical onset of cosmic consciousness in his own person which led him to investigate it in others. He has printed his conclusions in a highly interesting volume, from which I take the following account of what occurred to him : —

[1] Op. cit., pp. 256, 257, abridged.

[2] Cosmic Consciousness : a study in the evolution of the human Mind Philadelphia, 1901, p. 2.

" I had spent the evening in a great city, with two friends, reading and discussing poetry and philosophy. We parted at midnight. I had a long drive in a hansom to my lodging. My mind, deeply under the influence of the ideas, images, and emotions called up by the reading and talk, was calm and peaceful. I was in a state of quiet, almost passive enjoyment, not actually thinking, but letting ideas, images, and emotions flow of themselves, as it were, through my mind. All at once, without warning of any kind, I found myself wrapped in a flame-colored cloud. For an instant I thought of fire, an immense conflagration somewhere close by in that great city; the next, I knew that the fire was within myself. Directly afterward there came upon me a sense of exultation, of immense joyousness accompanied or immediately followed by an intellectual illumination impossible to describe. Among other things, I did not merely come to believe, but I saw that the universe is not composed of dead matter, but is, on the contrary, a living Presence; I became conscious in myself of eternal life. It was not a conviction that I would have eternal life, but a consciousness that I possessed eternal life then; I saw that all men are immortal; that the cosmic order is such that without any peradventure all things work together for the good of each and all; that the foundation principle of the world, of all the worlds, is what we call love, and that the happiness of each and all is in the long run absolutely certain. The vision lasted a few seconds and was gone; but the memory of it and the sense of the reality of what it taught has remained during the quarter of a century which has since elapsed. I knew that what the vision showed was true. I had attained to a point of view from which I saw that it must be true. That view, that conviction, I may say that consciousness, has never, even during periods of the deepest depression, been lost." [1]

We have now seen enough of this cosmic or mystic consciousness, as it comes sporadically. We must next

---

[1] Loc. cit., pp. 7, 8. My quotation follows the privately printed pamphlet which preceded Dr. Bucke's larger work, and differs verbally a little from the text of the latter.

pass to its methodical cultivation as an element of the religious life. Hindus, Buddhists, Mohammedans, and Christians all have cultivated it methodically.

In India, training in mystical insight has been known from time immemorial under the name of yoga. Yoga means the experimental union of the individual with the divine. It is based on persevering exercise; and the diet, posture, breathing, intellectual concentration, and moral discipline vary slightly in the different systems which teach it. The yogi, or disciple, who has by these means overcome the obscurations of his lower nature sufficiently, enters into the condition termed *samâdhi*, "and comes face to face with facts which no instinct or reason can ever know." He learns —

"That the mind itself has a higher state of existence, beyond reason, a superconscious state, and that when the mind gets to that higher state, then this knowledge beyond reasoning comes. . . . All the different steps in yoga are intended to bring us scientifically to the superconscious state or samâdhi. . . . Just as unconscious work is beneath consciousness, so there is another work which is above consciousness, and which, also, is not accompanied with the feeling of egoism. . . . There is no feeling of *I*, and yet the mind works, desireless, free from restlessness, objectless, bodiless. Then the Truth shines in its full effulgence, and we know ourselves — for Samâdhi lies potential in us all — for what we truly are, free, immortal, omnipotent, loosed from the finite, and its contrasts of good and evil altogether, and identical with the Atman or Universal Soul." [1]

The Vedantists say that one may stumble into superconsciousness sporadically, without the previous discipline, but it is then impure. Their test of its purity, like

[1] My quotations are from VIVEKANANDA, Raja Yoga, London, 1896. The completest source of information on Yoga is the work translated by VIHARI LALA MITRA : Yoga Vasishta Maha Ramayana, 4 vols., Calcutta, 1891–99.

our test of religion's value, is empirical : its fruits must be good for life. When a man comes out of Samâdhi, they assure us that he remains "enlightened, a sage, a prophet, a saint, his whole character changed, his life changed, illumined." [1]

The Buddhists use the word 'samâdhi' as well as the Hindus; but 'dhyâna' is their special word for higher states of contemplation. There seem to be four stages recognized in dhyâna. The first stage comes through concentration of the mind upon one point. It excludes desire, but not discernment or judgment : it is still intellectual. In the second stage the intellectual functions drop off, and the satisfied sense of unity remains. In the third stage the satisfaction departs, and indifference begins, along with memory and self-consciousness. In the fourth stage the indifference, memory, and self-consciousness are perfected. [Just what 'memory' and 'self-consciousness' mean in this connection is doubtful. They cannot be the faculties familiar to us in the lower life.] Higher stages still of contemplation are mentioned — a region where there exists nothing, and where the meditator says : "There exists absolutely nothing," and stops. Then he reaches another region where he says : "There are neither ideas nor absence of ideas," and stops again. Then another region where, "having reached the end of both idea and perception, he stops

---

[1] A European witness, after carefully comparing the results of Yoga with those of the hypnotic or dreamy states artificially producible by us, says : " It makes of its true disciples good, healthy, and happy men. . . . Through the mastery which the yogi attains over his thoughts and his body, he grows into a 'character.' By the subjection of his impulses and propensities to his will, and the fixing of the latter upon the ideal of goodness, he becomes a 'personality' hard to influence by others, and thus almost the opposite of what we usually imagine a 'medium' so-called, or 'psychic subject' to be." KARL KELLNER : Yoga : Eine Skizze, München, 1896, p. 21.

finally." This would seem to be, not yet Nirvâna, but as close an approach to it as this life affords.[1]

In the Mohammedan world the Sufi sect and various dervish bodies are the possessors of the mystical tradition. The Sufis have existed in Persia from the earliest times, and as their pantheism is so at variance with the hot and rigid monotheism of the Arab mind, it has been suggested that Sufism must have been inoculated into Islam by Hindu influences. We Christians know little of Sufism, for its secrets are disclosed only to those initiated. To give its existence a certain liveliness in your minds, I will quote a Moslem document, and pass away from the subject.

Al-Ghazzali, a Persian philosopher and theologian, who flourished in the eleventh century, and ranks as one of the greatest doctors of the Moslem church, has left us one of the few autobiographies to be found outside of Christian literature. Strange that a species of book so abundant among ourselves should be so little represented elsewhere — the absence of strictly personal confessions is the chief difficulty to the purely literary student who would like to become acquainted with the inwardness of religions other than the Christian.

M. Schmölders has translated a part of Al-Ghazzali's autobiography into French : [2] —

"The Science of the Sufis," says the Moslem author, " aims at detaching the heart from all that is not God, and at giving to it for sole occupation the meditation of the divine being. Theory being more easy for me than practice, I read [certain books] until I understood all that can be learned by study and

[1] I follow the account in C. F. KOEPPEN : Die Religion des Buddha, Berlin, 1857, i. 585 ff.

[2] For a full account of him, see D. B. MACDONALD : The Life of Al-Ghazzali, in the Journal of the American Oriental Society, 1899, vol. xx. p. 71.

hearsay. Then I recognized that what pertains most exclusively to their method is just what no study can grasp, but only transport, ecstasy, and the transformation of the soul. How great, for example, is the difference between knowing the definitions of health, of satiety, with their causes and conditions, and being really healthy or filled. How different to know in what drunkenness consists, — as being a state occasioned by a vapor that rises from the stomach, — and *being* drunk effectively. Without doubt, the drunken man knows neither the definition of drunkenness nor what makes it interesting for science. Being drunk, he knows nothing; whilst the physician, although not drunk, knows well in what drunkenness consists, and what are its predisposing conditions. Similarly there is a difference between knowing the nature of abstinence, and *being* abstinent or having one's soul detached from the world. — Thus I had learned what words could teach of Sufism, but what was left could be learned neither by study nor through the ears, but solely by giving one's self up to ecstasy and leading a pious life.

" Reflecting on my situation, I found myself tied down by a multitude of bonds — temptations on every side. Considering my teaching, I found it was impure before God. I saw myself struggling with all my might to achieve glory and to spread my name. [Here follows an account of his six months' hesitation to break away from the conditions of his life at Bagdad, at the end of which he fell ill with a paralysis of the tongue.] Then, feeling my own weakness, and having entirely given up my own will, I repaired to God like a man in distress who has no more resources. He answered, as he answers the wretch who invokes him. My heart no longer felt any difficulty in renouncing glory, wealth, and my children. So I quitted Bagdad, and reserving from my fortune only what was indispensable for my subsistence, I distributed the rest. I went to Syria, where I remained about two years, with no other occupation than living in retreat and solitude, conquering my desires, combating my passions, training myself to purify my soul, to make my character perfect, to prepare my heart for meditating on God — all according to the methods of the Sufis, as I had read of them.

" This retreat only increased my desire to live in solitude, and to complete the purification of my heart and fit it for meditation. But the vicissitudes of the times, the affairs of the family, the need of subsistence, changed in some respects my primitive resolve, and interfered with my plans for a purely solitary life. I had never yet found myself completely in ecstasy, save in a few single hours; nevertheless, I kept the hope of attaining this state. Every time that the accidents led me astray, I sought to return; and in this situation I spent ten years. During this solitary state things were revealed to me which it is impossible either to describe or to point out. I recognized for certain that the Sufis are assuredly walking in the path of God. Both in their acts and in their inaction, whether internal or external, they are illumined by the light which proceeds from the prophetic source. The first condition for a Sufi is to purge his heart entirely of all that is not God. The next key of the contemplative life consists in the humble prayers which escape from the fervent soul, and in the meditations on God in which the heart is swallowed up entirely. But in reality this is only the beginning of the Sufi life, the end of Sufism being total absorption in God. The intuitions and all that precede are, so to speak, only the threshold for those who enter. From the beginning, revelations take place in so flagrant a shape that the Sufis see before them, whilst wide awake, the angels and the souls of the prophets. They hear their voices and obtain their favors. Then the transport rises from the perception of forms and figures to a degree which escapes all expression, and which no man may seek to give an account of without his words involving sin.

" Whoever has had no experience of the transport knows of the true nature of prophetism nothing but the name. He may meanwhile be sure of its existence, both by experience and by what he hears the Sufis say. As there are men endowed only with the sensitive faculty who reject what is offered them in the way of objects of the pure understanding, so there are intellectual men who reject and avoid the things perceived by the prophetic faculty. A blind man can understand nothing of colors save what he has learned by narration and hearsay. Yet God

has brought prophetism near to men in giving them all a state
analogous to it in its principal characters. This state is sleep.
If you were to tell a man who was himself without experience
of such a phenomenon that there are people who at times swoon
away so as to resemble dead men, and who [in dreams] yet
perceive things that are hidden, he would deny it [and give his
reasons]. Nevertheless, his arguments would be refuted by
actual experience. Wherefore, just as the understanding is a
stage of human life in which an eye opens to discern various
intellectual objects uncomprehended by sensation; just so in
the prophetic the sight is illumined by a light which uncovers
hidden things and objects which the intellect fails to reach.
The chief properties of prophetism are perceptible only during the transport, by those who embrace the Sufi life. The
prophet is endowed with qualities to which you possess nothing
analogous, and which consequently you cannot possibly understand. How should you know their true nature, since one
knows only what one can comprehend? But the transport
which one attains by the method of the Sufis is like an immediate perception, as if one touched the objects with one's
hand." [1]

This incommunicableness of the transport is the keynote of all mysticism. Mystical truth exists for the individual who has the transport, but for no one else. In
this, as I have said, it resembles the knowledge given to
us in sensations more than that given by conceptual
thought. Thought, with its remoteness and abstractness,
has often enough in the history of philosophy been contrasted unfavorably with sensation. It is a commonplace
of metaphysics that God's knowledge cannot be discursive but must be intuitive, that is, must be constructed
more after the pattern of what in ourselves is called
immediate feeling, than after that of proposition and
judgment. But *our* immediate feelings have no content

---

[1] A. SCHMÖLDERS : Essai sur les écoles philosophiques chez les Arabes,
Paris, 1842, pp. 54–68, abridged.

but what the five senses supply ; and we have seen and shall see again that mystics may emphatically deny that the senses play any part in the very highest type of knowledge which their transports yield.

In the Christian church there have always been mystics. Although many of them have been viewed with suspicion, some have gained favor in the eyes of the authorities. The experiences of these have been treated as precedents, and a codified system of mystical theology has been based upon them, in which everything legitimate finds its place.[1] The basis of the system is ' orison ' or meditation, the methodical elevation of the soul towards God. Through the practice of orison the higher levels of mystical experience may be attained. It is odd that Protestantism, especially evangelical Protestantism, should seemingly have abandoned everything methodical in this line. Apart from what prayer may lead to, Protestant mystical experience appears to have been almost exclusively sporadic. It has been left to our mind-curers to reintroduce methodical meditation into our religious life.

The first thing to be aimed at in orison is the mind's detachment from outer sensations, for these interfere with its concentration upon ideal things. Such manuals as Saint Ignatius's Spiritual Exercises recommend the disciple to expel sensation by a graduated series of efforts to imagine holy scenes. The acme of this kind of discipline would be a semi-hallucinatory mono-ideism — an imaginary figure of Christ, for example, coming fully to

---

[1] GÖRRES's Christliche Mystik gives a full account of the facts. So does RIBET's Mystique Divine, 2 vols., Paris, 1890. A still more methodical modern work is the Mystica Theologia of VALLGORNERA, 2 vols., Turin, 1890.

occupy the mind. Sensorial images of this sort, whether
literal or symbolic, play an enormous part in mysticism.[1]
But in certain cases imagery may fall away entirely, and
in the very highest raptures it tends to do so. The state
of consciousness becomes then insusceptible of any verbal
description. Mystical teachers are unanimous as to this.
Saint John of the Cross, for instance, one of the best of
them, thus describes the condition called the 'union of
love,' which, he says, is reached by 'dark contemplation.'
In this the Deity compenetrates the soul, but in such a
hidden way that the soul —

"finds no terms, no means, no comparison whereby to render
the sublimity of the wisdom and the delicacy of the spiritual
feeling with which she is filled. . . . We receive this mystical
knowledge of God clothed in none of the kinds of images, in
none of the sensible representations, which our mind makes use
of in other circumstances. Accordingly in this knowledge,
since the senses and the imagination are not employed, we get
neither form nor impression, nor can we give any account or
furnish any likeness, although the mysterious and sweet-tasting
wisdom comes home so clearly to the inmost parts of our soul.
Fancy a man seeing a certain kind of thing for the first time in
his life. He can understand it, use and enjoy it, but he cannot
apply a name to it, nor communicate any idea of it, even though
all the while it be a mere thing of sense. How much greater
will be his powerlessness when it goes beyond the senses! This
is the peculiarity of the divine language. The more infused,
intimate, spiritual, and supersensible it is, the more does it
exceed the senses, both inner and outer, and impose silence
upon them. . . . The soul then feels as if placed in a vast and
profound solitude, to which no created thing has access, in an
immense and boundless desert, desert the more delicious the

---

[1] M. Récéjac, in a recent volume, makes them essential. Mysticism he
defines as "the tendency to draw near to the Absolute morally, *and by the aid
of Symbols.*" See his Fondements de la Connaissance mystique, Paris, 1897,
p. 66. But there are unquestionably mystical conditions in which sensible
symbols play no part.

more solitary it is. There, in this abyss of wisdom, the soul grows by what it drinks in from the well-springs of the comprehension of love, . . . and recognizes, however sublime and learned may be the terms we employ, how utterly vile, insignificant, and improper they are, when we seek to discourse of divine things by their means." [1]

I cannot pretend to detail to you the sundry stages of the Christian mystical life.[2]   Our time would not suffice, for one thing ; and moreover, I confess that the subdivisions and names which we find in the Catholic books seem to me to represent nothing objectively distinct. So many men, so many minds : I imagine that these experiences can be as infinitely varied as are the idiosyncrasies of individuals.

The cognitive aspects of them, their value in the way of revelation, is what we are directly concerned with, and it is easy to show by citation how strong an impression they leave of being revelations of new depths of truth. Saint Teresa is the expert of experts in describing such conditions, so I will turn immediately to what she says of one of the highest of them, the 'orison of union.'

"In the orison of union," says Saint Teresa, " the soul is fully awake as regards God, but wholly asleep as regards things of this world and in respect of herself. During the short time the union lasts, she is as it were deprived of every feeling, and even if she would, she could not think of any single thing.

---

[1] Saint John of the Cross : The Dark Night of the Soul, book ii. ch. xvii., in Vie et Œuvres, 3me édition, Paris, 1893, iii. 428–432. Chapter xi. of book ii. of Saint John's Ascent of Carmel is devoted to showing the harmfulness for the mystical life of the use of sensible imagery.

[2] In particular I omit mention of visual and auditory hallucinations, verbal and graphic automatisms, and such marvels as ' levitation,' stigmatization, and the healing of disease. These phenomena, which mystics have often presented (or are believed to have presented), have no essential mystical significance, for they occur with no consciousness of illumination whatever, when they occur, as they often do, in persons of non-mystical mind. Consciousness of illumination is for us the essential mark of ' mystical ' states.

Thus she needs to employ no artifice in order to arrest the use of her understanding: it remains so stricken with inactivity that she neither knows what she loves, nor in what manner she loves, nor what she wills. In short, she is utterly dead to the things of the world and lives solely in God. . . . I do not even know whether in this state she has enough life left to breathe. It seems to me she has not; or at least that if she does breathe, she is unaware of it. Her intellect would fain understand something of what is going on within her, but it has so little force now that it can act in no way whatsoever. So a person who falls into a deep faint appears as if dead. . . .

"Thus does God, when he raises a soul to union with himself, suspend the natural action of all her faculties. She neither sees, hears, nor understands, so long as she is united with God. But this time is always short, and it seems even shorter than it is. God establishes himself in the interior of this soul in such a way, that when she returns to herself, it is wholly impossible for her to doubt that she has been in God, and God in her. This truth remains so strongly impressed on her that, even though many years should pass without the condition returning, she can neither forget the favor she received, nor doubt of its reality. If you, nevertheless, ask how it is possible that the soul can see and understand that she has been in God, since during the union she has neither sight nor understanding, I reply that she does not see it then, but that she sees it clearly later, after she has returned to herself, not by any vision, but by a certitude which abides with her and which God alone can give her. I knew a person who was ignorant of the truth that God's mode of being in everything must be either by presence, by power, or by essence, but who, after having received the grace of which I am speaking, believed this truth in the most unshakable manner. So much so that, having consulted a half-learned man who was as ignorant on this point as she had been before she was enlightened, when he replied that God is in us only by 'grace,' she disbelieved his reply, so sure she was of the true answer; and when she came to ask wiser doctors, they confirmed her in her belief, which much consoled her. . . .

" But how, you will repeat, *can* one have such certainty in respect to what one does not see ? This question, I am powerless to answer. These are secrets of God's omnipotence which it does not appertain to me to penetrate. All that I know is that I tell the truth ; and I shall never believe that any soul who does not possess this certainty has ever been really united to God." [1]

The kinds of truth communicable in mystical ways, whether these be sensible or supersensible, are various. Some of them relate to this world, — visions of the future, the reading of hearts, the sudden understanding of texts, the knowledge of distant events, for example ; but the most important revelations are theological or metaphysical.

" Saint Ignatius confessed one day to Father Laynez that a single hour of meditation at Manresa had taught him more truths about heavenly things than all the teachings of all the doctors put together could have taught him. . . . One day in orison, on the steps of the choir of the Dominican church, he saw in a distinct manner the plan of divine wisdom in the creation of the world. On another occasion, during a procession, his spirit was ravished in God, and it was given him to contemplate, in a form and images fitted to the weak understanding of a dweller on the earth, the deep mystery of the holy Trinity. This last vision flooded his heart with such sweetness, that the mere memory of it in after times made him shed abundant tears." [2]

[1] The Interior Castle, Fifth Abode, ch. i., in Œuvres, translated by Bouix, iii. 421–424.

[2] BARTOLI-MICHEL : Vie de Saint Ignace de Loyola, i. 34–36. Others have had illuminations about the created world, Jacob Boehme, for instance. At the age of twenty-five he was " surrounded by the divine light, and replenished with the heavenly knowledge ; insomuch as going abroad into the fields to a green, at Görlitz, he there sat down, and viewing the herbs and grass of the field, in his inward light he saw into their essences, use, and properties, which was discovered to him by their lineaments, figures, and signatures." Of a later period of experience he writes : " In one quarter of an hour I saw and knew more than if I had been many years together at

Similarly with Saint Teresa. "One day, being in orison," she writes, "it was granted me to perceive in one instant how all things are seen and contained in God. I did not perceive them in their proper form, and nevertheless the view I had of them was of a sovereign clearness, and has remained vividly impressed upon my soul. It is one of the most signal of all the graces which the Lord has granted me. . . . The view was so subtile and delicate that the understanding cannot grasp it." [1]

She goes on to tell how it was as if the Deity were an enormous and sovereignly limpid diamond, in which all our actions were contained in such a way that their full sinfulness appeared evident as never before. On another day, she relates, while she was reciting the Athanasian Creed, —

"Our Lord made me comprehend in what way it is that one God can be in three Persons. He made me see it so clearly

an university. For I saw and knew the being of all things, the Byss and the Abyss, and the eternal generation of the holy Trinity, the descent and original of the world and of all creatures through the divine wisdom. I knew and saw in myself all the three worlds, the external and visible world being of a procreation or extern birth from both the internal and spiritual worlds ; and I saw and knew the whole working essence, in the evil and in the good, and the mutual original and existence ; and likewise how the fruitful bearing womb of eternity brought forth. So that I did not only greatly wonder at it, but did also exceedingly rejoice, albeit I could very hardly apprehend the same in my external man and set it down with the pen. For I had a thorough view of the universe as in a chaos, wherein all things are couched and wrapt up, but it was impossible for me to explicate the same." Jacob Behmen's Theosophic Philosophy, etc., by EDWARD TAYLOR, London, 1691, pp. 425, 427, abridged. So George Fox : "I was come up to the state of Adam in which he was before he fell. The creation was opened to me ; and it was showed me, how all things had their names given to them, according to their nature and virtue. I was at a stand in my mind, whether I should practice physic for the good of mankind, seeing the nature and virtues of the creatures were so opened to me by the Lord." Journal, Philadelphia, no date, p. 69. Contemporary 'Clairvoyance' abounds in similar revelations. Andrew Jackson Davis's cosmogonies, for example, or certain experiences related in the delectable ' Reminiscences and Memories of Henry Thomas Butterworth,' Lebanon, Ohio, 1886.

[1] Vie, pp. 581, 582.

that I remained as extremely surprised as I was comforted, . . . and now, when I think of the holy Trinity, or hear It spoken of, I understand how the three adorable Persons form only one God and I experience an unspeakable happiness."

On still another occasion, it was given to Saint Teresa to see and understand in what wise the Mother of God had been assumed into her place in Heaven.[1]

The deliciousness of some of these states seems to be beyond anything known in ordinary consciousness. It evidently involves organic sensibilities, for it is spoken of as something too extreme to be borne, and as verging on bodily pain.[2] But it is too subtle and piercing a delight for ordinary words to denote. God's touches, the wounds of his spear, references to ebriety and to nuptial union have to figure in the phraseology by which it is shadowed forth. Intellect and senses both swoon away in these highest states of ecstasy. "If our understanding comprehends," says Saint Teresa, "it is in a mode which remains unknown to it, and it can understand nothing of what it comprehends. For my own part, I do not believe that it does comprehend, because, as I said, it does not understand itself to do so. I confess that it is all a mystery in which I am lost."[3] In the condition called *raptus* or ravishment by theologians, breathing and circulation are so depressed that it is a question among the doctors whether the soul be or be not temporarily dissevered from the body. One must read Saint Teresa's descriptions and the very exact distinctions which she makes, to

---

[1] Loc. cit., p. 574.

[2] Saint Teresa discriminates between pain in which the body has a part and pure spiritual pain (Interior Castle, 6th Abode, ch. xi.). As for the bodily part in these celestial joys, she speaks of it as "penetrating to the marrow of the bones, whilst earthly pleasures affect only the surface of the senses. I think," she adds, "that this is a just description, and I cannot make it better." Ibid., 5th Abode, ch. i.

[3] Vie, p. 198.

persuade one's self that one is dealing, not with imaginary experiences, but with phenomena which, however rare, follow perfectly definite psychological types.

To the medical mind these ecstasies signify nothing but suggested and imitated hypnoid states, on an intellectual basis of superstition, and a corporeal one of degeneration and hysteria. Undoubtedly these pathological conditions have existed in many and possibly in all the cases, but that fact tells us nothing about the value for knowledge of the consciousness which they induce. To pass a spiritual judgment upon these states, we must not content ourselves with superficial medical talk, but inquire into their fruits for life.

Their fruits appear to have been various. Stupefaction, for one thing, seems not to have been altogether absent as a result. You may remember the helplessness in the kitchen and schoolroom of poor Margaret Mary Alacoque. Many other ecstatics would have perished but for the care taken of them by admiring followers. The 'other-worldliness' encouraged by the mystical consciousness makes this over-abstraction from practical life peculiarly liable to befall mystics in whom the character is naturally passive and the intellect feeble; but in natively strong minds and characters we find quite opposite results. The great Spanish mystics, who carried the habit of ecstasy as far as it has often been carried, appear for the most part to have shown indomitable spirit and energy, and all the more so for the trances in which they indulged.

Saint Ignatius was a mystic, but his mysticism made him assuredly one of the most powerfully practical human engines that ever lived. Saint John of the Cross, writing of the intuitions and 'touches' by which God reaches the substance of the soul, tells us that —

" They enrich it marvelously. A single one of them may be sufficient to abolish at a stroke certain imperfections of which the soul during its whole life had vainly tried to rid itself, and to leave it adorned with virtues and loaded with supernatural gifts. A single one of these intoxicating consolations may reward it for all the labors undergone in its life — even were they numberless. Invested with an invincible courage, filled with an impassioned desire to suffer for its God, the soul then is seized with a strange torment — that of not being allowed to suffer enough." [1]

Saint Teresa is as emphatic, and much more detailed. You may perhaps remember a passage I quoted from her in my first lecture.[2] There are many similar pages in her autobiography. Where in literature is a more evidently veracious account of the formation of a new centre of spiritual energy, than is given in her description of the effects of certain ecstasies which in departing leave the soul upon a higher level of emotional excitement?

" Often, infirm and wrought upon with dreadful pains before the ecstasy, the soul emerges from it full of health and admirably disposed for action . . . as if God had willed that the body itself, already obedient to the soul's desires, should share in the soul's happiness. . . . The soul after such a favor is animated with a degree of courage so great that if at that moment its body should be torn to pieces for the cause of God, it would feel nothing but the liveliest comfort. Then it is that promises and heroic resolutions spring up in profusion in us, soaring desires, horror of the world, and the clear perception of our proper nothingness. . . . What empire is comparable to that of a soul who, from this sublime summit to which God has raised her, sees all the things of earth beneath her feet, and is captivated by no one of them? How ashamed she is of her former attachments! How amazed at her blindness! What lively pity she feels for those whom she recognizes still shrouded in the darkness! . . . She groans at having ever been sensi-

[1] Œuvres, ii. 320.   [2] Above, p. 21.

tive to points of honor, at the illusion that made her ever see
as honor what the world calls by that name. Now she sees in
this name nothing more than an immense lie of which the world
remains a victim. She discovers, in the new light from above,
that in genuine honor there is nothing spurious, that to be
faithful to this honor is to give our respect to what deserves to
be respected really, and to consider as nothing, or as less than
nothing, whatsoever perishes and is not agreeable to God. . . .
She laughs when she sees grave persons, persons of orison,
caring for points of honor for which she now feels profoundest
contempt. It is suitable to the dignity of their rank to act
thus, they pretend, and it makes them more useful to others.
But she knows that in despising the dignity of their rank for
the pure love of God they would do more good in a single day
than they would effect in ten years by preserving it. . . . She
laughs at herself that there should ever have been a time in her
life when she made any case of money, when she ever desired
it. . . . Oh! if human beings might only agree together to
regard it as so much useless mud, what harmony would then
reign in the world! With what friendship we would all treat
each other if our interest in honor and in money could but disappear from earth! For my own part, I feel as if it would be a
remedy for all our ills." [1]

Mystical conditions may, therefore, render the soul
more energetic in the lines which their inspiration favors.
But this could be reckoned an advantage only in case
the inspiration were a true one. If the inspiration were
erroneous, the energy would be all the more mistaken
and misbegotten. So we stand once more before that
problem of truth which confronted us at the end of the
lectures on saintliness. You will remember that we
turned to mysticism precisely to get some light on truth.
Do mystical states establish the truth of those theological affections in which the saintly life has its root?

In spite of their repudiation of articulate self-descrip-

[1] Vie, pp. 229, 200, 231–233, 243.

tion, mystical states in general assert a pretty distinct
theoretic drift.   It is possible to give the outcome of the
majority of them in terms that point in definite philosophical directions.   One of these directions is optimism, and
the other is monism.   We pass into mystical states from
out of ordinary consciousness as from a less into a more,
as from a smallness into a vastness, and at the same time
as from an unrest to a rest.   We feel them as reconciling,
unifying states.   They appeal to the yes-function more
than to the no-function in us.   In them the unlimited
absorbs the limits and peacefully closes the account.
Their very denial of every adjective you may propose
as applicable to the ultimate truth, — He, the Self, the
Atman, is to be described by 'No! no!' only, say the
Upanishads,[1] — though it seems on the surface to be a
no-function, is a denial made on behalf of a deeper yes.
Whoso calls the Absolute anything in particular, or says
that it is *this*, seems implicitly to shut it off from being
that — it is as if he lessened it.   So we deny the 'this,'
negating the negation which it seems to us to imply, in
the interests of the higher affirmative attitude by which
we are possessed.   The fountain-head of Christian mysticism is Dionysius the Areopagite.   He describes the
absolute truth by negatives exclusively.

"The cause of all things is neither soul nor intellect; nor
has it imagination, opinion, or reason, or intelligence; nor is it
reason or intelligence; nor is it spoken or thought.   It is
neither number, nor order, nor magnitude, nor littleness, nor
equality, nor inequality, nor similarity, nor dissimilarity.   It
neither stands, nor moves, nor rests. . . . It is neither essence, nor eternity, nor time.   Even intellectual contact does
not belong to it.   It is neither science nor truth.   It is not
even royalty or wisdom; not one; not unity; not divinity

[1] MÜLLER's translation, part ii. p. 180.

or goodness; nor even spirit as we know it," etc., *ad libitum*.[1]

But these qualifications àre denied by Dionysius, not because the truth falls short of them, but because it so infinitely excels them. It is above them. It is *super*-lucent, *super*-splendent, *super*-essential, *super*-sublime, *super* everything that can be named. Like Hegel in his logic, mystics journey towards the positive pole of truth only by the ' Methode der Absoluten Negativität.'[2]

Thus come the paradoxical expressions that so abound in mystical writings. As when Eckhart tells of the still desert of the Godhead, " where never was seen difference, neither Father, Son, nor Holy Ghost, where there is no one at home, yet where the spark of the soul is more at peace than in itself."[3] As when Boehme writes of the Primal Love, that " it may fitly be compared to Nothing, for it is deeper than any Thing, and is as nothing with respect to all things, forasmuch as it is not comprehensible by any of them. And because it is nothing respectively, it is therefore free from all things, and is that only good, which a man cannot express or utter what it is, there being nothing to which it may be compared, to express it by."[4] Or as when Angelus Silesius sings : —

> " Gott ist ein lauter Nichts, ihn rührt kein Nun noch Hier ;
> Je mehr du nach ihm greiffst, je mehr entwind er dir."[5]

To this dialectical use, by the intellect, of negation as

---

[1] T. DAVIDSON'S translation, in Journal of Speculative Philosophy, 1893, vol. xxii. p. 399.

[2] " Deus propter excellentiam non immerito Nihil vocatur." Scotus Erigena, quoted by ANDREW SETH : Two Lectures on Theism, New York, 1897, p. 55.

[3] J. ROYCE : Studies in Good and Evil, p. 282.

[4] Jacob Behmen's Dialogues on the Supersensual Life, translated by BERNARD HOLLAND, London, 1901, p. 48.

[5] Cherubinischer Wandersmann, Strophe 25.

a mode of passage towards a higher kind of affirmation, there is correlated the subtlest of moral counterparts in the sphere of the personal will. Since denial of the finite self and its wants, since asceticism of some sort, is found in religious experience to be the only doorway to the larger and more blessed life, this moral mystery intertwines and combines with the intellectual mystery in all mystical writings.

" Love," continues Behmen, is Nothing, for " when thou art gone forth wholly from the Creature and from that which is visible, and art become Nothing to all that is Nature and Creature, then thou art in that eternal One, which is God himself, and then thou shalt feel within thee the highest virtue of Love. . . . The treasure of treasures for the soul is where she goeth out of the Somewhat into that Nothing out of which all things may be made. The soul here saith, *I have nothing*, for I am utterly stripped and naked; *I can do nothing*, for I have no manner of power, but am as water poured out: *I am nothing*, for all that I am is no more than an image of Being, and only God is to me I AM; and so, sitting down in my own Nothingness, I give glory to the eternal Being, and *will nothing* of myself, that so God may will all in me, being unto me my God and all things." [1]

In Paul's language, I live, yet not I, but Christ liveth in me. Only when I become as nothing can God enter in and no difference between his life and mine remain outstanding.[2]

[1] Op. cit., pp. 42, 74, abridged.

[2] From a French book I take this mystical expression of happiness in God's indwelling presence : —

"Jesus has come to take up his abode in my heart. It is not so much a habitation, an association, as a sort of fusion. Oh, new and blessed life ! life which becomes each day more luminous. . . . The wall before me, dark a few moments since, is splendid at this hour because the sun shines on it. Wherever its rays fall they light up a conflagration of glory ; the smallest speck of glass sparkles, each grain of sand emits fire ; even so there is a royal song of triumph in my heart because the Lord is there. My

This overcoming of all the usual barriers between the individual and the Absolute is the great mystic achievement. In mystic states we both become one with the Absolute and we become aware of our oneness. This is the everlasting and triumphant mystical tradition, hardly altered by differences of clime or creed. In Hinduism, in Neoplatonism, in Sufism, in Christian mysticism, in Whitmanism, we find the same recurring note, so that there is about mystical utterances an eternal unanimity which ought to make a critic stop and think, and which brings it about that the mystical classics have, as has been said, neither birthday nor native land. Perpetually telling of the unity of man with God, their speech antedates languages, and they do not grow old.[1]

'That art Thou!' say the Upanishads, and the Vedantists add : 'Not a part, not a mode of That, but identically That, that absolute Spirit of the World.' "As pure water poured into pure water remains the same, thus, O Gautama, is the Self of a thinker who knows.

days succeed each other ; yesterday a blue sky ; to-day a clouded sun ; a night filled with strange dreams ; but as soon as the eyes open, and I regain consciousness and seem to begin life again, it is always the same figure before me, always the same presence filling my heart. . . . Formerly the day was dulled by the absence of the Lord. I used to wake invaded by all sorts of sad impressions, and I did not find him on my path. To-day he is with me ; and the light cloudiness which covers things is not an obstacle to my communion with him. I feel the pressure of his hand, I feel something else which fills me with a serene joy ; shall I dare to speak it out ? Yes, for it is the true expression of what I experience. The Holy Spirit is not merely making me a visit ; it is no mere dazzling apparition which may from one moment to another spread its wings and leave me in my night, it is a permanent habitation. He can depart only if he takes me with him. More than that ; he is not other than myself : he is one with me. It is not a juxtaposition, it is a penetration, a profound modification of my nature, a new manner of my being." Quoted from the MS. 'of an old man' by WILFRED MONOD : Il Vit : six méditations sur le mystère chrétien, pp. 280-283.

[1] Compare M. MAETERLINCK : L'Ornement des Noces spirituelles de Ruysbroeck, Bruxelles, 1891, Introduction, p. xix.

Water in water, fire in fire, ether in ether, no one can distinguish them; likewise a man whose mind has entered into the Self." [1] " 'Every man,' says the Sufi Gulshan-Râz, ' whose heart is no longer shaken by any doubt, knows with certainty that there is no being save only One. . . . In his divine majesty the *me*, the *we*, the *thou*, are not found, for in the One there can be no distinction. Every being who is annulled and entirely separated from himself, hears resound outside of him this voice and this echo : *I am God:* he has an eternal way of existing, and is no longer subject to death.' " [2] In the vision of God, says Plotinus, "what sees is not our reason, but something prior and superior to our reason. . . . He who thus sees does not properly see, does not distinguish or imagine two things. He changes, he ceases to be himself, preserves nothing of himself. Absorbed in God, he makes but one with him, like a centre of a circle coinciding with another centre." [3] "Here," writes Suso, " the spirit dies, and yet is all alive in the marvels of the Godhead . . . and is lost in the stillness of the glorious dazzling obscurity and of the naked simple unity. It is in this modeless *where* that the highest bliss is to be found." [4] " Ich bin so gross als Gott," sings Angelus Silesius again, " Er ist als ich so klein ; Er kann nicht über mich, ich unter ihm nicht sein." [5]

In mystical literature such self-contradictory phrases as ' dazzling obscurity,' 'whispering silence,' teeming desert,' are continually met with. They prove that not conceptual speech, but music rather, is the element through which we

[1] Upanishads, M. MÜLLER's translation, ii. 17, 334.

[2] SCHMÖLDERS : Op. cit., p. 210.

[3] Enneads, BOUILLIER's translation, Paris, 1861, iii. 561. Compare pp. 473–477, and vol. i. p. 27.

[4] Autobiography, pp. 309, 310.

[5] Op. cit., Strophe 10.

are best spoken to by mystical truth. Many mystical scriptures are indeed little more than musical compositions.

"He who would hear the voice of Nada, 'the Soundless Sound,' and comprehend it, he has to learn the nature of Dhâranâ. . . . When to himself his form appears unreal, as do on waking all the forms he sees in dreams; when he has ceased to hear the many, he may discern the ONE — the inner sound which kills the outer. . . . For then the soul will hear, and will remember. And then to the inner ear will speak THE VOICE OF THE SILENCE. . . . And now thy *Self* is lost in SELF, *thyself* unto THYSELF, merged in that SELF from which thou first didst radiate. . . . Behold! thou hast become the Light, thou hast become the Sound, thou art thy Master and thy God. Thou art THYSELF the object of thy search: the VOICE unbroken, that resounds throughout eternities, exempt from change, from sin exempt, the seven sounds in one, the VOICE OF THE SILENCE. *Om tat Sat*." [1]

These words, if they do not awaken laughter as you receive them, probably stir chords within you which music and language touch in common. Music gives us ontological messages which non-musical criticism is unable to contradict, though it may laugh at our foolishness in minding them. There is a verge of the mind which these things haunt; and whispers therefrom mingle with the operations of our understanding, even as the waters of the infinite ocean send their waves to break among the pebbles that lie upon our shores.

"Here begins the sea that ends not till the world's end. Where we stand,
Could we know the next high sea-mark set beyond these waves that gleam,
We should know what never man hath known, nor eye of man hath
     scanned. . . .
Ah, but here man's heart leaps, yearning towards the gloom with venturous
     glee,
From the shore that hath no shore beyond it, set in all the sea." [2]

[1] H. P. BLAVATSKY: The Voice of the Silence.
[2] SWINBURNE: On the Verge, in 'A Midsummer Vacation.'

That doctrine, for example, that eternity is timeless, that our 'immortality,' if we live in the eternal, is not so much future as already now and here, which we find so often expressed to-day in certain philosophic circles, finds its support in a 'hear, hear!' or an 'amen,' which floats up from that mysteriously deeper level.[1] We recognize the passwords to the mystical region as we hear them, but we cannot use them ourselves; it alone has the keeping of 'the password primeval.'[2]

I have now sketched with extreme brevity and insufficiency, but as fairly as I am able in the time allowed, the general traits of the mystic range of consciousness. *It is on the whole pantheistic and optimistic, or at least the opposite of pessimistic. It is anti-naturalistic, and harmonizes best with twice-bornness and so-called otherworldly states of mind.*

My next task is to inquire whether we can invoke it as authoritative. Does it furnish any *warrant for the truth* of the twice-bornness and supernaturality and pantheism which it favors? I must give my answer to this question as concisely as I can.

In brief my answer is this,— and I will divide it into three parts:—

(1) Mystical states, when well developed, usually are, and have the right to be, absolutely authoritative over the individuals to whom they come.

(2) No authority emanates from them which should make it a duty for those who stand outside of them to accept their revelations uncritically.

---

[1] Compare the extracts from Dr. Bucke, quoted on pp. 398, 399.

[2] As serious an attempt as I know to mediate between the mystical region and the discursive life is contained in an article on Aristotle's Unmoved Mover, by F. C. S. SCHILLER, in Mind, vol. ix., 1900.

(3) They break down the authority of the non-mystical or rationalistic consciousness, based upon the understanding and the senses alone. They show it to be only one kind of consciousness. They open out the possibility of other orders of truth, in which, so far as anything in us vitally responds to them, we may freely continue to have faith.

I will take up these points one by one.

1.

As a matter of psychological fact, mystical states of a well-pronounced and emphatic sort *are* usually authoritative over those who have them.[1] They have been ' there,' and know. It is vain for rationalism to grumble about this. If the mystical truth that comes to a man proves to be a force that he can live by, what mandate have we of the majority to order him to live in another way? We can throw him into a prison or a madhouse, but we cannot change his mind — we commonly attach it only the more stubbornly to its beliefs.[2] It mocks our utmost efforts, as a matter of fact, and in point of logic it absolutely escapes our jurisdiction. Our own more ' rational ' beliefs are based on evidence exactly similar in nature to that which mystics quote for theirs. Our senses, namely, have assured us of certain states of fact; but mystical experiences are as direct perceptions

---

[1] I abstract from weaker states, and from those cases of which the books are full, where the director (but usually not the subject) remains in doubt whether the experience may not have proceeded from the demon.

[2] Example : Mr. John Nelson writes of his imprisonment for preaching Methodism : " My soul was as a watered garden, and I could sing praises to God all day long ; for he turned my captivity into joy, and gave me to rest as well on the boards, as if I had been on a bed of down. Now could I say, ' God's service is perfect freedom,' and I was carried out much in prayer that my enemies might drink of the same river of peace which my God gave so largely to me." Journal, London, no date, p. 172.

of fact for those who have them as any sensations ever were for us. The records show that even though the five senses be in abeyance in them, they are absolutely sensational in their epistemological quality, if I may be pardoned the barbarous expression, — that is, they are face to face presentations of what seems immediately to exist.

The mystic is, in short, *invulnerable*, and must be left, whether we relish it or not, in undisturbed enjoyment of his creed. Faith, says Tolstoy, is that by which men live. And faith-state and mystic state are practically convertible terms.

2.

But I now proceed to add that mystics have no right to claim that we ought to accept the deliverance of their peculiar experiences, if we are ourselves outsiders and feel no private call thereto. The utmost they can ever ask of us in this life is to admit that they establish a presumption. They form a consensus and have an unequivocal outcome ; and it would be odd, mystics might say, if such a unanimous type of experience should prove to be altogether wrong. At bottom, however, this would only be an appeal to numbers, like the appeal of rationalism the other way ; and the appeal to numbers has no logical force. If we acknowledge it, it is for ' suggestive,' not for logical reasons : we follow the majority because to do so suits our life.

But even this presumption from the unanimity of mystics is far from being strong. In characterizing mystic states as pantheistic, optimistic, etc., I am afraid I over-simplified the truth. I did so for expository reasons, and to keep the closer to the classic mystical tradition. The classic religious mysticism, it now must be confessed, is only a 'privileged case.' It is an *extract*, kept true to type by the selection of the fittest specimens and their preservation in 'schools.' It is carved out from a much larger mass ; and if we take the larger mass as seriously as religious mysticism has historically taken itself, we find that the supposed unanimity largely disappears. To begin with, even religious mysticism itself, the kind that accumulates traditions and makes schools, is much less unanimous than I have allowed. It has been both ascetic and antinomianly self-indulgent within the Christian church.[1] It is dualistic in Sankhya, and monistic in Vedanta philosophy. I called it pantheistic ; but the great Spanish mystics are anything but pantheists. They are with few exceptions non-metaphysical minds, for whom 'the category of personality' is absolute. The 'union' of man with God is for them much more like an occasional miracle than like an original identity.[2] How different again, apart from the happiness common to all, is the mysticism of Walt Whitman, Edward Carpenter, Richard Jefferies, and other naturalistic pantheists, from the more distinctively Christian sort.[3] The fact is that the mystical feeling of enlargement, union, and emancipation has no specific intellectual content whatever of its own. It is capable of forming matrimonial alliances with material furnished by the most diverse philosophies and theologies, provided only they

[1] RUYSBROECK, in the work which Maeterlinck has translated, has a chapter against the antinomianism of disciples. H. DELACROIX'S book (Essai sur le mysticisme spéculatif en Allemagne au XIVme Siècle, Paris, 1900) is full of antinomian material. Compare also A. JUNDT : Les Amis de Dieu au XIVme Siècle, Thèse de Strasbourg, 1879.

[2] Compare PAUL ROUSSELOT : Les Mystiques Espagnols, Paris, 1869, ch. xii.

[3] See CARPENTER'S Towards Democracy, especially the latter parts, and JEFFERIES'S wonderful and splendid mystic rhapsody, The Story of my Heart.

can find a place in their framework for its peculiar emotional mood. We have no right, therefore, to invoke its prestige as distinctively in favor of any special belief, such as that in absolute idealism, or in the absolute monistic identity, or in the absolute goodness, of the world. It is only relatively in favor of all these things — it passes out of common human consciousness in the direction in which they lie.

So much for religious mysticism proper. But more remains to be told, for religious mysticism is only one half of mysticism. The other half has no accumulated traditions except those which the text-books on insanity supply. Open any one of these, and you will find abundant cases in which 'mystical ideas' are cited as characteristic symptoms of enfeebled or deluded states of mind. In delusional insanity, paranoia, as they sometimes call it, we may have a *diabolical* mysticism, a sort of religious mysticism turned upside down. The same sense of ineffable importance in the smallest events, the same texts and words coming with new meanings, the same voices and visions and leadings and missions, the same controlling by extraneous powers; only this time the emotion is pessimistic: instead of consolations we have desolations; the meanings are dreadful; and the powers are enemies to life. It is evident that from the point of view of their psychological mechanism, the classic mysticism and these lower mysticisms spring from the same mental level, from that great subliminal or transmarginal region of which science is beginning to admit the existence, but of which so little is really known. That region contains every kind of matter: 'seraph and snake' abide there side by side. To come from thence is no infallible credential. What comes must be sifted and tested, and run the gauntlet of confrontation with the total context of experience, just like what comes from the outer world of sense. Its value must be ascertained by empirical methods, so long as we are not mystics ourselves.

Once more, then, I repeat that non-mystics are under no obligation to acknowledge in mystical states a superior authority conferred on them by their intrinsic nature.[1]

3.

Yet, I repeat once more, the existence of mystical states absolutely overthrows the pretension of non-mystical states to be the sole and ultimate dictators of what we may believe. As a rule, mystical states merely add a supersensuous meaning to the ordinary outward data of consciousness. They are excitements like the emotions of love or ambition, gifts to our spirit by means of which facts already objectively before us fall into a new expressiveness and make a new connection with our active life. They do not contradict these facts as such, or deny anything that our senses have immediately seized.[2] It is the rationalistic critic rather who plays the part of denier in

[1] In chapter i. of book ii. of his work Degeneration, 'MAX NORDAU' seeks to undermine all mysticism by exposing the weakness of the lower kinds. Mysticism for him means any sudden perception of hidden significance in things. He explains such perception by the abundant uncompleted associations which experiences may arouse in a degenerate brain. These give to him who has the experience a vague and vast sense of its leading further, yet they awaken no definite or useful consequent in his thought. The explanation is a plausible one for certain sorts of feeling of significance ; and other alienists (WERNICKE, for example, in his Grundriss der Psychiatrie, Theil ii., Leipzig, 1896) have explained ' paranoiac ' conditions by a laming of the association-organ. But the higher mystical flights, with their positiveness and abruptness, are surely products of no such merely negative condition. It seems far more reasonable to ascribe them to inroads from the subconscious life, of the cerebral activity correlative to which we as yet know nothing.

[2] They sometimes add subjective *audita et visa* to the facts, but as these are usually interpreted as transmundane, they oblige no alteration in the facts of sense.

the controversy, and his denials have no strength, for there never can be a state of facts to which new meaning may not truthfully be added, provided the mind ascend to a more enveloping point of view.   It must always remain an open question whether mystical states may not possibly be such superior points of view, windows through which the mind looks out upon a more extensive and inclusive world.   The difference of the views seen from the different mystical windows need not prevent us from entertaining this supposition.   The wider world would in that case prove to have a mixed constitution like that of this world, that is all.   It would have its celestial and its infernal regions, its tempting and its saving moments, its valid experiences and its counterfeit ones, just as our world has them; but it would be a wider world all the same.   We should have to use its experiences by selecting and subordinating and substituting just as is our custom in this ordinary naturalistic world; we should be liable to error just as we are now;   yet the counting in of that wider world of meanings, and the serious dealing with it, might, in spite of all the perplexity, be indispensable stages in our approach to the final fullness of the truth.

In this shape, I think, we have to leave the subject. Mystical states indeed wield no authority due simply to their being mystical states.   But the higher ones among them point in directions to which the religious sentiments even of non-mystical men incline.   They tell of the supremacy of the ideal, of vastness, of union, of safety, and of rest.   They offer us *hypotheses*, hypotheses which we may voluntarily ignore, but which as thinkers we cannot possibly upset.   The supernaturalism and optimism to which they would persuade us may, interpreted in one way or another, be after all the truest of insights into the meaning of this life.

" Oh, the little more, and how much it is ; and the little less, and what worlds away ! " It may be that possibility and permission of this sort are all that the religious consciousness requires to live on. In my last lecture I shall have to try to persuade you that this is the case. Meanwhile, however, I am sure that for many of my readers this diet is too slender. If supernaturalism and inner union with the divine are true, you think, then not so much permission, as compulsion to believe, ought to be found. Philosophy has always professed to prove religious truth by coercive argument ; and the construction of philosophies of this kind has always been one favorite function of the religious life, if we use this term in the large historic sense. But religious philosophy is an enormous subject, and in my next lecture I can only give that brief glance at it which my limits will allow.

LECTURE XVIII

PHILOSOPHY

THE subject of Saintliness left us face to face with the question, Is the sense of divine presence a sense of anything objectively true? We turned first to mysticism for an answer, and found that although mysticism is entirely willing to corroborate religion, it is too private (and also too various) in its utterances to be able to claim a universal authority. But philosophy publishes results which claim to be universally valid if they are valid at all, so we now turn with our question to philosophy. Can philosophy stamp a warrant of veracity upon the religious man's sense of the divine?

I imagine that many of you at this point begin to indulge in guesses at the goal to which I am tending. I have undermined the authority of mysticism, you say, and the next thing I shall probably do is to seek to discredit that of philosophy. Religion, you expect to hear me conclude, is nothing but an affair of faith, based either on vague sentiment, or on that vivid sense of the reality of things unseen of which in my second lecture and in the lecture on Mysticism I gave so many examples. It is essentially private and individualistic; it always exceeds our powers of formulation; and although attempts to pour its contents into a philosophic mould will probably always go on, men being what they are, yet these attempts are always secondary processes which in no way add to the authority, or warrant the veracity, of the sentiments from which they derive their own stimulus and borrow whatever glow of conviction they may themselves possess. In short, you suspect that I am planning to defend feeling at the expense of reason, to rehabilitate the primitive and unreflective, and to dissuade you from the hope of any Theology worthy of the name.

To a certain extent I have to admit that you guess rightly. I do believe that feeling is the deeper source of religion, and that philosophic and theological formulas are secondary products, like translations of a text into another tongue. But all such statements are misleading from their brevity, and it will take the whole hour for me to explain to you exactly what I mean.

When I call theological formulas secondary products, I mean that in a world in which no religious feeling had ever existed, I doubt whether any philosophic theology could ever have been framed. I doubt if dispassionate intellectual contemplation of the universe, apart from inner unhappiness and need of deliverance on the one hand and mystical emotion on the other, would ever have resulted in religious philosophies such as we now possess. Men would have begun with animistic explanations of natural fact, and criticised these away into scientific ones, as they actually have done. In the science they would have left a certain amount of ' psychical research,' even as they now will probably have to re-admit a certain amount. But high-flying speculations like those of either dogmatic or idealistic theology, these they would have had no motive to venture on, feeling no need of commerce with such deities. These speculations must, it seems to me, be classed as over-beliefs, buildings-out performed by the intellect into directions of which feeling originally supplied the hint.

But even if religious philosophy had to have its first hint supplied by feeling, may it not have dealt in a superior way with the matter which feeling suggested? Feeling is private and dumb, and unable to give an account of itself. It allows that its results are mysteries and enigmas, declines to justify them rationally, and on occasion is willing that they should even pass for paradoxical and absurd. Philosophy takes just the opposite attitude. Her aspiration is to reclaim from mystery and paradox whatever territory she touches. To find an escape from obscure and wayward personal persuasion to truth objectively valid for all thinking men has ever been the intellect's most cherished ideal. To redeem religion from unwholesome privacy, and to give public status and universal right of way to its deliverances, has been reason's task.

I believe that philosophy will always have opportunity to labor at this task.[1] We are thinking beings, and we cannot exclude the intellect from participating in any of our functions. Even in soliloquizing with ourselves, we construe our feelings intellectually. Both our personal ideals and our religious and mystical experiences must be interpreted congruously with the kind of scenery which our thinking mind inhabits. The philosophic climate of our time inevitably forces its own clothing on us. Moreover, we must exchange our feelings with one another, and in doing so we have to speak, and to use general and abstract verbal formulas. Conceptions and constructions are thus a necessary part of our religion; and as moderator amid the clash of hypotheses, and mediator among the criticisms of one man's constructions by another, philosophy will always have much to do. It would be strange if I disputed this, when these very lectures which I am giving are (as you will see more clearly

---

[1] Compare Professor W. WALLACE's Gifford Lectures, in Lectures and Essays, Oxford, 1898, pp. 17 ff.

from now onwards) a laborious attempt to extract from
the privacies of religious experience some general facts
which can be defined in formulas upon which everybody
may agree.

Religious experience, in other words, spontaneously
and inevitably engenders myths, superstitions, dogmas,
creeds, and metaphysical theologies, and criticisms of
one set of these by the adherents of another. Of late,
impartial classifications and comparisons have become
possible, alongside of the denunciations and anathemas
by which the commerce between creeds used exclusively
to be carried on. We have the beginnings of a 'Science
of Religions,' so-called; and if these lectures could ever
be accounted a crumb-like contribution to such a science,
I should be made very happy.

But all these intellectual operations, whether they
be constructive or comparative and critical, presuppose
immediate experiences as their subject-matter. They
are interpretative and inductive operations, operations
after the fact, consequent upon religious feeling, not
coördinate with it, not independent of what it ascertains.

The intellectualism in religion which I wish to discredit pretends to be something altogether different from
this. It assumes to construct religious objects out of
the resources of logical reason alone, or of logical reason
drawing rigorous inference from non-subjective facts. It
calls its conclusions dogmatic theology, or philosophy of
the absolute, as the case may be; it does not call them
science of religions. It reaches them in an a priori way,
and warrants their veracity.

Warranted systems have ever been the idols of aspiring
souls. All-inclusive, yet simple; noble, clean, luminous,
stable, rigorous, true; — what more ideal refuge could

there be than such a system would offer to spirits vexed by the muddiness and accidentality of the world of sensible things ? Accordingly, we find inculcated in the theological schools of to-day, almost as much as in those of the fore-time, a disdain for merely possible or probable truth, and of results that only private assurance can grasp. Scholastics and idealists both express this disdain. Principal John Caird, for example, writes as follows in his Introduction to the Philosophy of Religion : —

"Religion must indeed be a thing of the heart ; but in order to elevate it from the region of subjective caprice and waywardness, and to distinguish between that which is true and false in religion, we must appeal to an objective standard. That which enters the heart must first be discerned by the intelligence to be *true*. It must be seen as having in its own nature a *right* to dominate feeling, and as constituting the principle by which feeling must be judged.[1] In estimating the religious character of individuals, nations, or races, the first question is, not how they feel, but what they think and believe — not whether their religion is one which manifests itself in emotions, more or less vehement and enthusiastic, but what are the *conceptions* of God and divine things by which these emotions are called forth. Feeling is necessary in religion, but it is by the *content* or intelligent basis of a religion, and not by feeling, that its character and worth are to be determined."[2]

Cardinal Newman, in his work, The Idea of a University, gives more emphatic expression still to this disdain for sentiment.[3] Theology, he says, is a science in the strictest sense of the word. I will tell you, he says, what it is not — not 'physical evidences' for God, not 'natural religion,' for these are but vague subjective interpretations : —

[1] Op. cit., p. 174, abridged.
[2] Ibid., p. 186, abridged and italicized.
[3] Discourse II. § 7.

" If," he continues, " the Supreme Being is powerful or skill-
ful, just so far as the telescope shows power, or the microscope
shows skill, if his moral law is to be ascertained simply by the
physical processes of the animal frame, or his will gathered
from the immediate issues of human affairs, if his Essence is
just as high and deep and broad as the universe and no more;
if this be the fact, then will I confess that there is no specific
science about God, that theology is but a name, and a protest
in its behalf an hypocrisy. Then, pious as it is to think of
Him, while the pageant of experiment or abstract reasoning
passes by, still such piety is nothing more than a poetry of
thought, or an ornament of language, a certain view taken of
Nature which one man has and another has not, which gifted
minds strike out, which others see to be admirable and ingenious, and which all would be the better for adopting. It is but
the theology of Nature, just as we talk of the *philosophy* or
the *romance* of history, or the *poetry* of childhood, or the pic-
turesque or the sentimental or the humorous, or any other abstract quality which the genius or the caprice of the individual,
or the fashion of the day, or the consent of the world, recognizes in any set of objects which are subjected to its contemplation. I do not see much difference between avowing that there
is no God, and implying that nothing definite can be known
for certain about Him."

What I mean by Theology, continues Newman, is none of
these things: " I simply mean the *Science of God*, or the truths
we know about God, put into a system, just as we have a science of the stars and call it astronomy, or of the crust of the
earth and call it geology."

In both these extracts we have the issue clearly set
before us : Feeling valid only for the individual is pitted
against reason valid universally. The test is a perfectly
plain one of fact. Theology based on pure reason must
in point of fact convince men universally. If it did not,
wherein would its superiority consist? If it only formed
sects and schools, even as sentiment and mysticism form
them, how would it fulfill its programme of freeing us

from personal caprice and waywardness ?   This perfectly
definite practical test of the pretensions of philosophy
to found religion on universal reason simplifies my procedure to-day. I need not discredit philosophy by laborious criticism of its arguments. It will suffice if I show
that as a matter of history it fails to prove its pretension
to be ' objectively' convincing. In fact, philosophy does
so fail. It does not banish differences ; it founds schools
and sects just as feeling does. I believe, in fact, that
the logical reason of man operates in this field of divinity
exactly as it has always operated in love, or in patriotism,
or in politics, or in any other of the wider affairs of life,
in which our passions or our mystical intuitions fix our
beliefs beforehand. It finds arguments for our conviction, for indeed it *has* to find them. It amplifies and
defines our faith, and dignifies it and lends it words and
plausibility. It hardly ever engenders it ; it cannot now
secure it.[1]

Lend me your attention while I run through some of
the points of the older systematic theology. You find
them in both Protestant and Catholic manuals, best of all
in the innumerable text-books published since Pope Leo's
Encyclical recommending the study of Saint Thomas.
I glance first at the arguments by which dogmatic the-

---

[1] As regards the secondary character of intellectual constructions, and
the primacy of feeling and instinct in founding religious beliefs, see the
striking work of H. FIELDING, The Hearts of Men, London, 1902, which
came into my hands after my text was written. " Creeds," says the author,
"are the grammar of religion, they are to religion what grammar is to
speech. Words are the expression of our wants ; grammar is the theory
formed afterwards. Speech never proceeded from grammar, but the reverse. As speech progresses and changes from unknown causes, grammar
must follow" (p. 313). The whole book, which keeps unusually close to
concrete facts, is little more than an amplification of this text.

ology establishes God's existence, after that at those by
which it establishes his nature.[1]

The arguments for God's existence have stood for
hundreds of years with the waves of unbelieving criticism breaking against them, never totally discrediting
them in the ears of the faithful, but on the whole slowly
and surely washing out the mortar from between their
joints. If you have a God already whom you believe in,
these arguments confirm you. If you are atheistic, they
fail to set you right. The proofs are various. The 'cosmological' one, so-called, reasons from the contingence of
the world to a First Cause which must contain whatever
perfections the world itself contains. The 'argument
from design' reasons, from the fact that Nature's laws are
mathematical, and her parts benevolently adapted to each
other, that this cause is both intellectual and benevolent.
The 'moral argument' is that the moral law presupposes a
lawgiver. The 'argument *ex consensu gentium*' is that
the belief in God is so widespread as to be grounded in
the rational nature of man, and should therefore carry
authority with it.

As I just said, I will not discuss these arguments technically. The bare fact that all idealists since Kant have
felt entitled either to scout or to neglect them shows that
they are not solid enough to serve as religion's all-suffi-
cient foundation. Absolutely impersonal reasons would
be in duty bound to show more general convincingness.
Causation is indeed too obscure a principle to bear the
weight of the whole structure of theology. As for the

[1] For convenience' sake, I follow the order of A. STÖCKL'S Lehrbuch der
Philosophie, 5te Auflage, Mainz, 1881, Band ii. B. BOEDDER'S Natural
Theology, London, 1891, is a handy English Catholic Manual; but an
almost identical doctrine is given by such Protestant theologians as C.
HODGE : Systematic Theology, New York, 1873, or A. H. STRONG : Syste-
matic Theology, 5th edition, New York, 1896.

argument from design, see how Darwinian ideas have revolutionized it. Conceived as we now conceive them, as so many fortunate escapes from almost limitless processes of destruction, the benevolent adaptations which we find in Nature suggest a deity very different from the one who figured in the earlier versions of the argument.[1]

[1] It must not be forgotten that any form of *dis*order in the world might, by the design argument, suggest a God for just that kind of disorder. The truth is that any state of things whatever that can be named is logically susceptible of teleological interpretation. The ruins of the earthquake at Lisbon, for example : the whole of past history had to be planned exactly as it was to bring about in the fullness of time just that particular arrangement of débris of masonry, furniture, and once living bodies. No other train of causes would have been sufficient. And so of any other arrangement, bad or good, which might as a matter of fact be found resulting anywhere from previous conditions. To avoid such pessimistic consequences and save its beneficent designer, the design argument accordingly invokes two other principles, restrictive in their operation. The first is physical : Nature's forces tend of their own accord only to disorder and destruction, to heaps of ruins, not to architecture. This principle, though plausible at first sight, seems, in the light of recent biology, to be more and more improbable. The second principle is one of anthropomorphic interpretation. No arrangement that for *us* is 'disorderly' can possibly have been an object of design at all. This principle is of course a mere assumption in the interests of anthropomorphic Theism.

When one views the world with no definite theological bias one way or the other, one sees that order and disorder, as we now recognize them, are purely human inventions. We are interested in certain types of arrangement, useful, æsthetic, or moral, — so interested that whenever we find them realized, the fact emphatically rivets our attention. The result is that we work over the contents of the world selectively. It is overflowing with disorderly arrangements from our point of view, but order is the only thing we care for and look at, and by choosing, one can always find some sort of orderly arrangement in the midst of any chaos. If I should throw down a thousand beans at random upon a table, I could doubtless, by eliminating a sufficient number of them, leave the rest in almost any geometrical pattern you might propose to me, and you might then say that that pattern was the thing prefigured beforehand, and that the other beans were mere irrelevance and packing material. Our dealings with Nature are just like this. She is a vast *plenum* in which our attention draws capricious lines in innumerable directions. We count and name whatever lies upon the special lines we trace, whilst the other things and the untraced lines are neither named nor counted. There are in reality infinitely more things

The fact is that these arguments do but follow the combined suggestions of the facts and of our feeling. They prove nothing rigorously. They only corroborate our preexistent partialities.

If philosophy can do so little to establish God's existence, how stands it with her efforts to define his attributes? It is worth while to look at the attempts of systematic theology in this direction.

Since God is First Cause, this science of sciences says, he differs from all his creatures in possessing existence *a se*. From this ' a-se-ity ' on God's part, theology deduces by mere logic most of his other perfections. For instance, he must be both *necessary* and *absolute*, cannot not be, and cannot in any way be determined by anything else. This makes Him absolutely unlimited from without, and unlimited also from within; for limitation is non-being; and God is being itself. This unlimitedness makes God infinitely perfect. Moreover, God is *One*, and *Only*, for the infinitely perfect can admit no peer. He is *Spiritual*, for were He composed of physical parts, some other power would have to combine them into the total, and his aseity would thus be contradicted. He is therefore both simple and non-physical in nature. He is *simple metaphysically* also, that is to say, his nature and his existence can-

' unadapted ' to each other in this world than there are things 'adapted ' ; infinitely more things with irregular relations than with regular relations between them. But we look for the regular kind of thing exclusively, and ingeniously discover and preserve it in our memory. It accumulates with other regular kinds, until the collection of them fills our encyclopædias. Yet all the while between and around them lies an infinite anonymous chaos of objects that no one ever thought of together, of relations that never yet attracted our attention.

The facts of order from which the physico-theological argument starts are thus easily susceptible of interpretation as arbitrary human products. So long as this is the case, although of course no argument against God follows, it follows that the argument for him will fail to constitute a knockdown proof of his existence. It will be convincing only to those who on other grounds believe in him already.

not be distinct, as they are in finite substances which share their formal natures with one another, and are individual only in their material aspect. Since God is one and only, his *essentia* and his *esse* must be given at one stroke. This excludes from his being all those distinctions, so familiar in the world of finite things, between potentiality and actuality, substance and accidents, being and activity, existence and attributes. We can talk, it is true, of God's powers, acts, and attributes, but these discriminations are only 'virtual,' and made from the human point of view. In God all these points of view fall into an absolute identity of being.

This absence of all potentiality in God obliges Him to be *immutable*. He is actuality, through and through. Were there anything potential about Him, He would either lose or gain by its actualization, and either loss or gain would contradict his perfection. He cannot, therefore, change. Furthermore, He is *immense, boundless;* for could He be outlined in space, He would be composite, and this would contradict his indivisibility. He is therefore *omnipresent*, indivisibly there, at every point of space. He is similarly wholly present at every point of time, — in other words *eternal*. For if He began in time, He would need a prior cause, and that would contradict his aseity. If He ended, it would contradict his necessity. If He went through any succession, it would contradict his immutability.

He has *intelligence* and *will* and every other creature-perfection, for *we* have them, and *effectus nequit superare causam*. In Him, however, they are absolutely and eternally in act, and their *object*, since God can be bounded by naught that is external, can primarily be nothing else than God himself. He knows himself, then, in one eternal indivisible act, and wills himself with an infinite self-pleasure.[1] Since He must of logical necessity thus love and will himself, He cannot be called 'free' *ad intra*, with the freedom of contrarieties that characterizes finite creatures. *Ad extra*, however, or with respect to his creation, God is free. He cannot *need* to create, being perfect in being and in happiness already. He *wills* to create, then, by an absolute freedom.

---

[1] For the scholastics the *facultas appetendi* embraces feeling, desire, and will.

Being thus a substance endowed with intellect and will and freedom, God is a *person ;* and a *living* person also, for He is both object and subject of his own activity, and to be this distinguishes the living from the lifeless. He is thus absolutely *self-sufficient :* his *self-knowledge* and *self-love* are both of them infinite and adequate, and need no extraneous conditions to perfect them.

He is *omniscient,* for in knowing himself as Cause He knows all creature things and events by implication. His knowledge is *previsive,* for He is present to all time. Even our free acts are known beforehand to Him, for otherwise his wisdom would admit of successive moments of enrichment, and this would contradict his immutability. He is *omnipotent* for everything that does not involve logical contradiction. He can make *being* — in other words his power includes *creation.* If what He creates were made of his own substance, it would have to be infinite in essence, as that substance is; but it is finite; so it must be non-divine in substance. If it were made of a substance, an eternally existing matter, for example, which God found there to his hand, and to which He simply gave its form, that would contradict God's definition as First Cause, and make Him a mere mover of something caused already. The things he creates, then, He creates *ex nihilo,* and gives them absolute being as so many finite substances additional to himself. The forms which he imprints upon them have their prototypes in his ideas. But as in God there is no such thing as multiplicity, and as these ideas for us are manifold, we must distinguish the ideas as they are in God and the way in which our minds externally imitate them. We must attribute them to Him only in a *terminative* sense, as differing aspects, from the finite point of view, of his unique essence.

God of course is holy, good, and just. He can do no evil, for He is positive being's fullness, and evil is negation. It is true that He has created physical evil in places, but only as a means of wider good, for *bonum totius præeminet bonum partis.* Moral evil He cannot will, either as end or means, for that would contradict his holiness. By creating free beings He *permits* it only, neither his justice nor his goodness obliging

Him to prevent the recipients of freedom from misusing the gift.

As regards God's purpose in creating, primarily it can only have been to exercise his absolute freedom by the manifestation to others of his glory. From this it follows that the others must be rational beings, capable in the first place of knowledge, love, and honor, and in the second place of happiness, for the knowledge and love of God is the mainspring of felicity. In so far forth one may say that God's secondary purpose in creating is *love*.

I will not weary you by pursuing these metaphysical determinations farther, into the mysteries of God's Trinity, for example. What I have given will serve as a specimen of the orthodox philosophical theology of both Catholics and Protestants. Newman, filled with enthusiasm at God's list of perfections, continues the passage which I began to quote to you by a couple of pages of a rhetoric so magnificent that I can hardly refrain from adding them, in spite of the inroad they would make upon our time.[1] He first enumerates God's attributes sonorously, then celebrates his ownership of everything in earth and Heaven, and the dependence of all that happens upon his permissive will. He gives us scholastic philosophy 'touched with emotion,' and every philosophy should be touched with emotion to be rightly understood. Emotionally, then, dogmatic theology is worth something to minds of the type of Newman's. It will aid us to estimate what it is worth intellectually, if at this point I make a short digression.

What God hath joined together, let no man put asunder. The Continental schools of philosophy have too often overlooked the fact that man's thinking is organically connected with his conduct. It seems to me to be

[1] Op. cit., Discourse III. § 7.

the chief glory of English and Scottish thinkers to have kept the organic connection in view. The guiding principle of British philosophy has in fact been that every difference must *make* a difference, every theoretical difference somewhere issue in a practical difference, and that the best method of discussing points of theory is to begin by ascertaining what practical difference would result from one alternative or the other being true. What is the particular truth in question *known as?* In what facts does it result? What is its cash-value in terms of particular experience? This is the characteristic English way of taking up a question. In this way, you remember, Locke takes up the question of personal identity. What you mean by it is just your chain of particular memories, says he. That is the only concretely verifiable part of its significance. All further ideas about it, such as the oneness or manyness of the spiritual substance on which it is based, are therefore void of intelligible meaning; and propositions touching such ideas may be indifferently affirmed or denied. So Berkeley with his 'matter.' The cash-value of matter is our physical sensations. That is what it is known as, all that we concretely verify of its conception. That, therefore, is the whole meaning of the term 'matter' — any other pretended meaning is mere wind of words. Hume does the same thing with causation. It is known as habitual antecedence, and as tendency on our part to look for something definite to come. Apart from this practical meaning it has no significance whatever, and books about it may be committed to the flames, says Hume. Dugald Stewart and Thomas Brown, James Mill, John Mill, and Professor Bain, have followed more or less consistently the same method; and Shadworth Hodgson has used the principle with full explicitness. When all is

said and done, it was English and Scotch writers, and
not Kant, who introduced 'the critical method' into
philosophy, the one method fitted to make philosophy a
study worthy of serious men.   For what seriousness can
possibly remain in debating philosophic propositions that
will never make an appreciable difference to us in action?
And what could it matter, if all propositions were practically indifferent, which of them we should agree to call
true or which false?

An American philosopher of eminent originality, Mr.
Charles Sanders Peirce, has rendered thought a service by
disentangling from the particulars of its application the
principle by which these men were instinctively guided,
and by singling it out as fundamental and giving to it a
Greek name.   He calls it the principle of *pragmatism*,
and he defends it somewhat as follows : [1] —

Thought in movement has for its only conceivable
motive the attainment of belief, or thought at rest.   Only
when our thought about a subject has found its rest in
belief can our action on the subject firmly and safely
begin.   Beliefs, in short, are rules for action; and the
whole function of thinking is but one step in the production of active habits.   If there were any part of a
thought that made no difference in the thought's practical consequences, then that part would be no proper
element of the thought's significance.   To develop a
thought's meaning we need therefore only determine
what conduct it is fitted to produce; that conduct is for
us its sole significance; and the tangible fact at the root
of all our thought-distinctions is that there is no one of
them so fine as to consist in anything but a possible difference of practice.   To attain perfect clearness in our

[1] In an article, How to make our Ideas Clear, in the Popular Science
Monthly for January, 1878, vol. xii. p. 286.

thoughts of an object, we need then only consider what
sensations, immediate or remote, we are conceivably to
expect from it, and what conduct we must prepare in case
the object should be true. Our conception of these practical consequences is for us the whole of our conception
of the object, so far as that conception has positive significance at all.

This is the principle of Peirce, the principle of pragmatism. Such a principle will help us on this occasion
to decide, among the various attributes set down in the
scholastic inventory of God's perfections, whether some
be not far less significant than others.

If, namely, we apply the principle of pragmatism to
God's metaphysical attributes, strictly so called, as distinguished from his moral attributes, I think that, even
were we forced by a coercive logic to believe them, we
still should have to confess them to be destitute of all
intelligible significance. Take God's aseity, for example;
or his necessariness; his immateriality; his 'simplicity'
or superiority to the kind of inner variety and succession
which we find in finite beings, his indivisibility, and lack
of the inner distinctions of being and activity, substance
and accident, potentiality and actuality, and the rest;
his repudiation of inclusion in a genus ; his actualized
infinity; his 'personality,' apart from the moral qualities which it may comport; his relations to evil being
permissive and not positive ; his self-sufficiency, self-
love, and absolute felicity in himself : — candidly speaking, how do such qualities as these make any definite
connection with our life? And if they severally call for
no distinctive adaptations of our conduct, what vital difference can it possibly make to a man's religion whether
they be true or false?

For my own part, although I dislike to say aught that

may grate upon tender associations, I must frankly confess that even though these attributes were faultlessly
deduced, I cannot conceive of its being of the smallest
consequence to us religiously that any one of them
should be true.   Pray, what specific act can I perform in
order to adapt myself the better to God's simplicity ? Or
how does it assist me to plan my behavior, to know that
his happiness is anyhow absolutely complete ?   In the
middle of the century just past, Mayne Reid was the great
writer of books of out-of-door adventure. He was forever
extolling the hunters and field-observers of living animals' habits, and keeping up a fire of invective against
the ' closet-naturalists,' as he called them, the collectors
and classifiers, and handlers of skeletons and skins.
When I was a boy, I used to think that a closet-natural-
ist must be the vilest type of wretch under the sun.
But surely the systematic theologians are the closet-
naturalists of the deity, even in Captain Mayne Reid's
sense. What is their deduction of metaphysical attributes but a shuffling and matching of pedantic diction-
ary-adjectives, aloof from morals, aloof from human
needs, something that might be worked out from the
mere word ' God ' by one of those logical machines of
wood and brass which recent ingenuity has contrived as
well as by a man of flesh and blood. They have the
trail of the serpent over them. One feels that in the
theologians' hands, they are only a set of titles obtained
by a mechanical manipulation of synonyms; verbality has
stepped into the place of vision, professionalism into that
of life.   Instead of bread we have a stone ; instead of a
fish, a serpent. Did such a conglomeration of abstract
terms give really the gist of our knowledge of the deity,
schools of theology might indeed continue to flourish, but
religion, vital religion, would have taken its flight from

this world. What keeps religion going is something else than abstract definitions and systems of concatenated adjectives, and something different from faculties of theology and their professors. All these things are after-effects, secondary accretions upon those phenomena of vital conversation with the unseen divine, of which I have shown you so many instances, renewing themselves *in sæcula sæculorum* in the lives of humble private men.

So much for the metaphysical attributes of God! From the point of view of practical religion, the metaphysical monster which they offer to our worship is an absolutely worthless invention of the scholarly mind.

What shall we now say of the attributes called moral? Pragmatically, they stand on an entirely different footing. They positively determine fear and hope and expectation, and are foundations for the saintly life. It needs but a glance at them to show how great is their significance.

God's holiness, for example: being holy, God can will nothing but the good. Being omnipotent, he can secure its triumph. Being omniscient, he can see us in the dark. Being just, he can punish us for what he sees. Being loving, he can pardon too. Being unalterable, we can count on him securely. These qualities enter into connection with our life, it is highly important that we should be informed concerning them. That God's purpose in creation should be the manifestation of his glory is also an attribute which has definite relations to our practical life. Among other things it has given a definite character to worship in all Christian countries. If dogmatic theology really does prove beyond dispute that a God with characters like these exists, she may well claim to give a solid basis to religious sentiment. But verily, how stands it with her arguments?

It stands with them as ill as with the arguments for his existence. Not only do post-Kantian idealists reject them root and branch, but it is a plain historic fact that they never have converted any one who has found in the moral complexion of the world, as he experienced it, reasons for doubting that a good God can have framed it. To prove God's goodness by the scholastic argument that there is no non-being in his essence would sound to such a witness simply silly.

No! the book of Job went over this whole matter once for all and definitively. Ratiocination is a relatively superficial and unreal path to the deity: "I will lay mine hand upon my mouth; I have heard of Thee by the hearing of the ear, but now mine eye seeth Thee." An intellect perplexed and baffled, yet a trustful sense of presence — such is the situation of the man who is sincere with himself and with the facts, but who remains religious still.[1]

We must therefore, I think, bid a definitive good-by to dogmatic theology. In all sincerity our faith must do without that warrant. Modern idealism, I repeat, has said good-by to this theology forever. Can modern idealism give faith a better warrant, or must she still rely on her poor self for witness?

The basis of modern idealism is Kant's doctrine of the

[1] Pragmatically, the most important attribute of God is his punitive justice. But who, in the present state of theological opinion on that point, will dare maintain that hell fire or its equivalent in some shape is rendered certain by pure logic? Theology herself has largely based this doctrine upon revelation; and, in discussing it, has tended more and more to substitute conventional ideas of criminal law for a priori principles of reason. But the very notion that this glorious universe, with planets and winds, and laughing sky and ocean, should have been conceived and had its beams and rafters laid in technicalities of criminality, is incredible to our modern imagination. It weakens a religion to hear it argued upon such a basis.

Transcendental Ego of Apperception. By this formidable term Kant merely meant the fact that the consciousness 'I think them' must (potentially or actually) accompany all our objects. Former skeptics had said as much, but the 'I' in question had remained for them identified with the personal individual. Kant abstracted and depersonalized it, and made it the most universal of all his categories, although for Kant himself the Transcendental Ego had no theological implications.

It was reserved for his successors to convert Kant's notion of *Bewusstsein überhaupt,* or abstract consciousness, into an infinite concrete self-consciousness which is the soul of the world, and in which our sundry personal self-consciousnesses have their being. It would lead me into technicalities to show you even briefly how this transformation was in point of fact effected. Suffice it to say that in the Hegelian school, which to-day so deeply influences both British and American thinking, two principles have borne the brunt of the operation.

The first of these principles is that the old logic of identity never gives us more than a post-mortem dissection of *disjecta membra,* and that the fullness of life can be construed to thought only by recognizing that every object which our thought may propose to itself involves the notion of some other object which seems at first to negate the first one.

The second principle is that to be conscious of a negation is already virtually to be beyond it. The mere asking of a question or expression of a dissatisfaction proves that the answer or the satisfaction is already imminent; the finite, realized as such, is already the infinite *in posse.*

Applying these principles, we seem to get a propulsive force into our logic which the ordinary logic of a bare,

stark self-identity in each thing never attains to. The
objects of our thought now *act* within our thought, act as
objects act when given in experience. They change and
develop. They introduce something other than themselves along with them ; and this other, at first only ideal
or potential, presently proves itself also to be actual. It
supersedes the thing at first supposed, and both verifies
and corrects it, in developing the fullness of its meaning.

The program is excellent; the universe *is* a place
where things are followed by other things that both correct and fulfill them ; and a logic which gave us something like this movement of fact would express truth far
better than the traditional school-logic, which never gets
of its own accord from anything to anything else, and
registers only predictions and subsumptions, or static re-
semblances and differences. Nothing could be more unlike the methods of dogmatic theology than those of this
new logic. Let me quote in illustration some passages
from the Scottish transcendentalist whom I have already
named.

"How are we to conceive," Principal Caird writes, "of the
reality in which all intelligence rests?" He replies: "Two
things may without difficulty be proved, viz., that this reality
is an absolute Spirit, and conversely that it is only in communion with this absolute Spirit or Intelligence that the finite
Spirit can realize itself. It is absolute; for the faintest movement of human intelligence would be arrested, if it did not
presuppose the absolute reality of intelligence, of thought
itself. Doubt or denial themselves presuppose and indirectly
affirm it. When I pronounce anything to be true, I pronounce
it, indeed, to be relative to thought, but not to be relative to
my thought, or to the thought of any other individual mind.
From the existence of all individual minds as such I can abstract; I can think them away. But that which I cannot think
away is thought or self-consciousness itself, in its independence

and absoluteness, or, in other words, an Absolute Thought or Self-Consciousness."

Here, you see, Principal Caird makes the transition which Kant did not make : he converts the omnipresence of consciousness in general as a condition of ' truth ' being anywhere possible, into an omnipresent universal consciousness, which he identifies with God in his concreteness. He next proceeds to use the principle that to acknowledge your limits is in essence to be beyond them ; and makes the transition to the religious experience of individuals in the following words : —

" If [Man] were only a creature of transient sensations and impulses, of an ever coming and going succession of intuitions, fancies, feelings, then nothing could ever have for him the character of objective truth or reality. But it is the prerogative of man's spiritual nature that he can yield himself up to a thought and will that are infinitely larger than his own. As a thinking, self-conscious being, indeed, he may be said, by his very nature, to live in the atmosphere of the Universal Life. As a thinking being, it is possible for me to suppress and quell in my consciousness every movement of self-assertion, every notion and opinion that is merely mine, every desire that belongs to me as this particular Self, and to become the pure medium of a thought that is universal — in one word, to live no more my own life, but let my consciousness be possessed and suffused by the Infinite and Eternal life of spirit. And yet it is just in this renunciation of self that I truly gain myself, or realize the highest possibilities of my own nature. For whilst in one sense we give up self to live the universal and absolute life of reason, yet that to which we thus surrender ourselves is in reality our truer self. The life of absolute reason is not a life that is foreign to us."

Nevertheless, Principal Caird goes on to say, so far as we are able outwardly to realize this doctrine, the balm it offers remains incomplete. Whatever we may be *in posse*, the very best of us *in actu* falls very short of

being absolutely divine. Social morality, love, and self-
sacrifice even, merge our Self only in some other finite
self or selves. They do not quite identify it with the
Infinite. Man's ideal destiny, infinite in abstract logic,
might thus seem in practice forever unrealizable.

" Is there, then," our author continues, " no solution of the
contradiction between the ideal and the actual? We answer,
There is such a solution, but in order to reach it we are carried
beyond the sphere of morality into that of religion. It may be
said to be the essential characteristic of religion as contrasted
with morality, that it changes aspiration into fruition, anticipation into realization; that instead of leaving man in the inter-
minable pursuit of a vanishing ideal, it makes him the actual
partaker of a divine or infinite life. Whether we view religion
from the human side or the divine — as the surrender of the
soul to God, or as the life of God in the soul — in either aspect
it is of its very essence that the Infinite has ceased to be a far-
off vision, and has become a present reality. The very first
pulsation of the spiritual life, when we rightly apprehend its
significance, is the indication that the division between the
Spirit and its object has vanished, that the ideal has become
real, that the finite has reached its goal and become suffused
with the presence and life of the Infinite.

"Oneness of mind and will with the divine mind and will
is not the future hope and aim of religion, but its very beginning and birth in the soul. To enter on the religious life is to
terminate the struggle. In that act which constitutes the beginning of the religious life — call it faith, or trust, or self-surrender, or by whatever name you will — there is involved the
identification of the finite with a life which is eternally realized.
It is true indeed that the religious life is progressive; but
understood in the light of the foregoing idea, religious progress
is not progress *towards*, but *within* the sphere of the Infinite.
It is not the vain attempt by endless finite additions or incre-
ments to become possessed of infinite wealth, but it is the
endeavor, by the constant exercise of spiritual activity, to appropriate that infinite inheritance of which we are already in

possession. The whole future of the religious life is given in
its beginning, but it is given implicitly. The position of the
man who has entered on the religious life is that evil, error,
imperfection, do not really belong to him: they are excrescences which have no organic relation to his true nature : they
are already virtually, as they will be actually, suppressed and
annulled, and in the very process of being annulled they become
the means of spiritual progress. Though he is not exempt
from temptation and conflict, [yet] in that inner sphere in
which his true life lies, the struggle is over, the victory already
achieved. It is not a finite but an infinite life which the spirit
lives. Every pulse-beat of its [existence] is the expression and
realization of the life of God." [1]

You will readily admit that no description of the phenomena of the religious consciousness could be better than
these words of your lamented preacher and philosopher.
They reproduce the very rapture of those crises of conversion of which we have been hearing; they utter what
the mystic felt but was unable to communicate; and the
saint, in hearing them, recognizes his own experience.
It is indeed gratifying to find the content of religion
reported so unanimously. But when all is said and done,
has Principal Caird — and I only use him as an example
of that whole mode of thinking — transcended the sphere
of feeling and of the direct experience of the individual,
and laid the foundations of religion in impartial reason ?
Has he made religion universal by coercive reasoning,
transformed it from a private faith into a public certainty? Has he rescued its affirmations from obscurity
and mystery ?

I believe that he has done nothing of the kind, but
that he has simply reaffirmed the individual's experiences
in a more generalized vocabulary. And again, I can be

[1] John Caird : An Introduction to the Philosophy of Religion, London
and New York, 1880, pp. 243-250, and 291-299, much abridged.

excused from proving technically that the transcendental-ist reasonings fail to make religion universal, for I can point to the plain fact that a majority of scholars, even religiously disposed ones, stubbornly refuse to treat them as convincing. The whole of Germany, one may say, has positively rejected the Hegelian argumentation. As for Scotland, I need only mention Professor Fraser's and Professor Pringle-Pattison's memorable criticisms, with which so many of you are familiar.[1] Once more, I ask, if transcendental idealism were as objectively and abso-lutely rational as it pretends to be, could it possibly fail so egregiously to be persuasive?

What religion reports, you must remember, always pur-ports to be a fact of experience: the divine is actually present, religion says, and between it and ourselves rela-tions of give and take are actual. If definite percep-tions of fact like this cannot stand upon their own feet,

[1] A. C. FRASER : Philosophy of Theism, second edition, Edinburgh and London, 1899, especially part ii. chaps. vii. and viii. ; A. SETH [PRINGLE-PATTISON] : Hegelianism and Personality, Ibid., 1890, passim.

The most persuasive arguments in favor of a concrete individual Soul of the world, with which I am acquainted, are those of my colleague, Josiah Royce, in his Religious Aspect of Philosophy, Boston, 1885 ; in his Con-ception of God, New York and London, 1897 ; and lately in his Aberdeen Gifford Lectures, The World and the Individual, 2 vols., New York and London, 1901–02. I doubtless seem to some of my readers to evade the philosophic duty which my thesis in this lecture imposes on me, by not even attempting to meet Professor Royce's arguments articulately. I admit the momentary evasion. In the present lectures, which are cast throughout in a popular mould, there seemed no room for subtle metaphysical discussion, and for tactical purposes it was sufficient, the contention of philosophy being what it is (namely, that religion can be transformed into a universally con-vincing science), to point to the fact that no religious philosophy has actually convinced the mass of thinkers. Meanwhile let me say that I hope that the present volume may be followed by another, if I am spared to write it, in which not only Professor Royce's arguments, but others for monistic abso-lutism shall be considered with all the technical fullness which their great importance calls for. At present I resign myself to lying passive under the reproach of superficiality.

surely abstract reasoning cannot give them the support they are in need of. Conceptual processes can class facts, define them, interpret them; but they do not produce them, nor can they reproduce their individuality. There is always a *plus*, a *thisness*, which feeling alone can answer for. Philosophy in this sphere is thus a secondary function, unable to warrant faith's veracity, and so I revert to the thesis which I announced at the beginning of this lecture.

In all sad sincerity I think we must conclude that the attempt to demonstrate by purely intellectual processes the truth of the deliverances of direct religious experience is absolutely hopeless.

It would be unfair to philosophy, however, to leave her under this negative sentence. Let me close, then, by briefly enumerating what she *can* do for religion. If she will abandon metaphysics and deduction for criticism and induction, and frankly transform herself from theology into science of religions, she can make herself enormously useful.

The spontaneous intellect of man always defines the divine which it feels in ways that harmonize with its temporary intellectual prepossessions. Philosophy can by comparison eliminate the local and the accidental from these definitions. Both from dogma and from worship she can remove historic incrustations. By confronting the spontaneous religious constructions with the results of natural science, philosophy can also eliminate doctrines that are now known to be scientifically absurd or incongruous.

Sifting out in this way unworthy formulations, she can leave a residuum of conceptions that at least are possible. With these she can deal as *hypotheses*, testing them in all the manners, whether negative or positive, by which hypotheses are ever tested. She can reduce their number, as some are found more open to objection. She can perhaps become the champion of one which she picks out as being the most closely verified or verifiable. She can refine upon the definition of this hypothesis, distinguishing between what is innocent over-belief and symbolism in the expression of it, and what is to be literally taken. As a result, she can offer mediation between different believers, and help to bring about consensus of opinion. She can do this the more successfully, the better she discriminates the common and essential from the individual and local elements of the religious beliefs which she compares.

I do not see why a critical Science of Religions of this sort might not eventually command as general a public adhesion as is commanded by a physical science. Even the personally non-religious might accept its conclusions on trust, much as blind persons now accept the facts of optics — it might appear as foolish to refuse them. Yet as the science of optics has to be fed in the first instance, and continually verified later, by facts experienced by seeing persons; so the science of religions would depend for its original material on facts of personal experience, and would have to square itself with personal experience through all its critical reconstructions. It could never get away from concrete life, or work in a conceptual vacuum. It would forever have to confess, as every science confesses, that the subtlety of nature flies beyond it, and that its formulas are but approximations. Philosophy lives in words, but truth and fact well up into our lives in ways that exceed verbal formulation. There is in the living act of perception always something that glimmers and twinkles and will not be caught, and for which reflection comes too late. No one knows this as well as the philosopher. He must fire his volley of new vocables out of his conceptual shotgun, for his profession condemns him to this industry, but he secretly knows the hollowness and irrelevancy. His formulas are like stereoscopic or kinetoscopic photographs seen outside the instrument; they lack the depth, the motion, the vitality. In the religious sphere, in particular, belief that formulas are true can never wholly take the place of personal experience.

In my next lecture I will try to complete my rough description of religious experience; and in the lecture after that, which is the last one, I will try my own hand at formulating conceptually the truth to which it is a witness.

LECTURE XIX

OTHER CHARACTERISTICS

WE have wound our way back, after our excursion through mysticism and philosophy, to where we were before: the uses of religion, its uses to the individual who has it, and the uses of the individual himself to the world, are the best arguments that truth is in it. We return to the empirical philosophy: the true is what works well, even though the qualification ' on the whole ' may always have to be added. In this lecture we must revert to description again, and finish our picture of the religious consciousness by a word about some of its other characteristic elements. Then, in a final lecture, we shall be free to make a general review and draw our independent conclusions.

The first point I will speak of is the part which the æsthetic life plays in determining one's choice of a religion. Men, I said awhile ago, involuntarily intellectualize their religious experience. They need formulas, just as they need fellowship in worship. I spoke, therefore, too contemptuously of the pragmatic uselessness of the famous scholastic list of attributes of the deity, for they have one use which I neglected to consider. The eloquent passage in which Newman enumerates them [1] puts us on the track of it. Intoning them as he would intone a cathedral service, he shows how high is their æsthetic value. It enriches our bare piety to carry these exalted and mysterious verbal additions just as it enriches

[1] Idea of a University, Discourse III. § 7.

a church to have an organ and old brasses, marbles and frescoes and stained windows. Epithets lend an atmosphere and overtones to our devotion. They are like a hymn of praise and service of glory, and may sound the more sublime for being incomprehensible. Minds like Newman's [1] grow as jealous of their credit as heathen priests are of that of the jewelry and ornaments that blaze upon their idols.

Among the buildings-out of religion which the mind spontaneously indulges in, the æsthetic motive must never be forgotten. I promised to say nothing of ecclesiastical systems in these lectures. I may be allowed, however, to put in a word at this point on the way in which their satisfaction of certain æsthetic needs contributes to their hold on human nature. Although some persons aim most at intellectual purity and simplification, for others *richness* is the supreme imaginative requirement.[2] When one's mind is strongly of this type, an individual religion will hardly serve the purpose. The inner need is rather

---

[1] Newman's imagination so innately craved an ecclesiastical system that he can write : "From the age of fifteen, dogma has been the fundamental principle of my religion : I know no other religion ; I cannot enter into the idea of any other sort of religion." And again, speaking of himself about the age of thirty, he writes : "I loved to act as feeling myself in my Bishop's sight, as if it were the sight of God." Apologia, 1897, pp. 48, 50.

[2] The intellectual difference is quite on a par in practical importance with the analogous difference in character. We saw, under the head of Saintliness, how some characters resent confusion and must live in purity, consistency, simplicity (above, p. 280 ff.). For others, on the contrary, superabundance, over-pressure, stimulation, lots of superficial relations, are indispensable. There are men who would suffer a very syncope if you should pay all their debts, bring it about that their engagements had been kept, their letters answered, their perplexities relieved, and their duties fulfilled, down to one which lay on a clean table under their eyes with nothing to interfere with its immediate performance. A day stripped so staringly bare would be for them appalling. So with ease, elegance, tributes of affection, social recognitions — some of us require amounts of these things which to others would appear a mass of lying and sophistication.

of something institutional and complex, majestic in the hierarchic interrelatedness of its parts, with authority descending from stage to stage, and at every stage objects for adjectives of mystery and splendor, derived in the last resort from the Godhead who is the fountain and culmination of the system.   One feels then as if in presence of some vast incrusted work of jewelry or architecture ; one hears the multitudinous liturgical appeal ; one gets the honorific vibration coming from every quarter. Compared with such a noble complexity, in which ascending and descending movements seem in no way to jar upon stability, in which no single item, however humble, is insignificant, because so many august institutions hold it in its place, how flat does evangelical Protestantism appear, how bare the atmosphere of those isolated religious lives whose boast it is that "man in the bush with God may meet." [1]   What a pulverization and leveling of what a gloriously piled-up structure !   To an imagination used to the perspectives of dignity and glory, the naked gospel scheme seems to offer an almshouse for a palace.

It is much like the patriotic sentiment of those brought up in ancient empires.   How many emotions must be frustrated of their object, when one gives up the titles of dignity, the crimson lights and blare of brass, the gold embroidery, the plumed troops, the fear and trembling, and puts up with a president in a black coat who shakes hands with you, and comes, it may be, from a 'home' upon a veldt or prairie with one sitting-room and a Bible on its centre-table.   It pauperizes the monarchical imagination !

The strength of these æsthetic sentiments makes it

[1] In Newman's Lectures on Justification, Lecture VIII. § 6, there is a splendid passage expressive of this æsthetic way of feeling the Christian scheme.   It is unfortunately too long to quote.

rigorously impossible, it seems to me, that Protestantism, however superior in spiritual profundity it may be to Catholicism, should at the present day succeed in making many converts from the more venerable ecclesiasticism. The latter offers a so much richer pasturage and shade to the fancy, has so many cells with so many different kinds of honey, is so indulgent in its multiform appeals to human nature, that Protestantism will always show to Catholic eyes the almshouse physiognomy. The bitter negativity of it is to the Catholic mind incomprehensible. To intellectual Catholics many of the antiquated beliefs and practices to which the Church gives countenance are, if taken literally, as childish as they are to Protestants. But they are childish in the pleasing sense of 'childlike,' — innocent and amiable, and worthy to be smiled on in consideration of the undeveloped condition of the dear people's intellects. To the Protestant, on the contrary, they are childish in the sense of being idiotic falsehoods. He must stamp out their delicate and lovable redundancy, leaving the Catholic to shudder at his literalness. He appears to the latter as morose as if he were some hard-eyed, numb, monotonous kind of reptile. The two will never understand each other — their centres of emotional energy are too different. Rigorous truth and human nature's intricacies are always in need of a mutual interpreter.[1] So much for the æsthetic diversities in the religious consciousness.

[1] Compare the informality of Protestantism, where the 'meek lover of the good,' alone with his God, visits the sick, etc., for their own sakes, with the elaborate 'business' that goes on in Catholic devotion, and carries with it the social excitement of all more complex businesses. An essentially worldly-minded Catholic woman can become a visitor of the sick on purely coquettish principles, with her confessor and director, her 'merit' storing up, her patron saints, her privileged relation to the Almighty, drawing his attention as a professional *dévote*, her definite 'exercises,' and her definitely recognized social *pose* in the organization.

In most books on religion, three things are represented as its most essential elements. These are Sacrifice, Confession, and Prayer. I must say a word in turn of each of these elements, though briefly. First of Sacrifice.

Sacrifices to gods are omnipresent in primeval worship; but, as cults have grown refined, burnt offerings and the blood of he-goats have been superseded by sacrifices more spiritual in their nature. Judaism, Islam, and Buddhism get along without ritual sacrifice; so does Christianity, save in so far as the notion is preserved in transfigured form in the mystery of Christ's atonement. These religions substitute offerings of the heart, renunciations of the inner self, for all those vain oblations. In the ascetic practices which Islam, Buddhism, and the older Christianity encourage we see how indestructible is the idea that sacrifice of some sort is a religious exercise. In lecturing on asceticism I spoke of its significance as symbolic of the sacrifices which life, whenever it is taken strenuously, calls for.[1] But, as I said my say about those, and as these lectures expressly avoid earlier religious usages and questions of derivation, I will pass from the subject of Sacrifice altogether and turn to that of Confession.

In regard to Confession I will also be most brief, saying my word about it psychologically, not historically. Not nearly as widespread as sacrifice, it corresponds to a more inward and moral stage of sentiment. It is part of the general system of purgation and cleansing which one feels one's self in need of, in order to be in right relations to one's deity. For him who confesses, shams are over and realities have begun; he has exteriorized his rottenness If he has not actually got rid of it, he at least

[1] Above, p. 362 ff.

no longer smears it over with a hypocritical show of virtue — he lives at least upon a basis of veracity. The complete decay of the practice of confession in Anglo-Saxon communities is a little hard to account for. Reaction against popery is of course the historic explanation, for in popery confession went with penances and absolution, and other inadmissible practices. But on the side of the sinner himself it seems as if the need ought to have been too great to accept so summary a refusal of its satisfaction. One would think that in more men the shell of secrecy would have had to open, the pent-in abscess to burst and gain relief, even though the ear that heard the confession were unworthy. The Catholic church, for obvious utilitarian reasons, has substituted auricular confession to one priest for the more radical act of public confession. We English-speaking Protestants, in the general self-reliance and unsociability of our nature, seem to find it enough if we take God alone into our confidence.[1]

The next topic on which I must comment is Prayer, — and this time it must be less briefly. We have heard much talk of late against prayer, especially against prayers for better weather and for the recovery of sick people. As regards prayers for the sick, if any medical fact can be considered to stand firm, it is that in certain environments prayer may contribute to recovery, and should be encouraged as a therapeutic measure. Being a normal factor of moral health in the person, its omission would be deleterious. The case of the weather is different. Notwithstanding the recency of the opposite belief,[2]

---

[1] A fuller discussion of confession is contained in the excellent work by FRANK GRANGER : The Soul of a Christian, London, 1900, ch. xii.

[2] Example : " The minister at Sudbury, being at the Thursday lecture in

every one now knows that droughts and storms follow
from physical antecedents, and that moral appeals cannot
avert them.   But petitional prayer is only one department of prayer; and if we take the word in the wider
sense as meaning every kind of inward communion or
conversation with the power recognized as divine, we can
easily see that scientific criticism leaves it untouched.

Prayer in this wide sense is the very soul and essence
of religion.   " Religion," says a liberal French theologian, " is an intercourse, a conscious and voluntary relation, entered into by a soul in distress with the mysterious power upon which it feels itself to depend, and upon
which its fate is contingent.   This intercourse with God
is realized by prayer.   Prayer is religion in act; that is,
prayer is real religion.   It is prayer that distinguishes
the religious phenomenon from such similar or neighbor-
ing phenomena as purely moral or æsthetic sentiment.
Religion is nothing if it be not the vital act by which
the entire mind seeks to save itself by clinging to the
principle from which it draws its life.   This act is prayer,
by which term I understand no vain exercise of words,
no mere repetition of certain sacred formulæ, but the
very movement itself of the soul, putting itself in a personal relation of contact with the mysterious power of
which it feels the presence, — it may be even before it
has a name by which to call it.   Wherever this interior
prayer is lacking, there is no religion; wherever, on the
other hand, this prayer rises and stirs the soul, even in
the absence of forms or of doctrines, we have living religion.   One sees from this why ' natural religion,' so-

Boston, heard the officiating clergyman praying for rain.   As soon as the
service was over, he went to the petitioner and said, ' You Boston ministers, as soon as a tulip wilts under your windows, go to church and pray for
rain, until all Concord and Sudbury are under water.' "   R. W. EMERSON:
Lectures and Biographical Sketches, p. 363.

called, is not properly a religion. It cuts man off from prayer. It leaves him and God in mutual remoteness, with no intimate commerce, no interior dialogue, no interchange, no action of God in man, no return of man to God. At bottom this pretended religion is only a philosophy. Born at epochs of rationalism, of critical investigations, it never was anything but an abstraction. An artificial and dead creation, it reveals to its examiner hardly one of the characters proper to religion." [1]

It seems to me that the entire series of our lectures proves the truth of M. Sabatier's contention. The religious phenomenon, studied as an inner fact, and apart from ecclesiastical or theological complications, has shown itself to consist everywhere, and at all its stages, in the consciousness which individuals have of an intercourse between themselves and higher powers with which they feel themselves to be related. This intercourse is realized at the time as being both active and mutual. If it be not effective; if it be not a give and take relation; if nothing be really transacted while it lasts; if the world is in no whit different for its having taken place; then prayer, taken in this wide meaning of a sense that *something is transacting*, is of course a feeling of what is illusory, and religion must on the whole be classed, not simply as containing elements of delusion, — these undoubtedly everywhere exist, — but as being rooted in delusion altogether, just as materialists and atheists have always said it was. At most there might remain, when the direct experiences of prayer were ruled out as false witnesses, some inferential belief that the whole order of existence must have a divine cause. But this way of contemplating nature, pleasing as it would doubtless be

[1] AUGUSTE SABATIER : Esquisse d'une Philosophie de la Religion, 2me éd., 1897, pp. 24–26, abridged.

to persons of a pious taste, would leave to them but the spectators' part at a play, whereas in experimental religion and the prayerful life, we seem ourselves to be actors, and not in a play, but in a very serious reality.

The genuineness of religion is thus indissolubly bound up with the question whether the prayerful consciousness be or be not deceitful. The conviction that something is genuinely transacted in this consciousness is the very core of living religion. As to what is transacted, great differences of opinion have prevailed. The unseen powers have been supposed, and are yet supposed, to do things which no enlightened man can nowadays believe in. It may well prove that the sphere of influence in prayer is subjective exclusively, and that what is immediately changed is only the mind of the praying person. But however our opinion of prayer's effects may come to be limited by criticism, religion, in the vital sense in which these lectures study it, must stand or fall by the persuasion that effects of some sort genuinely do occur. Through prayer, religion insists, things which cannot be realized in any other manner come about: energy which but for prayer would be bound is by prayer set free and operates in some part, be it objective or subjective, of the world of facts.

This postulate is strikingly expressed in a letter written by the late Frederic W. H. Myers to a friend, who allows me to quote from it. It shows how independent the prayer-instinct is of usual doctrinal complications. Mr. Myers writes: —

"I am glad that you have asked me about prayer, because I have rather strong ideas on the subject. First consider what are the facts. There exists around us a spiritual universe, and that universe is in actual relation with the material. From the spiritual universe comes the energy which maintains the material ; the energy which makes the life of each individual spirit. Our spirits are supported by a perpetual indrawal of this energy, and the vigor of that indrawal is perpetually changing, much as the vigor of our absorption of material nutriment changes from hour to hour.

"I call these 'facts' because I think that some scheme of this kind is the only one consistent with our actual evidence ; too complex to summarize here. How, then, should we *act* on these facts? Plainly we must endeavor to draw in as much spiritual life as possible, and we must place our minds in any attitude which experience shows to be favorable to such indrawal. *Prayer* is the general name for that attitude of open and earnest expectancy. If we then ask to *whom* to pray, the answer (strangely enough) must be that *that* does not much matter. The prayer is not indeed a purely subjective thing ; — it means a real increase in intensity of absorption of spiritual power or grace ; — but we do not know enough of what takes place in the spiritual world to know how the prayer operates ; — *who* is cognizant of it, or through what channel the grace is given. Better let children pray to Christ, who is at any rate the highest individual spirit of whom we have any knowledge. But it would be rash to say that Christ himself *hears us ;* while to say that *God* hears us is merely to restate the first principle, — that grace flows in from the infinite spiritual world."

Let us reserve the question of the truth or falsehood of the belief that power is absorbed until the next lecture, when our dogmatic conclusions, if we have any, must be reached. Let this lecture still confine itself to the description of phenomena ; and as a concrete example of an extreme sort, of the way in which the prayerful life may still be led, let me take a case with which most of you must be acquainted, that of George Müller of Bristol, who died in 1898. Müller's prayers were of the crassest petitional order. Early in life he resolved on taking certain Bible promises in literal sincerity, and on letting himself be fed, not by his own worldly foresight, but by the Lord's hand. He had an extraordinarily active and successful career, among the fruits of which were the distribution of over two million copies of the Scripture text, in different languages; the equipment of several hundred missionaries; the circulation of more than a hundred and eleven million of scriptural books, pamphlets, and tracts; the building of five large orphanages, and the keeping and educating of thousands of orphans; finally, the establishment of schools in which over a hundred and twenty-one thousand youthful and adult pupils were taught. In the course of this work Mr. Müller received and administered nearly a million and a half of pounds sterling, and traveled over two hundred thousand miles of sea and land.[1] During the sixty-eight years of his ministry, he never owned any property except his clothes and furniture, and cash in hand; and he left, at the age of eighty-six, an estate worth only a hundred and sixty pounds.

His method was to let his general wants be publicly known, but not to acquaint other people with the details of his temporary necessities. For the relief of the latter, he prayed directly to the Lord, believing that sooner or later prayers are always answered if one have trust enough. "When I lose such a thing as a key," he writes, "I ask the Lord to direct me to it, and I look for an answer to my prayer; when a person with whom I have made an appointment does not come, according to the fixed time, and I begin to be inconvenienced by it, I ask the Lord to be pleased to hasten him to me, and I look for an answer; when I do not understand a passage of the word of God, I lift up my heart to the Lord that he would be pleased by his Holy Spirit to instruct me, and I expect to be taught, though I do not fix the time when, and the manner how it should be; when I am going to minister in the Word, I seek help from the Lord, and . . . am not cast down, but of good cheer because I look for his assistance."

[1] My authority for these statistics is the little work on Müller, by FREDERIC G. WARNE, New York, 1898.

Müller's custom was to never run up bills, not even for a
week. " As the Lord deals out to us by the day, . . . the
week's payment might become due and we have no money to
meet it; and thus those with whom we deal might be inconvenienced by us, and we be found acting against the commandment of the Lord: 'Owe no man anything.' From this day
and henceforward whilst the Lord gives to us our supplies by
the day, we purpose to pay at once for every article as it is
purchased, and never to buy anything except we can pay for
it at once, however much it may seem to be needed, and however much those with whom we deal may wish to be paid only
by the week."

The articles needed of which Müller speaks were the food,
fuel, etc., of his orphanages. Somehow, near as they often
come to going without a meal, they hardly ever seem actually
to have done so. " Greater and more manifest nearness of the
Lord's presence I have never had than when after breakfast
there were no means for dinner for more than a hundred persons; or when after dinner there were no means for the tea,
and yet the Lord provided the tea; and all this without one
single human being having been informed about our need. . . .
Through Grace my mind is so fully assured of the faithfulness
of the Lord, that in the midst of the greatest need, I am enabled in peace to go about my other work. Indeed, did not
the Lord give me this, which is the result of trusting in him, I
should scarcely be able to work at all; for it is now comparatively a rare thing that a day comes when I am not in need
for one or another part of the work." [1]

In building his orphanages simply by prayer and faith,
Müller affirms that his prime motive was " to have something
to point to as a visible proof that our God and Father is the
same faithful God that he ever was, — as willing as ever to
prove himself the living God, in our day as formerly, to all
that put their trust in him." [2] For this reason he refused to
borrow money for any of his enterprises. " How does it work

[1] The Life of Trust; Being a Narrative of the Lord's Dealings with
George Müller, New American edition, N. Y., Crowell, pp. 228, 194, 219.
[2] Ibid., p. 126.

when we thus anticipate God by going our own way? We certainly weaken faith instead of increasing it; and each time we work thus a deliverance of our own we find it more and more difficult to trust in God, till at last we give way entirely to our natural fallen reason and unbelief prevails. How different if one is enabled to wait God's own time, and to look alone to him for help and deliverance! When at last help comes, after many seasons of prayer it may be, how sweet it is, and what a present recompense! Dear Christian reader, if you have never walked in this path of obedience before, do so now, and you will then know experimentally the sweetness of the joy which results from it." [1]

When the supplies came in but slowly, Müller always considered that this was for the trial of his faith and patience. When his faith and patience had been sufficiently tried, the Lord would send more means. "And thus it has proved," — I quote from his diary, — "for to-day was given me the sum of 2050 pounds, of which 2000 are for the building fund [of a certain house], and 50 for present necessities. It is impossible to describe my joy in God when I received this donation. I was neither excited nor surprised; for I *look out* for answers to my prayers. *I believe that God hears me.* Yet my heart was so full of joy that I could only *sit* before God, and admire him, like David in 2 Samuel vii. At last I cast myself flat down upon my face and burst forth in thanksgiving to God and in surrendering my heart afresh to him for his blessed service." [2]

George Müller's is a case extreme in every respect, and in no respect more so than in the extraordinary narrowness of the man's intellectual horizon. His God was, as he often said, his business partner. He seems to have been for Müller little more than a sort of supernatural clergyman interested in the congregation of tradesmen and others in Bristol who were his saints, and in the orphanages and other enterprises, but unpossessed of

[1] Op. cit., p. 383, abridged.   [2] Ibid., p. 323.

any of those vaster and wilder and more ideal attributes with which the human imagination elsewhere has invested him. Müller, in short, was absolutely unphilosophical. His intensely private and practical conception of his relations with the Deity continued the traditions of the most primitive human thought.[1] When we compare a mind like his with such a mind as, for example, Emerson's or Phillips Brooks's, we see the range which the religious consciousness covers.

There is an immense literature relating to answers to petitional prayer. The evangelical journals are filled

[1] I cannot resist the temptation of quoting an expression of an even more primitive style of religious thought, which I find in Arber's English Garland, vol. vii. p. 440. Robert Lyde, an English sailor, along with an English boy, being prisoners on a French ship in 1689, set upon the crew, of seven Frenchmen, killed two, made the other five prisoners, and brought home the ship. Lyde thus describes how in this feat he found his God a very present help in time of trouble : —

"With the assistance of God I kept my feet when they three and one more did strive to throw me down. Feeling the Frenchman which hung about my middle hang very heavy, I said to the boy, 'Go round the binnacle, and knock down that man that hangeth on my back.' So the boy did strike him one blow on the head which made him fall. . . . Then I looked about for a marlin spike or anything else to strike them withal. But seeing nothing, I said, 'LORD! what shall I do?' Then casting up my eye upon my left side, and seeing a marlin spike hanging, I jerked my right arm and took hold, and struck the point four times about a quarter of an inch deep into the skull of that man that had hold of my left arm. [One of the Frenchmen then hauled the marlin spike away from him.] But through GOD's wonderful providence! it either fell out of his hand, or else he threw it down, and at this time the Almighty GOD gave me strength enough to take one man in one hand, and throw at the other's head : and looking about again to see anything to strike them withal, but seeing nothing, I said, 'LORD! what shall I do now?' And then it pleased GOD to put me in mind of my knife in my pocket. And although two of the men had hold of my right arm, yet GOD Almighty strengthened me so that I put my right hand into my right pocket, drew out the knife and sheath, . . . put it between my legs and drew it out, and then cut the man's throat with it that had his back to my breast : and he immediately dropt down, and scarce ever stirred after." — I have slightly abridged Lyde's narrative.

with such answers, and books are devoted to the subject,[1] but for us Müller's case will suffice.

A less sturdy beggar-like fashion of leading the prayerful life is followed by innumerable other Christians. Persistence in leaning on the Almighty for support and guidance will, such persons say, bring with it proofs, palpable but much more subtle, of his presence and active influence. The following description of a ' led ' life, by a German writer whom I have already quoted, would no doubt appear to countless Christians in every country as if transcribed from their own personal experience. One finds in this guided sort of life, says Dr. Hilty, —

" That books and words (and sometimes people) come to one's cognizance just at the very moment in which one needs them; that one glides over great dangers as if with shut eyes, remaining ignorant of what would have terrified one or led one astray, until the peril is past — this being especially the case with temptations to vanity and sensuality; that paths on which one ought not to wander are, as it were, hedged off with thorns; but that on the other side great obstacles are suddenly removed; that when the time has come for something, one suddenly receives a courage that formerly failed, or perceives the root of a matter that until then was concealed, or discovers thoughts, talents, yea, even pieces of knowledge and insight, in one's self, of which it is impossible to say whence they come; finally, that persons help us or decline to help us, favor us or refuse us, as if they had to do so against their will, so that often those indifferent or even unfriendly to us yield us the greatest service and furtherance. (God takes often their worldly goods, from those whom he leads, at just the right

---

[1] As, for instance, In Answer to Prayer, by the BISHOP OF RIPON and others, London, 1898 ; Touching Incidents and Remarkable Answers to Prayer, Harrisburg, Pa., 1898 (?) ; H. L. HASTINGS : The Guiding Hand, or Providential Direction, illustrated by Authentic Instances, Boston, 1898 (?).

moment, when they threaten to impede the effort after higher interests.)

" Besides all this, other noteworthy things come to pass, of which it is not easy to give account. There is no doubt whatever that now one walks continually through ' open doors ' and on the easiest roads, with as little care and trouble as it is possible to imagine.

" Furthermore one finds one's self settling one's affairs neither too early nor too late, whereas they were wont to be spoiled by untimeliness, even when the preparations had been well laid. In addition to this, one does them with perfect tranquillity of mind, almost as if they were matters of no consequence, like errands done by us for another person, in which case we usually act more calmly than when we act in our own concerns. Again, one finds that one can *wait* for everything patiently, and that is one of life's great arts. One finds also that each thing comes duly, one thing after the other, so that one gains time to make one's footing sure before advancing farther. And then everything occurs to us at the right moment, just what we ought to do, etc., and often in a very striking way, just as if a third person were keeping watch over those things which we are in easy danger of forgetting.

" Often, too, persons are sent to us at the right time, to offer or ask for what is needed, and what we should never have had the courage or resolution to undertake of our own accord.

" Through all these experiences one finds that one is kindly and tolerant of other people, even of such as are repulsive, negligent, or ill-willed, for they also are instruments of good in God's hand, and often most efficient ones. Without these thoughts it would be hard for even the best of us always to keep our equanimity. But with the consciousness of divine guidance, one sees many a thing in life quite differently from what would otherwise be possible.

" All these are things that every human being *knows*, who has had experience of them; and of which the most speaking examples could be brought forward. The highest resources of worldly wisdom are unable to attain that which, under divine leading, comes to us of its own accord." [1]

[1] C. HILTY: Glück, Dritter Theil, 1900, pp. 92 ff.

Such accounts as this shade away into others where the belief is, not that particular events are tempered more towardly to us by a superintending providence, as a reward for our reliance, but that by cultivating the continuous sense of our connection with the power that made things as they are, we are tempered more towardly for their reception. The outward face of nature need not alter, but the expressions of meaning in it alter. It was dead and is alive again. It is like the difference between looking on a person without love, or upon the same person with love. In the latter case intercourse springs into new vitality. So when one's affections keep in touch with the divinity of the world's authorship, fear and egotism fall away; and in the equanimity that follows, one finds in the hours, as they succeed each other. a series of purely benignant opportunities. It is as if all doors were opened, and all paths freshly smoothed. We meet a new world when we meet the old world in the spirit which this kind of prayer infuses.

Such a spirit was that of Marcus Aurelius and Epictetus.[1] It is that of mind-curers, of the transcendentalists, and of the so-called 'liberal' Christians. As an expres-

---

[1] "Good Heaven!" says Epictetus, "any one thing in the creation is sufficient to demonstrate a Providence, to a humble and grateful mind. The mere possibility of producing milk from grass, cheese from milk, and wool from skins; who formed and planned it? Ought we not, whether we dig or plough or eat, to sing this hymn to God? Great is God, who has supplied us with these instruments to till the ground; great is God, who has given us hands and instruments of digestion; who has given us to grow insensibly and to breathe in sleep. These things we ought forever to celebrate. . . . But because the most of you are blind and insensible, there must be some one to fill this station, and lead, in behalf of all men, the hymn to God; for what else can I do, a lame old man, but sing hymns to God? Were I a nightingale, I would act the part of a nightingale; were I a swan, the part of a swan. But since I am a reasonable creature, it is my duty to praise God . . . and I call on you to join the same song." Works, book i. ch. xvi., CARTER-HIGGINSON translation, abridged.

sion of it, I will quote a page from one of Martineau's sermons : —

" The universe, open to the eye to-day, looks as it did a thousand years ago : and the morning hymn of Milton does but tell the beauty with which our own familiar sun dressed the earliest fields and gardens of the world. We see what all our fathers saw. And if we cannot find God in your house or in mine, upon the roadside or the margin of the sea ; in the bursting seed or opening flower ; in the day duty or the night musing ; in the general laugh and the secret grief ; in the procession of life, ever entering afresh, and solemnly passing by and dropping off ; I do not think we should discern him any more on the grass of Eden, or beneath the moonlight of Gethsemane. Depend upon it, it is not the want of greater miracles, but of the soul to perceive such as are allowed us still, that makes us push all the sanctities into the far spaces we cannot reach. The devout feel that wherever God's hand is, *there* is miracle : and it is simply an indevoutness which imagines that only where miracle is, can there be the real hand of God. The customs of Heaven ought surely to be more sacred in our eyes than its anomalies ; the dear old ways, of which the Most High is never tired, than the strange things which he does not love well enough ever to repeat. And he who will but discern beneath the sun, as he rises any morning, the supporting finger of the Almighty, may recover the sweet and reverent surprise with which Adam gazed on the first dawn in Paradise. It is no outward change, no shifting in time or place ; but only the loving meditation of the pure in heart, that can reawaken the Eternal from the sleep within our souls : that can render him a reality again, and reassert for him once more his ancient name of 'the Living God.' " [1]

When we see all things in God, and refer all things to him, we read in common matters superior expressions of

[1] JAMES MARTINEAU : end of the sermon ' Help Thou Mine Unbelief,' in Endeavours after a Christian Life, 2d series. Compare with this page the extract from Voysey on p. 275, above, and those from Pascal and Madame Guyon on p. 286.

meaning. The deadness with which custom invests the familiar vanishes, and existence as a whole appears transfigured. The state of a mind thus awakened from torpor is well expressed in these words, which I take from a friend's letter : —

" If we occupy ourselves in summing up all the mercies and bounties we are privileged to have, we are overwhelmed by their number (so great that we can imagine ourselves unable to give ourselves time even to begin to review the things we may imagine *we have not*). We sum them and realize that *we are actually killed with God's kindness ;* that we are surrounded by bounties upon bounties, without which all would fall. Should we not love it; should we not feel buoyed up by the Eternal Arms ? "

Sometimes this realization that facts are of divine sending, instead of being habitual, is casual, like a mystical experience. Father Gratry gives this instance from his youthful melancholy period : —

" One day I had a moment of consolation, because I met with something which seemed to me ideally perfect. It was a poor drummer beating the tattoo in the streets of Paris. I walked behind him in returning to the school on the evening of a holiday. His drum gave out the tattoo in such a way that, at that moment at least, however peevish I were, I could find no pretext for fault-finding. It was impossible to conceive more nerve or spirit, better time or measure, more clearness or richness, than were in this drumming. Ideal desire could go no farther in that direction. I was enchanted and consoled; the perfection of this wretched act did me good. Good is at least possible, I said, since the ideal can thus sometimes get embodied." [1]

In Sénancour's novel of Obermann a similar transient lifting of the veil is recorded. In Paris streets, on a March day, he comes across a flower in bloom, a jonquil ·

[1] Souvenirs de ma Jeunesse, 1897, p. 122.

"It was the strongest expression of desire : it was the first perfume of the year. I felt all the happiness destined for man. This unutterable harmony of souls, the phantom of the ideal world, arose in me complete. I never felt anything so great or so instantaneous. I know not what shape, what analogy, what secret of relation it was that made me see in this flower a limitless beauty. . . . I shall never inclose in a conception this power, this immensity that nothing will express; this form that nothing will contain; this ideal of a better world which one feels, but which, it seems, nature has not made actual." [1]

We heard in previous lectures of the vivified face of the world as it may appear to converts after their awakening.[2] As a rule, religious persons generally assume that whatever natural facts connect themselves in any way with their destiny are significant of the divine purposes with them. Through prayer the purpose, often far from obvious, comes home to them, and if it be ' trial,' strength to endure the trial is given. Thus at all stages of the prayerful life we find the persuasion that in the process of communion energy from on high flows in to meet demand, and becomes operative within the phenomenal world. So long as this operativeness is admitted to be real, it makes no essential difference whether its immediate effects be subjective or objective. The fundamental religious point is that in prayer, spiritual energy, which otherwise would slumber, does become active, and spiritual work of some kind is effected really.

So much for Prayer, taken in the wide sense of any kind of communion. As the core of religion, we must return to it in the next lecture.

The last aspect of the religious life which remains for

[1] Op. cit., Letter XXX.
[2] Above, p. 248 ff. Compare the withdrawal of expression from the world, in Melancholiacs, p. 151.

me to touch upon is the fact that its manifestations so frequently connect themselves with the subconscious part of our existence. You may remember what I said in my opening lecture [1] about the prevalence of the psychopathic temperament in religious biography. You will in point of fact hardly find a religious leader of any kind in whose life there is no record of automatisms. I speak not merely of savage priests and prophets, whose followers regard automatic utterance and action as by itself tantamount to inspiration, I speak of leaders of thought and subjects of intellectualized experience. Saint Paul had his visions, his ecstasies, his gift of tongues, small as was the importance he attached to the latter. The whole array of Christian saints and heresiarchs, including the greatest, the Bernards, the Loyolas, the Luthers, the Foxes, the Wesleys, had their visions, voices, rapt conditions, guiding impressions, and 'openings.' They had these things, because they had exalted sensibility, and to such things persons of exalted sensibility are liable. In such liability there lie, however, consequences for theology. Beliefs are strengthened wherever automatisms corroborate them. Incursions from beyond the transmarginal region have a peculiar power to increase conviction. The inchoate sense of presence is infinitely stronger than conception, but strong as it may be, it is seldom equal to the evidence of hallucination. Saints who actually see or hear their Saviour reach the acme of assurance. Motor automatisms, though rarer, are, if possible, even more convincing than sensations. The subjects here actually feel themselves played upon by powers beyond their will. The evidence is dynamic; the God or spirit moves the very organs of their body.[2]

[1] Above, pp. 24, 25.

[2] A friend of mine, a first-rate psychologist, who is a subject of graphic

The great field for this sense of being the instrument of a higher power is of course 'inspiration.' It is easy to discriminate between the religious leaders who have been habitually subject to inspiration and those who have not. In the teachings of the Buddha, of Jesus, of Saint Paul (apart from his gift of tongues), of Saint Augustine, of Huss, of Luther, of Wesley, automatic or semi-automatic composition appears to have been only occasional. In the Hebrew prophets, on the contrary, in Mohammed, in some of the Alexandrians, in many minor Catholic saints, in Fox, in Joseph Smith, something like it appears to have been frequent, sometimes habitual. We have distinct professions of being under the direction of a foreign power, and serving as its mouthpiece. As regards the Hebrew prophets, it is extraordinary, writes an author who has made a careful study of them, to see —

"How, one after another, the same features are reproduced in the prophetic books. The process is always extremely different from what it would be if the prophet arrived at his insight into spiritual things by the tentative efforts of his own

automatism, tells me that the appearance of independent actuation in the movements of his arm, when he writes automatically, is so distinct that it obliges him to abandon a psychophysical theory which he had previously believed in, the theory, namely, that we have no feeling of the discharge downwards of our voluntary motor-centres. We must normally have such a feeling, he thinks, or the *sense of an absence* would not be so striking as it is in these experiences. Graphic automatism of a fully developed kind is rare in religious history, so far as my knowledge goes. Such statements as Antonia Bourignon's, that "I do nothing but lend my hand and spirit to another power than mine," is shown by the context to indicate inspiration rather than directly automatic writing. In some eccentric sects this latter occurs. The most striking instance of it is probably the bulky volume called, 'Oahspe, a new Bible in the Words of Jehovah and his angel ambassadors,' Boston and London, 1891, written and illustrated automatically by DR. NEWBROUGH of New York, whom I understand to be now, or to have been lately, at the head of the spiritistic community of Shalam in New Mexico. The latest automatically written book which has come under my notice is 'Zertoulem's Wisdom of the Ages,' by GEORGE A. FULLER, Boston, 1901.

genius. There is something sharp and sudden about it. He can lay his finger, so to speak, on the moment when it came. And it always comes in the form of an overpowering force from without, against which he struggles, but in vain. Listen, for instance, [to] the opening of the book of Jeremiah. Read through in like manner the first two chapters of the prophecy of Ezekiel.

" It is not, however, only at the beginning of his career that the prophet passes through a crisis which is clearly not self-caused. Scattered all through the prophetic writings are expressions which speak of some strong and irresistible impulse coming down upon the prophet, determining his attitude to the events of his time, constraining his utterance, making his words the vehicle of a higher meaning than their own. For instance, this of Isaiah's: 'The Lord spake thus to me with a strong hand,' — an emphatic phrase which denotes the overmastering nature of the impulse, — 'and instructed me that I should not walk in the way of this people.' . . . Or passages like this from Ezekiel: ' The hand of the Lord God fell upon me,' ' The hand of the Lord was strong upon me.' The one standing characteristic of the prophet is that he speaks with the authority of Jehovah himself. Hence it is thåt the prophets one and all preface their addresses so confidently, ' The Word of the Lord,' or ' Thus saith the Lord.' They have even the audacity to speak in the first person, as if Jehovah himself were speaking. As in Isaiah : ' Hearken unto me, O Jacob, and Israel my called ; I am He, I am the First, I also am the last,' — and so on. The personality of the prophet sinks entirely into the background ; he feels himself for the time being the mouth-piece of the Almighty." [1]

" We need to remember that prophecy was a profession, and that the prophets formed a professional class. There were schools of the prophets, in which the gift was regularly culti-vated. A group of young men would gather round some com-manding figure — a Samuel or an Elisha — and would not only record or spread the knowledge of his sayings and doings, but seek to catch themselves something of his inspiration. It

[1] W. Sanday : The Oracles of God, London, 1892, pp. 49–56, abridged.

seems that music played its part in their exercises. . . . It is perfectly clear that by no means all of these Sons of the prophets ever succeeded in acquiring more than a very small share in the gift which they sought. It was clearly possible to 'counterfeit' prophecy. Sometimes this was done deliberately. . . . But it by no means follows that in all cases where a false message was given, the giver of it was altogether conscious of what he was doing." [1]

Here, to take another Jewish case, is the way in which Philo of Alexandria describes his inspiration : —

"Sometimes, when I have come to my work empty, I have suddenly become full; ideas being in an invisible manner showered upon me, and implanted in me from on high; so that through the influence of divine inspiration, I have become greatly excited, and have known neither the place in which I was, nor those who were present, nor myself, nor what I was saying, nor what I was writing; for then I have been conscious of a richness of interpretation, an enjoyment of light, a most penetrating insight, a most manifest energy in all that was to be done; having such effect on my mind as the clearest ocular demonstration would have on the eyes." [2]

If we turn to Islam, we find that Mohammed's revelations all came from the subconscious sphere. To the question in what way he got them, —

"Mohammed is said to have answered that sometimes he heard a knell as from a bell, and that this had the strongest effect on him; and when the angel went away, he had received the revelation. Sometimes again he held converse with the angel as with a man, so as easily to understand his words. The later authorities, however, . . . distinguish still other kinds. In the Itgân (103) the following are enumerated: 1, revelations with

---

[1] Op. cit., p. 91. This author also cites Moses's and Isaiah's commissions, as given in Exodus, chaps. iii. and iv., and Isaiah, chap. vi.

[2] Quoted by AUGUSTUS CLISSOLD : The Prophetic Spirit in Genius and Madness, 1870, p. 67. Mr. Clissold is a Swedenborgian. Swedenborg's case is of course the palmary one of *audita et visa*, serving as a basis of religious revelation.

sound of bell, 2, by inspiration of the holy spirit in M.'s heart, 3, by Gabriel in human form, 4, by God immediately, either when awake (as in his journey to heaven) or in dream. . . . In Almawâhib alladunîya the kinds are thus given : 1, Dream, 2, Inspiration of Gabriel in the Prophet's heart, 3, Gabriel taking Dahya's form, 4, with the bell-sound, etc., 5, Gabriel in propriâ personâ (only twice), 6, revelation in heaven, 7, God appearing in person, but veiled, 8, God revealing himself immediately without veil. Others add two other stages, namely : 1, Gabriel in the form of still another man, 2, God showing himself personally in dream." [1]

In none of these cases is the revelation distinctly motor. In the case of Joseph Smith (who had prophetic revelations innumerable in addition to the revealed translation of the gold plates which resulted in the Book of Mormon), although there may have been a motor element, the inspiration seems to have been predominantly sensorial. He began his translation by the aid of the ' peepstones ' which he found, or thought or said that he found, with the gold plates, — apparently a case of ' crystal gazing.' For some of the other revelations he used the peep-stones, but seems generally to have asked the Lord for more direct instruction. [2]

---

[1] NÖLDEKE, Geschichte des Qorâns, 1860, p. 16. Compare the fuller account in Sir WILLIAM MUIR's Life of Mahomet, 3d ed., 1894, ch. iii.

[2] The Mormon theocracy has always been governed by direct revelations accorded to the President of the Church and its Apostles. From an obliging letter written to me in 1899 by an eminent Mormon, I quote the following extract : —

"It may be very interesting for you to know that the President [Mr. Snow] of the Mormon Church claims to have had a number of revelations very recently from heaven. To explain fully what these revelations are, it is necessary to know that we, as a people, believe that the Church of Jesus Christ has again been established through messengers sent from heaven. This Church has at its head a prophet, seer, and revelator, who gives to man God's holy will. Revelation is the means through which the will of God is declared directly and in fullness to man. These revelations are got through dreams of sleep or in waking visions of the mind, by

Other revelations are described as 'openings' — Fox's, for example, were evidently of the kind known in spiritistic circles of to-day as 'impressions.' As all effective initiators of change must needs live to some degree upon this psychopathic level of sudden perception or conviction of new truth, or of impulse to action so obsessive that it must be worked off, I will say nothing more about so very common a phenomenon.

When, in addition to these phenomena of inspiration, we take religious mysticism into the account, when we recall the striking and sudden unifications of a discordant self which we saw in conversion, and when we review the extravagant obsessions of tenderness, purity, and self-severity met with in saintliness, we cannot, I think, avoid the conclusion that in religion we have a department of human nature with unusually close relations to the transmarginal or subliminal region. If the word 'subliminal' is offensive to any of you, as smelling too much of psychical research or other aberrations, call it by any other name you please, to distinguish it from the level of full sunlit consciousness. Call this latter the A-region of personality, if you care to, and call the other the B-region. The B-region, then, is obviously the larger part of each of us, for it is the abode of everything that is latent and the reservoir of everything that passes unrecorded or unobserved. It contains, for example, such things as all our momentarily inactive memories, and it harbors the springs of all our obscurely motived passions, impulses, likes, dislikes, and prejudices. Our intuitions, hypotheses, fancies, superstitions, persuasions, convictions, and in general all our non-rational operations, come from it.

voices without visional appearance, or by actual manifestations of the Holy Presence before the eye. We believe that God has come in person and spoken to our prophet and revelator."

It is the source of our dreams, and apparently they may return to it. In it arise whatever mystical experiences we may have, and our automatisms, sensory or motor; our life in hypnotic and 'hypnoid' conditions, if we are subjects to such conditions; our delusions, fixed ideas, and hysterical accidents, if we are hysteric subjects; our supra-normal cognitions, if such there be, and if we are telepathic subjects. It is also the fountain-head of much that feeds our religion. In persons deep in the religious life, as we have now abundantly seen, — and this is my conclusion, — the door into this region seems unusually wide open; at any rate, experiences making their entrance through that door have had emphatic influence in shaping religious history.

With this conclusion I turn back and close the circle which I opened in my first lecture, terminating thus the review which I then announced of inner religious phenomena as we find them in developed and articulate human individuals. I might easily, if the time allowed, multiply both my documents and my discriminations, but a broad treatment is, I believe, in itself better, and the most important characteristics of the subject lie, I think, before us already. In the next lecture, which is also the last one, we must try to draw the critical conclusions which so much material may suggest.

LECTURE XX

CONCLUSIONS

THE material of our study of human nature is now spread before us; and in this parting hour, set free from the duty of description, we can draw our theoretical and practical conclusions. In my first lecture, defending the empirical method, I foretold that whatever conclusions we might come to could be reached by spiritual judgments only, appreciations of the significance for life of religion, taken 'on the whole.' Our conclusions cannot be as sharp as dogmatic conclusions would be, but I will formulate them, when the time comes, as sharply as I can.

Summing up in the broadest possible way the characteristics of the religious life, as we have found them, it includes the following beliefs : —

1. That the visible world is part of a more spiritual universe from which it draws its chief significance ;

2. That union or harmonious relation with that higher universe is our true end ;

3. That prayer or inner communion with the spirit thereof — be that spirit 'God' or 'law' — is a process wherein work is really done, and spiritual energy flows in and produces effects, psychological or material, within the phenomenal world.

Religion includes also the following psychological characteristics : —

4. A new zest which adds itself like a gift to life, and takes the form either of lyrical enchantment or of appeal to earnestness and heroism.

5. An assurance of safety and a temper of peace, and, in relation to others, a preponderance of loving affections.

In illustrating these characteristics by documents, we have been literally bathed in sentiment. In re-reading my manuscript, I am almost appalled at the amount of emotionality which I find in it. After so much of this, we can afford to be dryer and less sympathetic in the rest of the work that lies before us.

The sentimentality of many of my documents is a consequence of the fact that I sought them among the extravagances of the subject. If any of you are enemies of what our ancestors used to brand as enthusiasm, and are, nevertheless, still listening to me now, you have probably felt my selection to have been sometimes almost perverse, and have wished I might have stuck to soberer examples. I reply that I took these extremer examples as yielding the profounder information. To learn the secrets of any science, we go to expert specialists, even though they may be eccentric persons, and not to commonplace pupils. We combine what they tell us with the rest of our wisdom, and form our final judgment independently. Even so with religion. We who have pursued such radical expressions of it may now be sure that we know its secrets as authentically as any one can know them who learns them from another; and we have next to answer, each of us for himself, the practical question: what are the dangers in this element of life? and in what proportion may it need to be restrained by other elements, to give the proper balance?

But this question suggests another one which I will answer immediately and get it out of the way, for it has more than once already vexed us.[1] Ought it to be as-

---

[1] For example, on pages 135, 163, 333, above.

sumed that in all men the mixture of religion with other elements should be identical? Ought it, indeed, to be assumed that the lives of all men should show identical religious elements? In other words, is the existence of so many religious types and sects and creeds regrettable?

To these questions I answer 'No' emphatically. And my reason is that I do not see how it is possible that creatures in such different positions and with such different powers as human individuals are, should have exactly the same functions and the same duties. No two of us have identical difficulties, nor should we be expected to work out identical solutions. Each, from his peculiar angle of observation, takes in a certain sphere of fact and trouble, which each must deal with in a unique manner. One of us must soften himself, another must harden himself; one must yield a point, another must stand firm, — in order the better to defend the position assigned him. If an Emerson were forced to be a Wesley, or a Moody forced to be a Whitman, the total human consciousness of the divine would suffer. The divine can mean no single quality, it must mean a group of qualities, by being champions of which in alternation, different men may all find worthy missions. Each attitude being a syllable in human nature's total message, it takes the whole of us to spell the meaning out completely. So a 'god of battles' must be allowed to be the god for one kind of person, a god of peace and heaven and home, the god for another. We must frankly recognize the fact that we live in partial systems, and that parts are not interchangeable in the spiritual life. If we are peevish and jealous, destruction of the self must be an element of our religion; why need it be one if we are good and sympathetic from the outset? If we are sick souls, we require a religion of deliverance; but why think so much of deliverance, if we are healthy-minded?[1]   Unquestionably, some men have the completer experience and the higher vocation, here just as in the social world; but for each man to stay in his own experience, whate'er it be, and for others to tolerate him there, is surely best.

But, you may now ask, would not this one-sidedness be cured if we should all espouse the science of religions as our own religion?   In answering this question I must open again the general relations of the theoretic to the active life.

Knowledge about a thing is not the thing itself.   You remember what Al-Ghazzali told us in the Lecture on Mysticism, — that to understand the causes of drunkenness, as a physician understands them, is not to be drunk. A science might come to understand everything about the causes and elements of religion, and might even

[1] From this point of view, the contrasts between the healthy and the morbid mind, and between the once-born and the twice-born types, of which I spoke in earlier lectures (see pp. 162–167), cease to be the radical antagonisms which many think them. The twice-born look down upon the rectilinear consciousness of life of the once-born as being 'mere morality,' and not properly religion. "Dr. Channing," an orthodox minister is reported to have said, "is excluded from the highest form of religious life by the extraordinary rectitude of his character." It is indeed true that the outlook upon life of the twice-born — holding as it does more of the element of evil in solution — is the wider and completer. The 'heroic' or 'solemn' way in which life comes to them is a 'higher synthesis' into which healthy-mindedness and morbidness both enter and combine. Evil is not evaded, but sublated in the higher religious cheer of these persons (see pp. 47–52, 362–365). But the final consciousness which each type reaches of union with the divine has the same practical significance for the individual; and individuals may well be allowed to get to it by the channels which lie most open to their several temperaments. In the cases which were quoted in Lecture IV, of the mind-cure form of healthy-mindedness, we found abundant examples of regenerative process. The severity of the crisis in this process is a matter of degree. How long one shall continue to drink the consciousness of evil, and when one shall begin to short-circuit and get rid of it, are also matters of amount and degree, so that in many instances it is quite arbitrary whether we class the individual as a once-born or a twice-born subject.

decide which elements were qualified, by their general harmony with other branches of knowledge, to be considered true; and yet the best man at this science might be the man who found it hardest to be personally devout. *Tout savoir c'est tout pardonner.* The name of Renan would doubtless occur to many persons as an example of the way in which breadth of knowledge may make one only a dilettante in possibilities, and blunt the acuteness of one's living faith.[1] If religion be a function by which either God's cause or man's cause is to be really advanced, then he who lives the life of it, however narrowly, is a better servant than he who merely knows about it, however much. Knowledge about life is one thing; effective occupation of a place in life, with its dynamic currents passing through your being, is another.

For this reason, the science of religions may not be an equivalent for living religion; and if we turn to the inner difficulties of such a science, we see that a point comes when she must drop the purely theoretic attitude, and either let her knots remain uncut, or have them cut by active faith. To see this, suppose that we have our science of religions constituted as a matter of fact. Suppose that she has assimilated all the necessary historical material and distilled out of it as its essence the same conclusions which I myself a few moments ago pronounced. Suppose that she agrees that religion, wherever it is an active thing, involves a belief in ideal presences, and a belief that in our prayerful communion with them,[2] work is done, and something real comes to pass. She has now to exert her critical activity, and to decide how far, in the light of other sciences and in that of general philosophy, such beliefs can be considered *true.*

[1] Compare, e. g., the quotation from Renan on p. 37, above.
[2] 'Prayerful' taken in the broader sense explained above on pp. 463 ff.

Dogmatically to decide this is an impossible task. Not only are the other sciences and the philosophy still far from being completed, but in their present state we find them full of conflicts. The sciences of nature know nothing of spiritual presences, and on the whole hold no practical commerce whatever with the idealistic conceptions towards which general philosophy inclines. The scientist, so-called, is, during his scientific hours at least, so materialistic that one may well say that on the whole the influence of science goes against the notion that religion should be recognized at all. And this antipathy to religion finds an echo within the very science of religions itself. The cultivator of this science has to become acquainted with so many groveling and horrible superstitions that a presumption easily arises in his mind that any belief that is religious probably is false. In the 'prayerful communion' of savages with such mumbo-jumbos of deities as they acknowledge, it is hard for us to see what genuine spiritual work — even though it were work relative only to their dark savage obligations — can possibly be done.

The consequence is that the conclusions of the science of religions are as likely to be adverse as they are to be favorable to the claim that the essence of religion is true. There is a notion in the air about us that religion is probably only an anachronism, a case of 'survival,' an atavistic relapse into a mode of thought which humanity in its more enlightened examples has outgrown; and this notion our religious anthropologists at present do little to counteract.

This view is so widespread at the present day that I must consider it with some explicitness before I pass to my own conclusions. Let me call it the 'Survival theory,' for brevity's sake.

The pivot round which the religious life, as we have traced it, revolves, is the interest of the individual in his private personal destiny. Religion, in short, is a monumental chapter in the history of human egotism. The gods believed in — whether by crude savages or by men disciplined intellectually — agree with each other in recognizing personal calls. Religious thought is carried on in terms of personality, this being, in the world of religion, the one fundamental fact. To-day, quite as much as at any previous age, the religious individual tells you that the divine meets him on the basis of his personal concerns.

Science, on the other hand, has ended by utterly repudiating the personal point of view. She catalogues her elements and records her laws indifferent as to what purpose may be shown forth by them, and constructs her theories quite careless of their bearing on human anxieties and fates. Though the scientist may individually nourish a religion, and be a theist in his irresponsible hours, the days are over when it could be said that for Science herself the heavens declare the glory of God and the firmament showeth his handiwork. Our solar system, with its harmonies, is seen now as but one passing case of a certain sort of moving equilibrium in the heavens, realized by a local accident in an appalling wilderness of worlds where no life can exist. In a span of time which as a cosmic interval will count but as an hour, it will have ceased to be. The Darwinian notion of chance production, and subsequent destruction, speedy or deferred, applies to the largest as well as to the smallest facts. It is impossible, in the present temper of the scientific imagination, to find in the driftings of the cosmic atoms, whether they work on the universal or on the particular scale, anything but a kind of aimless weather, doing and

undoing, achieving no proper history, and leaving no
result.   Nature has no one distinguishable ultimate tendency with which it is possible to feel a sympathy.   In
the vast rhythm of her processes, as the scientific mind
now follows them, she appears to cancel herself.   The
books of natural theology which satisfied the intellects of
our grandfathers seem to us quite grotesque,[1] represent-

[1] How was it ever conceivable, we ask, that a man like Christian Wolff,
in whose dry-as-dust head all the learning of the early eighteenth century
was concentrated, should have preserved such a baby-like faith in the personal and human character of Nature as to expound her operations as he
did in his work on the uses of natural things ?   This, for example, is the
account he gives of the sun and its utility : —

"We see that God has created the sun to keep the changeable conditions
on the earth in such an order that living creatures, men and beasts, may
inhabit its surface.   Since men are the most reasonable of creatures, and
able to infer God's invisible being from the contemplation of the world, the
sun in so far forth contributes to the primary purpose of creation : without
it the race of man could not be preserved or continued. . . . The sun
makes daylight, not only on our earth, but also on the other planets ; and
daylight is of the utmost utility to us ; for by its means we can commodi-
ously carry on those occupations which in the night-time would either be
quite impossible, or at any rate impossible without our going to the expense
of artificial light.   The beasts of the field can find food by day which they
would not be able to find at night.   Moreover we owe it to the sunlight
that we are able to see everything that is on the earth's surface, not only
near by, but also at a distance, and to recognize both near and far things
according to their species, which again is of manifold use to us not only in
the business necessary to human life, and when we are traveling, but also
for the scientific knowledge of Nature, which knowledge for the most part
depends on observations made with the help of sight, and, without the sunshine, would have been impossible.   If any one would rightly impress on his
mind the great advantages which he derives from the sun, let him imagine
himself living through only one month, and see how it would be with all
his undertakings, if it were not day but night.   He would then be sufficiently convinced out of his own experience, especially if he had much work
to carry on in the street or in the fields. . . . From the sun we learn to recognize when it is midday, and by knowing this point of time exactly, we can
set our clocks right, on which account astronomy owes much to the sun.
. . . By help of the sun one can find the meridian. . . . But the meridian
is the basis of our sun-dials, and generally speaking, we should have no
sun-dials if we had no sun."   Vernünftige Gedanken von den Absichten
der natürlichen Dinge, 1782, pp. 74–84.

ing, as they did, a God who conformed the largest things of nature to the paltriest of our private wants. The

Or read the account of God's beneficence in the institution of "the great variety throughout the world of men's faces, voices, and handwriting," given in Derham's Physico-theology, a book that had much vogue in the eighteenth century. "Had Man's body," says Dr. Derham, "been made according to any of the Atheistical Schemes, or any other Method than that of the infinite Lord of the World, this wise Variety would never have been : but Men's Faces would have been cast in the same, or not a very different Mould, their Organs of Speech would have sounded the same or not so great a Variety of Notes ; and the same Structure of Muscles and Nerves would have given the Hand the same Direction in Writing. And in this Case, what Confusion, what Disturbance, what Mischiefs would the world eternally have lain under ! No Security could have been to our persons ; no Certainty, no Enjoyment of our Possessions ; no Justice between Man and Man ; no Distinction between Good and Bad, between Friends and Foes, between Father and Child, Husband and Wife, Male or Female ; but all would have been turned topsy-turvy, by being exposed to the Malice of the Envious and ill-Natured, to the Fraud and Violence of Knaves and Robbers, to the Forgeries of the crafty Cheat, to the Lusts of the Effeminate and Debauched, and what not ! Our Courts of Justice can abundantly testify the dire Effects of Mistaking Men's Faces, of counterfeiting their Hands, and forging Writings. But now as the infinitely wise Creator and Ruler hath ordered the Matter, every man's Face can distinguish him in the Light, and his Voice in the Dark ; his Hand-writing can speak for him though absent, and be his Witness, and secure his Contracts in future Generations. A manifest as well as admirable Indication of the divine Superintendence and Management."

A God so careful as to make provision even for the unmistakable signing of bank checks and deeds was a deity truly after the heart of eighteenth century Anglicanism.

I subjoin, omitting the capitals, Derham's 'Vindication of God by the Institution of Hills and Valleys,' and Wolff's altogether culinary account of the institution of Water : —

"The uses," says Wolff, " which water serves in human life are plain to see and need not be described at length. Water is a universal drink of man and beasts. Even though men have made themselves drinks that are artificial, they could not do this without water. Beer is brewed of water and malt, and it is the water in it which quenches thirst. Wine is prepared from grapes, which could never have grown without the help of water ; and the same is true of those drinks which in England and other places they produce from fruit. . . . Therefore since God so planned the world that men and beasts should live upon it and find there everything required for their necessity and convenience, he also made water as one means whereby

God whom science recognizes must be a God of universal laws exclusively, a God who does a wholesale, not a retail business. He cannot accommodate his processes to the

to make the earth into so excellent a dwelling. And this is all the more manifest when we consider the advantages which we obtain from this same water for the cleaning of our household utensils, of our clothing, and of other matters. . . . When one goes into a grinding-mill one sees that the grindstone must always be kept wet and then one will get a still greater idea of the use of water."

Of the hills and valleys, Derham, after praising their beauty, discourses as follows : "Some constitutions are indeed of so happy a strength, and so confirmed an health, as to be indifferent to almost any place or temperature of the air. But then others are so weakly and feeble, as not to be able to bear one, but can live comfortably in another place. With some the more subtle and finer air of the hills doth best agree, who are languishing and dying in the feculent and grosser air of great towns, or even the warmer and vaporous air of the valleys and waters. But contrariwise, others languish on the hills, and grow lusty and strong in the warmer air of the valleys.

"So that this opportunity of shifting our abode from the hills to the vales, is an admirable easement, refreshment, and great benefit to the valetudinarian, feeble part of mankind ; affording those an easy and comfortable life, who would otherwise live miserably, languish, and pine away.

"To this salutary conformation of the earth we may add another great convenience of the hills, and that is affording commodious places for habitation, serving (as an eminent author wordeth it) as screens to keep off the cold and nipping blasts of the northern and easterly winds, and reflecting the benign and cherishing sunbeams, and so rendering our habitations both more comfortable and more cheerly in winter.

"Lastly, it is to the hills that the fountains owe their rise and the rivers their conveyance, and consequently those vast masses and lofty piles are not, as they are charged, such rude and useless excrescences of our ill-formed globe ; but the admirable tools of nature, contrived and ordered by the infinite Creator, to do one of its most useful works. For, was the surface of the earth even and level, and the middle parts of its islands and continents not mountainous and high as now it is, it is most certain there could be no descent for the rivers, no conveyance for the waters ; but, instead of gliding along those gentle declivities which the higher lands now afford them quite down to the sea, they would stagnate and perhaps stink, and also drown large tracts of land.

"[Thus] the hills and vales, though to a peevish and weary traveler they may seem incommodious and troublesome, yet are a noble work of the great Creator, and wisely appointed by him for the good of our sublunary world."

convenience of individuals. The bubbles on the foam which coats a stormy sea are floating episodes, made and unmade by the forces of the wind and water. Our private selves are like those bubbles, — epiphenomena, as Clifford, I believe, ingeniously called them ; their destinies weigh nothing and determine nothing in the world's irremediable currents of events.

You see how natural it is, from this point of view, to treat religion as a mere survival, for religion does in fact perpetuate the traditions of the most primeval thought. To coerce the spiritual powers, or to square them and get them on our side, was, during enormous tracts of time, the one great object in our dealings with the natural world. For our ancestors, dreams, hallucinations, revelations, and cock-and-bull stories were inextricably mixed with facts. Up to a comparatively recent date such distinctions as those between what has been verified and what is only conjectured, between the impersonal and the personal aspects of existence, were hardly suspected or conceived. Whatever you imagined in a lively manner, whatever you thought fit to be true, you affirmed confidently ; and whatever you affirmed, your comrades believed. Truth was what had not yet been contradicted, most things were taken into the mind from the point of view of their human suggestiveness, and the attention confined itself exclusively to the æsthetic and dramatic aspects of events.[1]

[1] Until the seventeenth century this mode of thought prevailed. One need only recall the dramatic treatment even of mechanical questions by Aristotle, as, for example, his explanation of the power of the lever to make a small weight raise a larger one. This is due, according to Aristotle, to the generally miraculous character of the circle and of all circular movement. The circle is both convex and concave ; it is made by a fixed point and a moving line, which contradict each other ; and whatever moves in a circle moves in opposite directions. Nevertheless, movement in a circle is the most 'natural' movement ; and the long arm of the lever, moving, as

How indeed could it be otherwise? The extraordinary value, for explanation and prevision, of those mathemati-

it does, in the larger circle, has the greater amount of this natural motion, and consequently requires the lesser force. Or recall the explanation by Herodotus of the position of the sun in winter : It moves to the south because of the cold which drives it into the warm parts of the heavens over Libya. Or listen to Saint Augustine's speculations : " Who gave to chaff such power to freeze that it preserves snow buried under it, and such power to warm that it ripens green fruit ? Who can explain the strange properties of fire itself, which blackens all that it burns, though itself bright, and which, though of the most beautiful colors, discolors almost all that it touches and feeds upon, and turns blazing fuel into grimy cinders ? . . . Then what wonderful properties do we find in charcoal, which is so brittle that a light tap breaks it, and a slight pressure pulverizes it, and yet is so strong that no moisture rots it, nor any time causes it to decay." City of God, book xxi. ch. iv.

Such aspects of things as these, their naturalness and unnaturalness, the sympathies and antipathies of their superficial qualities, their eccentricities, their brightness and strength and destructiveness, were inevitably the ways in which they originally fastened our attention.

If you open early medical books, you will find sympathetic magic invoked on every page. Take, for example, the famous vulnerary ointment attributed to Paracelsus. For this there were a variety of receipts, including usually human fat, the fat of either a bull, a wild boar, or a bear ; powdered earthworms, the *usnia*, or mossy growth on the weathered skull of a hanged criminal, and other materials equally unpleasant — the whole prepared under the planet Venus if possible, but never under Mars or Saturn. Then, if a splinter of wood, dipped in the patient's blood, or the bloodstained weapon that wounded him, be immersed in this ointment, the wound itself being tightly bound up, the latter infallibly gets well, — I quote now Van Helmont's account, — for the blood on the weapon or splinter, containing in it the spirit of the wounded man, is roused to active excitement by the contact of the ointment, whence there results to it a full commission or power to cure its cousin-german, the blood in the patient's body. This it does by sucking out the dolorous and exotic impression from the wounded part. But to do this it has to implore the aid of the bull's fat, and other portions of the unguent. The reason why bull's fat is so powerful is that the bull at the time of slaughter is full of secret reluctancy and vindictive murmurs, and therefore dies with a higher flame of revenge about him than any other animal. And thus we have made it out, says this author, that the admirable efficacy of the ointment ought to be imputed, not to any auxiliary concurrence of Satan, but simply to the energy of the *posthumous character of Revenge* remaining firmly impressed upon the blood and concreted fat in the unguent. J. B. VAN HELMONT: A Ternary of Paracal and mechanical modes of conception which science uses, was a result that could not possibly have been expected in advance. Weight, movement, velocity, direction, position, what thin, pallid, uninteresting ideas! How could the richer animistic aspects of Nature, the peculiarities and oddities that make phenomena picturesquely striking or expressive, fail to have been first singled out and followed by philosophy as the more promising avenue to the knowledge of Nature's life? Well, it is still in these richer animistic and dramatic aspects that religion de-

doxes, translated by WALTER CHARLETON, London, 1650. — I much abridge the original in my citations.

The author goes on to prove by the analogy of many other natural facts that this sympathetic action between things at a distance is the true rationale of the case. "If," he says, "the heart of a horse, slain by a witch, taken out of the yet reeking carcase, be impaled upon an arrow and roasted, immediately the whole witch becomes tormented with the insufferable pains and cruelty of the fire, which could by no means happen unless there preceded a conjunction of the spirit of the witch with the spirit of the horse. In the reeking and yet panting heart, the spirit of the witch is kept captive, and the retreat of it prevented by the arrow transfixed. Similarly hath not many a murdered carcase at the coroner's inquest suffered a fresh hæmorrhage or cruentation at the presence of the assassin? — the blood being, as in a furious fit of anger, enraged and agitated by the impress of revenge conceived against the murderer, at the instant of the soul's compulsive exile from the body. So, if you have dropsy, gout, or jaundice, by including some of your warm blood in the shell and white of an egg, which, exposed to a gentle heat, and mixed with a bait of flesh, you shall give to a hungry dog or hog, the disease shall instantly pass from you into the animal, and leave you entirely. And similarly again, if you burn some of the milk either of a cow or of a woman, the gland from which it issued will dry up. A gentleman at Brussels had his nose mowed off in a combat, but the celebrated surgeon Tagliacozzus digged a new nose for him out of the skin of the arm of a porter at Bologna. About thirteen months after his return to his own country, the engrafted nose grew cold, putrefied, and in a few days dropped off, and it was then discovered that the porter had expired, near about the same punctilio of time. There are still at Brussels eye-witnesses of this occurrence," says Van Helmont; and adds, "I pray what is there in this of superstition or of exalted imagination?"

Modern mind-cure literature — the works of Prentice Mulford, for example — is full of sympathetic magic.

lights to dwell. It is the terror and beauty of phenomena, the 'promise' of the dawn and of the rainbow, the 'voice' of the thunder, the 'gentleness' of the summer rain, the 'sublimity' of the stars, and not the physical laws which these things follow, by which the religious mind still continues to be most impressed; and just as of yore, the devout man tells you that in the solitude of his room or of the fields he still feels the divine presence, that inflowings of help come in reply to his prayers, and that sacrifices to this unseen reality fill him with security and peace.

Pure anachronism! says the survival-theory; — anachronism for which deanthropomorphization of the imagination is the remedy required. The less we mix the private with the cosmic, the more we dwell in universal and impersonal terms, the truer heirs of Science we become.

In spite of the appeal which this impersonality of the scientific attitude makes to a certain magnanimity of temper, I believe it to be shallow, and I can now state my reason in comparatively few words. That reason is that, so long as we deal with the cosmic and the general, we deal only with the symbols of reality, but *as soon as we deal with private and personal phenomena as such, we deal with realities in the completest sense of the term.* I think I can easily make clear what I mean by these words.

The world of our experience consists at all times of two parts, an objective and a subjective part, of which the former may be incalculably more extensive than the latter, and yet the latter can never be omitted or suppressed. The objective part is the sum total of whatsoever at any given time we may be thinking of, the subjective part is the inner ' state' in which the thinking comes to pass. What we think of may be enormous, — the cosmic times and spaces, for example, — whereas the inner state may be the most fugitive and paltry activity of mind. Yet the cosmic objects, so far as the experience yields them, are but ideal pictures of something whose existence we do not inwardly possess but only point at outwardly, while the inner state is our very experience itself; its reality and that of our experience are one. A conscious field *plus* its object as felt or thought of *plus* an attitude towards the object *plus* the sense of a self to whom the attitude belongs — such a concrete bit of personal experience may be a small bit, but it is a solid bit as long as it lasts; not hollow, not a mere abstract element of experience, such as the ' object' is when taken all alone. It is a *full* fact, even though it be an insignificant fact; it is of the *kind* to which all realities whatsoever must belong; the motor currents of the world run through the like of it; it is on the line connecting real events with real events. That unsharable feeling which each one of us has of the pinch of his individual destiny as he privately feels it rolling out on fortune's wheel may be disparaged for its egotism, may be sneered at as unscientific, but it is the one thing that fills up the measure of our concrete actuality, and any would-be existent that should lack such a feeling, or its analogue, would be a piece of reality only half made up.[1]

If this be true, it is absurd for science to say that the egotistic elements of experience should be suppressed. The axis of reality runs solely through the egotistic

[1] Compare Lotze's doctrine that the only meaning we can attach to the notion of a thing as it is ' in itself ' is by conceiving it as it is *for* itself; i. e., as a piece of full experience with a private sense of ' pinch' or inner activity of some sort going with it.

places, — they are strung upon it like so many beads.
To describe the world with all the various feelings of
the individual pinch of destiny, all the various spiritual
attitudes, left out from the description — they being as
describable as anything else — would be something like
offering a printed bill of fare as the equivalent for a solid
meal. Religion makes no such blunder. The individual's religion may be egotistic, and those private realities
which it keeps in touch with may be narrow enough;
but at any rate it always remains infinitely less hollow
and abstract, as far as it goes, than a science which
prides itself on taking no account of anything private at
all.

A bill of fare with one real raisin on it instead of the
word 'raisin,' with one real egg instead of the word
'egg,' might be an inadequate meal, but it would at least
be a commencement of reality. The contention of the
survival-theory that we ought to stick to non-personal
elements exclusively seems like saying that we ought to
be satisfied forever with reading the naked bill of fare.
I think, therefore, that however particular questions connected with our individual destinies may be answered,
it is only by acknowledging them as genuine questions,
and living in the sphere of thought which they open
up, that we become profound. But to live thus is to
be religious; so I unhesitatingly repudiate the survival-
theory of religion, as being founded on an egregious
mistake. It does not follow, because our ancestors made
so many errors of fact and mixed them with their religion, that we should therefore leave off being religious
at all.[1] By being religious we establish ourselves in

[1] Even the errors of fact may possibly turn out not to be as wholesale as
the scientist assumes. We saw in Lecture IV how the religious conception
of the universe seems to many mind-curers 'verified' from day to day by

possession of ultimate reality at the only points at which reality is given us to guard. Our responsible concern is with our private destiny, after all.

You see now why I have been so individualistic throughout these lectures, and why I have seemed so bent on rehabilitating the element of feeling in religion and subordinating its intellectual part. Individuality is founded in feeling; and the recesses of feeling, the darker, blinder strata of character, are the only places in the world in which we catch real fact in the making, and

their experience of fact. ' Experience of fact ' is a field with so many things in it that the sectarian scientist, methodically declining, as he does, to recognize such ' facts' as mind-curers and others like them experience, otherwise than by such rude heads of classification as ' bosh,' ' rot,' ' folly,' certainly leaves out a mass of raw fact which, save for the industrious interest of the religious in the more personal aspects of reality, would never have succeeded in getting itself recorded at all. We know this to be true already in certain cases; it may, therefore, be true in others as well. Miraculous healings have always been part of the supernaturalist stock in trade, and have always been dismissed by the scientist as figments of the imagination. But the scientist's tardy education in the facts of hypnotism has recently given him an apperceiving mass for phenomena of this order, and he consequently now allows that the healings may exist, provided you expressly call them effects of ' suggestion.' Even the stigmata of the cross on Saint Francis's hands and feet may on these terms not be a fable. Similarly, the time-honored phenomenon of diabolical possession is on the point of being admitted by the scientist as a fact, now that he has the name of ' hystero-demonopathy ' by which to apperceive it. No one can foresee just how far this legitimation of occultist phenomena under newly found scientist titles may proceed — even 'prophecy,' even ' levitation,' might creep into the pale.

Thus the divorce between scientist facts and religious facts may not necessarily be as eternal as it at first sight seems, nor the personalism and romanticism of the world, as they appeared to primitive thinking, be matters so irrevocably outgrown. The final human opinion may, in short, in some manner now impossible to foresee, revert to the more personal style, just as any path of progress may follow a spiral rather than a straight line. If this were so, the rigorously impersonal view of science might one day appear as having been a temporarily useful eccentricity rather than the definitively triumphant position which the sectarian scientist at present so confidently announces it to be.

directly perceive how events happen, and how work is actually done.[1] Compared with this world of living individualized feelings, the world of generalized objects which the intellect contemplates is without solidity or life.   As in stereoscopic or kinetoscopic pictures seen outside the instrument, the third dimension, the movement, the vital element, are not there.   We get a beautiful picture of an express train supposed to be moving, but where in the picture, as I have heard a friend say, is the energy or the fifty miles an hour?[2]

[1] Hume's criticism has banished causation from the world of physical objects, and 'Science' is absolutely satisfied to define cause in terms of concomitant change — read Mach, Pearson, Ostwald.   The 'original' of the notion of causation is in our inner personal experience, and only there can causes in the old-fashioned sense be directly observed and described.

[2] When I read in a religious paper words like these : "Perhaps the best thing we can say of God is that he is *the Inevitable Inference*," I recognize the tendency to let religion evaporate in intellectual terms.   Would martyrs have sung in the flames for a mere inference, however inevitable it might be ?   Original religious men, like Saint Francis, Luther, Behmen, have usually been enemies of the intellect's pretension to meddle with religious things.   Yet the intellect, everywhere invasive, shows everywhere its shallowing effect.   See how the ancient spirit of Methodism evaporates under those wonderfully able rationalistic booklets (which every one should read) of a philosopher like Professor Bowne (The Christian Revelation, The Christian Life, The Atonement: Cincinnati and New York, 1898, 1899, 1900).   See the positively expulsive purpose of philosophy properly so called : —

"Religion," writes M. Vacherot (La Religion, Paris, 1869, pp. 313, 436, et passim), "answers to a transient state or condition, not to a permanent determination of human nature, being merely an expression of that stage of the human mind which is dominated by the imagination. . . . Christianity has but a single possible final heir to its estate, and that is scientific philosophy."

In a still more radical vein, Professor Ribot (Psychologie des Sentiments, p. 310) describes the evaporation of religion.   He sums it up in a single formula — the ever-growing predominance of the rational intellectual element, with the gradual fading out of the emotional element, this latter tending to enter into the group of purely intellectual sentiments. "Of religious sentiment properly so called, nothing survives at last save a vague respect for the unknowable x which is a last relic of the fear, and a certain attraction towards the ideal, which is a relic of the love, that characterized the earlier periods of religious growth.   To state this more

Let us agree, then, that Religion, occupying herself with personal destinies and keeping thus in contact with the only absolute realities which we know, must necessarily play an eternal part in human history. The next thing to decide is what she reveals about those destinies, or whether indeed she reveals anything distinct enough to be considered a general message to mankind. We have done as you see, with our preliminaries, and our final summing up can now begin.

I am well aware that after all the palpitating documents which I have quoted, and all the perspectives of emotion-inspiring institution and belief that my previous lectures have opened, the dry analysis to which I now advance may appear to many of you like an anticlimax, a tapering-off and flattening out of the subject, instead of a crescendo of interest and result. I said awhile ago that the religious attitude of Protestants appears poverty-stricken to the Catholic imagination. Still more poverty-stricken, I fear, may my final summing up of the subject appear at first to some of you. On which account I pray you now to bear this point in mind, that in the present part of it I am expressly trying to reduce religion to its lowest admissible terms, to that minimum, free from individualistic excrescences, which all religions contain as their nucleus, and on which it may be hoped that all religious persons may agree. That

simply, *religion tends to turn into religious philosophy.* — These are psychologically entirely different things, the one being a theoretic construction of ratiocination, whereas the other is the living work of a group of persons, or of a great inspired leader, calling into play the entire thinking and feeling organism of man."

I find the same failure to recognize that the stronghold of religion lies in individuality in attempts like those of Professor Baldwin (Mental Development, Social and Ethical Interpretations, ch. x.) and Mr. H. R. Marshall (Instinct and Reason, chaps. viii. to xii.) to make it a purely 'conservative social force.'

established, we should have a result which might be small, but would at least be solid ; and on it and round it the ruddier additional beliefs on which the different individuals make their venture might be grafted, and flourish as richly as you please. I shall add my own over-belief (which will be, I confess, of a somewhat pallid kind, as befits a critical philosopher), and you will, I hope, also add your over-beliefs, and we shall soon be in the varied world of concrete religious constructions once more. For the moment, let me dryly pursue the analytic part of the task.

Both thought and feeling are determinants of conduct, and the same conduct may be determined either by feeling or by thought. When we survey the whole field of religion, we find a great variety in the thoughts that have prevailed there ; but the feelings on the one hand and the conduct on the other are almost always the same, for Stoic, Christian, and Buddhist saints are practically indistinguishable in their lives. The theories which Religion generates, being thus variable, are secondary ; and if you wish to grasp her essence, you must look to the feelings and the conduct as being the more constant elements. It is between these two elements that the short circuit exists on which she carries on her principal business, while the ideas and symbols and other institutions form loop-lines which may be perfections and improvements, and may even some day all be united into one harmonious system, but which are not to be regarded as organs with an indispensable function, necessary at all times for religious life to go on. This seems to me the first conclusion which we are entitled to draw from the phenomena we have passed in review.

The next step is to characterize the feelings. To what psychological order do they belong?

The resultant outcome of them is in any case what Kant calls a 'sthenic' affection, an excitement of the cheerful, expansive, 'dynamogenic' order which, like any tonic, freshens our vital powers. In almost every lecture, but especially in the lectures on Conversion and on Saintliness, we have seen how this emotion overcomes temperamental melancholy and imparts endurance to the Subject, or a zest, or a meaning, or an enchantment and glory to the common objects of life.[1] The name of 'faith-state,' by which Professor Leuba designates it, is a good one.[2] It is a biological as well as a psychological condition, and Tolstoy is absolutely accurate in classing faith among the forces *by which men live*.[3] The total absence of it, anhedonia,[4] means collapse.

The faith-state may hold a very minimum of intellectual content. We saw examples of this in those sudden raptures of the divine presence, or in such mystical seizures as Dr. Bucke described.[5] It may be a mere vague enthusiasm, half spiritual, half vital, a courage, and a feeling that great and wondrous things are in the air.[6]

---

[1] Compare, for instance, pages 203, 219, 223, 226, 249 to 256, 275 to 278.

[2] American Journal of Psychology, vii. 345.

[3] Above, p. 184.

[4] Above, p. 145.

[5] Above, p. 400.

[6] Example : Henri Perreyve writes to Gratry : "I do not know how to deal with the happiness which you aroused in me this morning. It overwhelms me ; I want to *do* something, yet I can do nothing and am fit for nothing. . . . I would fain do *great things*." Again, after an inspiring interview, he writes : "I went homewards, intoxicated with joy, hope, and strength. I wanted to feed upon my happiness in solitude, far from all men. It was late ; but, unheeding that, I took a mountain path and went on like a madman, looking at the heavens, regardless of earth. Suddenly an instinct made me draw hastily back — I was on the very edge of a precipice, one step more and I must have fallen. I took fright and gave up

When, however, a positive intellectual content is associated with a faith-state, it gets invincibly stamped in upon belief,[1] and this explains the passionate loyalty of religious persons everywhere to the minutest details of their so widely differing creeds. Taking creeds and faith-state together, as forming ' religions,' and treating these as purely subjective phenomena, without regard to the question of their ' truth,' we are obliged, on account of their extraordinary influence upon action and endurance, to class them amongst the most important biological functions of mankind. Their stimulant and anæsthetic effect is so great that Professor Leuba, in a recent article,[2] goes so far as to say that so long as men can *use* their God, they care very little who he is, or even whether he is at all. " The truth of the matter can be put," says Leuba, " in this way : *God is not known, he is not understood ; he is used* — sometimes as meat-purveyor, sometimes as moral support, sometimes as friend, sometimes as an object of love. If he proves himself useful, the re-

my nocturnal promenade." A. GRATRY : Henri Perreyve, London, 1872, pp. 92, 89.

This primacy, in the faith-state, of vague expansive impulse over direction is well expressed in Walt Whitman's lines (Leaves of Grass, 1872, p. 190) : —

" O to confront night, storms, hunger, ridicule, accidents, rebuffs, as the trees and
　animals do. . . .
Dear Camerado ! I confess I have urged you onward with me, and still urge
　you, without the least idea what is our destination,
Or whether we shall be victorious, or utterly quell'd and defeated."

This readiness for great things, and this sense that the world by its importance, wonderfulness, etc., is apt for their production, would seem to be the undifferentiated germ of all the higher faiths. Trust in our own dreams of ambition, or in our country's expansive destinies, and faith in the providence of God, all have their source in that onrush of our sanguine impulses, and in that sense of the exceedingness of the possible over the real.

[1] Compare LEUBA : Loc. cit., pp. 346–349.

[2] The Contents of Religious Consciousness, in The Monist, xi. 536, July, 1901.

ligious consciousness asks for no more than that. Does God really exist? How does he exist? What is he? are so many irrelevant questions. Not God, but life, more life, a larger, richer, more satisfying life, is, in the last analysis, the end of religion. The love of life, at any and every level of development, is the religious impulse." [1]

At this purely subjective rating, therefore, Religion must be considered vindicated in a certain way from the attacks of her critics. It would seem that she cannot be a mere anachronism and survival, but must exert a permanent function, whether she be with or without intellectual content, and whether, if she have any, it be true or false.

We must next pass beyond the point of view of merely subjective utility, and make inquiry into the intellectual content itself.

First, is there, under all the discrepancies of the creeds, a common nucleus to which they bear their testimony unanimously?

And second, ought we to consider the testimony true?

I will take up the first question first, and answer it immediately in the affirmative. The warring gods and

---

[1] Loc. cit., pp. 571, 572, abridged. See, also, this writer's extraordinarily true criticism of the notion that religion primarily seeks to solve the intellectual mystery of the world. Compare what W. BENDER says (in his Wesen der Religion, Bonn, 1888, pp. 85, 38) : "Not the question about God, and not the inquiry into the origin and purpose of the world is religion, but the question about Man. All religious views of life are anthropocentric." "Religion is that activity of the human impulse towards self-preservation by means of which Man seeks to carry his essential vital purposes through against the adverse pressure of the world by raising himself freely towards the world's ordering and governing powers when the limits of his own strength are reached." The whole book is little more than a development of these words.

formulas of the various religions do indeed cancel each other, but there is a certain uniform deliverance in which religions all appear to meet.   It consists of two parts : —

1. An uneasiness ; and

2. Its solution.

1. The uneasiness, reduced to its simplest terms, is a sense that there is *something wrong about us* as we naturally stand.

2. The solution is a sense that *we are saved from the wrongness* by making proper connection with the higher powers.

In those more developed minds which alone we are studying, the wrongness takes a moral character, and the salvation takes a mystical tinge.   I think we shall keep well within the limits of what is common to all such minds if we formulate the essence of their religious experience in terms like these : —

The individual, so far as he suffers from his wrongness and criticises it, is to that extent consciously beyond it, and in at least possible touch with something higher, if anything higher exist.   Along with the wrong part there is thus a better part of him, even though it may be but a most helpless germ.   With which part he should identify his real being is by no means obvious at this stage ; but when stage 2 (the stage of solution or salvation) arrives,[1] the man identifies his real being with the germinal higher part of himself ; and does so in the following way.   *He becomes conscious that this higher part is conterminous and continuous with a MORE of the same quality, which is operative in the universe outside of him, and which he can keep in working touch with, and in a fashion get on board of and save himself when all his lower being has gone to pieces in the wreck.*

[1] Remember that for some men it arrives suddenly, for others gradually, whilst others again practically enjoy it all their life.

It seems to me that all the phenomena are accurately describable in these very simple general terms.[1] They allow for the divided self and the struggle; they involve the change of personal centre and the surrender of the lower self; they express the appearance of exteriority of the helping power and yet account for our sense of union with it;[2] and they fully justify our feelings of security and joy. There is probably no autobiographic document, among all those which I have quoted, to which the description will not well apply. One need only add such specific details as will adapt it to various theologies and various personal temperaments, and one will then have the various experiences reconstructed in their individual forms.

So far, however, as this analysis goes, the experiences are only psychological phenomena. They possess, it is true, enormous biological worth. Spiritual strength really increases in the subject when he has them, a new life opens for him, and they seem to him a place of conflux where the forces of two universes meet; and yet this may be nothing but his subjective way of feeling things, a mood of his own fancy, in spite of the effects produced. I now turn to my second question : What is the objective 'truth' of their content?[3]

The part of the content concerning which the question

[1] The practical difficulties are : 1, to 'realize the reality' of one's higher part ; 2, to identify one's self with it exclusively; and 3, to identify it with all the rest of ideal being.

[2] " When mystical activity is at its height, we find consciousness possessed by the sense of a being at once *excessive* and *identical* with the self : great enough to be God ; interior enough to be *me*. The 'objectivity' of it ought in that case to be called *excessivity*, rather, or exceedingness." RÉCÉJAC : Essai sur les fondements de la conscience mystique, 1897, p. 46.

[3] The word 'truth' is here taken to mean something additional to bare value for life, although the natural propensity of man is to believe that whatever has great value for life is thereby certified as true.

of truth most pertinently arises is that 'MORE of the same quality' with which our own higher self appears in the experience to come into harmonious working relation. Is such a 'more' merely our own notion, or does it really exist? If so, in what shape does it exist? Does it act, as well as exist? And in what form should we conceive of that 'union' with it of which religious geniuses are so convinced?

It is in answering these questions that the various theologies perform their theoretic work, and that their divergencies most come to light. They all agree that the 'more' really exists; though some of them hold it to exist in the shape of a personal god or gods, while others are satisfied to conceive it as a stream of ideal tendency embedded in the eternal structure of the world. They all agree, moreover, that it acts as well as exists, and that something really is effected for the better when you throw your life into its hands. It is when they treat of the experience of 'union' with it that their speculative differences appear most clearly. Over this point pantheism and theism, nature and second birth, works and grace and karma, immortality and reincarnation, rationalism and mysticism, carry on inveterate disputes.

At the end of my lecture on Philosophy [1] I held out the notion that an impartial science of religions might sift out from the midst of their discrepancies a common body of doctrine which she might also formulate in terms to which physical science need not object. This, I said, she might adopt as her own reconciling hypothesis, and recommend it for general belief. I also said that in my last lecture I should have to try my own hand at framing such an hypothesis.

The time has now come for this attempt. Who says

[1] Above, p. 455.

'hypothesis' renounces the ambition to be coercive in his arguments. The most I can do is, accordingly, to offer something that may fit the facts so easily that your scientific logic will find no plausible pretext for vetoing your impulse to welcome it as true.

The 'more,' as we called it, and the meaning of our 'union' with it, form the nucleus of our inquiry. Into what definite description can these words be translated, and for what definite facts do they stand? It would never do for us to place ourselves offhand at the position of a particular theology, the Christian theology, for example, and proceed immediately to define the 'more' as Jehovah, and the 'union' as his imputation to us of the righteousness of Christ. That would be unfair to other religions, and, from our present standpoint at least, would be an over-belief.

We must begin by using less particularized terms; and, since one of the duties of the science of religions is to keep religion in connection with the rest of science, we shall do well to seek first of all a way of describing the 'more,' which psychologists may also recognize as real. The *subconscious self* is nowadays a well-accredited psychological entity; and I believe that in it we have exactly the mediating term required. Apart from all religious considerations, there is actually and literally more life in our total soul than we are at any time aware of. The exploration of the transmarginal field has hardly yet been seriously undertaken, but what Mr. Myers said in 1892 in his essay on the Subliminal Consciousness [1] is

---

[1] Proceedings of the Society for Psychical Research, vol. vii. p. 305. For a full statement of Mr. Myers's views, I may refer to his posthumous work, 'Human Personality in the Light of Recent Research,' which is already announced by Messrs. Longmans, Green & Co. as being in press. Mr. Myers for the first time proposed as a general psychological problem the explora-

as true as when it was first written: " Each of us is in
reality an abiding psychical entity far more extensive
than he knows — an individuality which can never express
itself completely through any corporeal manifestation.
The Self manifests through the organism; but there is
always some part of the Self unmanifested; and always,
as it seems, some power of organic expression in abeyance or reserve." [1] Much of the content of this larger
background against which our conscious being stands out
in relief is insignificant. Imperfect memories, silly jin-
gles, inhibitive timidities, ' dissolutive' phenomena of various sorts, as Myers calls them, enter into it for a large
part. But in it many of the performances of genius
seem also to have their origin; and in our study of conversion, of mystical experiences, and of prayer, we have
seen how striking a part invasions from this region play
in the religious life.

Let me then propose, as an hypothesis, that whatever
it may be on its *farther* side, the ' more' with which
in religious experience we feel ourselves connected is on
its *hither* side the subconscious continuation of our conscious life. Starting thus with a recognized psychological fact as our basis, we seem to preserve a contact
with ' science' which the ordinary theologian lacks. At
the same time the theologian's contention that the religious man is moved by an external power is vindicated,
for it is one of the peculiarities of invasions from the

tion of the subliminal region of consciousness throughout its whole extent,
and made the first methodical steps in its topography by treating as a natural
series a mass of subliminal facts hitherto considered only as curious isolated
facts, and subjecting them to a systematized nomenclature. How important this exploration will prove, future work upon the path which Myers
has opened can alone show. Compare my paper: 'Frederic Myers's Services to Psychology,' in the said Proceedings, part xlii., May, 1901.

[1] Compare the inventory given above on pp. 483–4, and also what is said
of the subconscious self on pp. 233–236, 240–242.

subconscious region to take on objective appearances, and to suggest to the Subject an external control. In the religious life the control is felt as 'higher'; but since on our hypothesis it is primarily the higher faculties of our own hidden mind which are controlling, the sense of union with the power beyond us is a sense of something, not merely apparently, but literally true.

This doorway into the subject seems to me the best one for a science of religions, for it mediates between a number of different points of view. Yet it is only a doorway, and difficulties present themselves as soon as we step through it, and ask how far our transmarginal consciousness carries us if we follow it on its remoter side. Here the over-beliefs begin: here mysticism and the conversion-rapture and Vedantism and transcendental idealism bring in their monistic interpretations [1] and tell us that the finite self rejoins the absolute self, for it was always one with God and identical with the soul of the world.[2] Here the prophets of all the different religions

---

[1] Compare above, pp. 419 ff.

[2] One more expression of this belief, to increase the reader's familiarity with the notion of it : —

"If this room is full of darkness for thousands of years, and you come in and begin to weep and wail, 'Oh, the darkness,' will the darkness vanish? Bring the light in, strike a match, and light comes in a moment. So what good will it do you to think all your lives, 'Oh, I have done evil, I have made many mistakes'? It requires no ghost to tell us that. Bring in the light, and the evil goes in a moment. Strengthen the real nature, build up yourselves, the effulgent, the resplendent, the ever pure, call that up in every one whom you see. I wish that every one of us had come to such a state that even when we see the vilest of human beings we can see the God within, and instead of condemning, say, 'Rise, thou effulgent One, rise thou who art always pure, rise thou birthless and deathless, rise almighty, and manifest your nature.' . . . This is the highest prayer that the Advaita teaches. This is the one prayer : remembering our nature." . . . "Why does man go out to look for a God? . . . It is your own heart beating, and you did not know, you were mistaking it for something external. He, nearest of the near, my own self, the reality of my own life, my body and my come with their visions, voices, raptures, and other openings, supposed by each to authenticate his own peculiar faith.

Those of us who are not personally favored with such specific revelations must stand outside of them altogether and, for the present at least, decide that, since they corroborate incompatible theological doctrines, they neutralize one another and leave no fixed result. If we follow any one of them, or if we follow philosophical theory and embrace monistic pantheism on non-mystical grounds, we do so in the exercise of our individual freedom, and build out our religion in the way most congruous with our personal susceptibilities. Among these susceptibilities intellectual ones play a decisive part. Although the religious question is primarily a question of life, of living or not living in the higher union which opens itself to us as a gift, yet the spiritual excitement in which the gift appears a real one will often fail to be aroused in an individual until certain particular intellectual beliefs or ideas which, as we say, come home to him, are touched.[1] These ideas will thus be essential to

soul. — I am Thee and Thou art Me. That is your own nature. Assert it, manifest it. Not to become pure, you are pure already. You are not to be perfect, you are that already. Every good thought which you think or act upon is simply tearing the veil, as it were, and the purity, the Infinity, the God behind, manifests itself — the eternal Subject of everything, the eternal Witness in this universe, your own Self. Knowledge is, as it were, a lower step, a degradation. We are It already ; how to know It ? " Swami Vivekananda : Addresses, No. XII., Practical Vedanta, part iv. pp. 172, 174, London, 1897 ; and Lectures, The Real and the Apparent Man, p. 24, abridged.

[1] For instance, here is a case where a person exposed from her birth to Christian ideas had to wait till they came to her clad in spiritistic formulas before the saving experience set in : —

" For myself I can say that spiritualism has saved me. It was revealed to me at a critical moment of my life, and without it I don't know what I should have done. It has taught me to detach myself from worldly things and to place my hope in things to come. Through it I have learned to see in that individual's religion; — which is as much as to say that over-beliefs in various directions are absolutely indispensable, and that we should treat them with tenderness and tolerance so long as they are not intolerant themselves. As I have elsewhere written, the most interesting and valuable things about a man are usually his over-beliefs.

Disregarding the over-beliefs, and confining ourselves to what is common and generic, we have in *the fact that the conscious person is continuous with a wider self through which saving experiences come*,[1] a positive content of religious experience which, it seems to me, *is literally and objectively true as far as it goes*. If I now proceed to state my own hypothesis about the farther limits of this extension of our personality, I shall be offering my own over-belief — though I know it will appear a sorry under-belief to some of you — for which I can only bespeak the same indulgence which in a converse case I should accord to yours.

The further limits of our being plunge, it seems to me, into an altogether other dimension of existence from the sensible and merely 'understandable' world. Name it the mystical region, or the supernatural region, whichever you

all men, even in those most criminal, even in those from whom I have most suffered, undeveloped brothers to whom I owed assistance, love, and forgiveness. I have learned that I must lose my temper over nothing, despise no one, and pray for all. Most of all I have learned to pray ! And although I have still much to learn in this domain, prayer ever brings me more strength, consolation, and comfort. I feel more than ever that I have only made a few steps on the long road of progress ; but I look at its length without dismay, for I have confidence that the day will come when all my efforts shall be rewarded. So Spiritualism has a great place in my life, indeed it holds the first place there." Flournoy Collection.

[1] " The influence of the Holy Spirit, exquisitely called the Comforter, is a matter of actual experience, as solid a reality as that of electro-magnetism." W. C. BROWNELL, Scribner's Magazine, vol. xxx. p. 112.

choose. So far as our ideal impulses originate in this region (and most of them do originate in it, for we find them possessing us in a way for which we cannot articulately account), we belong to it in a more intimate sense than that in which we belong to the visible world, for we belong in the most intimate sense wherever our ideals belong. Yet the unseen region in question is not merely ideal, for it produces effects in this world. When we commune with it, work is actually done upon our finite personality, for we are turned into new men, and consequences in the way of conduct follow in the natural world upon our regenerative change.[1] But that which produces effects within another reality must be termed a reality itself, so I feel as if we had no philosophic excuse for calling the unseen or mystical world unreal.

God is the natural appellation, for us Christians at least, for the supreme reality, so I will call this higher part of the universe by the name of God.[2] We and God

[1] That the transaction of opening ourselves, otherwise called prayer, is a perfectly definite one for certain persons, appears abundantly in the preceding lectures. I append another concrete example to reinforce the impression on the reader's mind : —

"Man can learn to transcend these limitations [of finite thought] and draw power and wisdom at will. . . . The divine presence is known through experience. The turning to a higher plane is a distinct act of consciousness. It is not a vague, twilight or semi-conscious experience. It is not an ecstasy ; it is not a trance. It is not super-consciousness in the Vedantic sense. It is not due to self-hypnotization. It is a perfectly calm, sane, sound, rational, common-sense shifting of consciousness from the phenomena of sense-perception to the phenomena of seership, from the thought of self to a distinctively higher realm. . . . For example, if the lower self be nervous, anxious, tense, one can in a few moments compel it to be calm. This is not done by a word simply. Again I say, it is not hypnotism. It is by the exercise of power. One feels the spirit of peace as definitely as heat is perceived on a hot summer day. The power can be as surely used as the sun's rays can be focused and made to do work, to set fire to wood." The Higher Law, vol. iv. pp. 4, 6, Boston, August, 1901.

[2] Transcendentalists are fond of the term 'Over-soul,' but as a rule they

have business with each other; and in opening ourselves
to his influence our deepest destiny is fulfilled. The universe, at those parts of it which our personal being constitutes, takes a turn genuinely for the worse or for the
better in proportion as each one of us fulfills or evades
God's demands. As far as this goes I probably have you
with me, for I only translate into schematic language
what I may call the instinctive belief of mankind: God
is real since he produces real effects.

The real effects in question, so far as I have as yet admitted them, are exerted on the personal centres of energy
of the various subjects, but the spontaneous faith of most
of the subjects is that they embrace a wider sphere than
this. Most religious men believe (or 'know,' if they be
mystical) that not only they themselves, but the whole
universe of beings to whom the God is present, are secure
in his parental hands. There is a sense, a dimension,
they are sure, in which we are *all* saved, in spite of the
gates of hell and all adverse terrestrial appearances.
God's existence is the guarantee of an ideal order that
shall be permanently preserved. This world may indeed,
as science assures us, some day burn up or freeze; but
if it is part of his order, the old ideals are sure to be
brought elsewhere to fruition, so that where God is,
tragedy is only provisional and partial, and shipwreck
and dissolution are not the absolutely final things. Only
when this farther step of faith concerning God is taken,
and remote objective consequences are predicted, does
religion, as it seems to me, get wholly free from the first
immediate subjective experience, and bring a *real hypothesis* into play. A good hypothesis in science must have

use it in an intellectualist sense, as meaning only a medium of communion.
'God' is a causal agent as well as a medium of communion, and that is the
aspect which I wish to emphasize.

other properties than those of the phenomenon it is immediately invoked to explain, otherwise it is not prolific enough. God, meaning only what enters into the religious man's experience of union, falls short of being an hypothesis of this more useful order. He needs to enter into wider cosmic relations in order to justify the subject's absolute confidence and peace.

That the God with whom, starting from the hither side of our own extra-marginal self, we come at its remoter margin into commerce should be the absolute world-ruler, is of course a very considerable over-belief. Over-belief as it is, though, it is an article of almost every one's religion. Most of us pretend in some way to prop it upon our philosophy, but the philosophy itself is really propped upon this faith. What is this but to say that Religion, in her fullest exercise of function, is not a mere illumination of facts already elsewhere given, not a mere passion, like love, which views things in a rosier light. It is indeed that, as we have seen abundantly. But it is something more, namely, a postulator of new *facts* as well. The world interpreted religiously is not the materialistic world over again, with an altered expression; it must have, over and above the altered expression, *a natural constitution* different at some point from that which a materialistic world would have. It must be such that different events can be expected in it, different conduct must be required.

This thoroughly ' pragmatic ' view of religion has usually been taken as a matter of course by common men. They have interpolated divine miracles into the field of nature, they have built a heaven out beyond the grave. It is only transcendentalist metaphysicians who think that, without adding any concrete details to Nature, or subtracting any, but by simply calling it the expression of absolute spirit, you make it more divine just as it stands.

I believe the pragmatic way of taking religion to be the deeper way. It gives it body as well as soul, it makes it claim, as everything real must claim, some characteristic realm of fact as its very own. What the more characteristically divine facts are, apart from the actual inflow of energy in the faith-state and the prayer-state, I know not. But the over-belief on which I am ready to make my personal venture is that they exist. The whole drift of my education goes to persuade me that the world of our present consciousness is only one out of many worlds of consciousness that exist, and that those other worlds must contain experiences which have a meaning for our life also; and that although in the main their experiences and those of this world keep discrete, yet the two become continuous at certain points, and higher energies filter in. By being faithful in my poor measure to this over-belief, I seem to myself to keep more sane and true. I *can*, of course, put myself into the sectarian scientist's attitude, and imagine vividly that the world of sensations and of scientific laws and objects may be all. But whenever I do this, I hear that inward monitor of which W. K. Clifford once wrote, whispering the word 'bosh!' Humbug is humbug, even though it bear the scientific name, and the total expression of human experience, as I view it objectively, invincibly urges me beyond the narrow 'scientific' bounds. Assuredly, the real world is of a different temperament, — more intricately built than physical science allows. So my objective and my subjective conscience both hold me to the over-belief which I express. Who knows whether the faithfulness of individuals here below to their own poor over-beliefs may not actually help God in turn to be more effectively faithful to his own greater tasks?

POSTSCRIPT

IN writing my concluding lecture I had to aim so much at simplification that I fear that my general philosophic position received so scant a statement as hardly to be intelligible to some of my readers. I therefore add this epilogue, which must also be so brief as possibly to remedy but little the defect. In a later work I may be enabled to state my position more amply and consequently more clearly.

Originality cannot be expected in a field like this, where all the attitudes and tempers that are possible have been exhibited in literature long ago, and where any new writer can immediately be classed under a familiar head. If one should make a division of all thinkers into naturalists and supernaturalists, I should undoubtedly have to go, along with most philosophers, into the supernaturalist branch. But there is a crasser and a more refined supernaturalism, and it is to the refined division that most philosophers at the present day belong. If not regular transcendental idealists, they at least obey the Kantian direction enough to bar out ideal entities from interfering causally in the course of phenomenal events. Refined supernaturalism is universalistic supernaturalism; for the 'crasser' variety 'piecemeal' supernaturalism would perhaps be the better name. It went with that older theology which to-day is supposed to reign only among uneducated people, or to be found among the few belated professors of the dualisms which Kant is thought to have displaced. It admits miracles and providential leadings, and finds no intellectual difficulty in mixing the ideal and the real worlds together by interpolating influences from the ideal region among the forces that causally determine the real world's details. In this the refined supernaturalists think that it muddles disparate dimensions of existence. For them the world of the ideal has no efficient causality, and never bursts into the world of phenomena at particular points. The ideal world, for them, is not a world of facts, but only of the meaning of facts; it is a point of view for judging facts. It appertains to a different '-ology,' and inhabits a different dimension of being altogether from that in which existential propositions obtain. It cannot get down upon the flat level of experience and interpolate itself piecemeal between distinct portions of nature, as those who believe, for example, in divine aid coming in response to prayer, are bound to think it must.

Notwithstanding my own inability to accept either popular Christianity or scholastic theism, I suppose that my belief that in communion with the Ideal new force comes into the world, and new departures are made here below, subjects me to being classed among the supernaturalists of the piecemeal or crasser type. Universalistic supernaturalism surrenders, it seems to me, too easily to naturalism. It takes the facts of physical science at their face-value, and leaves the laws of life just as naturalism finds them, with no hope of remedy, in case their fruits are bad. It confines itself to sentiments about life as a whole, sentiments which may be admiring and adoring, but which need not be so, as the existence of systematic pessimism proves. In this universalistic way of taking the ideal world, the essence of practical religion seems to me to evaporate. Both instinctively and for logical reasons, I find it hard to believe that principles can exist which make no difference in facts.[1] But all facts are particular facts, and the whole interest of the question of God's existence seems to me to lie in the consequences for particulars which that existence may be expected to entail. That no concrete particular of experience should alter its complexion in consequence of a God being there seems to me an incredible proposition, and yet it is the thesis to which (implicitly at any rate) refined supernaturalism seems to cling. It is only with experience *en bloc*, it says, that the Absolute maintains relations. It condescends to no transactions of detail.

I am ignorant of Buddhism and speak under correction, and merely in order the better to describe my general point of view; but as I apprehend the Buddhistic doctrine of Karma, I agree in principle with that. All supernaturalists admit that facts are under the judgment of higher law ; but for Buddhism as I interpret it, and for religion generally so far as it remains unweakened by transcendentalistic metaphysics, the word 'judgment' here means no such bare academic verdict or platonic appreciation as it means in Vedantic or modern absolutist systems ; it carries, on the contrary, *execution* with it, is *in*

---

[1] Transcendental idealism, of course, insists that its ideal world makes *this* difference, that facts *exist*. We owe it to the Absolute that we have a world of fact at all. 'A world' of fact !— that exactly is the trouble. An entire world is the smallest unit with which the Absolute can work, whereas to our finite minds work for the better ought to be done within this world, setting in at single points. Our difficulties and our ideals are all piecemeal affairs, but the Absolute can do no piecework for us ; so that all the interests which our poor souls compass raise their heads too late. We should have spoken earlier, prayed for another world absolutely, before this world was born. It is strange, I have heard a friend say, to see this blind corner into which Christian thought has worked itself at last, with its God who can raise no particular weight whatever, who can help us with no private burden, and who is on the side of our enemies as much as he is on our own. Odd evolution from the God of David's psalms !

rebus as well as *post rem,* and operates 'causally' as partial factor in the total fact. The universe becomes a gnosticism[1] pure and simple on any other terms. But this view that judgment and execution go together is that of the crasser supernaturalist way of thinking, so the present volume must on the whole be classed with the other expressions of that creed.

I state the matter thus bluntly, because the current of thought in academic circles runs against me, and I feel like a man who must set his back against an open door quickly if he does not wish to see it closed and locked. In spite of its being so shocking to the reigning intellectual tastes, I believe that a candid consideration of piecemeal supernaturalism and a complete discussion of all its metaphysical bearings will show it to be the hypothesis by which the largest number of legitimate requirements are met. That of course would be a program for other books than this; what I now say sufficiently indicates to the philosophic reader the place where I belong.

If asked just where the differences in fact which are due to God's existence come in, I should have to say that in general I have no hypothesis to offer beyond what the phenomenon of 'prayerful communion,' especially when certain kinds of incursion from the subconscious region take part in it, immediately suggests. The appearance is that in this phenomenon something ideal, which in one sense is part of ourselves and in another sense is not ourselves, actually exerts an influence, raises our centre of personal energy, and produces regenerative effects unattainable in other ways. If, then, there be a wider world of being than that of our every-day consciousness, if in it there be forces whose effects on us are intermittent, if

[1] See my Will to Believe and other Essays in Popular Philosophy, 1897, p. 165.

one facilitating condition of the effects be the openness of the 'subliminal' door, we have the elements of a theory to which the phenomena of religious life lend plausibility. I am so impressed by the importance of these phenomena that I adopt the hypothesis which they so naturally suggest. At these places at least, I say, it would seem as though transmundane energies, God, if you will, produced immediate effects within the natural world to which the rest of our experience belongs.

The difference in natural 'fact' which most of us would assign as the first difference which the existence of a God ought to make would, I imagine, be personal immortality. Religion, in fact, for the great majority of our own race *means* immortality, and nothing else. God is the producer of immortality; and whoever has doubts of immortality is written down as an atheist without farther trial. I have said nothing in my lectures about immortality or the belief therein, for to me it seems a secondary point. If our ideals are only cared for in 'eternity,' I do not see why we might not be willing to resign their care to other hands than ours. Yet I sympathize with the urgent impulse to be present ourselves, and in the conflict of impulses, both of them so vague yet both of them noble, I know not how to decide. It seems to me that it is eminently a case for facts to testify. Facts, I think, are yet lacking to prove 'spirit-return,' though I have the highest respect for the patient labors of Messrs. Myers, Hodgson, and Hyslop, and am somewhat impressed by their favorable conclusions. I consequently leave the matter open, with this brief word to save the reader from a possible perplexity as to why immortality got no mention in the body of this book.

The ideal power with which we feel ourselves in connection, the 'God' of ordinary men, is, both by ordinary men and by philosophers, endowed with certain of those metaphysical attributes which in the lecture on philosophy I treated with such disrespect. He is assumed as a matter of course to be 'one and only' and to be 'infinite'; and the notion of many finite gods is one which hardly any one thinks it worth while to consider, and still less to uphold. Nevertheless, in the interests of intellectual clearness, I feel bound to say that religious experience, as we have studied it, cannot be cited as unequivocally supporting the infinitist belief. The only thing that it unequivocally testifies to is that we can experience union with *something* larger than ourselves and in that union find our greatest peace. Philosophy, with its passion for unity, and mysticism with its mono-ideistic bent, both 'pass to the limit' and identify the something with a unique God who is the all-inclusive soul of the world. Popular opinion, respectful to their authority, follows the example which they set.

Meanwhile the practical needs and experiences of religion seem to me sufficiently met by the belief that beyond each man and in a fashion continuous with him there exists a larger power which is friendly to him and to his ideals. All that the facts require is that the power should be both other and larger than our conscious selves. Anything larger will do, if only it be large enough to trust for the next step. It need not be infinite, it need not be solitary. It might conceivably even be only a larger and more godlike self, of which the present self would then be but the mutilated expression, and the universe might conceivably be a collection of such selves, of different degrees of inclusiveness, with no absolute unity realized in it at all.[1] Thus would a sort of

---

[1] Such a notion is suggested in my Ingersoll Lecture On Human Immortality, Boston and London, 1899.

polytheism return upon us—a polytheism which I do not on this occasion defend, for my only aim at present is to keep the testimony of religious experience clearly within its proper bounds. [Compare p. 132 above.]

Upholders of the monistic view will say to such a polytheism (which, by the way, has always been the real religion of common people, and is so still to-day) that unless there be one all-inclusive God, our guarantee of security is left imperfect. In the Absolute, and in the Absolute only, *all* is saved. If there be different gods, each caring for his part, some portion of some of us might not be covered with divine protection, and our religious consolation would thus fail to be complete. It goes back to what was said on pages 131–133, about the possibility of there being portions of the universe that may irretrievably be lost. Common sense is less sweeping in its demands than philosophy or mysticism have been wont to be, and can suffer the notion of this world being partly saved and partly lost. The ordinary moralistic state of mind makes the salvation of the world conditional upon the success with which each unit does its part. Partial and conditional salvation is in fact a most familiar notion when taken in the abstract, the only difficulty being to determine the details. Some men are even disinterested enough to be willing to be in the unsaved remnant as far as their persons go, if only they can be persuaded that their cause will prevail — all of us are willing, whenever our activity-excitement rises sufficiently high. I think, in fact, that a final philosophy of religion will have to consider the pluralistic hypothesis more seriously than it has hitherto been willing to consider it. For practical life at any rate, the *chance* of salvation is enough. No fact in human nature is more characteristic than its willingness to live on a chance. The existence of the chance makes the difference, as Edmund Gurney says, between a life of which the keynote is resignation and a life of which the keynote is hope.[1] But all these statements are unsatisfactory from their brevity, and I can only say that I hope to return to the same questions in another book.

[1] Tertium Quid, 1887, p. 99.   See also pp. 148, 149.

BIBLIOGRAPHICAL NOTES

James' bibliographical footnotes have been left intact in the foregoing text. A number of the most important books he refers to, while long out of print in the editions he refers to, have been recently reprinted. The author's lifelong interest in psychical research has been the aspect of his work least studied even by his admirers. Among the books listed below are (1) books containing material from the *Proceedings* of the Society for Psychical Research referred to in the foregoing text and (2) key works in psychical research, published by University Books, Inc.

PODMORE, Frank. Mediums of the 19th Century; Introduction by Eric J. Dingwall. index. xxvii + 720 pages, 2 volumes, bound in buckram and slipcased. 63-10384. $20.00   PARAPSYCH

PRINCE, Walter Franklin. Noted Witnesses for Psychic Occurrences; Introduction by Gardner Murphy. index. x-336 pp. 63-10387. $10.00   PARAPSYCH

FOX, Oliver. Astral Projection: A Record of Out-of-the-Body Experiences. xiii—160 pages. 62-19195. $5.00   OCCULT

SIDGWICK, Eleanor Mildred. Phantasms of the Living: Cases of Telepathy Printed in the Journal of the Society for Psychical Research During Thirty-Five Years; and Phantasms of the Living, by Edmund Gurnye, Frederic W. H. Myers & Frank Podmore; abridged & ed. by Eleanor Mildred Sidgwick. xxxvi, 462 + 520 pp. 62-17319. $15.00   PSYCH

MYERS, F. W. H. Human Personality and its Survival of Bodily Death; ed. by Susy Smith; fwd. by Aldous Huxley. index. 416 pp. 61-9319. $10.00
                                                    PARAPSYCH

OSBORN, Arthur W. The Future Is Now: the Significance of Precognition; intro. by Eileen J. Garrett. index. 254 pp. 61-9321. $6.00   PARAPSYCH

TYRRELL, G. N. M. Science and Psychical Phenomena, and Apparitions; 2 vols. bound as one; fwd. by Laura A. Dale; pref. by H. H. Price. appendixes. indexes. xxi + 379 pp., 127 pp. 61-8701. $7.50   PARAPSYCH

William James on Psychical Research. Compiled and Edited by Gardner Murphy and Robert O. Ballou. viii + 339 pp. 60-11807. $6.00. The Viking Press, distributed by Mystic Arts Book Society, New Hyde Park, N.Y.   PSYCH

BUCKE, Richard Maurice Bucke. Cosmic Consciousness, a Study in the Evolution of the Human Mind. xvii + 326 pp. 61-11100. $5.95   PSYCH

APPENDICES

ABBREVIATIONS

CER: *Collected Essays and Reviews,* New York, 1920

HI: *Human Immortality: Two Supposed Objections to the Doctrine,* Boston, 1898

LWJ: *William James, Letters of,* edited by his son Henry James, Boston, 1920

MS: *Memories and Studies,* New York, 1911

PP: *Principles of Psychology,* New York, 1890

PR: *Pragmatism: A New Name for Some Old Ways of Thinking,* New York, 1907

PU: *A Pluralistic Universe: Hibbert Lectures on the Present Situation in Philosophy,* New York, 1909

PY: R. B. Perry. *The Thought and Character of William Jones,* Boston, 1935

SPP: *Some Problems of Philosophy: A Beginning of an Introduction to Philosophy,* New York, 1911

WB: *The Will to Believe, and Other Essays in Popular Philosophy,* New York, 1897

APPENDIX I

THE PRATT QUESTIONNAIRE*

It is being realized as never before that religion, as one of the most important things in the life both of the community and of the individual, deserves close and extended study. Such study can be of value only if based upon the personal experiences of many individuals. If you are in sympathy with such study and are willing to assist in it, will you kindly write out the answers to the following questions and return them with this questionnaire, as soon as you conveniently can, to James B. Pratt, 20 Shepard Street, Cambridge, Mass.

Please answer the questions at length and in detail. Do not give philosophical generalizations, but your own personal experience.

1. What does religion mean to you personally? Is it
   (1) A belief that something exists? *Yes.*
   (2) An emotional experience? *Not powerfully so, yet a social reality.*
   (3) A general attitude of the will toward God or toward righteousness? *It involves these.*
   (4) Or something else?

If it has several elements, which is for you the most important? *The social appeal for corroboration, consolation, etc., when things are going wrong with my causes (my truth denied), etc.*

2. What do you mean by God? *A combination of Ideality and (final) efficacity.*
   (1) Is He a person — if so, what do you mean by His being a person? *He must be cognizant and responsive in some way.*
   (2) Or is He only a Force? *He must do.*
   (3) Or is God an attitude of the Universe toward you? *Yes, but more conscious. "God," to me, is not the only spiritual reality to believe in. Religion means primarily a universe of spiritual relations surrounding the earthly practical ones, not merely relations of "value," but agencies and their activities. I suppose that the chief premise for my hospitality towards the religious testimony of others is*

*From LWJ II:212-215. James's answers, printed in italics, were written sometime in the autumn of 1904.

*my conviction that "normal" or "sane" consciousness is
so small a part of actual experience. What e'er be true, it
is not true exclusively, as philistine scientific opinion assumes. The other kinds of consciousness bear witness to a
much wider universe of experiences, from which our belief selects and emphasizes such parts as best satisfy
our needs.*

How do you apprehend His relation to mankind and
to you personally?

                                             Uncertain

If your position on any of these matters is uncertain,
please state the fact.

  3. Why do you believe in God? Is it
     (1) From some argument? *Emphatically, no.*
Or (2) Because you have experienced His presence? *No, but
      rather because I need it so that it "must" be true.*
Or (3) From authority, such as that of the Bible or of some pro-
      phetic person? *Only the whole tradition of religious
      people, to which something in me makes admiring re-
      sponse.*
Or (4) From any other reason? *Only for the social reasons.*
      If from several of these reasons, please indicate carefully
      the order of their importance.
  4. Or do you not so much *believe* in God as want to *use* Him?
     I can't use him very definitely, yet I believe. Do you accept
     Him not so much as a real existent Being, but rather as an
     ideal to live by? *More as a more powerful ally of my own
     ideals.* If you should become thoroughly convinced that there
     was no God, would it make any great difference in your life —
     either happiness, morality, or in other respects? *Hard to say. It
     would surely make some difference.*
  5. Is God very real to you, as real as an earthly friend, though
     different? *Dimly [real]; not [as an earthly friend].*

Do you feel that you have experienced His presence? If so, please
describe what you mean by such an experience. *Never.*
How vague or how distinct is it? How does it affect you mentally
and physically?
If you have had no such experience, do you accept the testimony
of others who claim to have felt God's presence directly? Please
answer this question with special care and in as great detail as
possible. *Yes! The whole line of testimony on this point is so strong
that I am unable to pooh-pooh it away. No doubt there is a germ
in me of something similar that makes response.*

6. Do you pray, and if so, why? That is, is it purely from habit, and social custom, or do you really believe that God hears your prayers? *I can't possibly pray — I feel foolish and artificial.*
Is prayer with you one-sided or two-sided — i.e., do you sometimes feel that in prayer you receive something — such as strength or the divine spirit — from God? Is it a real communion?

7. What do you mean by "spirituality"? *Susceptibility to ideals, but with a certain freedom to indulge in imagination about them. A certain amount of "otherworldly" fancy. Otherwise you have mere morality, or "taste."*
Describe a typical spiritual person. *Phillips Brooks.*

8. Do you believe in personal immortality? *Never keenly; but more strongly as I grow older.* If so, why? *Because I am just getting fit to live.*

9. Do you accept the Bible as *authority* in religious matters? Are your religious faith and your religious life based on it? If so, how would your belief in God and your life toward Him and your fellow men be affected by loss of faith in the *authority of* the Bible? *No. No. No. It is so human a book that I don't see how belief in its divine authorship can survive the reading of it.*

10. What do you mean by a "religious experience"? *Any moment of life that brings the reality of spiritual things more "home" to one.*

APPENDIX II

LETTERS CONCERNING THE VARIETIES

1*

To Mrs. James:

Keene Valley, July 9, 1898

... I have had an eventful 24 hours, and my hands are so stiff after it that my fingers can hardly hold the pen. I left, as I informed you by post-card, the Lodge at seven, and five hours of walking brought us to the top of Marcy — I carrying 18 lbs. of weight in my pack.

My guide had to serve for the party, and quite unexpectedly to me the night turned out one of the most memorable of all my memorable experiences. I was in a wakeful mood before starting, having been awake since three, and I may have slept a little dur-

---

*From LWJ II:75-77, excerpt with inessentials of camping incidents eliminated. It was the strain of this two days' climb that caused a valvular lesion from which James never recovered. He did not give his condition the attention is required and strained himself again. (Editor's note.)

ing this night; but I was not aware of sleeping at all. My companions, except Waldo Adler, were all motionless. The guide had got a magnificent provision of firewood, the sky swept itself clear of every trace of cloud or vapor, the wind entirely ceased, so that the fire-smoke rose straight up to heaven. The temperature was perfect either inside or outside the cabin, the moon rose and hung above the scene before midnight, leaving only a few of the larger stars visible, and I got into a state of spiritual alertness of the most vital description. The influences of Nature, the wholesomeness of the people round me, especially the good Pauline, the thought of you and the children, dear Harry on the wave, the problem of the Edinburgh lectures, all fermented within me till it became a regular Walpurgis Nacht. I spent a good deal of it in the woods, where the streaming moonlight lit up things in a magical checkered play, and it seemed as if the Gods of all the nature-mythologies were holding an indescribable meeting in my breast with the moral Gods of the inner life. The two kinds of Gods have nothing in common — the Edinburgh lectures made quite a hitch ahead. The intense significance of some sort, of the whole scene, if one could only *tell* the significance; the intense inhuman remoteness of its inner life, and yet the intense *appeal* of it; its everlasting freshness and its immemorial antiquity and decay; its utter Americanism, and every sort of patriotic suggestiveness, and you, and my relation to you part and parcel of it all, and beaten up with it, so that memory and sensation all whirled inexplicably together; it was indeed worth coming for, and worth repeating year by year, if repetition could only procure what in its nature I suppose must be all unplanned for and unexpected. It was one of the happiest lonesome nights of my existence, and I understand now what a poet is. He is a person who can feel the immense complexity of influences that I felt, and make some partial tracks in them for verbal statement. In point of fact, I can't find a single word for all that significance, and don't know what it was significant of, so there it remains, a mere boulder of *impression*. Doubtless in more ways than one, though, things in the Edinburgh lectures will be traceable to it.

2*

Lamb House, Dec. 23, 1899
I have resigned my Gifford lectureship, but they will undoubtedly grant me indefinite postponement. I have also asked

*From LWJ II:111-112.

for a second year of absence from Harvard, which of course will be accorded. If I improve, I may be able to give my first Gifford course next year. I can do no work whatsoever at present, but through the summer and half through the fall was able to do a good deal of reading in religious biography. Since July, in fact, my only companions have been saints, most excellent, though sometimes rather lop-sided company. In a general manner I can see my way to a perfectly bully pair of volumes, the first an objective study of the "Varieties of Religious Experience," the second, my own last will and testament, setting forth the philosophy best adapted to normal religious needs. I hope I may be spared to get the thing down on paper. So far my progress has been rather downhill, but the last couple of days have shown a change which possibly may be the beginning of better things. I mean to take great care of myself from this time on.

3*

Castebelle, April 13, 1900

Six months ago, I shouldn't have thought it possible that a life deliberately founded on pottering about and dawdling through the day would be endurable or even possible. I have attained such skill that I doubt if my days ever at any time seemed to glide by so fast. But it corrodes one's soul nevertheless. I scribble a little in bed every morning, and have reached page 48 of my third Gifford lecture — though Lecture II, alas! must be rewritten entirely. The conditions don't conduce to an energetic grip of the subject, and I am afraid that what I write is pretty slack and not what it would be if my vital tone were different. The problem I have set myself is a hard one: *first,* to defend (against all the prejudices of my "class") "Experience" against "Philosophy" as being the real backbone of the world's religious life — I mean prayer, guidance, and all that sort of thing immediately and privately felt, as against high and noble general views of our destiny and the world's meaning; and *second,* to make the hearer or reader believe what I myself invincibly do believe, that although all the special manifestations of religion may have been absurd (I mean its creeds and theories), yet the life of it as a whole is mankind's most important function. A task well-nigh impossible, I fear, and in which I shall fail; but to attempt it is *my* religious act.

We got a visit the other day from (a Scottish couple here who have heard that I am to give the Gifford lectures); and two days

*From LWJ II:126-127.

ago went to afternoon tea with them at their hotel, next door. *She* enclosed a tract (by herself) in the invitation, and proved to be a (mass) of holy egotism and conceit based on professional invalidism and self-worship. I wish my sister Alice were there to "react" on her with a description! Her husband, apparently weak, and the slave of her. No talk but evangelical talk. It seemed assumed that a Gifford lecturer must be one of Moody's partners, and it gave me rather a foretaste of what the Edinburgh atmosphere may be like. Well, I shall enjoy sticking a knife into its gizzard — if atmospheres have gizzards? Blessed be Boston — probably the freest place on earth, that isn't merely heathen and sensual.

4*

To Henry W. Rankin:

Edinburgh, June 16, 1901

I have given nine of my lectures and am to give the tenth tomorrow. In these lectures the ground I am taking is this: The mother sea and fountainhead of all religions lie in the mystical experiences of the individual, taking the word mystical in a very wide sense. All theologies and all ecclesiasticisms are secondary growths superimposed; and the experiences make such flexible combinations with the intellectual prepossessions of their subjects, that one may almost say that they have no proper *intellectual* deliverance of their own, but belong to a region deeper, and more vital and practical, than that which the intellect inhabits. For this they are also indestructible by intellectual arguments and criticisms. I attach the mystical or religious consciousness to the possession of an extended subliminal self, with a thin partition through which messages make irruption. We are thus made convincingly aware of the presence of a sphere of life larger and more powerful than our usual consciousness, with which the latter is nevertheless continuous. The impressions and impulsions and emotions and excitements which we thence receive help us to live, they found invincible assurance of a world beyond the sense, they melt our hearts and communicate significance and value to everything and make us happy. They do this for the individual who has them, and other individuals follow him. Religion in this way is absolutely indestructible. Philosophy and theology give their conceptual interpretations of this experiential life. The farther margin of the subliminal field being unknown, it can be treated as by Transcendental idealism, as an Absolute mind with a part of which we coalesce, or by Christian theology, as a distinct deity acting on us. Something, not

*From LWJ II:149-150; one passage eliminated from excerpt.

our immediate self, does act on our life! So I seem doubtless to my audience to be blowing hot and cold, explaining away Christianity, yet defending the more general basis from which I say it proceeds. I fear that these brief words may be misleading, but let them go! When the book comes out, you will get a truer idea.

5*

Rye, N. Y., June 26, 1901

The audience was extraordinarily attentive and reactive — I never had an audience so keen to catch every point. I flatter myself that by blowing alternately hot and cold on their Christian prejudices I succeeded in baffling them completely till the final quarter-hour, when I satisfied their curiosity by showing more plainly my hand. Then, I think, I permanently dissatisfied both extremes, and pleased a mean numerically quite small. *Qui vivra verra.*

6*

Salisbury, Conn., August 24, 1904

Your third stricture, about Higher Powers, is also very important, and I am not at all sure that you may not be right. I have frankly to confess that my "Varieties" carried "theory" as far as I could then carry it, and that I can carry it no farther today. I can't see clearly over that edge. Yet I am sure that tracks have got to be made there — I think that the fixed point with me is the conviction that our "rational" consciousness touches but a portion of the real universe and that our life is fed by the "mystical" region as well. I have no mystical experience of my own, but just enough of the germ of mysticism in me to recognize the region from which their voice comes when I hear it.

I was much disappointed in Leuba's review of my book in the "International Journal of Ethics." . . . I confess that the way in which he stamps out all mysticism whatever, using the common pathological arguments, seemed to me unduly crude. I wrote him an expostulatory letter, which evidently made no impression at all, and which he possibly might send you if you had the curiosity to apply.

7*

DEAR LEUBA:

Cambridge, April 17, 1904

I have read your article with great interest, admiring its clear-

*From LWJ II:151.
*From LWJ II:210.
*From PY II:348-351, whole letter.

ness of statement, and rejoicing in the way in which you go to the heart of my contentions, straight and without floundering. Only of your characterization of my thesis as that of "spirit-intervention" do I complain.[1] No reader . . . could possibly guess that the only spirit that I contend for is "God." Unless he knows my book he will suppose that I am a "spiritist" out and out, which I am not. This is unfair.

I also find the same fault with this article that I have found with its predecessors. You hide your own religious cards, so that one does (not) know exactly how to reply to you. You may think there is no God, nothing but Nature, and that all these vague experiences are "poppy-cock" and nerves. Or you may think there is a God, but that the evidence for him must always be indirect — induction from sensations, or "philosophic" reasoning. Most readers, from your evident anti-"pathological" bias, would infer the former; and if that be your state of mind, reply to you is harder. If, however, you do concede the possibility of a God, and your final sentence is not merely diplomatic,[2] argument grows easier. For then, just as the foundation of "natural" knowledge is sensation, due to immediate non-rational influence of either body on body (or, if you are an idealist, of mental fact on mental fact), so there might be a similar direct influence from God, and our knowledge might be partly at least founded thereon. So far as the feelings of influence harmonized with the rational evidence, the hypothesis that God was the source of influence would be corroborated. Otherwise not. They are bound to harmonize in part, because the mystical and the rational spheres of life are not absolutely discontinuous. It is evident that our intellectual stock in trade plays a suggestive part in our mystical life, and that this suggestive part changes with the progress of our thoughts, so that Vedantic and Christian mysticism have slightly different forms.

If mystical states with all their differences have a common

---

[1] The original of this "expostulatory" letter is missing, and the following is made up of several fragmentary versions which have been found among the James papers. The passage to which James objects contains the statements that there are "spread throughout the book, with marvelous skill, the mysterious, imaginary shadows of spirit agents"; "the reader is almost unavoidably thrown into the temper of the materializing seance"; "ghosts pop out of the very places he has just shown you to be empty," etc. (*op. cit.*, 337).

[2] The concluding sentences are: "It may not be useless to add that the rejection of spirit-interference does in nowise commit one to Materialism. It leaves a clear field to Absolute, as well as to many forms of Pluralistic, Idealism."

nucleus, then this nucleus should be reckoned a coordinate factor with reason in the building of religious belief. The intellect is interpretative, and critical of its own interpretation, but there must have been a thesis to interpret, and that thesis seems to me to be the non-rational sense of a "higher" power. Religious men largely agree that this sense has been that of their "best" moments — best not only in passing, but when looked back upon. The notion of it has leaked into mankind from their authority, the rest of us being imitative, just as we are of scientific men's opinions. Now may not this mystical testimony that there is a God be true, even though his precise determinations, being so largely "suggestive" contributions of our rational factor, should widely differ? It seems to me that to throw out, as you do, the whole mystical life from a hearing, because of the facility with which it combines with discrepant interpretations, would be like throwing out the senses, for a similar reason, from recognition as factors of our "rational" knowledge. . . . It is evident that our data are complex, however we confine them, and that *sifting* is necessary, be the mystical door left open or kept closed. The truth is what will survive the sifting — sifting by successive generations, and "on the whole." Your critical method sifts out everything, lets nothing survive of mystical authority in God's favor, even though (let me suppose) you admit the possibility of a God.

I find it preposterous to suppose that if there be a feeling of unseen reality shared by large numbers of best men in their best moments, responded to by other men in their "deep" moments, good to live by, strength-giving — I find it preposterous, I say, to suppose that the goodness of that feeling for living purposes should be held to carry no objective significance, and especially preposterous if it combines harmoniously with our otherwise grounded philosophy of objective truth. *You* say we must consider it a purely subjective affection. But this opens the whole subject of what the word "truth" means, and I cannot enter that except to say that if inferences from "good for life" to "true" were on principle forbidden, not religion but the whole notion of truth would probably have to be the thing overhauled and revised.

My personal position is simple. I have no living sense of commerce with a God. I envy those who have, for I know that the addition of such a sense would help me greatly. The Divine, for my active life, is limited to impersonal and abstract concepts which, as ideals, interest and determine me, but do so but faintly in comparison with what a feeling of God might effect, if I had one. This, to be sure, is largely a matter of intensity, but a shade of intensity may make one's whole centre of moral energy shift. Now, although I am so devoid of *Gottesbewusstsein* in the directer and stronger sense, yet there is *something in me* which *makes response* when I hear utterances from that quarter made by others. I recognize the deeper voice. Something tells me: — *"thither lies truth"* — and I am sure it is not old theistic prejudices of infancy. Those in my case were Christian, but I have grown so out of Christianity that entanglement therewith on the part of a mystical utterance has to be abstracted from and overcome, before I can listen. Call this, if you like, my mystical *germ*. It is a very common germ. It creates the rank and file of believers. As it withstands in my case, so it will withstand in most cases, all purely atheistic criticism, but *interpretative* criticism (not of the mere "hysteria" and "nerves" order) it can energetically combine with.

Your criticism seems to amount to a pure *non possumus:* "Mystical deliverances must be infallible revelations in every particular, or nothing. Therefore they are *nothing,* for anyone else than their owner." Why may they not be *something,* although not everything? Your only consistent position, it strikes me, would be a dogmatic atheistic naturalism; and, without any mystical germ in us, that, I believe, is where we all should unhesitatingly be today. Once allow the mystical germ to influence our beliefs, and I believe that we are in my position. Of course the "subliminal" theory is an inessential hypothesis, and the question of pluralism or monism is equally inessential.

I am letting loose a deluge on you! Don't reply at length, or at all. *I* hate to reply to anybody, and will sympathize with your silence. But I had to restate my position more clearly.[3]

Yours truly, WM. JAMES

8*

To CHARLES A. STRONG:

Cambridge, Apr. 9, 1907

I am overwhelmed with duties, so I must be very brief *in re religionis*. Your warnings against my superstitious tendencies, for such I suppose they are — this is the second heavy one I remember — touch me, but not in the prophetic way, for they don't weaken my trust in the healthiness of my own attitude, which in part (I fancy) is less remote from your own than you suppose.

---

[3]The last two paragraphs are reprinted from LWJ, II:211-212.
*From LWJ II:269-270, excerpt whole. Although the reference of this letter is to PRAGMATISM, the defense James here makes of his religious views may, without distortion, be taken as a commentary on the VARIETIES. (Editor's note.)

For instance, my "God of things as they are," being part of a pluralistic system, is responsible for only such of them as he knows enough and has enough power to have accomplished. For the rest he is identical with your "ideal" God. The "omniscient" and "omnipotent" God of theology I regard as a disease of the philosophy-shop. But, having thrown away so much of the philosophy-shop, you may ask me why I don't throw away the whole? That would mean too strong a negative will-to-believe for me. It would mean a dogmatic disbelief in any extant consciousness higher than that of the "normal" human mind; and this in the teeth of the extraordinary vivacity of man's psychological commerce with something ideal that *feels as if* it were also actual (I have no such commerce — I wish I had, but I can't close my eyes to its vitality in others); and in the teeth of such analogies as Fechner uses to show that there may be other consciousness than man's. If other, then why not higher and bigger? Why *may* we not be in the universe as our dogs and cats are in our drawing-rooms and libraries? It's a will-to-believe on both sides: I am perfectly willing that others should disbelieve: why should you not be tolerantly interested in the spectacle of my belief? What harm does the little residuum or germ of actuality that I leave in God do? If ideal, why (except on epiphenomenist principles) may he not have got himself at least partly real by this time? I do not believe it to be healthy-minded to nurse the notion that ideals are self-sufficient and require no actualization to make us content. It is a quite unnecessarily heroic form of resignation and sour grapes. Ideals ought to aim at *transformation of reality* — no less! When you defer to what you suppose a certain authority in scientists as confirming these negations, I am surprised. Of all insufficient authorities as to the total nature of reality, give me the "scientists," from Münsterberg up, or down. Their interests are most incomplete and their professional conceit and bigotry immense. I know no narrower sect or club, in spite of their excellent authority in the lines of fact they have explored, and their splendid achievement there. Their only authority *at large* is for *method* — and the pragmatic method completes and enlarges them there. When you shall have read my whole set of lectures (now with the printer, to be out by June 1st) I doubt whether you will find any great harm in the God I patronize — the poor thing is so largely an ideal possibility. Meanwhile I take delight, or shall take delight, in any efforts you may make to negate all superhuman consciousness, for only by these counter-attempts can a finally satisfactory *modus vivendi* be reached.

APPENDIX III

CHRISTIANITY MONOTHEISM POLYTHEISM

1*

To Charles Renouvier:

Cambridge, Dec. 27, 1880

It is a strange thing, this resurrection of Hegel in England and here, after his burial in Germany. I think his philosophy will probably have an important influence on the development of our liberal form of Christianity. It gives a quasi-metaphysic backbone which this theology has always been in need of, but it is too fundamentally rotten and charlatanish to last long. As a reaction against materialistic evolutionism it has its use, only this evolutionism is fertile while Hegelism is absolutely sterile.

2*

To Thomas Davidson:

Cambridge, Jan. 8, 1882

Your letter just received, makes my heart glad. Next to a good theist, give me a good atheist; and that you seem to have become, whether in spite or in consequence of Rosmini, ignorance prevents me from deciding. To speak seriously, your blame is more agreeable to me than most all the praise I've got for that "address" ("Reflex Action and Theism"). The latter left me with my bad conscience increased; for the address was a curious composition on my part, the conclusions I believed in being forced by arguments which I cared little about, and which were used merely on account of their availability and *ad captandum* power. I wanted to show that physiology could send out an antimaterialistic blast as well as she had been supposed to emit materialistic ones. I wanted, too, to give popular form to my hobby of the ubiquitousness of emotional interests in the mind's operations. So I rather deliberately sacrificed accuracy to effectiveness in taking the reflex triad ready made from the physiologists, as if it were a truly *mental* analysis — and I reaped my reward in much applause. I

*From LWJ I:208.
*From PY 1:736-738.

have felt constrained to explain my errors to such correspondents as Hodgson and Renouvier. But you don't attack me for them, but for my conclusions, which I hold to.

It is a curious thing, this matter of God! I can sympathize perfectly with the most rabid hater of him and the idea of him, when I think of the use that has been made of him in history and philosophy as a *starting-point,* or premise for grounding deductions. But as an ideal to attain and make probable, I find myself less and less able to do without him. He need not be an *all*-including "subjective unity of the universe," as you suppose. In fact there is nothing I clasp hands with you so heartily in, as in defying the superstition of such a unity. It is only one possible hypothesis amid many and becomes (d--n my eyes, I must call my wife to write for me!) a pure superstition the moment it is treated dogmatically. All I mean is that there must be *some* subjective unity in the universe which has purposes commensurable with my own, and which is at the same time large enough to be, among all the powers that may be there, the strongest. I simply refuse to accept the notion of there being *no* purpose in the objective world. On the other hand, I cannot represent the existence of purpose except as based in a mind. The not-me, therefore, so far as it contains purpose, must spring from a mind; but not necessarily a *one and only* mind. In saying "God exists" all I imply is that my purposes are cared for by a mind so powerful as on the whole to control the drift of the universe. This is as much polytheism as monotheism. As a matter of fact it is neither, for it is hardly a speculative position at all, but a merely practical and emotional faith which I fancy even your Promethean *Gemüth* shares.

The only difficulties of theism are the moral difficulties and meannesses; and they have always seemed to me to flow from the gratuitous dogma of God being the all-exclusive reality. Once think possible a primordial pluralism of which he may be one member and which may have no single subjective synthesis, and piety forthwith ceases to be incompatible with manliness, and religious "faith" with intellectual rectitude. In short, the only theism I defend is that of simple unphilosophic mankind, to which numerical mysteries are added corruptions. If there be a God, how the devil can we know what difficulties he may have had to contend with? (This last remark is from my amanuensis spouse!) *Darauf kommt es an!* Possible difficulties! They save everything. But what are they but limitations to the all-inclusiveness of any single being?

3*

To Thomas Davidson:

Cambridge, Mar. 30, 1884

I had neither seen your article in the Unitarian Review nor heard of it, but ran for it as soon as I got your announcement of its existence. I know not what to think of it practically; though I confess the idea of engrafting the bloodless pallor of Boston Unitarianism on the Roman temperament strikes one at first sight as rather queer. Unitarianism seems to have a sort of moribund vitality here, because it is a branch of Protestantism and the tree keeps the branch sticking out. But whether it could be grafted on a Catholic trunk seems to me problematic. I confess I rather despair of any popular religion of a philosophic character; and I sometimes find myself wondering whether there can be any popular religion raised on the ruins of the old Christianity without the presence of that element which in the past has presided over the origin of all religions, namely, a belief in new *physical* facts and possibilities. Abstract considerations about the soul and the reality of a moral order will not do in a year what the glimpse into a world of new phenomenal possibilities enveloping those of the present life, afforded by an extension of our insight into the order of nature, would do in an instant. Are the much despised "Spiritualism" and the "Society for Psychical Research" to be the chosen instruments for a new era of faith? It would surely be strange if they were; but if they are not, I see no other agency that can do the work.

4*

To Henry W. Rankin:

Edinburgh, June 16, 1901

I believe myself to be (probably) permanently incapable of believing the Christian scheme of vicarious salvation, and wedded to a more continuously evolutionary mode of thought.

5*

To Henry W. Rankin:

Chocurua, June 10, 1903

Once more has my graphophobia placed me heavily in your debt. Your two long letters, though unanswered, were and are

*From LWJ I:236-237.
*From LWJ II:149.
*From LWJ II:196-197.

appreciated, in spite of the fact that, as you know, I do not (and I fear cannot) follow the gospel scheme as you do, and that the Bible itself, in both its testaments (omitting parts of John and the Apocalypse) seems to me, by its intense naturalness and humanness, the most fatal document that one can read against the orthodox theology, in so far as the latter claims the words of the Bible to be its basis. I myself believe that the orthodox theology contains elements that are permanently true, and that such writers as Emerson, by reason of their extraordinary healthy-mindedness and "once-born"-ness, are incapable of appreciating. I believe that they will have to be expressed in any ultimately valid religious philosophy; and I see in the temper of friendliness of such a man as you for such writings as Emerson's and mine *(magnus comp. parvo)* a foretaste of the day when the abstract essentials of belief will be the basis of communion more than the particular forms and concrete doctrines in which they articulate themselves. Your letter about Emerson seemed to me so admirably written that I was on the point of sending it back to you, thinking it might be well that you should publish it somewhere. I will still do so, if you ask me. I have myself been a little scandalized at the non-resisting manner in which orthodox sheets have celebrated his anniversary. An "Emerson number" of "Zion's Herald" strikes me as *tant soit peu* of an anomaly, and yet I am told that such a number appeared. Rereading him *in extenso,* almost *in toto,* lately, has made him loom larger than ever to me as a human being, but I feel the distinct lack in him of too little understanding of the morbid side of life.

6*

Not until those weeks at Oxford, and these days at Durham, have I had any sense of what a part the Church plays in the national life. So massive and all-pervasive, so authoritative, and on the whole so decent, in spite of the iniquity and farcicality of the whole thing. Never were incompatibles so happily yoked together. Talk about the genius of Romanism! It's nothing to the genius of Anglicanism, for Catholicism still contains some haggard elements that ally it with the Palestinian desert, whereas Anglicanism remains obese and round and comfortable and decent with this world's decencies, without an *acute* note in its whole life or history, in spite of the shrill Jewish words on which its ears are

*From LWJ II:305-306.

fed, and the nitroglycerine of the Gospels and Epistles which has been injected into its veins. Strange feat to have achieved! Yet the success is great — the whole Church-machine makes for all sorts of graces and decencies, and is not incompatible with a high type of Churchman; high, that is, on the side of moral and worldly virtue.

APPENDIX IV
THE HUMAN SOUL
1
AN ILLUSORY TERM*

The theory of the Soul is the theory of popular philosophy and of scholasticism, which is only popular philosophy made systematic. It declares that the principle of individuality within us must be *substantial,* for psychic phenomena are activities, and there can be no activity without a concrete agent. This substantial agent cannot be the brain but must be something *immaterial;* for its activity, thought, is both immaterial and takes cognizance of immaterial things, and of material things in general and intelligible, as well as in particular and sensible ways — all which powers are incompatible with the nature of matter, of which the brain is composed. Thought moreover is simple, whilst the activities of the brain are compounded of the elementary activities of each of its parts. Furthermore, thought is spontaneous or free, whilst all material activity is determined *ab extra;* and the will can turn itself against all corporeal goods and appetites, which would be impossible were it a corporeal function. For these objective reasons the principle of psychic life must be both immaterial and simple as well as substantial, must be what is called *a Soul.* The same consequence follows from subjective reasons. Our consciousness of personal identity assures us of our essential simplicity: the owner of the various constituents of the self, as we have seen them, the hypothetical Arch-Ego whom we provisionally conceived as possible, is a real entity of whose existence self-consciousness makes us directly aware. No material agent could thus turn round and grasp *itself* — material activities always grasp something else than the agent. And if a brain *could* grasp itself and be self-conscious, it would be conscious of itself *as* a brain

*From PP I:343-350.

and not as something of an altogether different kind. The Soul then exists as a simple spiritual substance in which the various psychic faculties, operations, and affections inhere.

If we ask what a Substance is, the only answer is that it is a self-existent being, or one which needs no other subject in which to inhere. At bottom its only positive determination is Being, and this is something whose meaning we all realize even though we find it hard to explain. The Soul is moreover an *individual* being, and if we ask what that is, we are told to look in upon our Self, and we shall learn by direct intuition better than through any abstract reply. Our direct perception of our own inward being is in fact by many deemed to be the original prototype out of which our notion of simple active substance in general is fashioned. The *consequences* of the simplicity and substantiality of the Soul are its incorruptibility and natural *immortality* — nothing but God's direct *fiat* can annihilate it — and its *responsibility* at all times for whatever it may have ever done.

This substantialist view of the Soul was essentially the view of Plato and of Aristotle. It received its completely formal elaboration in the middle ages. It was believed in by Hobbes, Descartes, Locke, Leibnitz, Wolf, Berkeley, and is now defended by the entire modern dualistic or spiritualistic or common-sense school. Kant held to it while denying its fruitfulness as a premise for deducing consequences verifiable here below. Kant's successors, the absolute idealists, profess to have discarded it — how that may be we shall inquire ere long. Let us make up our minds what to think of it ourselves.

It is at all events needless for expressing the actual subjective phenomena of consciousness as they appear. We have formulated them all without its aid, by the supposition of a stream of thoughts, each substantially different from the rest, but cognitive of the rest and 'appropriative' of each other's content. At least, if I have not already succeeded in making this plausible to the reader, I am hopeless of convincing him by anything I could add now. The unity, the identity, the individuality, and the immateriality that appear in the psychic life are thus accounted for as phenomenal and temporal facts exclusively, and with no need of reference to any more simple or substantial agent than the present Thought or 'section' of the stream. We have seen it to be single and unique in the sense of having no *separable* parts — perhaps that is the only kind of simplicity meant to be predicated of the Soul. The present Thought also has being — at least all believers in the Soul believe so — and if there be no other Being in which it 'inheres,' it ought itself to be a 'substance.' If *this* kind of simplicity and substantiality were all that is predicated of the Soul, then it might appear that we had been talking of the Soul all along, without knowing it, when we treated the present Thought as an agent, an owner, and the like. But the Thought is a perishing and not an immortal or incorruptible thing. Its successors may continuously succeed to it, resemble it, and appropriate it, but they *are* not it, whereas the Soul-Substance is supposed to be a fixed unchanging thing. By the Soul is always meant something *behind* the present Thought, another kind of substance, existing on a non-phenomenal plane.

When we brought in the Soul as an entity which the various brain-processes were supposed to affect simultaneously, and which responded to their combined influence by single pulses of its thought, it was to escape integrated mind-stuff on the one hand, and an improbable cerebral monad on the other. But when (as now, after all we have been through since that earlier passage) we take the two formulations, first of a brain to whose processes pulses of thought *simply* correspond, and second, of one to whose processes pulses of thought *in a Soul* correspond, and compare them together, we see that at bottom the second formulation is only a more roundabout way than the first, of expressing the same bald fact. That bald fact is that *when the brain acts, a thought occurs.* The spiritualistic formulation says that the brain-processes knock the thought, so to speak, out of a Soul which stands there to receive their influence. The simpler formulation says that the thought simply *comes.* But what positive meaning has the Soul, when scrutinized, but the *ground of possibility* of the thought? And what is the 'knocking' but the *determining of the possibility to actuality?* And what is this after all but giving a sort of concreted form to one's belief that the coming of the thought, when the brain-processes occur, has *some* sort of ground in the nature of things? If the word Soul be understood merely to express that claim, it is a good word to use. But if it be held to do more, to gratify the claim — for instance, to connect rationally the thought which comes with the processes which occur, and to mediate intelligibly between their two disparate natures — then it is an illusory term. It is, in fact, with the word Soul as with the word Substance in general. To say that phenomena inhere in a Substance is at bottom only to record one's protest against the notion that the bare existence of the phenomena is the total truth. A phenomenon would not itself be, we insist, unless there were something *more* than the phenomenon. To the more we give the provisional name of Substance. So, in the present instance, we ought certainly to admit that there is more than the bare fact of coexistence of a passing thought with a passing brain-state. But we do not answer the question 'What is that more?' when we say that it is a 'Soul' which the brain-state affects. This kind of more *explains* nothing; and when we are once trying metaphysical explanations we are foolish not to go as far as we can. For my own part I confess that the moment I become metaphysical and try to define the more, I find the notion of some sort of an *anima mundi* thinking in all of us to be a more promising hypothesis, in spite of all its difficulties, than that of a lot of absolutely individual souls. Meanwhile, as *psychologists,* we need not be metaphysical at all. The phenomena are enough, the passing Thought itself is the only *verifiable* thinker, and its empirical connection with the brain-process is the ultimate known law.

To the other arguments which would prove the need of a Soul, we may also turn a deaf ear. The argument from free-will can convince only those who believe in free-will; and even they will have to admit that spontaneity is just as possible, to say the least, in a temporary spiritual agent like our 'Thought' as in a permanent one like the supposed Soul. The same is true of the argument from the kinds of things cognized. Even if the brain could not cognize universals, immaterials, or its 'Self,' still the 'Thought' which we have relied upon in our account *is not* the brain, closely as it seems connected with it; and after all, if the brain could cognize at all, one does not well see why it might not cognize one sort of thing as well as another. The great difficulty is in seeing how a thing can cognize *anything.* This difficulty is not in the least removed by giving to the thing that cognizes the name of Soul. The Spiritualists do not deduce any of the properties of the mental life from otherwise known properties of the Soul. They simply find various characters ready-made in the mental life, and these they clap into the Soul, saying, "Lo! behold the source from whence they flow!" The merely verbal character of this 'explanation' is obvious. The Soul invoked, far from making the phenomena more intelligible, can only be made intelligible itself by borrowing their form — it must be represented, if at all, as a transcendent stream of consciousness duplicating the one we know.

Altogether, the Soul is an outbirth of that sort of philosophizing whose great maxim, according to Dr. Hodgson, is: "Whatever you are *totally* ignorant of, assert to be the explanation of everything else."

Locke and Kant, whilst still believing in the Soul, began the work of undermining the notion that we know anything about it. Most modern writers of the mitigated, spiritualistic, or dualistic philosophy — the Scotch school, as it is often called among us — are forward to proclaim this ignorance, and to attend exclusively to the verifiable phenomena of self-consciousness, as we have laid them down. Dr. Wayland, for example, begins his Elements of Intellectual Philosophy with the phrase, "Of the essence of Mind we know nothing," and goes on: "All that we are able to affirm of it is that it is *something* which perceives, reflects, remembers, imagines, and wills; but what that something *is* which exerts these energies we know not. It is only as we are conscious of the action of these energies that we are conscious of the existence of mind. It is only by the exertion of its own powers that the mind becomes cognizant of their existence. The cognizance of its powers, however, gives us no knowledge of that essence of which they are predicated. In these respects our knowledge of mind is precisely analogous to our knowledge of matter." This analogy of our two ignorances is a favorite remark in the Scotch school. It is but a step to lump them together into a single ignorance, that of the 'Unknowable', to which anyone fond of superfluities in philosophy may accord the hospitality of his belief, if it so please him, but which anyone else may as freely ignore and reject.

The Soul-theory is, then, a complete superfluity, so far as accounting for the actually verified facts of conscious experience goes. So far, no one can be compelled to subscribe to it for definite scientific reasons. The case would rest here, and the reader be left free to make his choice, were it not for other demands of a more practical kind.

The first of these is *Immortality,* for which the simplicity and substantiality of the Soul seem to offer a solid guarantee. A 'stream' of thought, for aught that we see to be contained in its essence, may come to a full stop at any moment; but a simple substance is incorruptible and will, by its own inertia, persist in Being so long as the Creator does not by a direct miracle snuff it out. Unquestionably this is the stronghold of the spiritualistic belief — as indeed the popular touchstone for all philosophies is the question, "What is their bearing on a future life?"

The Soul, however, when closely scrutinized, guarantees no immortality of a sort *we care for*. The enjoyment of the atom-like simplicity of their substance *in secula seculorum* would not to most people seem a consummation devoutly to be wished. The substance must give rise to a stream of consciousness continuous with the present stream, in order to arouse our hope, but of this the mere persistence of the substance *per se* offers no guarantee. Moreover, in the general advance of our moral ideas, there has come to be something ridiculous in the way our forefathers had of grounding their hopes of immortality on the simplicity of their substance. The demand for immortality is nowadays essentially teleological. We believe ourselves immortal because we believe ourselves *fit* for immortality. A 'substance' ought surely to perish, we think, if not worthy to survive, and an insubstantial 'stream' to prolong itself, provided it be worthy, if the nature of Things is organized in the rational way in which we trust it is. Substance or no substance, soul or 'stream,' what Lotze says of immortality is about all that human wisdom can say:

"We have no other principle for deciding it than this general idealistic belief: that every created thing will continue whose continuance belongs to the meaning of the world, and so long as it does so belong; whilst everyone will pass away whose reality is justified only in a transitory phase of the world's course. That this principle admits of no further application in human hands need hardly be said. *We* surely know not the merits which may give to one being a claim on eternity, nor the defects which would cut others off." *

A second alleged necessity for a soul-substance is our forensic responsibility before God. Locke caused an uproar when he said that the unity of *consciousness* made a man the same *person,* whether supported by the same *substance* or no, and that God would not, in the great day, make a person answer for what he remembered nothing of. It was supposed scandalous that our forgetfulness might thus deprive God of the chance of certain retributions, which otherwise would have enhanced his 'glory.' This is certainly a good speculative ground for retaining the Soul — at least for those who demand a plenitude of retribution. The mere stream of consciousness, with its lapses of memory, cannot possibly be as 'responsible' as a soul which *is* at the judgment day all that it ever was. To modern readers, however, who are less insatiate for retribution than their grandfathers, this argument will hardly be as convincing as it seems once to have been.

One great use of the Soul has always been to account for, and at the same time to guarantee, the closed individuality of each personal consciousness. The thoughts of one soul must unite into one self, it was supposed, and must be eternally insulated from those of every other soul. But we have already begun to see that,

---

*Metaphysik, §245 *fin*. This writer, who in his early work, the Medizinische Psychologie, was (to my reading) a strong defender of the Soul-Substance theory, has written in §§243-5 of his Metaphysik the most beautiful criticism of this theory which exists.

although unity is the rule of each man's consciousness, yet in some individuals, at least, thoughts may split away from the others and form separate selves. As for insulation, it would be rash, in view of the phenomena of thought-transference, mesmeric influence and spirit-control, which are being alleged nowadays on better authority than ever before, to be too sure about that point either. The definitively closed nature of our personal consciousness is probably an average statistical resultant of many conditions, but not an elementary force or fact; so that, if one wishes to preserve the Soul, the less he draws his arguments from *that* quarter the better. So long as our self, on the whole, makes itself good and practically maintains itself as a closed individual, why, as Lotze says, is not that enough? And why is the *being*-an-individual in some inaccessible metaphysical way so much prouder an achievement?*

My final conclusion, then, about the substantial Soul is that it explains nothing and guarantees nothing. Its successive thoughts are the only intelligible and verifiable things about it, and definitely to ascertain the correlations of these with brain-processes is as much as psychology can empirically do. From the metaphysical point of view it is true that one may claim that the correlations have a rational ground; and if the word Soul could be taken to mean merely some such vague problematic ground, it would be unobjectionable. But the trouble is that it professes to give the ground in positive terms of a very dubiously credible sort. I therefore feel entirely free to discard the word Soul from the rest of this book. If I ever use it, it will be in the vaguest and most popular way. The reader who finds any comfort in the idea of the Soul, is, however, perfectly free to continue to believe in it; for our reasonings have not established the non-existence of the Soul; they have only proved its superfluity for scientific purposes.

2

STILL AN ILLUSORY TERM*

It is not for idle or fantastical reasons that the notion of the substantial soul, so freely used by common men and the more popular philosophies, has fallen upon such evil days, and has no prestige in the eyes of critical thinkers. It only shares the fate of other unrepresentable substances and principles. They are

*On the empirical and transcendental conceptions of the self's unity, see Lotze, Metaphysik, §244.
*From PU 209-211.

without exception all so barren that to sincere inquirers they appear as little more than names masquerading — *Wo die begriffe fehlen da stellt ein wort zur rechten zeit sich ein.* You see no deeper into the fact that a hundred sensations get compounded or known together by thinking that a 'soul' does the compounding than you see into a man's living eighty years by thinking of him as an octogenarian, or into our having five fingers by calling us pentadactyls. Souls have worn out both themselves and their welcome, that is the plain truth. Philosophy ought to get the manifolds of experience unified on principles less empty. Like the word 'cause,' the word 'soul' is but a theoretic stop-gap — it marks a place and claims it for a future explanation to occupy.

Some day, indeed, souls may get their innings again in philosophy — I am quite ready to admit that possibility — they form a category of thought too natural to the human mind to expire without prolonged resistance. But if the belief in the soul ever does come to life after the many funeral-discourses which Humeian and Kantian criticism have preached over it, I am sure it will be only when someone has found in the term a pragmatic significance that has hitherto eluded observation. When that champion speaks, as he well may speak some day, it will be time to consider souls more seriously.

APPENDIX V

COSMIC SOULS: CONCERNING FECHNER*

Among the philosophic cranks of my acquaintance in the past was a lady all the tenets of whose system I have forgotten except one. The world, she said, is composed of only two elements, the Thick, namely, and the Thin. No one can deny the truth of this analysis, as far as it goes (though in the light of our contemporary knowledge of nature it has itself a rather 'thin' sound), and it is nowhere truer than in that part of the world called philosophy.

Fechner's thickness is a refreshing contrast to the thin, abstract, indigent, and threadbare appearance, the starving, school-room aspect, which the speculations of most of our absolutist philosophers present.

There is something really weird and uncanny in the contrast between the abstract pretensions of rationalism and what rationalistic methods concretely can do. If the 'logical prius' of our

*From PU 135-136, 144-156, 168-176, 297-312, abridged.

mind were really the 'implicit presence' of the whole 'concrete
universal,' the whole of reason, or reality, or spirit, or the absolute
idea, or whatever it may be called, in all our finite thinking, and
if this reason worked (for example) by the dialectical method,
doesn't it seem odd that in the greatest instance of rationalization
mankind has known, in 'science,' namely, the dialectical method
should never once have been tried? Not a solitary instance of the
use of it in science occurs to my mind. Hypotheses, and deductions from these, controlled by sense-observations and analogies
with what we know elsewhere, are to be thanked for all of
science's results.

Fechner used no methods but these latter ones in arguing for
his metaphysical conclusions about reality.

The original sin, according to Fechner, of both our popular
and our scientific thinking, is our inveterate habit of regarding
the spiritual not as the rule but as an exception in the midst of
nature. Instead of believing our life to be fed at the breasts of
the greater life, our individuality to be sustained by the greater
individuality, which must necessarily have more consciousness
and more independence than all that it brings forth, we habitually
treat whatever lies outside of our life as so much slag and ashes
of life only; or if we believe in a Divine Spirit, we fancy him
on the one side as bodiless, and nature as soulless on the other.
What comfort, or peace, Fechner asks, can come from such a
doctrine? The flowers wither at its breath, the stars turn into
stone; our own body grows unworthy of our spirit and sinks to
a tenement for carnal senses only. The book of nature turns into
a volume on mechanics, in which whatever has life is treated as a
sort of anomaly; a great chasm of separation yawns between
us and all that is higher than ourselves; and God becomes a thin
nest of abstractions.

Fechner's great instrument for vivifying the daylight view is
analogy; not a rationalistic argument is to be found in all his
many pages — only reasonings like those which men continually
use in practical life. For example: My house is built by someone, the world too is built by someone. The world is greater than
my house, it must be a greater someone who built the world.
My body moves by the influence of my feeling and will; the sun,
moon, sea, and wind, being themselves more powerful, move by
the influence of some more powerful feeling and will. I live now,
and change from one day to another; I shall live hereafter, and
change still more, etc.

Bain defines genius as the power of seeing analogies. The num-

ber that Fechner could perceive was prodigious; but he insisted
on the differences as well. Neglect to make allowance for these,
he said, is the common fallacy in analogical reasoning. Most of
us, for example, reasoning justly that, since all the minds we
know are connected with bodies, therefore God's mind should be
connected with a body, proceed to suppose that that body must
be just an animal body over again, and paint an altogether human
picture of God. But all that the analogy comports is *a* body — the
particular features of *our* body are adaptations to a habitat so
different from God's that if God have a physical body at all, it
must be utterly different from ours in structure. Throughout his
writing Fechner makes difference and analogy walk abreast, and
by his extraordinary power of noticing both, he converts what
would ordinarily pass for objections to his conclusions into factors of their support.

The vaster orders of mind go with the vaster orders of body.
The entire earth on which we live must have, according to
Fechner, its own collective consciousness. So must each sun,
moon, and planet; so must the whole solar system have its own
wider consciousness, in which the consciousness of our earth plays
one part. So has the entire starry system as such its consciousness;
and if that starry system be not the sum of all that *is,* materially
considered, then that whole system, along with whatever else may
be, is the body of that absolutely totalized consciousness of the
universe to which men give the name of God.

Speculatively Fechner is thus a monist in his theology; but
there is room in his universe for every grade of spiritual being
between man and the final all-inclusive God; and in suggesting
what the positive content of all this super-humanity may be, he
hardly lets his imagination fly beyond simple spirits of the
planetary order. The earth-soul he passionately believes in; he
treats the earth as our special human guardian angel; we can
pray to the earth as men pray to their saints; but I think that in
his system, as in so many of the actual historic theologies, the
supreme God marks only a sort of limit of enclosure of the
worlds above man. He is left thin and abstract in his majesty,
men preferring to carry on their personal transactions with the
many less remote and abstract messengers and mediators whom
the divine order provides.

Altho the type of reasoning he employs is almost childlike for
simplicity, and his bare conclusions can be written on a single
page, the *power* of the man is due altogether to the profuseness
of his concrete imagination, to the multitude of the points which

he considers successively, to the cumulative effect of his learning, of his thoroughness, and of the ingenuity of his detail, to his admirably homely style, to the sincerity with which his pages glow, and finally to the impression he gives of a man who doesn't live at second-hand, but who *sees,* who in fact speaks as one having authority, and not as if he were one of the common herd of professorial philosophic scribes.

Abstractly set down, his most important conclusion for my purpose in these lectures is that the constitution of the world is identical throughout. In ourselves, visual consciousness goes with our eyes, tactile consciousness with our skin. But altho neither skin nor eye knows aught of the sensations of the other, they come together and figure in some sort of relation and combination in the more inclusive consciousness which each of us names his *self.* Quite similarly, then, says Fechner, we must suppose that my consciousness of myself and yours of yourself, altho in their immediacy they keep separate and know nothing of each other, are yet known and used together in a higher consciousness, that of the human race, say, into which they enter as constituent parts. Similarly, the whole human and animal kingdoms come together as conditions of a consciousness of still wider scope. This combines in the soul of the earth with the consciousness of the vegetable kingdom, which in turn contributes its share of experience to that of the whole solar system, and so on from synthesis to synthesis and height to height, till an absolutely universal consciousness is reached.

A vast analogical series, in which the basis of the analogy consists of facts directly observable in ourselves.

The special thought of Fechner's with which I have most practical concern, is his belief that the more inclusive forms of consciousness are in part *constituted* by the more limited forms. Not that they are the mere sum of the more limited forms. As our mind is not the bare sum of our sights plus our sounds plus our pains, but in adding these terms together also finds relations among them and weaves them into schemes and forms and objects of which no one sense in its separate estate knows anything, so the earth-soul traces relations between the contents of my mind and the contents of yours of which neither of our separate minds is conscious. It has schemes, forms, and objects proportionate to its wider field, which our mental fields are far too narrow to cognize. By ourselves we are simply out of relation with each other, for it we are both of us there, and *different* from each other, which is a positive relation. What we are without knowing, it knows that we are. We are closed against its world, but that world is not closed against us. It is as if the total universe of inner life had a sort of grain or direction, a sort of valvular structure, permitting knowledge to flow in one way only, so that the wider might always have the narrower under observation, but never the narrower the wider.

Fechner's great analogy here is the relation of the senses to our individual minds. When our eyes are open their sensations enter into our general mental life, which grows incessantly by the addition of what they see. Close the eyes, however, and the visual additions stop, nothing but thoughts and memories of the past visual experiences remain — in combination of course with the enormous stock of other thoughts and memories, and with the data coming in from the senses not yet closed. Our eye-sensations of themeselves know nothing of this enormous life into which they fall. Fechner thinks, as any common man would think, that they are taken into it directly when they occur, and form part of it just as they are. They don't stay outside and get represented inside by their copies. It is only the memories and concepts of them that are copies; the sensible perceptions themselves are taken in or walled out in their own proper persons according as the eyes are open or shut.

Fechner likens our individual persons on the earth unto so many sense-organs of the earth's soul. We add to its perceptive life so long as our own life lasts. It absorbs our perceptions, just as they occur, into its larger sphere of knowledge, and combines them with the other data there. When one of us dies, it is as if an eye of the world were closed, for all *perceptive* contributions from that particular quarter cease. But the memories and conceptual relations that have spun themselves round the perceptions of that person remain in the larger earth-life as distinct as ever, and form new relations and grow and develop throughout all the future, in the same way in which our own distinct objects of thought, once stored in memory, form new relations and develop throughout our whole finite life. This is Fechner's theory of immortality.

We rise upon the earth as wavelets rise upon the ocean. We grow out of her soil as leaves grow from a tree. The wavelets catch the sunbeams separately, the leaves stir when the branches do not move. They realize their own events apart, just as in our own consciousnss, when anything becomes emphatic, the background fades from observation. Yet the event works back upon the background, as the wavelet works upon the waves, or as the leaf's movements work upon the sap inside the branch. The whole sea and the whole tree are registers of what has happened, and are different for the wave's and the leaf's action having occurred. A grafted twig may modify its stock to the roots: — so our out-lived private experiences, impressed on the whole earth-mind as memories, lead the immortal life of ideas there, and become parts of the great system, fully distinguished from one another, just as we ourselves when alive were distinct, realizing themselves no longer isolatedly, but along with one another as so many partial systems, entering thus into new combinations, being affected by the perceptive experiences of those living then, and affecting the living in their turn — altho they are so seldom recognized by living men to do so.

If you imagine that this entrance after the death of the body into a common life of higher type means a merging and loss of our distinct personality, Fechner asks you whether a visual sensa-tion of our own exists in any sense *less for itself* or *less distinctly,* when it enters into our higher relational consciousness and is there distinguished and defined.

— But here I must stop my reporting and send you to his volumes. Thus is the universe alive, according to this philosopher! I think you will admit that he makes it more *thickly* alive than do the other philosophers who, following rationalistic methods solely, gain the same results, but only in the thinnest outlines. Both Fechner and Professor Royce, for example, believe ultimately in one all-inclusive mind. Both believe that we, just as we stand here, are constituent parts of that mind. No other *content* has it than us, with all the other creatures like or unlike us, and the relations which it finds between us. Our eaches, collected into one, are substantively identical with its all, tho the all is perfect while no each is perfect, so that we have to admit that new qualities as well as unperceived relations accrue from the col-lective form. It is thus superior to the distributive form. But having reached this result, Royce (tho his treatment of the subject on its moral side seems to me infinitely richer and thicker than that of any other contemporary idealistic philosopher) leaves us very much to our own devices. Fechner, on the contrary, tries to trace the superiorities due to the more collective form in as much detail as he can. He marks the various intermediary stages and halting places of collectivity — as we are to our separate senses, so is the earth to us, so is the solar system to the earth, etc. — and if, in order to escape an infinitely long summation, he posits a complete God as the all-container and leaves him about as in-definite in feature as the idealists leave their absolute, he yet provides us with a very definite gate of approach to him in the shape of the earth-soul, through which in the nature of things we must first make connexion with all the more enveloping superhuman realms, and with which our more immediate religious commerce at any rate has to be carried on.

Ordinary monistic idealism leaves everything intermediary out. It recognizes only the extremes, as if, after the first rude face of the phenomenal world in all its particularity, nothing but the supreme in all its perfection could be found. First, you and I, just as we are in this room; and the moment we get below that surface, the unutterable absolute itself! Doesn't this show a singularly indigent imagination? Isn't this brave universe made on a richer pattern, with room in it for a long hierarchy of beings? Materialistic science makes it infinitely richer in terms, with its molecules, and ether, and electrons, and what not. Absolute idealism, thinking of reality only under intellectual forms, knows not what to do with *bodies* of any grade, and can make no use of any psychophysical analogy or correspondence. The resultant thinness is startling when compared with the thickness and articulation of such a universe as Fechner paints. May not satisfaction with the rationalistic absolute as the alpha and omega, and treatment of it in all its abstraction as an adequate religious object, argue a certain native poverty of mental demand? Things reveal themselves soonest to those who most passionately want them, for our need sharpens our wit. To a mind content with little, the much in the universe may always remain hid.

To be candid, one of my reasons for saying so much about Fechner has been to make the thinness of our current transcendentalism appear more evident by an effect of contrast. Scholasticism ran thick; Hegel himself ran thick; but English and American transcendentalisms run thin. If philosophy is more a matter of passionate vision than of logic — and I believe it is, logic only finding reasons for the vision afterwards — must not such thinness come either from the vision being defective in the disciples, or from their passion, matched with Fechner's or with Hegel's own passion, being as moonlight unto sunlight or as water unto wine?

The numerous facts of divided or split human personality which the genius of certain medical men, as Janet, Freud, Prince, Sidis, and others, have unearthed were unknown in Fechner's time, and neither the phenomena of automatic writing and speech, nor of mediumship and 'possession' generally, had been recognized or studied as we now study them, so Fechner's stock of analogies is scant compared with our present one. He did the best with what

he had, however. For my own part I find in some of these abnormal or supernormal facts the strongest suggestions in favor of
a superior co-consciousness being possible. I doubt whether we
shall ever understand some of them without using the very letter
of Fechner's conception of a great reservoir in which the memories
of earth's inhabitants are pooled and preserved, and from which,
when the threshold lowers or the valve opens, information ordinarily shut out leaks into the mind of exceptional individuals
among us. But those regions of inquiry are perhaps too spook-
haunted to interest an academic audience, and the only evidence
I feel it now decorous to bring to the support of Fechner is
drawn from ordinary religious experience. I think it may be asserted that there *are* religious experiences of a specific nature,
not deducible by analogy or psychological reasoning from our
other sorts of experience. I think that they point with reasonable
probability to the continuity of our consciousness with a wider
spiritual environment from which the ordinary prudential man
(who is the only man that scientific psychology, so called, takes
cognizance of) is shut off.

The Athenians thought that the very gods must admire the
rectitude of Phocion and Aristides; and those gentlemen themselves were apparently of much the same opinion. Cato's veracity
was so impeccable that the extremest incredulity a Roman could
express of anything was to say, 'I would not believe it even if
Cato had told me.' Good was good, and bad was bad, for these
people. Hypocrisy, which church-Christianity brought in, hardly
existed; the naturalistic system held firm; its values showed no
hollowness and brooked no irony. The individual, if virtuous
enough, could meet all possible requirements. The pagan pride
had never crumbled. Luther was the first moralist who broke with
any effectiveness through the crust of all this naturalistic self-
sufficiency, thinking (and possibly he was right) that Saint Paul
had done it already. Religious experience of the Lutheran type
brings all our naturalistic standards to bankruptcy. You are
strong only by being weak, it shows. You cannot live on pride or
self-sufficingness. There is a light in which all the naturally
founded and currently accepted distinctions, excellences, and safeguards of our characters appear as utter childishness. Sincerely
to give up one's conceit or hope of being good in one's own
right is the only door to the universe's deeper reaches.

These deeper reaches are familiar to evangelical Christianity
and to what is nowadays becoming known as 'mind-cure' religion
or 'new thought.' The phenomenon is that of new ranges of life

succeeding on our most despairing moments. There are resources in us that naturalism with its literal and legal virtues never recks of, possibilities that take our breath away, of another kind of happiness and power, based on giving up our own will and letting something higher work for us, and these seem to show a world wider than either physics or philistine ethics can imagine. Here is a world in which all is well, in *spite* of certain forms of death, indeed *because* of certain forms of death — death of hope, death of strength, death of responsibility, of fear and worry, competency and desert, death of everything that paganism, naturalism, and legalism pin their faith on and tie their trust to.

Reason, operating on our other experiences, even our psychological experiences, would never have inferred these specifically religious experiences in advance of their actual coming. She could not suspect their existence, for they are discontinuous with the 'natural' experiences they succeed upon and invert their values. But as they actually come and are given, creation widens to the view of their recipients. They suggest that our natural experience, our strictly moralistic and prudential experience, may be only a fragment of real human experience. They soften nature's outlines and open out the strangest possibilities and perspectives.

This is why it seems to me that the logical understanding, working in abstraction from such specifically religious experiences, will always omit something, and fail to reach completely adequate conclusions. Death and failure, it will always say, *are* death and failure simply, and can nevermore be one with life; so religious experience, peculiarly so called, needs, in my opinion, to be carefully considered and interpreted by everyone who aspires to reason out a more complete philosophy.

The sort of belief that religious experience of this type naturally engenders in those who have it is fully in accord with Fechner's theories. To quote words which I have used elsewhere, the believer finds that the tenderer parts of his personal life are continuous with a *more* of the same quality which is operative in the universe outside of him and which he can keep in working touch with, and in a fashion get on board of and save himself, when all his lower being has gone to pieces in the wreck. In a word, the believer is continuous, to his own consciousness, at any rate, with a wider self from which saving experiences flow in. Those who have such experiences distinctly enough and often enough to live in the light of them remain quite unmoved by criticism, from whatever quarter it may come, be it academic or scientific, or be it merely the voice of logical common sense. They have had their vision and they *know* — that is enough — that we inhabit an invisible spiritual environment from which help comes, our soul being mysteriously one with a larger soul whose instruments we are.

One may therefore plead, I think, that Fechner's ideas are not without direct empirical verification. There is at any rate one side of life which would be easily explicable if those ideas were true, but of which there appears no clear explanation so long as we assume either with naturalism that human consciousness is the highest consciousness there is, or with dualistic theism that there is a higher mind in the cosmos, but that it is discontinuous with our own. It has always been a matter of surprise with me that philosophers of the absolute should have shown so little interest in this department of life, and so seldom puts its phenomena in evidence, even when it seemed obvious that personal experience of some kind must have made their confidence in their own vision so strong. The logician's bias has always been too much with them. They have preferred the thinner to the thicker method, dialectical abstraction being so much more dignified and academic than the confused and unwholesome facts of personal biography.

In spite of rationalism's disdain for the particular, the personal, and the unwholesome, the drift of all the evidence we have seems to me to sweep us very strongly towards the belief in some form of superhuman life with which we may, unknown to ourselves, be co-conscious. We may be in the universe as dogs and cats are in our libraries, seeing the books and hearing the conversation, but having no inkling of the meaning of it all. The intellectualist objections to this fall away when the authority of intellectualist logic is undermined by criticism, and then the positive empirical evidence remains. The analogies with ordinary psychology and with the facts of pathology, with those of psychical research, so called, and with those of religious experience, establish, when taken together, a decidedly *formidable* probability in favor of a general view of the world almost identical with Fechner's. The outlines of the superhuman consciousness thus made probable must remain, however, very vague, and the number of functionally distinct 'selves' it comports and carries has to be left entirely problematic. It may be polytheistically or it may be monotheistically conceived of. Fechner, with his distinct earth-soul functioning as our guardian angel, seems to me clearly polytheistic; but the word 'polytheism' usually gives offence, so perhaps it is better not to use it. Only one thing is certain: the only way to escape from the paradoxes and perplexities that a consistently thought-out monistic universe suffers from as from a species of antointoxication — the mystery of the 'fall' namely, of reality lapsing into appearance, truth into error, perfection into imperfection; of evil, in short; the mystery of universal determinism, of the block-universe eternal and without a history, etc.; — the only way of escape, I say, from all this is to be frankly pluralistic and assume that the superhuman consciousness, however vast it may be, has itself an external environment, and consequently is finite. Why should we envelop our many with the 'one' that brings so much poison in its train?

The line of least resistance, then, as it seems to me, both in theology and in philosophy, is to accept, along with the superhuman consciousness, the notion that it is not all-embracing, the notion, in other words, that there is a God, but that he is finite, either in power or in knowledge, or in both at once. These, I need hardly tell you, are the terms in which common men have usually carried on their active commerce with God; and the monistic perfections that make the notion of him so paradoxical practically and morally are the colder addition of remote professorial minds operating in *distans* upon conceptual substitutes for him alone.

APPENDIX VI
HUMAN IMMORTALITY

EDITOR'S NOTE:

In the text of the VARIETIES (the official twenty Gifford Lectures) James ignores the question of immortality. In the "Postscript" he explains why: "it seems a secondary point" and "it is eminently a case for facts to testify." (524) Matters of fact are properly the subject matter of scientific investigation; hence James's support of the Society for Psychical Research. What James has to say about the "fact" is contained in Appendix VII.

When James sent Bergson a copy of his Ingersoll Lecture on *Human Immortality*, he wrote in his accompanying letter that he proposes "no positive theory but merely an *argumentum ad hominem* for the ordinary cerebralistic objection — in which it may amuse you to see a formulation like your own that the brain is an organ of *filtration* for spiritual life." (LWJ, II, 180) James makes no mention of the "second objection" he removes. James's attack on the cerebralistic objection is Fechnerian. More than one-third of the space given over to "Notes" is devoted to quotations from Fechner. These have been entirely omitted, James's exposition of Fechnerian doctrine in Appendix V being far more than an adequate substitute.

The natural place for a "Preface" is at the beginning of a book. But in this Appendix the natural place for James's Preface to the Second Edition is at the end, which is where the reader will find it.

1*

There are two difficulties which our modern culture finds in the old notion of a life hereafter — difficulties that I am sure rob the notion of much of its old power to draw belief, in the scientifically cultivated circles to which this audience belong.

A. THE FIRST DIFFICULTY: STATED AND REMOVED

The first of these difficulties is relative to the absolute dependence of our spiritual life, as we know it here, upon the brain. Physiological psychology is what is supposed to bar the way to the old faith. And it is now as a physiological psychologist that I ask you to look at the question with me a little more closely.

It is indeed true that physiological science has come to the conclusion cited; and we must confess that in so doing she has only carried out a little farther the common belief of mankind. Everyone knows that arrests of brain development occasion imbecility, that blows on the head abolish memory or consciousness, and that brain-stimulants and poisons change the quality of our ideas. The anatomists, physiologists, and pathologists have only shown this generally admitted fact of a dependence to be detailed and minute.

The assurance that observation will go on to establish them ever more and more minutely is the inspirer of all contemporary research. And almost any of our young psychologists will tell you that only a few belated scholastics, or possibly some crack-brained theosophist or psychical researcher, can be found holding back, and still talking as if mental phenomena might exist as independent variables in the world.

For the purposes of my argument, now, I wish to adopt this general doctrine as if it were established absolutely, with no possibility of restriction: the great psycho-physiological formula: *Thought is a function of the brain.*

The question is then, does this doctrine logically compel us

*From HI text, abridged.

to disbelieve in immortality? Ought it to force every truly consistent thinker to sacrifice his hopes of an hereafter to what he takes to be his duty of accepting all the consequences of a scientific truth?

I believe that it has in strict logic no deterrent power. The fatal consequence is not coercive, as is commonly imagined, even though our soul's life (as here below it is revealed to us) may be in literal strictness the function of a brain that perishes, yet it is not at all impossible, but on the contrary quite possible, that the life may still continue when the brain itself is dead.

The supposed impossibility of its continuing comes from too superficial a look at the admitted fact of functional dependence.

When the physiologist who thinks that his science cuts off all hope of immortality pronounces the phrase, "Thought is a function of the brain," he thinks of the matter just as he thinks when he says, "Steam is a function of the tea-kettle," "Light is a function of the electric circuit," "Power is a function of the moving waterfall." In these latter cases the several material objects have the function of inwardly creating or engendering their effects, and their function must be called *productive* function. Just so, he thinks, it must be with the brain. Of course, if such production be the function, then when the organ perishes, since the production can no longer continue, the soul must surely die. Such a conclusion as this is indeed inevitable from that particular conception of the facts.

But in the world of physical nature, productive function of this sort is not the only kind of function with which we are familiar. We have also releasing or permissive function; and we have transmissive function.

The trigger of a crossbow has a releasing function: it removes the obstacle that holds the string, and lets the bow fly back to its natural shape.

In the case of a colored glass, a prism, or a refracting lens, we have transmissive function. Similarly, the keys of an organ have only a transmissive function. The voices of the various pipes are constituted by the columns of air trembling as they emerge. But the air is not engendered in the organ. The organ proper, as distinguished from its air-chest, is only an apparatus for letting portions of it loose upon the world in these peculiarly limited shapes.

My thesis now is this: that, when we think of the law that thought is a function of the brain, we are not required to think of productive function only; *we are entitled also to consider per-*

missive or transmissive function. And this the ordinary psycho-physiologist leaves out of his account.

Suppose, for example, that the whole universe of material things — the furniture of earth and choir of heaven — should turn out to be a mere surface-veil of phenomena, hiding and keeping back the world of genuine realities. Such a supposition is foreign neither to common sense nor to philosophy. Common sense believes in realities behind the veil even too superstitiously; and idealistic philosophy declares the whole world of natural experience, as we get it, to be but a time-mask, shattering or refracting the one infinite Thought which is the sole reality into those millions of finite streams of consciousness known to us as our private selves.

Admit now that *our brains* are such thin and half-transparent places in the veil. What will happen? The life of souls as it is in its fullness will break through our several brains into this world in all sorts of restricted forms, and with all the imperfections and queernesses that characterize our finite individualities here below.

According to the state in which the brain finds itself, the barrier of its obstructiveness may also be supposed to rise or fall. It sinks so low, when the brain is in full activity, that a comparative flood of spiritual energy pours over. At other times, only such occasional waves of thought as heavy sleep permits get by. And when finally a brain stops acting altogether, or decays, that special stream of consciousness which it subserved will vanish entirely from this natural world. But the sphere of being that supplied the consciousness would still be intact; and in that more real world with which, even whilst here, it was continuous, the consciousness might, in ways unknown to us, continue still.

You see that, on all these suppositions, our soul's life, as we know it, would none the less in literal strictness be the function of the brain. The brain would be the independent variable, the mind would vary dependently on it. But such dependence on the brain for this natural life would in no wise make immortal life impossible — it might be quite compatible with supernatural life behind the veil hereafter.

As I said, then, the fatal consequence is not coercive, the conclusion which materialism draws being due solely to its one-sided way of taking the word 'function.' And, whether we care or not for immortality in itself, we ought, as mere critics doing police duty among the vagaries of mankind, to insist on the illogicality of a denial based on the flat ignoring of a palpable alternative.

How much more ought we to insist, as lovers of truth, when the denial is that of such a vital hope of mankind!

In strict logic, then, the fangs of cerebralistic materialism are drawn. My words ought consequently already to exert a releasing function on your hopes. You *may* believe henceforward, whether you care to profit by the permission or not.

All abstract hypotheses sound unreal; and the abstract notion that our brains are colored lenses in the wall of nature, admitting light from the super-solar source, but at the same time tingeing and restricting it, has a thoroughly fantastic sound. What is it, you may ask, but a foolish metaphor? And how can such a function be imagined? Isn't the common materialistic notion vastly simpler? Is it not more rigorously scientific to treat the brain's function as function of production?

The immediate reply is that, in strict science, we can only write down the bare fact of concomitance; and all talk about either production or transmission, as the mode of taking place, is pure superadded hypothesis, and metaphysical hypothesis at that, for we can frame no more notion of the details on the one alternative than on the other. Ask for any indication of the exact process either of transmission or of production, and Science confesses her imagination to be bankrupt. She has, so far, not the least glimmer of a conjecture or suggestion — not even a bad verbal metaphor or pun to offer. Into the mode of production of steam in a tea-kettle we have conjectural insight, for the terms that change are physically homogeneous one with another, and we can easily imagine the case to consist of nothing but alterations of molecular motion. But in the production of consciousness by the brain, the terms are heterogeneous natures altogether; and as far as our understanding goes, it is as great a miracle as if we said, Thought is 'spontaneously generated,' or 'created out of nothing.'

The theory of production is therefore not a jot more simple or credible in itself than any other conceivable theory. It is only a little more popular.

But if we consider the theory of transmission in a wider way, we see that it has certain positive superiorities, quite apart from its connection with the immortality question.

Consciousness in this process does not have to be generated *de novo* in a vast number of places. It exists already, behind the scenes, coeval with the world. The transmission-theory not only avoids in this way multiplying miracles, but it puts itself in touch with general idealistic philosophy better than the production-theory does. It should always be reckoned a good thing when science and philosophy thus meet.

It puts itself also in touch with the conception of a 'threshold' — a word with which, since Fechner wrote his book called 'Psychophysik,' the so-called 'new Psychology' has rung.

The transmission-theory also puts itself in touch with a whole class of experiences that are with difficulty explained by the production-theory. I refer to those obscure and exceptional phenomena reported at all times throughout human history, which the 'psychical-researchers,' with Mr. Frederick Myers at their head, are doing so much to rehabilitate; such phenomena, namely, as religious conversions, providential leadings in answer to prayer, instantaneous healings, premonitions, apparitions at time of death, clairvoyant visions or impressions, and the whole range of mediumistic capacities, to say nothing of still more exceptional and incomprehensible things.

The ordinary production-theory of consciousness is knit up with a peculiar notion of how brain-action *can* occur — that notion being that all brain-action, without exception, is due to a prior action, immediate or remote, of the bodily sense-organs *on* the brain. As transmissionists, we also must admit this to be the condition of all our usual thought. But, in the mysterious phenomena to which I allude, it is often hard to see where the sense-organs can come in. On the production-theory, one does not see from what sensations such odd bits of knowledge are produced. On the transmission-theory, they don't have to be 'produced' — they exist ready-made in the transcendental world, and all that is needed is an abnormal lowering of the brain-threshold to let them through. All such experiences, quite paradoxical and meaningless on the production-theory, fall very naturally into place on the other theory. We need only suppose the continuity of our consciousness with a mother sea, to allow for exceptional waves occasionally pouring over the dam. Of course the causes of these odd lowerings of the brain's threshold still remain a mystery on any terms.

Add, then, this advantage to the transmission-theory — an advantage which I am well aware that some of you will not rate very high — and also add the advantage of not conflicting with a life hereafter, and I hope you will agree with me that it has many points of superiority to the more familiar theory.

But still, you will ask, in what positive way does this theory help us to realize our immortality in imagination? What we all wish to keep is just these individual restrictions, these selfsame tendencies and peculiarities that define us to ourselves and others, and constitute our identity, so called. Our finitenesses and limitations seem to be our personal essence; and when the finiting organ drops away, and our several spirits revert to their original source and resume their unrestricted condition, will they then be anything like those sweet streams of feeling which we know, and which even now our brains are sifting out from the great reservoir for our enjoyment here below? Such questions are truly living questions, and surely they must be seriously discussed. But into these higher and more transcendental matters I refuse to enter upon this occasion.

B. THE SECOND DIFFICULTY: STATED AND REMOVED

My second point is relative to the incredible and intolerable number of beings which, with our modern imagination, we must believe to be immortal, if immortality be true. I cannot but suspect that this, too, is a stumbling-block to many. And it is a stumbling-block which I should thoroughly like to clear away.

It is, I fancy, a stumbling-block of altogether modern origin, due to the strain upon the quantitative imagination which recent scientific theories, and the moral feelings consequent upon them, have brought in their train.

For our ancestors the world was a small, and — compared with our modern sense of it — a comparatively snug affair. Six thousand years at most it had lasted. In its history a few particular human heroes, kings, ecclesiarchs, and saints stood forth very prominent, overshadowing the imagination with their claims and merits, so that not only they, but all who were associated familiarly with them, shone with a glamour which even the Almighty, it was supposed, must recognize and respect. The whole scene of eternity (so far, at least, as Heaven and not the nether place was concerned in it) never struck the believer's fancy as an overwhelmingly large or inconveniently crowded stage. One might call this an aristocratic view of immortality; the immortals — I speak of Heaven exclusively, for an immortality of torment need not now concern us — were always an élite, a select and manageable number.

But, with our own generation, an entirely new quantitative imagination has swept over our western world. The theory of evolution now requires us to suppose a far vaster scale of times, spaces, and numbers than our forefathers ever dreamed the cosmic process to involve. Human history grows continuously out of animal history, and goes back possibly even to the tertiary epoch. From this there has emerged insensibly a democratic view, instead of the old aristocratic view, of immortality. For our minds, though in one sense they may have grown a little cynical, in another they have been made sympathetic by the evolutionary perspective. Bone of our bone and flesh of our flesh are these half-brutish prehistoric brothers. They ever rescued triumphantly from the jaws of ever-imminent destruction the torch of life, which, thanks to them, now lights the world for us. We grow humble and reverent as we contemplate the prodigious spectacle. Not our differences and distinctions — we feel — no, but our common animal essence of patience under suffering and enduring effort must be what redeems us in the Deity's sight. An immense compassion and kinship fill the heart. An immortality from which these inconceivable billions of fellow-strivers should be excluded becomes an irrational idea for us. And a modern mind, expanded as some minds are by cosmic emotion, by the great evolutionist vision of universal continuity, hesitates to draw the line even at man. If any creature lives forever, why not all? — why not the patient brutes? So that a faith in immortality, if we are to indulge it, demands of us nowadays a scale of representation so stupendous that our imagination faints before it, and our personal feelings refuse to rise up and face the task. The supposition we are swept along to is too vast, and, rather than face the conclusion, we abandon the premise from which it starts. Life is a good thing on a reasonably copious scale; but the very heavens themselves, and the cosmic times and spaces, would stand aghast, we think, at the notion of preserving eternally such an ever-swelling plethora and glut of it.

Having myself, as a recipient of modern scientific culture, gone through a subjective experience like this, I feel sure that it must also have been the experience of many, perhaps of most, of you who listen to my words. But I have also come to see that it harbors a tremendous fallacy.

It is the most obvious fallacy in the world, and the only wonder is that all the world should not see through it. It is the result of nothing but an invincible blindness from which we suffer, an insensibility to the inner significance of alien lives, and a conceit that would project our own incapacity into the vast cosmos, and measure the wants of the Absolute by our own puny needs. Our Christian ancestors dealt with the problem more easily than we do. We, indeed, lack sympathy; but they had a positive antipathy for these alien human creatures, and they naïvely supposed the Deity to have the antipathy, too. Being, as they were, 'heathen,' our forefathers felt a certain sort of joy in thinking that their

Creator made them as so much mere fuel for the fires of hell. Our culture has humanized us beyond that point, but we cannot yet conceive them as our comrades in the fields of heaven. We have, as the phrase goes, *no use for them,* and it oppresses us to think of their survival. God himself, you think, can have no use for them. An immortality of every separate specimen must be to him and to the universe as indigestible a load to carry as it is to you.

But is not such an attitude due to the veriest lack and dearth of your imagination? You take these swarms of alien kinsmen as they are *for you:* an external picture painted on your retina, representing a crowd oppressive by its vastness and confusion. As they are for you, so you think they positively and absolutely are. *I* feel no call for them, you say; therefore there *is* no call for them. But all the while, beyond this externality which is your way of realizing them, they realize themselves with the acutest internality, with the most violent thrills of life. 'Tis you who are dead, stone-dead and blind and senseless, in your way of looking on. You open your eyes upon a scene of which you miss the whole significance. Each of these grotesque or even repulsive aliens is animated by an inner joy of living as hot or hotter than that which you feel beating in your private breast. The sun rises and beauty beams to light his path. To miss the inner joy of him, as Stevenson says, is to miss the whole of him.

That you have a saturation-point of interest tells us nothing of the interests that absolutely are. The Universe, with every living entity which her resources create, creates at the same time a call for that entity, and an appetite for its continuance — creates it, if nowhere else, at least within the heart of the entity itself. It is absurd to suppose, simply because our private power of sympathetic vibration with other lives gives out so soon, that in the heart of infinite being itself there can be such a thing as plethora, or glut, or supersaturation. It is not as if there were a bounded room where the minds in possession had to move up or make place and crowd together to accommodate new occupants. Each new mind brings its own edition of the universe of space along with it, its own room to inhabit; and these spaces never crowd each other — the space of my imagination, for example, in no way interferes with yours. The amount of possible consciousness seems to be governed by no law analogous to that of the so-called conservation of energy in the material world. When one man wakes up, or one is born, another does not have to go to sleep, or die, in order to keep the consciousness of the universe a constant quantity. There seems no formal limit to the positive increase of being in spiritual respects; and since spiritual being, whenever it comes, affirms itself, expands and craves continuance, we may justly and literally say, regardless of the defects of our own private sympathy, that the supply of individual life in the universe can never possibly, however immeasurable it may become, exceed the demand. The demand for that supply is there the moment the supply itself comes into being, for the beings supplied demand their own continuance.

I hope now that you agree with me that the tiresomeness of an over-peopled Heaven is a purely subjective and illusory notion, a sign of human incapacity, a remnant of the old narrow-hearted aristocratic creed. The Deity that suffers us, we may be sure, can suffer many another queer and wondrous and only half-delightful thing.

For my own part, then, so far as logic goes, I am willing that every leaf that ever grew in this world's forests and rustled in the breeze should become immortal. It is purely a question of fact: are the leaves so, or not? Abstract quantity, and the abstract need-lessness in our eyes of so much reduplication of things so much alike, have no connection with the subject. For bigness and number and generic similarity are only manners of our finite way of thinking; and, considered in itself and apart from our imagination, one scale of dimensions and of numbers for the Universe is no more miraculous or inconceivable than another, the moment you grant to a universe the liberty to be at all, in place of the Non-entity that might conceivably have reigned.

The heart of being can have no exclusions akin to those which our poor little hearts set up. The inner significance of other lives exceeds all our powers of sympathy and insight. If we feel a significance in our own life which would lead us spontaneously to claim its perpetuity, let us be at least tolerant of like claims made by other lives, however numerous, however unideal they may seem to us to be. Let us at any rate not decide adversely on our own claim, whose grounds we feel directly, because we cannot decide favorably on the alien claims, whose grounds we cannot feel at all. That would be letting blindness lay down the law to sight.

2*

NOTE A: DENIAL OF IMMORTALITY
ON PHYSIOLOGICAL GROUNDS

So widespread is this conclusion in positivistic circles, so abundantly is it expressed in conversation, and so frequently

*From HI: Note 2; quotations abridged.

implied in things that are written, that I confess that my surprise was great when I came to look into books for a passage explicitly denying immortality on physiological grounds, which I might quote to make my text more concrete. I was unable to find anything blunt and distinct enough to serve. I looked through all the books that would naturally suggest themselves, with no effect; and I vainly asked various psychological colleagues. And yet I should almost have been ready to take oath that I had read several such passages of the most categoric sort within the last decade. Very likely this is a false impression, and it may be with this opinion as with many others. The atmosphere is full of them; many a writer's pages logically presuppose and involve them; yet, if you wish to refer a student to an express and radical statement that he may employ as a text to comment on, you find almost nothing that will do. In the present case there are plenty of passages in which, in a general way, mind is said to be conterminous with brain-function, but hardly one in which the author thereupon explicitly denies the possibility of immortality. The best one I have found is perhaps this: "Not only consciousness, but every stirring of life depends on functions that go out like a flame when nourishment is cut off. . . . The phenomena of consciousness correspond, element for element, to the operations of special parts of the brain. . . . The destruction of any piece of the apparatus involves the loss of some one or other of the vital operations; and the consequence is that, as far as life extends, we have before us only an organic function, not a *Ding-an-sich,* or an expression of that imaginary entity the Soul. This fundamental proposition . . . carries with it the denial of the immortality of the soul, since, where no soul exists, its mortality or immortality cannot be raised as a question." [*E. Duhring: der Werth des Lebens,* 3d edition, pp. 48, 168.]

NOTE B: POSSIBLE THEORIES
OF THE BRAIN'S FUNCTION*

The philosophically instructed reader will notice that I have all along been placing myself at the ordinary dualistic point of view of natural science and of common sense. From this point of view mental facts like feelings are made of one kind of stuff or substance, physical facts of another. An absolute phenomenism, not believing such a dualism to be ultimate, may possibly end by

*From HI: Note 3; quotations abridged.

solving some of the problems that are insoluble when propounded in dualistic terms. Meanwhile, since the physiological objection to immortality has arisen on the ordinary dualistic plane of thought, and since absolute phenomenism has as yet said nothing articulate enough to count about the matter, it is proper that my reply to the objection should be expressed in dualistic terms — leaving me free, of course, on any later occasion to make an attempt, if I wish, to transcend them and use different categories.

Now, on the dualistic assumption, one cannot see more than two really different sorts of dependence of our mind on our brain: Either

(1) The brain brings into being the very stuff of consciousness of which our mind consists; or else

(2) Consciousness preëxists as an entity, and the various brains give to it its various special forms.

If supposition 2 be the true one, and the stuff of mind preëxists, there are, again, only two ways of conceiving that our brain confers upon it the specifically human form. It may exist

(a) In disseminated particles; and then our brains are organs of concentration, organs for combining and massing these into resultant minds of personal form. Or it may exist

(b) In vaster unities (absolute 'world-soul,' or something less); and then our brains are organs for separating it into parts and giving them finite form.

There are thus three possible theories of the brain's function, and no more. We may name them, severally —

1. The theory of production;
2a. The theory of combination;
2b. The theory of separation.

In the text of the lecture, theory number 2b (specified more particularly as the transmission-theory) is defended against theory number 1. Theory 2a, otherwise known as the mind-dust or mind-stuff theory, is left entirely unnoticed for lack of time. I also leave it uncriticised in these notes, having already considered it, as fully as the so-far published forms of it may seem to call for, in my work, *The Principles of Psychology*, New York, Holt & Co., 1892, chapter VI. I may say here, however, that Professor W. K. Clifford, one of the ablest champions of the combination-theory, and originator of the useful term 'mind-stuff,' considers that theory incompatible with individual immortality, and in his review of Stewart's and Tait's book, *The Unseen Universe*, thus expresses his conviction:—

"Consciousness is a complex thing made up of elements, a

stream of feelings. The action of the brain is also a complex thing made up of elements, a stream of nerve-messages. For every feeling in consciousness there is at the same time a nerve-message in the brain. If individual feeling always goes with individual nerve-message, if combination or stream of feelings always goes with stream of nerve-messages, does it not follow that, when the stream of nerve-messages is broken up, the stream of feelings will be broken up also, will no longer form a consciousness? The force of this evidence is not to be weakened by any number of spiritual bodies. Inexorable facts connect our consciousness with this body that we know; and that not merely as a whole, but the parts of it are connected severally with parts of our brain-action. If there is any similar connection with a spiritual body, it only follows that the spiritual body must die at the same time with the natural one." [*Lectures and Essays,* vol. i. p. 247-49. Compare also passages of similar purport in vol. ii, pp. 65-70.]

NOTE C: FORMULATIONS OF PRODUCTION THEORY*

The theory of production, or materialistic theory, seldom ventures to formulate itself very distinctly. Perhaps the following passage from Cabanis is as explicit as anything one can find:—

"To acquire a just idea of the operations from which thought results, we must consider the brain as a particular organ specially destined to produce it; just as the stomach and intestines are destined to operate digestion. The impressions, arriving in the brain, force it to enter into activity; just as the alimentary materials, falling into the stomach, excite it to a more abundant secretion of gastric juice, and to the movements which result in their own solution.

"Do you say that the organic movements by which the brain exercises these functions are unknown? I reply that the action by which the nerves of the stomach determine the different operations which constitute digestion, are equally hidden from our scrutiny. We see the food-materials fall into this viscus with their own proper qualities; we see them emerge with new qualities, and we infer that the stomach is really the author of this alteration. Similarly we see the impressions reaching the brain by the intermediation of the nerves; it acts upon them, and soon it emits [*renvoie*] them metamorphosed into ideas, to which the language of physiognomy or gesture, or the signs of speech and writing, give an outward expression. We conclude, then, with an equal certitude, that the brain digests, as it were, the impressions; that

*From HI: Note 4; quotations abridged.

it performs organically the secretion of thought." [*Rapports du Physique et du Moral,* 8th edition, 1844, p. 137.]

It is to the ambiguity of the word 'impression' that such an account owes whatever plausibility it may seem to have. More recent forms of the production-theory have shown a tendency to liken thought to a 'force' which the brain exerts, or to a 'state' into which it passes. Herbert Spencer, for instance, writes:—

"The law of metamorphosis, which holds among the physical forces, holds equally between them and the mental forces. . . . How this metamorphosis takes place; how a force existing as motion, heat, or light can become a mode of consciousness; how it is possible for aerial vibrations to generate the sensation we call sound, or for the forces liberated by chemical changes in the brain to give rise to emotion — these are mysteries which it is impossible to fathom. But they are not profounder mysteries than the transformations of the physical forces into each other." [*First Principles,* 2nd Edition, p. 217.]

So Büchner says: "Thinking must be regarded as a special mode of general natural motion. . . . That thinking is and must be a mode of motion is not merely a postulate of logic, but a proposition which has of late been demonstrated experimentally. . . . Various ingenious experiments have proved that the swiftest thought that we are able to evolve occupies at least the eighth or tenth part of a second." [*Force and Matter,* New York, 1891, p. 241.]

Heat and light, being modes of motion, 'phosphorescence' and 'incandescence' are phenomena to which consciousness has been likened by the production-theory. Mr. Percival Lowell writes: "When we have, as we say, an idea, what happens inside of us is probably something like this: the neural current of molecular change passes up the nerves, and through the ganglia reaches at last the cortical cells. . . . When it reaches the cortical cells, it finds a set of molecules which are not so accustomed to this special change. The current encounters resistance, and in overcoming this resistance it causes the cells to glow. This white-heating of the cells we call consciousness. Consciousness, in short, is probably nerve-glow." [*Occult Japan,* Boston, 1895, p. 311.]

NOTE D: TRANSMISSION-THEORY AND TRANSCENDENTALISM*

The transmission-theory connects itself very naturally with that whole tendency of thought known as transcendentalism. Emerson,

*From HI: Note 5

for example, writes: "We lie in the lap of immense intelligence, which makes us receivers of its truth and organs of its activity. When we discern justice, when we discern truth, we do nothing of ourselves, but allow a passage to its beams." [*Self-Reliance*, p. 56.] But it is not necessary to identify the consciousness postulated in the lecture, as preëxisting behind the scenes, with the Absolute Mind of transcendental Idealism, although, indeed, the notion of it might lead in that direction. The absolute Mind of transcendental Idealism is one integral Unit, one single World-mind. For the purposes of my lecture, however, there might be many minds behind the scenes as well as one. All that the transmission-theory absolutely requires is that they should transcend *our* minds — which thus come from *something* mental that preëxists, and is larger than themselves.

NOTE E: BLINDNESS OF MEN*

I beg the reader to peruse R. L. Stevenson's magnificent little essay entitled 'The Lantern Bearers,' reprinted in the collection entitled *Across the Plains*. The truth is that we are doomed, by the fact that we are practical beings with very limited tasks to attend to, and special ideals to look after, to be absolutely blind and insensible to the inner feelings, and to the whole inner significance of lives that are different from our own. Our opinion of the worth of such lives is absolutely wide of the mark, and unfit to be counted at all.

3

PREFACE TO SECOND EDITION

So many critics have made one and the same objection to the doorway to immortality which my lecture claims to be left open by the "transmission-theory" of cerebral action, that I feel tempted, as the book is again going to press, to add a word of explanation.

If our finite personality here below, the objectors say, be due to the transmission through the brain of portions of a preëxisting larger consciousness, all that can remain after the brain expires is the larger consciousness itself as such, with which we should henceforth be perforce reconfounded, the only means of our existence in finite personal form having ceased.

But this, the critics continue, is the pantheistic idea of immortality, survival, namely, in the soul of the world; not the

*From HI: Note 10.

Christian idea of immortality, which means survival in strictly personal form.

In showing the possibility of a mental life after the brain's death, they conclude, the lecture has thus at the same time shown the impossibility of its identity with the personal life, which is the brain's function.

Now I am myself anything but a pantheist of the monistic pattern; yet for simplicity's sake I did in the lecture speak of the "mother-sea" in terms that must have sounded pantheistic, and suggested that I thought of it myself as a unit. The interpretation of my critics was therefore not unnatural; and I ought to have been more careful to guard against its being made.

In note [D] I partially guarded against it by saying that the "mother-sea" from which the finite mind is supposed to be strained by the brain, need not be conceived of in pantheistic terms exclusively. There might be, I said, many minds behind the scenes as well as one. The plain truth is that *one may conceive the mental world behind the veil in as individualistic a form as one pleases, without any detriment to the general scheme by which the brain is represented as a transmissive organ.*

If the extreme individualistic view were taken, one's finite mundane consciousness would be an extract from one's larger, truer personality, the latter having even now some sort of reality behind the scenes. And in transmitting it — to keep to our extremely mechanical metaphor, which confessedly throws no light on the actual *modus operandi* — one's brain would also leave effects upon the part remaining behind the veil; for when a thing is torn, both fragments feel the operation.

And just as (to use a very coarse figure) the stubs remain in a check-book whenever a check is used, to register the transaction, so these impressions on the transcendent self might constitute so many vouchers of the finite experiences of which the brain had been the mediator; and ultimately they might form that collection within the larger self of memories of our earthly passage, which is all that, since Locke's day, the continuance of our personal identity beyond the grave has by psychology been recognized to mean.

It is true that all this would seem to have affinities rather with preëxistence and with possible reincarnations than with the Christian notion of immortality. But my concern in the lecture was not to discuss immortality in general. It was confined to showing it to be *not incompatible* with the brain-function theory of our present mundane consciousness. I hold that it is so compatible, and compatible moreover in fully individualized form. The reader would be in accord with everything that the text of my lecture intended to say, were he to assert that every memory and affection of his present life is to be preserved, and that he shall never *in secula seculorum* cease to be able to say to himself: "I am the same personal being who in old times upon the earth had those experiences."

APPENDIX VII
PSYCHICAL RESEARCH*

For twenty-five years I have been in touch with the literature of psychical research, and have had acquaintance with numerous "researchers." I have also spent a good many hours (though far fewer than I ought to have spent) in witnessing (or trying to witness) phenomena. Yet I am theoretically no "further" than I was at the beginning; and I confess that at times I have been tempted to believe that the Creator has eternally intended this department of nature to remain *baffling,* to prompt our curiosities and hopes and suspicions all in equal measure, so that, although ghosts and clairvoyances, and raps and messages from spirits, are always seeming to exist and can never be fully explained away, they also can never be susceptible of full corroboration.

The peculiarity of the case is just that there are so many sources of possible deception in most of the observations that the whole lot of them *may* be worthless, and yet that in comparatively few cases can aught more fatal than this vague general possibility of error be pleaded against the record. Science meanwhile needs something more than bare possibilities to build upon; so your genuinely scientific inquirer — I don't mean your ignoramus "scientist" — has to remain unsatisfied. It is hard to believe, however, that the Creator has really put any big array of phenomena into the world merely to defy and mock our scientific tendencies; so my deeper belief is that we psychical researchers have been too precipitate with our hopes, and that we must expect to mark progress not by quarter-centuries, but by half-centuries or whole centuries.

Fraud, conscious or unconscious, seems ubiquitous throughout the range of physical phenomena of spiritism, and false pretense, prevarication, and fishing for clues are ubiquitous in the mental manifestations of mediums. If it be not everywhere fraud simulat-

*From MS:176-206, abridged.

ing reality, one is tempted to say, then the reality (if any reality there be) has the bad luck of being fated everywhere to simulate fraud. The suggestion of humbug seldom stops, and mixes itself with the best manifestations. Mrs. Piper's control, "Rector," is a most impressive personage, who discerns in an extraordinary degree his sitter's inner needs, and is capable of giving elevated counsel to fastidious and critical minds. Yet in many respects he is an arrant humbug—such he seems to me at least—pretending to a knowledge and power to which he has no title, nonplussed by contradiction, yielding to suggestion, and covering his tracks with plausible excuses. Now the non-"researching" mind looks upon such phenomena simply according to their face-pretension and never thinks of asking what they may signify below the surface. Since they profess for the most part to be revealers of spirit life, it is either as being absolutely that, or as being absolute frauds, that they are judged. The result is an inconceivably shallow state of public opinion on the subject. One set of persons, emotionally touched at hearing the names of their loved ones given, and consoled by assurances that they are "happy," accept the revelation, and consider spiritualism "beautiful." More hard-headed subjects, disgusted by the revelation's contemptible contents, outraged by the fraud, and prejudiced beforehand against all "spirits," high or low, avert their minds from what they call such "rot" or "bosh" entirely. Thus do two opposite sentimentalisms divide opinion between them!

Meanwhile the first thing that anyone learns who attends seriously to these phenomena is that their causation is far too complex for our feelings about what is or is not romantic enough to be spiritual to throw any light upon it. The causal factors must be carefully distinguished and traced through series, from their simplest to their strongest forms, before we can begin to understand the various resultants in which they issue.

"Psychics" form indeed a special branch of education, in which experts are only gradually becoming developed. The phenomena are as massive and widespread as is anything in nature, and the study of them is as tedious, repellent, and undignified. To reject it for its unromantic character is like rejecting bacteriology because *penicillium glaucum* grows on horse-dung and *bacterium termo* lives in putrefaction. Scientific men have long ago ceased to think of the dignity of the materials they work in. When imposture has been checked off as far as possible, when chance coincidence has been allowed for, when opportunities for normal knowledge on the part of the subject have been noted, and skill in "fishing" and following clues unwittingly furnished by the voice or face of by-standers have been counted in, those who have the fullest acquaint-ance with the phenomena admit that in good mediums *there is a residuum of knowledge displayed* that can only be called super-normal: the medium taps some source of information not open to ordinary people. Myers used the word "telepathy" to indicate that the sitter's own thoughts or feelings may be thus directly tapped. Mrs. Sidgwick has suggested that if living minds can be thus tapped telepathically, so possibly may the minds of spirits be similarly tapped—if spirits there be. On this view we should have one dis-tinct theory of the performances of a typical test-medium. They would be all originally due to an odd *tendency to personate,* found in her dream life as it expresses itself in trance. (Most of us reveal such a tendency whenever we handle a "ouija-board" or a "plan-chette," or let ourselves write automatically with a pencil.) The result is a "control," who purports to be speaking; and all the resources of the automatist, including his or her trance faculty of telepathy, are called into play in building this fictitious personage out plausibly. On such a view of the control, the medium's *will to personate* runs the whole show; and if spirits be involved in it at all, they are passive beings, stray bits of whose memory she is able to seize and use for her purposes, without the spirit being any more aware of it than the sitter is aware of it when his own mind is similarly tapped.

This is one possible way of interpreting a certain type of psychical phenomenon. It uses psychological as well as "spiritual" factors, and quite obviously it throws open for us far more questions than it answers, questions about our subconscious con-stitution and its curious tendency to humbug, about the telepathic faculty, and about the possibility of an existent spirit world.

I do not instance this theory to defend it, but simply to show what complicated hypotheses one is inevitably led to consider, the moment one looks at the facts in their complexity and turns one's back on the *naïve* alternative of "revelation or imposture," which is as far as either spiritist thought or ordinary scientist thought goes. The phenomena are endlessly complex in their factors, and they are so little understood as yet that offhand judgments, whether of "spirits" or of "bosh," are the one as silly as the other. When we complicate the subject still further by considering what connec-tion such things as rappings, apparitions, poltergeists, spirit photo-graphs, and materializations may have with it, the bosh end of the scale gets heavily loaded, it is true, but your genuine inquirer still is loath to give up. He lets the data collect, and bides his time.

He believes that "bosh" is no more an ultimate element in nature, or a really explanatory category in human life, than "dirt" is in chemistry. Every kind of "bosh" has its own factors and laws; and patient study will bring them definitely to light.

The only way to rescue the "pure bosh" view of the matter is one which has sometimes appealed to my own fancy, but which I imagine few readers will seriously adopt. If, namely, one takes the theory of evolution radically, one ought to apply it not only to the rock-strata, the animals and the plants, but to the stars, to the chemical elements, and to the laws of nature. There must have been a far-off antiquity, one is then tempted to suppose, when things were really chaotic. Little by little, out of all the haphazard possibilities of that time, a few connected things and habits arose, and the rudiments of regular performance began. Every variation in the way of law and order added itself to this nucleus, which inevitably grew more considerable as history went on; while the aberrant and inconstant variations, not being similarly preserved, disappeared from being, wandered off as unrelated vagrants, or else remained so imperfectly connected with the part of the world that had grown regular as only to manifest their existence by occasional lawless intrusions, like those which "psychic" phenomena now make into our scientifically organized world. On such a view, these phenomena ought to remain "pure bosh" forever, that is, they ought to be forever intractable to intellectual methods, because they should not yet be organized enough in themselves to follow any laws. Wisps and shreds of the original chaos, they would be connected enough with the cosmos to affect its periphery every now and then, as by a momentary whiff or touch or gleam, but not enough ever to be followed up and hunted down and bagged. Their relation to the cosmos would be tangential solely.

Looked at dramatically, most occult phenomena make just this sort of impression. They are inwardly as incoherent as they are outwardly wayward and fitful. If they express anything, it is pure "bosh," pure discontinuity, accident, and disturbance, with no law apparent but to interrupt, and no purpose but to baffle. They seem like stray vestiges of that primordial irrationality, from which all our rationalities have been evolved.

To settle dogmatically into this bosh-view would save labor, but it would go against too many intellectual prepossessions to be adopted save as a last resort of despair. Your psychical researcher therefore bates no jot of hope, and has faith that when we get our data numerous enough, some sort of rational treatment of them will succeed.

Someone said to me a short time ago that after my twenty-five years of dabbling in "Psychics," it would be rather shameful were I unable to state any definite conclusions whatever as a consequence. I had to agree; so I now proceed to take up the challenge and express such convictions as have been engendered in me by that length of experience, be the same true or false ones. I may be dooming myself to the pit in the eyes of better-judging posterity; I may be raising myself to honor; I am willing to take the risk, for what I shall write is *my* truth, as I now see it.

I began this article by confessing myself baffled. I *am* baffled, as to spirit return, and as to many other special problems. I am also constantly baffled as to what to think of this or that particular story, for the sources of error in any one observation are seldom fully knowable. But weak sticks make strong faggots; and when the stories fall into consistent sorts that point each in a definite direction, one gets a sense of being in the presence of genuinely natural types of phenomena. As to there being such real natural types of phenomena ignored by orthodox science, I am not baffled at all, for I am fully convinced of it. One cannot get demonstrative proof here. One has to follow one's personal sense, which, of course, is liable to err, of the dramatic probabilities of nature. Our critics here obey their sense of dramatic probability as much as we do. Take "raps," for example, and the whole business of objects moving without contact. "Nature," thinks the scientific man, is not so unutterably silly. The cabinet, the darkness, the tying, suggest a sort of human rat-hole life exclusively and "swindling" is for him the dramatically sufficient explanation. It probably is, in an indefinite majority of instances; yet it is to me dramatically improbable that the swindling should not have accreted round some originally genuine nucleus. If we look at human imposture as a historic phenomenon, we find it always imitative. One swindler imitates a previous swindler, but the first swindler of that kind imitated someone who was honest. You can no more create an absolutely new trick than you can create a new word without any previous basis. You don't know how to go about it. Try, reader, yourself, to invent an unprecedented kind of "physical phenomenon of spiritualism." When *I* try, I find myself mentally turning over the regular medium-stock, and thinking how I might improve some item. This being the dramatically probable human way, I think differently of the whole type, taken collectively, from the way in which I may think of the single instance. I find myself believing that there is "something in" these never ending reports of physical phenomena, although I haven't yet the least positive notion of the something. It becomes to my mind simply a very worthy problem for investigation. Either I or the scientist is of course a fool, with our opposite views of probability here; and I only wish he might feel the liability, as cordially as I do, to pertain to both of us.

I fear I look on nature generally with more charitable eyes than his, though perhaps he would pause if he realized, as I do, how vast the fraudulency is which in consistency he must attribute to her. Nature is brutal enough, Heavens knows; but no one yet has held her non-human side to be *dishonest,* and even in the human sphere deliberate deceit is far rarer than the "classic" intellect, with its few and rigid categories, was ready to acknowledge. There is a hazy penumbra in us all where lying and delusion meet, where passion rules beliefs as well as conduct, and where the term "scoundrel" does not clear up everything to the depths as it did for our forefathers. The first automatic writing I ever saw was forty years ago. I unhesitatingly thought of it as deceit, although it contained vague elements of supernormal knowledge. Since then I have come to see in automatic writing one example of a department of human activity as vast as it is enigmatic. Every sort of person is liable to it, or to something equivalent to it; and whoever encourages it in himself finds himself personating someone else, either signing what he writes by fictitious name, or spelling out, by ouija board or table-tips, messages from the departed. Our subconscious region seems, as a rule, to be dominated either by a crazy "will to make-believe," or by some curious external force impelling us to personation. The first difference between the psychical researcher and the inexpert person is that the former realizes the commonness and typicality of the phenomenon here, while the latter, less informed, thinks it so rare as to be unworthy of attention. *I wish to go on record for the commonness.*

The next thing I wish to go on record for is *the presence,* in the midst of all the humbug, *of really supernormal knowledge.* By this I mean knowledge that cannot be traced to the ordinary sources of information—the senses, namely, of the automatist. In really strong mediums this knowledge seems to be abundant, though it is usually spotty, capricious, and unconnected. Really strong mediums are rarities; but when one starts with them and works downwards into less brilliant regions of the automatic life, one tends to interpret many slight but odd coincidences with truth as possibly rudimentary forms of this kind of knowledge.

What is one to think of this queer chapter in human nature? It is odd enough on any view. If all it means is a preposterous and inferior monkey-like tendency to forge messages, systematically embedded in the soul of all of us, it is weird; and weirder still that it should then own all this supernormal information. If on the other hand the supernormal information be the key to the phenomenon, it ought to be superior; and then how ought we to account for the "wicked partner," and for the undeniable mendacity and inferiority of so much of the performance? We are thrown, for our conclusions, upon our instinctive sense of the dramatic probabilities of nature. My own dramatic sense tends instinctively to picture the situation as an interaction between slumbering faculties in the automatist's mind and a cosmic environment of *other consciousness* of some sort which is able to work upon them. If there were in the universe a lot of diffuse soul-stuff, unable of itself to get into consistent personal form, or to take permanent possession of an organism, yet always craving to do so, it might get its head into the air, parasitically, so to speak, by profiting by weak spots in the armor of human minds, and slipping in and stirring up there the sleeping tendency to personate. It would induce habits in the subconscious region of the mind it used thus, and would seek above all things to prolong its social opportunities by making itself agreeable and plausible. It would drag stray scraps of truth with it from the wider environment, but would betray its mental inferiority by knowing little how to weave them into any important or significant story.

This, I say, is the dramatic view which my mind spontaneously takes, and it has the advantage of falling into line with ancient human traditions. The views of others are just as dramatic, *for the phenomenon is actuated by will of some sort anyhow,* and wills give rise to dramas. The spiritist view, as held by Messrs. Hyslop and Hodgson, sees a "will to communicate," struggling through inconceivable layers of obstruction in the conditions. I have heard Hodgson liken the difficulties to those of two persons who on earth should have only dead-drunk servants to use as their messengers. The scientist, for his part, sees a "will to deceive," watching its chance in all of us, and able (possibly?) to use "telephathy" in its service.

Which kind of will, and how many kinds of will are most inherently probable? Who can say with certainty? The only certainty is that the phenomena are enormously complex, especially if one includes in them such intellectual flights of mediumship as Swedenborg's, and if one tries in any way to work the physical phenomena in. That is why I personally am as yet neither a convinced believer in parasitic demons, nor a spiritist, nor a scientist, but still remain a psychical researcher waiting for more facts before concluding.

Out of my experience, such as it is (and it is limited enough), one fixed conclusion dogmatically emerges, and that is this, that we with our lives are like islands in the sea, or like trees in the forest. The maple and the pine may whisper to each other with their leaves, and Conanicut and Newport hear each other's foghorns. But the trees also commingle their roots in the darkness underground, and the islands also hang together through the ocean's bottom. Just so there is a continuum of cosmic consciousness, against which our individuality builds but accidental fences, and into which our several minds plunge as into a mother-sea or reservoir. Our "normal" consciousness is circumscribed for adaptation to our external earthly environment, but the fence is weak in spots, and fitful influences from beyond leak in, showing the otherwise unverifiable common connection. Not only psychic research, but metaphysical philosophy, and speculative biology are led in their own ways to look with favor on some such "panpsychic" view of the universe as this. Assuming this common reservoir of consciousness to exist, this bank upon which we all draw, and in which so many of earth's memories must in some way be stored, or mediums would not get at them as they do, the question is, What is its own structure? What is its inner topography? This question, first squarely formulated by Myers, deserves to be called "Myers's problem" by scientific men hereafter. What are the conditions of individuation or insulation in this mother-sea? To what tracts, to what active systems functioning separately in it, do personalities correspond? Are individual "spirits" constituted there? How numerous, and of how many hierarchic orders may these then be? How permanent? How transient? And how confluent with one another may they become?

What, again, are the relations between the cosmic consciousness and matter? Are there subtler forms of matter which upon occasion may enter into functional connection with the individuations in the psychic sea, and then, and then only, show themselves?—so that our ordinary human experience, on its material as well as on its mental side, would appear to be only an extract from the larger psychophysical world?

Vast, indeed, and difficult is the inquirer's prospect here, and the most significant data for his purpose will probably be just these dingy little mediumistic facts which the Huxleyan minds of our time find so unworthy of their attention. But when was not the science of the future stirred to its conquering activities by the little rebellious exceptions to the science of the present? Hardly, as yet, has the surface of the facts called "psychic" begun to be scratched for scientific purposes. It is through following these facts, I am persuaded, that the greatest scientific conquests of the coming generation will be achieved. *Kühn ist das Mühen, herrlich der Lohn!*

APPENDIX VIII
A SUGGESTION ABOUT MYSTICISM*

Much interest in the subject of religious mysticism has been shown in philosophic circles of late years. Most of the writings I have seen have treated the subject from the outside, for I know of no one who has spoken as having the direct authority of experience in favor of his views. I also am an outsider, and very likely what I say will prove the fact loudly enough to readers who possibly may stand within the pale. Nevertheless, since between outsiders one is as good as another, I will not leave my suggestion unexpressed.

The suggestion, stated very briefly, is that states of mystical intuition may be only very sudden and great extensions of the ordinary "field of consciousness." Concerning the causes of such extensions I have no suggestion to make; but the extension itself would, if my view be correct, consist in an immense spreading of the margin of the field, so that knowledge ordinarily transmarginal would become included, and the ordinary margin would grow more central. Fechner's "wave-scheme" will diagrammatize the alteration, as I conceive it, if we suppose that the wave of present awareness, steep above the horizontal line that represents the plane of the usual "threshold," slopes away below it very gradually in all directions. A fall of the threshold, however caused, would, under these circumstances, produce the state of things which we see on an unusually flat shore at the ebb of a spring-tide. Vast tracts usually covered are then revealed to view, but nothing rises more than a few inches above the water's bed, and great parts of the scene are submerged again, whenever a wave washes over them.

Some persons have naturally a very wide, others a very narrow, field of consciousness. The narrow field may be represented by an unusually steep form of the wave. When by any accident the threshold lowers, in persons of this type—I speak here from direct

*From CER:500-513. The whole article. It was written about six months before James's death.

personal experience—so that the field widens and the relations of its centre to matters usually subliminal come into view, the larger panorama perceived fills the mind with exhilaration and sense of mental power. It is a refreshing experience; and—such is now my hypothesis—we only have to suppose it to occur in an exceptionally extensive form, to give us a mystical paroxysm, if such a term be allowed.

A few remarks about the field of consciousness may be needed to give more definiteness to my hypothesis. The field is composed at all times of a mass of present sensation, in a cloud of memories, emotions, concepts, etc. Yet these ingredients, which have to be named separately, are not separate, as the conscious field contains them. Its form is that of a much-at-once, in the unity of which the sensations, memories, concepts, impulses, etc., coalesce and are dissolved. The present field as a whole came continuously out of its predecessor and will melt into its successor as continuously again, one sensation-mass passing into another sensation-mass and giving the character of a gradually changing *present* to the experience, while the memories and concepts carry time-coefficients which place whatever is present in a temporal perspective more or less vast.

When, now, the threshold falls, what comes into view is not the next mass of *sensation;* for sensation requires new physical stimulations to produce it, and no alteration of a purely mental threshold can create these. Only in case the physical stimuli were already at work subliminally, preparing the next sensation, would whatever sub-sensation was already prepared reveal itself when the threshold fell. But with the memories, concepts, and conational states, the case is different. Nobody knows exactly how far we are "marginally" conscious of these at ordinary times, or how far beyond the "margin" of our present thought transmarginal consciousness of them may exist.[1] There is at any rate no definite bound set between what is central and what is marginal in consciousness, and the margin itself has no definite bound *a parte foris.* It is like the field of vision, which the slightest movement of the eye will extend, revealing objects that always stood there

[1]Transmarginal or subliminal, the terms are synonymous. Some psychologists deny the existence of such consciousness altogether (A. H. Pierce, for example, and Münsterberg apparently). Others, *e.g.,* Bergson, make it exist and carry the whole freight of our past. Others again (as Myers) would have it extend (in the "telepathic" mode of communication) from one person's mind into another's. For the purposes of my hypothesis I have to postulate its existence; and once postulating it, I prefer not to set any definite bounds to its extent.

to be known. My hypothesis is that a movement of the threshold downwards will similarly bring a mass of subconscious memories, conceptions, emotional feelings, and perceptions of relation, etc., into view all at once; and that if this enlargement of the nimbus that surrounds the sensational present is vast enough, while no one of the items it contains attracts our attention singly, we shall have the conditions fulfilled for a kind of consciousness in all essential respects like that termed mystical. It will be transient, if the change of threshold is transient. It will be of reality, enlargement, and illumination, possibly rapturously so. It will be of unification, for the present coalesces in it with ranges of the remote quite out of its reach under ordinary circumstances; and the sense of *relation* will be greatly enhanced. Its form will be intuitive or perceptual, not conceptual, for the remembered or conceived objects in the enlarged field are supposed not to attract the attention singly, but only to give the sense of a tremendous *muchness* suddenly revealed. If they attracted attention separately, we should have the ordinary steep-waved consciousness, and the mystical character would depart.

Such is my suggestion. Persons who *know* something of mystical experience will no doubt find in it much to criticize. If any such shall do so with definiteness, it will have amply served its purpose of helping our understanding of mystical states to become more precise.

The notion I have tried (at such expense of metaphor) to set forth was originally suggested to me by certain experiences of my own, which could only be described as very sudden and incomprehensible enlargements of the conscious field, bringing with them a curious sense of cognition of real fact. All have occurred within the past five years; three of them were similar in type; the fourth was unique.

In each of the three like cases, the experience broke in abruptly upon a perfectly commonplace situation and lasted perhaps less than two minutes. In one instance I was engaged in conversation, but I doubt whether the interlocutor noticed my abstraction. What happened each time was that I seemed all at once to be reminded of a past experience; and this reminiscence, ere I could conceive or name it distinctly, developed into something further that belonged with it, this in turn into something further still, and so on, until the process faded out, leaving me amazed at the sudden vision of increasing ranges of distant fact of which I could give no articulate account. The mode of consciousness was perceptual, not conceptual — the field expanding so fast that there seemed

no time for conception or identification to get in its work. There
was a strongly exciting sense that my knowledge of past (or present?) reality was enlarging pulse by pulse, but so rapidly that my
intellectual processes could not keep up the pace. The *content* was
thus entirely lost to retrospection — it sank into the limbo into
which dreams vanish as we gradually awake. The feeling — I won't
call it belief — that I had had a sudden *opening,* had seen through
a window, as it were, distant realities that incomprehensibly belonged with my own life, was so acute that I cannot shake it
off to-day.

This conviction of fact-revealed, together with the perceptual
form of the experience and the inability to make articulate report,
are all characters of mystical states. The point of difference is
that in my case certain special directions only, in the field of
reality, seemed to get suddenly uncovered, whereas in classical
mystical experiences it appears rather as if the whole of reality
were uncovered at once. *Uncovering* of some sort is the essence
of the phenomenon, at any rate, and is what, in the language
of the Fechnerian wave-metaphor, I have used the expression
"fall of the threshold" to denote.

My fourth experience of uncovering had to do with dreams. I
was suddenly intromitted into the cognizance of a pair of dreams
that I could not remember myself to have had, yet they seemed
somehow to connect with me. I despair of giving the reader any
just idea of the bewildering confusion of mind into which I was
thrown by this, the most intensely peculiar experience of my whole
life. I wrote a full memorandum of it a couple of days after it
happened, and appended some reflections. Even though it should
cast no light on the conditions of mysticism, it seems as if this
record might be worthy of publication, simply as a contribution
to the descriptive literature of pathological mental states. I let it
follow, therefore, as originally written, with only a few words
altered to make the account more clear.

"San Francisco, Feb. 14th, 1906. — The night before last, in my
bed at Stanford University, I woke at about 7:30 A.M., from a
quiet dream of some sort, and whilst gathering my waking wits,
seemed suddenly to get mixed up with reminiscences of a dream
of an entirely different sort, which seemed to telescope, as it
were, into the first one, a dream very elaborate, of lions, and
tragic. I concluded this to have been a previous dream of the same
sleep; but the apparent mingling of two dreams was something
very queer, which I had never before experienced.

"On the following night (Feb. 12-13) I awoke suddenly from

my first sleep, which appeared to have been very heavy, in the middle of a dream, in thinking of which I became suddenly confused by the contents of two other dreams that shuffled themselves abruptly in between the parts of the first dream, and of which I couldn't grasp the origin. Whence come *these dreams?* I asked. They were close to *me,* and fresh, as if I had just dreamed them; and yet they were far away *from the first dream.* The contents of the three had absolutely no connection. One had a cockney atmosphere, it had happened to someone in London. The other two were American. One involved the trying on of a coat (was this the dream I seemed to wake from?) the other was a sort of nightmare and had to do with soldiers. Each had a wholly distinct emotional atmosphere that made its individuality discontinuous with that of the others. And yet, in a moment, as these three dreams alternately telescoped into and out of each other, and I seemed to myself to have been their common dreamer, they seemed quite as distinctly *not* to have been dreamed in succession, in that one sleep. *When,* then? Not on a previous night, either. *When,* then, and *which* was the one out of which I had just awakened? *I could no longer tell:* one was as close to me as the others, and yet they entirely repelled each other, and I seemed thus to belong to three different dream-systems at once, no one of which would connect itself either with the others or with my waking life. I began to feel curiously confused and *scared,* and tried to wake myself up wider, but I seemed already wide-awake. Presently cold shivers of dread ran over me: *am I getting into other people's dreams?* Is this a 'telepathic' experience? Or an invasion of double (or treble) personality? Or is it a thrombus in a cortical artery? and the beginning of a general mental 'confusion' and disorientation which is going on to develop who knows how far?

"Decidedly I was losing hold of my 'self,' and making acquaintance with a quality of mental distress that I had never known before, its nearest analogue being the sinking, giddying anxiety that one may have when, in the woods, one discovers that one is really 'lost.' Most human troubles look towards a terminus. Most fears point in a direction, and concentrate towards a climax. Most assaults of the evil one may be met by bracing oneself against something — one's principles, one's courage, one's will, one's pride. But in this experience all was diffusion from a centre, and foot-hold swept away, the brace itself disintegrating all the faster as one needed its support more direly. Meanwhile vivid perception (or remembrance) of the various dreams kept coming over me in alternation. Whose? *whose?* WHOSE? Unless I can *attach* them, I am swept out to sea with no horizon and no bond, getting *lost*. The idea aroused the 'creeps' again, and with it the fear of again falling asleep and renewing the process. It had begun the previous night, but then the confusion had only gone one step, and had seemed simply curious. *This* was the second step — where might I be after a third step had been taken? My teeth chattered at the thought.

"At the same time I found myself filled with a new pity towards persons passing into dementia with *Verwirrtheit,* or into invasions of secondary personality. *We* regard them as simply *curious;* but what *they* want in the awful drift of their being out of its customary self, is any principle of steadiness to hold on to. We ought to assure them and reassure them that we will stand by them, and recognize the true self in them to the end. We ought to let them know that we are with *them* and not (as too often we must seem to them) a part of the world that but confirms and publishes their deliquescence.

"Evidently I was in full possession of my reflective wits; and whenever I thus objectively thought of the situation in which I was, my anxieties ceased. But there was a tendency to relapse into the dreams and reminiscences, and to relapse vividly; and then the confusion recommenced, along with the emotion of dread lest it should develop farther.

"Then I looked at my watch. Half-past twelve! Midnight, therefore. And this gave me another reflective idea. Habitually, on going to bed, I fall into a very deep slumber from which I never naturally awaken until after two. I never awaken, therefore, from a midnight dream, as I did to-night, so of midnight dreams my ordinary consciousness retains no recollection. My sleep seemed terribly heavy as I woke to-night. Dream states carry dream memories — why may not the two succedaneous dreams (whichever two of the three *were* succedaneous) be memories of *twelve o'clock dreams of previous nights,* swept in, along with the just-fading dream, into the just-waking system of memory? Why, in short, may I not be tapping, in a way precluded by my ordinary habit of life, *the midnight stratum* of my past experiences?

"This idea gave great relief — I felt now as if I were in full possession of my *anima rationalis.* I turned on my light, resolving to read myself to sleep. But I didn't read, I felt drowsy instead, and, putting out the light, soon was in the arms of Morpheus.

"I woke again two or three times before daybreak with no dream-experiences, and finally, with a curious, but not alarming, confusion between two dreams, similar to that which I had had the previous morning, I awoke to the new day at seven.

"Nothing peculiar happened the following night, so the thing seems destined not to develop any further."[2]

The distressing confusion of mind in this experience was the exact opposite of mystical illumination, and equally unmystical was the definiteness of what was perceived. But the exaltation of the sense of relation was mystical (the perplexity all revolved about the fact that the three dreams *both did and did not belong in the most intimate way together);* and the sense that *reality was being uncovered* was mystical in the highest degree. To this day I feel that those extra dreams were dreamed in reality, but when, where, and by whom, I cannot guess.

In the *Open Court* for December, 1909, Mr. Frederick Hall narrates a fit of ether-mysticism which agrees with my formula very well. When one of his doctors made a remark to the other, he chuckled, for he realized that these friends "believed they saw real things and causes, but they *didn't,* and I did. . . . I was where the causes *were* and to see them required no more mental ability than to recognize a color as blue. . . . The knowledge of how little [the doctors] actually did see, coupled with their evident feeling that they saw all there was, was funny to the last degree. . . . [They] knew as little of the real causes as does the child who, viewing a passing train and noting its revolving wheels, supposes that they, turning of themselves, give to coaches and locomotive

---

[2] I print the rest of my memorandum in the shape of a note:—

"Several ideas suggest themselves that make the observation instructive.

"First, the general notion, now gaining ground in mental medicine, that certain mental maladies may be foreshadowed in dream-life, and that therefore the study of the latter may be profitable.

"Then the specific suggestion, that states of 'confusion,' loss of personality, *apraxia,* etc., so often taken to indicate cortical lesion or degeneration of dementic type, may be very superficial functional affections. In my own case the confusion was *foudroyante*—a state of consciousness unique and unparalleled in my sixty-four years of the world's experience; yet it alternated quickly with perfectly rational states, as this record shows. It seems, therefore, merely as if the threshold between the rational and the morbid state had, in my case, been temporarily lowered, and as if similar confusions might be very near the line of possibility in all of us.

"There are also the suggestions of a telepathic entrance into someone else's dreams, and of a doubling up of personality. In point of fact I don't know now 'who' had those three dreams, or which one 'I' first woke up from, so quickly did they substitute themselves back and forth for each other, discontinuously. Their discontinuity was the pivot of the situation. My sense of it was as 'vivid' and 'original' an experience as anything Hume could ask for. And yet they kept telescoping!

"Then there is the notion that by waking at certain hours we may tap distinct strata of ancient dream-memory."

their momentum. Or imagine a man seated in a boat, surrounded
by dense fog, and out of the fog seeing a flat stone leap from the
crest of one wave to another. *If he had always sat thus,* his
explanations must be very crude as compared with those of a man
whose eyes could pierce fog, and who saw upon the shore the boy
skipping stones. In some such way the remarks of the two
physicians seemed to me like the last two 'skips' of a stone
thrown from my side. . . . All that was essential in the remark
I knew before it was made. Thus to discover convincingly and for
myself, that the things which are unseen are those of real importance, this was sufficiently stimulating."

It is evident that Mr. Hall's marginal field got enormously enlarged by the ether, yet so little defined as to its particulars that
what he perceived was mainly the thoroughgoing causal inte-
gration of its whole content. That this perception brought with
it a tremendous feeling of importance and superiority is a matter
of course.

I have treated the phenomenon under discussion as if it consisted
in the uncovering of tracts of *consciousness.* Is the consciousness
already there waiting to be uncovered? and is it a veridical revelation of reality? These are questions on which I do not touch.
In the subjects of the experience the "emotion of conviction" is
always strong, and sometimes absolute. The ordinary psychologist
disposes of the phenomenon under the conveniently "scientific"
head of *petit mal,* if not of "bosh" or "rubbish." But we know so
little of the noetic value of abnormal mental states of any kind
that in my opinion we had better keep an open mind and collect
facts sympathetically for a long time to come. We shall not
understand these alterations of consciousness either in this generation or in the next.

APPENDIX IX
FAITH: ITS PLACE, FUNCTIONS AND RIGHTS

1

GENERAL PHILOSOPHIC ATTITUDE*

Were I obliged to give a short name to my philosophic
attitude, I should call it that of *radical empiricism,* in spite of the
fact that such brief nicknames are nowhere more misleading than

*From WB: Preface, vii-xiii.

in philosophy. I say 'empiricism," because it is contented to regard its most assured conclusions concerning matters of fact as hypotheses liable to modification in the course of future experience; and I say 'radical,' because it treats the doctrine of monism itself as an hypothesis, and, unlike so much of the half-way empiricism that is current under the name of positivism or agnosticism or scientific naturalism, it does not dogmatically affirm monism as something with which all experience has got to square. The difference between monism and pluralism is perhaps the most pregnant of all the differences in philosophy. *Primâ facie* the world is a pluralism; as we find it, its unity seems to be that of any collection; and our higher thinking consists chiefly of an effort to redeem it from that first crude form. Postulating more unity than the first experiences yield, we also discover more. But absolute unity, in spite of brilliant dashes in its direction, still remains undiscovered, still remains a *Grensbegriff*. "Ever not quite" must be the rationalistic philosopher's last confession concerning it. After all that reason can do has been done, there still remains the opacity of the finite facts as merely given, with most of their peculiarities mutually unmediated and unexplained. To the very last, there are the various 'points of view' which the philosopher must distinguish in discussing the world; and what is inwardly clear from one point remains a bare externality and datum to the other. The negative, the alogical, is never wholly banished. Something — "call it fate, chance, freedom, spontaneity, the devil, what you will" — is still wrong and other and outside and unincluded, from *your* point of view, even though you be the greatest of philosophers. Something is always mere fact and *givenness;* and there may be in the whole universe no one point of view extant from which this would not be found to be the case. "Reason," as a gifted writer says, "is but one item in the mystery; and behind the proudest consciousness that ever reigned, reason and wonder blushed face to face. The inevitable stales, while doubt and hope are sisters. Not unfortunately the universe is wild — game-flavored as a hawk's wing. Nature is miracle all; the same returns not save to bring the different. The slow round of the engraver's lathe gains but the breadth of a hair, but the difference is distributed back over the whole curve, never an instant true — ever not quite."[1]

This is pluralism, somewhat rhapsodically expressed. He who takes for his hypothesis the notion that it is the permanent form

[1] B. P. Blood: The Flaw in Supremacy: Published by the Author, Amsterdam, N. Y., 1893.

of the world is what I call a radical empiricist. For him the crudity of experience remains an eternal element thereof. There is no possible point of view from which the world can appear an absolutely single fact. Real possibilities, real indeterminations, real beginnings, real ends, real evil, real crises, catastrophes, and escapes, a real God, and a real moral life, just as common-sense conceives these things, may remain in empiricism as conceptions which that philosophy gives up the attempt either to 'overcome' or to reinterpret in monistic form.

Many of my professionally trained *confrères* will smile at the irrationalism of this view, and at the artlessness of my essays in point of technical form. But they should be taken as illustrations of the radically empiricist attitude rather than as argumentations for its validity. That admits meanwhile of being argued in as technical a shape as anyone can desire, and possibly I may be spared to do later a share of that work. Meanwhile these essays seem to light up with a certain dramatic reality the attitude itself, and make it visible alongside of the higher and lower dogmatisms between which in the pages of philosophic history it has generally remained eclipsed from sight.

The first four essays are largely concerned with defending the legitimacy of religious faith. To some rationalizing readers such advocacy will seem a sad misuse of one's professional position. Mankind, they will say, is only too prone to follow faith unreasoningly, and needs no preaching nor encouragement in that direction. I quite agree that what mankind at large most lacks is criticism and caution, not faith. Its cardinal weakness is to let belief follow recklessly upon lively conception, especially when the conception has instinctive liking at its back. I admit, then, that were I addressing the Salvation Army or a miscellaneous popular crowd it would be a misuse of opportunity to preach the liberty of believing as I have in these pages preached it. What such audiences most need is that their faiths should be broken up and ventilated, that the northwest wind of science should get into them and blow their sickliness and barbarism away. But academic audiences, fed already on science, have a very different need. Paralysis of their native capacity for faith and timorous *abulia* in the religious field are their special forms of mental weakness, brought about by the notion, carefully instilled, that there is something called scientific evidence by waiting upon which they shall escape all danger of shipwreck in regard to truth. But there is really no scientific or other method by which men can steer safely between the opposite dangers of believing too little or of believing too much. To face such dangers is apparently our duty, and to hit the right channel between them is the measure of our wisdom as men. It does not follow, because recklessness may be a vice in soldiers, that courage ought never to be preached to them. What *should* be preached is courage weighted with responsibility — such courage as the Nelsons and Washingtons never failed to show after they had taken everything into account that might tell against their success, and made every provision to minimize disaster in case they met defeat. I do not think that anyone can accuse me of preaching reckless faith. I have preached the right of the individual to indulge his personal faith at his personal risk. I have discussed the kinds of risk; I have contended that none of us escape all of them; and I have only pleaded that it is better to face them open-eyed than to act as if we did not know them to be there.

After all, though, you will say, Why such an ado about a matter concerning which, however, we may theoretically differ, we all practically agree? In this age of toleration, no scientist will ever try actively to interfere with our religious faith, provided we enjoy it quietly with our friends and do not make a public nuisance of it in the market-place. But it is just on this matter of the market-place that I think the utility of such essays as mine may turn. If religious hypotheses about the universe be in order at all, then the active faiths of individuals in them, freely expressing themselves in life, are the experimental tests by which they are verified, and the only means by which their truth or falshood can be wrought out. The truest scientific hypothesis is that which, as we say, 'works' best; and it can be no otherwise with religious hypotheses. Religious history proves that one hypothesis after another has worked ill, has crumbled at contact with a widening knowledge of the world, and has lapsed from the minds of men. Some articles of faith, however, have maintained themselves through every vicissitude, and possess even more vitality to-day than ever before: it is for the 'science of religions' to tell us just which hypotheses these are. Meanwhile the freest competition of the various faiths with one another, and their openest application to life by their several champions, are the most favorable conditions under which the survival of the fittest can proceed. They ought therefore not to lie hid each under its bushel, indulged-in quietly with friends. They ought to live in publicity, vying with each other; and it seems to me that (the régime of tolerance once granted, and a fair field shown) the scientist has nothing to fear for his own interests from the liveliest possible state of fermentation in the religious world of his time. Those faiths will best stand the test which adopt also his hypotheses, and make them integral elements of their own. He should welcome therefore every species of religious agitation and discussion, so long as he is willing to allow that some religious hypothesis *may* be true. Of course there are plenty of scientists who would deny that dogmatically, maintaining that science has already ruled all possible religious hypotheses out of court. Such scientists ought, I agree, to aim at imposing privacy on religious faiths, the public manifestation of which could only be a nuisance in their eyes. With all such scientists, as well as with their allies outside of science, my quarrel openly lies; and I hope that my book may do something to persuade the reader of their crudity, and range him on my side. Religious fermentation is always a symptom of the intellectual vigor of a society; and it is only when they forget that they are hypotheses and put on rationalistic and authoritative pretensions, that our faiths do harm. The most interesting and valuable things about a man are his ideals and over-beliefs. The same is true of nations and historic epochs; and the excesses of which the particular individuals and epochs are guilty are compensated in the total, and become profitable to mankind in the long run.

2

FAITH, THE WILL TO ACT AND REALITY*

Religion has meant many things in human history; but when from now onward I use the word I mean to use it in the supernaturalist sense, as declaring that the so-called order of nature, which constitutes this world's experience, is only one portion of the total universe, and that there stretches beyond this visible world an unseen world of which we now know nothing positive, but in its relation to which the true significance of our present mundane life consists. A man's religious faith (whatever more special items of doctrine it may involve) means for me essentially his faith in the existence of an unseen order of some kind in which the riddles of the natural order may be found explained. In the more developed religions the natural world has always been regarded as the mere scaffolding or vestibule of a truer, more eternal world, and affirmed to be a sphere of education, trial, or redemption. In these religions, one must in some fashion die to the natural life before one can enter into life eternal. The notion

*From WB ("Is Life Worth Living?"): 51-62.

that this physical world of wind and water, where the sun rises and the moon sets, is absolutely and ultimately the divinely aimed-at and established thing, is one which we find only in very early religions, such as that of the most primitive Jews. It is this natural religion (primitive still, in spite of the fact that poets and men of science whose good-will exceeds their perspicacity keep publishing it in new editions tuned to our contemporary ears) that, as I said a while ago, has suffered definitive bankruptcy in the opinion of a circle of persons, among whom I must count myself, and who are growing more numerous every day. For such persons the physical order of nature, taken simply as science knows it, cannot be held to reveal any one harmonious spiritual intent. It is mere *weather,* as Chauncey Wright called it, doing and undoing without end.

Now, I wish to make you feel, if I can in the short remainder of this hour, that we have a right to believe the physical order to be only a partial order; that we have a right to supplement it by an unseen spiritual order which we assume on trust, if only thereby life may seem to us better worth living again. But as such a trust will seem to some of you sadly mystical and execrably unscientific, I must first say a word or two to weaken the veto which you may consider that science opposes to our act.

There is included in human nature an ingrained naturalism and materialism of mind which can only admit facts that are actually tangible. Of this sort of mind the entity called 'science' is the idol. Fondness for the word 'scientist' is one of the notes by which you may know its votaries; and its short way of killing any opinion that it disbelieves in is to call it 'unscientific.' It must be granted that there is no slight excuse for this. Science has made such glorious leaps in the last three hundred years, and extended our knowledge of nature so enormously both in general and in detail; men of science, moreover, have as a class displayed such admirable virtues — that it is no wonder if the worshippers of science lose their head. In this very University, accordingly, I have heard more than one teacher say that all the fundamental conceptions of truth have already been found by science, and that the future has only the details of the picture to fill in. But the slightest reflection on the real conditions will suffice to show how barbaric such notions are. They show such a lack of scientific imagination, that it is hard to see how one who is actively advancing any part of science can make a mistake so crude. Think how many absolutely new scientific conceptions have arisen in our own generation, how many new problems have been formulated that were never thought of before, and then cast an eye upon the brevity of science's career. It began with Galileo, not three hundred years ago. Four thinkers since Galileo, each informing his successor of what discoveries his own lifetime had seen achieved, might have passed the torch of science into our hands as we sit here in this room. Indeed, for the matter of that, an audience much smaller than the present one, an audience of some five or six score people, if each person in it could speak for his own generation, would carry us away to the black unknown of the human species, to days without a document or monument to tell their tale. Is it credible that such a mushroom knowledge, such a growth overnight as this, *can* represent more than the minutest glimpse of what the universe will really prove to be when adequately understood? No! our science is a drop, our ignorance a sea. Whatever else be certain, this at least is certain — that the world of our present natural knowledge *is* enveloped in a larger world of *some* sort of whose residual properties we at present can frame no positive idea.

Agnostic positivism, of course, admits this principle theoretically in the most cordial terms, but insists that we must not turn it to any practical use. We have no right, this doctrine tells us, to dream dreams, or suppose anything about the unseen part of the universe, merely because to do so may be for what we are pleased to call our highest interests. We must always wait for sensible evidence for our beliefs; and where such evidence is inaccessible we must frame no hypotheses whatever. Of course this is a safe enough position *in abstracto*. If a thinker had no stake in the unknown, no vital needs, to live or languish according to what the unseen world contained, a philosophic neutrality and refusal to believe either one way or the other would be his wisest cue. But, unfortunately, neutrality is not only inwardly difficult, it is also outwardly unrealizable, where our relations to an alternative are practical and vital. This is because, as the psychologists tell us, belief and doubt are living attitudes, and involve conduct on our part. Our only way, for example, of doubting, or refusing to believe, that a certain thing *is,* is continuing to act as if it were *not.* If, for instance, I refuse to believe that the room is getting cold, I leave the windows open and light no fire just as if it still were warm. If I doubt that you are worthy of my confidence, I keep you uninformed of all my secrets just as it you were *un*worthy of the same. If I doubt the need of insuring my house, I leave it uninsured as much as if I believed there were no need. And so if I must not believe that the world is divine, I can only express that refusal by declining ever to act distinctively as if it were so, which can only mean acting on certain critical occasions as if it were *not* so, or in an irreligious way. There are, you see, inevitable occasions in life when inaction is a kind of action, and must count as action, and when not to be for is to be practically against; and in all such cases strict and consistent neutrality is an unattainable thing.

And, after all, is not this duty of neutrality where only our inner interests would lead us to believe, the most ridiculous of commands? Is it not sheer dogmatic folly to say that our inner interests can have no real connection with the forces that the hidden world may contain? In other cases divinations based on inner interests have proved prophetic enough. Take science itself! Without an imperious inner demand on our part for ideal logical and mathematical harmonies, we should never have attained to proving that such harmonies lie hidden between all the chinks and interstices of the crude natural world. Hardly a law has been established in science, hardly a fact ascertained, which was not first sought after, often with sweat and blood, to gratify an inner need. Whence such needs come from we do not know: we find them in us, and biological psychology so far only classes them with Darwin's 'accidental variations.' But the inner need of believing that this world of nature is a sign of something more spiritual and eternal than itself is just as strong and authoritative in those who feel it, as the inner need of uniform laws of causation ever can be in a professionally scientific head. The toil of many generations has proved the latter need prophetic. Why *may* not the former one be prophetic, too? And if needs of ours outrun the visible universe, why *may* not that be a sign that an invisible universe is there? What, in short, has authority to debar us from trusting our religious demands? Science as such assuredly has no authority, for she can only say what is, not what is not; and the agnostic "thou shalt not believe without coercive sensible evidence" is simply an expression (free to anyone to make) of private personal appetite for evidence of a certain peculiar kind.

Now, when I speak of trusting our religious demands, just what do I mean by 'trusting'? Is the word to carry with it license to define in detail an invisible world, and to anathematize and excommunicate those whose trust is different? Certainly not! Our faculties of belief were not primarily given us to make orthodoxies and heresies withal; they were given us to live by. And to trust our religious demands means first of all to live in the light of them, and to act as if the invisible world which they suggest were

real. It is a fact of human nature, that men can live and die by
the help of a sort of faith that goes without a single dogma or
definition. The bare assurance that this natural order is not ultimate
but a mere sign or vision, the external staging of a many-storied
universe, in which spiritual forces have the last word and are
eternal — this bare assurance is to such men enough to make life
seem worth living in spite of every contrary presumption suggested by its circumstances on the natural plane. Destroy this
inner assurance, however, vague as it is, and all the light and
radiance of existence is extinguished for these persons at a stroke.
Often enough the wild-eyed look at life — the suicidal mood —
will then set in.

And now the application comes directly home to you and me.
Probably to almost everyone of us here the most adverse life
would seem well worth living, if we only could be *certain* that our
bravery and patience with it were terminating and eventuating and
bearing fruit somewhere in an unseen spiritual world. But grant-
ing we are not certain, does it then follow that a bare trust in
such a world is a fool's paradise and lubberland, or rather that
it is a living attitude in which we are free to indulge? Well, we
are free to trust at our own risks anything that is not impossible,
and that can bring analogies to bear in its behalf. That the world
of physics is probably not absolute, all the converging multitude
of arguments that make in favor of idealism tend to prove; and
that our whole physical life may lie soaking in a spiritual atmosphere, a dimension of being that we at present have no organ for
apprehending, is vividly suggested to us by the analogy of the life
of our domestic animals. Our dogs, for example, are in our human
life but not of it. They witness hourly the outward body of events
whose inner meaning cannot, by any possible operation, be revealed to their intelligence — events in which they themselves often
play the cardinal part. My terrier bites a teasing boy, for example,
and the father demands damages. The dog may be present at
every step of the negotiations, and see the money paid, without
an inkling of what it all means, without a suspicion that it has
anything to do with *him;* and he never *can* know in his natural
dog's life. Or take another case which used greatly to impress me
in my medical-student days. Consider a poor dog whom they are
vivisecting in a laboratory. He lies strapped on a board and
shrieking at his executioners, and to his own dark consciousness
is literally in a sort of hell. He cannot see a single redeeming ray
in the whole business; and yet all these diabolical-seeming events
are often controlled by human intentions with which, if his poor

benighted mind could only be made to catch a glimpse of them, all that is heroic in him would religiously acquiesce. Healing truth, relief to future sufferings of beast and man, are to be bought by them. It may be genuinely a process of redemption. Lying on his back on the board there he may be performing a function incalculably higher than any that prosperous canine life admits of; and yet, of the whole performance, this function is the one portion that must remain absolutely beyond his ken.

Now turn from this to the life of man. In the dog's life we see the world invisible to him because we live in both worlds. In human life, although we only see our world, and his within it, yet encompassing both these worlds a still wider world may be there, as unseen by us as our world is by him; and to believe in that world *may* be the most essential function that our lives in this world have to perform. But *"may* be! *may* be!" one now hears the positivist contemptuously exclaim; "what use can a scientific life have for maybes?" Well, I reply, the 'scientific' life itself has much to do with maybes, and human life at large has everything to do with them. So far as man stands for anything, and is productive or originative at all, his entire vital function may be said to have to deal with maybes. Not a victory is gained, not a deed of faithfulness or courage is done, except upon a maybe; not a service, not a sally of generosity, not a scientific exploration or experiment or textbook, that may not be a mistake. It is only by risking our persons from one hour to another that we live at all. And often enough our faith beforehand in an uncertified result *is the only thing that makes the result come true.* Suppose, for instance, that you are climbing a mountain, and have worked yourself into a position from which the only escape is by a terrible leap. Have faith that you can successfully make it, and your feet are nerved to its accomplishment. But mistrust yourself, and think of all the sweet things you have heard the scientists say of *maybes,* and you will hesitate so long that, at last, all unstrung and trembling, and launching yourself in a moment of despair, you roll in the abyss. In such a case (and it belongs to an enormous class), the part of wisdom as well as of courage is to *believe what is in the line of your needs,* for only by such belief is the need fulfilled. Refuse to believe, and you shall indeed be right, for you shall irretrievably perish. But believe, and again you shall be right, for you shall save yourself. You make one or the other of two possible universes true by your trust or mistrust — both universes having been only *maybes,* in this particular, before you contributed your act.

Now, it appears to me that the question whether life is worth living is subject to conditions logically much like these. It does, indeed, depend on you *the liver*. If you surrender to the nightmare view and crown the evil edifice by your own suicide, you have indeed made a picture totally black. Pessimism, completed by your act, is true beyond a doubt, so far as your world goes. Your mistrust of life has removed whatever worth your own enduring existence might have given to it; and now, throughout the whole sphere of possible influence of that existence, the mistrust has proved itself to have had divining power. But suppose, on the other hand, that instead of giving way to the nightmare view you cling to it that this world is not the *ultimatum*. Suppose you find yourself a very well-spring, as Wordsworth says, of —

> "Zeal, and the virtue to exist by faith
> As solders live by courage; as, by strength
> Of heart, the sailor fights with roaring seas."

Suppose, however thickly evils crowd upon you, that your unconquerable subjectivity proves to be their match, and that you find a more wonderful joy than any passive pleasure can bring in trusting ever in the larger whole. Have you not now made life worth living on these terms? What sort of a thing would life really be, with your qualities ready for a tussle with it, if it only brought fair weather and gave these higher faculties of yours no scope? Please remember that optimism and pessimism are definitions of the world, and that our own reactions on the world, small as they are in bulk, are integral parts of the whole thing, and necessarily help to determine the definition. They may even be the decisive elements in determining the definition. A large mass can have its unstable equilibrium overturned by the addition of a feather's weight; a long phrase may have its sense reversed by the addition of the three letters *n-o-t*. This life *is* worth living, we can say, *since it is what we make it, from the moral point of view;* and we are determined to make it from that point of view, so far as we have anything to do with it, a success.

Now, in this description of faiths that verify themselves I have assumed that our faith in an invisible order is what inspires those efforts and that patience which make this visible order good for moral men. Our faith in the seen world's goodness (goodness now meaning fitness for successful moral and religious life) has verified itself by leaning on our faith in the unseen world. But will our faith in the unseen world similarly verify itself? Who knows?

Once more it is a case of *maybe;* and once more *maybes* are the essence of the situation. I confess that I do not see why the very existence of an invisible world may not in part depend on the personal response which any one of us may make to the religious appeal. God himself, in short, may draw vital strength and increase of very being from our fidelity. For my own part, I do not know what the sweat and blood and tragedy of this life mean, if they mean anything short of this. If this life be not a real fight, in which something is eternally gained for the universe by success, it is no better than a game of private theatricals from which one may withdraw at will. But it *feels* like a real fight — as if there were something really wild in the universe which we, with all our idealities and faithfulnesses, are needed to redeem; and first of all to redeem our own hearts from atheisms and fears. For such a half-wild, half-saved universe our nature is adapted. The deepest thing in our nature is this *Binnenleben* (as a German doctor lately has called it), this dumb region of the heart in which we dwell alone with our willingnesses and unwillingnesses, our faiths and fears. As through the cracks and crannies of caverns those waters exude from the earth's bosom which then form the fountain-heads of springs, so in these crepuscular depths of personality the sources of all our outer deeds and decisions take their rise. Here is our deepest organ of communication with the nature of things; and compared with these concrete movements of our soul all abstract statements and scientific arguments — the veto, for example, which the strict positivist pronounces upon our faith — sound to us like mere chatterings of the teeth. For here possibilities, not finished facts, are the realities with which we have actively to deal; and to quote my friend William Salter, of the Philadelphia Ethical Society, "as the essence of courage is to stake one's life on a possibility, so the essence of faith is to believe that the possibility exists."

Be not afraid of life. Believe that life *is* worth living, and your belief will help create the fact. The 'scientific proof' that you are right may not be clear before the day of judgment (or some stage of being which that expression may serve to symbolize) is reached. But the faithful fighters of this hour, or the beings that then and there will represent them, may then turn to the faint-hearted, who here decline to go on, with words like those with which Henry IV greeted the tardy Crillon after a great victory had been gained: "Hang yourself, brave Crillon! we fought at Arques, and you were not there."

3

SOME BASIC DISTINCTIONS*

Let us give the name of *hypothesis* to anything that may be proposed to our belief; and just as the electricians speak of live and dead wires, let us speak of any hypothesis as either *live* or *dead*. A live hypothesis is one which appeals as a real possibility to him to whom it is proposed. If I ask you to believe in the Mahdi, the notion makes no electric connection with your nature — it refuses to scintillate with any credibility at all. As an hypothesis it is completely dead. To an Arab, however (even if he be not one of the Mahdi's followers), the hypothesis is among the mind's possibilities: it is alive. This shows that deadness and liveness in an hypothesis are not intrinsic properties, but relations to the individual thinker. They are measured by his willingness to act. The maximum of liveness in an hypothesis means willingness to act irrevocably. Practically, that means belief; but there is some believing tendency wherever there is willingness to act at all.

Next, let us call the decision between two hypotheses an *option*. Options may be of several kinds. They may be — 1, *living* or *dead;* 2, *forced* or *avoidable;* 3, *momentous* or *trivial;* and for our purposes we may call an option a *genuine* option when it is of the forced, living, and momentous kind.

1. A living option is one in which both hypotheses are live ones. If I say to you: "Be a theosophist or be a Mohammedan," it is probably a dead option, because for you neither hypothesis is likely to be alive. But if I say: "Be an agnostic or be a Christian," it is otherwise: trained as you are, each hypothesis makes some appeal, however small, to your belief.

2. Next, if I say to you: "Choose between going out with your umbrella or without it," I do not offer you a genuine option, for it is not forced. You can easily avoid it by not going out at all. Similarly, if I say, "Either love me or hate me," "Either call my theory true or call it false," your option is avoidable. You may remain indifferent to me, neither loving nor hating, and you may decline to offer any judgment as to my theory. But if I say, "Either accept this truth or go without it," I put on you a forced option, for there is no standing place outside of the alternative. Every dilemma based on a complete logical disjunction, with no possibility of not choosing, is an option of this forced kind.

3. Finally, if I were Dr. Nansen and proposed to you to join my

*From WB ("The Will to Believe"): 2-4, 17-19, 8-11, slightly abridged.

North Pole expedition, your option would be momentous; for this would probably be your only similar opportunity, and your choice now would either exclude you from the North Pole sort of immortality altogether or put at least the chance to it into your hands. He who refuses to embrace a unique opportunity loses the prize as surely as if he tried and failed. *Per contra,* the option is trivial when the opportunity is not unique, when the stake is insignificant, or when the decision is reversible if it later prove unwise. Such trivial options abound in the scientific life. A chemist finds an hypothesis live enough to spend a year in its verification: he believes in it to that extent. But if his experiments prove inconclusive either way, he is quit for his loss of time, no vital harm being done.

There are two ways of looking at our duty in the matter of opinion — ways entirely different, and yet ways about whose difference the theory of knowledge seems hitherto to have shown very little concern. *We must know the truth;* and *we must avoid error* — these are our first and great commandments as would-be knowers; but they are not two ways of stating an identical commandment, they are two separable laws. Although it may indeed happen that when we believe the truth *A,* we escape as an incidental consequence from believing the falsehood *B,* it hardly ever happens that my merely disbelieving *B* we necessarily believe *A.* We may in escaping *B* fall into believing other falsehoods, *C* or *D,* just as bad as *B;* or we may escape *B* by not believing anything at all, not even *A.*

Believe truth! Shun error! — these, we see, are two materially different laws; and by choosing between them we may end by coloring differently our whole intellectual life. We may regard the chase for truth as paramount, and the avoidance of error as secondary; or we may, on the other hand, treat the avoidance of error as more imperative, and let truth take its chance. Clifford in the instructive passage which I have quoted*, exhorts us to th

*"Belief is desecrated when given to unproved and unquestioned ste-ments for the solace and private pleasure of the believer ... Whoso yuld deserve well of his fellows in this matter will guard the purity of his elief with a very fanaticism of jealous care, lest at any time it should st on an unworthy object, and catch a stain which can never be wipe away. ... If [a] belief has been accepted on insufficient evidence [eve though the belief be true, as Clifford on the same page explains] the p asure is a stolen one.... It is sinful because it is stolen in defiance of o duty to mankind. That duty is to guard ourselves from such beliefs s from a pestilence which may shortly master our own body and then s ead to the rest of the town.... It is wrong always, everywhere, and f everyone, to believe anything upon insufficient evidence."

latter course. Believe nothing, he tells us, keep your mind in suspense forever, rather than by closing it on insufficient evidence incur the awful risk of believing lies. You, on the other hand, may think that the risk of being in error is a very small matter when compared with the blessings of real knowledge, and be ready to be duped many times in your investigation rather than postpone indefinitely the chance of guessing true. I myself find it impossible to go with Clifford. We must remember that these feelings of our duty about either truth or error are in any case only expressions of our passional life. Biologically considered, our minds are as ready to grind out falsehood as veracity, and he who says, "Better go without belief forever than believe a lie!" merely shows his own preponderant private horror of becoming a dupe. He may be critical of many of his desires and fears, but this fear he slavishly obeys. He cannot imagine any one questioning its binding force. For my own part, I have also a horror of being duped; but I can believe that worse things than being duped may happen to a man in this world: so Clifford's exhortation has to my ears a thoroughly fantastic sound. It is like a general informing his soldiers that it is better to keep out of battle forever than to risk a single wound. Not so are victories either over enemies or over nature gained. Our errors are surely not such awfully solemn things. In a world where we are so certain to incur them in spite of all our caution, a certain lightness of heart seems healthier than this excessive nervousness on their behalf. At any rate, it seems the fittest thing for the empiricist philosopher.

The thesis I defend is, briefly stated, this: *Our passional nature not only lawfully may, but must, decide an option between propositions, whenever it is a genuine option that cannot by its nature be decided on intellectual grounds; for to say, under such circumstances, "Do not decide, but leave the question open," is itself a passional decision — just like deciding yes or no — and is attended with the same risk of losing the truth.*

4*

FAITH AND THE RIGHT TO BELIEVE[1]

'Intellectualism' is the belief that our mind comes upon a world complete in itself, and has the duty of ascertaining its contents;

*From Sp: 221-231.
[1][The following pages, part of a syllabus printed for the use of students in an introductory course in philosophy, were found with the MS. of this book, with the words, 'To be printed as part of the Introduction to Philosophy,' noted thereon in the author's handwriting.]

but has no power of re-determining its character, for that is already given.

Among intellectualists two parties may be distinguished. Rationalizing intellectualists lay stress on deductive and 'dialectic' arguments, making large use of abstract concepts and pure logic (Hegel, Bradley, Taylor, Royce). Empiricist intellectualists are more 'scientific,' and think that the character of the world must be sought in our sensible experiences, and found in hypotheses based exclusively thereon (Clifford, Pearson).

Both sides insist that in our conclusions personal preferences should play no part, and that no argument from what *ought to be* to what *is,* is valid. 'Faith,' being the greeting of our whole nature to a kind of world conceived as well adapted to that nature, is forbidden, until purely intellectual *evidence* that such *is* the actual world has come in. Even if evidence should eventually prove a faith true, the truth, says Clifford, would have been 'stolen,' if assumed and acted on too soon.

Refusal to believe anything concerning which 'evidence' has not yet come in, would thus be the rule of intellectualism. Obviously it postulates certain conditions, which for aught we can see need not necessarily apply to all the dealings of our minds with the Universe to which they belong.

1. It postulates that *to escape error* is our paramount duty. Faith *may* grasp truth; but also it *may* not. By resisting it always, we are sure of escaping error; and if by the same act we renounce our chance at truth, that loss is the lesser evil, and should be incurred.

2. It postulates that in every respect the universe is finished in advance of our dealings with it;

That the knowledge of what it thus is, is best gained by a passively receptive mind, with no native sense of probability, or good-will towards any special result;

That 'evidence' not only needs no good-will for its reception; but is able, if patiently waited for, to neutralize ill-will;

Finally, that our beliefs and our acts based thereupon, although they are parts of the world, and although the world without them is unfinished, are yet such mere externalities as not to alter in any way the significance of the rest of the world when they are added to it.

In our dealings with many details of fact these postulates work well. Such details exist in advance of our opinion; truth concerning them is often of no pressing importance; and by believing nothing, we escape error while we wait. But even here we often *cannot* wait but must act, somehow; so we act on the most *probable* hypothesis, trusting that the event may prove us wise. Moreover, not to act on one belief, is often equivalent to acting as if the opposite belief were true, so inaction would not always be as 'passive' as the intellectualists assume. It is one attitude of will.

Again, Philosophy and Religion have to interpret the total character of the world, and it is by no means clear that here the intellectualist postulates obtain. It may be true all the while (even though the evidence be still imperfect) that, as Paulsen says, 'the natural order is at bottom a moral order.' It may be true that work is still doing in the world-process, and that in that work we are called to bear our share. The character of the world's results may in part depend upon our acts. Our acts may depend on our religion — on our not-resisting our faith-tendencies, or on our sustaining them in spite of 'evidence' being incomplete. These faith-tendencies in turn are but expressions of our good-will towards certain forms of result.

Such faith-tendencies are extremely active psychological forces, constantly outstripping evidence. The following steps may be called the 'faith-ladder':

1. There is nothing absurd in a certain view of the world being true, nothing self-contradictory;
2. It *might* have been true under certain conditions;
3. It *may* be true, even now;
4. It is *fit* to be true;
5. It *ought* to be true;
6. It *must* be true;
7. It *shall* be true, at any rate true for *me*.

Obviously this is no intellectual chain of inferences, like the *sorites* of the logic-books. Yet it is a slope of good-will on which in the larger questions of life men habitually live.

Intellectualism's proclamation that our good-will, our 'will to believe,' is a pure disturber of truth, is itself an act of faith of the most arbitrary kind. It implies the will to insist on a universe of intellectualist constitution, and the willingness to stand in the way of a pluralistic universe's success, such success requiring the good-will and active faith, theoretical as well as practical, of all concerned, to make it 'come true.'

Intellectualism thus contradicts itself. It is a sufficient objection to it, that if a 'pluralistically' organized, or 'co-operative' universe or the 'melioristic' universe above, were really here, the veto of intellectualism on letting our good-will ever have any vote would debar us from ever admitting that universe to be true.

Faith thus remains as one of the inalienable birthrights of our mind. Of course it must remain a practical, and not a dogmatic attitude. It must go with toleration of other faiths, with the search for the most probable, and with the full consciousness of responsibilities and risks.

It may be regarded as a formative factor in the universe, if we be integral parts thereof, and co-determinants, by our behavior, of what its total character may be.

HOW WE ACT ON PROBABILITIES

In most emergencies we have to act on probability, and incur the risk of error.

'Probability' and 'possibility' are terms applied to things of the conditions of whose coming we are (to some degree at least) ignorant.

If we are entirely ignorant of the conditions that make a thing come, we call it a 'bare' possibility. If we know that some of the conditions already exist, it is for us in so far forth a 'grounded' possibility. It is in that case *probable* just in proportion as the said conditions are numerous, and few hindering conditions are in sight.

When the conditions are so numerous and confused that we can hardly follow them, we treat a thing as probable in proportion to the *frequency* with which things of that *kind* occur. Such frequency being a fraction, the probability is expressed by a fraction. Thus, if one death in 10,000 is by suicide, the antecedent probability of my death being a suicide is 1-10,000th. If one house in 5,000 burns down annually, the probability that my house will burn is 1-5,000th, etc.

Statistics show that in most kinds of thing the frequency is pretty regular. Insurance companies bank on this regularity, undertaking to pay (say) 5,000 dollars to each man whose house burns, provided he and the other house-owners each pay enough to give the company that sum, plus something more for profits and expenses.

The company, hedging on the large number of cases it deals with, and working by the long run, need run no risk of loss by the single fires.

The individual householder deals with his own single case exclusively. The probability of his house burning is only 1-5,000, but if that lot befall he will lose everything. He has no 'long run' to go by, if his house takes fire, and he can't hedge as the company does, by taxing his more fortunate neighbors. But in this particular kind of risk, the company helps him out. It translates his one chance in 5,000 of a big loss, into a certain loss 5,000 times smaller, and the bargain is a fair one on both sides. It is clearly better for the man to lose *certainly,* but *fractionally,* than to trust to his 4,999 chances of no loss, and then have the improbable chance befall.

But for most of our emergencies there is no insurance company at hand, and fractional solutions are impossible. Seldom can we *act* fractionally. If the probability that a friend is waiting for you in Boston is 1-2, how should you act on that probability? By going as far as the bridge? Better stay at home! Or if the probability is 1-2 that your partner is a villain, how should you act on that probability? By treating him as a villain one day, and confiding your money and your secrets to him the next? That would be the worst of all solutions. In all such cases we must act wholly for one *or* the other horn of the dilemma. We must go in for the more probable alternative as if the other one did not exist, and suffer the full penalty if the event belie our faith.

Now the metaphysical and religious alternatives are largely of this kind. We have but this one life in which to take up our attitude towards them, no insurance company is there to cover us, and if we are wrong, our error, even though it be not as great as the old hell-fire theology pretended, may yet be momentous. In such questions as that of the *character* of the world, of life being moral in its essential meaning, of our playing a vital part therein, etc., it would seem as if a certain *wholeness* in our faith were necessary. To calculate the probabilities and act fractionally, and treat life one day as a farce, and another day as a very serious business, would be to make the worst possible mess of it. Inaction also often counts as action. In many issues the inertia of one member will impede the success of the whole as much as his opposition will. To refuse, *e.g.,* to testify against villainy, is practically to help it to prevail.[2]

THE PLURALISTIC OR MELIORISTIC UNIVERSE

Finally, if the 'melioristic' universe were *really* here, it would require the active good-will of all of us, in the way of belief as well as of our other activities, to bring it to a prosperous issue.

The melioristic universe is conceived after a *social* analogy, as a pluralism of independent powers. It will succeed just in pro-

[2] Cf. Wm. James: *The Will to Believe,* etc., pp. 1-31, and 90-110.

portion as more of these work for its success. If none work, it will fail. If each does his best, it will not fail. Its destiny thus hangs on an *if,* or on a lot of *ifs* — which amounts to saying (in the technical language of logic) that, the world being as yet unfinished, its total character can be expressed only by *hypothetical* and not by *categorical* propositions.

(Empiricism, believing in possibilities, is willing to formulate its universe in hypothetical propositions. Rationalism, believing only in impossibilities and necessities, insists on the contrary on their being categorical.)

As individual members of a pluralistic universe, we must recognize that, even though we do *our* best, the other factors also will have a voice in the result. If they refuse to conspire, our goodwill and labor may be thrown away. No insurance company can here cover us or save us from the risks we run in being part of such a world.

We *must* take one of four attitudes in regard to the other powers: either

1. Follow intellectualist advice: wait for evidence; and while waiting, do nothing; or

2. *Mistrust* the other powers and, sure that the universe will fail, *let* it fail; or

3. *Trust* them; and at any rate do *our* best, in spite of the *if;* or, finally,

4. *Flounder,* spending one day in one attitude, another day in another.

This 4th way is no systematic solution. The 2d way spells faith in failure. The 1st way may in practice be indistinguishable from the 2d way. The 3d way seems the only wise way.

'*If* we do *our* best, *and* the other powers do *their* best, the world will be perfected' — this proposition expresses no actual fact, but only the complexion of a fact thought of as eventually possible. As it stands, *no* conclusion can be positively deduced from it. *A conclusion would require another premise of fact, which only we can supply. The original proposition* per se *has no pragmatic value whatsoever, apart from its power to challenge our will to produce the premise of fact required.* Then indeed the perfected world emerges as a logical conclusion.

We can *create* the conclusion, then. We can and we may, as it were, jump with both feet off the ground into or towards a world of which we trust the other parts to meet our jump — and *only so* can the *making* of a perfected world of the pluralistic pattern ever take place. Only through our precursive trust in it can it come into being.

There is no inconsistency anywhere in this, and no 'vicious circle' unless a circle of poles holding themselves upright by leaning on one another, or a circle of dancers revolving by holding each other's hands, be 'vicious.'

The faith circle is so congruous with human nature that the only explanation of the veto that intellectualists pass upon it must be sought in the offensive character *to them* of the faiths of certain concrete persons.

Such possibilities of offense have, however, to be put up with on empiricist principles. The long run of experience may weed out the more foolish faiths. Those who held them will then have failed: but without the wiser faiths of the others the world could never be perfected.

(Compare G. Lowes Dickinson: "Religion, a Criticism and a Forecast," N. Y. 1905, Introduction; and chaps. iii, iv.)

APPENDIX X

PRAGMATISTIC OR MELIORISTIC RELIGION*

What does it pragmatically mean to say that the salvation of the world is possible? It means that some of the conditions of the world's deliverance do actually exist. The more of them there are existent, the fewer preventing conditions you can find, the better-grounded is the salvation's possibility, the more *probable* does the fact of the deliverance become.

Now it would contradict the very spirit of life to say that our minds must be indifferent and neutral in questions like that of the world's salvation. Any one who pretends to be neutral writes himself down here as a fool and a sham. We all do wish to minimize the insecurity of the universe; we are and ought to be unhappy when we regard it as exposed to every enemy and open to every life-destroying draft. Nevertheless there are unhappy men who think the salvation of the world impossible. Theirs is the doctrine known as pessimism.

Optimism in turn would be the doctrine that thinks the world's salvation inevitable.

Midway between the two there stands what may be called the doctrine of meliorism, tho it has hitherto figured less as a doctrine

*From PR:284-301, with a few inconsequential deletions.

than as an attitude in human affairs. Optimism has always been the regnant *doctrine* in European philosophy. Pessimism was only recently introduced by Schopenhauer and counts few systematic defenders as yet. Meliorism treats salvation as neither necessary nor impossible. It treats it as a possibility, which becomes more and more of a probability the more numerous the actual conditions of salvation become.

It is clear that pragmatism must incline towards meliorism. Some conditions of the world's salvation are actually extant, and she can not possibly close her eyes to this fact: and should the residual conditions come, salvation would become an accomplished reality. Naturally the terms I use here are exceedingly summary. You may interpret the word 'salvation' in any way you like, and make it as diffuse and distributive, or as climacteric and integral a phenomenon as you please.

Take, for example, any one of us in this room with the ideals which he cherishes and is willing to live and work for. Every such ideal realized will be one moment in the world's salvation. But these particular ideals are not bare abstract possibilities. They are grounded, they are *live* possibilities, for we are their live champions and pledges, and if the complementary conditions come and add themselves, our ideals will become actual things. What now are the complementary conditions? They are first such a mixture of things as will in the fulness of time give us a chance, a gap that we can spring into, and, finally, *our act*.

Does our act then *create* the world's salvation so far as it makes room for itself, so far as it leaps into the gap? Does it create, not the whole world's salvation of course, but just so much of this as itself covers of the world's extent?

Here I take the bull by the horns, and in spite of the whole crew of rationalists and monists, of whatever brand they be, I ask *why not?* Our acts, our turning-places, where we seem to ourselves to make ourselves and grow, are the parts of the world to which we are closest, the parts of which our knowledge is the most intimate and complete. Why should we not take them at their face-value? Why may they not be the actual turning-places and growing-places which they seem to be, of the world — why not the workshop of being, where we catch fact in the making, so that nowhere may the world grow in any other kind of way than this?

Irrational! we are told. How can new being come in local spots and patches which add themselves or stay away at random, independently of the rest? There must be a reason for our acts, and where in the last resort can any reason be looked for save in the material pressure or the logical compulsion of the total nature of the world? There can be but one real agent of growth, or seeming growth, anywhere, and that agent is the integral world itself. It may grow all-over, if growth there be, but that single parts should grow *per se* is irrational.

But if one talks of rationality — and of reasons for things, and insists that they can't just come in spots, what *kind* of a reason can there ultimately be why anything should come at all? Talk of logic and necessity and categories and the absolute and the contents of the whole philosophical machine-shop as you will, the only *real* reason I can think of why anything should ever come is that *someone wishes it to be here.* It is *demanded* — demanded, it may be, to give relief to no matter how small a fraction of the world's mass. This is *living reason,* and compared with it material causes and logical necessities are spectral things.

In short the only fully rational world would be the world of wishing-caps, the world of telepathy, where every desire is fulfilled instanter, without having to consider or placate surrounding or intermediate powers. This is the Absolute's own world. He calls upon the phenomenal world to be, and it *is,* exactly as he calls for it, no other condition being required. In our world, the wishes of the individual are only one condition. Other individuals are there with other wishes and they must be propitiated first. So Being grows under all sorts of resistances in this world of the many, and, from compromise to compromise, only gets organized gradually into what may be called secondarily rational shape. We approach the wishing-cap type of organization only in a few departments of life. We want water and we turn a faucet. We want a kodak-picture and we press a button. We want information and we telephone. We want to travel and we buy a ticket. In these and similar cases, we hardly need to do more than the wishing — the world is rationally organized to do the rest.

But this talk of rationality is a parenthesis and a digression. What we were discussing was the idea of a world growing not integrally but piecemeal by the contributions of its several parts. Take the hypothesis seriously and as a live one. Suppose that the world's author put the case to you before creation, saying: "I am going to make a world not certain to be saved, a world the perfection of which shall be conditional merely, the condition being that each several agent does its own 'level best.' I offer you the chance of taking part in such a world. Its safety, you see, is unwarranted. It is a real adventure, with real danger, yet it may win through. It is a social scheme of co-operative work genuinely to be done. Will you join the procession? Will you trust yourself and trust the other agents enough to face the risk?"

Should you in all seriousness, if participation in such a world were proposed to you, feel bound to reject it as not safe enough? Would you say that, rather than be part and parcel of so fundamentally pluralistic and irrational a universe, you preferred to relapse into the slumber of nonentity from which you had been momentarily aroused by the tempter's voice?

Of course if you are normally constituted, you would do nothing of the sort. There is a healthy-minded buoyancy in most of us which such a universe would exactly fit. We would therefore accept the offer — "Top! *und schlag auf schlag!*" It would be just like the world we practically live in; and loyalty to our old nurse Nature would forbid us to say no. The world proposed would seem 'rational' to us in the most living way.

Most of us, I say, would therefore welcome the proposition and add our *fiat* to the *fiat* of the creator. Yet perhaps some would not; for there are morbid minds in every human collection, and to them the prospect of a universe with only a fighting chance of safety would probably make no appeal. There are moments of discouragement in us all, when we are sick of self and tired of vainly striving. Our own life breaks down, and we fall into the attitude of the prodigal son. We mistrust the chances of things. We want a universe where we can just give up, fall on our father's neck, and be absorbed into the absolute life as a drop of water melts into the river or the sea.

The peace and rest, the security desiderated at such moments is security against the bewildering accidents of so much finite experience. Nirvana means safety from this everlasting round of adventures of which the world of sense consists. The Hindoo and the Buddhist, for this is essentially their attitude, are simply afraid, afraid of more experience, afraid of life.

And to men of this complexion, religious monism comes with its consoling words: "All is needed and essential — even you with your sick soul and heart. All are one with God, and with God all is well. The everlasting arms are beneath, whether in the world of finite appearance you seem to fail or to succeed." There can be no doubt that when men are reduced to their last sick extremity absolutism is the only saving scheme. Pluralistic moralism simply makes their teeth chatter, it refrigerates the very heart within their breast.

So we see concretely two types of religion in sharp contrast. Using our old terms of comparison, we may say that the ab-

solutistic scheme appeals to the tender-minded while the pluralistic
scheme appeals to the tough. Many persons would refuse to call
the pluralistic scheme religious at all. They would call it moralistic,
and would apply the word religious to the monistic scheme alone.
Religion in the sense of self-surrender, and moralism in the sense
of self-sufficingness, have been pitted against each other as incompatibles frequently enough in the history of human thought.

We stand here before the final question of philosophy: the
monistic-pluralistic alternative, the deepest and most pregnant
question that our minds can frame. Can it be that the disjunction
is a final one? that only one side can be true? Are a pluralism and
monism genuine incompatibles? So that, if the world were really
pluralistically constituted, if it really existed distributively and
were made up of a lot of eaches, it could only be saved piecemeal
and *de facto* as the result of their behavior, and its epic history
in no wise short-circuited by some essential oneness in which the
severalness were already 'taken up' beforehand and eternally 'overcome'? If this were so, we should have to choose one philosophy or
the other. We could not say 'yes, yes' to both alternatives. There
would have to be a 'no' in our relations with the possible. We
should confess an ultimate disappointment: we could not remain
healthy-minded and sick-minded in one indivisible act.

Of course as human beings we can be healthy minds on one
day and sick souls on the next; and as amateur dabblers in
philosophy we may perhaps be allowed to call ourselves monistic
pluralists, or free-will determinists, or whatever else may occur
to us of a reconciling kind. But as philosophers aiming at clearness
and consistency, and feeling the pragmatistic need of squaring
truth with truth, the question is forced upon us of frankly adopting either the tender or the robustious type of thought. In particular *this* query has always come home to me: May not the
claims of tender-mindedness go too far? May not the notion of
a world already saved *in toto* anyhow, be too saccharine to stand?
May not religious optimism be too idyllic? Must *all* be saved? Is
no price to be paid in the work of salvation? Is the last word
sweet? Is all 'yes, yes' in the universe? Doesn't the fact of 'no'
stand at the very core of life? Doesn't the very 'seriousness' that
we attribute to life mean that ineluctable noes and losses form
a part of it, that there are genuine sacrifices somewhere, and that
something permanently drastic and bitter always remains at the
bottom of its cup?

I can not speak officially as a pragmatist here; all I can say is
that my own pragmatism offers no objection to my taking sides

with this more moralistic view, and giving up the claim of total reconciliation. The possibility of this is involved in the pragmatistic willingness to treat pluralism as a serious hypothesis. In the end it is our faith and not our logic that decides such questions, and I deny the right of any pretended logic to veto my own faith. I find myself willing to take the universe to be really dangerous and adventurous, without therefore backing out and crying 'no play.' I am willing to think that the prodigal-son attitude, open to us as it is in many vicissitudes, is not the right and final attitude towards the whole of life. I am willing that there should be real losses and real losers, and no total preservation of all that is. I can believe in the ideal as an ultimate, not as an origin, and as an extract, not the whole. When the cup is poured off, the dregs are left behind for ever, but the possibility of what is poured off is sweet enough to accept.

As a matter of fact countless human imaginations live in this moralistic and epic kind of a universe, and find its disseminated and strung-along successes sufficient for their rational needs. There is a finely translated epigram in the Greek anthology which admirably expresses this state of mind, this acceptance of loss as unatoned for, even though the lost element might be one's self:

> "*A shipwrecked sailor, buried on this coast,*
> *Bids you set sail.*
> *Full many a gallant bark, when we were lost,*
> *Weathered the gale.*"

Those puritans who answered 'yes' to the question: Are you willing to be damned for God's glory? were in this objective and magnanimous condition of mind. The way of escape from evil on this system is *not* by getting it 'aufgehoben,' or preserved in the whole as an element essential but 'overcome.' *It is by dropping it out altogether, throwing it overboard and getting beyond it, helping to make a universe that shall forget its very place and name.*

It is then perfectly possible to accept sincerely a drastic kind of a universe from which the element of 'seriousness' is not to be expelled. Whoso does so is, it seems to me, a genuine pragmatist. He is willing to live on a scheme of uncertified possibilities which he trusts; willing to pay with his own person, if need be, for the realization of the ideals which he frames.

What now actually *are* the other forces which he trusts to co-operate with him, in a universe of such a type? They are at least his fellow men, in the stage of being which our actual universe has reached. But are there not superhuman forces also, such as religious men of the pluralistic type we have been considering have always believed in? Their words may have sounded monistic when they said "there is no God but God"; but the original polytheism of mankind has only imperfectly and vaguely sublimated itself into monotheism, and monotheism itself, so far as it was religious and not a scheme of classroom instruction for the metaphysicians, has always viewed God as but one helper, *primus inter pares,* in the midst of all the shapers of the great world's fate.

I have shown small respect indeed for the Absolute, but the Absolute has nothing but its superhumanness in common with the theistic God. On pragmatistic principles, if the hypothesis of God works satisfactorily in the widest sense of the word, it is true. Now whatever its residual difficulties may be, experience shows that it certainly does work, and that the problem is to build it out and determine it so that it will combine satisfactorily with all the other working truths. I can not start upon a whole theology at the end of this lecture; but when I tell you that I have written a book on men's religious experience, which on the whole has been regarded as making for the reality of God, you will perhaps exempt my own pragmatism from the charge of being an atheistic system. I firmly disbelieve, myself, that our human experience is the highest form of experience extant in the universe. I believe rather that we stand in much the same relation to the whole of the universe as our canine and feline pets do to the whole of human life. They inhabit our drawing-rooms and libraries. They take part in scenes of whose significance they have no inkling. They are merely tangent to curves of history the beginnings and ends and forms of which pass wholly beyond their ken. So we are tangent to the wider life of things. But, just as many of the dog's and cat's ideals coincide with our ideals, and the dogs and cats have daily living proof of the fact, so we may well believe, on the proofs that religious experience affords, that higher powers exist and are at work to save the world on ideal lines similar to our own.

You see that pragmatism can be called religious, if you allow that religion can be pluralistic or merely melioristic in type. But whether you will finally put up with that type of religion or not is a question that only you yourself can decide. Pragmatism has to postpone dogmatic answer, for we do not yet know certainly which type of religion is going to work best in the long run. The various overbeliefs of men, their several faith-ventures, are in fact what are needed to bring the evidence in. You will probably make your own ventures severally. If radically tough, the hurly-burly of the sensible facts of nature will be enough for you, and you will need no religion at all. If radically tender, you will take up with the more monistic form of religion: the pluralistic form, with its reliance on possibilities that are not necessities, will not seem to afford you security enough.

But if you are neither tough nor tender in an extreme and radical sense, but mixed as most of us are, it may seem to you that the type of pluralistic and moralistic religion that I have offered is as good a religious synthesis as you are likely to find. Between the two extremes of crude naturalism on the one hand and transcendental absolutism on the other, you may find that what I take the liberty of calling the pragmatistic or melioristic type of theism is exactly what you require.

INDEX

Absolute, oneness with the, 419.
Abstractness of religious objects, 53.
ACHILLES, 86.
ACKERMANN, MADAME, 63.
Adaptation to environment, of things, 438; of saints, 374–377.
Æsthetic elements in religions, 460.
Alacoque, 310, 344, 413.
Alcohol, 387.
AL-GHAZZALI, 402.
ALI, 341.
ALLEINE, 228.
ALLINE, 159, 217.
Alternations of personality, 193.
ALVAREZ DE PAZ, 116.
AMIEL, 394.
Anæsthesia, 288.
Anæsthetic revelation, 387–393.
ANGELUS SILESIUS, 417.
Anger, 181, 264.
' Anhedonia,' 145.
Aristocratic type, 371.
ARISTOTLE, 495.
Ars, le Curé d', 302.
Asceticism, 273, 296–310, 360–365.
Aseity, God's, 439, 445.
Atman, 400.
Attributes of God, 440; their æsthetic use, 458.
AUGUSTINE, SAINT, 171, 361, 496.
AURELIUS, see MARCUS.
Automatic writing, 62, 478.
Automatisms, 234, 250, 478–483.

BALDWIN, 347, 503.
BASHKIRTSEFF, 83.
BEECHER, 256.
BEHMEN, see BOEHME.
Belief, due to non-rationalistic impulses, 73.
BESANT, MRS., 23, 168.
Bhagavad-Gita, 361.
BLAVATSKY, MADAM, 421.
BLOOD, 389.
BLUMHARDT, 113.
BOEHME, 410, 417, 418.
BOOTH, 203.
BOUGAUD, 344.
BOURGET, 263.
BOURIGNON, 321.

BOWNE, 502.
BRAINERD, 212, 253.
BRAY, 249, 256, 290.
BROOKS, 512.
BROWNELL, 515.
BUCKE, 398.
Buddhism, 31, 34, 522.
Buddhist mysticism, 401.
BULLEN, 287.
BUNYAN, 157, 160.
BUTTERWORTH, 411.

CAIRD, EDWARD, 106.
CAIRD, J., on feeling in religion, 434; on absolute self, 450; he does not prove, but reaffirms, religion's dicta, 453.
CALL, 289.
CARLYLE, 41, 300.
CARPENTER, 319.
Catharine, Saint, of Genoa, 289.
Catholicism and Protestantism compared, 114, 227, 336, 461.
Causality of God, 517, 522.
Cause, 502.
CENNICK, 301.
Centres of personal energy, 196, 267, 523.
Cerebration, unconscious, 207.
Chance, 526.
CHANNING, 300, 488.
CHAPMAN, 324.
Character, cause of its alterations, 193; scheme of its differences of type, 197, 214.
Causes of its diversity, 261; balance of, 340.
Charity, 274, 278, 310, 355.
Chastity, 310.
Chiefs of tribes, 371.
Christian Science, 106.
Christ's atonement, 129, 245.
Churches, 335, 460.
CLARK, 389.
CLISSOLD, 481.
COE, 240.
Conduct, perfect, 355.
Confession, 462.
Consciousness, fields of, 231; subliminal, 233.

621

Library of the Mystic Arts
A LIBRARY OF ANCIENT AND MODERN CLASSICS

BIRREN, Faber. Color Psychology and Color Therapy: A Factual Study of the Influence of Color on Human Life; intro. by Felix Morrow. ill. photogs. biblio. index. xv — 302pp. 61-14266. $7.50

PSYCH

"Faber Birren is a consultant on the use of color in industrial and other applications, and perhaps without a peer in this field. The book, however, goes much farther than the mere applications and their psychology. There is fascinating detail from historical, medical, occult, physiological sources as well — fascinating and documented . . . Recommended." — LIBRARY JOURNAL

THE BOOK OF THE DEAD: the Hieroglyphic Transcript of the Papyrus of ANI; tr. and intro. by E. A. Wallis Budge. ill. appendixes. index. xiv + 704pp. 60-12165. $12.50 REL
This is the collection of texts which the ancient Egyptian scribes composed for the benefit of the dead. A book-length introduction by Sir Wallis Budge, late Keeper of the Egyptian and Assyrian Antiquities in the British Museum, gives us its history and theology. This is an exact reproduction of the famous Medici Society edition of 1911 except that the original two volumes are here bound as one.

BUDGE, E. A. Wallis. Amulets and Talismans. ill. b/w 22 plates, 300 ill. index. xxxix + 543pp. 61-7163. $10.00 REL/ARCHEOL.
"This encyclopedic volume represents years of research and an extensive knowledge of ancient civilizations. The author, as teacher at Cambridge University and curator of the British Museum, has accumulated a wealth of data dealing with demonology, divination, astrology, numerology and the belief in the prophylactic properties of the gems prevalent among the people of the ancient civilizations of Sumer, Babylon, Persia, Egypt and others. The author throws new light on many passages in early biblical writings which will give the student of the Old Testament often a clearer meaning of the archaic sense of the text. 'Amulets and Talismans' is a reliable reference book of lasting value." — THE LUTHERAN

BUDGE, E. A. Wallis. Egyptian Magic. ill. xv + 234pp. 58-8302. $5.00 REL
The Egyptian priest made darkness as well as light his realm; his power was exercised by names, spells, enchantments, amulets, pictures and ceremonies accompanied by potent words to be spoken in a certain manner.

BUDGE, E. A. Wallis. Egyptian Religion. ill. 224pp. 59-8616. $5.00 REL
Many illustrations from the collection of the author have been added to the original edition to make this as much a picture story as it is an exposition. Much of the book consists of selections from the celebrated *Book of the Dead*.

BUDGE, E. A. Wallis. Osiris; the Egyptian Religion of Resurrection; 2 vols. bound as one; intro. by Jane Harrison. ill. 14 b/w plates, 212 line cuts. appendix. index. xliii + 440pp. 404pp. 61-10531. $15. REL
"In this full-length study, Dr. Wallis Budge, the late Keeper of the Egyptian and Assyrian Antiquities in the British Museum, interprets Osiris as a year-god who dies and lives again. In contradistinction to Frazer, he dwells on the

native African origins of this ancient Egyptian cult and avoids the obvious parallels with the mid-Eastern gods Attis and Adonis ... His work will be read with profit and enjoyment by all students of· comparative religion."
— LIBRARY JOURNAL

CAMMELL, Charles Richard. Aleister Crowley: The Man: The Mage: The Poet; intro. by John C. Wilson. ill. bibliog. index. 236pp. 62-12565. $6   BIOG
A quiet and dignified life of Crowley (1875-1947) written not in a spirit of polemic, but to introduce Crowley anew for what he really was — a great poet and mystic — and not the "great beast" portrayed by the yellow press.

CONYBEARE, F. C. The Origins of Christianity; intro. by Joel Carmichael. index. xxx + 382 pp. 58-8305. $6.   REL
It was not until the end of thé eighteenth century that the attempt was made to ascertain the historical facts behind the apotheosized figure of Jesus and extricate the man himself from the web of tradition, myth, and faith that had enveloped him. This absorbing volume, one of the finest fruits of this campaign of historical reinterpretation, takes a bold course away from the traditional and conventional story of Jesus; Paul's decisive role is made clear.

DANIELOU, Alain. Yoga; The Method of Re-integration. ills. appendixes. ix + 165pp. $3.75. YOGA
Yoga as defined in the Hindu Scriptures, with an appendix of Sanskrit text. Processes by which the subconscious may be controlled are treated at length. These processes can lead to unusual attainments, both spiritually and intellectually.

DAVID-NEEL, Alexandra. Magic and Mystery in Tibet; intro. by Aaron Sussman. photogs. xiv + 320pp. 56-13013. $6.   OCCULT
"Precisely the person to explore Tibet ... absolutely fearless. Her accounts of Tibetan religious ceremonies and beliefs are the fullest and best we have."
— THE NEW YORKER

DAY, Harvey. The Study and Practice of Yoga. ill. bibliog. index. 160pp. 56-7836. $3.75.   YOGA
A practical manual on Yoga postures and exercises which are within the capabilities of any individual. It shows how this ancient science helps to induce clear thinking, control weight and aid in preserving a youthful appearance and physique.

FODOR, Nandor. The Haunted Mind: A Psychoanalyst Looks at the Supernatural. index. v + 314pp. 59-15675. $5.   PARAPSYCH
From his practice as a psychoanalyst and psychic researcher, Dr. Fodor has selected some 20 cases as the most interesting. They include mediumship, levitation, communication after death.

FRAZER, James George. Adonis Attis Osiris; 2 vols. bound as one; intro. by Sidney Waldron. ill. b/w 15pp. plates. index. xxviii + 321pp., 317pp. 61-15336. $10.   REL
The book that has most influenced modern literature is Frazer's *Golden Bough,* and this influence comes mainly from Frazer's writings on the year-gods, Adonis, Attis and Osiris. These two unabridged volumes (bound as one) constitute Part IV of the thirteen volumes of the unabridged *Golden Bough.* A new introduction by the anthropologist Sidney Waldron defends Frazer against his critics.

GOLDBERG, B. Z. The Sacred Fire: the Story of Sex in Religion; intro. by Dr. Charles Francis Potter. ill. bibliog. index. 288pp. 58-13358. $7.50.   REL/ANTHROP
The sexual symbolism underlying expressions of faith from prehistoric

farmers to present-day evangelists is examined in the light of wide anthropological and historical evidence.

GRILLOT DE GIVRY, Emile Angelo. A Pictorial Anthology of Witchcraft, Magic and Alchemy. 376 ills. index. 395pp. 58-11782. $10.   OCCULT
Graphic illustration is the author's successful answer to the knotty problem of explaining occult concepts. The author makes clear what the alchemist was searching for, what his various tools looked like, and how they were made and used. He does the same for the other occult practitioners. Perhaps the rarest illustrations are in the section on Kabbalah.

GUIGNEBERT, Charles. Ancient, Medieval and Modern Christianity: The Evolution of a Religion; fwd. by John C. Wilson. xxxii + 507pp. 61-15334. $7.50   REL
The late Professor of the History of Christianity at the Sorbonne here applies the theory of evolution to Christianity itself. The author believes that every religion is born, develops, adapts and transforms itself, grows old and dies. Guignebert warms his scientific truths, which may be unpleasant to professing Christians, by his fervent belief that the honest study of religion is "the mother of tolerance and religious peace." "Always provocative, it does stimulate constructive thinking. And those who seriously enter these pages, will also be stimulated to discover answers to many of the charges and facts that may have profoundly moved and disturbed them." — *Daniel A. Poling* in THE CHRISTIAN HERALD

GUIGNEBERT, Charles. Jesus; fwd. by Joel Carmichael. bibliog. index. xv + 560pp. 56-7837. $7.50.   REL
"The virtue of Professor Guignebert's venture lies in his comprehensive analysis of the scholarship of the past decades in this field. The specialists are acquainted with all the evidence which he analyzes. But there is no book of recent years which will give the interested layman a more comprehensive account of what has been written and said about the life of Jesus and a fairer estimate of conflicting evidence. Naturally, the author has a position of his own to maintain, but the reader is permitted to see how he arrives at it and with what cogency and plausibility he defends it against contrasting views. On the whole his own position is strongly influenced by the eschatological emphasis which was introduced into New Testament criticism by Albert Schweitzer." — *Reinhold Niebuhr*

GUIGNEBERT, Charles. The Jewish World in the Time of Jesus; fwd. by Charles Francis Potter. bibliog. index. xiii + 288pp. 59-14528. $6.   REL
The Old Testament closes hundreds of years before Jesus, the New is written long after his death. What, then, do most of us know about his Jewish world? Most of us do not know that world — its Essenes, gnostics, magicians, angels and demons, hermetic books and Messiahs, none of them to be found in the Old Testament. In the New Testament, written from an anti-Jewish bias, there is already a distorted picture of the Jewish world of Jesus. Here it is vividly reconstructed for us.

HUYSMANS, Joris-Karl. La Bas: Down There: a Study in Satanism; intro. by Robert Baldick. xxviii + 317pp. 56-13015. $5.   OCCULT
Presented as a novel, this book can also serve as a reference on satanism. Huysmans made excellent use of the documents on sorcery, alchemy and satanism as well as of conversations he had had with people intimately acquainted with occult practices.

MALORY, Thomas. Le Morte D'Arthur: the Book of King Arthur and his Knights of the Round Table: 2 vols. bound as one; intro. by John C. Wilson. index. xxxix + 432pp., 530pp. 61-18526. $15. LIT
This is the complete, unexpurgated text; the only liberty taken with the original has been to modernize the spelling to make it easily readable. The

text is that of A. W. Pollard as finally revised in his Medici Society edition of 1920. Only in this uncut version does it become clear how the lighthearted journeys build up to the journeys of the soul, that they were not really journeys on horseback and clothed in armor, but journeys of the spirit. "Here is an important segment of our English heritage in unexpurgated form. A Must for all libraries." — VIRGINIA KIRKUS SERVICE

MEAD, G. R. S. Fragments of a Faith Forgotten: the Gnostics: a Contribution to the Study of the Origins of Christianity; intro. by Kenneth Rexroth. ill. bibliog. index. lxvii + 633pp. 60-15310. $10.
REL
"This re-issue of a classic is a real service to modern religious thinkers because it makes available between two covers many widely scattered sources for the study of mystery religions, Gnosticism and even modern theosophical as well as syncretistic trends in religion." — CHURCH MANAGEMENT
"A monumental work. A definitive scholarly and intensely interesting contribution to the vast study of the origins of Christianity. A synopsis of contents and the index are a major contribution to the study. There at once is a profound study with a wealth of culture satisfaction written with distinguished scholarship." — *Daniel A. Poling* in THE CHRISTIAN HERALD

MYERS, F. W. H. Human Personality and its Survival of Bodily Death; ed. by Susy Smith; fwd. by Aldous Huxley. index. 416pp. 61-9319. $10.
PARAPSYCH
"This often quoted, and much respected work (at least among psychic researchers) was first published in 1903. Now it is being offered in one volume rather than two, and with all the Victorian wordiness removed . . . A felicitous foreword by Aldous Huxley has been included, too. The excisions have improved the readability immeasurably, and Huxley's blessing should attract not only those who are convinced that the exploration of the human mind is our last frontier, but also many skeptical seekers after truth. Rereading and comparing this work with the original edition was a fascinating task. Myers' investigations and his case records of abnormal psychology, genius, sleep, hypnotism, automatism, trance, and ecstasy, among other subjects, make adventurous reading. Every library should buy it, not only as a pioneer work in the field of psychic research, but also because little convincing material beyond it exists as of the present time." — LIBRARY JOURNAL

OSBORN, Arthur W. The Future Is Now: the Significance of Precognition; intro. by Eileen J. Garrett. index. 254pp. 61-9321. $6.
PARAPSYCH
Precognition is the most baffling of all paranormal phenomena even though the most abundantly documented and established. Clairvoyance and telepathy at least occur in our present time field. But precognition "transmits" information not only across space but across time fields. The author's case histories (including personal experiences of his wife and himself) range through precognitive warnings, precognition of death, of trivial events, of significant events, and longer-range precognition.

OUSPENSKY, P. D. Strange Life of Ivan Osokin. 166pp. 62-13501. $5.00
FICTION
The famous exiled Russian psychologist, author of *Tertium Organum* and *A New Model of the Universe,* turns to the novel form to put flesh and blood on his esoteric science. The author personally supervised the English version of his novel.

PIRENNE, Henri. A History of Europe from the Invasions to the XVIth century; intro. by Dr. Jan-Albert Goris; tr. by Bernard Miall. xxii + 625pp. $7.50
HIST
"This edition, translated from the 8th French edition, and first printed in England in 1938, is here available in a photo-offset edition. A supplement contains a number of errors which, it is said, could not be corrected owing to the offset method of printing of the present edition. The new introduction does not deal specifically with this book, which is sufficiently well established to need no editorial comment, but presents a brief biography of Pirenne,